THE CLASH

ALSO BY WALTER LAFEBER

The American Age: U.S. Foreign Policy at Home and Abroad Since 1750

Inevitable Revolutions: The United States in Central America

America, Russia and the Cold War, 1945–1996

The American Search for Opportunity, 1865–1913

The New Empire

The Panama Canal; the Crisis in Historical Perspective

THE CLASH

U.S.–Japanese

Relations throughout History

WALTER LaFEBER

W · W · NORTON & COMPANY

NEW YORK   LONDON

For information about permission to reproduce selections from this book, write to
Permissions, W. W. Norton & Company, Inc., 500 Fifth Avenue,
New York, NY 10110.

The text of this book is composed in 11/13 Fairfield LH Light
with the display set in Lucian BT Roman
Composition and Manufacturing by The Maple-Vail Book Manufacturing Group
Book design and title page illustration by Margaret M. Wagner
Cartography by Jacques Chauzaud

Library of Congress Cataloging-in-Publication Data
LaFeber, Walter.
        The clash : U.S.-Japan relations throughout
history / Walter LaFeber.
        p.   cm.
        Includes bibliographical references (p.   ) and
index.
        ISBN 0-393-31837-0 (pbk.)
        1. United States—Foreign relations—Japan.
2. Japan—Foreign relations—United States.
I. Title.
E183.8.J3L34   1998
327.73052'09—dc21   98-34387
                                                                                              CIP

W. W. Norton & Company, Inc., 500 Fifth Avenue, New York, N.Y. 10110
www.wwnorton.com

W. W. Norton & Company Ltd., 10 Coptic Street, London WC1A 1PU

2 3 4 5 6 7 8 9 0

THIS BOOK IS DEDICATED TO

Dale and Nellie Corson   *Frank and Rosa Rhodes*

JAPANESE names are usually given in Japanese form, that is, surname first (for example, Yoshida Shigeru). Exceptions are made when Japanese authors publish in English and give their surname last (as in American usage), so readers can more easily track down these references if they wish. In accordance with many English-language works, long vowel marks have been omitted from Japanese words.

The term "Americans," with apologies to neighbors north and south, is used synonymously with U.S. citizens for purposes of word variation and succinctness.

Contents

"I DO BELIEVE we [in the United States and Japan] do practice differ-ent forms of capitalism. The differences, I think, are increasingly famil-iar. What is needed, I think, is a harmonization to some degree, but not a homogenization."

—U.S. Ambassador to Japan
MICHAEL ARMACOST, June 1993

"RECENT international trends indicate that racial rivalry has yearly become more intense. It is a striking fact that the Turkish and Balkan wars of the past . . . all had their origins in racial rivalry and hatred. Furthermore, the exclusion of Japanese in the state of California . . . and the discrimination against Indians in British Africa are also manifesta-tions of the racial problem. . . . [After the war in Europe is over] the rivalry between the white and colored peoples will intensify; and perhaps it will be a time when the white races will all unite to oppose the colored peoples."

—YAMAGATA ARITOMO, August 1914

"IN THE FAR EAST, peace can be permanently secured only if the two great Powers lying on either side of the Pacific work together in harmony and understanding. . . . The first evidence of this should be our common attitude towards the Chinese nation."

—THOMAS LAMONT, operating head of
J. P. Morgan, in Japan, March 1920

"THE QUESTION of Sino-Japanese relations is always the essential pre-occupation of Japan's foreign affairs."

—PIERRE RENOUVIN, La Question
d'Extrême-Orient, 1840–1940 (1946)

"HE POINTED OUT that policy is really a series of responses to chal-lenges, and that the responses are largely determined by, first, our own principles of conduct and ethics, and, secondly, our concept of ourselves as a nation and its past in the world."

—Confidential record of GEORGE KENNAN
speaking to U.S. ambassadors, 1950

Preface

On December 7, 1964, the New York Council on Foreign Relations commemorated the twenty-third anniversary of the Japanese attack on Pearl Harbor by convening a private meeting to discuss U.S.-Japan relations. An exchange developed among John K. Emmerson (longtime State Department expert on Japan), Professor James Morley (a distinguished Columbia University analyst of East Asian affairs), and Robert W. Barnett (a top State Department specialist on Asia):

> Mr. Emmerson thinks it important that recently the Japanese are not sure whether to call themselves Far East or Far West. They talk about themselves as a bridge between Communist China and the West. To Mr. Morley, the Japanese regard themselves as hanging between two cultures, rather than identifying with either one.
>
> Mr. Barnett expressed hope that both of the above analyses were right, but feared they might be wrong. He had never seen a Japanese, he said, who talked about China without (1) a feeling of admiration for the long Chinese tradition, and (2) a feeling that any Japanese could outsmart any Chinese over any issue.[1]

Significantly, the discussion occurred as the Japanese economic "miracle" was beginning—that is, as Japan surprisingly emerged to challenge a U.S. industrial powerhouse that had dominated international markets since the end of World War II. The exchange also took place as American fear of Communist China was peaking. China had exploded its first atomic device earlier in 1964 and was condemned by U.S. officials for stoking, if not actually controlling, the wearisome war in Vietnam.

These words of December 7, 1964, illustrate the three themes of this book. First, although (with the significant exception of 1931 to 1945) Americans and Japanese have generally seen each other as partners in most East Asian affairs, they have in truth endured a series of some-times highly dangerous clashes during their 150-year relationship. The conflict began at the beginning: U.S. Commodore Matthew Perry used cannon to open a highly reluctant Japan to U.S. interests in 1853. The clash extended into the 1990s, when public opinion polls revealed that with the end of the Cold War, Japanese and Americans saw the other—rather than the Soviet military—as now posing the greatest threat to themselves.

A second theme is that at the root of these problems has been, and continues to be, a clash between two different forms of capitalism. A powerful Japanese finance ministry official explained the difference in the 1990s by declaring that the United States followed capitalist market policies, while Japan followed a non-capitalist market policy. This exag-geration made the point: some four hundred years of Japanese history formed a compact, homogeneous, closely knit society that, for good reason, is terrified of disorder. It has sought to avoid disorder with a strong central government, which guides the subtle, informal networks that run the economy. For some two hundred years, on the other hand, American history has formed a sprawling, pluralistic, open-ended soci-ety that, for good reason, is terrified of economic depressions and sought to avoid them by creating an open international marketplace. In the late eighteenth and early nineteenth century, "international" meant the frontier, the western part of the North American continent, as well as Europe and Latin America. After the 1840s, "international" has also meant what Emmerson and other prominent Americans called the "Far West"—that is, Asia.

Thus the book's third theme; the clash of the two capitalisms has focused on China. Perry forced Japan open because Washington offi-cials wanted it as a strategic way station to the potentially rich Chinese markets. For their part, the Japanese, as Robert Barnett indicated, have seen China as both a source of their culture and as their own frontier of opportunity. Through the late nineteenth century, Japan and the United States cooperated in their China policies. They cooperated largely because both so feared the Russian Empire's advance into North China. After Japan defeated the Russians in 1904–05—as a yellow race triumphed over a white race with an efficiency that stunned Americans and Europeans—the Japanese set about establishing their own empire on the Asian mainland. By 1915–20, Washington approached flashpoint with Tokyo over Japan's pressures on China and intervention in Siberia.

The Washington Conference of 1921–22—one of the most significant, and overlooked, diplomatic meetings in American history—resolved these conflicts. But only temporarily. The conference worked out a deal: Japan received de facto naval superiority in the western Pacific in return for agreeing to work with New York bankers in developing parts of China. Even during the 1920s, this deal brought order neither to Japan nor to an increasingly revolutionary China. After 1929, the agreement crashed as its foundation, the dollar, collapsed.

Japan's military then took matters into its own hand. The *zaibatsu*—those immense, family-based industrial-banking combinations that powered the economy—cooperated with the military to try to break free of dependence on the West. The *zaibatsu,* as always, received help from an extraordinary government bureaucracy. As the Canadian diplomat E. H. Norman explained in a pioneering book published on the eve of World War II, this military-industrial-governmental phalanx came together not in the 1930s but during the Tokugawa (1603–1867) and especially Meiji (1868–1912) eras.[2]

The United States had deployed powerful governmental-mercantilist measures of its own—tariffs, immense subsidies to producers and railway builders, currency manipulation—to become the globe's premier economic power by World War I. Once they climbed to that pinnacle, however, Americans, not surprisingly, were determined to open up world markets so their booming factories and farms could find profits and their burgeoning, pluralistic population could find employment. They, like the Japanese, focused a business eye on the Asian mainland, even as Japan moved to seal off parts of that vast market.

Unlike the Japanese, however, Americans viewed Asia as only part of a larger opportunity. While Japan historically stressed the importance of East and Southeast Asia for its survival, the United States developed a global vision that saw those Asians as part of a much larger structure. Americans and Japanese clashed not only because of China questions, but because Japan saw the Asian mainland as all-important, while the United States saw as all-important an open global system that could be undermined unless East and Southeast Asia became integrated into that system. In the end, Americans went to war in 1941 because they could not resolve their differences with Japan over China, especially how China was to be integrated into a global marketplace.

The dollar's collapse in the 1930s and then World War II's horrors only confirmed to Americans that their global vision had to be made real after 1945. Their domestic order and prosperity rested on it. And by the mid-1940s, they finally seemed to hold the power to realize such a vision. A fundamental step was the occupation and restructuring of a devastated Japan. But, in one of the many entertaining ironies in U.S.-Japanese relations, Washington officials concluded that Japan could only survive—and be saved from communism—if it developed a great export trade. That decision, in turn, led to the American-supported re-creation of industrial-banking combinations that could produce competitive exports. It also led to the re-creation of a powerful government bureaucracy to guide these combinations and gear the overall economy to meet the needs of this trade. The Japanese, under the leadership of Prime Minister Yoshida Shigeru, used the U.S. occupation for their own purposes. As Yoshida observed, "History provides examples of winning by diplomacy after losing in war."[3]

The pivotal part of Japan's policy proved to be control of capital and, as it turned out, virtual exclusion of U.S. investment. Americans learned from the 1930s that closed economic blocs (as in Japan and Germany) led to war, and that appeasement (such as the deal made in 1938 at Munich with Hitler) only encouraged aggressors. Japanese, however, learned two quite different lessons from the 1930s: they should never again be dependent on outsiders for capital; and that means other than militarism must be found to exploit frontiers of economic opportunity in East Asia.

The ironies did not end there. Japanese exporters required both raw materials and markets. By the late 1940s, U.S. officials had decided that Southeast Asia would best fulfill both requirements. That these officials had gone to war with Japan in 1941 in part because Tokyo insisted on creating a closed "co-prosperity sphere" in Southeast Asia was now irrelevant. If Japan did not have an open Southeast Asia, then, as John Foster Dulles and other top officials warned, it would either be forced to dump products on the United States, or—even worse—begin making deals with Communist China. Out of this U.S. approach came the commitment to Vietnam. Out of this approach also came a bitter American-Japanese clash over policy toward Vietnam and China in the 1960s and after.

While the United States bogged down in the Southeast Asian quagmire, Japan opened trade relations with the North Vietnamese Communist regime, made billions of dollars by supplying the U.S.–South Vietnam war effort, and began moving back into China. Richard Nixon's historic trip to Beijing in 1972 was like a starter's pistol that set off Americans on yet another race for the China market. After economic reforms began in 1978, China promised to be the world's largest economy in the early twenty-first century. Intense competition for this market was obscured—in part by a growing outcry over Japan's immense favorable trade balance with the United States, in part by the common interests of the U.S.-Japanese security partnership that targeted the Soviets and allowed Japan to maintain a small, relatively cheap military establishment.

Nixon's closest foreign policy adviser, Henry Kissinger, hoped to play China off against Japan for American benefit, even if it meant Japan might build nuclear weapons. The Japanese, he was recorded as telling the U.S. Joint Chiefs of Staff, "are mean and treacherous but they pursue their own interest." They "will go nuclear at some time. . . . He said that the Chinese would worry if the Japanese began to increase their defense expenditures. He said that it is all right. . . . He said it is good to keep the Chinese concerned."[4]

A series of events in 1989–91 once again changed the relationship. First, China's massacre of dissidents in Tiananmen Square in early June 1989 revealed important differences between the American and Japanese views of whether human rights should receive priority over trading privileges. Second, the crisis in the Persian Gulf during 1990–91 deeply embittered the relationship when Japan refused to reverse its post-1945 anti-military policy and help the United States. Even its considerable financial aid was sent reluctantly, which was not surprising given the growing differences between American and Japanese interests in the Middle East. Third, the Liberal Democratic Party (LDP) that had ruled Japan since 1955 fell apart, the victim of corruption and inept leadership. Fourth, the post-1960 economic "miracle" ended as a result of overspeculation and, as some would have it, of overregulation by the powerful Ministry of Finance and Ministry of International Trade and Industry (MITI). Fifth, the death of the Soviet Union on December 25, 1991, removed the common enemy that helped Americans and Japanese ignore their differences. Trade and China questions moved to the forefront—so much so that they became weapons used by Bill Clinton to defeat George Bush in the 1992 election, and then shaped Clinton's own foreign policies.[5]

Through all this turmoil, Japan's economic policies changed remarkably little. It continued to guard jealously its capital sources and regulatory society. As U.S. Ambassador Michael Armacost observed, while Japanese invested hundreds of billions of dollars in American property and Treasury securities, all foreign investments in Japan amounted to only 0.3 percent of gross national product—and were falling. While Japanese automakers built vast plants in the United States, less than half the Fortune 500 companies had a presence in Japan, and frequently those only held a minority stake in a joint venture. The Japanese systematically gained access to U.S. technology, but meanwhile ensured that foreigners had little access to their own. A critical part of their technology was designed for dual use (both civilian and military). Until 1983, Tokyo used legalistic excuses even to prevent export of its defense technology to its protector, the United States.[6]

The post–Cold War policies of the two nations will necessarily blend the new and the old. The new is the redefinition of their security treaty so it will counter the powerful centrifugal forces that threaten the relationship. For Americans, the security arrangement gives them their most effective lever to influence Asian developments. For Japanese, it allows them to depend on the United States for protection (especially against a militarizing China), while pouring investment into profitable civilian goods rather than into military budgets. For Chinese and Southeast Asians, the treaty also provides security—against the possibility of a remilitarized Japan.

Americans have thus stationed nearly fifty thousand troops and overwhelming naval and airpower in and around Japan to protect their foremost economic competitor and help give that competitor easier access to a reassured East and Southeast Asia. Such policies (and ironies) are deeply rooted in—and can only be understood in the context of—150 years of U.S.-Japan relations. The differing economic and social systems, competition over China, the U.S. attempts to integrate Japan into a Western system on Western terms, often blatant racism—all go back to the beginnings of the relationship. So does the ongoing argument over interpreting the relationship's history. The embittered debates in 1995 over how to view the atomic bombings of Hiroshima and Nagasaki fifty years before exemplified how history was manipulated by both Americans and Japanese to justify their own policies past and present.

No one author has examined the entire post-1850s relationship in a single volume for several decades. This book attempts to do that and, in addition, to present a quite different history of the relationship than was provided by the 1995 debates. William Faulkner famously observed that "The past is never dead. It is not even the past."[7] He could have been explaining the clashes between the United States and Japan.

THE CLASH

I

Irresistible Force, Immovable Object

Two Peoples

AMERICANS, as usual, were on the move. "Before him lies a boundless continent, and he surges onward as if time pressed and he was afraid of finding no room for his exertions," wrote the observant French visitor, Alexis de Tocqueville, as he minutely examined the American in the early 1830s. These people "daily quit the spots which gave them birth, to acquire extensive domains in a remote region," he noted with awe. "Millions of men are marching at once towards the same horizon; their language, their religion, their manners differ; their object is the same. Fortune has been promised to them somewhere in the West, and to the West they go to find it."[1]

By 1850, this landed West had largely been claimed by the Americans. A war for conquest against Mexico between 1846 and 1848 brought California and much of the Southwest into the Union. A near war with Great Britain, and then panicked negotiations by U.S. officials, had added the Oregon Territory. Suddenly possessing some of the world's finest harbors on the Pacific Ocean's eastern rim, Americans now looked toward a new West— the islands of the Pacific and the countries of East Asia, where vast populations promised opportunity for trade and profit.

Tocqueville had understood this destiny nearly a generation before the United States occupied the continent's west coast. "The Americans [are] destined by nature to be a great maritime people, . . . They will become, like the English, the commercial agents of a great portion of the world." he wrote. They produced more than they needed, they enjoyed superb ports, and they employed cheaper ships and better sailors than other nations. Moreover, they were already beating the British in Asian trade, especially in a race for the greatest of all Asian markets, China:

> The European navigator touches at different ports in the course of a long voyage; he loses precious time in making the harbor or in waiting for a favorable wind. . . . [But] the American starts from Boston to purchase tea in China; he arrives at Canton, stays there a few days, and then returns. In less than two years he has sailed as far as the entire circumference of the globe and has seen land but once. It is true that during a voyage of eight or ten months he has drunk brackish water and lived on salt meat; that he has been in a continual contest with the sea, with disease, and with weariness, but upon his return he can sell a pound of his tea for a halfpenny less than the English merchant, and his purpose is accomplished.

In all, Tocqueville summarized with both accuracy and sarcasm, Americans "do for cheapness what the French did for conquest"—that is, develop it into a national system. The Frenchman's sketching of the U.S.-China trade was largely accurate, although many ships did stop in California or Hawaii for rest and more trading.[2] Notably, the United States did not open formal diplomatic relations with China until 1844, about a decade after Tocqueville wrote.

After forging this link with China and occupying the west coast springboard, American attention to Asia intensified. New technology, especially the primitive railroads that sped internal commerce to ports, and the beautiful clipper ships that cut sailing time across oceans, further riveted this Far Eastern focus. The British called this region "the Far East." Washington officials continued to use the term, but in the ever-expanding arena of American history, it was clearly more accurate and revealing to think of it as the Far West. A popular American magazine wrote in 1852 that "Twenty years ago the 'far west' was a fixed idea resting upon a fixed extent of territory"; but now U.S. officials had discovered "a 'far west' on the isles of the Japanese Empire and on the shores of China." One editor directly linked the Indians and Japanese:

"The same law of civilization that has compelled the red men . . . to retire before the superior hardihood of our pioneers will require the people of the Japanese empire to abandon their . . . cruelty."[3]

Americans tended to think of Japan and China as two distinct countries linked for U.S. traders in one common opportunity. At first the interest in Japan was not solely for trade, but for using the islands as a way station to the already mystical markets of China. Sailors washed ashore from the wrecks of ships once involved in China trade or the equally lucrative whaling business would be better treated than had their unfortunate predecessors if the Japanese were taught civilized manners. From the beginning of this relationship, Americans saw Japan as part of a giant triangle, with China as the third point. The Japanese came to view the United States and China similarly. This perspective shaped Japanese and U.S. foreign policies for the next 150 years.

By the early 1850s, Tocqueville's "great maritime people" thus were focusing on a civilization profoundly unlike their own. The United States occupied much of the North American continent; Japan was an island nation one-twenty-fifth the size. (In the twentieth century, four of the fifty American states were each larger than Japan.) The American continent held great mineral wealth and natural resources; the Japanese islands were extremely poor except for coal. The United States was about 75 years old; Japan's state could be traced back unbroken over 2,500 years to 660 B.C. when, as history and mythology held, the first emperor, Jimmu Tenno, sat on the throne. Over the centuries, and especially between A.D. 600 and 800, Japan adopted Buddhism, Confucianism, language, and even administrative practices from the great Chinese civilization. Americans adopted Christianity, language, and governmental principles from a Western Europe transformed by the post-1400 Renaissance and Reformation. The Japanese language, while grown from Chinese roots, was extremely difficult to learn, especially in its written form, and related little to other languages; Americans used English, and sometimes German, Italian, Spanish, or variants of French—all related to languages understood over large areas of both the so-called Old and New worlds. The languages revealed a specially divisive characteristic: while Japan's people were homogeneous—less than 1 percent being non-Japanese—the American teemed with peoples from many European, Latin American, African, and, especially after 1860, Asian cultures. In the United States the melting pot had not melted and blurred those cultures, but produced a mosaic of peoples. In Japan, the melting pot never needed to be turned on.[4]

Perhaps, however, an equally great difference between the two peoples in the nineteenth century (and indeed, long after) lay in their views of order and, as a corollary, their views of the role their national governments played in maintaining that order. Tocqueville was amazed at the ever restless, ever-climbing-upward Americans: "All are constantly seeking to acquire property, power, and reputation," but "few contemplate these things on a great scale." The poet Walt Whitman bragged in midcentury that "Yankeedoodledom is going ahead with the resistless energy of a sixty-five-hundred-thousand-horsepower steam engine." Seldom, if ever, was American society more changing, expansive, explosively pluralistic, and open to the different cultures and practices of new immigrants. Americans, indeed, not only rushed westward, but rushed toward civil war.[5]

They were free to follow this headlong pursuit of wealth for a number of reasons. Americans believed they had quite literally been born free— that is, that they were born, or had come to live, in a land free of feudal institutions (guilds, orders, religious and governmental institutions) and other restraints found in Europe after 1200. Lacking a feudal history, Americans wondered why peoples in Europe or Asia were not similarly unrestrained. Moreover, Americans in the mid-nineteenth century ruled a vast land that seemed endlessly open for settlement and exploitation. Several million Indians had stood in the way, but they were being systematically exterminated or contained on reservations. The central government's role in all this was not to regulate, restrain, or harmonize the society, but to release it—to provide the highways, canals, currency policy, tariffs, and military protection required for the expansion of Whitman's "Yankeedoodledom." Midcentury America reveled in the relentless, individualistic, acquisition-for-ascent that Tocqueville had recorded with jaw-dropping wonder.[6]

Japan belonged to a different world. A Japanese "constitution" of 604, attributed to Prince Shotoku, stated in its first article that harmony, above all, was most to be valued. That early—and forever after—Japanese emphasized harmony, or wa, over acquisition-for-ascent. Not that passivity was tolerated. Prince Shotoku's document had as Article VIII: "Let the ministers and functionaries attend the court early in the morning and retire late. The business of the State does not admit remissness, and the whole day is hardly enough for its accomplishments." For more than a thousand years Japanese practiced a strong work ethic. It was an ethic, unlike the American, exercised within feudal institutions that formed during the next twelve hundred years, and over a constricted territory rather than limitless frontiers. Within this space and these institutions, Japanese leaders believed, wa alone held back disorder, anarchy, and destruction.[7]

Not that disorder disappeared. Japanese history is pockmarked by uprisings, riots, and assassinations. In 1942, a *New York Times* reporter entitled a book about Japan *Government by Assassination*. For fifteen years after Japan opened to the West, periodic wars, even civil war, occurred—one reason why then and later leading Japanese linked Western influence and internal disorder. But before and after that era, the Japanese fervently assumed that society and their own happiness advanced on the wheels of consensus and harmony, much as Americans credited their success to openness and acquisition-for-ascent. The Americans liked to say, "The squeaking wheel gets the grease." The Japanese proverb ran, "The nail that sticks up will be hammered down." Long before 1800, officials had discouraged nails from sticking up. As Buddhism grew after its introduction from China in the seventh century, so too did its principles of discipline and mediation. By 1100 a new military class, the *samurai* ("one who serves"), became the right hand of the Shogun, a military ruler living in Edo, the present Tokyo. The Shogun was the center of power. But he and all Japanese swore their allegiance to the Emperor, whose divine origins extended back to Jimmu Tenno, although his actual power—exercised from his throne in the magnificent and isolated city of Kyoto—was mostly ceremonial. The Shogun presided over a system whose key agents were about 260 feudal lords, or *daimyo,* who ruled over provincial centers where Japanese daily life was both focused and governed.[8]

First Encounters with a New West

Propelled outward by the search for gold and Christian converts, and often guided by the technological discoveries of the Renaissance, explorers from a new Western Europe moved across the globe in the early sixteenth century. In 1542, storm-tossed Portuguese sailors landed in southern Kyushu. They carried firearms which Japanese had never seen. Seven years later, Jesuit missionaries appeared; the Japanese allowed them to proselytize. By 1582, the missionaries claimed 150,000 converts, despite considerable language barriers. Suddenly in 1587 the great military ruler Hideyoshi threw out the missionaries. To make his point clear, he crucified both foreign and Japanese Christians. Hideyoshi then tightened his political links with the samurai and undertook a "sword hunt" in which all weapons were seized from everyone except the samurai. Forever after, the holding of firearms by private citizens was considered unacceptable by the society, and one crucial contribution to *wa* was in place.[9]

In 1603 the powerful Tokugawa family began its rule as Shogun, a rule that lasted for two and a half centuries. In 1640, as if by premonition, the Tokugawas decided that *wa* could best be maintained by closing Japan to the West. Any Japanese trying to leave or return to the islands could receive the death penalty. To lessen the temptation further, the Shogun ended all construction of oceangoing ships. Other than selected Asians, only a few Dutch traders were allowed contact, and then only through the artificial island of Deshima, built offshore near Nagasaki. Trade with China did continue, and government-to-government relations developed with Korea. Otherwise the Japanese followed the "closed country" (*sakoku*) policy. A trigger for this rapid closing had been a revolt of 1637–38 led by Japanese Roman Catholics. Trade and Christianity were now defined as disruptive and evil.

As a century of contact with the new Western Europe suddenly stopped, an interesting paradox appeared: the vigorous people of an island nation, surrounded by water and possessing ships comparable to Europe's finest, voluntarily gave up trade routes that already stretched into Southeast Asia and the Indian Ocean, outlawed the making of profit (or the taking of new weapons) from Westerners, and largely closed itself off for the sake of internal peace. This closing off, however, did not mean stagnation. To the contrary: the Tokugawa energetically set about defining an orderly Japanese society as the center of Asia; scholars now see the Tokugawa era as the base of post-1890s, and especially 1930s, Japanese expansion over Asia. As the less civilized Manchus swept over China in the seventeenth century, Japan saw itself as the old China, that is, as Japan-as-central-kingdom. The Tokugawas gave refuge to Chinese scholars, and even set up a form of tribute system in which Korean, Ryukyu, and Dutch envoys paid homage to the Shogun. Japanese self-isolation before the 1850s thus ironically led to a self-definition and identity in the handling of foreign relations that helped propel Japanese expansion over Asia after the 1890s.[10]

The Tokugawa Shogun based his power largely on military capability and control of about one-quarter of the nation's rice crop. Peace was so rampant throughout the land that the samurai, with Tokugawa encouragement, evolved from uneducated, brave warriors into learned and highly competitive bureaucrats. This pillar of post-1868 Japan thus began forming a century earlier. But the bureaucracy and the polity of *sakoku* did not mean a lack of creativity. A flourishing middle-class culture bloomed that produced Kabuki theater, imaginative fashions, influential painters, and lasting poetry. Important parts of this culture were centralized in Nagasaki, where Japanese officials kept track of Western developments through the Dutch traders.[11]

Until 1800, foreign powers all but ignored Japan. The most aggressive and powerful, Great Britain, disdained the tea and silk trade conducted by the Dutch, a trade paltry compared with the British profits from India, the Americas, and parts of Southeast Asia. In 1814, one British official examined the record and flatly declared "that the Trade with Japan can never become an object of attention for the Manufactures and produce of Great Britain." Other foreign warships, however, now cruised Japan's coasts, and the captains were not primarily interested in trade.

Most ominous were the Russians. As they moved across Siberia into the Amur River region and over to Alaska during the eighteenth and early nineteenth centuries, they clashed with fishermen from Japan's northern islands. Both the Kurile Islands and Sakhalin were soon contested by Russians and Japanese. In 1804 the Russian-American Company asked officials at Nagasaki for permission to trade with Japan so the company could supply the expanding Russian settlements to the north. The Japanese flatly rejected the request. The Russians decided during 1806–07 to teach the Tokugawa a lesson by raiding villages in the northern islands. The Japanese did not back down. Instead, they captured a Russian official in 1811 and held him for two years until the tsar's officials finally apologized for the raids. Meanwhile, Japanese writers began to warn that Russia posed the major threat to their country's security. By the 1840s and 1850s, this feeling grew intense as Japan watched the Europeans exploit China. After Great Britain's victory over China in the 1840–42 Opium War, a war that unsettled much of the Pacific's western rim, the powers scrambled for concessions. The Russians dispatched Rear Admiral Evfimii Putiatin in 1842–43 to open trade with Japan, but Japanese resistance and the trade's skimpy rewards led Putiatin to put his considerable talents to work elsewhere. Ten years later, Putiatin was again ordered to open Japan. When he entered Nagasaki Harbor in August 1853, he found he was too late. The Americans had sailed into the bay at Edo two weeks earlier.[12]

The Appearance of the Americans

These visitors had been propelled across the Pacific by their national credo of "manifest destiny," their growing desire to conquer Asian markets, and—paradoxically—a fear of deepening internal crisis. The slogan of "manifest destiny" had appeared in a feverishly expansionist Democratic Party newspaper in 1845 that demanded the conquering of Oregon, even if it meant war with Great Britain which also claimed the territory. The slogan came to mean that Americans ("with the calm confidence of a Christian holding 4 aces," as frontier writer Mark Twain later phrased it) believed they had God-given rights to spread both their new political institutions and successful commerce across the continent, then into Latin America, and to uplift, among others, the benighted Europeans and Asians.

Driven by principle, Americans aimed also to gain profits. God and Mammon, the larger purpose and the individual's earthly success, were seldom far apart in mainstream American society. (In Japan, to the contrary, when a larger purpose—a Japanese manifest destiny—did emerge, it was seldom confused with individual acquisition.)

Between 1790 and 1853 at least twenty-seven U.S. ships (including three warships) visited Japan, only to be turned away. In 1832, as part of his epochal navigation of the Pacific, Edmund Roberts received orders from the Andrew Jackson administration to make a treaty with Japan, but he died before reaching the islands. Five years later, the *Morrison,* owned by Americans in Canton, tried to enter Japan with the excuse that it was returning shipwrecked Japanese sailors. The crew, however, hoped to Christianize Japanese as well as "trade a little." When shore cannon opened fire, the *Morrison* beat it back to China. In 1846, Commodore James Biddle, head of the newly created U.S. East Asia squadron, carried on heated talks with Japanese officials near Tokyo Bay, only to have them emphasize they had no interest in trading with him and that he need not try a second time. To demonstrate their point, when Biddle tried to force his way onto a Japanese ship a crew member knocked him down.[13]

Meanwhile U.S. whaling vessels worked the rich Japanese coastal waters and often (as in 1848) forced their shipwrecked sailors on the unkind mercies of Japanese villagers. Whaling became a metaphor for the American crossing of the last great frontier of the Pacific, and the hubris that compelled individuals to challenge those frontiers, when Herman Melville published *Moby-Dick* in 1851. (Later, when Commodore Matthew C. Perry wanted a writer to tell the story of how he opened Japan to the West, Nathaniel Hawthorne recommended Melville. Some 140 years later, Melville's work shaped both United States and Japanese literary studies.)[14]

Japan moved into still sharper focus after 1840 when Shanghai was opened to trade. U.S. ship captains followed the shorter way from California to Shanghai via the north circle route that brought them close to Japan. The 1846–48 conquests of California ports, along with an accelerating industrial and agricultural economic revolution, opened a historic opportunity—but also a potential trap. The opportunity was noted by Secretary of the Treasury Robert Walker in 1848: "By our recent acquisitions in the Pacific, Asia has suddenly become our neighbor, with a placid intervening ocean inviting our steamships upon the track of a commerce greater than that of all Europe combined." In 1851, *Hunt's Merchant Magazine* warned that U.S. production was already furnishing "us with a potential danger: constantly augmenting capital that must seek for new channels of employment." The showdown, *Hunt's* believed, would be against the equally aggressive British and result, happily, in American control of "the whole Oriental trade."[15]

But manifest destiny had its dark side. As vast new territory was rapidly annexed, bitter debate erupted between a pro-slave South and anti-slave North over which section would control the newly conquered West and its ports. When Congress passed the Compromise of 1850, the problem seemed resolved. But many, including Secretary of State Daniel Webster, feared the crisis had been only papered over. In 1850–51, Webster even resorted to blowing up a very minor problem with Austria into a diplomatic crisis so, as he later admitted, he could take American minds off internal dangers and put them on less divisive foreign problems. Webster, moreover, had long been a leader of the Whig Party, whose most powerful members included large mercantile houses deeply involved in international trade. During earlier debates over whether to annex Texas, Webster caught Whig foreign policy priorities perfectly when he proclaimed that one San Francisco was worth twenty Texases. Using U.S. ports as the springboards to Asia became a Websterian principle. As Secretary of State in 1843, he had written the instructions that led to the first U.S. trade treaty with China in 1844. In 1842, moreover, he had penned a declaration, duly announced by President John Tyler, that Hawaii was to be treated by other powers as a special U.S. reserve. Webster was creating the first American policy for the Pacific and China. Japan was next.[16]

In May 1851, Webster heard from Captain John H. Aulick, who was to take command of the East Asia squadron, that the return of seventeen shipwrecked Japanese then in San Francisco might provide the opportunity for "opening commercial relations with Japan." The Secretary of State put Aulick in charge of the mission. Captain James Glynn, an experienced Asian hand, gave President Millard Fillmore and Aulick good advice: do not treat Japanese "as being less civilized than ourselves," do not get into arguments over treatment of U.S. sailors, and do focus only on obtaining a trade treaty. Moreover, Glynn shrewdly added, do not ask for exclusive U.S. privileges, but for access to Japan for all nations. Thus the powerful British will have reason to support, rather than oppose, the American demands.[17]

On May 10, 1851, Webster drafted a letter from President Fillmore to the Japanese Emperor. Assuring the Emperor that Aulick was on no religious enterprise, the letter asked for "friendship and commerce," as well as help (especially coal) for ships that used the northern route to China. Of special interest, Webster's draft of the note emphasized recent U.S. triumphs on land and in technology:

> You know [Fillmore told the Emperor] that the United States of America now extend from sea to sea; that the great countries of Oregon & California are parts of the United States; and that from these countries, which are rich in gold & silver & precious stones, our steamers can reach the shores of your happy land in less than twenty days. . . .
>
> [These ships] must pass along the Coast of your Empire; storms & winds may cause them to be wrecked on your shores, and we ask & expect from your kindness & your greatness, kindness for our men. . . . We wish that our people may be permitted to trade with your people, but we shall not authorize them to break any laws of your Empire. . . .
>
> Your Empire has a great abundance of coal; this is an article which our Steamships, in going from California to China, must use.

Or, as Webster phrased it to Aulick, "The moment is near, when the last link in the chain of oceanic steam-navigation is to be formed," and "our enterprising merchants [should] supply [that] last link in that great chain, which unites all nations of the world." Such a dream propelled many powerful Americans westward across the Pacific after as well as before 1900.[18]

The opening of Japan thus resulted from both the U.S. quest for China's trade and the technological breakthroughs (especially steam) of the 1840s. Japan, as Webster nicely phrased it to a friend, was the key because God had placed coal "in the depths of the Japanese islands for the benefit of the human family." Aulick, however, fumbled his chance to become famous. Charged with mistreating a Brazilian diplomat, Aulick was replaced by Fillmore with Commodore Matthew C. Perry. The commodore initially protested: he preferred commanding the U.S. Mediterranean squadron instead of trying to make yet another attempt to open Japan. Born in Rhode Island in 1794, Perry had served in the War of 1812 under his famous brother, Oliver Hazard Perry (who after one battle in 1813, issued the succinct, soon-to-be-famous announcement: "We have met the enemy, and they are ours"). By 1837 Matthew had risen through the ranks and commanded one of the first U.S. steam warships. During the Mexican War he won some fame for helping to conquer Vera Cruz.

After overcoming his reluctance to become Webster's battering ram against Japan, Perry prepared thoroughly. He especially carried on extensive talks with business figures interested in Asian trade. The commodore also demanded greater latitude in his orders from Webster, a demand the Secretary of State granted just before his death in October 1852. Perry sailed for Japan with "full and discretionary powers," in Webster's words, but the commodore was to "be held to a strict responsibility" for his actions. The "discretionary powers" included possible use of force if the Japanese tried to treat him as they had the unfortunate Commodore Biddle.[19]

Perry's four ships, the *Susquehanna, Mississippi* (both the new steam type), *Plymouth,* and *Saratoga,* took the long traditional route along the Atlantic, around the Cape of Good Hope, through the Indian Ocean, then to Singapore, Hong Kong, and Shanghai, before approaching Japan. Then they returned briefly to the China coast and, finally, moved into Edo (Tokyo) Bay on July 8, 1853. The Dutch had warned the Shogun's government, the *bakufu,* that Americans were coming, but the Japanese were nevertheless surprised that Perry appeared so soon. Their surprise mounted when the commodore ignored low-level officials and insisted—pointedly as he stood beneath the cannons of his warship—on dealing only with *bugyo* (that is, someone given specific powers directly by the Shogun). Their surprise changed into near horror when they further learned that President Fillmore's letter was addressed to the Emperor as if Emperor Komei were a mere equal. The stunned *bakufu* decided to play for time by sending two *bugyo* to accept the letter on July 14. They also used their women to appease and distract the powerful. One U.S. officer recorded that "the inhabitants . . . by the most unmistakable signs invited our intercourse with their women." As the historian Ian Buruma explains, "The Americans had guns, the Japanese lifted their skirts." (A similar drama would be played out in late 1945.) Despite the diversion, Perry rightly feared that the Japanese might stall until he ran short of water and provisions; he would then have to sail away in disgrace. The commodore therefore declared he was departing for China, but promised to return a year later—with force—to receive the Japanese response.[20]

The next move was up to Abe Masahiro, leader of the Shogun's council. A *daimyo* (and hence known and trusted by most other powerful lords of these more than one hundred fiefdoms), Abe was a gentle, well-liked man so shrewd that he had entered the council at age twenty-four in 1843. A politician who sometimes bent too easily and quickly to prevailing political winds, he carefully sounded out the *daimyo* about the proper response to Perry. These men divided. Some knew nothing of dangerous international situations in the western Pacific. But all seemed to agree that under no circumstances could Japan open its empire to foreign traders; their goods would upset the nation's internal order. But how to inform Perry of this when he returned with his warships? Some of the more powerful *daimyo* advised stalling while the *bakufu* built a modern military to deal with the commodore on Japanese terms. A number, indeed, were willing to go to war with the United States—after proper preparations.

These *daimyo* demonstrated a fascinating confidence that Japan could quickly match the West's military technology, as well as perhaps profit from that technology in international trade. ("We have reason to believe that the Americans and Russians have recently learned the art of navigation," a typically confident *daimyo* told Abe; "in what way would the keen and wise men of our empire appear inferior to the Westerners if they got into training from today?") Abe knew that the West, most immediately Perry, would not give Japan the needed time. Any doubt of that disappeared when Admiral Putiatin again led his four Russian ships into Nagasaki harbor just after Perry left Edo. The convenient death of the Shogun gave Abe an excuse to put off Putiatin's demands for a treaty. At the same time, however, Abe removed a two-century rule against building large ships and named an admiral of the new Shogun's navy. A different Japan was beginning to stir.[21]

Putiatin finally departed just before Perry reappeared on February 24, 1854. This time he brought seven impressive ships and sailed straight into sight of Edo—before the edgy Japanese talked him into moving some forty-five miles west to Kanagawa. As the *bakufu* examined the commodore's demands, the two sides demonstrated their friendship by exchanging gifts. Perry's legendary gifts included a telegraph machine, books, maps, and a miniature steam train that the Japanese delighted in operating. On the last day of March 1854, Perry and the Japanese signed a treaty of Kanagawa that contained a dozen provisions. The first promised eternal peace between Japan and America. Another clause opened to U.S. vessels two ports, Shimoda and Hakodate, where shipwrecked sailors could also be taken in. Americans could move around within a roughly fifty-mile radius of these two ports.

The *bakufu* agreed to accept a U.S. consul in Japan. But—pointedly— nothing was stated explicitly about trade. Allowing entry into Japan's market was so complex, the Shogun's officials told Perry, that a decision required a great deal of time. The Japanese, in other words, had no intention of following the downhill slide of China into dependency on the wishes and products of foreigners.[22]

After two centuries of dealing only with the Dutch, the 250-year-old Tokugawa Shogunate opened itself—carefully, narrowly, and fearfully— to the recently born United States. In late 1854, the British, Russians, and Dutch issued successful demands for access to ports that would allow them to match Perry's victory. Again, however, the Europeans received no trading rights. (When Putiatin had to build a vessel to replace one of his Russian warships damaged at sea, the Japanese watched intently and soon afterward produced an exact copy.) The news of Perry's success reached the United States via the *Saratoga,* which made the fastest trip yet between Japan and America. The *New York Times* bragged that the United States had opened Japan to the West, and upstaged the Europeans as well, by using "peaceful diplomacy, to overcome obstacles hitherto considered insurmountable," despite "the sneers, the ridicule, and the contempt" of shortsighted European and American newspapers.[23]

The *Times,* however, was also puzzled. The Japanese "seemed remarkably conversant with the affairs of the United States—knew all about the Mexican War, its occasion and results." Quite true. Even when Perry felt, in the words of a later historian, "like a combination Santa Claus and conjurer" as he demonstrated the toy railroad, the Japanese actually knew all about railways from the *Illustrated London News,* to which the Shogun himself regularly subscribed.[24]

More important, the Japanese had kept up with American affairs since 1797 when officials discovered that the Dutch, short of their own ships, were sneaking U.S. vessels into Nagasaki under the Dutch flag. The Shogunate demanded information about these Americans. The Dutch responded with history lessons that featured the revolt against the British in 1776 (because, the Dutch emphasized, of cruel treatment by the British), the 1787 Constitution, the great George Washington ("a very capable general" whose name has been given to "a new city"), and Thomas Jefferson. The Dutch had supported the new nation in the 1770s, so the Shogun heard a pro-American version of the history. By the 1840s, Japanese used the Dutch to acquire good world geographies, as well as histories, and exploited their contacts with China, where U.S. missionaries were publishing material, to obtain fresh information.

Then, too, a few Japanese who had lived in the United States returned home and, as one reported in 1851, announced that Americans were "lewd by nature, but otherwise well-behaved." Japan might have chosen isolation, but its people, including peasants, were about as well educated as the British (and more so than the general French population), and in reality they were not isolated. By 1839 one group of intellectuals was so active in learning from the Dutch and spreading the information that several committed suicide fearing their activities embarrassed their *daimyo* master in the eyes of the Shogun.[25]

The tension illustrated by these suicides—the tension created between the seeking of outside news to protect Japan, yet the fear that spreading of such foreign influence could create disorder, perhaps civil war—shaped the background that foreigners such as Perry never understood. For two centuries, after all, the Tokugawa Shogun had assumed that the tightest relationship existed between foreign and domestic policies. The government had announced, on the basis of its bitter sixteenth-century experience, that Japan's survival and the maintenance of internal order required cutting off the inherently disorderly—and usually uncontrollable—affairs of the outside world. A powerful and influential argument was made by a scholar from the domain of Mito, two days travel from Edo. In 1825, Aizawa Seishisai wrote *New Proposals* (*Shinron*). His work had been triggered by a Shogunate decree that again, to Aizawa's great satisfaction, banned foreign ships. Aizawa warned that Japanese weakness "for novel gadgets" could "lure ignorant people" to the spell of "treacherous foreigners." The result, he concluded, would be the internal corruption and decay of Japanese society, or outright foreign conquest.[26]

Aizawa had reason to worry. Not only were foreigners trying to penetrate Japan. Of equal importance, his own domain of Mito had long suffered from low agricultural production, natural disasters, and increased taxation. Famine and revolt threatened to spread. After 1750 especially, these economic problems, including natural disasters, forced the Shogun (who was living beyond his means anyway) to tax and borrow. The *daimyo* did the same, and thus the peasants and samurai paid and suffered even more exploitation. A new merchant class (*chonin*) meanwhile arose to provide goods for the nation's growing population— and also make loans to the once-proud samurai. The *chonin* began to break apart the feudal restrictions on trade, land transfer, and certain kinds of new production. Mito's changes and unrest encapsulated only a small case study of immense Japanese social problems by 1850. The samurai, for example, became dissatisfied and restless as the Shogun turned them into bureaucrats. *Chonin* also grew restless; they wanted to rupture the feudal restraints of the *daimyo*. Thus even as Americans, Russians, and British approached from the outside, Tokugawa rule was being internally undermined by spreading frustrations as well as by a rising price inflation caused in part by the Shogun's own over-spending.[27]

An intense debate was therefore erupting just as Perry demanded entrance. By the mid-1850s, his appearance helped turn a central part of that debate into the highly dangerous question of how Japan must change in order to deal with "the barbarians." The shock of Perry's timing and success, moreover, transformed a once-restricted discussion into an explosive public argument. The political stakes rose dramatically as several fiefs that had never been fully controlled by the Shogun or the *bakufu* seized on the debate to challenge the *bakufu* and try to solve their growing economic crises by transforming themselves to make their own domains more efficient. The Shogunate began to endure exactly what it had long feared: opening Japan to foreign influences was helping undermine Tokugawa rule and destroying social harmony.

Harris's Triumphs, Ii's Assassination

The clash between Japanese and American systems therefore occurred initially not in Manchuria in 1910, or China in the 1930s, or the international market of the 1980s. The clash came with the first appearance of Americans in Edo Bay during 1853–54. The Tokugawa rule had long been under attack. The Americans did not cause these fundamental economic and social problems that struck Japan, but they accelerated the problems and, of special note, created a new and more dangerous political environment in which the *bakufu* had to deal with the crises. For nothing less was happening than an assault on a centuries-old feudal structure that many Japanese assumed to be fundamental for their own happiness. Americans were the cutting edge of a new world, a world that had little use for feudal order; a world that valued social harmony less than individual acquisition; and a world that (unlike the Shogun's) saw its survival resting not on exclusion, but on a manifest destiny that required the opening of ports and markets everywhere.[28]

Abe found himself trying to steer a weakening Japan around a radical turn in its history. He had to steer, moreover, as competing groups grabbed for control. On one side was the Shogun Iesada (1853–58) who, out of a sense for survival, wanted to exclude the Americans while

building up military power at home. (The term *Shogūn* could be translated as "barbarian-fighting general.") He was supported by his only
superior, Emperor Komei (who ruled in 1846–67). Komei's ardent xenophobia merely moderated in the 1860s. On the other side were Ii Naosuke, a tough, powerful *daimyo* of Hikone, and Hotta Masayoshi,
daimyo of Shimoda. They believed that increased contacts, even treaties, with foreigners were inevitable, so should be turned to advantage.
Amid this power struggle, another more serious fight intensified: outlying areas, especially Choshu, in the extreme west, and Satsuma, in the
far south, had never been fully integrated into Tokugawa Japan. Led by
Choshu, these areas began a major assault on the weakened *bakufu*'s
powers. The challenges to the central government were supported by
some intellectuals and political activists who saw the American Revolution as exemplifying the kind of radical change needed to replace the
decaying Shogunate. Many of these writers wished to work with the
Americans. But some (like Nakaoka Shintaro) thought the 1776 Revolution simply a splendid example of how to expel foreigners.[29]

Abe and the Shogun thus not only had to deal with the Westerners
but to develop a policy that stood the beliefs of two centuries on their
head—that is, deal with foreigners without bringing about a war while
reconciling the internal debates and facing down the Choshu-Satsuma
challenge. All of this suddenly came to a head on August 21, 1856,
when a U.S. consul, Townsend Harris, appeared at Shimoda. Harris
announced that the Japanese must now sign a trade agreement with
the United States.

The bland failures of Harris's previous fifty-three years of life gave
no hint that he would succeed in opening Japan to trade after the
world's leading empires had failed. With little formal schooling, he had
risen in New York City business circles and even persuaded the city's
Board of Education to establish a school for poor boys that later became
City College of New York. In 1848, however, his mother died, his china-
importing company began to lose money, and he apparently was drinking heavily. Never married, he had few ties left in New York, so Harris
invested in a ship that took him to the Philippines, India, and China's
open ports. As his business prospects darkened, he asked for a U.S.
consul's job at Hong Kong or Canton, then requested that he be allowed
to join the Perry mission. Harris received none of these appointments.
Although he was finally offered the consul's position at the backwater
port of Ningpo, Harris turned down its pitiful salary. At this point, he
heard about the possible consul's job at Shimoda. Backed by New York
friends, but hounded by stories of his drinking, he decided to take the

long journey back to convince President Franklin Pierce of his abilities and sobriety. Harris won the appointment, left in October 1855, and arrived in Japan ten months later. On the way, he had finally renegotiated a trade treaty with Siam that left him tired and bitter ("the proper way to negotiate with the Siamese," he concluded, "is to send two or three men-of-war").[30]

Harris was thus no innocent as he approached Shimoda. "I have a perfect knowledge of the social banishment I must endure while in Japan," he had written Pierce, "and the mental isolation in which I must live. . . . I am a single man, without any ties to cause me to look anxiously to my home, or to become impatient in my new one." But not even Harris was prepared for the next fourteen months. As he stepped off the U.S. warship, the *San Jacinto,* that brought him from China, Harris realized that Shimoda, a small, isolated town, had no housing for him. Local officials who greeted him with surprise told him they understood the 1854 treaty provided for a U.S. consul only if both nations wanted one—and Japan decidedly did not. When Harris insisted on staying, the officials put him and his translator, Henry C. J. Heusken, a Dutch American hired in New York, in a broken-down temple five miles from town. "Bats in rooms. See enormous tête de mort spider; the legs extended five and a half inches as the insect stood," Harris recorded. "Unpleasant discovery of large rats in numbers, running about the house."

He came both to appreciate and be befuddled by the Japanese. They "are a *clean* people. Everyone bathes every day," Harris wrote admiringly. But poorer classes "of both sexes, old and young, enter the same bathroom and there perform their ablutions in a state of perfect nudity. I cannot account for so indelicate a proceeding on the part of a people so generally correct." Harris was partially reassured only when Japanese friends told him that "the chastity of their females" was protected by "this very exposure [that] lessens the desire that owes much of its power to mystery and difficulty." Plagued, as he admitted, by too much smoking and exotic food, Harris quit smoking, took long walks, and learned to appreciate the wild game the Japanese began to bring to him. Heusken, who refused to stop smoking, grew increasingly prickly.[31]

But Harris's central problem was somehow to reach the Shogun's officials who could make decisions. Stalling, the Japanese told him that Edo was too distant for him to visit. At one point, believing he was being lied to by officials and spied on by servants, he shook the Japanese by picking up a stove (*hibachi*) and flinging it against the wall. According to legend, Shimoda officials appeased Harris by giving him a geisha named Okichi-san as a mistress. Heusken also supposedly received a mistress. Stories passed down relate that Okichi was then shunned by her own people for living intimately with a white man. She took to drinking and finally drowned herself. Nothing in official records supports these accounts, but Okichi's birthplace in Shimoda became a tourist attraction, at least five plays were written about her, and in 1958 Hollywood immortalized her in the film *The Barbarian and the Geisha.*[32]

Whether Okichi was a reason or not, Harris grew to admire the Japanese. "I do not think the world contains a people so truly frugal and plain in matters of diet and dress as the Japanese" he wrote in early 1857. "No jewelry is ever seen on a man. . . . They are a people of but few wants." Admiration, however, led to no diplomatic breakthroughs. Those came from Harris's stubbornness, Japanese internal divisions, and the *bakufu's* sound information that British warships were again blasting China open in 1857 and when finished might well use their cannon to impose ugly trade terms on Japan. Harris's arrival had driven even deeper fissures between those Japanese who wanted to stall the foreigners and others who believed that the best possible deal should be made—while quickly copying the West's weaponry.[33]

The key official who was to deal with Harris belonged to the second camp. Hotta Masayoshi, soon to be the most powerful member of the *bakufu,* was also one of the more moderate. Hotta had somehow gained extensive knowledge of "Dutch studies"—that is, events in the West. He wrote later in 1857 that "military power always springs from national wealth," and that such wealth could be found "principally in trade and commerce." Japan consequently had "to conclude friendly alliances . . . send ships to foreign countries everywhere and . . . copy the foreigners where they are at their best and so repair our own shortcomings." By March 1857, Hotta's approach led to the first substantive talks with Harris. The consul was plagued by cholera, little medical help, no news from U.S. ships on the China coast, and no assistance whatever from Washington. He nevertheless warned the Shimoda officials that he had been instructed to tell them that if they continued to delay, the President would ask Congress for the authority to use "arguments . . . they [the Japanese] could not resist." In June, Harris excitedly recorded that he had broken through. Shimoda officials agreed to a convention that opened Nagasaki to U.S. ships, allowed American residency and a vice consul at Hakodate, enabled Harris to move around Japan more freely, and settled the exchange rate for Japanese money at a more favorable level. But this agreement only prepared the way for the most difficult step: traveling to Edo and negotiating a full trade treaty with Hotta.[34]

In November 1857, Harris and Heusken approached Edo in a spectacular caravan that aimed to convince all onlookers that Americans were not to be trifled with. Made up of 250 persons, including 12 guardsmen, two standard-bearers, two shoe and fan carriers, two grooms, 40 porters carrying Harris's luggage and household goods, and 20 bearers of the sedan chairs on which Harris and Heusken rode, the procession finally entered Edo on November 30. Always sharply aware of his possible place in history, the consul wrote that the entry "will form an important epoch in my life, and a still more important one" for the Japanese, for "I have forced this singular people to acknowledge the *rights of embassy*"—formal diplomatic relations with the United States.[35]

On December 7, 1857, Harris had a brief, formal, historic meeting with the Shogun, who expressed pleasure with the consul's presence and declared, according to the interpreter, that "intercourse shall be continued forever." But detailed talks with officials on December 12 turned frustrating. Harris notably opened them by explaining two of the beliefs that drove U.S. policy, then and since: because of the technological breakthrough (of steam locomotion), "Japan would be forced to abandon her exclusive policy"; her wealth and happiness would grow most rapidly "when developed by the action of free trade." Otherwise the powers would "send powerful fleets" to force Japan open. Hotta thanked Harris for the thoughts, then added "that the Japanese never acted as promptly on business of importance as the Americans" because "many persons had to be consulted." Weeks dragged by. Harris began to complain that Heusken could not solve the mysteries of the Japanese language: it "does not possess either singular or plural, has no relative pronoun, nor is the use of the antecedent known. . . . I never shall get to the bottom of the deceptions of the Japanese." (Later observers also helped explain Harris's frustration by noting that, having considerable mistrust of verbal skills, a Japanese preferred to communicate feeling indirectly and even without language. If these signals were communicated, the receiver, not the sender, was blamed for lacking sensitivity and intelligence if they were not picked up.)[36]

Finally in March 1858, agreement was nearly complete, a result of Hotta's influence and ominous British and French warmaking in China, when again Japanese internal divisions stalled the talks. In June, Hotta carried the day. The treaty, signed initially on July 29, 1858, opened five ports to trade between then and 1863, including Nagasaki and Kanagawa (later Yokohama); allowed foreigners into Osaka and Edo; permitted a resident minister in Edo and a Japanese minister in Washington with each country's consuls at the other's open ports; protected Americans through extraterritoriality (that is, they would be tried only in American courts); and imposed an import and export tariff that was fixed extremely low so the Japanese could not manipulate it to keep out foreign goods. Americans could enjoy freedom of religion as well as own land for business, residential, and even religious purposes. (Later, in 1859, Harris tried to obtain a provision guaranteeing religious freedom for the Japanese themselves, but the *bakufu* quickly rejected it.) Oddly, one of the great U.S. diplomatic principles, that of most-favored-nation—that any trading rights Japan gave to one nation automatically went to others—was not included. (This omission was remedied in August when the British, using Harris's secretary and treaty, opened trade relations with Japan and obtained most-favored-nation rights.)

Of special significance was a provision in Article III:

> Americans may freely buy from Japanese and sell to them any articles that either may have for sale, without the intervention of any Japanese officers in such purchase or sale.

Not for the last time, Americans, with deep suspicions about state power, tried to remove that power as much as possible in their commerce with Japan. They enjoyed little success in this attempt. Nor could they become involved in Japan's internal commerce, for foreign traders were mostly confined to a residential area near the ports.

The Dutch and Russians as well as the British followed Harris into the Japanese market during August 1858. The American, meanwhile, followed up his triumph by having a physical breakdown that had been building since August 1856. Delirious for days, he was probably saved because the Shogun ordered Japan's best physicians to attend him. Harris nevertheless had his historic treaty and even a letter for President James Buchanan from the Shogun, the first letter sent by a Shogun to a foreign leader in 240 years.[37]

Harris knew his demands had divided the *bakufu*, but he did not realize he was helping to destroy the 250-year-old Tokugawa rule itself. For his demands, coupled with the growing internal unrest, had led to a crisis and Hotta's removal in June 1858. He was replaced by Ii Naosuke (1815–1860), a powerful *daimyo* of Hikone. Tough, determined, relentless, Ii became a virtual dictator of the *bakufu*. Assuming power in mid-1858, he discovered that the Emperor, sitting in his majesty at Kyoto, feared the proposed treaty. "The American affair is a great sorrow to our divine land," he had told Hotta. The treaty "would disturb the ideas of our people and make it impossible to preserve lasting tranquillity." Many *daimyo* sided with the Emperor. But most of them, Ii learned, believed the treaty to be inevitable. The alternative of war with the Western powers was unthinkable.[38]

Ii, moreover, heard in July 1858 that British and French warships had finished their work in China and might be heading for Japan. He decided therefore to sign the treaty with Harris in July. The Emperor had not changed his mind, but he reluctantly went along out of fear that the Westerners would play on the divisions between his court in Kyoto and the Shogun in Edo. The rebels who hoped to keep out the "hairy barbarians" and weaken the Shogun never forgave Ii for easing the foreigners' entry into Japan. On March 3, 1860, eighteen samurai from the rebellious *daimyo* at Mito, assisted by Shinto priests, attacked Ii outside the Imperial Palace. Because it was raining, Ii's sixty guards had covered their sword hilts. Before they could uncover their swords, Ii lay dead and four guards were dying. The attackers were killed or captured, but the death of the decisive Ii left a power vacuum that soon proved fatal for the Shogun himself. Harris's treaty was already casting long shadows.[39]

The Americans and the Birth of Modern Japan

On February 13, 1860, after many postponements, a Japanese diplomatic mission of seventy-seven persons left on a U.S. warship for Washington where formal ratifications of the treaty were to be exchanged. It was the first such trip anywhere by a Japanese diplomatic delegation of this size after two hundred years of seclusion. The trip was difficult. Few Japanese cared to speak English—too difficult—and so spoke only Dutch other than their native language. Not many Americans knew Dutch. The mission included spies who reported on other members. U.S. sailors found soy sauce and fish foul-smelling and so threw out most of the Japanese food, forcing the diplomats to eat meat, cheese, and bread, which they hated.

The high point of the mission's visit was its arrival on June 16 in New York Harbor. In November 1858, the *New York Times* had carried an account from a reporter traveling with Harris who had seen a Japanese steamer. He asked his readers "to stop here a moment, reflect upon the strangeness of such a thing." Such a steamer had not existed when

Perry arrived five years earlier. Now this state-of-the-art vessel not only existed, it "could capture any Portuguese man-of-war of her class." In 1860, the *Times* did not yet want to say that a new era had opened between "Western Christendom" and the "heathen East." But this "England of the Pacific," as Japan was now commonly called, could nevertheless cause a spectacle even in New York City where tens of thousands went on holiday to welcome the stolid visiting diplomats. The *Times* nicely added, moreover, that it was only fitting that the trip climax in New York, rather than in "more provincial cities [that is, Washington] through which they have been dragged as a kind of vulgar show." For New York, after all, "represents the full grandeur of that mighty American commerce," which had beaten the military of the "more arrogant powers" in opening "the hitherto impregnable East."[40]

A more exalted and memorable response came from Walt Whitman, a New Yorker who had come to see the growing U.S.-Asia ties in mystical terms, yet with words that nicely captured central themes of U.S. diplomacy. The *New York Times* published his long poem, "The Errand-Bearers," on June 27, 1860, to commemorate the Japanese delegation's visit:

Superb-faced Manhattan,
Comrade Americanos—to us, then, at last, the Orient comes. . . .

The Originatress comes. . . .
Florid with blood, pensive, rapt with musing, hot with passion,
Sultry with perfume, with ample and flowing garments. . . .

I, too, raising my voice, bear an errand,
I chant the World on my Western Sea. . . .
I chant the new empire, grander than any before—As in a vision it comes
    to me:
I chant America, the Mistress—I chant a greater supremacy. . . .
I chant commerce opening, the sleep of ages have done its work—races,
    reborn, refreshed.

The Japanese were not as happy with the moment as was Whitman. Americans often shouted insults, as in Philadelphia where one cried out to a U.S. naval officer, ". . . is that your monkey you have got with you?" The puritanical, male-dominated Japanese were notably stunned by American women, who, as one of the mission noted during a dance, "were nude from shoulders to arms. . . . The way men and women, both young and old, mixed in the dance, was simply insufferable to watch." One Japanese compared American couples to "butterflies crazed by the sight of flowers," especially when the men actually gave their chairs to women.[41]

Whitman's "new empire" nevertheless seemed to be booming by 1860. As Perry and Harris opened Japan to Western trade, Lieutenant John Rodgers led a U.S. survey expedition through the waters surrounding Japan and along China's coasts between 1853 and 1856. After thoroughly investigating this Great Circle route, Rodgers concluded that the "commercial possibilities [of Asia] are so vast as to dazzle sober calculation." At the same time, American merchants and the U.S. minister to China pushed Washington to seize Taiwan, both as a strategic base and as leverage with which to beat down Chinese opposition to Western trade. In 1854 to 1860, Russia began to discuss the sale of its Alaska territory to the Americans. The U.S. Civil War stalled the talks until 1867, when the Russians recognized the reality—Americans already controlled the commerce around the region—and sold Alaska for $7.2 million. Holding Alaska and with formal entry into Japan, the United States grabbed a secure hold on the Great Circle route to Asia's markets.[42]

But Japan itself seemed much less secure. Ii's murder in 1860 occurred in a wave of assassinations that finally washed over foreigners. Harris noted that gangs of Japanese roamed the streets at night; seven killings of Westerners occurred in eighteen months. Many of these murders were done by the hands of *ronin,* that is, samurai who had broken loyalty to their *daimyo* and now, in a Japan coming apart, committed crimes from political or economic motives. In January 1861, Heusken, Harris's translator, was killed when he made the mistake of walking home from the Prussian legation in the dark. The foreign diplomats demanded retribution, as did U.S. Secretary of State William H. Seward, just newly appointed by President Abraham Lincoln. But Harris successfully held out against any retaliation. He instead blamed Heusken, who "should have known better" than to be on foot after dark. The consul quieted the issue by accepting a $10,000 indemnity from the *bakufu* for Heusken's mother, an amount one-tenth the indemnity the British collected after one of their officials was murdered by Satsuma samurai. Harris doggedly remained in Edo even when the other diplomats left after the British legation was attacked and burned in 1862.[43]

Much as the Emperor had feared, the West's intrusions were undermining Japanese order. Foreigners bought up Japanese gold coins and resold them in China at great profit. When the *bakufu* threatened to stop the traffic, Western officials threatened war. The *bakufu* therefore minted cheaper coins, debased the money, and triggered rapid inflation that devastated the mass of Japanese. Foreign demand for tea and silk pushed up prices for Japan's people. The Shogun's sudden desire for Western arms, and the reparations the *bakufu* had to pay the West for the murders of the foreigners, drained the country of good money. The view that the Shogun was becoming a mere frontman for the Westerners, mistaken as it was, fatally infected the *bakufu*'s legitimacy. Japan's first extensive contact with the West was turning into a catastrophe.[44]

Worn down, Harris returned finally to a United States, itself torn by civil war, in 1862. He was thus not present to soften the crisis that erupted between the Westerners and the Tokugawa regime in 1863–64—a crisis that led to bloodshed. By 1863, the Shogun's policy of reluctantly agreeing to the foreigners' demands had created a loose alliance of various *daimyo* at the Emperor's court in Kyoto. The alliance was led by the distant clans of Choshu and Satsuma. The group aimed at undermining the Shogun's power and driving out the foreigners. The objectives were two sides of the same policy. As the Shogun's government in Edo weakened, the *ronin* became more vicious and the distant *daimyo* more daring. On May 24, 1863, the U.S. legation in Edo was gutted by fire. The new U.S. minister, Robert H. Pruyn (an Albany Republican politician who had taken the post at the begging of his close friend, Secretary of State Seward), wanted to believe the fire was accidental; yet, after all, "repeated attempts have been made to induce me to leave." Then word circulated that the embattled *bakufu* was about to go back on its agreements, close the ports, and regain its power by moving decisively against the foreigners. Pruyn's response was direct: "Even to propose such a measure is an insult to my country and equivalent to a declaration of war." The Edo government strongly denied any idea of going back on its commitments, but it was clear that the Shogun was losing control.[45]

On June 25, 1863, the small U.S. steamer *Pembroke* was fired upon by the Choshu when it tried to pass through the Straits of Shimonoseki. French and Dutch vessels also received fire. On July 16, the U.S. warship *Wyoming* was hit before its cannon sank several Japanese boats; five Americans and an undetermined number of Japanese lost their lives. Ten years after Perry, the first Americans and Japanese had fired at each other. The Western diplomats decided to cut through the frustrating Japanese politics to teach their hosts a lesson. Pruyn asked Seward for instructions.[46]

Seward's responses formed a new U.S. policy toward Asia. The Secretary of State's views, moreover, shaped U.S. approaches toward much of Asia until World War II. Japan, it turned out, was to serve as a laboratory case study. Indeed, Seward treated the Japanese even more brutally than he did the Chinese. And if it were his policies that guided U.S. diplomatic activities for the next three-quarters of a century, it was also his policy that the Japanese vowed to destroy inasmuch as it applied to them.

Seward had begun his obsession with Asia in the early 1850s (just as Perry was setting out for the new West), when he was a Whig senator. Believing that the American continent was soon to become the center of the world's production and communications, he urged Americans to take their eyes off the western hemisphere where, he was sure, the United States was inevitably going to be supreme, and focus on the incredible potential of Asia, "the prize," "the chief theatre of events in the world's great hereafter," as he termed it. The key to Asia was commerce, "which [,] surviving dynasties and empires . . . continues, as in former ages, to be a chief fertilizer" for both Europe and Asia. If commerce was the "fertilizer," then missionaries often acted as the plow. Not especially religious himself, Seward developed a fixation on prosletyzing in, of all places, Japan. Not only were "the simple people of Japan" to be made to respect "the institutions of Christianity"; their attacks and limitations imposed on Christians were not to be tolerated. He even urged what his biographer termed a "holy war." Japan's attempts to recover its internal harmony by moving against Christians "will only prepare the way for fearful and bloody convulsions. . . ," Seward wrote the U.S. minister in Edo in 1868. "Humanity indeed demands and expects a continually extending sway for the Christian religion."[47]

To achieve these objectives of expanding commerce and Christianity, Seward did nothing less than reverse the decades-old principles of U.S. policy in Asia. Traditionally, the Americans had acted alone (so as not to be tarnished by acting with European imperialists), and largely stayed away from the use of force. Competitive goods and peaceful relations, not gunboats, were to win over Asian souls and money. Seward, however, believed that the Western powers shared interests in China and Japan; cooperation could best advance those interests. Given the distraction of their civil war, in any case, Americans needed all the foreign help they could find to hold on to their Asian trophies. That belief led as well to the reversal of the second principle: Seward now believed that U.S. military power had to be applied. His close friend, Minister Pruyn, understood the Secretary of State's mind perfectly. It was not any Japanese respect for the "public good" that had opened the country, the minister wrote Seward in 1863; it had been "the silent but no less potent utterances of bayonet and wide-mouthed cannon [that] burst away the barriers of isolation." Now, he added, "our foothold here can be maintained . . . with the hand on the sword."[48]

Seward, resembling many U.S. leaders before and after, believed that having been born free of feudalism themselves, Americans were destined to free others of feudal institutions. Then the ever-moving hand of Western capitalism and Christianity could justly enjoy access. He instructed Pruyn to help any *daimyo* who favored Western trade, "and thus lead to the ultimate revoking of the feudal system, and of the exclusive theory of Japan." In the same instruction, Seward ordered Pruyn to work with the other foreign governments. The Secretary of State realized that Western policies could destroy traditional Japanese society and create large-scale disorder. Not for the first or last time, U.S. officials willingly accepted disorder, perhaps even civil war, for the sake of obtaining access for Western goods and missionaries. After all, Seward candidly wrote, "One can hardly expect anything less than serious political changes as a consequence of the sudden entrance by Japan into relations with the other nations." The idea that Americans always valued order more than the opportunity of profit is, as Seward illustrated, a myth.[49]

Weeks after arriving in Japan, Pruyn believed that "all the officers of the Western Powers in Japan are sentinels in the outposts of civilization. It is here as with our Indian tribes"—strike or be struck. Given these racial and ideological views, Seward and Pruyn not surprisingly agreed in early 1864 to commit U.S. force to an international flotilla that would teach Choshu hard lessons about the power of Western technology, while opening forever the Straits of Shimonoseki. Officials in London were even more enthusiastic about using such force, for British citizens had been especially targeted by *ronin*. In Japan, the British minister, Sir Rutherford Alcock, vigorously agreed with Pruyn that all policy toward "Asiatics" had to "rest on a solid substratum of force," in Alcock's words. He led the preparations for an attack on Choshu. The only problem for Seward and Pruyn was they had little naval power to commit. The major ships were at home fighting the South. Pruyn finally found a small sailing boat, the *Jamestown,* to accompany seventeen powerful ships dispatched by the British, French, and Dutch. The *Jamestown,* however, could not keep up with the fleet, so Pruyn had to charter a privately owned ship, install on it a 600-pound cannon from the *Jamestown,* and send it off to uphold American honor. After four days of bombarding Choshu and suffering a dozen killed in September 1864, the Westerners seized Choshu's cannon and the straits were open. The Japanese had indeed been taught a lesson they would not forget, although it was not precisely the lesson Seward and Pruyn had hoped they would learn.[50]

The *New York Times* reporter in Japan thought the Japanese should actually thank Seward, Alcock, and other Western officials for disciplining Choshu and enabling the Shogun to meet his obligations. The *Times* correspondent nevertheless had to admit, "It will take a long time . . . to break down the prejudices of millions of the non-ruling classes, who have for generations looked upon seclusion as their peculiar institution [a reference to the American South calling slavery its "peculiar institution"], and who, in their ignorance and superstition," would blame the West for Japan's ills. "The masses," he told his readers, "must be made to feel the benefits arising from trade and contact with civilization." The Japanese did quickly feel such "benefits." Immediately after the flotilla attacked, the *bakufu* agreed to pay a $3 million indemnity for past attacks by Japan. The Americans, with the smallest ship, received the smallest share. (It was therefore not onerous in 1883 when the United States returned the indemnity to warm relations with a different, now respected, Japan.)[51]

In the Convention of 1866 the powers forced Japan to fix tariff duties for the foreigners' long-term advantage. But of special significance, Japan had to promise that its traders would deal with foreign merchants directly—that is, without the support of the government—not only in Japan but everywhere. The *bakufu* also had to agree to reverse 250 years of policy by allowing Japanese to travel abroad.[52]

The treaties of 1858 and after were transformed by the enemies of the Shogun and the Western powers into weapons to destroy both the Shogun and the influence of the powers. "Revere the Emperor and expel the barbarian" became the motto for the rebels at Mito and many other places. Choshu, despite (or because of) the powers' attack of 1864, regrouped, joined Satsuma in 1867, and helped lead the drive to destroy the Tokugawa Shogun. In March 1868, an imperial army, led by Choshu and Satsuma, moved out of Edo to defeat the Shogun's forces. It occupied Edo in April. The Shogun resigned. A fifteen-year-old emperor began to rule as well as reign by a proclamation of October 23, 1868. The powers officially remained neutral through the fighting. In reality, Pruyn sympathized with the Shogun, who had, after all, worked (albeit most reluctantly) with Perry and Harris. Alcock ironically backed Choshu.[53]

The victors declared not the creation of a new nation, but the "restoration" of a Japan that had allegiance to the Emperor, whose lineage, they claimed, went back to Jimmu Tenno. Or, as Robert Smith has summarized their feat, "Seeking nationalist revolution, they called it imperial restoration." The restorationists moved to switch the allegiance of the Japanese people away from the feudal *daimyo*, now on their way to extinction, and toward the Emperor. This was accomplished in part by taking up the long practice of ancestor worship—arguing that all Japanese were descended through the centuries from the imperial family, and concluding that hence all Japanese were related.[54]

Until 1868 emperors had been considered so divine that their persons were not allowed to touch the earth and their subjects could not look upon them. During the Tokugawa years of 1626 to 1863, no emperor had even left the palace at Kyoto unless forced out by fire or other emergencies. But the young Emperor traveled in April 1869 from Kyoto to his new capital at Edo (now renamed Tokyo, the nation's commercial as well as political center). He took the name of Meiji, or "enlightened rule." When the Emperor emerged from his Tokyo palace, he was dressed in foreign-style clothes and rode in an open carriage for all to see. Having established a vital link with the Japanese past through the Emperor, the victors were nevertheless pointing toward a very different future. The Charter Oath, signed by the Emperor in April 1868, declared that councils for discussion of the public's needs would be established, a declaration that quieted samurai who opposed the new regime. The Charter Oath also proclaimed that "knowledge shall be sought throughout the world"—but the objective was "to strengthen the foundations of imperial rule," not to become Westernized.[55]

Restoration paradoxically led to great innovation. Japan meant to avoid the Chinese example of subjection to foreign powers. The Japanese instead intended to join the powers, but on their own terms, not the West's. Harmony and a traditional community were to be restored along with the Emperor's authority. In 1860, an observant visitor noted the dividing line between Japan and the West: "It is a singular fact that in Japan, where the individual is sacrificed to the community, he would seem perfectly happy and contented; while in America, where exactly the opposite takes place, and the community is sacrificed to the individual, the latter is in a perpetual state of uproarious clamor for his rights."[56]

Tocqueville could not have stated it better. Between 1853 and 1868 the relentless American determination to break feudal barriers and gain access for every individual—whether merchant, diplomat, or missionary—had encountered a centuries-old and apparently immovable culture of Tokugawa Japan. The irresistible force nonetheless helped destroy the shell of the unmovable object. A new capitalism triumphed over an old regime. Now it was to be decided: could a different Japanese political system—one that continued to value harmony at home and a strong relationship between the individual and the state—adapt rapidly enough to obtain Western industrial and military power while retaining Japanese forms of society? And would this make Americans happy? Or would they push Japan's society further, to fit the principles of American capitalism? And how would the Japanese respond to such pressures? Around these questions, the conflict between Americans and Japanese built over the next century and a half.

II

Joining the Club (1868–1900)

Two Systems

IN 1881, a foreigner wrote in a Yokohama newspaper that "the Japanese are a happy race, and being content with little, are not likely to achieve much." The degree of his error grew as the sentence progressed. In a little more than thirty years, between 1868 and 1900, the Japanese built both a nation and an empire. It was revealing that when a visiting Japanese student at Rutgers University literally studied himself to death, he became a national hero in Japan. When, however, the Japanese were about to reap the harvest of their discipline in 1895–96, they were slammed back to reality by European powers. U.S. officials notably refused to join the powers in humiliating Japan. American-Japanese relations would never be better than they were between 1868 and 1900.[1]

In part, these warm feelings benefited from lack of contact. In a rather remarkable parallel development, both nations turned inward to rebuild societies after each suffered enormous trauma and destruction in the 1860s. The U.S. Civil War killed 600,000 people, destroyed much of the South, and caused massive economic shifts. Suddenly millions of African Americans were thrown from slavery into a free labor market. And a president lay murdered. In Japan, the decline of the Tokugawa Shogun, and the harsh demands of foreigners backed by cannon, led to civil war, foreign military intervention, and terrorism. Gone was a 250-year-old ruling house in a society whose harmony and legitimacy depended on tradition. Fortunately for Japan, the supposedly 2,500-year-old institution of the Emperor easily replaced the Shogun as the center for social harmony, national unity, and political legitimacy.

Americans suffered the horrors of civil war, but at least the majority, northerners, emerged triumphant. Indeed, they emerged doubly triumphant—their own system vindicated by blood and then that system transformed into a powerful industrial complex. The United States usually emerges from its wars more powerful than before. The Civil War exemplified this rule. The nation's centralization, at the expense of states' rights, was reaffirmed. Supreme Court decisions, banking and currency acts, ever-rising national tariffs, a new rail and communications system largely paid for by the Washington government—all led to the concentration of incredible power between 1865 and 1900.

During those years, Americans performed the amazing feat of becoming a great global power while simultaneously settling more land on their own continent than they had in the previous three hundred years. The two expansionist acts were intimately related. The U.S. Census Bureau announced in 1890 that the four hundred-year-old "frontier" of white settlement had finally disappeared. Americans turned outward, especially to Asia, to find in the Far East what many termed a new western frontier. At the same time, the United States grew into the world's greatest economic power. Fearful Europeans warned at century's turn of an "American invasion" attacking their markets. Before the Civil War, 31 million Americans produced $3 billion of manufactures but virtually no steel. In 1900, 75 million Americans produced five times more manufactures and dominated the world's markets for steel (and oil, the other critical need of twentieth-century societies).[2]

This climb up the world's economic ladder cost Americans dearly. In 1873, rampant manipulation of New York banks and exchanges triggered panic in capital markets. The economy plummeted, laborers lost jobs, deflation struck. Optimists viewed all this as only another postwar recession so typical in the American experience. By 1877, however, the slump had worsened. Laborers suffering massive unemployment waged the nation's first general strike; it paralyzed much of the Midwest. In the Pennsylvania coal fields, ten "Molly Maguires"—Irish workers protesting the horrible conditions and ethnic discrimination in the mines— were hanged after terrorizing the area.

This was not at all the usual postwar depression. It proved to be the birth labor of the new U.S. industrial complex. The depression lasted not several years but a quarter century, finally releasing its grip in 1896–97. Strikes spread until in 1894 President Grover Cleveland decided he could restore order in Chicago only by dispatching federal troops. Secretary of State Walter Quintin Gresham worried in 1893–94 that such events "portend revolution." Historians now label this era the second industrial revolution. The first, during the 1840s and 1850s, involved steam, coal, and railways. The second was driven by electricity, steel, and finally automobiles and telephones. The first relied on small, household-type firms. The second emerged from an incredibly high savings and investment rate that produced huge amounts of capital for national, even new multinational, corporations. The first led to Americans opening relations with China and Japan. The second led Americans into clashes with Japan over China.[3]

Capitalists such as Andrew Carnegie defined the problem as overproduction. The steelmaker profited handsomely by equipping his steel mills with the most recent technology bought during the depths of the deflationary depressions. Carnegie's cheap steel drove competitors to the wall. On the other hand, a labor leader such as Samuel Gompers of the new American Federation of Labor traced the crisis to underconsumption and urged that laborers' buying power be jacked up. U.S. government officials greatly preferred Carnegie's analysis. These leaders vowed to find foreign markets for the overproduction. When the United States finally emerged from the twenty-five-year-old nightmare in 1897, many concluded that burgeoning American exports sounded the wake-up call. Vital exports, especially industrial goods, were indeed flowing in increasing amounts to Asia.

Superficially, Japan seemed to be enduring similar political, economic, and social experiences. But it did so for different reasons and much earlier in its industrialization process. Japanese leaders emerging from their civil war in 1867–68 began to dismantle the Shoguns' old scaffolding of power. By late 1871, the *daimyo* had become governors appointed from Tokyo, and their fiefs reduced to districts. They were bought off with government bonds that made them affluent and gave them strong reasons for helping the new government survive. To further weaken feudal traditions, legal equality was declared. In 1873, the Gregorian Calendar was adopted. New laws were promulgated and carried out by samurai who had led the fight against the Shogun. A superb bureaucracy was thus present from the start to supervise modern Japan.

To check opposition and to give opportunity to those with talent (rather than to those merely well born), the new government destroyed the traditional, perpetual military class. Instead, universal conscription began in 1873. The father of the modern Japanese army, Yamagata Aritomo, appointed trusted officers from his native Choshu. After 1878, this core evolved into an efficient army consciously patterned after the Prussian model. Yamagata's fellow Satsuma victors of the 1867–68 wars created a modern battle fleet modeled on the British Royal Navy. Dismissing fealty to the *daimyo,* who now largely existed in history books, the new military pledged fidelity to the Emperor.[4]

The early Meiji government and its military paid bills by confiscating the defeated Shogun's wealth, and, especially, by raising taxes. The taxes notably fell on the peasants, who already saw themselves as unwilling targets of the conscription law. In 1871, the Meiji further unified the country by declaring the yen to be the common currency. Brutal economic shifts and price deflations that afflicted the United States similarly created unrest in Japan. Amid economic and social turmoil, however, the Tokyo government drove ahead by extending telegraph service nationwide, building the first railways, and giving massive state support to industry. Again, the pattern followed the United States and other industrializing nations. Factories included government-run munitions and weapons complexes built to break the country's dependence on foreign suppliers. The Japanese were determined to copy—not become subject to—the West. But the 1866 tariff treaty and indemnities imposed by foreigners at the point of their naval cannon sent money flowing out of Japan. As the West grew richer, Japanese grew money-poor. Still an undeveloped economy (its main products were rice and handicrafts-made textiles), the government had few alternatives but to raise money needed for the military by imposing taxes on rice and land.[5]

Such pressure finally created an explosion: the Satsuma Rebellion in 1877 (which erupted in the same year as the U.S. general strike). Fueled by peasant unrest and the frustration of conservatives in Tokyo, the discontent owed something to the U.S. rebellion of 1776. "Let us be Patrick Henrys," proclaimed an article of the "Freedom and People's Rights Movement." "We might perish, but the unjust laws shall perish with us!" If the Meiji government looked to the West for inspiration, such use of Patrick Henry was decidedly not what the Meiji had in mind. Notably, Saigo Takamori, who led the rebels, had been a hero of the Meiji Restoration and had helped the Emperor destroy the feudal clans. But the new government was not to Saigo's liking, especially its reluctance to attack Korea. The rebels declared they were acting in the name, and for the sake, of the Emperor. Also in the name of the Emperor, and with more effect, the government dispatched the new army to smash the revolt. Saigo was beheaded, at his own request, by a friend on the battlefield. For the first time, the military's power combined with the Emperor's authority to uphold the bureaucracy's actions. That victory also embossed legitimacy on the military ("the Emperor's soldiers and officials," as they became known) that made criticism of it nearly impossible.[6]

Disdaining Patrick Henry, Japan made better use of other chapters of recent Western history. Japanese soon became famous for copying Western machines and some institutions, much as Americans had copied (the British preferred to call it stealing) industrial processes they saw in England. The Shogun Iemochi sounded the alarm in 1865 when he concluded that Japan must follow "the example of foreigners in using the profits from trade to construct many ships and guns, adopting the strategy of using the barbarian to subdue the barbarian." During the previous twelve hundred years, the "foreigner" the Japanese had copied was China. By the 1870s, however, they viewed the Chinese as corrupt, backward, and bending fatally before the West—the results of a long decline the Japanese believed had begun some two hundred years earlier. Now attention focused on Europe and the United States. Two objectives ranked highest: to build a military and industrial complex that could protect Japan from the West's demands; and—closely related—to destroy the unequal treaties imposed by the Westerners by demonstrating that Japanese could be responsible, and as orderly and modern as Westerners themselves.[7]

The most popular voice urging this turn to the West was Fukuzawa Yukichi, an intellectual landmark in Japan's history. Born in 1835, he had studied Dutch, then learned English when he understood the meaning of Perry's and Harris's successes. After seeing Europe and the United States in the 1860s, he returned to write a best-selling book on the importance for Japan of Western accomplishments. Fukuzawa flatly believed that Japan must "quit Asia," that is, turn away from Asia and learn from the "civilized" West. He translated and introduced the text of the American Declaration of Independence and the Constitution to the Japanese. "Heaven," he concluded, "did not create a man above or below another man." Fukuzawa lauded Americans' patriotism, their "sturdy spirit of independence." He praised Benjamin Franklin (who became a popular figure in the onward-and-upward society of Meiji Japan) for living frugally, sleeping little, and seizing opportunities relentlessly.

Then, like a thunderclap, Fukuzawa pointed to the fate of the American Indians. They were an early victim of Western imperialism. "Among the countries touched by the Westerners," he asked rhetorically, "was any able to maintain real independence?" "[N]ow their expansion threatens East Asia like a spreading fire," Fukuzawa warned. The line was starkly drawn: "We want our learning independent, not licking up the lees and scum of the westerner. We want our commerce independent, not dominated by them." And that led him back to Asia, for once Japan renewed itself, it could find its mission in revitalizing and exploiting nearby areas—above all, Korea. Fukuzawa thus instructed his many readers how to learn from the West even while Japan's mission was to focus on Asia.[8]

This most popular and understanding of Japanese writers who closely studied the West followed the motto, "Japanese spirit, Western things." Americans only comprehended half that motto. By 1871, U.S. reporters in Japan had been stunned by the changes of the past several years. Railways, schools, colleges, even the once-feudal society itself, had all suddenly opened. Clearly, these observers concluded, the Japanese must want American-style democracy and capitalism. The foreigners noted how Japanese newspapers urged *rikisha* men no longer to strip to loincloths when working, and to put partitions in public bathhouses to separate the sexes, because "you must not be laughed at by foreigners." In reality, the Japanese aimed to convince the West to terminate the unequal treaties. But Americans instead concluded that, inexorably, the gates of the East were about to swing wide to Western trade and Christian morals. "The opening of the whole country to foreign trade is now probable," one correspondent informed his American readers, "even without a formal demand from any foreign power."[9]

This observer had not been paying attention to leading Japanese politicians. A representative figure was Iwakura Tomomi (1825–1883). As a young adult, Iwakura was ardently anti-foreign, then turned more realistic. He understood that opposition to the foreigners could lead Westerners to force their way in and "interfere in our domestic politics" while seizing "such territory as they covet." By 1868, the fifteen-year-old Emperor Meiji listened to Iwakara, who had helped destroy the Shogun's power—and had helped remove the uncooperative, anti-foreign former Emperor by poisoning him. Serving as foreign minister in 1871, Iwakura became the government's power center. In 1873, he led an eighteen-month expedition of notables to Europe and the United States. The group spent the longest time, some seven months, in America. That Iwakura and such other central figures as Ito Hirobumi left Japan for so long at such a delicate, dangerous point in Japan's history revealed how important they and the Emperor considered the journey. The trip's purposes were several, Iwakura told his companions: negotiate to remove the unequal trade treaties and obtain useful knowledge. He utterly failed to gain the first objective, although the group made highly favorable impressions in Washington and London.

Knowing he had to adapt to some Western habits, Iwakura made it a point not to take along soy sauce, sandals, kimonos, or pickles. (At one point in the trip, a delegate, driven by hunger for home food, broke into Iwakura's hotel room to take a jar of pickles presented as a gift by their hosts.) Iwakura made the single mistake of wearing a traditional silk kimono for a formal negotiating session with President Ulysses S. Grant. Realizing his error in wearing "what to our eyes appeared a grotesque costume," as one Washington observer recorded, the delegation never again appeared in, as the American termed it, "feminine garments of silks and satins." Instead, he concluded, the Japanese wore Western suits, and "the gravity of their dusky visages commanded respect."[10]

In a historic speech before the U.S. House of Representatives in 1873, Iwakura declared, "We came for enlightenment and we gladly find it here." He believed Americans and Japanese destined to be linked by cords of trade: "In the future an extended commerce will unite our national interests in a thousand forms, as drops of water will commingle, flowing from our several rivers to that common ocean that divides our countries." But such trade and friendship, the Iwakura group concluded privately, was to be developed on Japan's terms.[11]

That conclusion became clear when the official record of the remarkable journey written by a Confucian scholar named Kume Kunitake became public in 1878. Kume had read widely about his Western hosts. One source was *A Brief Account of the United States* by Elijah C. Bridgman, a U.S. missionary in China whose translated work circulated widely in both China and Japan. Kume's 1878 account ranked Great Britain, France, and the United States as the world's three greatest nations, and Germany just below. Russia was ranked dead last. A division of labor, he believed, was taking shape. The British were admired for their navy and political institutions, the Americans for their business skills, the French for their literature and philosophy. His admiration, however, was highly selective. While noting that Americans maintained only a small, cheap military force, and that they denounced even that outfit for milking the Treasury, the Japanese also observed that Americans, unlike themselves, were not surrounded by ambitious imperialist powers. Westerners were polite, but they did not hesitate to use force. The American Indians, Kume declared in an echo of Fukuzawa's insight, had too much trusted "Christians who preached, 'Love your enemy.' " Japan should instead trust its military.[12]

The important political lesson learned on the journey was the value of laws that Westerners called constitutions. These the delegates viewed as the key to maintaining order because the documents spelled out rights and responsibilities. Not that the U.S. Constitution fitted Japan; to the contrary, it allowed too much individualism, corruption, and influence by wealthy interests. Democracy "tends to pit the people against their prince." Once this occurs, Kume believed, it is "difficult to restore social and political stability." France was the first victim of this evil in the 1790s. It was a recipe for disorder—or worse: "In a republican form of government, the power of the people gradually expands, and the power of the government must yield to it. . . . [If] the people stretch, the . . . government must shrink. If there is a keen desire for liberty, there will be a neglect of law." Tocqueville had seldom been more concise about the problems democracy faced.[13]

In the economic realm, the Japanese admired American and British skills. But they also heard speech after speech in the United States and Great Britain instructing them to be open to trade and show faith in a monotheistic god of profit. These speeches, the Japanese decided, did not ring true. American industry and farms boomed behind a protective tariff raised ever higher during the previous dozen years. The Japanese saw, moreover, that the U.S. government was everywhere—enforcing contracts, passing laws to subsidize production, creating government agencies to help farmers and manufacturers develop the latest technologies, and even (Kume might have noted) giving away the land, the nation's greatest treasure, so private capitalists could rapidly exploit its wealth. The Japanese group, prudish and Victorian, was, as the historian Marlene Mayo observes, "rather terrified by the boldness and coquetry of American women." The wide-open, acquisition-for-ascent U.S. society allowed too much public kissing, too vague a boundary between male and female responsibilities. In Japan, the women were responsible for the home, the men for the world outside the home. A man, Kume emphasized, had greater obligations to his parents than to his wife and children. An intelligent person could thus also learn from the West what not to do to create a secure, orderly Japan.[14]

Above all, Iwakura concluded that rapid internal development had to receive top priority. He and other Tokyo leaders received considerable help in this domestic effort from the United States. The northern island of Hokkaido was developed in the 1870s with extensive assistance from American experts, who taught new farming methods and brought in fresh breeds of livestock. Banking laws for the nation borrowed heavily from U.S. statutes. Japanese diplomacy was influenced by U.S. legal advisers such as Erasmus Peshine Smith, Henry Willard Denison, and

Durham White Stevens, who were to work with the Japanese foreign ministry. More specifically, once the 1877 rebellion was quelled, Iwakura and his successors determined to create a Japanese constitution— but not along the lines of the U.S. document.[15]

Given by the Emperor to his people in 1889, the new Constitution established a two-house parliament that could grant individual rights. (In the United States, on the other hand, individual rights were assumed—all "were created equal"—and the state was then charged by the Constitution to protect these rights, not create them.) Suffrage in Japan was so limited that the elected lower house, the House of Commons, was chosen by 1 percent of the population. Not even universal male suffrage was given until 1925. The Constitution was handed down on February 11, 1889, considered the 2,549th anniversary of the founding of the Japanese state, and so it was not unexpected when Article I declared: "The Empire of Japan shall be reigned over and governed by a line of Emperors unbroken for ages eternal." Article XIII stated: "The Emperor declares war, makes peace, and concludes treaties." Sacred and sovereign, the Emperor held supreme command over the military, but such a line of authority also provided army and navy leaders with direct access to the throne. The Diet's responsibilities lay almost wholly in the domestic arena. Both at home and abroad, however, only the Emperor could make the ultimate decision. But such simplicity (much as did the simplicity of the U.S. Constitution's language) badly misled. The central question was, who would shape the Emperor's decision? Below the throne, factions based on clans (such as groups from Choshu and Satsuma), and function (as military versus civilian), soon multiplied with near-American rapidity. The making of foreign policy in Japan, like its creation in the United States, became an invitation for struggle.[16]

Japan's Constitution was written in secret by a small group of men and put into force without public debate or vote. It nevertheless seemed to accomplish quickly some of its authors' main objectives as the Japanese, now more secure at home, moved rapidly to join the Western imperialists' exclusive club.

Two Systems, Two Imperialisms

American and Japanese successes in nation building during the 1870s and 1880s were not isolated events. After 1860, Germany and Italy also ated, and they, along with France, put into place new central ents. By the 1880s, great prizes were falling to peoples with the most powerful industries and armies, and with the most centralized regimes for conducting imperial policy. After 1500, when nearly five hundred separate countries and nation-states could be counted, the number dropped, until by the 1860–1914 era no more than fifty existed. A handful of nations put together the skills and aggressiveness to create concentrated industrial plants whose products and profits translated into military power. The resulting new imperialism of the post-1860 years redrew the maps of Africa and Asia. But Asia, unlike Africa, endured direct attack from every major imperialist power: Great Britain, France, Germany, Russia, Japan, and the United States.

The last two arrived relatively late (in the 1880s and 1890s), but with a sledgehammer impact. By 1910, if not as early as 1902, European nations were measuring the ground on their own continent for war among themselves. It thus began to appear that the fate of China and Northeast Asia might be decided by agreement—or a contest— between the United States and Japan. The clash lay well into the future. In the immediate post-1868 years, the two peoples seemed to be moving along roughly parallel, rather than converging, paths.

The differences between Japan and the United States, however, help explain why within a generation they would move onto a collision course. Americans were being driven outward by growing surpluses of production, as well as by domestic riots caused by overproduction and deflation. This drive was reinforced by a long tradition of American racism and missionary impulses, two traits that helped rationalize the opening and subjection of other, differently colored societies. Japan, on the other hand, struggled with a relatively primitive economy in the 1870s and 1880s. It was driven toward imperialism by different impulses: the well-justified fears that Westerners were creeping uncomfortably close to the home islands, and that these outsiders intended to dominate Japanese trade. One distinguished historian of Japanese foreign policy, Ian Nish, even believes that Japan's view of "this threat became something of a national neurosis."[17]

Meiji Japan heeded also a second set of impulses: the need to overcome dangerous internal unrest by focusing people's attention on overseas problems. Japan passed through the most dangerous dissension by the late 1880s. With the smashing of the Satsuma Rebellion and the issuing of the Constitution, a Japanese consensus was created in—and imposed on—the society. Most notably, at the center of this system sat the Emperor with his ancient legitimacy. The throne was undergirded by National Shinto as a state religion, propagated between 1868 and 1875 by new shrines and priests. All-important to Shintoism was the

Emperor himself. An education system was developed that systematically and uncritically taught the virtues of patriotism and allegiance to the Emperor. Not even this carefully mixed formula of worldly and other-worldly controls, however, could stamp out the ultranationalist groups, even assassinations of leading officials, that contually haunted Japanese foreign policy.[18]

Driven, then, by different impulses and systems, the two nations nevertheless sailed in the same directions by the 1880s—that is, toward Korea, China (especially northeast China or Manchuria), Hawaii, and strategic western Pacific islands. In those regions, imperial struggles raged. On one historic principle, both nations' leaders did agree, and fervently: domestic stability and foreign policy successes were becoming intimately related. In the United States, policymakers from Seward to Gresham and beyond assumed that the nation's future had to be worked out in a global arena. Overseas successes could ease domestic distresses. As for Japanese officials, they knew that if they misestimated the Westerners as had the Shogun, they, like he, would not survive.

In 1871–73 these officials tried to renegotiate the unequal treaties, then dispatched the Iwakura mission to accomplish the all-important task. Both approaches failed. In 1873 Judge John A. Bingham of Ohio became the U.S. minister. Astute, sympathetic, proper, Bingham began to work on easing the tariff treaties. In 1878, his patience paid off. The United States broke away from the other powers and agreed to restore tariff decision-making to Japan whenever the other nations made a similar concession. Secretary of State William M. Evarts, a New Yorker and disciple of Seward, hoped this policy would make Japan friendlier toward American merchants.[19]

Cooperation between the two nations extended to a number of levels. The Japanese had asked the Massachusetts Agricultural College to set up a school and experimental farm in Hokkaido. The Americans taught not only new farming techniques but also the virtues of Christianity, military drill, U.S.-style houses, and the motto, "Be Ambitious." Several of these teachings were already proving to be redundant in Japan. Philadelphia's great Centennial Exposition of 1876 had as one of its themes the need to trade abroad "to prevent continued depression." Asia received much attention. Elegant Japanese exhibits were praised for their beauty and order but also because, as a Philadelphia newspaper observed, "The Japanese have already adopted the American costume in dress, and the progressive spirit pervading the Old World is inclining her people to adopt American ideas and American machinery." (Notably, then and later, U.S. observers assumed that their machinery and their ideas were natural traveling companions. Few Japanese made such an assumption.)[20]

Apparently developing along parallel tracks, the two peoples also seemed to follow similar expansionist paths. For their part, the Japanese settled a delicate boundary question in 1875 by annexing the Kurile Islands in the northeast in exchange for giving Russia the island of Sakhalin, off Siberia's coast. The deal helped secure Japan's northern borders; it also marked Japan's first dealings on equal terms with a Western power. Tokyo's attention now focused on Korea. In the seventh century the first war between Japan and China had erupted over Korea. In the thirteenth century, Chinese and Korean troops tried to invade Japan through the Korean Peninsula. Three hundred years later the Japanese did invade Korea, although the results were slight (other than recharging Korean hatred for Japan). Then, with the Tokugawa's isolationist policies, Korean-Japanese relations settled into one of their few eras of tranquility. When the Tokugawa fell, the Koreans refused to recognize the Meiji regime in 1870–71—especially when they realized the new Tokyo leaders fully intended to limit Korea's long-profitable trade with Japan.

In 1873, as Japanese grew less patient with Korea—this "stagnant, stubborn, and shrewd country," as it was viewed—Saigo Takamori offered to invade the neighbor by himself so that when Koreans killed him, Japan would have reason to declare war. Iwakura sensibly put a stop to this (and Saigo instead moved toward his own beheading in the 1877 uprising). Iwakura's pivotal ally, Okubo Toshimichi, captured the moment by arguing powerfully that the war's expenses could lead to economic dependence on foreigners while wasting money needed for domestic development.[21]

Saigo's career was decapitated, but Japan's preoccupation with Korea grew and intensified. Again the interweaving of domestic and foreign affairs became clear. The 1873 debate over Korea (and, obviously, over much else as well) has been termed the "great divide" in Meiji policy. It turned the leaders who had triumphed with the Meiji Restoration in 1868 against one another. It deeply affected domestic policies. The passion of one debate over Korea even ruptured a blood vessel in the brain of Prime Minister Sanjo Sanetomi. Iwakura himself was attacked and severely wounded by persons determined to conquer Korea; the attackers were captured and executed.[22]

But for all the smoke and fire, the initial steps toward an imperialist foreign policy were measured. In 1871, fifty-four persons from the Liu-chi'iu islands (or the Ryukyus), which both Japan and China claimed, were killed by an aboriginal tribe when shipwrecked off Formosa. Charles W. LeGendre, an American and a former Civil War officer, was advising the Japanese foreign ministry. He urged the conquest of Formosa and brutally avenging the murders. In mid-1874, Japan landed three thousand troops to discipline the tribes on Formosa. The Japanese, who had devotedly studied Western international law since Townsend Harris had introduced it to them, nicely cited appropriate provisions to show China that it lacked jurisdiction. The Chinese replied they were governed only by "truth," not by an international law that was a device recently cooked up by Westerners. In 1879, Japan demonstrated (to paraphrase Napoleon) that truth and law were on the side of the largest artillery. A Japanese force seized the Ryukyus, including the chain's largest island of Okinawa.[23]

Korea might well have been the next landing site. In 1874, however, when Koreans slaughtered the crew of a Japanese ship, the news was overshadowed by a domestic uproar: the beheading, and public display of the heads, of leaders of a rebellion against the Tokyo government. The rebels had, among other aims, demanded the conquest of Korea. In 1876, the Japanese satisfied themselves by sending two warships and four transports full of soldiers to enforce new demands: that Korea be an "independent nation" free of the Chinese relationship; that Japanese-Korean diplomatic relations begin; and that three ports be opened to trade. Japan clearly was challenging the Chinese Empire as well as the Korean kingdom. The 1876 treaty marked Japan's first post-1868 step onto the Asian mainland.[24]

Into this cauldron of Asian crises stepped the United States. Americans had taken notice of Korea in 1871 when President Grant, avenging the Korean slaughter of a U.S. naval crew, sent warships into a Korean river. After the ships were fired on, the American cannon killed two hundred Koreans. Japan's more constructive success in 1876 encouraged U.S. officials to put relations with Korea on a happier, more profitable basis. Expansionists from the California business community and the U.S. Congress pushed Secretary of State Evarts to dispatch Commodore Robert N. Shufeldt to negotiate with Korea. Reflecting on the economic crisis of the 1870s, Shufeldt noted that "at least one-third of our mechanical and agricultural products are in excess of our own wants, and we *must* export these products." The commodore also pointed the direction: "the Pacific Ocean is to become at no distant day the commercial domain of America." In both 1867 and 1880, Shufeldt had tried to work directly with the Koreans to open their country, only to have his ambition of becoming the Commodore Perry of Korea deflated by the hostile Seoul regime. In 1882, Shufeldt pointedly opened talks with the Chinese before approaching Korea. The Chinese seemed friendly, and he explained why to the State Department: a U.S. treaty with Korea made with China's help "would tend to check the encroachment of Japan."[25]

The Shufeldt treaty of 1882, the first such pact Korea signed with a Western nation, opened the country to trade and residence for foreigners, while granting Americans commercial privileges. Shufeldt coldly rejected the Chinese demand that the treaty explicitly recognize Korean dependence on China. Having used the Chinese, he now refused to allow them to use him.

Japan was not pleased that China had been Shufeldt's ticket into Korea. But Tokyo officials thought that given China's decline, they enjoyed the best position for the newly opened race to exploit Korea. Or so some Japanese leaders dreamed.

Joining the Imperialists' Club:
Ito, Gresham, and the
"Pigtail War"

Japan had traveled far since 1868, but not nearly as far as most Japanese believed. The rampant nationalisms of the nineteenth century (and the resulting tragedies of the twentieth) had need of certain components: a strong sense of cultural nationhood ("manifest destiny" in the United States, for example), an efficient central government controlling the means of violence, a national army that could wield that violence to attain governmental objectives, and a growing industrial base that produced both manufactured exports and arms. By the 1880s, Japan possessed all but the industrial base.[26]

Matsukata Masayoshi intended to remedy this problem. After becoming finance minister in 1881, he destroyed inflation with a convertible currency, a 20 percent reduction in the quantity of money, new taxes, and a slashing of public expenditures. Reductions included closing, or turning over to private individuals, the public operation of factories and mines. In 1885, the Bank of Japan was created to oversee these policies. It did so with brutal efficiency. As governmental savings leaped upward, Japan found capital for its military.[27]

It also found capital for internal development. The manufacturing complex was premodern: food (especially brewing) and textiles accounted for two-thirds of all manufactures. True, by 1893 the country had built basic infrastructure (2,000 miles of railroads, 4,000 miles of telegraph lines, 100,000 tons of steam vessels as part of a fast-growing merchant marine). But Japan was using up its one major home-produced mineral, coal, and needed imports from Korean and Manchurian mines. Pig iron and steel production remained pitifully small until the new century. The most important exports included silk, half of which went to the United States, and cheaper cotton goods, which were shipped mainly to China and Korea. Japan somewhat resembled the American South at this point: a world player in cheaper textiles, but still in the low minor leagues when it came to iron and steel, two products that separated the real from the aspiring powers. Compared with the Western Europeans or the northern United States, Japan was an immature imperialist.[28]

One difference, however, sharply separated Japan from the American South. The former Confederacy's factories (not to mention some of its schools) had been built by the North's carpetbagging capital. The South was, in this and other respects, a colony. Japan, however, followed a fixed, single-minded determination not to become dependent on foreign investors. Hence Matsukata's boot-camp regimen for the economy in the 1880s. Hence the diversion of agricultural products abroad for profit rather than for use at home. Hence the forced savings. Hence the passion for destroying the unequal treaties. (And hence American experiences with Japanese trade and investment practices a century later.) Japan intended to join the Westerners, not invite them in.[29]

If Matsukata built the economic foundations, Ito Hirobumi was crucial in building political foundations. Born of low-ranking samurai in 1841, Ito ranked as one of the most colorful of this generation's leaders. His personal life was the history of Japan between 1860 and his murder in 1909. In the 1860s, he had been a Choshu youngster who joined in the cry, "Honor the Emperor, Expel the Barbarians!" Then, however, he was chosen to study abroad. His first sight of British warships made him think realistically. He concluded the "Barbarians" could not be quickly expelled, only copied until they had to treat Japan as an equal. Ever after, Ito was sensitive and shrewd in handling foreigners. These qualities became highly polished when Iwakura took him on the eighteen-month "knowledge-seeking" mission of 1871–73, and again in 1882–83 when Ito went to Europe for firsthand study of constitutions.[30]

By the 1880s, he was a pivotal figure in the highly centralized decision making that formed the 1889 Constitution. As Ito wrote Iwakura in 1882, the Emperor must be "a cornerstone, secure in his grasp of sovereign power." But as Japan's first significant prime minister in the 1890s, Ito also demonstrated a common touch. Unlike his peers, he paid little attention to tea ceremonies or Noh drama. "I am content with little and give absolutely no thought [to] saving money," he admitted. "What I like best is a geisha companion to entertain me after work." When he died, many women from restaurants and red-light districts recalled their friendships with Ito. His passions were the new Japan and women. One biographer believes Ito was described by a traditional song: "Drunk, my head pillowed on a beauty's lap; awake and sober, grasping power to govern the nation."[31]

Ito's major opponent was Yamagata Aritomo, founder of the post-1868 Japanese military. Schooled with Ito, the reserved, severe Yamagata acted like a soldier even when serving as prime minister. Yamagata was pivotal in winning the top military officers special access to the Emperor under the new Constitution. At the same time, he detested political parties and determined not to have them infect the armed forces. Thus in 1890, as Yamagata desired, voting rights were specifically denied to priests, the military, and the insane. Elected civilians therefore found themselves with little power over the military. Venerating the Emperor, Yamagata was an expansionist who believed in the traditional imperial slogan that the throne brought "the four corners of the world under one roof." No corner was more important to Yamagata (or Ito) than Korea. For here, as Yamagata's Prussian military mentors taught him in the 1870s, was the touchstone of Japan's security. And, as he had also concluded in the 1870s, Russia posed the great danger to this security. By 1894, Yamagata could put a quarter-million men in the field. The navy numbered twenty-eight steamships and owned facilities to build modern vessels and weapons.[32]

Foreign threats, in Japanese eyes, did not include the United States. This omission was notable. Americans, after all, had quickly pushed on the Korean door that Shufeldt opened. King Kojong believed (tragically, as it turned out) that Americans were committed to his nation's best interests: independence and protection against Japan and China. Some of the U.S. diplomats who reinforced Kojong's misperception were irresponsible and incompetent: one was a hopeless drunk, another a retired school superintendent ignorant of diplomatic responsibilities, and most had been political hacks back home.[33]

An exception was Horace Allen, a Presbyterian missionary who arrived as the secretary of the U.S. legation in 1884. He became the U.S. minister a decade later, and finally had to be pried out of Korea in 1905. Allen and other Americans worked with the Japanese during the years before 1894 in supporting Korean reformers intent on creating a fully independent Korea. The missionary-diplomat meanwhile used his access to the king to enrich Americans with lush concession contracts for railways and some of Asia's most promising gold mines. Kojong made all this possible. In his view, Americans were preferable to the neighboring predators, Russia or the historic enemy, Japan. American missionaries—largely excluded from Japan, discriminated against in China, and with their faith under bombardment from Darwinism at home—flooded into Korea to find their own market. Koreans may have massacred Western missionaries a generation earlier, but now it was in Korea's interest to use Americans to separate the peninsula's politics from Chinese control.[34]

The moment of truth struck in mid-1894. Ito and his foreign minister, Mutsu Munemitsu, occupied one side of the debate in Tokyo, Yamagata the other. In July 1894, Ito and Mutsu set the stage when they scored one of Japan's great diplomatic victories of the Meiji era by convincing Great Britain to end the unequal treaties. It is notable that, say, unlike the Soviet Bolsheviks later, the Meiji had not begun to reign by refusing to recognize treaties already in force. The Japanese instead had accepted them, then set out to destroy the pacts. Extraterritoriality was to be abolished in 1899; Japan was to enjoy full control over its own tariffs after 1911. Just two weeks after signing the British agreement, the Japanese moved to become a full-fledged member in the imperialists' club. Japan's fleet sank Chinese ships off the Korean coast. Within a week, Japanese troops moved in mass onto the peninsula.[35]

The war had been triggered by an uprising within Korea against King Kojong, who then asked China for assistance. The rioters (an outlawed group, the Tonghaks) were quickly smashed by Korean forces without China's help. Japan, however, claimed that the Chinese had abrogated the 1885 Sino-Japanese treaty that promised cooperation in any such military operations in Korea. More directly, the Tonghak outbreak was a mere pretext for Japan. Yamagata and his military associates had eyed the land beyond the Shimonoseki Straits since the 1870s. In 1892, when the Russians began building their great Trans-Siberian Railway into Northeast Asia, Yamagata warned the Emperor that the railway would bring Russian power dangerously close to Japan and create a crisis with St. Petersburg. Japan's military, along with civilian officials, had also been searching for a club to beat down political unrest, even rioting, arising from economic problems. A Japanese official in Washington admitted to Secretary of State Gresham that the "situation at home is critical, and war with China would improve it" by "more strongly attaching the people to the government"—a remark that stunned and angered the American. Intellectuals such as Fukuzawa fueled the fire by urging that Japan no longer associate with a declining Asia, but prove its modernity by treating Asians the way the West treated Japanese.[36]

As pro-war passion grew, Ito tried to avoid a conflict while simultaneously wringing quick concessions out of China. But the Chinese, with a larger military ready to fight (about 350,000 regulars), would not back down. Ito lost his struggle especially after Foreign Minister Mutsu moved toward Yamagata's hawkish position. War offered too much— peace at home, secure markets and strategic points in Korea, checkmating a Russian movement south, and membership in the imperialists' club. On July 24, 1894, Japan sank a Chinese transport, killing over a thousand men and (according to European advisers who survived) machine-gunning many of the victims in the water. Interestingly, few Americans blamed Japan for this attack. They preferred the westernizing Japan to the disintegrating but defiant Chinese. Japan now set out to show, as one of the nation's pro-war voices phrased it, that "civilization is not a monopoly of the white man."[37]

King Kojong brandished Shufeldt's 1882 treaty, in which Americans had solemnly promised to exert their "good offices" if Korea faced danger from a third party. Gresham, however, now flatly refused to respond. He only declared, lamely, that he hoped Japan would not wage an unjust war. That same day he told the Japanese privately he had no intention of helping Korea. As war had approached in July, the British asked Gresham and President Grover Cleveland to join Europeans in mediating the conflict. The Americans politely declined. They did not intend to cooperate publicly with the British unless U.S. interests in Asia required protection. Such interests certainly existed, but they were mainly China's market and missionary outposts. For their sake, Cleveland (the son of a Presbyterian minister and notably sensitive about missionaries in Asia) increased the U.S. Asian Fleet from one to eight ships. Gresham, it seemed, had only one major worry: that Japan's reach would exceed its grasp. He repeatedly warned the Japanese government that demanding too much from Korea would invite a European counterstroke. Such a response, U.S. officials feared (correctly, as it turned out), could climax in an imperialist scramble throughout Asia threatening the traditional U.S. open-door policy of keeping China whole and open to the business people of all nations on equal terms. A loss of that potentially bottomless market amid the 1890s economic crisis could be disastrous.[38]

Not for the last time in U.S.-Japan relations, Washington officials therefore stepped aside while Japan used force. Most Americans seemed to approve. "Japan, the Great Britain of Asia" (that is, an island nation that could sway a neighboring continent) became a common phrase. So was "Yankees of the East." "Everybody wanted to know, and knowing, liked the Japs," wrote one observer. The Japanese Secret Service built on this goodwill by hiring the highly effective Edward H. House, an American editor of the *Tokyo Times,* to propagandize Japan's views in the United States. When the Japanese attacked the vital Manchurian base of Port Arthur in November 1894, they discovered the Chinese had hung heads of Japanese prisoners at the main entry. The invading troops, in the words of an American reporter, "killed everything they saw, including children, and beheaded many." This sensational story oddly strengthened U.S.-Japanese friendship: Americans blamed the slaughter on Chinese barbarism and compared it to the Native American savagery that U.S. soldiers had faced.[39]

Washington officials nevertheless realized that dealing with these "Yankees" required the most careful calibration. Too little support, and Japan could be humiliated. Too much support, and Korea, perhaps even China, could shatter, with Europeans rushing in to claim the pieces. Gresham consequently warned Tokyo again to be careful or "other powers" could "demand a settlement not favorable to Japan's . . . well-being." His approach won some early rewards. China and Japan each asked Americans to oversee its property and diplomatic business in the other's country during the war. But Gresham could not finally protect Japan from the Europeans. By March 1895, Japan had overwhelmed the larger Chinese forces. It controlled not only Korea, but the Liaotung Peninsula that opened into the lush markets and mineral wealth of Manchuria.

Since August 1894, the confident foreign ministry under Mutsu had been considering its demands on China, beginning with the control of railways. As their military triumphs mounted, however, so did these officials' appetites, until by early 1895 Mutsu intended to take Formosa and strategic ports in South Manchuria as well as to control Korea. He calculated that the British and Americans would not object. After all, under their most-favored-nation treaties with China, these Westerners would enjoy any access into Manchuria obtained by Japan. And indeed, in March 1895, Gresham acted as go-between to expedite the Chinese acceptance of these terms, plus the Japanese demand of a $135 million indemnity from China. Russians and Germans, however, proved to be another matter. The tsar's regime wanted no other government in Manchuria close to its Trans-Siberian Railway. The kaiser's government meanwhile sought outright colonies and naval bases, not merely the open-door right to compete with the highly efficient Americans and British for markets.[40]

On April 23, 1895, the Russians and Germans struck. Joined by the French, they "advised" Mutsu to return the Liaotung Peninsula to China. Ito's cabinet stalled, tried to suggest a compromise, then suddenly backed down on May 5. Ito feared that the Russians, at least, were prepared to use force. The Japanese business community wanted no more war, and the prime minister doubted Japan could survive such a conflict, especially since the British and Americans had become emphatic in their silence. As consolation, Japan demanded and received a $200 million indemnity from China. On May 8, the Treaty of Shimonoseki ended the war on terms dictated by the Triple Intervention of Russia, Germany, and France.[41]

It was a bitter blow for Japan. The war had been so popular that even political squabbling in Tokyo had quieted. In October 1895, Japanese officials in Korea tried to counterattack by destroying Russian influence. They directed a revolt against the Korean court. Queen Min was killed. Americans, including Horace Allen, had, for the sake of their concessions, switched sides to Russia. Now they tried to help King Kojong against the pro-Japanese rebels. But again, the State Department ordered Allen to back away and scolded him for being involved in internal Korean politics. Embarrassingly disguised as a coolie, King Kojong sought refuge in the Russian (not American) legation. The Japanese coup was quelled, Russian influence grew. Allen moved to make the most of it. He obtained Korea's richest gold mine, the Un-san, for a U.S. company. From 1897 until 1939 the American owners earned $15 million of profit from the Un-san mine, despite the post-1905 Japanese control and annexation of Korea.[42]

For a moment in 1896, it indeed seemed that Americans might obtain more from the 1894–95 war than would the victors. When the Japanese government tried to talk its bankers into investing in Korean railways, the response was cool. The Mitsui Company expressed interest in Manchuria's soy beans, not its minerals. Japanese businessmen, in other words, wanted trade, not investment opportunities. This was most frustrating for an Ito government that hoped the war would finally produce long-term profits for investments as well as strategic security. Now the conflict threatened to produce neither. Japanese business lacked the capital and interest to build abroad. Russians and Americans were left to exploit Korea.

Ito's government had to resign in 1896. Public outrage over the

Korean debacle had risen to such explosive levels that the Emperor issued an imperial edict demanding quiet. By late 1895, Tokyo officials were already preparing for the next war by building four battleships. U.S. shipbuilders and steelmakers swarmed over Japan to obtain contracts.[43]

Irony abounded. Amid rioting and economic crisis at home, and while the State Department followed a hands-off policy, Americans moved to make fortunes from Korean, Chinese, and Japanese markets. This sudden emergence of U.S. influence opened a pivotal chapter of U.S.-Asian relations in a matter of months in 1895–96. Nevertheless, Japan, despite the Triple Intervention, emerged the real victor. It gained the strategic island of Formosa, (or "beautiful") as named by Portuguese explorers, but claimed by China for two centuries. The decision to annex occurred after bitter internal bureaucratic struggles. The navy believed the island to be worth much more than Manchurian territory, a belief that gained weight as Yamagata's projects collapsed under European pressure. So began a highly difficult fifty-five-year rule over Taiwan, as China called it. The beginnings of the rule were ominous: native Taiwanese quickly, and unsuccessfully, attempted to block the takeover by declaring their island a republic.[44]

At home, wartime spending and the Chinese indemnity fueled economic good times. The government used the indemnity to build the large Yawata Iron Works, soon a fount for the nation's arsenal. Yawata was one of many plants that exploited Western technology to bolster both economic and military prowess. Watching all this, Americans were mightily impressed. Not even the Triple Intervention seemed to do more than temporarily slow up the Japanese. "Americans cannot but wish them success," the Philadelphia *Press* declared in December 1895. "Nippon is indeed the day-star of the East." The American Medical Association surveyed the highly efficient military field hospitals and announced that "truly the Japanese is a wonderful man." A widely noted book of 1896 formally bestowed the ultimate compliment: the Japanese were *The Yankees of the East*.[45]

Lafcadio Hearn rang changes on this theme in "The Genius of Japanese Civilization," published in *Atlantic Monthly* and reprinted elsewhere. Hearn, born in Greece, had emigrated to the United States to be a reporter, but after difficult, drunken times in New Orleans, he headed for Japan in 1890. There he lived like a Japanese, married a Japanese wife, took a Japanese name, and became perhaps the best-known interpreter of Japan to Americans between the 1890s and his death in 1904. "Without losing a single ship or a single battle," Hearn wrote in late 1895, "Japan has broken down the power of China, made a new Korea, enlarged her own territory, and changed the whole political face of the East." All this was "astonishing," but equally so, he thought, was that even as the Japanese powerfully wielded "Western industrial invention," they changed little inwardly and emotionally. They remained Japanese. Their laborers continued to get along in clothes that cost 75 cents and with belongings that "can be put into a handkerchief." Yet these people had been "highly civilized" for a thousand years. Americans, Hearn warned, required too much: "We must have meat . . . glass windows and fire; hats, white shirts, and woolen underwear . . . all of which a Japanese can do without and is really better off without." Hearn then drew a conclusion: "Hence his present capacity to threaten Western manufacturers."[46]

Clash Over Hawaii

Hearn's gentle warning about a future conflict quickly came true, but not quite in the form he prophesied. Indeed, the turn of American attitudes toward Japan was remarkable—and ominous. Consider Hawaii.

The first U.S. settlers reached the islands in 1820. Missionaries and ship crews working the profitable Pacific whaling industry, they rapidly infiltrated the economy and politics. The Kanakas (native Hawaiians) soon sarcastically termed Americans "the Missionary Party." A U.S. consul, deeply disturbed that the missionaries were using tricks to buy up native-owned land, called them "bloodsuckers," who lived "like lords in this luxurious land disturbing the minds of these children of Nature with the idea that they are to be eternally damned unless they think and act as they [the missionaries] do." The major turn occurred in the 1860s–70s when whaling declined and a sugar industry developed. In 1875–76, a U.S.-Hawaiian reciprocity treaty was signed. It opened the vast U.S. market to Hawaii's sugar. An economic boom now reshaped the islands' society.[47]

Vigorously growing sugar exports required ever larger amounts of cheap labor. Chinese were the first imports, but racial tensions developed, along with a fear they were too apt to abandon the sugar plantations to set up their own shops in towns. In 1868, the initial Japanese laborers arrived, thanks to a direct agreement between the Hawaiian and Japanese governments. The Japanese emigration might have ended there, for most poorer Japanese did not wish to leave their ancestors' lands. But the situation changed in the 1880s when Matsukata's economic policies disciplined Japan's economy into recession and unrest. Looking for their own new frontier, and encouraged by Tokyo officials who began to envision Hawaii as well as Korea as Japan's new outposts, the number of Japanese in Hawaii leaped from a few to 24,400 in 1896. Both Americans and Japanese had converged on Hawaii after the 1870s because economic conditions at home pushed them out on this Pacific frontier. U.S. interest further intensified when the reciprocity treaty was renewed in 1886 and contained the added provision that Americans would gain access to the potentially magnificent harbor on the Pearl River. Now more than sugar was involved. As President Grover Cleveland declared, "Those islands, on the highway of Oriental and Australasian traffic, are virtually an outpost of American commerce and the stepping-stone to the growing trade of the Pacific."[48]

The islands had been integrated into the American commercial drive westward. An earlier drive had produced Perry's confrontation with the Japanese. After 1877, a more sophisticated and powerful thrust, generated by new industrialism, turmoil, and riots at home, was climaxing in another confrontation, but with quite a different Japan.

By the 1890s, Tokyo officials, who had cooperated in moving emigrants into Hawaii, knew their people were suffering humiliating discrimination, were waging strikes and enduring arrests, because of bad wages and working conditions. Between 1890 and 1893, those conditions worsened in Hawaii for everyone: a U.S. reciprocity act of 1890 allowed Cuban sugar into the United States at a more favorable cost than Hawaiian. As political tensions grew, white planter interests struck in February 1893 to overthrow Hawaii's Queen Liliuokalani. At the climactic moment, the feverishly pro-annexationist U.S. minister, John Stevens, ordered 150 sailors to land from the USS *Boston* to help the plotters. The new government quickly negotiated annexation to the United States. American economic power in the mid-Pacific had grown to the point that simply by manipulating tariff rates, Washington officials could ignite a revolution.[49]

President Cleveland and Secretary of State Gresham inherited this crisis when they entered office in March 1893. Cleveland had been forced out of the presidency between 1889 and 1893 by Benjamin Harrison, whose administration had been ready to annex Hawaii in early 1893. Cleveland and Gresham were not ready. They feared the U.S. Constitution could not extend that far across water into predominantly non-Anglo-Saxon regions, without snapping. Moreover, they wanted no colonies, especially colonies redolent of Republican gunboat diplomacy.

Besides, they had what they wanted without the headaches of daily governing: a white man's government, control of the economy, and de facto possession of the islands' most promising harbor. The Democratic *New York World* caught the policy exactly: "Annexation in any real sense is not necessary or desirable," for a simple protectorate could secure "the interests of our citizens there and the convenience of our commerce."[50]

Racism also infected U.S. policies. All imperialism contained some racism, but in the United States variety it cut in two directions: anti-imperialists argued that Caribbean or Central American areas should not be annexed because the United States already had enough problems absorbing people with brown or black skins, while imperialists insisted that Hawaii must be annexed to protect American whites far outnumbered by Hawaii's major racial groups—Hawaiians, Chinese, Japanese, and Portuguese. Some 7,200 white Americans lived amidst a total population of 109,000. The past commander of the U.S. Asiatic squadron, George Belknap, was "convinced . . . that Japan was anxious to enlarge her [possessions] and find colonial homes for some of her surplus population." He quoted a Japanese naval officer as saying, "We aim to make Japan the England of the Pacific." The new Honolulu government vowed not to let that occur. Apparently only one Japanese, a policeman, was allowed the right to vote in all Hawaii.[51]

In March–April 1897, two events threw Japan and the United States into direct conflict. First, the white Hawaiian government turned back two shiploads of Japanese immigrants on the grounds they were outside the islands' laws. Tokyo bitterly protested such treatment to the point that a battleship sailed in April to protect Japanese citizens. The Hawaiian foreign minister shot back that his country had the right to stop any "individuals dangerous to the community in its moral, sanitary, and economic interests." Realizing such words went too far, the regime tried to cool Tokyo down by turning the crisis over to arbitration. Then the second blow struck. A new President, William McKinley, picked up where his Republican predecessor had left off in 1893. McKinley moved to annex Hawaii. Believing in the exercise of strong central governmental powers, Republicans had little fear the Constitution might be over-stretched. McKinley and his advisers, moreover, never concealed their ambition to make Americans supreme in world markets. Hawaii held a key to Asian markets. U.S. officials, led by the young Assistant Secretary of the Navy Theodore Roosevelt, carefully noted who was sending a warship to keep that key out of American hands.[52]

McKinley and Roosevelt fully realized that annexation could create a flashpoint with Japan. In the spring of 1897, Roosevelt rushed ships toward Hawaii while warning McKinley about the power of Tokyo's fleet. On June 21, 1897, the Japanese foreign minister told Americans that annexation could disturb "the general status quo in the Pacific" and "endanger the actual and important treaty rights of Japan in Hawaii." While denying that Japan held any "designs" on the islands, he indirectly blamed Americans for circulating "mischievous reports" about Tokyo's intentions. McKinley flatly denied each statement. The U.S. Fleet went on alert. It received orders to stop the Japanese if they tried to use force to take Hawaii. The response could include extending the Navy's own "protectorate" over the islands. In Japan itself, U.S. sailors on leave were attacked by angry Japanese. McKinley's annexation treaty, however, became entangled in partisan politics and fights over a new tariff bill. It failed to obtain the necessary two-thirds vote in the Senate during 1897.[53]

The crisis, as both sides knew, had only quieted, not ended. "The United States," Roosevelt told an Ohio audience, "is not in a position which requires her to ask Japan, or any other foreign power, what territory it shall or shall not acquire." During one of their regular carriage rides around Washington, the usually cautious McKinley surprised Roosevelt in September by telling him that he had been "quite right" in publicly criticizing the Japanese.[54]

Roosevelt now pushed the administration to build six more battleships, in part so the U.S. Pacific Fleet could "constantly be kept above that of Japan." He received vibrant public support from the nation's best-regarded naval strategist, Alfred Thayer Mahan. In June 1895, Mahan had publicly observed that Japan's sudden appearance "as a strong ambitious state" not only "fairly startled the world," but deserved attention because Hawaii was "occupied largely by Japanese and Chinese." In a private letter to his good friend Roosevelt on May 1, 1897, Mahan was more explicit: Japan's navy directly threatened Hawaii; U.S. future interests were to face greater dangers in the Pacific than the Atlantic. It was, moreover, in the interest of the Russians (whom Mahan especially feared and despised) to have the United States and Japan at each other's throats. And so Mahan nicely instructed Roosevelt: "Do nothing unrighteous; but as regards the problem take the islands first and solve afterwards" any political and constitutional problems. Roosevelt told the new U.S. Naval War College that it should study a specific war problem: "Japan makes demands on Hawaiian Islands," and the United States responds with force while experiencing "complications" with Spanish-held Cuba.[55]

Suddenly on December 22, 1897, Japan withdrew its protest against possible U.S. annexation, but asked that its citizens' rights be protected on the islands. Two weeks later, the State Department thanked Japan while saying nothing about Japanese rights. The threat of a clash over Hawaii ebbed, but its root causes—a struggle for control of the Pacific and the treatment of Japanese citizens—lingered. Why had Tokyo backed down? Because a new crisis stood virtually on its doorstep. As for McKinley, he faced three crises, two on his own doorstep and one nearly on Japan's.

Joining the Imperialists' Club: The "Splendid Little War" and a Not-So-Splendid War

McKinley's first crisis was the birth cry of America's industrial power-house. Rapid growth in the production of U.S. goods had created a deflationary economic depression whose depths were reached in 1893–96. By early 1897, as McKinley and his near-senile Secretary of State, John Sherman of Ohio, entered office, the economy seemed to be recovering. Given the previous twenty-five years of economic hell, however, few were confident. McKinley quickly moved to protect the domestic U.S. market, while creating sticks and carrots to force other nations to accept American exports, in the 1897 Dingley Tariff.

One target was Japan. By 1894–95, observers warned of a Japanese invasion, with the light infantry being silks, linens, and cheap textiles that flowed out of Japan's factories. Higher duties were quickly imposed so that, as one Paterson, New Jersey, silk manufacturer said, "underval-ued Japanese goods could be kept out of the country."[56]

Merely stopping the influx of cheaper Japanese goods, however, was no solution for a twenty-five-year depression. That solution popped up in 1897 when gold was discovered in Alaska and South Africa (so the amount of money circulating in the United States began to increase), and when exports accelerated—especially in such prime second indus-trial revolution products as steel and locomotives.

The economic relief allowed McKinley to concentrate on his second crisis, a revolution in Cuba. Its roots reached back to 1868, when Cubans rebelled against a corrupt, declining, slave-ridden Spanish colo-nialism. That upheaval was finally quelled by 1878. Then in 1894 when a mere U.S. tariff change discriminated against Cuban sugar exports, the island's economy slumped, unemployment rose, and revolution erupted in 1895—this time with vocal support and financing from private U.S. citizens. As the revolution intensified, $50 million of American property was threatened. When Spain clearly could not keep order in Havana during early 1898, McKinley sent a warship, the *Maine*, to anchor off the capital. In February, a mysterious explosion blew up the ship and killed 250 U.S. sailors. McKinley reacted carefully. It was not clear the tragedy had been caused by Spain (later investigations indicated it probably had not), and the U.S. military was not quite prepared for war. The President moved toward a showdown, but at his own pace and after being certain that war expenses would not push the nation back into depression.[57]

By early 1898, McKinley faced a third critical problem, the problem that also confronted Japan. In 1897, after two of its missionaries were killed in China, Germany demanded as indemnity a major Chinese port, Kiaochou, on the strategic Shantung Peninsula, long desired by Japan. Germany received the port, as well as valuable railway and mineral concessions. The kaiser thereby unleashed an imperialist scramble to bite off other choice portions of the dying Chinese Empire. Russia consolidated its position in Manchuria and tried to increase its influence in Korea. Ito, again holding power in Tokyo, was relatively pro-Russian compared with other Japanese leaders (especially those in the military), but his approach to St. Petersburg was largely rebuffed. So Ito joined the race and asked for a sphere of influence in Fukien Province (that faced Japan's new colony of Taiwan), as well as railway concessions. France continued to nibble away at China's southeastern boundary. Then the major question arose: What would the world's greatest power, Great Britain, do—especially since it controlled 70 percent of China's trade and preferred to keep the Chinese market whole, not chopped off and colonized by London's imperial rivals?[58]

The British had one possible ally—the United States—in keeping China undivided. In January to March 1898, they approached McKinley for cooperation. Americans now realized they had a large stake in Asian developments. Literally hundreds of newspaper and journal articles trumpeted the vast importance of U.S. industrial exports moving into China. In some instances, the argument ran, entire factories—like the giant 25,000-spindle textile plant in Cordova, Alabama—totally depended on the China market. These economic demands were loudly seconded by missionary interests proclaiming that "God has placed us, like Israel of old, in the center of nations" to awaken Asia "out of sleep," so it can "combine with America to make the Pacific Ocean the chief highway of the world's commerce." Less noted was that Japan had become the more profitable market for Americans, and without help from missionaries. U.S. exports to Japan amounted to $20 million, more than twice those to China. On average, each Japanese bought $9.60 in American goods annually, each Chinese 9 cents' worth. But then, China's potential market for U.S. industrial goods was much greater than Japan's, and certainly China (through no wish of its own) was much more open to the missionary word.[59]

McKinley understood all of this. During 1897, his administration labored to open China's interior to U.S. business and missionaries. The President sharply separated friends from enemies. As his mouthpiece, the powerful *New York Tribune,* phrased it in mid-March 1898: "As between Russian rule and Japanese rule, a large share of the civilized world would choose the latter every time. Slav-Tartar-Cossack rule means tyranny, ignorance, reaction. Japanese rule means freedom, enlightenment, progress." U.S. officials, moreover, were convinced that sheer desperation had forced Japan to desert the open-door approach and join the race for colonies. If the United States and Great Britain provided help, the Japanese would work to prop the door back open. Given the Cuban crisis, however, McKinley could not join the British and Japanese—at least not yet. In mid-March, Washington told London that no cooperation was possible until Cuba was pacified. In April, to McKinley's horror, the British carved off the Chinese port of Weihaiwei for themselves to counter the German and Russian moves.[60]

Late that month, McKinley and the Congress declared war on Spain. The President quickly delivered one swift strike to deal with his problems both on the doorstep and in the Pacific. From the start, he eyed Spain's colony in the southwestern Pacific, the Philippines. He and the young Roosevelt had fully discussed the Philippines' possibilities during their buggy rides. Left alone in the Navy Department on February 25, 1898, the hyperactive Roosevelt sent orders to U.S. ships to prepare for war. The next day a surprised president rescinded most of the orders, but not the directive to Admiral George Dewey, commander of the U.S. Pacific Fleet then in Hong Kong. McKinley's decision was not accidental. The plans sent Dewey had been carefully created by U.S. naval planners (not Roosevelt) over several years and personally approved by the President. The war against Spain set these plans in motion. The outbreak of fighting in Cuba generated great support. "Even Bostonians have at last a chance to show they have emotions," wrote a skeptical Henry Adams. Those emotions reached high pitch when Americans learned that Dewey's ships had—with little effort and quite inaccurate

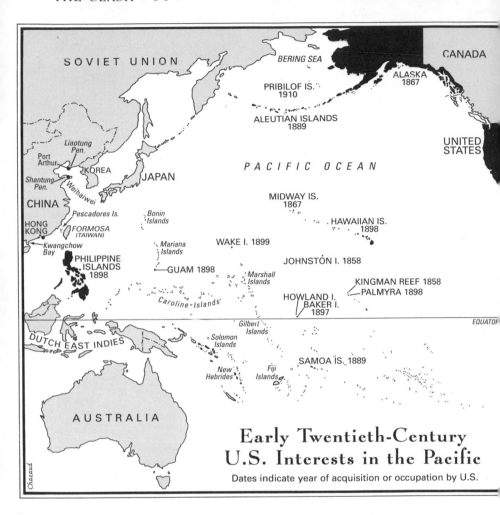

Early Twentieth-Century U.S. Interests in the Pacific

Dates indicate year of acquisition or occupation by U.S.

shooting—destroyed the decrepit Spanish flotilla in Manila Bay on May 1, 1898.[61]

Even before receiving official word from Dewey, an anxious McKinley dispatched twelve thousand troops to occupy Manila. The President also moved quickly to annex Hawaii. "We need Hawaii just as much and a good deal more than we did California," he told his private secretary. "It is manifest destiny." Senate opponents raged that the Philippines and "parts of Asia" would be next: "this Hawaiian scheme is but the entering wedge that cleaves a way open for empire." The critics were correct, but McKinley outfoxed them by skirting the Senate and asking instead for annexation by a joint resolution—a procedure requiring only a simple majority of the House and Senate. Hawaii was annexed in June 1898.[62]

By August, Spain had surrendered. In September, McKinley appointed John Hay Secretary of State. Returning from London where he was serving as U.S. ambassador, Hay intimately knew what was required to reopen the door to China. Having served as Abraham Lincoln's private secretary, and then becoming a wealthy industrialist, Hay also was highly sensitive to the political and economic meanings of foreign policy for Americans. Finally, in late autumn 1898, McKinley ordered the U.S. Peace Commission in Paris to demand that Spain surrender not only Cuba and Puerto Rico but all the Philippines as well. As a result of the "splendid little war" (Hay's phrase), the United States now controlled the strategic Philippines that were to be "the pickets of the Pacific, standing guard at the entrances to trade with the millions of China and Korea, French Indo-China, the Malay Peninsula, and the islands of Indonesia." Or so said the powerful New York banker, and McKinley's assistant secretary of the Treasury, Frank Vanderlip.[63]

But there was a problem. McKinley's attempt to extend formal U.S. power across thousands of miles of water and over millions of non-whites raised storms of protests. The President's fight to obtain Senate ratification for his peace treaty was therefore touch and go until the evening of February 4, 1899, when the White House telegraph informed him that Filipino nationalists had fired on U.S. troops. Even riding a new wave of patriotism, the treaty barely obtained the needed two-thirds vote in the Senate several days later. McKinley suddenly found himself enmeshed in an escalating war that lasted more than three years, took the lives of several thousand Americans and several hundred thousand Filipinos, and, at times, was fought on a subhuman scale.

U.S. policy in Asia now rested on a naval base at Manila and an informal alliance with Japan and Great Britain, the only other two powers interested in the open door. Or as Mahan portrayed the developing global power struggle, the seapowers of Great Britain, Japan, and the United States were pitted against the land powers of Russia, Germany, and France. For Americans, it was a contest of good traders versus evil colonizers.[64]

U.S. policy required a cooperative Japan. During the war of 1898, the Japanese had been preoccupied with German and Russian moves in nearby Manchuria, but worked to stay on good terms with Washington. Ambassador Komura Jutaro, one of Japan's most distinguished diplomats, moved easily in America as he enjoyed strong friendships from his three years at Harvard Law School and an internship at a New York City law firm in the 1870s. A former American teacher of Komura's during the 1870s in Japan told much about Komura—and the American view of Japanese—when he wrote that the diplomat was "a typical product of the new Japan." Thanks to Perry, the teacher rejoiced, the Japanese were now "a rejuvenated race." Heavily involved in pushing Japan into war with China in 1894, Komura knew Asian affairs intimately. In Washington he tried, without success, to guarantee the rights of Japanese in Hawaii and California. Komura also attempted to protect his nation's trading rights in Hawaii. But U.S. officials had decided that the open door no longer applied to the newly annexed islands.[65]

Komura's major task, however, was to pour oil on the friction arising from McKinley's annexation of the Philippines. When the 1898 war erupted, Japan had declared neutrality (its first such declaration in the post-1853 era). Tokyo nevertheless leaned toward the United States, especially in May, when it appeared for an instant that Dewey's fleet in Manila Bay might have to fight not Spain but a German flotilla. The kaiser had designs on the islands. Given the humiliating encounter with the Triple Intervention and the kaiser's grab for Manchurian ports, Germany was, along with Russia, the last nation Japan wanted to hold the Philippines. During a critical moment in the summer, a Japanese warship moved to the side of Dewey's vessels to show friendship. The act received much applause in the United States. When, however, McKinley hesitated in mid-1898 to annex the Philippines, Japan made a move. After all, some of the islands were closer to Japan's new outpost of Formosa than was Cuba to the United States. In September 1898, Tokyo not only asked McKinley that its "immediate concern" be considered, but gently offered to be "associated" in any American plans for the islands. With equal gentleness, the President rejected the offer. Japan accepted the result, given the German alternative. In Formosa, moreover, the Japanese had their hands full pacifying the indigenous people. When Filipinos took up arms against Americans in early 1899, Japan—despite the rebels' pleas to Tokyo for help—did nothing to hurt the new colonizers.[66]

When Americans and Japanese Were Friends

The quarter century after 1873 was pockmarked in both Japan and the United States with economic and social crises. It also was highlighted by both nations' emergence into the inner circle of imperialists. America's leading political humorist, Finley Peter Dunne, had his sage Irish character, "Mr. Dooley," comment on the results of Commodore Perry's 1853 exploits: "Th' throuble is whin the gallant Commodore kicked opn th' door, we didn't go in. They come out." The Japanese coming out was driven by fears of insecurity, especially along the Sea of Japan, and by state-devised policies for economic self-sufficiency—policies about which, in such crucial regions as Formosa and even Korea, the private Japanese business community demonstrated little interest.[67]

Americans meanwhile were driven by their second industrial revolution (that after 1873 produced wondrous amounts of both goods and labor upheavals), and a racism that helped justify actions in Hawaii, the Philippines, and China. During this era of their hectic relationship, Japanese and Americans were attracted to each other by common interests in opening China, working with Great Britain, checking and turning back German and Russian colonialism, and working out solutions to problems in Hawaii and the Philippines. So far, Washington and Tokyo officials had gotten along because of these common interests, and also because whenever a clash loomed, Japan retreated.

By 1900, common interests went beyond common imperial objectives. During the post–Civil War era, and especially in the depression-ridden 1890s, Americans went overboard for sports—college football, basketball (invented in 1891), and, above all, baseball. Historians have explained such enthusiasm in terms of rapid urbanization, which created critical masses of participants and audiences, new transportation systems, and a displacement that transferred economic and social frustrations into sport. An 1877 listing of the most popular sports in Yokohama, Kobe, Tokyo, and Nagasaki listed racing, cricket, yachting, rowing, track and field. But baseball, professionalized in the United States only eight years earlier, was already widely known. The Yokohama Cricket and Athletic Club, with a lineup of entirely English names, was an early baseball powerhouse. In 1873, Horace Wilson introduced the game at what is now Tokyo University. Hiroaki Hiroshi, who had studied in Boston so was already a doomed Red Sox fan, put together the first regular Japanese team in 1878 from Shimbashi railway employees. By the 1890s, Tokyo schoolboys were challenging the Yokohama Club. The Americans first condescendingly refused, then finally agreed to play—and were humiliated by the schoolboys 29–4, 32–9, and 22–6. Only when the Americans brought in ringers from visiting U.S. warships did they finally win. Baseball had captured and captivated Japan, as it had the United States.[68]

That both peoples shared such common passions and emerged as fellow members of the imperialists' club, however, hardly meant they were thinking alike. In 1896, Lafcadio Hearn concluded a study of American and Japanese pictures by observing that "Japanese art reflects the . . . perception of natural law in form and color, the perception of natural law in change, and the sense of life made harmonious by social order and by self-expression." But Western art "reflects the thirst of pleasure" and "the unamiable qualities which are indispensable to success in the competitive struggle." Hearn had "gone Japanese," according to some Western readers.[69]

Even so, his words rang true. As Japan vigorously moved into late nineteenth-century capitalism and imperialism, profound differences remained between that island nation and the Western members of the club. Within just seven years, those differences led officials in Tokyo and Washington to contemplate war between the United States and Japan.

III

The Turn (1900–1912)

In a mere twelve years, between 1900 and 1912, the United States and Japan turned from friendship to rivalry. The reasons for the historic turn were blatant racism and more subtle differences over imperialism. In 1900, the two nations' soldiers stood side by side in the bloody, shell-pockmarked streets of Peking. By 1912, Japan had sealed off Korea and much of South Manchuria while angry Washington officials vowed to pry open those closed doors. Each began to see the other as a probable enemy in a not-distant war. And for the first time in any significant fashion, questions about the all-important arena of China divided, rather than united, Americans and Japanese.

Powers and the Boxers

Americans emerged from their blink-of-an-eye war against a hollow Spanish Empire with their sense of destiny gorged. They now held Hawaiian and the Philippine bases to realize their manifest destiny in Asia. The way finally lay open to exploit the long-sought China market. Their closest allies in the quest were Japan and Great Britain, both sharing a professed devotion to the open-door approach instead of the colonial policies followed by Germany,

Russia, and France. Great Britain, however, was becoming suspect to some U.S. observers. For one thing, London primarily valued India, the jewel in the British crown, and was willing to bargain over China in order to protect that jewel. For another, the British seemed to be on the downward slope of world power. Their surprising defeats at the hands of South Africa's Boers in 1899–1900 stunned pro-British officials in Washington and Tokyo. "The American calf is now too old to get much nourishment from sucking the dry teats of the British cow," Henry Adams chuckled after the 1898 war. That view of Great Britain, however, was not shared by the Japanese.[1]

U.S. interests in China were growing. During the new century's first decade, Americans sent nearly 3,800 Protestant missionaries to spread the gospel around the world; 3,100 were in China. Most missionary organizations had supported the war against Roman Catholic Spain and now wanted the fruits of that effort. "God is beating down the long-closed doors," declared the non-sectarian *Christian Missionary Alliance* triumphantly in April 1898.

Trade seemed to follow U.S. missionaries rather than simply follow the flag, as it did in the case of Japanese and some European imperialism. Exports to China remained at roughly 1 percent of all U.S. exports ($14 million out of $1.2 billion exports in 1899), but observers stressed three features of this trade. First, China seemed to hunger for the products of the burgeoning U.S. industrial complex. More than 90 percent of American exports to China were manufactured goods, a percentage unobtainable in industrializing markets such as Western Europe or Japan. Second, China's potential, the apparently bottomless needs of its 400 million people, could be the world's great market in the new century—if China escaped the heavy hand of European colonization. U.S.-manufactured exports had astonishingly multiplied four times between 1895 and 1890. Third, some industries completely depended on China's market. One South Carolina cotton mill owner told Secretary of State John Hay that either China remained open or textile factories would endure cutthroat competition in the American market: "You can at once see what the importance of the China trade is to us. It is everything." Investors were also being sucked in. Railroad baron James J. Hill planned to make his Great Northern rail system a funnel to Oriental markets. President Cleveland was surprised to discover that Hill knew more about Japan and China than anyone the President had met. And no wonder. Cleveland learned that Hill "had spent more money than the government in sending competent men to Japan and China to study the need of those countries."[2]

In 1899–1900, as the great powers circled around the dying Manchu dynasty in Peking, American popular and business journals sprouted stories about China's future. Doubters were few, but well placed. Worthington C. Ford, a former U.S. Treasury official, argued in 1899 that the Chinese market could never amount to much because purchasing power, not mere numbers, counted. Besides, Ford suggested ominously, if China did develop, its cheap labor could bankrupt Western factories. The large majority of observers, however, agreed with Brooks Adams, a grandson of John Quincy Adams, the eccentric brother of Henry, and a close friend of the up-and-coming Theodore Roosevelt. Brooks was convinced that he had discovered a "law" of history. He concluded that whichever nation controlled the centers of money exchange also controlled the world power. In a widely read essay published just after the 1898 war, he warned that whoever controlled Chinese markets could control the exchanges. The battle was "between the maritime and the unmaritime races" (that is, between the Americans, the Japanese, and the British, on one side, the Russians, French, and Germans on the other). The United States had to have China's markets "or run the risk of suffocation."[3]

Japanese officials agreed in gentler terminology. Between 1898 and 1900, three different cabinets came to power in Tokyo, then disappeared just as China seemed about to dissolve in anti-foreign revolution. Not even the venerated general, Yamagata Aritomo, could provide decisiveness and continuity. In late 1900, Ito Hirobumi regained power. This time he led a political party, the Seiyukai, that added a new, highly unpredictable feature to Tokyo's politics. Ito's innovation infuriated Yamagata and others (especially in the military) who believed that national welfare was too important to be left to such bizarre political factions. All the governments, however, reached some agreement on the central foreign policy question: Should Japan concentrate on China, where the economic payoff could be rich, or on Korea, where the strategic security payoff could be high? In 1898–1901, these officials chose China over Korea.[4]

The choice was made for a number of reasons. Japan, resembling the United States, had discovered profits in the China market. Since the 1880s, Japan had transformed itself from a relatively undeveloped agricultural society into a rapidly industrializing complex. The implications for foreign relations were immense: the percentage of overseas trade to gross national expenditure doubled to 23 percent, and while the bulk of that trade in the 1880s had been with the West, by 1900 about half was with Asia. In Asia, unlike trade with the West, Japan was becoming the industrial center, the profitable hub of the system. During 1895 to 1900 alone, Japan's exports to China, especially in cotton yarn, more than tripled. Japanese surplus capital remained small, but its surplus products were growing and hence becoming dependent (as were some of America's) on keeping the Chinese market open to all on equal terms. When the brilliant diplomat Komura Jutaro returned from his posts in Washington and St. Petersburg to take over the foreign ministry in 1901, he argued that the government must strive to protect and support Japanese involved in the China trade. This led to another reason why China was given preference over Korea: Japan lacked the capital to exploit Korea. Fearful, moreover, that any further move across the Japan Sea could alienate Great Britain while infuriating Russia, Tokyo governments wisely decided to cooperate with the powers in China. Russia, as Yamagata and others had long argued, would have to be dealt with sometime, but not now, given the crises in China. Ito had long argued that Russia was to be stroked, not taunted. Korea, in turn, was to be handled with caution, given the memory of the Triple Intervention against Japan in 1895–96.[5]

Americans and Japanese thus shared some common interests when the Boxer uprising paralyzed parts of China and killed foreign missionaries and diplomats in 1899–1900. The Boxers (more fully, Boxers United in Righteousness) grew out of anti-foreign movements that multiplied in the post-1860 years when China was victimized by the powers. The Boxers especially targeted missionaries and the railway schemes that aimed to place these arteries under foreign control. Thus the revolt also targeted the collapsing Qing (Manchu) dynasty that foreigners pressured into handing out the concessions. The powers' scramble for Chinese territory in 1897–98 was the final straw. Comprised mostly of peasants, and including militant women's groups, the Boxers moved toward Peking, murdering Christian missionaries and converts along the way.[6]

The uprising complicated an already growing crisis for Americans and Japanese in China. In April 1899, the British and Russians had given themselves zones for railway monopolies. Russia also threatened to discriminate against non-Russian shipments over its railways in North China. The U.S. legation in Peking warned Hay that "the situation for China grows more critical, day by day." Panicked messages from U.S. exporters reached the McKinley administration. The Secretary of State had to act. Hay believed fervently in the marketplace's power to produce a happy society run by aristocrats-by-merit like himself. Hating both the new labor unions and the irresponsible rich who wanted to fix (rather than expand) the marketplace, Hay saw China as the ultimate test. His successes as a politician, author, industrialist, and diplomat had gained admirers among fellow aristocrats. "You have indeed led a life eminently worth living, oh writer of books and doer of deeds!" Theodore Roosevelt wrote his good friend in 1899, "and, in passing, builder of beautiful houses and father of strong sons and fair daughters."[7]

Between September 6 and November 21, 1899, Hay set a landmark in American history by sending the powers "a Declaration for an Open-Door Policy with Respect to Trade with China." The Secretary of State asked that within each power's sphere in China, "equal treatment in trade and navigation for the commerce and industry of the United States and all other nations be guaranteed." This first open-door note, the Japanese government decided, was welcome. As the Tokyo cabinet observed, "the monopoly of interests in China by a few powers will be eliminated and the territorial integrity of China will be preserved." But the cabinet carefully added that Japan would accept Hay's terms only if the other powers agreed to abide by them. Such agreement appeared unlikely. Great Britain had earlier pleaded for U.S. cooperation in China. Now it disliked Hay's lone ranger approach and the implied threat to British rail monopolies. Even so, with slight enthusiasm and various qualifications, the British, Germans, Russians, French, and Italians did join the Japanese in accepting Hay's note by April 1900.[8]

Meanwhile, parts of China burst into flames. "Boxers increasing," U.S. Minister Edwin Conger wired Washington in May 1900. "Nine Methodist converts brutally murdered . . . the movement has developed into open rebellion. . . . Many [Chinese] soldiers disloyal." Between June and early August 1900, the Boxers laid siege to the foreign compounds in Peking while killing the German minister and other foreigners. The powers finally decided to send in troops. President William McKinley, amid his own reelection campaign, used his newly acquired base at Manila to send 2,500 soldiers to Peking. This act set a crucial constitutional precedent, for McKinley deployed the troops and warships without congressional authorization, and not merely to protect U.S. citizens but to punish a foreign government. Since the Manchus had joined the Boxers, the Chinese government responded by declaring war on the United States—a declaration ignored by the United States, which did not deign to reply.[9]

Tokyo's initial response was more cautious than McKinley's, even after the Boxers killed a high Japanese official in Peking. Three times the British asked Japan to send military help before the cabinet responded. It finally dispatched the largest number of troops (22,000), and they fought the most effectively of all foreign contingents to lift the siege, at last, on August 14, 1900. Some 76 foreigners (out of nearly 1,000) had lost their lives; about 180 others were wounded. Japan emerged heroic. "What extraordinary soldiers those little Japs are!" Vice President-elect Theodore Roosevelt exulted privately in late 1900. "Our own troops out in China write grudgingly that they think the Japs did better than any of the allied forces." Unfortunately, Roosevelt later added, "The American, German, and English troops are the only ones that have not committed cruel and wanton outrages on women and children." The Japanese were "very callous in their cruelty," although "their commanders took more pains to stop the cruelty" than did other officers. As for the Russians, Roosevelt's dislike poured out: they were "brutal rather than cruel, showing themselves to be heavy animals rather than fiends."[10]

U.S. officials' fixation on Russia was becoming all-consuming. As thousands of the tsar's troops headed toward Peking in July 1900, both Washington and Tokyo intensely debated how to get them back beyond Chinese boundaries once the Boxers were destroyed. On July 3, 1900, Hay sent a second open-door note. This time he asked that all powers observe and uphold "Chinese territorial and administrative" integrity—in other words, that Russia not seize the opportunity to colonize parts of Manchuria. To Hay's surprise, all the powers, including Russia, agreed to the note. Agreement, of course, did not mean observance. Russian officials were deeply divided between war and peace factions, so much so that they too had hesitated before dispatching troops. Senator Henry Cabot Lodge of Massachusetts, a Roosevelt intimate, told the State Department's Asian expert, William W. Rockhill, that "The most significant thing about it [the Chinese crisis] to my mind is the break down of Russia." By late August, however, Russian troops were refusing to leave Manchuria. The situation swung dangerously just as McKinley entered the final weeks of his reelection campaign against the charismatic Democratic Party nominee, William Jennings Bryan of Nebraska.[11]

For 150 years, Americans' belief in the open-door policy—that is, as Hay once defined it, a fair field and no favor for all traders—has been as firm and fundamental as American love of sports (where again, the playing field is supposed to be fair to all). Tokyo, however, has blown hot and cold in its response. This difference readily explains the enmity after 1905, as well as why the two nations heatedly disagreed after the 1960s. But for several pressure-packed months in mid-1900, McKinley nearly ditched the hallowed principle.

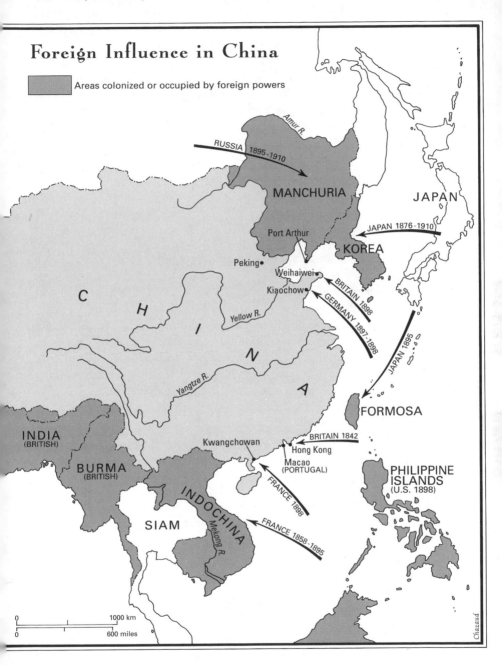

Foreign Influence in China

■ Areas colonized or occupied by foreign powers

RUSSIA 1895-1910
Amur R.
MANCHURIA
JAPAN
Port Arthur
JAPAN 1876-1910
KOREA
Peking•
Weihaiwei•
Kiaochow•
BRITAIN 1898
GERMANY 1897-1898
C
H
Yellow R.
I
N
A
Yangtze R.
JAPAN 1895
FORMOSA
INDIA
(BRITISH)
Kwangchowan
BRITAIN 1842
Hong Kong
Macao
(PORTUGAL)
PHILIPPINE
ISLANDS
(U.S. 1898)
BURMA
(BRITISH)
INDOCHINA
FRANCE 1898
SIAM
Mekong R.
FRANCE 1858-1895

0 ___ 1000 km
0 ___ 600 miles

Chazaud

The reasons were both domestic and foreign. At home, Bryan and the Democrats blasted the President's use of troops to keep China open. If U.S. traders and investors moved into China, the Democrats warned, China's cheap labor would mean that she *"would . . . become the great workshop to fill the markets of the United States,"* while U.S. capital would hire Chinese labor instead of "American labor." Americans who love " 'the open door' . . . would see western civilization crippled." Bryan called imperialism the central campaign issue. He had Andrew Carnegie's millions to back up his assault on McKinley's policies. "Mr. Dooley" sarcastically supported Bryan in the widely read humor column written by Finley Peter Dunne: "We ar-re th' advance guard iv Western Civilization . . . and we're goin' to give ye [Chinese] a railroad so ye can go swiftly to places that ye don't want to see. . . . A counthry that has no railroads is beneath contempt."[12]

In China itself, Russia and Britain maneuvered to partition choice portions of the dying empire. McKinley considered grabbing a strategic slice himself to protect the growing U.S. interests. From a sickbed in Newport, Rhode Island, Hay pulled the President back from the edge. The United States had no alternative, the Secretary of State instructed McKinley, but to play for all China by cooperating, especially with the British and Japanese, in maintaining the open door. Believing that U.S. interests could be protected by "moral" power or American forces alone was "mere flap-doodle." At the same moment, Italy proposed a face-saving compromise that calmed the rivalry in Peking and provided the tsar with an excuse to retreat in Manchuria. McKinley stayed with the open-door principle, the crisis passed, Bryan fumbled away his campaign while the Republicans ran a well-financed race, and the President won reelection in a landslide.[13]

But Hay, it turned out, wanted the best of both worlds, colonial and open door. While supporting his notes, the Secretary of State, apparently without embarrassment, sounded out Japan to see whether it would oppose a U.S. lease on Samsah Bay, in Fukien Province. Japan had tried to obtain rights in Fukien, especially because the province faced its newly seized colony of Formosa. Hay's approach not surprisingly hit a solid wall in Tokyo. Cool officials quoted back to the Americans the open-door principles that prohibited such leases. Hay backed off, then redoubled his efforts to push out the Russians and prop up a crumbling China. In the Boxer Protocol of September 7, 1901, ten Western powers plus Japan forced China to pay a $318 million indemnity, and worse, to accept foreign troops to be permanently stationed in Peking's foreign quarter and other strategic areas throughout the country. The United States tried to reduce the indemnity. Such a large amount left China open to financial pressure from the powers who wanted to finance it. In the end, the American share was largely used to help educate Chinese students in the United States. Japan received relatively little out of the settlement, given its large military commitment. Short of capital, as usual, the Japanese could not join others in the profitable financing of China's bonds to pay the indemnity. They went along with the deal anyway to show a cooperative spirit with the imperial powers.[14]

Ito, indeed, seemed nearly frantic to demonstrate that spirit. "One says that the Japanese and Chinese are of another race and that the yellow race will always have a tendency to draw together and unite against the white race," the prime minister told the Belgian ambassador in 1901. "Nothing is farther from the truth or more absurd." Japan wanted to establish a "progressive government in China," but "in cooperation with the European nations. . . . Our interests in China are identical with those of the industrial powers of both worlds. All our efforts are directed toward the development of our trade and industry, and the big [China] market which is at our door must be open wide to us." McKinley had not said it better. But in September 1901 the President was killed in Buffalo, New York, by an assassin's bullet. In 1909, a Korean nationalist assassinated Ito in Manchuria. By 1909 their successors were talking much less about American-Japanese cooperation.[15]

Yamagata, Roosevelt, and the Russo-Japanese War

The Chinese Empire was gravely weakened by the Boxer intervention (or the "foreign intervention," as Chinese later termed the Boxer episode). The remains were rapidly filling with Chinese nationalism and explosive big-power rivalry. One of the worst fates that can befall a nation befell China: it became utterly unpredictable. Some astute Japanese officials believed the upshot would be "a complete change of government" in China. Western observers more dimly saw a possible radical turn in Chinese affairs. Like the Japanese, Westerners most cared about maintaining foreign rights in Chinese markets. The powers thus faced an awful dilemma when dealing with China before 1949: they wanted to make continual demands on a Chinese government they hoped could deliver concessions, but do so without it becoming a Chinese government that because of the concessions became a target of its people's xenophobia. The West and Japan thus tried to figure out how to have it both ways: a China weak enough to be dominated by foreigners, but strong enough to resist the demands of its own people.[16]

The United States and Japan dealt with this dilemma differently, and, for all the talk about open doors, for different reasons. Americans wanted markets. Japanese wanted markets and security. Americans cared most about open economic competition in Asia. Japanese cared most about Russian military forces. U.S. officials found the worst of their domestic upheavals behind them, in the horrors of the 1890s, and sought economic expansion to keep such protests in the past. Japanese officials feared that without changes the worst of their public protests lay ahead. Japan had to open mainland markets, control and exploit the long-despised Koreans, and drive back Russian forces who refused to keep their agreements of 1901 to evacuate Manchuria. Indeed, in a secret deal that the Japanese discovered, China and Russia had agreed that if the tsar's troops left Peking, China would help Russia build railways in Manchuria that linked up with the great Trans-Siberian railroad system. With China's help, Russia was practically settling on Japan's doorstep.

Japanese officials discussed this growing danger amid unpredictability at home. Since 1868, the Emperor Meiji had been guided by a group of elder statesmen known as the *genro*. From Satsuma and Choshu (the two provinces that led in the overthrow of the Shogun), the five remaining *genro* in 1904 averaged sixty-six years of age. In 1901, for the first time, they failed to solve a political crisis by putting a *genro* member in the prime minister's chair. One *genro,* Ito, stepped down while another (and Ito's longtime political opponent), Yamagata, finally was able to place of his younger followers, Katsura Taro, in the top governmental position. Even as this generational change threatened to shake Japanese politics, Ito tried to counterattack by using his Seiyukai political party as a base. The party had little support from the public. Bearing small resemblance to grass-roots American parties, Seiyukai was made by, for, and with elite officials. But some of the elites, especially Yamagata, hated such parties. In a cunning move during 1903, Yamagata politically beheaded the Seiyukai by having Ito promoted to the Emperor's Privy Council, a job that forced Ito to cut party ties.[17]

Yamagata also moved to strengthen the military's hand in this transitional period. In 1900, the prime minister established the principle that only high, active-service officers could serve as ministers of the army and navy. He excluded civilians from overseeing the military and gave the military a virtual veto power over Japanese politics. Yamagata further checked civilian politicians by helping to insulate the bureaucracy against them. The Civil Service examinations, begun in the 1880s, had created an elite, powerful corps of bureaucrats. By passing through the so-called Dragon Gate into government, this elite saw itself as "servants of the Emperor." By 1900, the best and brightest of Japanese men (quite unlike those in the United States) wanted careers not in law or business but in government. As bureaucrats, they would enjoy enormous prestige, power, and a status above that of most politicians. Yamagata's moves between 1900 and 1904 significantly shaped Japanese politics for nearly the next half century.[18]

More immediately, he shaped those politics by helping Katsura stay in power as prime minister from 1901 to 1906. Member of a Choshu samurai family, Katsura had closely studied the new German military, then distinguished himself as an officer under Yamagata in the 1894–95 war. Named a viscount and a general by 1898, Katsura was nevertheless looked upon as a temporary prime minister in 1901. This view suddenly changed when, to the surprise of many, Komura Jutaro quickly accepted his offer to become foreign minister. The rising star in the foreign policy firmament, fresh from diplomatic successes in Washington and the Boxer crisis in Peking, the Harvard-educated Komura was on his way to becoming perhaps the greatest twentieth-century Japanese diplomat.[19]

Komura had close ties to the United States, and he held great respect for British tradition. (When he died in 1911 at age fifty-seven, the two books on his bedside table were Tennyson and the *Oxford Book of English Verse*.) Above all, however, he was a Japanese nationalist and expansionist. Komura believed that Japan needed Manchuria, both to block Russian power and to exploit the markets. He also concluded that the open door was not the answer. Japan remained too weak to compete: "our commercial capitalists have not yet reached the stage of development at which they could compete equally with those of other countries under such new privileges." The open-door principles were fine for Americans and British. Their industrialization enjoyed a head start over Japan's and they had access to rich raw materials. Open doors did not work as well for Japan. Komura's thinking marked a historic transition in Japanese diplomacy from a willingness to work with the United States along Hay's principles, to a realization that being able to exploit those principles was beyond Japan's power. And that thinking was shaped by Komura's reading of the new industrial revolution.[20]

Between 1901 and early 1904 an epic struggle erupted between Ito's group and the Katsura-Komura government. Ito feared war with Russia and deplored dependence on Great Britain and the United States. He thus advocated "exchanging Korea for Manchuria"—that is, Japan would receive a free hand in Korea in return for recognizing Russia's free hand in Manchuria. On the other hand, Komura's policy aimed at obtaining rights in both Korea and Manchuria. He thought a confrontation with Russia was inevitable. Any deal with the tsar, as Ito urged, would necessarily only be a "short-term remedy." To clear the way, and establish the necessary power alignment, Komura aimed for a formal alliance with Great Britain and an informal understanding with the United States. He knew all about the U.S. aversion to formal alliances. Since the near-disastrous alliance with the French between 1778 and 1800, Americans had kept free of overseas ties so they could freely pursue their own interests. Such going-it-alone was the real definition of their own "isolationism." In early 1904, a U.S. reporter asked Komura whether an American-Japan deal could be worked out so "the Philippine Islands could be the garden, Japan the factory, China the market, and the United States the banker." Komura replied that Japan was fully ready to intensify its manufacturing. He added that the Japanese badly needed Philippine products, especially tobacco and sugar. The foreign minister politely did not add that such a neatly integrated operation was to be worked out on Japanese terms, not necessarily on those of the banker.[21]

Komura's aggressive approach triumphed on January 30, 1902, when Great Britain and Japan signed an alliance that shook the international terrain. The treaty, recognizing Japan's special interest in Korea, further provided that if other powers attacked one of the signatories, the other would come to its aid. In a stroke, Komura put Korea at Japan's disposal. He also prevented any more Triple Interventions from robbing Japan of its conquests, and began to integrate the world's greatest navy with Japan's fleet in war planning along the western Pacific. For their part, the British forestalled a possible Japanese-German deal. They could now preoccupy Russia with Japan in Northeast Asia so the tsar would have less time to pressure Afghanistan and threaten India.[22]

The surprised Russians began to bend by evacuating some troops from Manchuria in 1902. By 1903, however, the retreat stopped. Japan and Great Britain quietly urged Chinese officials to put more pressure on the Russians. The United States, already recognized as an informal member of the Anglo-Japanese alliance, also pushed the Chinese—who instead backed away. "We have done the Chinks a great service, which they don't seem to recognize," declared the State Department's ranking Asian expert William Rockhill. "It will never do to let them imagine they can treat us as they please." After all, "the only power they need fear is Russia."[23]

The Katsura-Komura government meanwhile accelerated war preparations. To ensure a consensus in the cabinet, Komura approached St. Petersburg for a settlement. Russia did not respond for fifty-two days. When the answer appeared in October 1903, it was sobering: the tsar demanded complete freedom of action in Manchuria while limiting Japan's in Korea. Even Ito and the (relative) pro-Russian faction lost patience. Katsura's patron, Yamagata, at last had his chance to seize Korea and drive back Russia, objectives he had harbored since the 1870s. He now presided over a powerful military. Between 1890 and 1919, these forces consumed about 30 to 50 percent of Japan's annual budgets (some 10 to 20 percent of total national income). The policy acclaimed by nearly all officials was *fukoku kyohei,* or "enrich the nation and strengthen its army."

The business community was less united. Sounding much like American business just before the 1898 war, many Japanese worried that war would further destabilize an already depressed economy. But others, especially cotton textile producers, demanded Manchurian markets and were willing to fight Russia for them. Again sounding like U.S. business in early 1898, one newspaper finally decided in early 1904 that this "endless 'uneasy peace' " was "worse than . . . a temporary war." Japanese resembled some Americans in yet another way: while deeply divided over the importance of the new Darwinian and social Darwinian beliefs, a number of expansionists cited them to demonstrate Japanese superiority. Pulling themselves up by their own bootstraps since 1868, the Japanese had shown they were the fittest, that they stood atop the evolutionary ladder along with a few other great powers. Further expansion (especially over the less fortunate Chinese) was in a future that all enlightened and worthy people could glimpse.[24]

By early 1904, Japan was in a war frenzy. U.S. Minister Lloyd Griscom reported to Washington that "The Japanese nation is now worked up to a high pitch of excitement." If no war occurred, "it will be a severe disappointment to the Japanese individual of every walk of life. The people are under such a strain that the present condition cannot last long." A Japanese war song chanted that Great Britain, "Lion, Lion, the king to the Beasts," now "approves of us, and America sympathizes with us in the war for civilization." The lyrics were correct: Komura had carefully kept President Roosevelt and Secretary of State Hay informed about his talks with Russia. He knew that the Americans quietly, but fully, supported Japan. Yet on February 4, 1904, when the Imperial Conference decided to wage war, it was not done without fear. The army figured it had only a fifty-fifty chance of defeating Russia; the navy expected to lose half its fleet. To avoid such disaster, the government launched a surprise strike that destroyed part of the Russian fleet at Port Arthur, and landed troops in Korea before the tsar received a declaration of war. Americans and British applauded such ingeniousness. U.S. Minister Horace Allen told Washington that since "These people [Koreans] cannot govern themselves," a "civilized race" like Japan should take over "these kindly Asiatics for the good of the people and . . . the establishment of order and the development of commerce." Of course, Allen was confident Japan would keep Korea "open" to all for "development of commerce."[25]

At the same time, Japan dispatched an old friend of Roosevelt's Harvard days, Kaneko Kentaro, to Washington for talks with the President about how the conflict could end. As the historian Shumpei Okamoto observes, Japanese officials thus were "thinking of ending the war at the time of beginning it." Roosevelt and most Americans thoroughly sympathized with the Japanese position. At the 1904 Louisiana Purchase Exposition in St. Louis, the Japanese, one reporter wrote, were no longer seen as "half-developed, peculiar people" who made "toys and knickknacks," but as "one of the first nations of the world." Another writer breathlessly explained in Darwinian terms that Japan's quick triumphs over Russia were understood by anthropologists as resulting from "the complexity of the blood." Resembling Anglo-Saxons, Japanese were "the most complex" people in Asia. (The writer also admitted that anthropologists actually knew little about Japanese.) At the Portland Exposition in 1905, a journalist fantasized over the profits to be made from 800 million Asians, "half of the population of the entire world," when "they wake up after the Russo-Japanese war. . . . The day when the Pacific shall be transformed into an American lake will come even earlier than Seward's prophetic vision grasped." Such optimism rested on one assumption: that a victorious Japan would open Asian markets to Americans.[26]

Not everyone trusted the Japanese. U.S. investors poured $55 million into Russia by 1906. Some made fortunes in helping build the Trans-Siberian and other transportation networks. Powerful Republican Party figures, including Civil War hero and railway entrepreneur James Harrison Wilson and New York attorney John J. McCook, tried to persuade McKinley and Roosevelt that Russia could be a more profitable and less dangerous partner than Japan. The two presidents were not moved. The arch-expansionist Republican senator from Indiana, Albert J. Beveridge, then warned that if the Japanese and British gained control of Asia, American goods would be shut out. Only Russia's market and cooperation, the Hoosier senator argued, could make U.S. involvement worthwhile. Roosevelt's close friend Henry Adams took another, more ominous, approach: "Everybody is interested, and excited, and all are anti-Russian, almost to a dangerous extent [Adams wrote privately in 1904 as the Russo-Japanese War erupted]. I am the only—relative— Russian afloat, and only because I am half-crazy with the fear that Russia is sailing straight into another French revolution which may upset all Europe and us too. A serious disaster to Russia might smash the whole civilized world."

Adams understood a fundamental fact about this era that too few others saw. Japan and Russia were both backward, brittle societies, compared with the rapidly industrializing Americans and West Europeans, and given the terrible precariousness of each of these societies, any setback could trigger a string of internal catastrophes. Americans were being driven outward by their successes and divisions at home, but both Japanese and Russians were being driven outward by weakness and divisions at home. Adams's choice was not merely to be friendly toward Russia. He wanted to quit the search for Asian markets. Adams suggested building a tariff wall around the United States to shut out cheap Asian goods. Perhaps then, he speculated, Asians could sort things out for Asia, while Americans could keep their system going at least several more generations.[27]

The ebullient occupant of the White House pooh-poohed his friend's dark outlook. Roosevelt had closely studied America's Asian destiny. He had also been tutored by Brooks Adams and Alfred Thayer Mahan on the need to develop and protect (by force if necessary) Asian markets. His country was entering the Pacific Century, Roosevelt passionately believed, and Japan was fighting America's fight against Russia.

Although heavily racist (when he especially wanted to demean someone he called them a "Chinese"), and believing that race was a primary determinant in history, TR had little belief in social Darwinism. The President recalled that social Darwinism could be championed by ardent anti-imperialists (as William Graham Sumner), as well as by imperialists. He preferred Lamarckianism, with its suggestion that superior races could improve the characteristics of the inferior. Social Darwinism in the United States (and Japan) was too complex to lend itself as an easy explanation for imperialism or anti-imperialism. Certainly Roosevelt considered it unimportant that the "Japanese are of an utterly different race from ourselves and . . . the Russians are of the same race." As he had earlier noted, Russians posed a "more serious problem" to future Americans than did even Germany, while "Russians and Americans . . . have nothing whatsoever in common." Roosevelt even later bragged that in 1904 he had warned France and Germany not to interfere against Japan, a boast without documentary evidence.[28]

At the same time, Roosevelt understood he was dealing with dynamite. As he wrote in one letter: "if the Japanese win out, not only the Slav, but all of us will have to reckon with a great new force in eastern Asia. . . . If, moreover, Japan seriously starts in to reorganize China and makes headway, there will result a real shifting of the center of equilibrium as far as the white races are concerned." In another letter of mid-1904, he wrote that over lunch he had told his old friend, Baron Kaneko, that Japan "might get the 'big head' and enter into a general career of insolence and aggression" that could turn out to be "very unpleasant for Japan." Roosevelt apparently suggested to Kaneko that Japan follow its own Monroe Doctrine in Asia—that is, civilize and order, but not conquer, the region. (In the 1930s these alleged Rooseveltian remarks were resurrected by an imperialist Japan.) The President also told Kaneko that Americans could learn from Japan about how to deal with "the misery in our great cities," but the Japanese "had to learn from us the ideal of the proper way of treating womanhood." Kaneko agreed. In all, the President noted to his intimate friend, British Ambassador Cecil Spring Rice, in June 1904, if the Japanese "win out it may possibly mean a struggle between them and us in the future; but I hope not and believe not."[29]

How to avoid the "struggle" haunted Roosevelt during the next four years of his presidency. He failed to find an answer, other than retreating from Asia and leaving it to the Japanese. Not wanting either the "despicable" Russians or the Japanese with their "big head" to triumph, TR hoped "that the two powers will fight until both are fairly well exhausted." The peace terms would then "not mean the creation of either a yellow peril or a Slav peril." It was a pious hope. The well-drilled front-line Japanese forces overran ill-prepared Russian reservists, then in early 1905 won tougher battles at Port Arthur and Mukden. Mukden cost Japan at least 41,000 casualties and Russia nearly 60,000. But Russian resources seemed limitless; Japan's were not. "While the enemy still has his powerful forces in its [sic] home country," Yamagata warned, "we have already exhausted ours."[30]

Some Americans stepped forward to help replenish Japan's resources. They were led by leading Jewish investment bankers in New York City who had witnessed, or personally endured, the atrocities com mittcd by Russians against Jews, especially between the early 1880s and the Kishinev Massacre of 1903. These pogroms produced both a wave of Jewish immigration into the United States and anti-Russian measures by the U.S. Congress, including economic retaliation. Roosevelt, who valued Jewish friends and political support, condemned the tsar's brutalities, although more privately than publicly.

After the already-strapped Japanese treasury failed to float large loans in London and New York during April 1904, Jacob Schiff, the powerful head of the Kuhn, Loeb investment bank, took charge. He worked with his friend, Lord Rothschild, of the great European banking house, to block Russian loans in London and Paris. Schiff then put together for Japan the first major flotation of foreign securities successfully offered in New York City. In all, Schiff helped Japan sell Americans four bond issues that totaled nearly $350 million, or almost half the cost of the entire war for Tokyo. For the third loan, Kuhn, Loeb sought $95 million for Japanese war bonds, but received $500 million in subscriptions in only several hours. These loans marked the birth of Wall Street as a force in international diplomacy. One journal noted that it had "never known a conflict in which the United States was not an active participant wherc there was anything like the unanimity of opinion or intensity of sympathy which is felt in the republic for Japan."[31]

Despite Schiff's herculean efforts, by April 1905 Japanese officials found themselves in a bind. On the one hand, Katsura and especially Komura had enlarged the primary objective from Korea solely to Korea and Manchuria. Elated and overconfident, they aimed, yes, to remove the Russian danger from South Manchuria, but also replace it with Japanese power. They believed they could do this without stepping on the considerable U.S. economic interests in Manchuria. Throughout 1904–05, Komura reassured Roosevelt that Japan only wanted to defeat Russia; otherwise Tokyo would accept the Asian status quo. (Komura especially pushed this line after the Russians told the President that once Japan obtained Korea, the Philippines would be next.) Komura was not being quite straight with the person whom the Japanese hoped might mediate their victory. But his government's bind was tighter. For as their victories grew in number, and as the Japanese endured the terrible financial and social strains (not to mention 81,000 dead), they came to expect riches from the war—that is, they expected a large indemnity as well as territory from the tsar. Katsura and Komura knew better. Japanese officials realized they now faced a Russian army three times the size of Japan's. The tsar had used the Trans-Siberian line to move fourteen trains a day and transfer 500,000 troops from Europe.[32]

As early as March 8, 1905, Japan had quietly approached Roosevelt for his good offices to help end the war. The tsar, however, was not ready to deal. Despite the Bloody Sunday outbreak in January at St. Petersburg, a violence that anticipated the outbreak of the Russian Revolution, the tsar awaited the climatic battle of his Baltic fleet. For nearly eight months those ships had sailed eighteen thousand miles from the Baltic Sea, around Europe and Africa, then through the Indian Ocean, to engage Japan's in the Battle of the Japan Sea on May 27–28. To the world's amazement, the Japanese won a complete victory. Roosevelt believed that "Even the Battle of Trafalgar could not match this. I could not believe it myself. . . . I grew so excited that I myself became almost like a Japanese, and I could not attend to official duties." The President now pressed Tsar Nicholas (this "preposterous little creature" who was "unable to make war" and "is now unable to make peace") to negotiate. But the initiative for Roosevelt's good offices, unknown to the Japanese people, came from Japan.[33]

For his part, Roosevelt wanted that war ended quickly before "Japan will drive Russia out of East Asia." It was "best," he told Senator Henry Cabot Lodge, that Russia "be left face to face with Japan so that each may have a moderative action on the other." In a June 16, 1905, letter to his British friend, Spring Rice, Roosevelt described the victors: "What wonderful people the Japanese are! They are quite as remarkable industrially as in warfare." He acutely noted two unusual features of Japan's effort. Even while fighting Russians, the Japanese were able to increase their exports into the China market. Moreover, their new steamers carrying this export trade were wondrous: they "are not allowed to compete with one another," but only with foreign ships, and the Japanese usually won. Roosevelt then expressed fear: "In a dozen years the English, Americans and Germans, who now dread one another as rivals in the trade of the Pacific, will have each to dread the Japanese more than they do any other nation."[34]

Roosevelt did not attend the peace conference at Portsmouth, New Hampshire, in July and August 1905. From Washington and his home, Sagamore Hill on Long Island, however, he oversaw every detail. The Russian delegation was headed by Count Sergei Witte, the creator of the Trans-Siberian rail system and highly respected by U.S. leaders. Komura led Japan's group, but only after Ito turned down the job, probably because as a skilled politician he knew the Japanese people were going to be furious about the results. Komura also understood the dilemma. He agreed with an aide who noted the people were sending them off with cries of *"Banzai!"*, but the return cry could be *"Bakayaro"*

(You fool!). Military leaders mistrusted Komura, and with good reason: they had wanted peace before Russia's sheer numbers ground down their forces. But Komura wanted empire. They won their demands that the skillful foreign minister must not exceed his instructions and had to remain in close touch with Tokyo. His instructions listed "absolutely essential" items that were to be obtained: a free hand in Korea and control of South Manchuria, including the key railway. "Comparatively essential" demands were to obtain an indemnity and all of Sakhalin. Once Komura obtained the former demands, he could give up the latter group, if necessary, to obtain peace.[35]

For Komura, one issue shaped the conference and, indeed, much of the U.S.-Japan relationship that followed: the Japanese need to become financially independent so they could expand on the Asian mainland, especially in Manchuria, on their own terms. To have such freedom, a Russian indemnity was absolutely necessary. Otherwise, Japan would have to continue borrowing in New York and London, both to pay the ruinous war expenses and to have capital for projects in Korea and Manchuria. One question burned: Could Japan develop an Asian empire on its own terms, or must it bow to the open-door, non-colonization terms of Washington? The foreign minister believed there was no choice.

Roosevelt tried to set the tone at his first meeting with Komura and Witte when he cut through a fight over protocol by grabbing each man by the arm and taking them through a doorway to dinner at the same time, then making everyone stand up while eating from a round table. Komura, given the results on battlefields and oceans, believed he should be treated more equally than Witte. The foreign minister quickly wrested Russia's agreement to the "absolutely essential" demands for Korea and Manchuria. But on the orders of the tsar, who believed that Russia might have lost some battles but had certainly not lost the war, Witte stood fast: no indemnity ("Russia will not pay even a kopeck," the tsar exclaimed), no cession of Sakhalin, no limiting of Russia's fleet in the western Pacific.[36]

Komura publicly prepared to break up the conference and return to Japan. At the last minute he was overruled by the military and the *genro,* including Ito, who instructed him to compromise. On August 29, Komura proposed giving up the indemnity if Russia left Sakhalin. After a long silence during which Komura's bitterness no doubt grew, Witte accepted. Japan now held Korea, South Manchuria as a protectorate, the southern half of Sakhalin, and had removed Russian power from the Japan Sea. Roosevelt, it turned out, won the Nobel Peace Prize for his efforts—a prize that the critics of the war-loving, big-game-killing Roosevelt found richly ironic, if not flabbergasting.[37]

But no more flabbergasting than the Japanese people found the peace terms. When they learned there was to be no indemnity, offices were hung with mourning crepe. Chanting "Constitutional Government at Home, Imperialism Abroad," even relative moderates expressed outrage. In September 1905, anti-peace riots rocked Tokyo. How much they were fueled by anti-Americanism is in dispute, but Japanese police records revealed that mobs surrounded the U.S. legation, and Americans were attacked at the Imperial Hotel. When a gruesome picture of the heads of Komura and Roosevelt dripping with blood appeared, the crowd cheered. Komura quietly returned to Tokyo, fearing for his life. Admiral Togo Heihachiro, hero of the naval battles, was welcomed by cheering throngs.[38]

Manchuria: The First Clash

During his several months in the United States, Komura grew even more fearful of American open-door principles. They would not make Japan more self-sufficient inside an Asian empire. Important American opinion, moreover, had cooled toward Japan. The *Florida Times-Union* captured the essence of other editorials, including those in New York City newspapers, by writing that, "Japan may not want the earth, but her plenipotentiaries have evidently made a pretty good break at it." Roosevelt remained outwardly friendly. His desire to balance Russia against Japan was known, however. During the war his feelings became clearer when he wrote privately, "I am not at all sure that the Japanese people draw any distinctions between the Russians and other foreigners, including ourselves. I have no doubt that they include all white men as being people who, as a whole, they dislike, and whose past arrogance they resent; and doubtless they believe their own yellow civilization to be better. . . . Japan is an oriental nation, and the individual standard of truthfulness in Japan is low." The President concluded that Americans, in the end, had to depend not on Great Britain ("she is pretty flabby"), but on the U.S. Fleet. He consequently reinforced units in the Philippines. TR also worried over Japanese in Hawaii, who outnumbered the white population. According to the U.S. governor of the territory, they were becoming "insolent" because of Japan's military victories.[39]

On the immediate question of Korea, however, Roosevelt quickly made a deal that helped seal that nation's fate. Forgotten were the 1882 American assurances to Korea that "if other Powers deal unjustly or oppressively with either Government, the other will exert its good offices . . . to bring about an amicable arrangement." No matter that Minister Horace Allen had assured Korea's Kojong, now a self-styled emperor, that Americans would not leave him in the lurch. At least by early 1905, Roosevelt had decided that Japan might better be engrossed in Korea than in China or California. In mid-1905 he dispatched Secretary of War William Howard Taft for an inspection trip to the Philippines, with a detour to Tokyo. Taft was accompanied by Roosevelt's spectacular twenty-one-year-old daughter Alice. She loved to shock onlookers by smoking in public and wearing a boa constrictor around her neck. Once when a friend criticized Roosevelt for not making his daughter behave, TR responded, "I can be President of the United States—or . . . I can attend to Alice." Not even the energetic Roosevelt could do both. Alice was a reporter's dream. As Taft, Alice, and their eighty-person entourage docked at Yokohama in July 1905, they expected the usual stiff, polite greetings the always-correct Japanese bestowed on foreign dignitaries. Instead, they were met by huge fireworks displays, vast crowds of people waving flags, and bands playing American songs. Lodged at an imperial home, they were given the unparalleled honor of being shown the Emperor's gardens. Reporters from both the United States and Japan followed Alice everywhere.

The reporters made a mistake. While Alice was attracting crowds, Taft met quietly with Prime Minister Katsura on July 27. Taft began by declaring that Americans discounted those "pro-Russians" who warned that Japan would next attack the Philippines. He knew the Japanese wanted the islands under a friendly nation rather than an "unfriendly European power." Katsura agreed "in the strongest terms," then added that all these stories about "the yellow peril" threatening California and U.S. interests in China were "malicious and clumsy slanders." He added that he hoped the United States, Great Britain, and Japan could formally ally. Katsura understood, however, that this was not in accord with American tradition. True, Taft replied, but the United States wanted to work with its two friends "as confidently as if [it] were under treaty obligations." Seizing the opening, Katsura said that something had to be done about Korea. There would be no Asian peace if that nation fell "into her former condition." Taft jumped in: in his opinion "Japanese troops" should establish a "suzerainty" over Korea so Japan would control its foreign relations.

Out of this exchange came the Taft-Katsura agreement that Roosevelt approved four days later: the Japanese recognized America's hold on the Philippines while the United States recognized Japan's full control of Korea. This executive agreement, one of the first important such agreements made by a president on his own, avoided possibly embarrassing ratification debates in the U.S. Senate. The agreement was also sealed in secrecy. The Taft-Katsura deal was not known publicly until the historian Tyler Dennett discovered Taft's memorandum in the Roosevelt Papers nearly twenty years later. The United States, the first Western nation to recognize Korea in 1882, became—at Japan's request, which Roosevelt immediately met—the first nation to withdraw its diplomats from Korea in 1905. The young romantic secretary of the departing U.S. legation in Seoul, Willard Straight, was enamored of Alice, but not of her father's policy, which he compared to "the stampede of rats from a sinking ship." Straight found himself "hating the Japanese more than anything in the world." In a few years he was in the forefront of the American drive to block Japanese expansionism in Manchuria.[40]

More immediately, Foreign Minister Komura began to block the United States in Manchuria. He was now supported by Yamagata, and the army, who meant to ensure that Russians never again threatened Korea. Roosevelt had suggested strongly to Japan that Manchuria should be fully returned to China and open to all on a fair-field-and-no-favor basis. Komura assured both Washington and London he agreed. He significantly added, however, that "peace and order" had to be guaranteed, and he implied the Chinese could not provide such a guarantee.

In October 1905, the great U.S. railway builder Edward H. Harriman appeared in Tokyo to take advantage of Japan's financial dilemma by offering to buy the South Manchurian Railway. He planned to place it under joint U.S.-Japanese control and make it a pivotal section of a globe-girdling transportation network. Prime Minister Katsura, as well as officials of the Mitsui and Mitsubishi *zaibatsu*, liked Harriman's offer. They saw him as a pipeline to American money; they also believed the Russians would never challenge a U.S.-Japanese partnership. But Komura, freshly returned from Portsmouth, strongly dissented. He warned that Harriman's ties to Wall Street capital made him much the stronger partner. The foreign minister urged that Japan instead raise its own money and work with the disintegrating Chinese government to ensure Japan's hold on South Manchuria. Komura then killed Harriman's proposal with a disingenuous argument: Since Japan was not sovereign in South Manchuria, it could not enter into such an agreement with the American. The foreign minister next strong-armed the Chinese into ceding the South Manchurian Railway to Japan in December 1905. A frustrated Harriman angrily compared Komura with Machiavelli.[41]

One voice issued a warning: given its dependence on Great Britain and the United States, Japan was moving too rapidly. Ito Hirobumi had earlier worried to his private secretary about "the attitudes of our people." For if Japan "ignores the proper rights and interests of other nations and behaves outrageously . . . national ruin is certain. . . . Our people must constantly be warned that 'the high tree encounters strong wind.'" He fought Komura's aggressive foreign policies, only to be named in 1906 as Japan's first consul general over Korea. On May 22, 1906, Ito lectured the new cabinet of his protégé, Prime Minister Saionji Kimmochi, that in recent days both U.S. and British officials had vigorously protested because Manchuria under Japanese control was less open to Western goods than it had been when under Russian. Ito warned that if this Manchurian problem was mishandled, the penalties could be severe: Koreans would seize the chance "by reaching out to Russia, as Japan has yet to win over their hearts and souls."

In a prophetic moment, Ito added that Japan had to work with, not exclude, China in Manchuria. A hostile policy could trigger Chinese "nationalist intentions" and "xenophobia." Finally, in another war against Russia or China, "Japan needs to keep the British and Americans happy and sympathetic towards us for financial reasons." Convinced, the Saionji cabinet decided to reopen parts of Manchuria and replace Japanese military administration with Chinese. Japan's business community was notably relieved; its links to China and Western money markets were reinforced. Japan's military was not relieved. Its ambitions had grown since 1904, and its officers believed that Manchuria had to be fully controlled for strategic and economic reasons.[42]

Ito's temporary victory proved pyrrhic. While traveling through Manchuria in 1909, he was killed by a young Korean nationalist. After learning the assassin's motives, Ito's last words were "what a fool." The next year Japan completed its annexation of Korea. After 1945, when Korea finally became free of Japan, Ito's assassin was immortalized by having his statue erected in front of Ito's former Korean residence.[43]

The Crisis in California—and Beyond

By 1906, Americans marveled at Japan's triumphs in Korea and South Manchuria. So did others. The British, Germans, French, and Americans raised Japan's diplomatic standing from legations to the top rung of "embassy." Japanese diplomats were to be recognized as ambassadors rather than mere ministers. Ito may have feared for Japan's future, but not many Americans agreed. They instead agreed with Finley Peter Dunne's Mr. Dooley, who thought the Japanese had become almost supernatural: "[A] Jap'nese rowboat cud knock to pieces th' whole [US] Atlantic squadron. . . . They use guns that shoot around th' corner. . . . On land they ar're even more tur'rible. A Jap'nese sojer can march three hundhred miles a day an'subsist on a small piece iv chewein' gum. . . . Above all, th' Jap'nese is most to be feared because iv his love iv home an' his almost akel [equal] love iv death. He is so happy in Japan that he wud rather die somewhere's else. Most sojers don't like to be kilt. A Jap'nese sojer prefers it." It was not the last time Americans caricatured Japanese abilities. But in this humor column, Mr. Dooley was much closer to the truth when he observed, "A subjick race is on'y funny whin it's raaly subjek. About three years ago [1904] I stopped laughin' at Japanese jokes."[44]

Californians shared both Mr. Dooley's racism and his failure to find Japanese funny. Problems in the Golden State had begun in 1882 when the U.S. Congress for the first time restricted immigration, but only from China. By 1891, Chinese labor was being replaced by the thousand and more Japanese who entered the United States each year. In 1890, about 2,000 Japanese lived in California; by 1900, there were 24,000, many flowing out of the new U.S. territory of Hawaii. Japanese from Hawaii (and Canada) swamped a 1900 Gentlemen's Agreement in which Tokyo officials had promised to curtail emigration. The *San Francisco Chronicle*, prodded by the Japanese and Korean Exclusion League, began to warn of a growing "Yellow Peril," especially those foreigners whom Californians condemned for offering "labor for less than a white man can live on." The immigrants from Japan, moreover, were condemned for staying in their own neighborhoods, reading their own newspapers, strongly supporting their own people, and, in all, not assimilating. This "Yellow Peril," however, seemed limited to northern California. Oregon, Washington, and especially southern California condemned the growing anti-Asian agitation, not least because, as the *Los Angeles Times* noted, these areas needed farm and orchard labor. In early 1906, James J. Hill, president of the Great Northern Railroad, told Japanese officials he was employing over twelve hundred of their citizens and wanted three to five thousand more. The officials replied they were trying to limit emigration to improve relations with the United States, but Hill continued to advertise in California and Hawaii for Japanese labor.[45]

That same year, 1906, the great San Francisco earthquake destroyed many schools. In October the Board of Education ordered, allegedly because of lack of space, that all Chinese, Japanese, and Korean children go (sometimes at a great distance) to a segregated Oriental Public School. The timing was not thoughtful: Japan's Red Cross had just sent a quarter-million dollars to help California's earthquake victims. The Japanese government strongly protested the segregation of its citizens. A leading Tokyo newspaper cried: "Stand up, Japanese nation! Our countrymen have been HUMILIATED. . . . Why do we not insist on sending [war]ships?" Roosevelt was furious at the "idiots" in California. The tension over Portsmouth, and especially Manchuria, the defeat of the white race in 1904–05 by Asians, the realization that Japan could easily endanger the Philippines—all this sharpened the President's tart-tongued views about parochial Americans. In his annual message of 1906 he called the school board's act "a wicked absurdity."[46]

The President and Secretary of State Elihu Root summoned San Francisco school officials to the White House, where Roosevelt dictated a deal: the segregation order was to be rescinded in return for the Japanese promise (the so-called Gentlemen's Agreement of 1907) to allow only non-labor relatives of laborers already in America, or laborers who owned property, to leave for the United States. Roosevelt helped quiet Californians by issuing a proclamation barring Japanese laborers in Mexico, Canada, or Hawaii from the United States mainland.

In a letter of 1905 to his close friend Senator Lodge, the President condemned California's action—"as foolish as if conceived by the mind of a Hottentot." He moved on to discuss growing Japanese power, the intensifying competition over "oriental markets," and concluded—as he did in a number of personal letters at this time—by expressing confidence in the U.S. battleship fleet. During 1905 to 1908, the possibility of war between Americans and Japanese was much in the air. Since 1900, the U.S. Navy had risen from the world's seventh to the third or second largest, just behind Great Britain and probably Germany. Japan's ranked fifth. The Americans, however, had to patrol two oceans and were presiding over a large number of Marine Corps interventions in the Caribbean region. Japan could concentrate its forces in the western Pacific. The Panama Canal, which Roosevelt had begun to build in a fit of expansionism in 1903, would not be usable until 1914. Rumors flew that Japan might attack the Canal before it opened. Those rumors were unfounded, but in 1907—as anti-Asian riots again erupted in California—Japanese naval planners carefully reexamined the importance of the future Canal. The Imperial Defense planners saw the United States as a primary potential enemy. They feared, moreover, that the Canal would allow Americans to move more efficiently into China's market.[47]

In 1906, Roosevelt and his military advisers began their first systematic planning for war against Japan—War Plan ORANGE. It concluded that, first, Japan was now a possible enemy in the Pacific; and second, U.S. forces could probably defend Guam and Hawaii, but not the Philippines. In one sense, Roosevelt now found himself back with Lincoln and Seward: the nation's open-door interests in China and Manchuria had to be protected by cooperative diplomatic and military efforts with allies, not by the world's second-greatest fleet, which lacked the power to act unilaterally in Asia. The United States, in other words, seemed as dependent on Japan for the maintenance of stability and openness in Asia, as Japan was dependent on the United States for capital. Certainly Roosevelt, to his embarrassment, found himself having to change his mind about the Philippines. As a Republican vice-presidential candidate in 1900, he had condemned the anti-annexationists with such fervor that he lost his voice. Just seven years later, the Philippines, as Roosevelt admitted, "form our heel of Achilles. They are all that make the present situation dangerous."[48]

For months, however, the President fought the notion that historic U.S. interests in Asia depended increasingly on Japanese cooperation. He hoped that the U.S. Fleet would give him and his successors the power to deal with an uncooperative Japan, while—unilaterally if necessary—protecting American interests in the trans-Pacific West. To demonstrate this unilateral power in the late spring of 1907, he decided to send the fleet on an around-the-world cruise.

A majority of American newspapers favored this showing of the flag, although the *New York Evening Post* warned it could "heighten the bad feeling against the Japanese . . . and . . . encourage the talk of war." Other critics worried that Japan would seize the moment to invade Hawaii, or perhaps even attack California. The problem, however, was not to project U.S. power into California, but 5,000 miles away into Asia. The Japanese cordially invited the warships to visit. The "Great White Fleet" finally arrived in Tokyo during October 1908, after a ten-month voyage. The sixteen first-class cruisers were greeted tumultuously, not by the suspicious anti-foreignism that had tormented Perry and Harris, but by hundreds of thousands of Japanese waving the Stars and Stripes and singing "The Star-Spangled Banner"—in English. Over the 434 days of sailing, the ships spent more power in salutes than had been shot off in the entire 1898 war. But the Asian balance of power never changed. Moreover, Roosevelt was embarrassed to learn that it was now clear that U.S. posts in the Pacific could not adequately ser-

vice the fleet in wartime. During the cruise, the ships even had to borrow coal from the British.[49]

The fleet's cruise merely highlighted American problems with Japan
rather than solving them. For example, fear was rising, not only from
Californians but from U.S. missionaries in Japan. When the Japanese
Edict of Toleration in 1873 legitimated Christian proselytizing, the missionaries took it as a sign of coming conversions rather than for what it
was: a move to appease the Western powers so they would dismantle
the unequal treaties and treat Japan as an equal. The 138 American
missionaries of 1883 grew to 723 in 1900, but Japanese Christians systematically took over the movement from Westerners. The Emperor's
1890 Rescript on Morals, moreover, emphasized how much more
acceptable were Shinto and Confucian values for the state. Fifteen
years later, Japan no longer had to appease the missionaries. John R.
Mott, the hyperactive evangelist who founded the Young Men's Christian Association, worried about Japan's "almost insane patriotism," then
pointedly asked, "Japan is leading the Orient—but where?" Mott's
warnings were counterbalanced in 1907 when a group of prominent
Americans led by Lindsay Russell, an attorney, and his friend Hamilton
Holt, founded the Japan Society to develop understanding between the
two countries.[50]

Russell and Holt had their work cut out. The 1905 triumph, in the
words of a later scholar, "had made imperialists of all Japanese, even
those as yet unborn, who were to learn of the glory of the Japanese
victory from their primary school books." That imperialism, however,
focused on nearby Asian regions, not Hawaii or California. Foreign
Minister Komura embodied this view. Believing that Japan had become
a "semi-continental power" in Asia, he warned that "we should avoid
scattering our people in the foreign countries [such as the United
States] where they are lost."[51]

Roosevelt gradually acknowledged the inevitable: Japan controlled
South Manchuria. His moment of truth arose in late 1908. Willard
Straight, still detesting Japan after serving as U.S. consul general in
Harbin, Manchuria, tried to work with Chinese officials to build a
South Manchurian bank-rail system to counter the Japanese railroads.
The twenty-eight-year-old diplomat was driven not only by his racism
but by a romantic determination to win—in Kipling's phrase—"the
great game of empire." Straight excitedly rushed back to Washington to
obtain Roosevelt's agreement to build the competing rail line. But the
Japanese, who had been watching Straight, reached the White House
first. In November 1908, Secretary of State Elihu Root and Japanese

Ambassador Takahira Kogoro agreed to maintain the status quo in the Pacific and respect China's independence and "integrity." In his instructions to Takahira, however, Komura deliberately refused to use John Hay's open-door phrase of China's "territorial integrity." Komura cleverly argued that such a phrase was unnecessary and, indeed, insulted China. In reality, the omission meant that Japan kept its hands free to carve off South Manchuria from China's rule. Straight's dreams of checking Japan in Manchuria were becoming nightmares.[52]

Roosevelt and Root knew that particular game was up. The Secretary of State favored the Japanese position. Perhaps the most powerful corporation lawyer in the country before he entered government, Root loved order and industrialization. Japan, he believed, represented both. China represented neither. In 1907, moreover, Russia and France had already moved to recognize Japan's control of both Korea and South Manchuria. Root now joined the Europeans by signing another executive agreement with Japan. When the Secretary of State suggested the Root-Takahira agreement might be given to the Senate at least for comment, TR was direct: "Why invite the expression of views with which we may not agree?" Roosevelt's response rephrased his earlier remark: "I do not much admire the Senate because it is such a helpless body when efficient work for good is to be done."[53]

Manchuria: The Second Clash

During 1908, Roosevelt quietly pulled the fleet back to Hawaii, thus giving up hope of defending the Philippines. Two years later, a U.S. Army officer reported to his brother from Manila that "The Blue foxes, Americans, are defending the islands against the Red foxes, Japanese." The war games' results reinforced Roosevelt's conclusions. "The Japanese could land 100,000 men in a week," the officer worried, "and not miss them," so the maneuvers were "somewhat out of proportion."[54]

The military imbalance in the western Pacific was half of Washington's problem in the region. The other half, closely related, was the belief that Asian markets were essential if the terrors of the 1890s were not to be repeated, but the reality that Japan was closing off some of those markets. This was a terrible dilemma that Roosevelt left for his handpicked successor, William Howard Taft.[55]

As Roosevelt's one-time diplomatic troubleshooter, Taft had visited Japan four times and China three. The new President's Secretary of State, Philander C. Knox, was also experienced. Knox had been a pow-

erful Pittsburgh corporate lawyer who helped put together the first bil-
lion-dollar corporation, U.S. Steel, before serving in the Senate
between 1904 and 1909. Knox intimately knew the needs of America's
second industrial revolution that had appeared after the Civil War. Both
men believed U.S. productivity required open Asian markets. They also
assumed that the government must help American financiers and producers compete with the great business-government cartels of Germany, Japan, Great Britain, and France for international markets. Taft
reorganized the Department of State and gave it the modern face by
setting up specialized geographical bureaus (such as assistant secretary
for the Far East). As Taft said, it was to be "a thoroughly efficient instru-
ment in the furtherance of foreign trade and of American interest
abroad." The Taft-Knox approach became famous as "dollar diplomacy"—or "substituting dollars for bullets," as the administration came
to define it. Willard Straight, at age twenty-nine the first holder of the
new State Department's Far East bureau, nicely defined "dollar diplomacy" as "the financial expression of John Hay's 'Open Door' " to protect
"China's integrity."[56]

With these policies, Taft, Knox, and Straight were on a collision
course with Japan. The Japanese economic machine was heading full-
tilt for the Asian mainland. The key industrial sector, textiles, targeted
Manchurian as well as other Chinese markets. Japan was finally accumulating some surplus capital of its own. Most notably, the government
helped set up the South Manchurian Railway Company in 1906: 99,000
shares were for sale, but more than 109,000 bid. The center of capital
holdings concentrated on a few rich merchant bankers, led by Iwasaki,
Mitsui, and Sumitomo. These firms had helped the government in the
late nineteenth-century wars and now, in turn, were being helped by
the government.[57]

This intimate relationship had deep roots that went back at least to
Tokugawa Japan when the Shogun had granted trading monopolies. By
the turn of the twentieth century, these powerful financial houses, or
zaibatsu, were becoming powers in Asia. They remained, however, at
least a generation behind the United States (not to mention Great Britain) in accumulating capital resources. The sale of the South Manchurian Railway shares was a success story because the government
handsomely supported these ventures with subsidies and contracts.[58]

In June 1907, Japan signed a fisheries agreement with Russia that
contained a secret provision: Russia recognized Japan's special interests
in Korea and South Manchuria, while Japan recognized Russia's special
interests in northern Manchuria and Outer Mongolia. Despite this deal,

military officials in Tokyo continued to believe that another Russian war was only a matter of time. By 1914, nearly half the government's budget would go to the military and war debt service. Japan, historians have noted, seemed to be developing two governments, one military and one civilian.[59]

Komura brilliantly moved to shape a consensus foreign policy between the two factions on September 25, 1908. He succeeded, notably, as the U.S. Fleet steamed toward Japan and as China turned more unpredictable. Amid a whirl of change, Komura laid out his strategy to the cabinet. He first assumed that the alliance with Great Britain "is the main pillar of this empire's foreign policy." As for Russia, its power had declined and the tsar could well join in a deal to divide Manchuria permanently. Komura and the cabinet then agreed that Manchuria was to be held. No "third country," that is, the United States, was to be allowed to be "tempted to intervene" in that region. Discussing the United States specifically, Komura emphasized that given its "importance to our own commerce," friendship was necessary—despite "a handful of [American] figures" who were "suspicious" of Japanese intentions. Above all, the festering immigration problem should be resolved so it would not poison relations with Washington over larger Asian questions.[60]

Komura's aim was obvious: Develop South Manchuria and check Russia, but go to all lengths to retain British and American friendship and—more specifically—access to the capital surpluses in the City of London and Wall Street. Hence the pivotal importance of the new Root-Takahira understanding. Komura became one of the long line of Japanese officials who emphasized, in his words, that "What this empire needs most is the import of capital and technology." The cabinet consequently endorsed "joint ventures with westerners."[61]

In 1909, Japan further closed off Manchuria by obtaining new rail and mineral concessions from China. The most active U.S. business group on Asian affairs, the American Asiatic Association, and its mouthpiece, the *New York Commercial,* stepped up their condemnation of Japan's activities in Manchuria. A widely known mining executive and investor, John Hays Hammond, warned that American's economic interests "run counter to those of Japan." Once established in Korea and perhaps Manchuria, Hammond added, the Japanese would be "our most formidable competitor in the Far East." At the same time, a skillful publicist, Homer Lea, spread his ardent anti-Japanese beliefs in *The Valor of Ignorance;* other widely read books followed his lead. William Philipps, an expert Asian observer, summed it up in 1908: "Shall the

United States use its influence to preserve the integrity of China or shall we let Manchuria go to Russia and Japanese influence?"[62]

For Taft and Knox, this was a rhetorical question. Since 1905, when he had visited Asia and become well acquainted with E. H. Harriman's grandiose plans for Manchuria, Taft understood the enormous stakes being played for the imperial powers. For his part, Knox believed that only when U.S. capital gained a central role in the rail systems could the indispensable open door be guaranteed in China and Manchuria. Roosevelt might be willing to retreat before Japan's immediate military strength and political position. Taft and Knox, however, decided to play for one of the richest of all prizes, the whole of Manchuria. Straight— ever the anti-Japanese agent, ever the imperial dreamer—rushed back once again to China as a representative for a U.S. banking group (that included J. P. Morgan and Kuhn, Loeb) to help Taft and Knox win the great game of empire in northern China.[63]

Straight quickly obtained Chinese approval to build a railway that would directly compete with Japan's South Manchurian line. The Chinese of course saw Straight as the perfect foil to check both Russia and Japan. But not even the Chinese were prepared for what happened next.

In November–December 1909, Knox sent notes to Japan, Russia, France, Germany, and Great Britain that tried to use Straight's project as a weapon directly to threaten the Russian and Japanese positions in Manchuria. Knox demanded that St. Petersburg and Tokyo allow their railways in Manchuria to be placed under both international control and the open-door principle. In one of the more breathtaking proposals in twentieth-century American diplomacy, Knox challenged Japan's and Russia's expanding colonial empires with American open-market capitalism. Knox defined the stakes to Komura on December 18, 1909: the U.S. government had decided "that the most effective way" to preserve China's control in Manchuria, and thus to have *all* China "under the practical application of the open door and equal opportunity, would be to combine all Manchurian railways under an economic, scientific, and impartial administration." In a press statement, Knox went further. Nothing would afford "so impressive an object lesson to China and the world," he declared, as "the sight of the four great capitalist nations— Great Britain, Germany, France, and the United States—standing together for equality of commercial opportunity." Komura must have understood that with that sentence Knox apparently saw Japan as a threat to—rather than a member of—the club of "great capitalist nations."[64]

Knox and Taft's miscalculation was truly of heroic proportions. Any hope for taking a step toward this neutralization plan depended on the cooperation of the British, Japan's great and explicit ally. Privately, the Foreign Office in London blasted Knox's interference as an "ill-considered and fantastic proposal." For its part, Japan told Knox that its position in South Manchuria, after all, resulted in part from Roosevelt's good offices in 1905 and had been reconfirmed by Root in 1908. But for Knox the unkindest cut of all occurred on July 4, 1910, when Japan and Russia reached a new agreement. It divided Manchuria into a Russian sphere in the north and a Japanese sphere in the south. Knox had driven the two former enemies into an embrace. As one historian later observed, in his quest for the open door, Knox had "nailed that door closed with himself on the outside."[65]

Japan could annex "South Manchuria to-morrow," a top British diplomat told his Foreign Office colleagues, and no European power could prevent it. Nor should the British try, given their alliance with Japan, and given that southern Manchuria already was "a Japanese province." Only "the regeneration of China" could stop Japan, this official concluded, and that "prospect seems infinitely remote." Theodore Roosevelt agreed. In personal exchanges with Knox and Taft, he condemned their policies for worsening an already shaky U.S.-Japan relationship. The influential naval strategist Alfred Thayer Mahan, a close friend of Roosevelt's, also came to terms with the new Japan. Before 1907, Mahan had admired how the Japanese blocked the Russians, upheld open-door principles, and heaped praise on his naval theories; he assumed they shared U.S. policies about the open door. They were "the grain of mustard seed," Mahan said of the Japanese, a "regenerating force" for Asia. By 1910, however, Japan had become a "problem state" that threatened Asia. Mahan now suggested that the United States not seek "the object of supremacy in the Pacific," but draw a line along the Hawaiian Islands and use the Navy to defend the U.S. interests eastward from Hawaii. How such a fleet would ensure entry into the vast Asian markets for the growing glut of American production—a problem that had obsessed Mahan in the 1890s—he now left unasked.[66]

Japan followed up its victory in Manchuria with the full annexation of Korea in 1910. Then came another triumph in 1911. For nearly a half century its officials had worked to destroy the treaties imposed on them in the 1860s that robbed Japan of the right to control its own tariffs and some of its ports. In 1911, Japan approached the British for a revision of their commercial treaties. When London officials raised complications, the Japanese shrewdly switched and began talking with the United

States, where the immigration problem continued to fester. A treaty was worked out in February 1911: the Americans gave concessions on tariffs while the Japanese promised to continue to restrict emigration to the United States. The British and the other powers quickly followed the American lead. Japan finally regained full control over its foreign trade.[67]

The 1900 to 1912 years provided a string of horrors for U.S. hopes in Asia. By the time he left office after his doomed reelection bid in 1912, Taft had little else to show for his efforts than the 1911 treaty. "Taken as a whole," British Ambassador James Bryce told the Foreign Office in London, the President's annual message in December 1912 "has almost as little value as an exposition of the broad and general lines of the United States policy as it has of literary excellence." The new President, Woodrow Wilson, was not nearly as experienced in or knowledgeable about foreign policy as Taft, but understood that the U.S. approach to Asia, especially Japan, demanded a fundamental rethinking—something Wilson thought he was eminently qualified to do regardless of his ignorance about Asia.[68]

Japan was also at a crossroads in 1912. The Emperor Meiji died after a reign of forty-four years. It had been a triumphant era: victories over China and Russia, the annexation öf Korea, a protectorate over South Manchuria, near realization of the long quest for economic autonomy, freedom from foreign-imposed treaties, the writing of a constitution patterned after European models but protecting Japanese traditions necessary for preserving (or restoring) harmony within the society. The distinguished Western scholar of Japan, Sir George Sansom, observed that in the Meiji era, "power was now in the hands of men who had been brought up as soldiers and were schooled to drastic action. . . . Most foreign observers who were acquainted with the great figures of the Meiji period are agreed in thinking that there was a great fall in the quality of statesmanship after they had departed from that stage."[69]

Leaders of Japan's new industrial-banking giants, such as Mitsubishi and Mitsui, agreed with powerful government officials that the West's technology might be borrowed and adapted. The West's capitalism and its attendant social and cultural values, however, could not be safely accepted. Control was all-important: expansion abroad in quasi-Western style for harmony at home Japanese-style. The Japanese saw no contradiction. As they consolidated their gains in Korea and Manchuria, for example, they passed the Factory Law in 1911 that legislated a weak minimum-age protection. Corporations meanwhile instituted paternalistic programs ensuring a laborer's loyalty to a single firm. The "uniquely Japanese style" of utilizing labor began not after 1951, but a half century earlier.

Despite the triumphs of the Meiji era, however, two enormous problems remained. First, Japanese society was not harmonious. It endured constant upheaval, not least from assassinations, public protests (as in 1905), and civilian-military rivalry. Second, Japanese expansionism might have resembled European imperialism, but Americans saw no resemblance to their own expansionism—an expansionism which disavowed colonialism on the Asian mainland and pledged itself to Chinese territorial integrity. Taft, Knox, Straight, and now Woodrow Wilson intended to contain Japanese expansionism in Asia—and elsewhere, including parts of Latin America.

The United States, after all, thought its domestic system unique as well, a system that produced the incredible wealth and social fluidity so valued by Americans. Indeed, American society had become so fluid and disorderly after 1873 that it also became imperialistic abroad to restore order at home. One difference stood out: while Americans believed their exceptionalism could be exported—whether by missionaries, corporate leaders, or education advisers—the Japanese saw themselves as too unique to be such proselytizers. Japan thus preferred colonialism, for that strategy fixed markets, solved security questions, and allowed the colonizers to adjust other cultures forcefully but quietly behind high political walls.

The great clash between the Americans and Japanese systems thus began over China—a China careening toward revolution.

IV

Revolution, War, and Race (1912–1920)

An Old Europe, a New Asia

BETWEEN 1914 and 1918, European civilization nearly destroyed itself. No nation gained so much so cheaply from the carnage as Japan. The acceleration of its imperialism was phenomenal. That imperialism, however, ran headlong into a newly powerful United States that—as Europe verged on suicide—was replacing the British as the globe's leading economic and military power. For both Americans and Japanese, war was indeed the health of the state.

As the two non-European imperial powers began reshaping global relations, they also moved toward conflict over China and with each other. China, for its part, began the era with a three-century-old monarchy, and ended, in 1920, enduring the convulsions of a great twentieth-century revolution. U.S. and Japanese leaders feared, but little understood, the upheaval's dimensions. Japan had the most to lose. When the Manchu dynasty collapsed in February 1912, the Japanese industrial economy was being driven by textile exports. China, along with Hong Kong and Kwantung Leased Territory, took three-quarters of Japan's cotton goods exports. By 1910, overall trade with China was five times that with Korea and Taiwan combined.

Japan's triumph in conquering China's profitable cotton yarn market provided a case study of new Asian capitalism. Japan won out over American exporters not because of superior technology or availability of raw materials. It won because direct help from the Tokyo government manipulated currency so Japanese investors enjoyed a competitive edge. It also succeeded because Japanese did not follow Western-style vertical integration that combined purchasing, manufacturing, and marketing under single ownership (the kind of integration that made Carnegie Steel and Standard Oil giants). Instead, "Japanese-style vertical integration, " as the historian Sherman Cochran calls it, was developed: coordinating the entire process from a central office, but leaving factory ownership in China to Japanese on the spot who exploited the local family networks by hiring Chinese to run the factory. Asian family ties proved to be more powerful than American capital ties. The Chinese and Japanese economies seemed to grow symbiotic: China supplied vast amounts of raw materials for Japan's heavy industry, then took back much of that industry's production and absorbed Japanese investment. Of China's nearly 1 million textile spindles in 1913, Japanese owned about 250,000.[1]

The China market grew in significance just as some Tokyo officials feared that the opening of the Panama Canal in 1914 would allow the United States to accelerate its invasion of Asian markets. That fear of an economic Armageddon, moreover, arose amid economic crises in Japan itself. Between 1904 and 1913, the Japanese suffered a severe unfavorable balance of trade. The gap was covered in part by foreign loans and printing of currency. These Band-Aids did little to halt the inflation that by 1913 brought the nation to the edge of disaster. As the situation deteriorated, the army and navy competed bitterly for increased budgets. The struggle brought down several governments between 1911 and 1914. Military expenditures were becoming overwhelming; they amounted to 15 percent of the total budget in the 1880s, then reached 48 percent during the period 1901–10. A major boost came from naval officers' fears that competition over China, immigration issues, and the opening of the Panama Canal were rapidly leading to war with the United States.[2]

Across the Pacific, Americans were also waging an intense debate over their politics, economy, and China policy. But as their system differed from Japan's, so did their debate. The differences can be understood by comparing the policies of Yamagata Aritomo and Woodrow Wilson.

Yamagata, Wilson, and the "Frontier" of a Revolutionary China

Born in 1838, Yamagata was shaped by his military experiences during the upheavals of the 1860s. His success at uniting the anti-Tokugawa clans, Satsuma and Choshu, and then establishing a military system that enjoyed virtual veto power over civilian cabinets, laid two foundation stones for the Japan of 1868 to 1945. Before 1912, Yamagata twice headed governments. After 1912 he wielded immense power as one of the few remaining, venerated, elder statesmen, or *genro*, from the Meiji era. (In his magnificent seaside villa at Odawara, the general built a shrine to the Meiji Emperor's spirit.) He also venerated the bureaucracy—an agent, in his view, for loyally carrying out the Emperor's wishes and for blocking the new political parties, which he viewed as corrupt mouthpieces of a dangerous public opinion. His foreign policies were shaped by a fixation on seizing parts of Asia that would make Japan both strategically secure and economically independent. Hence the seventy-four-year-old's demand in 1912 that Japan (especially the army) profit from China's upheaval by formally occupying southern Manchuria. When the Saionji cabinet refused, Yamagata told Katsura, "I am truly and mightily indignant for the sake of our country."[3]

In 1912, many Japanese, led by intellectuals, workers, and some businessmen, hoped the new Taisho era (the name given the 1912–26 reign of Emperor Yoshihito, who replaced the Meiji Emperor) would usher in more open, less military-dominated governments. These groups believed a major generational change was at hand. In 1913, as it became clear that Yamagata's generation was holding on to power, rioters took to the streets. They forced the resignation of the government. For the first time, masses played a decisive role in bringing down a cabinet.

Japan had taken its first tentative steps toward a Taisho democracy that marked the next dozen years. Yamagata, other *genro*, and especially the military hated the turbulence, which they blamed on the political parties. And they feared the disorder because it struck just as China and Europe were edging toward explosions of their own. Yamagata was convinced that Japan was being sucked into a worldwide race war:

Recent international trends indicate that racial rivalry has yearly become more intense [he told the government in August 1914]. It is a striking fact that the Turkish and Balkan wars of the past . . . all had their origins in racial rivalry and hatred. Furthermore, the exclusion of Japanese in the state of California . . . and the discrimination against Indians in British Africa are also manifestations of the racial problem. . . . [After the war in Europe is over] the rivalry between the white and colored peoples will intensify; and perhaps it will be a time when the white races will all unite to oppose the colored peoples.

After all, if the European bloodshed was "a struggle between the Slavic and Germanic races," one could "imagine how much more fierce the struggle between the yellow and white races will be." Yamagata hoped to exploit, if not avert, this tragedy by drawing "closer to China," and, in the meantime, strengthening Anglo-Japanese ties. Improving relations with the United States was important, but ranked a distant third on his priority list.[4]

Woodrow Wilson, Virginia-born in 1856, then raised in Georgia, also grew up amid war, racism, and political upheaval—in his case, the Civil War and the bitterness of Reconstruction. Wilson's and Yamagata's worlds then moved farther apart. Yamagata's political center was the Emperor, Wilson's his conception of American individualism. Yamagata saw the danger as civilian political partisanship, Wilson the new industrial and banking corporations that threatened to strangle the individual. If Yamagata's policies were fueled by a passion to use the army to find security and independence for Japan, Wilson passionately hoped to use a more democratic government to reform (or, as he liked to say, "restore") the economic world of corporate America before class warfare erupted. "For whatever we say of other motives," the American declared when he was a well-known political scientist in 1898, "we must never forget that in the main the ordinary conduct of men is determined by economic motives." Or, as he phrased it as a reform governor of New Jersey in 1911, "A new economic society has sprung up, and we must effect a new set of adjustments." "Adjustments" in this different, post-1890s imperial America required active government led by a powerful president: "It is evident that empire is an affair of strong government."[5]

Wilson knew he worked inside a developing American empire. The turn, he calculated, occurred with the War of 1898, when the nation found its landed frontier disappearing after four hundred years of continual expansion, then "turned from developing its own resources to make conquests of the markets of the world." Resembling Yamagata, Wilson viewed the world as infected and made more explosive by the question of race. As a white man raised in the South and elected by a Democratic Party that depended on all-white southern (and some northern) political machines, his racism was not exceptional. Indeed, it was so traditional that Wilson focused on what he believed to be a new, more dangerous problem: a growing "empire" whose economic system threatened to destroy American society as it rushed from individualistic nineteenth-century competition on a continent to giant twentieth-century corporations dividing global markets.[6]

Wilson intended to discipline corporations and avoid class war by waging peaceful economic warfare abroad. When he entered the presidency in 1913, he knew little else about foreign policy. During the 1912 campaign, Wilson declared in several speeches that U.S. industries had "expanded to such a point that they will burst their jackets if they cannot find a free outlet to the markets of the world." As he had earlier noted, Asia was pivotal, "the market for which statesmen as well as merchants must plan and play their game of competition, the market to which diplomacy, and if need be power, must make an open way."[7]

Taking that remarkable statement to its logical conclusion, Wilson declared that the open-door policy had been "not the open door to the rights of China but the open door to the good of America." Wilson and Theodore Roosevelt grew to hate each other for personal and policy reasons, but on Asian issues they agreed, as Roosevelt phrased it, that Americans were witnessing the "expansion of the frontier of the United States westward to the interior of China."[8]

In March 1913, Wilson began trying to use China as a tool to reform corporate America. He faced the question of whether he would stay in the six-power consortium, as William Howard Taft and Willard Straight had pieced it together in 1911–12, so U.S. banks would enjoy equal rights with the other five powers in developing China. In 1913, however, a new China was coming under the control of a military strongman, Yuan Shih-k'ai. Believing that Yuan favored "the development of China by foreign capital," Straight hoped that Wilson would keep Americans inside the consortium. Straight was even prepared to cooperate with the despised Japanese: "We might all be better off if these little devils had charge of China's destiny after all," he wrote only half in jest. "They could not run any monopoly game and then, like the Manchus, they would be so corrupt after a few generations and so softened by riches . . . that they would no longer be a military menace to us honest folks."[9]

Wilson rejected Straight's views. Two reasons for his decision stood out: the consortium was dominated by giant bankers who had shut out smaller firms, and the United States could not control the consortium. The President preferred returning to a traditional go-it-alone policy that allowed many American firms to compete for all of China's development projects while remaining separated from Japanese and European imperialists.[10]

The President destroyed the consortium without consulting either the other five powers or his State Department's Asian experts. Only Secretary of State William Jennings Bryan, appointed for his political importance despite Wilson's disdain for his intellect, knew about and sympathized with the President's decision before its announcement. The radical nature of Wilson's new direction was limited. He recognized Yuan as the Chinese leader despite the military man's disinterest in democracy, and stayed with Yuan even after he declared himself the new Emperor. Wilson thus joined a long line of U.S. officials who held contradictory hopes: that China would somehow become a democracy, but also remain orderly and whole for the sake of foreign interests. Straight, furious, concluded that the China market had been lost. A State Department memorandum of August–September 1913, however, declared the U.S. intention to develop Sino-American trade "to the fullest extent." U.S. firms "should have opportunity everywhere to compete for contractual favors on the same footing as any foreign competition." Wilson was hardly pulling out of China. The United States and Japan remained on a collision course.[11]

California: "Another Race Problem"

Within two months after Wilson deserted the consortium, that collision seemed so imminent that U.S. naval officers prepared for war. Tension had built for months. Early in 1912, rumor spread that Japanese business interests were purchasing a strategic area of Mexico's Baja California. Japan's government denied any such purchase. William Randolph Hearst's anti-Japanese newspapers nevertheless loudly rang the alarm. In the Senate, Henry Cabot Lodge wheeled out a large cannon from the nation's diplomatic arsenal—the Monroe Doctrine—aimed it at Japan, and loosed the charge with what came to be known as the Lodge Corollary to the doctrine. In 1823, the senator announced, President James Monroe had banned further foreign "colonization" in this hemisphere. "By the word 'colonization' we also cover action by companies or corporations by citizens or subjects of a foreign state which might do . . . what the Monroe Doctrine was intended to prevent." The Senate roared through his resolution 51–4. During the next two decades, the State Department deployed Lodge's Corollary at least four times. In every instance it aimed to stop Japanese from obtaining Mexican land.[12]

Lodge spoke as his intimate friend, Theodore Roosevelt, embarked on a losing presidential election campaign against Wilson and Taft. "Japan-bashing," as it was later termed, was featured in the campaign, especially because California had begun to debate laws to ban Japanese from owning land. Since the 1907 Gentlemen's Agreement, immigration from Japan had declined. Only about fifty thousand Japanese lived in the state. Many were welcomed for providing reliable field labor. Some, however, scrimped and saved enough to purchase their own land. Such success honored a great American tradition, but one California Democratic Party leader called Japanese "a non-assimilable people, clever and industrious," who take "farms from . . . white men in destructive competition" and threaten to make California "a Japanese plantation" where "republican institutions [will] perish."

Similar words were heard from a strong Wilson supporter, James D. Phelan, wealthy real estate speculator, former mayor of San Francisco, and later a U.S. senator. Phelan warned Wilson to make his views clear if he hoped to carry California. In May 1912, the New Jersey governor wrote Phelan that he favored "exclusion (or restricted immigration). The whole question is one of assimilation of diverse races. We cannot make a homogeneous population out of people who do not blend with the caucasian race." "Their lower standard of living as laborers," Wilson added," will crowd out the white agriculturalist and is, in other fields, a most serious industrial menace. . . . Oriental coolieism will give us another race problem to solve, and surely we have had our lesson." Phelan brandished Wilson's letter during the campaign.[13]

When California moved to ban Japanese from owning land, the newly elected President dispatched Bryan to talk sense with the state legislators. The Secretary of State had little luck. Wilson tried to suggest wording that would accomplish the legislature's goal without offending Japan, but Californians refused to cooperate. Most American journals repeated the New York World's opinion that the state's legislation was "ridiculous" and out of proportion to the problem. Again, however, Hearst's newspapers loved the law and whipped up anti-Japanese feelings.[14]

U.S. naval officials' apprehension grew. In Tokyo, a crowd of twenty thousand cheered as a politician urged that the Imperial Fleet steam to California to protect Japan's citizens and dignity. Stories spread that the fleet was preparing to seize Hawaii and the Philippines. Repeated complaints by Americans that, after all, Japan barred U.S. citizens from owning land in Japan produced no effect on Tokyo officials. In mid-May 1913, Admiral Bradley A. Fiske, a naval operation planner, told

Navy Secretary Josephus Daniels that "war is not only possible but even probable." The admirals asked permission to move more ships into the Philippine and Hawaiian areas. Wilson flatly refused. He wanted to do nothing that might further alarm Japan. The Joint Board of the Army and Navy insisted, then a leak appeared in newspapers that revealed the admirals' request. Furious, Wilson abolished the Joint Board. Tensions cooled, but California's Webb-Heney Alien Land Act of May 9, 1913, became law. Yamagata's views on the importance of race were reinforced.[15]

At a press conference in May, Wilson declared his admiration for Japanese achievements. A military mortality rate of only 2 percent from disease in the 1904–05 war, for example, demonstrated a "scientific superiority over any other modern nation" that "impresses the imagination." Moreover, "they can adapt what they take to their own uses so perfectly." On the other hand, the President added, the California legislation arose because "we do not want to have intimate association in our life with the Japanese." He noted a "feeling on our part that they are not on the same plane with us. That, of course, is something that diplomacy itself cannot handle."[16]

The Two-Front War: 1914–1918

Wilson admired the Japanese, but preferred they not live in California. He also concluded that fewer Japanese ought to work in revolution-torn China. Between 1914 and 1918, he and Japan waged a two-front war. One they fought together, finally, against Germany. The other they fought diplomatically against each other. The first war was over Germany's place in world affairs. The second was over China's place in the development of the Japanese and American systems.

The second war's intensity could be partly explained by economic problems afflicting Japan and the United States when Europe walked into the abyss during August 1914. Bedeviled by inflation and long-term unfavorable foreign trade balances, the Japanese economy was finally accelerated by the selling of vast amounts of goods to European belligerents and by rushing into Asian markets suddenly deserted by Western imperial powers. Tokyo also moved to intensify development in Manchuria, Korea, and Taiwan.

The United States economy suffered from shorter-term problems as it spiraled downward in mid-1914. At first, Americans lent to neither side. Money was the "worst of all contrabands because it commands everything else," moralized Bryan. Within fourteen months, however, Americans grew rich by loaning money and selling food, clothing, and arms to anyone with enough credit—which meant largely the Allied powers of Great Britain, France, and Russia. Japan prospered and the United States emerged as the globe's center for capital.

The war, however, would end someday soon, while the China market would supposedly go on forever. And as Americans positioned themselves to exploit the European war, Japanese moved to exploit the Chinese upheaval. Some such as Straight even viewed the Chinese revolution as largely a Japanese invention. In 1896, the first thirteen Chinese students had arrived in Tokyo; by 1914, many more Chinese were studying in Japan (in 1905, eight thousand arrived). A Pan-Asianist movement hatched in Tokyo, nourished by the defeat of the Russians in 1905 and now inspiring revolutionaries who hated the West, seemed to be rising in the far U.S. frontier. The "Yellow Peril" in California or Hawaii was small change compared with events in China. In Tokyo, meanwhile, out of near political chaos Okuma Shigenobu emerged as prime minister in 1914 to seize the opportunities presented by the European war. Okuma was championed by Yamagata and the army.[17]

Now seventy-six years old, this son of a samurai had learned to admire the U.S. Constitution—but not individualistic American society—from an American missionary during the 1860s. At first opposed to military conquests in the 1870s, Okuma soon pushed for seizing Taiwan, Manchuria, and Korea. Ironically, he also became head of the Chinese Peace Society. Finance minister from age thirty-four to forty-three, Okuma became rich from military contracts supplying the forces that quelled the 1877 rebellion. Later he forged close ties with the Mitsubishi *zaibatsu*. When revelations of corruption drove him from office in the early 1890s, he helped build a political party that ultimately propelled him back into power as premier in 1898. From that height, Okuma opposed the U.S. annexation of Hawaii, which he had targeted as a Japanese protectorate. Corruption charges again drove him from power, this time for sixteen years. Okuma occupied himself by founding Waseda University, soon to be a distinguished institution free of government oversight. In 1914, the Emperor and *genro* turned to him as a last resort. He brought with him a checkered political past, close ties to the Iwasaki family that owned Mitsubishi, great vanity, a rampant Pan-Asianism (he once claimed, to the anger of British officials, that even India looked to Japan for deliverance), and a marked dislike and fear of the United States.[18]

Between 1914 and 1916, Okuma and his foreign minister, Kato Komei, dominated policymaking. Born with the next generation of leaders in 1860, Kato, unlike Okuma, was a professional diplomat who enjoyed a meteoric rise to become minister to Great Britain at age thirty-four, then foreign minister in 1900 and again in 1906. He, like Okuma, married into the Iwasaki family. He also shared Okuma's short temper, belief in Japan's manifest destiny, and willingness to use force in China.[19]

Kato's mistakes soon turned out to be as large as his ambition. He believed he could ignore the *genro* and take the British for granted as he moved to put all China under a de facto Japanese protectorate. Such a protectorate would also destroy the U.S. open-door policy once and for all. His first steps were taken in 1911–13. As ambassador to Great Britain, Kato thought he and Foreign Secretary Sir Edward Grey agreed that Japan must expand. Sir Edward, however, had Manchuria in mind, not central China, where British interests profited. Kato either misunderstood Grey or, more likely, thought that in the right circumstances the British would acquiesce when Japan imposed order on China.[20]

The golden opportunity opened with the European war. Japan first declared its neutrality. Then the British asked for naval protection in the Pacific. Kato successfully argued that joining the British could produce rich rewards; these included the seizure of German possessions in China and the Pacific. Thus occurred the long-awaited revenge for Germany directing the Triple Intervention twenty years earlier. The Japanese seized the strategic German base at Kiaochou on the Shantung Peninsula (and deployed German prisoners to breweries where Asahi beer was born). They then invaded the kaiser's colonial possessions in the northern Pacific—the Mariana, Marshall, and Caroline Islands. Another white nation stood humiliated. Japanese power was poised to strike south and west. Ambitious Tokyo students began to study the Malay and Dutch languages. Highly impressed, the British asked Kato for military help in Europe. He flatly refused.[21]

Japan fought World War I for its Asian interests, not for its allies' survival. In early 1916, for example, when Okuma thought Germany might have something attractive to offer, Japan secretly talked with Berlin officials about a separate peace. "When there is a fire in a jeweller's shop, the neighbors cannot be expected to refrain from helping themselves," a Tokyo official had explained in 1914. Wilson and the State Department were not amused. When war began, a frightened China had asked Washington to protect the status quo in the Pacific. Bryan duly issued such a request of the powers. Only Germany agreed. As Japan seized German possessions north of the equator, the British took those to the south. China again complained, but State Department Counselor Robert Lansing—a conservative New York lawyer who had little sympathy for disorderly, disintegrating empires—told the Chinese that while American friendship for them was "sincere," it "would be quixotic in the extreme" for the United States to become entangled in Asia over Japan's anti-German actions.[22]

Kato and Okuma's stars also seemed to be perfectly aligning in China itself. When the Chinese Revolution appeared in 1911, two leaders were in the forefront. Sun Yat-sen moved from the south while Yuan Shih-k'ai used his military forces to control the north. Japanese policy also divided. Tokyo officials disliked the radicals around Sun and, like Woodrow Wilson, preferred a predictable monarchy over the unknown republic that Sun championed. Giant *zaibatsu*, however, led by Mitsui and Mitsubishi, funneled arms and money to Sun in return for a promise of future economic concessions. Sun ultimately became the revered godfather of the Chinese Revolution, but in 1912–14 Yuan twice blocked him, seized full power for himself, and forced Sun and other southern leaders to find refuge in Japan.[23]

As the cannons roared in Europe, Yuan listened politely while the Japanese explained their interest in Kiaochou and additional Manchurian railways. Yuan replied diplomatically and insincerely that yellow races should not "make friends of Europeans and Americans who are of the white race"—that is, those who will be "powerful white adversaries" after the war. Kato put such remarks together with his own belief that the British would tolerate Japanese expansion in China. The result was an integrated, detailed set of demands drawn up by Kato and his subordinates.

In January 1915, Kato, trying to maintain utmost secrecy, handed these so-called Twenty-one Demands to Yuan's regime. The list was impressive. Japan would acquire all German rights in Shantung (Kiaochou); receive vast concessions in South Manchuria and Inner Mongolia, including an additional ninety-nine-year lease to the South Manchurian Railway; control a rich iron and coal company in central China; and obtain essential control of Fukien Province just across from Taiwan. The final, or fifth, set of demands was the most stunning: China was to hire Japanese political, financial, and military advisers; give Japanese the right to build temples and schools; and grant permission to Tokyo to construct three railways between the pivotal Yangtze River area and the southern coast.[24]

The most dangerous Far East crisis of World War I was at hand. Kato believed neither Europeans nor Americans could stop this diplomatic

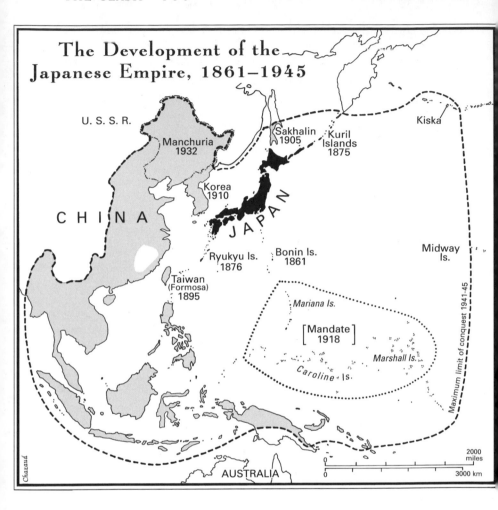

The Development of the Japanese Empire, 1861–1945

U. S. S. R.

Manchuria 1932

Sakhalin 1905

Kuril Islands 1875

Kiska

Korea 1910

CHINA

JAPAN

Ryukyu Is. 1876

Bonin Is. 1861

Midway Is.

Taiwan (Formosa) 1895

Mariana Is.

[Mandate 1918]

Marshall Is.

Caroline Is.

Maximum limit of conquest 1941-45

2000 miles

3000 km

AUSTRALIA

Chazaud

strike. With Japan's leases on Manchuria's railway lapsing between 1923 and 1940, moreover, this might be the last opportunity to save them on Tokyo's terms. Of course, the secrecy did not hold. U.S. Minister to China Paul Reinsch learned about the demands in late January 1915.

A noted scholar of China from the University of Wisconsin, Reinsch was a tough, passionate defender of China and an outspoken critic of Japan. Believing that only the United States could safely bring China into the twentieth century, he saw the Japanese (and, to only a slightly lesser extent, their partners the British) as the villains. The Twenty-one Demands were the "greatest crisis yet experienced in China," Reinsch instructed Wilson and Bryan. If Kato succeeded, the open door would close forever: "The independence of China and equal opportunity of western nations are at stake." Wilson paid little attention. He was caught up in defending U.S. neutrality, mourning the death of his first wife, and ardently courting his second. The President, moreover, saw little wrong with the more civilized (as he defined them) helping out disorderly neighbors. After all, he had sent, or was about to send, U.S. troops into Mexico, Haiti, Santo Domingo, and Nicaragua. Bryan did ask Japanese Ambassador Count Chinda about the fifth set of demands. Chinda, an experienced diplomat who had gone to school in the United States, denied this set existed. Bryan's long political relations with Tammany Hall should have taught him better, but he nevertheless declared, "I trust the Japanese Ambassador."[25]

On February 18, 1915, China published the fifth set of demands. In London, Grey was appalled. He ratcheted up the pressure on Tokyo until in May Kato finally dropped the fifth set. Wilson and Bryan, meanwhile, excoriated Japan for lying. But they knew they needed Japanese cooperation in Asia, Europe, and, not least, California. They also had no military force to face down Japan in China. In the game for the open door, Wilson held few good cards.

On March 13, the Americans consequently accepted the first four sets of demands (and thus Japan's new hold on Manchuria and even Shantung) by using a fateful phrase. The United States recognized that "territorial contiguity creates special relations between Japan and these districts." The phrase had been suggested by Lansing, who hoped that in return Japan would cooperate in California and drop the fifth set of demands. By early May, Wilson believed Japan was not backing down. On May 5, Bryan sent a tough note warning Japan and the other powers that Washington would not surrender its rights in China. Six days later, he reaffirmed loudly "the international policy . . . commonly known as the open door."[26]

The Chinese accepted most of the first four sets of demands, but rejected the fifth set. Despite this limited victory, Kato was in deep trouble at home. He had issued the demands without consulting with the *genro,* who, he believed, were too old and too cautious. The elder statesmen, however, still commanded the Emperor's ear and were furious that after they had spent forty years courting the West, Kato's bumbling diplomacy threatened to cancel their efforts—and embitter the British—in a single strike. In May 1915, they forced Kato to resign. The episode had already further poisoned Japanese-American relations. Reinsch's anti-Japanese warnings seemed validated. The Hearst newspapers trumpeted a series of articles entitled "Japan's Plans to Invade and Conquer the United States." The contents of the series were pirated from a Japanese novel, while accompanying pictures were highly doctored photos from the Sino-Japanese conflict of 1894–95. Readers knew none of this. Other than Hearst, Wilson and Bryan seemed to be the big winners. They thought their tough notes had saved China and doomed Kato. In truth, it had been Grey, using his leverage within the Anglo-Japanese alliance, who had forced the *genro* to act.[27]

U.S. officials nevertheless deplored Grey's behavior and grew deeply suspicious about the Anglo-Japanese alliance. The British, after all, had shown little interest in the open door until their interests in central China were directly endangered. Nor had Grey gone out of his way to support the Americans, doubtless because a real open door in China could undermine British as well as Japanese holdings. Grey even bluntly told Wilson's closest adviser, Edward M. House, in May 1915 that Japan required Manchuria since "North and South America, Africa and the British colonies were closed against her citizens."[28]

A wonderful irony threatened: acting as a supposed ally, Japan was using the European war as cover for destroying seventy-five years of U.S. policy in Asia and creating a "Yellow Peril" beyond even Hearst's imagination. Formulating a response fell to Lansing. In June 1915, the suave New Yorker became Secretary of State when Bryan resigned after a dispute with Wilson over handling German submarine warfare. Lansing, unlike Bryan, wanted the United States to enter the war on the side of the British. By 1916, Wilson understood the country would probably have to fight, even as his supporters reelected him with the slogan, "He kept us out of war." For Lansing, therefore, the pivotal problem in Asia was how to contain Japan once Americans became enmeshed in European war.

Wilson and Lansing devised two containment policies. First, they swallowed hard and admitted that Wilson's go-it-alone policy of 1913, which aimed at wrecking the six-power consortium, had only left the Japanese to go-it-alone. By 1916, Japan was accelerating its economic offensive in China with a massive set of loans. The President knew the consortium had to be rebuilt, although its walls could now be only four-sided (the United States, Great Britain, France, and Japan). Reinsch vigorously opposed the plan. He urged that Americans use their new war-gotten wealth unilaterally and drive Japan back in a kind of holy war for the open door.

In the history of American diplomacy, unilateralism—or isolationism, as it is usually called—has always been a tactic, not an immutable prin-

*With his Black Ships and their cannon hovering in
the background, Commodore Perry deployed his men
to meet the Japanese commissioners at Yokohama on
March 8, 1854. (Library of Congress)*

Commodore Perry, in the flesh, was a reserved,
distinguished-looking naval officer. But, as this
Japanese drawing illustrates, his involuntary hosts
had a quite different view of him. (Corbis-Bettmann
and Asahi Shimbun Publishing)

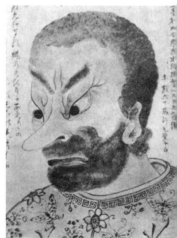

ABOVE. Perry, his officers, and crew give a formal dinner, complete with toasts, for the Japanese commissioners. Note the cannon and the band. (Library of Congress)

LEFT. A portrait of Townsend Harris, painted by James Bogle in 1855, the year he was appointed consul general to Japan. (City College, New York)

The first Japanese mission to the
United States in 1860 took particular
interest in American technology.
(Library of Congress)

*OPPOSITE. Yamagata Aritomo—the father
of Japanese militarism and strategist of his
nation's expansionism onto the Asian
mainland between the 1870s and World
War I. (Library of Congress)*

Artist's rendition of marines
defending the U.S. Legation
in Peking. (AP/Wide World
Photos)

OPPOSITE ABOVE. During their widely noted visit to Japan in
summer 1905, Alice Roosevelt (the President's daughter) enraptured the press, but, quietly, William Howard Taft (at her left)
reshaped U.S.-Japan-Korean relations. Here they leave the
Resting Palace in Yokohama en route to Tokyo. (Library of
Congress)

OPPOSITE BELOW. Count Sergei Witte, Baron Rosen, President
Roosevelt, Baron Komura Jutaro, and Takahira Kogoro at the
1905 peace negotiations. (Underwood & Underwood/ Corbis-
Bettmann)

ABOVE LEFT. *Elihu Root, the father of the American "establishment," tried to cement U.S.-Japanese friendship, especially in 1908 and at the 1921–22 Washington Conference. (Corbis-Bettmann)*

RIGHT. *Baron Saionji—adviser to emperors, the last of the genro who created modern Japan—in 1920, on the eve of the Washington Conference. (Library of Congress)*

ABOVE RIGHT. *Skilled gambler, fully aware of U.S. power, Yamamoto Isoroku planned the Pearl Harbor attack reluctantly. Here he is shown as Japan's naval attaché in Washington, February 1926. (Library of Congress)* ciple. Americans have usually joined multilateral efforts when they held control. Wilson quit the consortium in 1913 because he could not control it. By 1917, he and Lansing recreated the consortium because they thought Americans could control it.

In mid-1918, Lansing explained to Wilson that China desperately needed money, and given the wartime circumstances, "That leaves Japanese capital in control." U.S. money had to go in to counter the Japanese. Since sufficient amounts of dollars would enter China only when Wilson offered his full support, the President gave it. If the plan worked out, results could be mind-boggling. Because the British and French were bankrupting themselves to fight the war, they would be dependent on U.S. capital. In a new consortium, Americans could control three votes to one for Japan. Money was gushing into New York City, moreover, in amounts the Japanese could not match. At first, Tokyo officials, not blind to these circumstances, opposed joining the new consortium. As the Japanese press put it, the powers were using the United States "as a check" on Japan. British pressure and American power, however, proved to be too much. Wilson bluntly announced in 1916 that having become "the creditors of the world," Americans "can determine to a large extent who is to be financed and who is not to be financed." By mid-1918, the American Group—led by J. P. Morgan, the Rockefellers' National City Bank, and twenty-nine smaller banks whose inclusion satisfied Wilson's desire for a more open capitalist system—was inside the new consortium.[29]

Wilson's growing fear of Japan, as well as his racism, dramatically appeared during the historic weeks of early 1917 when he agonized over whether to ask Americans to die in Europe. On the one hand, he had to respond to Germany's all-out submarine offensive that was sinking U.S. ships. Moreover, he knew he had to enter the war if he hoped to enter the peace negotiations as an equal after the conflict.[30]

On the other hand, Wilson knew that American entry could win an all-out victory for the Allies, who by no means shared his vision for a different, more democratic postwar world. That point was driven home in 1915–16 when the Allies signed a series of secret treaties that divided German possessions among themselves. Americans were not consulted as Europeans formally gave Japan most of what it wanted of German territory in the Pacific theater. Of particular interest, Wilson began to worry aloud about the damage to "white civilization" if Americans died alongside Europeans. Or, as he told the cabinet on February 5, 1917, if "in order to keep the white race or part of it strong to meet the yellow race—Japan, for instance, in alliance with Russia, dominating China—

it was wise to do nothing, he would do nothing, and would submit to
. . . any imputations of weakness or cowardice." Lansing tried to push
Wilson forward and over the edge to war by arguing another perspective: if Germany won, it would join Russia and Japan—"which are
almost as hostile to democracy as Germany and which have similar
ambitions of territorial expansion"—and then divide up the globe, with
Japan targeting the west coast of the United States.[31]

Either way, Wilson's decision for war rested in part on his evaluation
of how best to protect the interest of "white races" against Japanese
power. In the end, Lansing's arguments and Wilson's urge to mediate
the postwar peace prevailed. The President tried to innoculate himself
against his Allies, however, with a remarkable speech in Congress on
January 22, 1917. He demanded a "peace without victory," a peace that
replaced a world of imperialism with "a community of power." The President declared that he sought a globe free of "entangling alliances"
(such as the Allies' secret treaties?). He asked that all nations "adopt
the doctrine of President Monroe," by which he meant that "no nation
should seek to extend its polity over any other nation or people." In
April, he finally joined Japan and its European Allies in war, but only,
he emphasized, as an "associated power" because "we have no allies."
Wilson thus went to war to win a military victory with the Allies, but
more importantly to win a new world after the war despite the Allies.
It would be a neat trick.[32]

His reference to the Monroe Doctrine rang false. The Japanese,
resembling every other nation except the United States, viewed the
doctrine as a convenient rationale for controlling neighboring territory.
After all, that was how Americans long treated neighbors in Latin
America. Tokyo officials had become transfixed with the idea of the
doctrine because they believed they had a right to employ a similar
doctrine in their region. Again, Japan wanted not only to join the imperialists but obtain all the rights and privileges of the club.

No Japanese wanted to join the club more than did Viscount Ishii
Kikujiro. He arrived in Washington during September 1917 to exchange
"frank views concerning problems in China," as he later phrased it in
his memoirs. In distinction and diplomatic experience, Ishii was unsurpassed in Japan. Born in 1866, graduated from the prestigious Law
School of Tokyo Imperial University, he became a protégé of Komura.
On this fast track he served in Korea, in China during the Boxer uprising, in California when the immigration issue exploded, as ambassador
to France, and, finally, as Kato's successor as foreign minister during
1915–16. Fluent in English, well connected in New York, the urbane

Ishii had scored with Wilson and Lansing in 1916 when rumors flew that if Mexico—whose revolution Wilson had tried to control until he even sent in U.S. troops—went to war with the United States, Japan would help the Mexicans. Ishii flatly declared that any such aid "is out of the question and absurd." He was, after all, sensitive to the meaning of the Monroe Doctrine. He also understood the importance of American public opinion. The *New York Times* lauded the viscount's skill at billiards and even his singing as a "parlor entertainer."[33]

The newspaper would have been less enchanted if it had heard Ishii and Lansing argue over China. The Secretary of State planned to tie up Japan politically, as well as with the consortium, while Americans sank deeper into the European bloodbath. He therefore asked Japan to reaffirm the open door and disavow closed spheres of interests in China. Ishii had no intention of taking such vows, especially after Japan's secret pacts with the allies cemented its hold on Manchuria. Foreign Minister Motono Ichiro, moreover, ordered Ishii to "secure, in whatever form, America's clear understanding of Japan's special position in China." New York capital was welcome in Manchuria and Inner Mongolia, but only if it passed through Japanese hands. Ishii thus now argued that his nation's rights in China resembled U.S. rights under the Monroe Doctrine: they "exist regardless of the recognition of other nations." Japan wanted recognition as well of its "paramount interests" in Manchuria.[34]

Lansing asked whether the term "peculiar interests" could be substituted. The entire China market could in time became a Japanese-controlled arena if "paramount interests" were admitted. "Paramount interests," Ishii replied, was the term U.S. officials had used to justify their interests in Mexico. "As there was no difference . . . between Japan's interests in China and the interests of the United States in Mexico," the viscount thought his own words appropriate. No record has been found of Lansing's facial expression at that point, but he managed to say that the phrase was too radical. He also probably knew that Japan had used the "paramount interests" phrase in an Anglo-Japanese treaty about Korea—just before Tokyo fully annexed Korea.

On November 2, 1917, the dueling halted and a formula developed that from the American view became the second containment policy to control Japan. The Lansing-Ishii agreement, expressed in a letter from the former to the latter, declared that "territorial propinquity creates special relations" between countries. Given Motono's instructions, Ishii had performed this part of his job well. The United States recognized that Japan had "special interests" in China, especially in those areas "to which her possessions are contiguous," which meant Manchuria (and also the freshly seized Shantung?). In return, Ishii joined Lansing in declaring that China's sovereignty must not be impaired. They promised to "adhere to the principle of the so-called 'open-door' or equal opportunity for commerce and industry in China." Lansing and Wilson, however, demanded more. In a secret protocol, not published until 1938 (when the State Department released it amid an even greater crisis with Japan over China), both nations agreed not to take "advantage" of the European war "to seek special rights or privileges which would abridge the rights of subjects of other nations." Thus Japan promised to keep its hands off U.S. and Allied interests in China during the conflict.[35]

Lansing was satisfied. Willard Straight was ecstatic. He declared the agreement to be the "most constructive thing" since Hay's open-door notes of 1899–1900. Reinsch and the Chinese, who knew nothing about the secret protocol, were not ecstatic. Lansing heard from the U.S. post in Peking during 1918 that "The present government is so much under Japanese influence" that the Secretary of State would have to "bring pressure on Japan" if he hoped to save anything in China. As the American and Japanese systems maneuvered for advantage in Asia, Wilson could conclude that the consortium and the Lansing-Ishii agreement were not sufficient as ties that bound.[36]

Siberia: The Bitter Choice

If the struggle over China were not enough, by late 1918 Wilson faced a more immediate crisis with Japan. It erupted in Russia and its results helped shape U.S.-Japanese relations, as well as the larger international arena, for much of the twentieth century.

In February 1917, the tsar had been overthrown by a social democratic regime that could not both fight Germany and reform Russia— tasks truly beyond any mortals. The regime deteriorated until November 1917, when it became the victim of a Bolshevik takeover led by V. I. Lenin and Leon Trotsky. Wilson and Lansing approved of the February regime, but quickly feared and hated the Bolsheviks. Lansing concluded they mainly appealed to "the ignorant and mentally deficient." Such hatred heightened when Lenin damned the Europeans and Japanese by publishing the secret treaties that divided up the postwar world, and when—even worse in Wilson's mind—Lenin moved to make peace with Germany.[37]

These political earthquakes shook Allied capitals in quite different ways. In Washington, Wilson saw Lenin as a fellow visionary, but one who had a radically different and revolutionary plan for the postwar world. During January 1918, the President answered the challenge with the Fourteen Points speech that outlined his own hopes for the peace. He treated Russia as he and Lansing had tried to treat China when they dealt with Ishii: the Allied handling of Russia "will be the acid test of their good will," and the country was not to be carved up by Germany or any other neighboring predators. In London, British officials feared a "Germanized" Russia and the loss of the region's immense resources. They therefore asked their alliance partner in Tokyo to take over the Trans-Siberian Railway, a daring move that Lansing immediately condemned as the first Anglo-Japanese giant step to dominate Russia.[38]

In Tokyo, most officials viewed the British proposal as heavensent: in one stroke, the Japanese army could create a huge buffer zone for Manchuria while seizing one of the world's richest raw material banks, and thus—finally—move the empire to economic independence. But arguments over how and when to deal such a stroke deeply divided the shaky government of Terauchi Masatake, a career army officer and another protégé of Prince Yamagata. In June 1917, Terauchi tried to impose some order on policymaking by creating a Foreign Affairs Advisory Council of nine members who supposedly spoke for the military, the leading clans, bureaucrats, conservatives, and liberals. The advisory council became a vital—sometimes the only—channel for moderates to restrain militants. But it worsened an already ramshackle decision-making process. At times the advisory council divided between go-it-alone anti-Russian military (led by Yamagata) and more cautious civilians (led by Saionji, one of the few remaining *genro*). As Tokyo governments suffered paralysis, the military, especially the army, seized the day.[39]

In January 1918, London proposed that the Allies land forces at Murmansk in northern Russia—to keep caches of weapons out of German hands—and at Vladivostok on Siberia's Pacific coast. Six months of agonizing debate now tormented Tokyo and Washington. The Japanese army quickly forwarded a plan to secure the Trans-Siberian Railroad. The government, led by Terauchi and Yamagata, also wanted to move quickly, but warned that Japan had to follow the American lead. Wilson's cold response to the British proposal was a yellow light. His and Lansing's public lectures about the evils of slicing up China or Russia soon turned yellow to red. On March 5, 1918, the State Department bluntly told Tokyo that intervention could generate "hot resentment" inside Russia and play to the "enemies of Russia" both inside and outside. As Yamagata warned his government, Japan had to be careful because "I regret to say that we . . . count greatly" on Americans and British for money and material. The effect of the United States cutting off steel shipments to Japan in 1917 (to conserve steel for the American war effort) made the prince's point unanswerable. Japan was becoming the great Asian power, but it still needed the Americans.[40]

The Allies now waited for Wilson's decision. The President was convinced that keeping Russia whole, while not doing anything that gave the Bolsheviks new reasons for rallying Russians against the capitalist nations, remained the "acid tests" of policy. He turned back at least six Allied requests for intervention between January and July 1918. On March 3, 1918, however, Lenin and Trotsky made peace with Germany at Brest Litovsk. Fear spread through the West that the Bolsheviks planned to use Russia as a springboard for launching revolutions abroad while (somewhat contradictorily) they opened their resources to German exploitation.

Lansing and Wilson's views hardened. Having urged a "peace without victory" a year earlier, the President furiously demanded on April 6, 1918, "Force, Force to the utmost" against Germany. "Force without stint or limit, the righteous and triumphant Force which shall make Right the law of the world." Wilson's counsels, however, were split over where to apply this force. Lansing urged intervention against the Bolsheviks. Colonel House urged caution. House had a personal network of young liberals scattered strategically throughout Washington, and one of them, William Christian Bullitt—a wealthy, handsome mainline Philadelphian working in the State Department—rained messages on House demanding that he restrain Wilson. "I am sick at heart because I feel that we are about to make one of the most tragic blunders in the history of mankind," Bullitt wrote his mentor. A U.S. landing at Vladivostok, as the British urged, would lead to bloodshed and chaos, then the use of massive force, and at the end, "the Germans will control European Russia and the Japanese will control Siberia." Bullitt believed that only Wilson, by aligning with Lenin, could keep Russia whole and out of the hands of Germany and Japan. Baldly put, Bolshevism was preferable to Japanese imperialism.[41]

Wilson suffered as the Allies screwed up the pressure. "I have been sweating blood over the question of what is right and feasible to do in Russia," he told House. "It goes to pieces like quicksilver under my touch." In May, the quicksilver was transforming into steel. Sixty thousand Czech troops, who had been fighting the Germans, began moving eastward after the Brest Litovsk treaty so they could find transportation to the Western Front. As they and Bolsheviks clashed in Siberia on July 2, the Czechs asked for outside help. Fifteen days later, Wilson announced that U.S. troops would enter Russia in a limited intervention. About five thousand were to join British forces at Archangel to guard Allied stores. Some seven thousand others were to enter Vladivostok, ostensibly to help the Czechs reach the Western Front. Clearly, however, Wilson also intended that the troops watch the Japanese, who would now surely come in and, as well, help anti-Bolshevik forces. The President's decision closed the divided ranks in Tokyo. Despite blunt U.S. signals that any Japanese intervention should be limited, Prime Minister Terauchi disingenuously construed Wilson's response as giving Japan the green light to send troops beyond Vladivostok, and to "reinforce our troops depending on the developments of the situation." Thus was sown, in the words of the historian Hosoya Chihiro, "another seed of trouble . . . which grew into the Pacific War" of 1941.[42]

The original seven thousand Japanese troops who landed in Siberia during August 1918 soon multiplied to eighty thousand. When confronted about the high number, Japan's foreign minister answered, "Force is spirit!"—an answer one Japanese historian describes as so "Orientally mystic" that the U.S. ambassador could make no sense of it. Japan's army chief of staff issued orders quite different from Wilson's. The troops, he secretly ruled, were to create "a nucleus of anti-Bolshevik elements," help Japanese civilians who were in the region for "the development of natural resources," and—above all—keep the U.S. and other foreign troops as far as possible from Manchuria. A first Japanese target was the Chinese Eastern Railway, once controlled by Russia in northern Manchuria and now, in 1918, operated by an Allied group led by an American. By August 19, 1918, as the U.S. troops arrived, the Czech forces had largely left the region. The Americans and Japanese nevertheless remained, for their true missions (watching each other and helping anti-Bolsheviks) clearly were more important than their ostensible mission (helping Czechs).[43]

In Washington, Viscount Ishii, now Japan's ambassador, worked feverishly to keep rising tensions from boiling over into a full-fledged crisis. It proved difficult, for by early 1919 Tokyo officials aimed, in their words, to "develop to the utmost the autonomous organization in Siberia" and "remove . . . existing restrictions", not only on exploiting natural resources but the "operation of industry." William Bullitt was beside himself. Everything had gone wrong. Lenin and Trotsky remained in power. The Japanese remained entrenched in Siberia. U.S. troops were mired in Russia long after the war ended on November 11, 1918, and

Woodrow Wilson arrived in Paris two months later to create a new world. U.S.-Japanese relations were clearly most awkward starting points for such a creation.[44]

Paris

Tension between the United States and Japan during the war was exemplified by the film *Patria*, which President and Mrs. Wilson saw in Washington during March 1917. Produced by William Randolph Hearst, *Patria* showed Japanese and Mexican troops looting, murdering, and raping as they invaded the United States. Wilson told the film distributor that the movie was "extremely unfair to the Japanese." He asked that it not be screened at such a delicate time. The film continued to run.[45]

In addition to the differences over Siberia and Shantung, Japan was also using the war as an opportunity to undercut Americans and Europeans in profitable Asian markets, especially in textiles and sometimes through corrupt means. Japanese producers, for example, won cigarette-paper markets by perfectly copying the paper that had dominated those markets, even down to the "Made in Austria" on the label. Much worse lay ahead at Paris.

Preparing for the conference, Japan was again of two minds. In one, Japanese were rightly proud that they attended as one of the five great powers. More specifically, they were the first non-white race recognized by the white nations to deserve top-five ranking. Japan's wartime exploits gave white powers little choice. Besides seizing strategic territory, imposing many of the Twenty-one Demands, and occupying parts of Siberia, Japan's trade boomed as exports quadrupled between 1914 and 1917. As its industrial population nearly doubled during those years, Japan strengthened its role as the manufacturing hub of that half of the globe stretching from the western Pacific across China to the Urals and the Black Sea. Nearly 80 percent of Japanese continued to work the land, but their capitalist economy was transforming from commercial to industrial.[46]

But another mind also existed. This one was in continual turmoil as debates raged over whether the military, bureaucrats, new political parties, or shifting coalitions of all three were to rule the country. In September 1918, the fresh capital inflow, rampant speculation, and the needs of troops in Siberia raised costs until riots over rice prices toppled the Terauchi government. The riots spread to mining areas. Even with their new economic prowess, moreover, Japanese knew they remained dependent on Americans for capital and such vital products as steel. The new prime minister, Hara Takashi (also known as Hara Kei), understood the vulnerability. Soon admired as the "Commoner" because of his newspaper background and leadership of the popular Seiyukai political party, the sixty-two-year-old Hara was also an ultimate insider who had brokered and calmed the intense rivalry between the army and navy over budgets between 1914 and 1918. Sometimes compared with the British prime minister, David Lloyd George, as a political genius, he also seemed to emulate Lloyd George's personal life by leaving his wife and living with a courtesan in a seaside villa.[47]

As his diaries revealed, Hara understood that Japan needed the United States. He went out of his way to reassure American visitors about Shantung and Siberia. His words were carefully phrased. Shantung, for example, was to be discussed after the peace treaty was written. Japanese forces were to evacuate Siberia after they and the Americans agreed on mutual withdrawal. Of particular importance, Hara told U.S. Ambassador Roland Morris that he wanted to cooperate in China. Morris, however, also cabled Lansing in late 1918 that the Japanese wished the peace conference to recognize, explicitly, "the equality of the yellow race." The demand created consternation in European capitals that ruled over millions of non-white peoples. Nor was it well received in Washington, where a southern-based Democratic Party ruled over a segregated nation and racist Californians.

Hara entrusted the sensitive mission to Paris to seventy-year-old Prince Saionji Kimmochi, one of the five remaining *genro*. Saionji departed for Paris with his mistress, two attending physicians, and the head chef of his favorite restaurant. He had been the first noble to wear Western clothes at the Imperial Palace, one of the first to cut his hair short in Western style, had studied law in France, and enjoyed extensive contacts because of his diplomatic service in Europe. In Paris, Saionji's role turned out to be largely ceremonial. He left negotiations to others, especially Prince Chinda, the ambassador to Great Britain. In truth, Hara and the advisory council were, with good reason, so fearful of a possible explosion at home and so sensitive to the immense stakes in China that they dictated policy almost daily to the Japanese delegates.[48]

The center of U.S. power, on the other hand, lay in Paris itself, once Woodrow Wilson arrived in triumph. He took little advice from anyone, other than Lansing and House. The President's main concern, indeed his obsession, was to create a League of Nations that would right the wrongs of the war and keep the peace thereafter. He obtained his

League, finally, when it was April in Paris. But negotiations since January had been so protracted and bitter that his health was breaking. He probably suffered a small stroke in April. The British, French, Italians, and Japanese could then focus on their main objective: dividing up the German Empire and ensuring that that empire would never again threaten them. Wilson fully understood that Hara and Saionji aimed to secure Japan's hegemony in East Asia. Thus Japan would remain in Shantung and the northern Pacific islands, perhaps Siberia. Thanks to the secret treaties, the British and French would support Japan's claims.[49]

The President did have cards to play. The Japanese need for capital, especially to develop Manchuria, Taiwan, and Korea, led them to New York City's newly rich banks. In 1916, moreover, the President—nearly as angry at the British-Japanese alliance as at German submarine attacks—proposed the largest naval building program in history with words privately uttered to House, "Let us build a navy bigger than [Great Britain's] and do what we please." Just as he boarded the *George Washington* to steam to Paris in late 1918, he proposed building ten more battleships and 146 smaller vessels. Pointedly, the fleet's biggest ships were dispatched to Pacific stations. As new docking facilities went up at Hawaii's Pearl Harbor, the Navy said it was ready for "any movement, offensive or defensive, across the Pacific." Naval planners prophesied that in another conflict, "the most probable combination against us would be Germany, Austria, and Japan." (At the same time, Japanese naval planners viewed the United States as their most likely enemy in a new war.) To do battle with the giant banking-industrial combines, the *zaibatsu,* as well as with the great European cartels, Wilson had also pushed through legislation giving U.S. corporations new weapons to fight for foreign markets. The weapons included the Federal Reserve Act and the Webb-Pomerene Act allowing businesses to combine to conquer markets abroad in ways that would be illegal at home.[50]

Wilson's major problem at Paris, however, turned out to be whether any amount of power could tame Japanese, British, and French policies. Wilson found himself now controlling the world's greatest economic and military power; but it was not enough to have his way with Japan.

His two closest advisers gave Wilson quite different opinions about how to deal with this problem. House had long hoped that the great nations could work out a neat partnership for dividing up the less efficient, unruly parts of the world (including China), then develop these areas, profit from them, and "civilize" them. This self-styled "Colonel" from Texas was only an informal adviser, but he knew how to work on

Wilson. "Never begin by arguing," House once observed, but "discover a common hate . . . get the President warmed up, and then start on your business." Another successful tactic was flattery, House's specialty and Wilson's addiction. The colonel combined this art with a global view that impressed the President. The Japanese could only be brought into a Wilsonian world order, House declared, by helping them develop Asia and recognizing that their place in the "East . . . is in some degree superior to that of the western powers." Otherwise, he warned, "there will be a reckoning."[51]

Lansing's advice was quite different. He urged reducing Japanese influence in China until it was at least no greater than that of the white powers. He wanted Japan largely out of China not because he took seriously Wilson's emphasis on "self-determination," a Wilsonian principle that had captured the world's imagination. Lansing knew that neither Wilson nor House nor any of House's bright young men (such as Bullitt or Walter Lippmann) had ever thought through the term's implications. As a lawyer and conservative, Lansing indeed feared the infinite meanings of self-determination, especially when the explosive term was combined with the collapse of centuries-old European empires. Lansing worried about Shantung less because of any Chinese right to self-determination than because pushing the Japanese out would weaken their position throughout Asia. He agreed with Reinsch in Peking that "the Japanese military masters" not only endangered U.S. short-term commercial interests but were clumsily fueling anti-foreign feelings among Chinese. "Mr. Lansing observed that the attitude of the Japanese was extremely disquieting, particularly in . . . China," minutes of a January 1919 meeting of the U.S. delegates in Paris read, "and that he felt that this was the time for us to have it out once and for all with Japan."[52]

Given conflicting if passionate advice, faced with a possible breakup of the conference over a wondrous number of issues, and sometimes confined to bed by his physician because of exhaustion, Wilson faced a determined Japan. The Japanese, moreover, now raised perhaps the most explosive question: the racial equality clause. The demand did not only arise from Japan's acute sensitivity to the issue of race (or as the historian Shimazu Naoko later wrote, "Japanese sought to gain the status of honorary whites and nothing more"). Tokyo officials also feared that Wilson's League was itself a suspect organization—suspect because Wilson and Lansing might use the League to butt into Japan's business in Asia. If they could not stop its creation, the Japanese were intent on limiting the League's capacity as a troublemaker. Hara thus tried to insert the racial equality principle into the League's Covenant itself. House privately lobbied the Japanese, tried to moderate their demands, and finally succeeded in removing "race" from the resolution. On April 11, 1919, the Japanese proposed that the League of Nations Commission include in the Covenant's preamble "the principle of the equality of Nations and the just treatment of their nationals."[53]

Immediately, Lord Robert Cecil rose to speak for the white nations of the British Empire, especially Australia, whose prime minister raged against such proposals. Cecil declared he personally agreed with the Japanese. He "realised the importance of the racial question"; the proposal, however, "opened the door to serious controversy and to interference in the domestic affairs" of member nations. The "claims of the International Council of Women," Cecil noted, could not be included in the Covenant for precisely the same reasons. Viscount Chinda shrewdly responded that Japan had said nothing about "race" or "immigration," but only about "the equality of nations." Japanese opinion was so strong, Chinda added, that Japan might not join the League "unless satisfied on this point." Wellington Koo, China's delegate, supported Japan.

The appearance of a yellow race coalition may have been more than enough for Wilson. He announced his opposition to the proposal because, he declared, the Covenant already recognized the equality of nations. Baron Makino, of the Japanese delegation, failed to see what Wilson saw and demanded a vote. The Japanese amendment passed 11–6. Wilson, chairing the commission, then ruled that the amendment failed because it "had not received unanimous support." As the President quickly admitted, other provisions had passed by a mere majority, but such "strong opposition" existed against Chinda's proposal that the measure should not be declared approved. Wilson doubtless had in mind the "strong opposition" that would appear in the U.S. Senate that was going to have to ratify the Covenant. Wilson's sensitivity was keen; after all, as President he had begun formal segregation in the federal government. He and Cecil probably also had in mind the first Pan-African Congress, then meeting in Paris, which was plumping for an end to discrimination and colonialism. Its fifty-seven delegates included sixteen from the United States, one of them W. E. B. DuBois. Chinda played to this global audience when he demanded that the vote and Wilson's ruling be on the public record. The Japanese did win this point.[54]

Chinda then dug in for another fight—one he was going to win, or, again the Japanese threatened, they would not join the League. This struggle was over the rich economic and railway concessions seized from the Germans in Shantung. They were willing to return sovereignty over the area to China sometime in the future, the Japanese argued, but they intended first to exploit the prize. Their position seemed impregnable. As Baron Makino directly told Wilson, Sino-Japanese treaties of 1915 and 1918, as well as the Allies' secret treaties, had endorsed Tokyo's view. The Chinese delegation claimed the 1915 treaty had been extracted at gunpoint, but the Europeans, especially the British, decided the real choice was between Japanese order and friendship or Chinese chaos and xenophobia. Nor did House seem to disagree with that formulation.[55]

Wilson nevertheless valiantly attempted to push Japan out of Shantung. He even hoped to use such a precedent to weaken British and French claims in China as well—the reason, no doubt, why Britain's Lloyd George and France's Georges Clemenceau now let Wilson fight alone. Japan must follow not its "rights" but its "duties to China," Wilson began his sermon to the Japanese on April 22, 1918. They therefore "might forego the special position they had acquired and . . . China might be put on the same footing as other nations. . . . There was a lot of combustible material in China and if the flames were put to it the fire could not be quenched for China had a population of four hundred million people." Yes, Makino answered coolly, Japan appreciated "the 'open door,'" but—as he neatly alluded to the Europeans humiliating Japan in 1895–97—not everyone had shown such appreciation for open doors in the past.

"They are not bluffers," the President worried privately, "and they will go home unless we give them what they should not have." So Wilson surrendered. He argued that a League with Japan in it could better straighten affairs out later. Lansing, who viewed the fight as disaster for the open door, condemned the deal as peeling off the "shell" of sovereignty to China while giving the "economic control, the kernel . . . to Japan." Young liberals on the U.S. team, led by Bullitt and Herbert Hoover, prepared to resign. In China, students and intellectuals moved into the streets on May 4, 1919, to protest the decisions at Paris. The Chinese Revolution entered a new phase. "Of all the defeats of President Wilson," wrote the acute young British official Harold Nicolson, the Shantung settlement was "the most flagrant."[56]

Wilson had yet one more clash with the Japanese. They demanded that they be allowed to keep the former German islands. London agreed, in return for Tokyo's agreement that the British Empire could control former German colonies south of the equator and in parts of

Africa. The President did not consider these colonies ready for self-determination, but neither did he want the imperialist nations to own them outright. In the end, a mandate system evolved: Japan, Great Britain, and other powers could run the colonies. They did so, however, under League mandates that gave the organization the right to check on the possessions. As the *New York Times* admitted, control of the island chain from the Kuriles to Taiwan "via Bonin, the Ladrones, Mariane and Caroline Islands" gave Japan, "according to the highest military circles . . . control over the whole Pacific Ocean front of Asia."[57]

House tried to buck up Wilson by admitting that the deals with Japan were indeed "all bad," but also necessary to clear out "a lot of old rubbish with the least friction and let the League of Nations and the new era do the rest." The President said he had done all he could with the "dirty past." For many, however, Wilson's scrubbing left far too much dirt. In Korea, for example, hope had risen when the President proclaimed the principle of self-determination, then fallen when he paid no attention to Korea's independence proclamation. The declaration drowned in blood when a Japanese army stopped an uprising with killing and burning. That American missionaries worked with the rebels doubtless did not escape Tokyo's attention.[58]

The bitterest blow to Wilson's dream was delivered in Washington. Senator Henry Cabot Lodge, chair of the Foreign Relations Committee that had to act on the President's handiwork, headed the largest group of opponents. Calling Japan "the coming danger of the world" and "the Prussia of the Far East," Lodge damned the Shantung deal as "one of the blackest things in the history of diplomacy." The powerful Republican had long hated (and envied) Wilson on a personal level, but many leaders, such as Elihu Root and Philander C. Knox, joined Lodge to pour condemnation on the Paris agreements—especially Article X of Wilson's Covenant. This provision appeared to commit the members to protect the status quo. If such an interpretation were correct, it meant members might be obligated to send their own troops to preserve Japan's hold on Shantung, or the Japanese and British hold on their new colonies.[59]

These conservatives were joined by two other sets of opponents. "Irreconcilables," led by Progressive Republican William Borah of Idaho, wanted nothing to do with a League in any form, but, especially in Borah's case, disliked and feared Japan as much as Lodge. The other set, the young liberals, were led by Bullitt, Hoover, and Lippmann. Lansing returned to Washington to tell Lodge's committee quietly that he, like Bullitt, thought Japan had received too much simply to keep it in a League that was (as Bullitt publicly quoted Lansing as saying) "entirely useless." In 1920, Wilson fired his Secretary of State.[60]

By 1921, the Senate had twice voted on and twice rejected Wilson's League. A major link uniting the President's wildly different opponents was a fear and dislike of Japan. Wilson had failed—not surprisingly since he attempted to create a new order in a world based on the old order existing in Japan, the British Empire, France, Italy, and the United States. The greater threat to that old order was not Wilson, but revolution in Russia and China.[61]

The brilliant anti-war voice, Randolph Bourne, had the last word. "If the war is too strong for you [Wilson] to prevent," Bourne asked in 1918, "how is it going to be weak enough for you to control and mold to your liberal purposes?" Disciplining an ambitious Japan was left to the very forces Wilson thought he had brought under control—Wall Street and Charles Evans Hughes, Wilson's Republican opponent in the 1916 election. These forces set about building a new order on the foundation of the dollar, rather than of the League. The new structure received rave reviews from other wealthy architects, but, as they all soon learned, it had been built on sand.[62]

V

Creating the New Era: From Washington to Mukden (1921–1931)

Hoover, Lamont, and the New Era

"DURING the whole of my six years of service at Tokyo I never remember an interval of any long duration in the controversies between America and Japan," British Ambassador Sir Conyngham Greene told his colleagues in London in September 1920. The Japanese fought against U.S. immigration policies and believed the Americans were blocking them in Asia, Greene wrote. On the United States side, "there was, and is, the very general American dislike and distrust of Japanese Imperialism, militarism and treatment of subject races, such for example, as Korea, together with a widespread suspicion as to Japan's ultimate aims in connection with the control of the Pacific." Washington officials would not have disagreed with this assessment, nor would they have disagreed with the Canadian prime minister who told the British Imperial Conference some months later that only "three major powers" remained in the world—the United States, Great Britain, and Japan. The difficulty was, U.S. officials concluded, that their problems with Japan in Asia came out of the unfortunate fact that two of those three "major powers" were allied. Japan could act irresponsibly in Asia because it enjoyed protection from its alliance with the British. If war flashed over China (as it had twice in recent memory, 1894 and 1900), Americans could find themselves squeezed from both East and West by the two allies.[1]

In the minds of U.S. officials, however, such an alliance was even more evil because it had been precisely such blocs of power that had collided and caused the 1914 to 1918 cataclysm, then, at Paris, spewed out the wartime secret treaties—like so many distorted offspring from hideous parents—that ate away and finally destroyed Woodrow Wilson's dreams of a better world. In 1921, Wilson lay slowly dying in his Washington, D.C., home, but American dreams of a better world, including an orderly and open China, were not dying with him. It quickly became apparent that the new Republican administration of Warren G. Harding had definite ideas about destroying what Harding disparaged as the "old order" so it could create what came to be known in the 1920s as the "new era."

The new world order was to be based on the dollar, as the President's prize catch for his cabinet, Secretary of Commerce Herbert Hoover, repeatedly explained. Orphaned at age seven in 1881, the Quaker-born Iowan graduated from the new Stanford University and then quickly became a multimillionaire engineering and business executive by developing enterprises in such distant areas as China and Russia. He gained an international reputation as a highly successful U.S. Food Administrator during World War I and then as an adviser to Wilson at Paris. He was, as observers concluded, one of the few participants at the peace conference who survived with his reputation enhanced. Hoover was a walking example of the enlightened American capitalist who served what he considered to be the world's higher purposes, whether those purposes involved distributing food to the starving in wartorn Europe or helping to stop the spread of Bolshevism in 1919 by threatening not to distribute food to East Europeans who voted for Communists.

Hoover personified his own philosophy of "American Individualism," as he entitled a widely noted essay of 1922. Traditional virtues of individualism, he emphasized, were to be preserved in the new era of industrialism and capitalism by a voluntary cooperation among entrepreneurs, who would stand up to the "emery wheel of competition," as Hoover phrased it, and not look to the state for bailouts or unfair advantages. It was a set of views that had little in common with the recent development of Japan's society. Both in his theories and in his actions first as Commerce Secretary and then as President between 1929 and 1933,

Hoover was the central figure in the American attempt to create a better world order.[2]

The relationship of Americans to that world, he stressed, had to be intimate. There was no other choice. As the country's economy sank into a postwar recession in December 1920, the newly appointed cabinet member told the American Bankers Association that "our welfare is no longer isolated from the welfare of the world." The "vicious economic circles" of boom and bust could "be broken in one way only. That is by the establishment of credits abroad. . . . We have reached the position of many European states before the war," Hoover lectured, "that if we would continue our advancement and prosperity we must enter upon foreign enterprise." The credits underwriting that "foreign enterprise" naturally had to come from the private marketplace. Government's involvement "would lead to evil ends," such as "political pressures by foreign countries and by nationals within the U.S."[3]

The United States could largely shape the terms of how the globe would develop after the war, Hoover told Secretary of State Charles Evans Hughes in early 1922, because "America is practically the final reservoir of international capital." An early test for his worldview occurred in U.S.-Japanese relations between 1920 and 1923, when it turned out that the "reservoir" was difficult to pump, if not too polluted for use. The drawer from this particular part of the reservoir was Thomas Lamont, the operating head of the J. P. Morgan banking firm in New York and, as it turned out, the key to the second consortium's operation that was set up by Wilson and Robert Lansing in 1918. Raised in a Hudson Valley Methodist parsonage and graduated from Harvard in 1892, Lamont rocketed upward in the New York City banking world, especially after he was persuaded to join Morgan in 1911. At the end of his life in 1946 he could say he still knew little about "the techniques of banking," but with his sharp mind tempered by an "unconventional" but "engaging personality" (as one friend put it), Lamont knew how to conduct economic diplomacy. The Morgan house itself had garnered immense power by using its ties to London's capital sources to develop the post–Civil War U.S. industrial and transportation complexes. Now in the 1920s, as Hoover indicated, Morgan and Lamont, not London, seemed in command of the world's financial reservoir.[4]

To Lamont and Wilson's anger, however, the Japanese refused to drink except on their own terms. In early 1920 U.S.-Japan relations had again grown tense over Shantung, the racial equality clause, the Siberian interventions, ominous measures by both nations to build great fleets of warships, and—as usual—Japanese moves in China. The consortium, Lamont noted during 1919 in Paris where he was advising Wilson, seemed to be "the one practical thing left which is going to prevent Japan from having a free hand in China. . . . I have had any number of people say to me that unless the Consortium actually functioned as outlined, our hope for any kind of square deal in the Far East was gone." Certainly the American Group—made up of New York City's most powerful banks along with those of Boston, Chicago, Pittsburgh, and other cities—was an impressive weapon.[5]

The Japanese, however, were less impressed. When Lamont and his peers from Great Britain, France, and Japan sat down to work out the details of the consortium, Japan quickly moved to exclude Manchuria and Mongolia from the new group's reach. Tokyo officials saw the value of melting in with their Western colleagues for handling deals in central China, where growing revolution targeted foreign properties, but they were not about to help the other three powers—especially the capital-rich Americans—reopen the door to southern Manchuria. An angry Lamont responded that "The Consortium had no plans whatsoever" for Manchuria and Mongolia, but to exclude the two regions explicitly could destroy the members' pledge (in which Japan joined) not to "attempt to cultivate special spheres of influence."

Lamont's fears were not veiled: "In the Far East, peace can be permanently secured only if the two great Powers lying on either side of the Pacific work together in harmony and understanding. . . . The first evidence of this should be in their common attitude towards the Chinese nation. . . . On this point, America . . . offers to become Japan's partner."[6]

The State Department tried to help by threatening Japan with the release of the still-secret protocol of the Lansing-Ishii agreement in which the Japanese had promised not to gain privileges in China at the expense of the other powers. Tokyo was unmoved. Lamont then threatened to drop Japan and have a three-power consortium, only to be stopped by the British, who understandably feared the "excommunication" (as they phrased it) of their best friend in the Far East. The New Yorker privately told the British he had "great disappointment with the . . . unbusiness-like methods" of the Japanese, and expressed "amazement at Japan being treated as a first-rate Power instead of being regarded as a third-rate Power, which in his opinion be nearer the truth." His British listener, Ambassador B. Alston, agreed on Japan's "dilatory ways" and lack of efficiency everywhere but in the military. Government officials in Tokyo seemed "overworked and worn out." "Super-efficiency is perhaps the prize myth of Japan," Alston believed, "but it is foreign writers, not Japanese, and visitors and self-styled investigators who have created the myth."[7]

Lamont finally worked out a compromise: the bankers would recognize Japan's economic interests in Manchuria and Mongolia, but governments would not. State Department officials killed the compromise: they refused to allow the explicit recognition of any part of China, even South Manchuria, as being outside the reach of the open-door policy. Lamont was now as furious with U.S. as with Japanese officials. It was clear, however, that the bankers were willing to overlook Manchuria while playing for the rest of China, but the State Department—led by young officials such as Stanley K. Hornbeck, who had been alienated at Paris by Japanese policies—insisted on playing for all of China. On May 11, 1920, Lamont and Kajiwara Nakaji, president of the Yokohama Specie Bank (Japan's central institution for conducting overseas business), exchanged letters that contained a workable compromise: instead of crossing off Manchuria, the bankers simply promised not to interfere with the Japanese-owned railroads that actually controlled the region's affairs.[8]

The Lamont-Kajiwara discussions had been well oiled by magnificent parties hosted by such *zaibatsu* as the Mitsui and Mitsubishi combines, and climaxed by a visit to the twenty-five-acre estate of lakes and gardens owned by Baron and Baroness Iwasaki (the family that founded Mitsubishi) in the very center of Tokyo. True, the Japanese had set spies on Lamont to the extent that they once took hotel rooms on both sides of his, and another time he simply handed a cable to a spy who was straining to look over his shoulder during a train trip. But the Morgan firm now had links with Japan that exceeded its ties with China and approached those with Great Britain. The path had been cleared for a massive flow of capital from New York to Tokyo, not—as it turned out—for the development of China, but for the development of Japanese holdings in Manchuria. When Hoover began to glimpse this result, he had second thoughts about the virtues of unbounded individualism. Nevertheless, the Lamont-Kajiwara agreement opened the way for the most important diplomatic conference of the 1920 to 1941 era, a conference that marked the high tide of U.S.-Japan relations during the first half of the twentieth century.[9]

Treaties of Washington, Black Chambers of New York City

Both Americans and Japanese grew wealthy from World War I, but by 1921 both suffered from a postwar economic recession. The Japanese not only suffered more, but felt considerably more insecure than the Americans. The 1918 rice riots, involving at least 700,000 protesters, indicated the mass reaction that could occur among an increasingly politicized population. In 1920–21, as war demand disappeared, prices fell severely, especially for raw silk producers (whose largest foreign market was the recession-plagued United States) and rice growers.[10]

The economy rebounded only after the terrible 1923 earthquake, when government spending rebuilt devastated cities. Meanwhile, "the rise of the masses," as the historian Bamba Nobuya has called it, accelerated. Individualism, or "the awakening of individuality," had entered Japan in part when Japanese compared the militarism of the German kaiser with the writings of Rousseau and Locke of Western Europe. The comparison was notably appreciated by a middle class that had emerged during the previous generation and was well educated (between 1895 and 1925 the number of high school students increased nearly ten times, and the number of universities shot up from two to thirty-four). In Osaka and Kobe, amusement parks appeared, as did new theater in which women played the roles—in contrast to classical *Noh* theater where men took all the parts.

Accompanying these transformations was the rapid growth of mass media. As magazines, journals, and newspapers multiplied in number and sold by the millions, radio broadcasting began in 1925. Westernization appeared in clothing styles and in "hiding-the-ear" hairstyles that replaced traditional upswept hair. A democratic surge was reflected in the growing power of political parties which, while not comparable in organization and effectiveness to the two U.S. parties, exerted considerably more influence than they had a generation earlier. The *genro* (the elder statesmen who had advised the Meiji Emperor) meanwhile were dying off. By late 1924, only Saionji Kimmochi remained. Demands for universal male suffrage intensified, demands that Hara Takashi's government and Seiyukai Party refused to meet in 1920–21. Hara, known as the "Commoner" because of his political skills, wanted nothing to do with democracy American-style (a style, that to the puzzlement of many Japanese leaders, had just given the suffrage to American women).[11]

The rise of the masses, as Hara well knew, was part of a global movement let loose in part during 1917–20 by Lenin's and Wilson's principles. In Japan, this trend was accelerated by a new American Studies program at Tokyo University led by Natabe Inazo, who argued that the spread of democratic thought made the analysis of the United States "a very important task for the Japanese." Such developments posed a terrible dilemma for Japan's leaders. Their analyses of World War I clearly demonstrated that Germany, with all its vaunted military power, had finally failed because of political reasons. Now Japan's domestic politics seemed to be increasingly chaotic. Tokyo officials could not protect their society by following the Tokugawa example and withdrawing from the world. In any case, the world war had dramatized how Japan now depended on the wider world for its existence, not least in that the conflict demonstrated that future naval power was to be driven by oil, not coal—and Japan had no oil.[12]

Japan faced severe internal crises by 1921. Further, it was also clearly overextended abroad. On January 9, 1920, the United States finally announced it was pulling out of Siberia, which had proven to be uncontrollable, and pressured the Japanese to follow its example. Tokyo officials replied that they intended to remain. Irritated Americans warned they would not tolerate any Japanese attempts to take over Siberian railways. Under continual pressure, Hara finally was planning to remove troops from Siberia when in March 1920 the Bolsheviks massacred 122 Japanese soldiers and civilians at Nikolaevsk. The cabinet bitterly divided over how to respond. Hara finally appeased the militants by ordering a costly intervention on the Siberian coast.

Foreign policy problems were getting out of hand. Japanese troops were fanning out in expensive, unprofitable operations. Anti-military feelings boiled up among the Japanese people. Draft evasion reached record heights. Some officers quietly refused to wear their uniforms on their way to work. Cries of political corruption meanwhile rang out against Hara and his colleagues. Ties with *zaibatsu* pocketbooks became so blatant that Hara's Seiyukai Party regime was known as the "Mitsui Cabinet" (ministers of the Kenseikai Party, when in power, were termed the "Mitsubishi Cabinets"). But some of the *zaibatsu* were ready to be more realistic about military spending, given the bubbling disorder at home, and they were helped by smaller businesses, especially in the Osaka area, which attacked Hara for not vigorously working to cut back arms spending. At no point did serious debate touch on Japan's control of South Manchuria or its growing ambitions in central China. The debate centered on the best and cheapest means to protect these vital interests.[13]

Lamont's visit had signaled a brilliant solution: Cooperate with the United States to gain access to its reservoir of dollars. By late 1920, U.S. politicians, moved by their own nation's economic problems and disillusionment with war, were ready to join business in working out a new peacetime order. The catalyst was the sudden realization in 1920–21 that the major powers were embarked on a costly race to build battleships fleets. In December 1918, Wilson had asked Congress to build 156 new ships; two years later, the Japanese and British announced they intended to try to keep up with the Americans. None, not even the United States, could afford such a race. The new League of Nations declared that it planned to hold a conference to limit arms. This announcement struck fear in the hearts of Senator William Borah (R: ID) and others who had just fought Wilson and had succeeded in keeping the United States free of the League. On December 14, 1920, Borah made headlines by introducing a joint resolution that proposed talks with the British and Japanese aimed at reducing naval building over the next five years by 50 percent. "Japan sincerely desires to support" disarmament, Borah declared, "but can not in safety to herself do so on account of the attitude and building program of this [U.S.] government." In mid-1921, the Senate and House overwhelmingly passed Borah's motion, as peace groups mobilized on Capitol Hill to shape the foreign policy of the new Harding administration. The President, Secretary of State Hughes, and the powerful Senator Henry Cabot Lodge (R: MA), chair of the Senate Foreign Relations Committee, had rather different ideas, however.[14]

Lodge agreed with New England friends who wanted Japanese neither emigrating to the United States nor controlling the western Pacific. There was "not the slightest danger" of war with Japan, the senator believed, "if Japan understands that she cannot get control of the Pacific." Lodge and Hughes's conclusions meshed with those of the U.S. Navy's War Plan ORANGE of 1919, which concluded that Japan posed no danger to the United States itself, but was in a position to close the open door to China and endanger much of Southeast Asia. The Navy separated company from the civilians, however, on the question of how to handle Japan. Hughes believed that a naval-building race could not protect U.S. interests. He instead aimed to limit arms while destroying the Anglo-Japanese alliance. Both the Japanese and the British could then be made dependent on U.S. cooperation. Washington officials understood, moreover, that London would probably go along with this policy because its valued dominions—led by Australia, New Zealand, and Canada—feared that the alliance was becoming nothing more than a shield behind which Japan made forays into Siberia, Shantung, and even central China.

On July 8, 1921, Hughes preempted the British, and raised Japanese suspicions, by calling for a conference in Washington to deal with a wide range of arms and diplomatic issues. Hara quickly tried to exclude Asian questions from the agenda. Hughes had already ruled out discussing immigration, but he would go no farther. Fearful that the conference was for "the arraignment of Japan," and that the Anglo-Saxons were preparing to gang up on them, the Japanese stalled. But the pressures at home and from Washington were too much. In late July 1921, Hara agreed to send a delegation.[15]

When Hara pressed him for specifics, Hughes continued to be irritatingly vague, but the Secretary of State was making very careful preparations. He asked E. I. Neville, a State Department expert on Japan, to brief him on Tokyo's policies. On June 15, Neville responded with a twenty-four-page memorandum. It stated flatly that Japan intended to control Chinese affairs and prevent the disintegration of China. The Twenty-one Demands, Neville noted, demonstrated these intentions. Across the Pacific lay a different world: "Japan and the Orient generally . . . have no desire to be known as Christian nations. They are Buddhists and ancestor worshippers. . . . As a principle of state policy," they want no "such revolutionary doctrine as the personal salvation of Christianity. Buddhism in Japan is a chauvinistic, militant and proselytizing force of no mean proportions." An object of this "force" was to control China and "her industrial resources," even if it required war, for Japan— Neville was convinced—"is determined to work out her salvation and that of China as well upon the basis of 'Asia for the Asiatics.' "

Neville believed such militant, nationalist groups as the Black Dragon Society exemplified this strain in the society. Japan "needs the resources locked up in the mainland of China, and perhaps of Siberia as well," for otherwise it faced "industrial ruin, and even starvation." Japan never was enthusiastic about John Hay's open-door policy, the adviser emphasized, and, he believed, the Japanese could only be stopped by "superior force." They did confront a central problem: Japan "has not the money to develop these concessions. She needs western help." Once Japanese had capital, however, "they will then be in the position of mediator between West and East, and will control both the investments in China, and the products which the investments have created. . . . No other nation, since the collapse of Russia . . . is in any position to dispute Japan's political, military and economic position in the Far East."[16]

Hughes accepted Neville's assumptions (Japan intended to dominate Asian affairs), but not his conclusions (no nation could dispute Japan's position in the Far East). By late summer his strategy was formed. First, the Anglo-Japanese alliance had to be destroyed. In 1920–21, Japanese and British officials began discussing the renewal of the pact. The outgoing Wilson administration seemed willing to accept the renewal with some changes. Hughes, however, so strongly opposed it that when the British ambassador made the mistake of referring to the treaty, the distinguished Secretary of State launched a temper tantrum: the shaken ambassador reported he had "never heard anything like Mr. Hughes's excited tirade outside of a madhouse." The United States, the Secretary of State warned, would see any renewal as aimed at itself, and renewal would only encourage Japanese imperialism. The British tactfully replied by noting that "when they had a bad elephant in India, they put him between two good elephants to make him behave, and this might be tried in the case of Japan." But Hughes wanted no one else in the center ring cracking the whip, especially if the other trainer might threaten to side with the elephant. He intended to ensure that in any crisis, the British were free to side with the Americans—and especially to side with their interpretation of the open-door policy rather than with Tokyo's version that always seemed to end with a "special position" for Japan.

Once the 1902 alliance was buried, Hughes could move to his next objective: roll back the race in naval armaments. U.S. naval planners had concluded that war might well erupt with Japan, and they had worked out detailed, and expensive, battle plans. With Borah's onslaught, and Hughes's removal of the Anglo-Japanese alliance danger, such planning could be scaled back. The planners, moreover, were embarrassed in January 1921 when, after Billy Mitchell and others argued that airpower would soon dominate over seapower, an airplane actually sunk a former German battleship in a demonstration off North Carolina. The final blow came when Lodge privately told officials that given other pressures, Congress would not spend the money to build a huge Pacific fleet.[17]

On November 11, 1921, a day that Harding proclaimed to be a national holiday, Hughes and the other conference delegates from nine invited nations (not, notably, including the Soviet Union) attended the burial of the Unknown Soldier at Arlington Cemetery. The solemn ceremonies made vivid the waste and folly of war. The next day, Hughes arose at the conference's opening session and stunned the world by proposing "a naval holiday," in which "for a period of not less than ten years there should be no further construction of capital ships." Ships under current construction were to be scrapped. He then provided carefully worked out, highly precise figures on how much tonnage each nation should destroy. His arithmetic added up to 500,000 tons remaining for Great Britain and the United States, and 300,000 tons for Japan. The galleries, populated especially by members of Congress, exploded in a "tornado of cheering," according to one observer. The loudest U.S. peace advocate, William Jennings Bryan, burst into tears. The British, led by Foreign Minister Arthur Balfour, soon joined what was now a Hughes bandwagon.[18]

The Japanese refused to get on board. Politely but insistently they demanded at least a 10:10:7 ratio, rather than the 10:10:6 proposed by Hughes. Their naval officers had decided that this higher ratio was required to protect Japan's interests in Asia, especially if the alliance with London expired. The naval plans and budget had been agreed upon only after tough political fights. Hara exhibited great skill in hammering out compromises among the military. Now Hughes threatened to blow up the results. He, like Perry nearly seventy years earlier, was the outsider threatening Japan's delicate political order.

Especially for three reasons, however, Hughes, like Perry, succeeded in having his way. First, Japan's naval officers were themselves badly divided over spending priorities. With good reason, they feared that if they dug in their heels, Hara would join with the army and further reduce the navy's share of a shrinking economic pie. They knew, moreover, from their own analyses that they could never win a naval race against the Americans. (Harding was indeed ready for such a race. "It all comes down to this," he said privately. "We'll talk sweetly and patiently to them [Japan and the other powers] at first, but if they don't agree then we'll say 'God damn you, if it's a race then the United States is going to go to it.'") Especially aware of this danger was a leader of Japan's delegation, Admiral Kato Tomosaburo, who was ready to accept 10:10:6, but only if the United States further limited its own military buildup in the Pacific.[19]

Kato's position indicated a second reason for Japan's final acceptance. Its delegation was led by men who believed that the powers had entered a postwar world that demanded an end to the old, pre-Wilson– pre-Lenin imperialism. New tactics had to be tooled to realize Japan's objectives. These men did not generally differ from militant factions who targeted Manchuria and China for Japanese interests, but they differed from those groups by emphasizing the need for cooperation with the West and using instruments of trade, rather than going-it-alone with the instruments of war. Kato was a fringe member of this group. Several years earlier he had believed the United States was Japan's great enemy in Asia; but by 1921, while fearing U.S. power, he concluded that adapting to the new world was necessary. The best-known examplar of the fresh approach was Shidehara Kijuro, Japan's ambassador to the United States and chief delegate to the conference. Indeed, his influence was such that the 1920s became tagged as the "Shidehara era" of Japan's diplomatic history.

Born in 1872 and graduated from prestigious Tokyo University, Shidehara rose rapidly in the diplomatic service through his talents and his marriage to the daughter of Iwasaki Yataro, founder of the Mitsubishi *zaibatsu*. Shidehara's mastery of English and wide contacts throughout the West made him a favorite in the United States. He was committed to advancing Japan's power into Asia, but wanted, if at all possible, to work with the Americans. He thus astutely supported Hughes by helping to write an amorphous Four-Power Treaty (signed by the United States, Great Britain, France, and Japan) that replaced the Anglo-Japanese alliance. The treaty bound the four signatories only to "consult" in case of a crisis in the Pacific. Shidehara also helped out by convincing Admiral Kato, austere, reserved, to wear civilian clothes and wave to American crowds. Kato hated every minute of it, but newspapers soon complimented the "charming admiral." Another delegate was ninety-year-old Baron Shibusawa, Japan's leading financier. When aged fourteen, he later claimed, he swam out to sink Perry's ship with a knife borne in his mouth. Since then, he had grown considerably more sophisticated. Resembling Kato, Shidehara, and many other Japanese, Shibuzawa feared future conflict with the United States, especially over China. Thus this Japanese trinity of admiral, statesman, and financier worked with Hughes to build a new Pacific order.[20]

Just as the conference was to begin, Hara was assassinated (stabbed in the heart) at the Tokyo Railway Station. The young murderer represented a group of Japanese that condemned the government's corruption, including involvement in opium smuggling and scandals in the South Manchurian Railway. Tokyo's politics again turned chaotic, but its policymaking did not, in part because of the trinity's leadership in Washington. Hughes was aware of Japan's policy discussions, because he was reading the most important messages being sent between the delegates and Tokyo.

These interceptions of the secret Japanese messages were a third reason why Hughes largely obtained his objectives. The intercepts were the work of Herbert O. Yardley—born in the tiny town of Worthington, Indiana, a dropout from the University of Chicago after one year, then an extraordinary poker player and railway telegraph operator in Worthington until he decided to take the train to Washington, D.C. He arrived during World War I, so quickly obtained a government job sending cable messages. Yardley swiftly proved to awestruck superiors that he could easily decode supposedly top-secret messages coming into President

Wilson. Soon the young Hoosier was set up on 38th Street in New York City, in part for secrecy, in part because the State Department budget was not supposed to be spent within the District of Columbia for such a residence. He had access to all the cable traffic touching the United States. In this house—which became known as the "Black Chamber"— Yardley and his staff decoded thousands of messages to and from embassies in Washington during the war and also during the conference in Paris.[21]

Threatened with being one of the many postwar unemployed, in early 1920 Yardley scored what he considered to be his greatest triumph: he cracked the highly complex Japanese code. Indeed, Yardley deciphered at least eleven different codes the Japanese used, as they sometimes jumped from one to another in mid-sentence. Thus Hughes read the secret Japanese message of July 15, 1921, in which Hara said his government would participate in the conference and, most reluctantly, discuss China but not Manchuria. After Hughes set up a special New York–Washington courier service, U.S. officials "read the messages" of Japan "before they have their morning coffee," Yardley proudly wrote. In all, his team decoded sixteen hundred cables during the conference. On November 28, 1921, he deciphered the telegram he considered "the most important and far-reaching that ever passed through [Black Chamber's] doors." It was Tokyo's first indication to the Japanese delegates that they could accept Hughes's insistence on a 10:10:6 ratio in battleships, if Hughes continued to pressure them to accept, if the newly completed giant battleship *Matsu* could be saved from the scrapheap, and if the United States promised not to fortify further its bases in the Pacific. As Yardly noted, Hughes now only had to maintain the pressure: "stud poker is not a very difficult game after you've seen your opponent's hòle card."

On December 12, 1921, the deal was struck. Japan accepted the 10:10:6 ratio and Hughes accepted the *Matsu* as an exception while agreeing not further to fortify U.S. bases in the Pacific—although he carefully exempted Hawaii from the agreement and also insisted on a formal end to the Anglo-Japanese alliance. He made the agreement after Lodge and other senators assured him that "Congress would never consent to spend the vast sums required in adequately fortifying these islands." When U.S. naval officers protested, Hughes silenced them. He had been helped by Herbert Yardley, but also by Thomas Lamont. Admiral Kato's decision to compromise turned on the central question of where Japan could obtain enough money for development, even war: "The answer is that there is no country other than America that could oblige Japan with the foreign credit required—and this would obviously not be forthcoming if America were the enemy. . . . At all costs Japan should avoid war with America."[22]

The Five-Power Treaty finally set the ratios at 5:5:3:1.7:1.7 for the heaviest ships of the United States, Great Britain, Japan, France, and Italy, respectively. Thus for every 5 tons of U.S. or British warships, Japan could have 3 tons of warships, while France and Italy could each control 1.7 tons. The agreement allowed Hughes to destroy the Anglo-Japanese alliance with the Four-Power Treaty agreed upon the next day, December 13. Throughout the arguments over ship ratios, the British had angered Japan by siding with Hughes. A badly wounded lion after World War I, Great Britain had begun reducing commitments in the Pacific and—especially at the urging of its dominions—was increasingly depending on the United States for security, not Japan. (Indeed, by mid-1922, Balfour and other top British officials feared that war with an expansionist Japan could break out in two or three years.) The alliance had outlived its original purposes, especially that of ganging up on Russia, which was now absorbed at home with its own revolution. With the new treaty replacing the alliance, Hughes, as Lodge phrased it, "substituted a four-power agreement to talk for a two-power agreement to fight."[23]

The stage was now set for the climax of the conference, a nine-power pact (signed by the Five-Power Treaty signatories plus the Netherlands, Belgium, Portugal, and China). This agreement incorporated formally for the first time John Hay's open-door policy into international law. The treaty was not a favor granted to China. Indeed, U.S. and Japanese delgates treated the Chinese as third-class participants who were continually informed, not consulted, about decisions. The 1919 revolution remained threatening as Sun Yat-sen's movement controlled China's south, and Hughes carefully refused even to recognize that Sun existed. The Chinese leader responded by refusing to accept any of the conference's decisions. Former Secretary of State Elihu Root, now a powerful elder statesman and a leader of the U.S. delegation, bluntly declared that China was not a full-fledged member of the family of nations. Strongly pro-Japanese, Root fervently believed that the United States would never use force to maintain the open door in China—a major reason why Japan received de facto naval superiority in the western Pacific from the Five-Power Treaty.[24]

Hughes agreed fully that Americans would never be willing to die for China's territorial integrity. He was determined, however, to use all means short of force to keep Japan from closing off more of China. He came up with an ingenious solution by asking Japan to sign in public what it had signed secretly in the Lansing-Ishii agreement of 1918—that is, that the Japanese would not seek any special rights in China at other nations' expense. Root, who drafted much of the Nine-Power Treaty, then demonstrated why he was perhaps the country's best lawyer. He accepted Hughes's proposal to protect China and coupled it with a line from the Lamont-Kajiwara deal of 1920 that exempted Manchuria from the open-door principles. The Japanese were then prepared to sign the pact. Under Hughes's unrelenting pressure, they also agreed to return Shantung to China, although continuing to hold the region's key railroad. The Chinese bitterly and unsuccessfully protested the entire arrangement, but since they had no alternative, they also finally signed. The Nine-Power Treaty did not protect China. It only protected the right of the other signatories to exploit China according to certain understood rules. The powers continued to control Chinese tariffs, treaty ports, and key rivers (where they kept their own warships).[25]

With the rules for the interwar game in the Pacific and Asia worked out, the powers then disposed of lesser, but nevertheless irritating, questions. Yap, a former German island taken from Japan, was seven hundred miles from the Philippines and in a strategic position to control trans-Pacific cable traffic. After U.S. protests and more pressure from Hughes, Tokyo agreed to allow the Americans and Dutch to use the island for their own private cable systems. The Secretary of State was also determined to evict Japan from Siberia, especially after Tokyo officials began dropping the phrase about their "special interests" in Russia's East—the same phrase used when they took over South Manchuria. Hughes warned Japan the United States would not recognize "any claim or title arising out of the present occupation." Japan agreed to pull out.[26]

Finally, the Japanese even agreed to "throw open" to the second consortium options on loans, including to railways, in Manchuria and Inner Mongolia. They thus surrendered much of the point that had nearly destroyed the consortium (and Lamont's temper) in 1919–20. They could do so now, however, because the Washington Conference agreements were in place. The Five-Power Treaty gave them naval superiority in the western Pacific. The Nine-Power Treaty (through Root's courtesy especially) recognized their hold on Manchuria. Before the conference, one Japanese delegate feared that it would be "an attempt to oppress the non-Anglo-Saxon races, especially the coloured races, by the two English-speaking countries." The conference instead turned out to be a contest between several races to decide how China could best and most safely be exploited.[27]

Everyone except China went home with reasons to be satisfied. With their naval superiority in East Asia and the U.S. pledge not to fortify further western Pacific holdings, the Japanese were safe from American attack across the central Pacific. But because Japan could not fortify its own Pacific islands (the Caroline, Marshall, and Mariana group), the Philippines, Hawaii, and California also seemed safe. For everyone except some frustrated U.S. naval officers, Hughes emerged as the hero who in a single stroke saved governments billions of dollars in arms expenditures, institutionalized the open door, destroyed the Anglo-Japanese alliance, and settled the problems of Shantung, Siberia, and Yap— all areas in which, notably, Woodrow Wilson had failed. And the United States had not had to make a single political alliance. (Indeed, the word "isolation" was first used to describe U.S. foreign policy when a British reporter, Edward Price Bell, wrote in November 1922 that American policy was moving gradually "from isolation into partnership." As is well known, however, partnership does not necessarily mean commitment.)[28]

The success of the Washington Conference ultimately was to rest not on the ability of the diplomats to manipulate the treaties' terms, but on the talents of the private bankers, such as Lamont and Shibusawa, to maintain an international flow of dollars. In 1922, the consortium, led by Lamont, declared that its purpose now was to carry out the Nine-Power Treaty and help China find "a settled state of government." Thus the bankers, in both Manchuria and China, also believed they had won at Washington.

Indeed, other than China, the only loser at the conference was Herbert Yardley. As peace set in, his Black Chamber lost its governmental funding. By 1931 he supported himself by writing books that revealed a past that not even 1930s movies could top. In one 900-page book, Yardley revealed every Japanese message decoded for the Washington Conference. The U.S. government immediately confiscated the book, keeping it partly censored for more than sixty years and passing laws (still in force) that prevent such revelations. Yardley worked in 1938 for the Chinese secret police (a posting where the young Theodore White recalled him as a man of "unrestrained enthusiasms," including "drink, gambling, and women"), helped the U.S. government during World War II, and at the end of his life supported himself by publishing a bestseller, *The Education of a Poker Player, Including Where and How One Learns to Win.* The book, unlike the Washington treaties, long remained highly influential.[29]

"The Tranquillizing Processes of Reason": The 1924 Immigration Act

A proud Secretary of State declared in 1923 that "we are seeking to establish a *Pax Americana* maintained not by arms but by mutual respect and good will and the tranquillizing processes of reason." Hughes's "reason" no doubt referred to the Washington treaties and their economic corollary, the Lamont-Kajiwara agreement. The term had no relevance to the growing American debate over immigration, which climaxed with the 1924 Exclusion Act, a measure that poisoned U.S.-Japanese relations for decades. The act was fathered by Congressman Albert Johnson (R: WA), who declared that "our capacity to maintain our cherished institutions stands diluted by a stream of alien blood." It was signed by President Calvin Coolidge, who, as Harding's Vice President, had published an essay praising Nordic supremacy and claiming that when "Nordics" intermarried with lesser ethnic groups, their children were degenerate.[30]

The 1924 act arose out of fears that immigrants such as Asians and Eastern Europeans were about to flood into the country again after the hiatus of World War I. In the decade before 1914, the highest numbers of immigrants (until 1989) arrived at U.S. shores. An act of 1917 imposed literacy tests, and a 1921 act for the first time set numerical quotas. For the exclusionists, however, these barriers were hardly high enough. The 1920s were a "verdant springtime of American racism," as two historians have aptly characterized a decade introduced in 1919–20 by bloody race riots in several cities, then contaminated by agricultural and mining recessions that threw millions of Americans, especially African Americans, out of work and into cities. A new Ku Klux Klan targeted Jews and Roman Catholics in the North and West. Out of this witch's brew came Johnson's proposals that resulted in the 1924 legislation, also known as the National Origins Act because it allowed new immigration on the basis of the origins of those already in the United States. Since those origins were carefully based on the 1890 Census, it blatantly discriminated against Poles, Italians, Asians, and East European and Russian Jews who had arrived in large numbers after 1890.[31]

For the Japanese, it was known as the Exclusion Act, because for them it went beyond numerical quotas to exclude directly "aliens ineligible for citizenship"—code words meaning only the Japanese. Hughes tried to stop this blatant discrimination by writing Johnson that "the Japanese are a sensitive people and unquestionably would regard [such a law] as fixing a stigma upon them." The Secretary of state warned that the act "would largely undo the work of the Washington Conference." He pointed out that if the Japanese were at least given quotas as were all other groups, even fewer (about 250 per year) would be admitted than were entering under the 1907 Gentlemen's Agreement. His words had no effect.

Japanese Ambassador Hanihara Masanao tried to help by writing a polite but firm letter of protest. This was done in part at Hughes's suggestion. The Secretary of State read and approved the letter, which included the phrase that "grave consequences" could result from the law. U.S. newspapers and such anti-Japanese senators as Lodge cried that the two words were a "veiled threat" to the United States. The law then was whipped through Congress (323–71 in the House; 76–2 in the Senate). An embarrassed Hanihara was quickly replaced as ambassador by the redoubtable Viscount Ishii. "I am greatly depressed," Hughes wrote a friend. "Japan cannot threaten anybody" because of its economic dependence on Americans and others. But the Senate had "in a few minutes spoiled the work of years and done a lasting injury."[32]

Hughes's opposition to the law actually attracted much support in the United States. That support simply was not in Congress. San Francisco newspapers, and especially the business community, took up the Japanese cause, but they were overwhelmed by California labor's and the Hearst newspapers' anti-Japanese cries. Most of the east coast opposed the law, and twenty-four prominent Americans—led by Thomas Lamont—publicly apologized for the legislation to the Japan Society in New York City. Missionaries, especially Sidney L. Gulick, who had long worked in Japan and America for closer relations, lobbied for a new act to rectify the old. Gulick was so effective that numerous anti-Japanese groups mobilized in opposition to his work during 1925 to 1930. The groups stopped any attempted revision of the exclusion provision, and the onset of the depression in 1929–30 ended any hope of changing the law.[33]

The Japanese saw the 1924 act as reaffirming their conclusion drawn from the clash with Wilson over the racial equality clause in 1919: Americans preached universal principles but practiced national discrimination. The act especially hurt Shidehara, who became foreign minister in the June 1924 cabinet of Premier Kato Takashi. Perhaps the leading Japanese voice to urge the new diplomacy of peaceful trade expansion and cooperation, especially with the United States, Shidehara was at long last in the position where he could break down Japanese militarism, parochialism, and nationalism. Instead, on July 1, 1924, when Shidehara made his maiden speech as foreign minister, the 1924 act went into effect and mobs tore down the Stars and Stripes at the U.S. Embassy. Shidehara had to apologize to the Americans, then track down the culprits. One Japanese committed *seppuku* in front of the U.S. Embassy; another tried to murder the American consul in Yokohama.[34]

Shidehara attempted to put the best face on the crisis by telling the Diet, not quite accurately, that Americans only wanted to exclude Japanese (because "Japanese are to Americans what oil is to water"), and did not mean to imply Japanese were inferior. He also noted that the United States had the right to control its immigration—a remark that doubtless reminded his listeners that they too prohibited foreigners from owning land, kept out Chinese laborers, and discriminated heavily against many non-Japanese, including other Asians. Many nevertheless took quite a different view. One author wrote that the 1924 act was the "most unprecedented humiliation in the recent fifty years of Japanese history," and argued that "rampant Americanism," not Bolshevism, most endangered Japan. Some were so angry that they tried to organize a boycott of American movies. But here Japanese—especially the young, who wore Harold Lloyd glasses and styled their hair like Clara Bow and Mary Pickford—drew the line. The boycott was an abysmal failure.[35]

The act had the effect of a ticking time bomb on Japan's policies. At one level, many Japanese who wished to emigrate looked elsewhere, especially toward Brazil, where they created a large colony in the 1920s. The Tokyo government worked closely to help these emigrants with subsidies and schools, even after anti-Japanese acts began to appear in Brazil by the decade's end. On another level, American racism led Japan back to the Asian mainland: if the United States wanted to play by such rules, conservative Japanese argued, they should instead work with the "colored races in Asia." In 1928, the first Manchuria Youth Congress called for a "Manchuria-Mongolia autonomous state" built on "racial harmony" of Japanese and Manchurians (but not Chinese). The 1924 Exclusion Act turned into a pivot that swiveled Americans inward, while pushing the Japanese away from Shidehara's cooperative policy of the 1920s toward the Kwantung Army's conquests of the 1930s.[36]

China Once Again

In the end, of course—in 1941—it was the question of China that led the United States and Japan into war. Both Hughes and Shidehara understood during the 1920s that they were dealing with a different, deeply divided, and less controllable China; but neither diplomat tried to limit the expansion of his nation's interests into China.

In 1922, China was torn by warlords who controlled various parts of the vast country. The gods of history, however, were to smile on Sun Yat-sen's Kuomindong movement in the south. Since he had helped set off the revolution in 1911–12, Sun had tried to work with both Japanese and Americans; but in 1922, as Hughes refused to deal with him, he was driven out of his stronghold at Canton. Sun and his brilliant young military aide, Chiang Kai-shek, turned to the Soviets. The Chinese Communist Party was born. Meanwhile, in 1923, Sun demanded China's control of its own customhouses and foreign trade. Hughes went to President Calvin Coolidge for consultation, and the President, in a Coolidge-like response, tersely said, "I think the naval units should be sent." U.S. warships joined those of other powers in a naval demonstration not because the United States feared communism, but because the Coolidge administration was determined to maintain imperialist controls over China's trade. Otherwise, U.S. attention fixed on economic opportunities. Between 1914 and 1930, U.S. investments in China tripled, to $155 million. In 1931, the United States replaced the Japanese as the leading supplier of goods to the Chinese. American missionary and philanthropic enterprises accounted for an abnormally large part ($69.3 million in 1926) of the U.S. overall investment. "The importance of the Rockefeller Foundation [deeply involved in educational and medical projects] is not to be underestimated in China," Hoover was told.[37]

Notably, little American attention was on the now-famous consortium. "The object of the old consortium" of 1911–13, a British official later wrote, "was to save China from foreign aggression. The object of the new consortium was to save China from herself." As a friend once unsuccessfully tried to explain to Woodrow Wilson, however, the most one can do is to help others; they have to save themselves. So it proved to be in China. Refusing "to be persuaded that foreigners knew better than they did what was good for China," as the British official noted, the Chinese ignored the consortium. The banking group did not make one major loan to China after 1922. Which does not mean that dollars were not going into China. They were, but under the control of individual banks, or—as U.S. officials looked on with some horror—through Japanese who were moving into Manchuria and North China.[38]

Such use of dollars fit in well with the Shidehara approach. As Prime Minister Takahashi summarized in 1922, "Armed competition has become obsolete, but economic competition is growing in intensity." The objectives—control of China's markets and raw materials, espe cially in its northern and central provinces—remained traditional, but the Japanese tried new tactics of trade, investment, and cooperation with the United States and other Western powers. As Taisho democracy reached its peak, Shidehara's policies went on the offensive in South-east Asia, the Middle East, and—especially—China to "develop oppor-tunities for expansion for our nationals abroad," as he phrased it. It was a climactic test for a highly delicate democracy and foreign policy that were closely related. And it proved to be a tragedy of Japanese history that these highest stakes rested in part on developments in China and the dollar in the United States. For as Shidehara took power, the Chi-nese Revolution moved into a new, brutal, anti-foreign phase, and the dollar became wildly unpredictable.[39]

Americans remained Japan's best customer through the 1920s by tak-ing about 40 percent of its exports. Much of that, however, was in silk and silk goods, while China—whose overall trade doubled during the decade (was the long-mythical China market finally becoming real?)—absorbed Japan's rising stream of industrial exports. In 1926–27, Japa-nese trade with China finally exceeded Great Britain's. China was becoming the profitable market that allowed the Japanese to import the foodstuffs and raw materials on which their prosperity depended. Shidehara thus believed that while Manchuria was vital, Japanese inter-ests in that area could not be allowed to endanger the tremendous opportunities further south. So he was a China-firster, as he explained in a speech in 1924:

> [On] our restricted islands we suffer from a population increase of 700,000–800,000 annually. There is, therefore, no alternative but to proceed with our industrialization. It follows from this that it is essential to secure overseas markets and this can only be done by adopting an economic diplomacy. If we try to cure our economic problems by territorial expansion, we will merely destroy interna-tional cooperation. Japan, being closest to China, has an advantage by way of transport costs and she has also the greatest competitive power because of her wages. It must therefore be a priority for Japan to maintain the great market of China.[40]

It is ironic that Shidehara's tenets of cooperation and economic expansion actually offended U.S. officials. For his idea of cooperation meant, in part, cooperation with the Soviet Union, which the Americans so detested that they had refused to recognize that the Communist regime officially existed. A Soviet-Chinese courtship of 1923–24 had angered Washington policymakers, but it stunned those in Tokyo.

The new Soviet presence directly challenged the Washington agreement on China. By 1925, Japan quickly adjusted by leaving northern Sakhalin, making trade agreements, and then restoring diplomatic relations with Moscow. The growing China-Russia-Japan coalition led one U.S. official to warn "that there is a menace to the entire West in such a combination seems self-evident." A few, such as Senator Borah, understood that the State Department's fear and dislike of the Soviets made impossible any hope of using them to contain Japanese expansionism. But Shidehara's idea of cooperation posed another dilemma as well to Americans, for he also intended to cooperate, to some degree, with the Chinese Revolution. In 1925 and 1927, when the powers discussed possible intervention to stop Chinese attacks on foreigners, Shidehara was reluctant to go along. He did not want Western power to move between Japan and China—nor, especially, to turn angry Chinese Nationalists toward retaliation by boycotting foreign goods.[41]

If Shidehara's ideas about cooperation offended Washington officials, his (and Wall Street's) views of economic cooperation drove those officials to frustration. As Lamont had demonstrated, and Hoover knew in detail, the Japanese wanted to work with the United States "to develop China" (as an aide told Hoover in 1921) because "they are convinced that they are not in a position to do it without assistance." Tokyo–Wall Street ties were indeed tight. After the massive earthquake of 1923, in which over a hundred thousand Japanese died, J. P. Morgan handled a $150 million earthquake loan and led private efforts to send assistance. Japan's powerful *zaibatsu,* the House of Mitsui, rebuilt its bank in the image of Morgan's building at 23 Wall Street. But the Americans went farther. Throughout the 1920s they floated loan after loan to Japan, and to Hoover and the State Department's anger, much of this money went to build Japanese railways and plants in Manchuria and China.[42]

Wall Street, Hoover and the State Department's Far East experts charged, was doing nothing less than using U.S. dollars to help the Japanese close the door to Manchuria and perhaps even central China. Hoover had told Hughes in 1922 that he wanted American money to develop industries at home, not used for bailing out "unbalanced budgets or the support of armies" abroad. Nor was it to be loaned to foreigners unless U.S. "contractors and builders of equipment" have "an equal chance to compete on equal terms with other foreigners." Hoover and Hughes tried to pressure Wall Street into clearing its foreign loans in

Washington to ensure that the money supported, rather than undercut, U.S. foreign policies. The attempt to bring the bankers in line with the policies was a failure. Hoover and Hughes were in a terrible dilemma, Hoover because according to his own view of capitalism too much government interference could lead to fascism or socialism; Hughes because too much interference would alienate the Japanese—needed to carry out the provisions of the Washington treaties—or the bankers—needed to carry out his reconstruction plan for Europe.[43]

State Department officials responsible for the Far East were beside themselves. They wanted the bankers to use the consortium (where the Japanese could be closely watched) to advance U.S. interests and China's development. Instead, the financiers ignored the consortium, ignored China (where risk-free money could hardly be made amid the revolution), to work bilaterally with the Japanese in Manchuria and northern China. Wall Street had no "adequate conception of the present as a special moment . . . to build a great financial port of entry for American influence and commerce in the new 'far West' of Eastern Asia," State Department expert Stanley Hornbeck lamented. By the mid-1920s, the historian of J. P. Morgan writes, the bank's new clients were Japan, Germany, and Italy: "It was strictly by chance that the bank became involved with three future enemies." Hoover and Hornbeck, among others, would have doubted whether chance had much to do with it.[44]

Shidehara, unlike Hoover, was finally undone not by Wall Street, but by economic malaise at home, the Japanese army's growing restlessness over his China-first instead of a Manchuria-first policy, and the Chinese Revolution. In 1927, Chiang Kai-shek's Kuomindong forces moved out of the south, consolidated their power over much of China, and marched into Nanking, where they destroyed foreign property, murdered foreigners (including a U.S. citizen who was vice president of Nanking University), and were stopped only after American and British gunboats opened fire. The United States, Japan, and Great Britain demanded that Chiang pay a large indemnity while promising never again to harm foreigners. He flatly refused, turning instead to his first order of business, which was the killing of all the Communists he could discover within the Kuomindong. Washington refused to recognize Chiang's government. Amid these crises, Shidehara's party fell from power in 1927. He was bitterly attacked for not involving Japan with an international force that was to teach the Kuomindong respect for foreigners and their property.[45]

In 1926, the Emperor Taisho had died. His son, the young Emperor

Hirohito, began the Showa era that was to stretch through most of the twentieth century. In 1927, General Tanaka Giichi's Seiyukai Party swept into office. Tanaka became prime minister and also replaced Shidehara as foreign minister. Born in the resurgent province of Choshu in 1863, a protégé of Yamagata's, he was a military man who had little respect either for politicians (although he was a political leader himself) or for diplomats (although he had served in the legation in St. Petersburg). Tanaka knew the United States and admired Germany, but it was his experiences in Russia that made him a leading advocate of the Siberian intervention of 1918, and—like most of his army colleagues—a fervent voice for controlling Manchuria as a barrier against Soviet expansion. His Manchuria-first policy was also driven by his hatred for Communist revolution (he suddenly arrested a thousand suspected Japanese Communists and radicals in early 1928), and his fear of Chiang Kai-shek's move northward after 1926.

Tanaka damned Shidehara as "weak-kneed," and worse, for his 1924 to 1927 China policy. The general was not wholly adverse to cooperating with the powers. In 1928, for example, he agreed to sign the Kellogg-Briand pact that artlessly outlawed war. Tanaka knew, of course, that the United States had stripped away the original French proposal, which had been aimed at Germany, until the remains left in the treaty were lifeless. Signing it was not for either Japan or the United States a major step toward international cooperation. As a disciple of Yamagata's, schooled by ex-samurai in the highly nationalist idea of *kokutai* (the national weal—literally, the national body) that became personified in the Emperor, Tanaka became a pivotal link between the Meiji expansionists of 1894 to 1912 and the Showa militarists of the 1930s and 1940s.[46]

This linkage was demonstrated in June 1927, when Tanaka's policy toward Asia was announced: as long as Japanese interests were not harmed, the Chinese could put their country in order as they thought best; in Manchuria, however, Japan had a special "obligation" to maintain peace and order. Part of the "obligation" required fresh talks with J. P. Morgan to obtain capital. Before going to Tokyo, Thomas Lamont believed he had obtained a green light from Secretary of State Frank Kellogg to make a $30 million loan that clearly was going to be used by the South Manchuria Railway Company. But when the deal became public, the Chinese government protested, and some American newspapers loudly warned that Lamont was helping Japan close the door in Manchuria. The head of Morgan attempted to launch a propaganda campaign of his own, but the State Department advised that the loan be postponed. Tanaka simply went instead to National City Bank and obtained $20 million for the Oriental Development Company, which, despite its more neutral name, was immersed in Manchurian business. Few newspapers noticed. Hoover had long since given up trying to bring Wall Street into line with U.S. policies, and State Department experts, such as Hornbeck, concentrated on China while largely accepting Japanese power in Manchuria—especially if the alternative was the antiforeign, highly unpredictable, revolutionary regime of Chiang.[47]

That kind of reasoning was to paralyze U.S. officials in 1931 when Japan's military finally seized Manchuria. In 1928, similar silence pervaded Washington when Tanaka moved to discipline Chinese forces in Shantung by sending in twenty thousand Japanese troops for a stay of several weeks. The Chinese asked for help from the League of Nations, which, as Japanese militarists doubtless noted, made no important response. U.S. silence also rang out in May 1928 when Tanaka decided to fix the northern warlord, Chang Tso-lin (Zhang Zuolin), whose armies were trying to link Manchuria with North China. Chang was threatening Japan's interests in Manchuria and endangering the ambitions of Chiang Kai-shek, who moved his armies northward to deal with the problem. Intent that neither Chinese leader would have his way in the north, Tanaka ordered Japanese troops to disarm Chang's troops in a key part of Manchuria. As Chang moved from Peking to Manchuria for a discussion of the problem, he died when his train was blown up on June 4, 1928. Japan's Kwantung Army, whose officers feared Tanaka would be too lenient in handling Chang, assassinated the Chinese leader, then brazenly tried to cover it up by claiming to have found some dead Chinese who had set off the bomb. When General Tanaka moved gingerly in punishing the Kwantung Army, the new young Emperor, for one of the few times in twentieth-century Japanese history, subtly intervened and forced the prime minister to resign.[48]

Tanaka's attempt to control Manchuria had turned out to be a disaster. The Kwantung Army demonstrated that it could act with virtual impunity against the wishes of Tokyo officials, even against a distinguished general. The murdered Chang was replaced by his son, Chang Hsueh-liang (Zhang Xueliang), who defied Japanese plans by pledging loyalty to Chiang Kai-shek. Chiang now stood on the brink of uniting all of North China. In December 1929, his Kuomindong flags flew over Manchuria's important government buildings. Chinese who had long hated Japan's pressure began to fuel anti-Tokyo activities. The Kwantung Army, determined not to take mere half-measures when the next opportunity arose, replaced its leader with Itagaki Seishiro and Ishiwara

Kanji, both of whom were prepared to act on their own and with force. Into this cauldron came Shidehara in 1929 for his final term as foreign minister.[49]

Broken in spirit and body, Tanaka died in 1929, shortly after leaving power. He was to be remembered later by Americans of the 1930s and 1940s for the so-called Tanaka Memorial, a document in which the general supposedly laid out Japan's plans for conquering China. In reality, the Memorial was a highly successful piece of Chinese propaganda. Tanaka nevertheless remained a link that helps explain how Meiji Japan transformed into the Japan of the 1930s. As for Shidehara, he was to be remembered as an instructive aberration, a "might-have-been" if only his world had not begun to disappear in 1929. But then, many people's worlds began to disappear that year.[50]

"They Still Need Us—and That Is Probably What Annoys Them": 1929–1931

By 1930, Japan's decade-long moves toward mass democracy and Shidehara's commercial foreign policies were buried under an avalanche of economic disasters. In the United States, another era was also ending beneath the collapse of a corrupt New York stock market and a thimble-rigged banking system. The 1920s could have been called the private-dollar era, for U.S. bankers, led by international figures such as Lamont, had been relied on by U.S. officials to rebuild wartorn Europe, cement good relations with a democratic Japan, undercut Chinese (and other) revolution with development, and all the while make the United States the hub of world production. As Hoover and Hornbeck lamented as early as 1922, the bankers were not cooperative, for large loans went to Germany, Japan, and Latin America for increasingly dubious ventures, while American farms, mines, and some specific industries (such as textiles) lost their competitive advantage and suffered throughout the decade. This suffering meant that millions of Americans lost their purchasing power. As the gap between poor and rich widened, bankers sent hundreds of millions of dollars abroad, often in get-rich schemes that quickly collapsed. By 1927–28, as overseas opportunities dwindled, investors turned to the New York stock market, where they boosted prices by pouring in millions of dollars they had borrowed.

It was the last rosy glow of a body before it bursts an artery. When investors could not cover loans in 1929, stock prices plummeted 50 percent in four months. Economic downturn had already begun abroad,

especially in Western Europe, and also in Japan, which had been borrowing from the Americans. The more dramatic decline was to occur
in 1930–31, after the American fall was fully felt. U.S. unemployment
was at 3 percent (1.5 million) in 1929 and climbed until it reached 25
percent (12.6 million) in 1933. As the gross national product sank unbe-
lievably from $104 billion in 1929 to $56 billion in 1933, Congress tried
to lift the economy by its bootstraps when it passed the Smoot-Hawley
Tariff Act in July 1930 that imposed the highest rates on imports in the
twentieth century. Exports from Japan were suddenly hit with a rate
rise of 23 percent, and this market was sliced at the same time that the
United States was overtaking Japan in trade with China. At Washington
and New York's demand, the diplomacy of the 1920s had largely rested
on dollars. Now, other nations could neither obtain dollars from the
bankers nor earn dollars from sales to Americans. The foundation of
U.S. post–World War I diplomacy washed away in a tide of bank failures and protectionism.[51]

Newly elected President Hoover did not know which way to turn. In
1926, he had argued that with the end of the four hundred-year frontier,
Americans must look abroad: "Our exports will tend to decrease
because our easily cultivable [sic] land is now well occupied. The day
of unlimited lands is over. If we are to maintain the total volume of our
exports and consequently our buying power for imports, it must be by
steady pushing of our manufactured goods." By 1930, however, many
world markets were mired in depression. As U.S. tariffs rose, so did
anti-American policies abroad. Even in 1928, U.S.-British relations had
been so bad that one high British diplomat believed that "war is *not*
unthinkable between the two countries." Two years later, it seemed they
verged on declaring economic war on each other. Hoover's hope that
Americans could lift themselves up to prosperity by selling abroad rapidly disappeared.

In 1931, Hoover argued that the United States was more self-con-
tained than any other power, so if it could "get its own house in order,"
affairs internationally would improve. But that solution implied quick
governmental help, and the President continued to agonize over how
far "the state" could become involved before it corrupted "the development of the individual." After lunching with Hoover, close friend and
Assistant Secretary of State William Castle recorded in mid-1930 that
"He looks pretty worn. . . . He says that the present Senate pretty nearly
represents the breakdown of representative government. . . . He is tired
and fairly discouraged." On New Year's eve, 1930, Castle observed,
"Someone said to someone else, 'I hope that 1931 will be better than

1930,' and the answer was, 'If it is not it will be non-existent.' " Castle added: "The poor President could hardly be in a worse state."[52]

By mid-1931, Hoover held tight to two hopes: that the depression was only an extra-sharp swing of the business cycle in which an equally sharp upward turn would propel him to reelection in 1932; and that the few remaining overseas friends—above all, Japan—would remain cooperative. He especially hoped, as he said in one speech, that such friends would help in quelling the political instability that now affected three-quarters of the world's population. Both hopes were utterly destroyed within months. The depression was not a working out of the business cycle but the result of massive problems in U.S. and world economies that were to be solved only with the next world war. And a frustrated, depression-wracked Japan was preparing to turn violently against the West.[53]

During 1927–28, most major world economies had enjoyed a boom—except those of Great Britain and Japan. The Japanese were recovering from their 1923 earthquake disaster when major scandals paralyzed their banking system. Due to failures, the number of banks suddenly plummeted 25 percent, to about one thousand. The *zaibatsu* profited as Mitsui, for example, bought up assets cheaply while greatly enlarging its already vast influence. As economic power concentrated, in early 1930 Finance Minister Inoue Junnosuke decided (in part because of persistent U.S. demands) to put Japan on the gold standard, the same standard that regulated most of the other industrialized nations' economies, led by the American. His timing could not have been worse. As Asia fell into revolution and depression, vital Japanese markets disappeared. When the American economy sank, so did Japan's leading customer. In 1929, the United States (with 43 percent) and China together absorbed 67 percent of Japan's exports. But most parts of China that were not chaotic were anti-Japanese, while increasing numbers of Americans had little money with which to purchase Japanese goods.

Having promised to support the yen with gold, Inoue now watched hopelessly as Japan's trade lost a full 60 percent of its specie reserves as gold flowed overseas. In 1929–31, U.S. prices fell 27 percent; but Japanese prices dropped 35 percent. These were led by all-important prices of silk, which depended on the American market and made up two-thirds of Japan's exports that earned dollars in the United States. Silk prices sank 50 percent in 1930 alone, and the all-important cotton textile price dropped nearly as much.[54]

Having tied itself to Wall Street and the U.S. market in the 1920s, Japan's economy now found itself tied to sinking stones. Two out of every five Japanese families depended on silk for cash income. As the value of silk exports was almost slashed in half, some Japanese families faced starvation. The many who grew rice, the price of which similarly fell by nearly half in 1929–30, also faced ruin. The crisis of the peasant class directly affected the army because it was largely recruited from this class. Some peasants tried to find work in manufacturing. They became part of a massive influx into urban centers that had begun before World War I. Militant labor leaders tried to organize this mass in the 1920s, but got nowhere. Low-wage female textile operators were impossible to organize, as were male peasants who did not like unions. Supply, in any case, more than met labor demand. And businessmen emphasized that unions were not necessary anyway: "In our country," the Tokyo Chamber of Commerce bragged, "relations between employers and employees are just like those within a family." This was known as the "warm-feeling principle," or as one observer phrase it, "a sort of benevolent despotism."[55]

Whenever leaders of any organization begin talking about "family," it is advisable for all other members to be on guard. Having in many cases been promised job security, Japanese workers discovered in 1930 that the number of their unemployed had shot upward 47.5 percent since 1925, to 323,000. One summary of the economic scene noted the precipitous fall-off of exports, then added that Japanese government figures showed that "an average of 500 people had committed suicide in Japan during each month in 1930. The major cause was believed to be the lack of employment." The government itself resembled Hoover's: it did little. More accurately, its resources were put at the disposal of the largest industrial-banking families, the *zaibatsu*, while small business people, workers, and farmers faced, alone, an increasingly vicious marketplace.

A stunned American author in the *New York Times Magazine* of March 2, 1930, had discovered that in late 1929 more than eight hundred Japanese were political prisoners, locked up "for the expression of radical opinions or for plans or acts to carry those opinion into effect." The author, James T. Shotwell, a distinguished political scientist, noted that these figures revealed "the extent of social and political unrest," and had been a "revelation" to most Japanese. He believed the unrest could mushroom, especially among the young, who had to make "an apparently impossible adjustment between an industrially modernized nation and a philosophy of life which connects nation and family with a mythological past," particularly the past represented by Shintoism and its "divine Emperor." Younger Chinese, Shotwell argued, could rally around a radical twentieth-century nationalism, but their Japanese counterparts had to reconcile a 2,500-year mythical past with the terrible realities of a turbulent, industrialized present that destroyed the traditional values and village life embodying that past.[56]

In early 1932, a fanatical young nationalist from one of those villages gunned down Inoue. The murderer told police he did the deed because the finance minister's deflationary policies had destroyed rural society. Several weeks later, another of Thomas Lamont's friends, Baron Dan Takuma—who had built the financial base for Mitsu zaibatsu—was shot by another member of an ultranationalist brotherhood. This assassin, also from a rural area, apparently acted because Baron Dan and Mitsui had made tens of millions of dollars by betting against their own nation's currency in international markets. Both killers received light sentences and were out of jail in several years.

During early 1930, William Castle glimpsed another side of this nationalism and mistrust of the West. American executives of General Electric and Truscon Steel told the State Department official that "There is clearly a strong tendency to get rid of foreign management in Japan. . . . More and more the Japanese want to get all manufacturing into their own hands without any outside help at all." After personally visiting GE and Ford plants in Japan, Castle concluded that the Japanese campaign to buy only homemade goods "is really the culmination of anti-foreign feeling which has grown for years. . . . It is obvious that they still need us—and that is probably what annoys them."[57]

Against this darkening background, Shidehara, who had returned as foreign minister in July 1929, made one last effort to rekindle the hopes of 1921–22 and reverse the disastrous policies Tanaka had tried in 1927–28. In his old spirit of cooperation, Shidehara even ordered Japanese gunboats to join U.S. and British vessels that intervened jointly during 1930 at Changsha to protect foreigners from Communist attacks. He also moved to follow the Americans and British by recognizing China's tariff autonomy in return for trade concessions to Japan. Throughout, officials in the navy, and especially the army, damned Shidehara for moving too slowly and being too much in lockstep with the West.[58]

Shidehara and Prime Minister Hamaguchi Osachi's greatest diplomatic triumph (as well as President Hoover's) occurred at the 1930 London Naval Conference. The Washington agreements had not placed limits on cruisers and other auxiliary ships. When the three powers met at Geneva in 1927 to set such limits, the British and Japanese proposed ratios that the Americans quickly rejected. After the other two delegations refused to budge, angry U.S. congressmen agreed with their naval officers' requests and passed bills to build fifteen heavy cruisers. The depression, however, forced Hoover to cut spending, especially naval appropriations, and with Shidehara now in power, prospects brightened for a deal.

Japan demanded a 10:10:7 ratio. Negotiations resulted in agreement on 10:10:6 in heavy cruisers with the possibility of Japan rising to 70 percent in 1935. There was to be equality among the three powers in submarines. Japan's naval officers protested strongly, but Shidehara and Hamaguchi (fresh from an overwhelming election victory) overruled them and ordered acceptance of the ratio. Economic constraints and the need for cooperation with the West required acceptance. Castle had hoped to make the pill sweeter for Tokyo by fashioning a fresh immigration treaty to replace the hated 1924 act (this "blot on America's reputation for fairness," Castle called it), but Congress was not agreeable. On the other side, Shidehara admitted that regardless of the ratio, Japan would not attack the Philippines, for "even if an initial attack were successful it would be the beginning only of a war which in the end must be the ruin of Japan."[59]

Castle placed his finger on the point that was now shaping relations with the Japanese: "Japan [that is, the military, the mass newspapers, and much of the public] believes—not the Government, perhaps—that we are building our navy with the thought in mind that we shall have to fight Japan on account of China." U.S. military planners accepted the point even if Castle did not. Japanese strategists such as Admiral Kato Kanji (who remarked, "We must . . . gain control over the Manchurian government in preparation for war with the United States") also accepted the point even if Shidehara and Inoue did not. The foreign minister plainly defined the relationship between the growing economic depression and Japan's naval plans: "we will not sacrifice our plans for a tax reduction in order to build warships, particularly in view of the fact that our revenues are decreasing." On October 27, 1930, Hamaguchi joined Hoover and British Prime Minister Ramsay MacDonald in a historic international radio hookup to applaud the London agreement. They had "opened a new chapter in the history of human civilization," Hamaguchi declared.[60]

Japanese naval officers launched a savage propaganda campaign against Hamaguchi. They cried that he had violated the right of the divine Emperor and themselves to determine military questions. Such accusations, and Inoue's financial policies, which seemed to be worsening the economy by sacrificing military expansion to budget cutting, poisoned the political air. On November 14, 1930, a twenty-three-year-old member of an ultranationalist society condemned both Inoue's policies and restraints on Japan's military, approached Hamaguchi in Tokyo Station, saluted, then shot him in the stomach. In April 1931, the badly wounded Hamaguchi finally resigned. And in August this victim of the London Naval Conference and the economic depression died. Shidehara remained foreign minister, but radical military officers had proved their point. A military made up of men from the suffering villages was ready to follow those officers.

Amid these and other disasters, Castle believed that Hoover "probably feels like getting tight," but because of Prohibition, which the President himself supported, he "has not the wherewithal." Everywhere Hoover looked, traditional American policies—whether arms limits, open-door cooperation with Japan, or the temperance movement— seemed to be conspiring against him. Amid all this came yet another great disaster: Mukden.[61]

√I

The Slipknot: Part 1
From Mukden . . .

The 1930s as a Model for U.S.-Japan Relations

For the United States and Japan, World War II's roots ran back to September 1931, when the Kwantung Army struck to place all Manchuria under Japanese control. The causes and results of that invasion exemplified the major themes of U.S.-Japan relations after Perry's arrival at Edo Bay. In the years before the attack, U.S. officials had tried to integrate Japan into the Western system on largely Western terms. The Lamont-Kajiwara and Washington Conference agreements of the early 1920s acted as gangplanks which Japan used to board the ship of American capitalism. By 1931, that ship not only threatened to sink but the ship's officers seemed to be trying to keep passengers from the lifeboats, porous as they were.

Some Japanese, having long doubted the ship's seaworthiness, had been building their own vessel. For example, the military, cooperating with *zaibatsu* and smaller businesses, moved to fashion a different capitalism (indeed, some thought it anti-capitalist), which integrated Japanese values into an economic system that challenged, not complemented, the American system. The military's effort was hardly new. Since the 1860s, Japanese leaders had tried to create a self-sufficient system. What was new in the 1930s (unlike the 1850s–60s, 1918–22, 1970s, or 1990s) was that it ended not in compromise or silent surrender but in a *Gotterdäm-merung*.

And once again this clash of different systems occurred in large part over the question of how, and by whom, China was to be developed and made orderly. As Perry's mission arose out of U.S. interests in China, as the Washington Conference arose out of the need to regulate clashes in a revolutionary China, as the need to revive Japan rapidly after 1947 arose out of the necessity of dealing with a China turned Communist, so World War II in the Pacific arose from the inability of either Japanese or Americans to resolve the central question of China. Even when bitterly divided, partly revolutionary, quasi-Fascist, quite corrupt, and wholly uncooperative, the Chinese, during the 1930s, were the Sirens whose song lured American and Japanese mariners to their fates.

The Crises in Wall Street and Manchuria

Manchuria was comprised of China's three northeastern provinces. Its 413,000 square miles made it more than one and a half times larger than Texas. Its Liaotung Peninsula, repeatedly fought over by the powers, opened into a vast region bordered on the east and north by the Soviet Union, the west by Mongolia, and the west and south by China itself. Political control of Manchuria since 1907 had been divided between the Russian operation of the Chinese Eastern Railway in the north, and the Japanese control of the South Manchurian rail system in the south. By 1931, both were coming under attack from Chiang Kai-shek's Chinese Nationalists, who intended to reclaim the region. Japan's Kwantung Army was the barrier Chiang had to breach.

The Japanese were highly dependent on Manchuria by 1931. They had over a half-billion dollars of investment; nearly seven hundred miles of rails that carried lumber and especially coal and ores on which Japan's industry relied; and several ingenious operations to draw oil from shale and coal which the navy helped develop for its ever-growing needs. As Japan's overall exports fell a disastrous 43 percent in value during 1929–31, Manchuria and its 30 million people took on enormous importance for both raw materials and markets for Japanese goods. That importance ramified as the rest of Japan's traditional overseas market— above all, the United States—sank further into depression, and as Chiang Kai-shek's forces stirred up the 29 million Chinese who made up 90 percent of Manchuria's population. Observers noted by 1931 that while Japanese trade with these areas had declined since 1929, commerce with Formosa and Korea, which Tokyo completely controlled, had risen dramatically. One lesson seemed to be that trade followed political power. By 1931 the slogan "Export or Die" never had more meaning for Japanese.[1]

The Kwantung Army understood that lesson, especially since its commanders through the late 1920s had been closely tied to the Mitsui *zaibatsu.* But to understand how Japan came to invade Manchuria, and transform its own government in Tokyo from civilian-controlled to military-dominated, requires understanding two other developments that prepared Japan for its rendezvous with tragedy.

The first was the idea known as "total mobilization." This idea arose in part out of the realization that World War I had been won by nations that had most effectively created self-sufficient industrial economies. Germany, long a model for Japanese military and political experts, had not organized itself as well as the United States or Great Britain. Some in Japan believed the Germans had gone to war too early, well before they had control over raw materials and industrial operations needed to fight total war. "Total mobilization" also arose out of the grinding economic decline that wore down Japan in the 1920s and seemed to climax with the bank panic of 1927. In 1925, under the leadership of Takahashi Korekiyo, the government established the Ministry of Commerce and Industry (MCI) that was to be central in industrial planning. Educated in part in the United States during the late 1860s when still in his teens, Takahashi intimately knew how Americans had used tariffs, subsidies, and other state devices to create their second industrial revolution. MCI, however, went far beyond the Americans' development of state power. It recruited some of the best and brightest graduates of Tokyo University, who pushed laws through the Diet that allowed the setting up of giant state-licensed cartels to accelerate exporting. Many officials who shaped Japan's industrial offensive in the 1950s and 1960s first appeared as staff for MCI and other governmental agencies in the 1920s, including future prime ministers such as Kishi Nobusuke.[2]

This new industrial policy pulled state and private corporations into a symbiotic relationship that focused especially on military production. In 1927, a breakthrough occurred. In return for helping the government retrench by cutting four divisions, the army won the establishment of a central planning agency, the Cabinet Resources Bureau, that exercised authority over every corner in Japan for industrial mobilization. The Bureau quickly worked out programs that would be required by two years of total war. During a ten-day test run in 1929, the Japanese military actually took over the plants, and much of the politics, in three large industrial centers, including Osaka. A network for economic control by the military was being created even as Foreign Minister Shidehara tried to limit the military's influence over foreign policy.[3]

This growing military influence was a second development of the 1920s that explained the Japan of the 1930s. Since the late nineteenth century no civilians had been allowed to lead the army and navy ministries. The military continued to exercise virtual veto power over the formation of new cabinet governments. Even in civilian posts, the military occupied about 28 percent of the positions between 1885 and 1945. By 1924, only one elderly *genro*, Saionji Kimmochi, remained to counter the armed forces' pressures. The Imperial Military Reserve Association, created in 1910, became by the 1930s perhaps the most powerful patriotic lobbying group. This grass-roots organization was especially strong in the depression-hit rural areas. One of its major goals became organizing campaigns urging leniency for the assassins of leaders such as Hara, Inoue, and Dan, whose patriotism was suspect. The army started a National Defense Women's Association in 1932. If there was effective public opinion, it tended to support highly nationalist, aggressive policies rather than the cautious approaches of those such as Shidehara.[4]

When the worldwide depression struck full force, Japan had already been suffering considerably. The future did not seem bright. "Japan's possibilities for industrialization are limited," one Western expert wrote in 1930, "and there seems to be no prospect that Japan can attain a position of major importance as a manufacturing nation." But analyses of the economic crisis had been started by the nationalists, and the military had established institutions to support alternative policies. Matsuoka Yosuke, soon to become a central figure in the U.S.-Japanese tragedy over the next decade, told the Diet in early 1931, "The economic warfare of the world is tending to create large economic blocs." In Japan, Matsuoka declared, "we feel suffocated as we observe internal and external situations. What we are seeking is that which is minimal for living beings. . . . We are seeking room that will let us breathe." The Kwantung Army was prepared to find the room.[5]

That army was named after the tip of the strategic Liaotung Peninsula, which Japan had held since 1905. By 1931, this force was not only a highly self-conscious military unit but a tight-knit seminar that under its leading staff officers, Colonel Itagaki Seishiro and Lieutenant Colonel Ishiwara Kanji, developed its own ideology. After studying in Germany between 1922 and 1925, Ishiwara became known as the army's leading theorist on strategy. He was not, however, the usual by-the-book strategist. A devoted follower of the thirteenth-century Buddhist priest

Nichiren, who persistently defied authorities with his teachings but accurately predicted foreign invasions, Ishiwara believed that 2,500 years after Buddha's death, or around the year 2000, a world government would come into being. It would appear, however, only after unprecedented horrors of war resulting from foreign threats to Japan's existence. Borrowing from a contemporary teacher, Kita Ikki, Ishiwara concluded that Japan was to be saved not by the corrupt *zaibatsu* or politicians but by its military. Saionji noted the military's assumption: "We say never rely on parliamentary policies." The army would create a greater Japan, one that conquered the resources needed for prosperity, and in which the state used these resources to help the proletariat and limit incomes of the rich. By 1928, middle-ranking army officers, influenced by Ishiwara and determined to gain economic self-sufficiency for Japan, came together in an association called the *Isseki-kai* (literally, one-stone [for two birds?] organization).[6]

Many in the *Isseki-kai*, again following Ishiwara, believed their vision faced both long-term and short-term enemies. The long-term enemy was the United States—the only power, they believed, which possessed the resources and manifest destiny to carry it into a global conflagration with Japan over the question of who was to control Asia. But that was in the distant future. The immediate enemy was China. This was a switch; until the late 1920s, Russia had been considered the main menace. The Soviets, however, had turned inward under Joseph Stalin (although Kwantung leaders did believe that later the Russians would try to avenge the 1904–05 war). Now Chiang Kai-shek's Kuomindong was driving northward to reclaim the railways and other concessions seized by Japan after 1905. The growing Sino-Japanese confrontation centered on the South Manchuria Railway, where each side persistently probed the other's intentions.[7]

In early September 1931, rumors of possible war swept Tokyo. Led by Shidehara and Saionji, government officials told senior army officials to cool the situation. Tatekawa Yoshitsugu of the General Staff was instructed to carry the message to the Kwantung Army. Tatekawa arrived in Mukden (the provincial capital and military center) on September 18. He went with other officers to the Kikubun, a Japanese restaurant, where he drank until, according to some accounts, he was lying on the floor. Other accounts, noting that Tatekawa shared Ishiwara and Itagaki's views—and perhaps even forewarned them of the message he was carrying—believe the staff officer faked his drunkenness so he did not have to deliver the message. Tatekawa might have even actually helped plant the explosion that rocked the railway at Mukden

Manchuria—Target of Imperial Rivalry until 1949

that September night. Fighting broke out between Japanese and Chinese troops. By morning, the Kwantung Army held Mukden and was expanding its control over surrounding territory. Its officers claimed that the bomb had been set by the Chinese and even conveniently spread several Chinese bodies around the explosion site. But authorities in Tokyo and other world capitals quickly concluded that the army had blown up its own railway tracks as an excuse to conquer Manchuria.[8]

So, Saionji recorded bitterly in his diary, "it had finally happened." The government divided bitterly. A shocked Shidehara understood the army's new conquests could not be handed back to a Manchurian government that was coming under Chiang's influence. The high command was split; civilians and military alike nevertheless worked feverishly to keep Kwantung troops out of North Manchuria, where they could clash with the Soviet army. The Emperor equivocated. Saionji feared advising him to call back the army because the Manchurian officers might not obey. Shidehara and Inoue condemned the attack, but by the end of September units from Korea—clearly moving with the central military command's approval—helped Kwantung forces fan out over much of Manchuria. Kwantung officers now planned to announce that Manchuria was to be absorbed by Japan. The uproar in Tokyo and Nanking, however, instead led the officers to set up a multi-racial, autonomous state of Manchukuo, ostensibly under the control of Manchurians, actually under the aegis of the Kwantung Army.[9]

For Americans who had recently fought a "war to end all wars," the invasion was confusing, its brutality shocking. U.S. missionaries and journalists in Mukden sent back gruesome stories about Chinese onlookers being shot in cold blood. The Hoover administration issued statements asking that the fighting stop and the Japanese retreat. In truth, U.S. officials were paying little attention to Manchuria. They had more immediate crises on their mind. "He pointed out," recorded Assistant Secretary of State William Castle after an August 1931 talk with Hoover, "that Chicago today could not pay its bills or its wages." Detroit and Los Angeles seemed on the verge of economic panic. "There seems to be no light through the clouds in any direction," Castle concluded nine days before the Kwantung Army struck. The British went off the gold standard in September, thereby destroying any hope Hoover had of uniting the most powerful industrial nations' policies against the depression. From now on, it was everyone for themselves, politically and economically. Secretary of State Henry Stimson, with his eyes on Latin American revolutions and European economic disasters, simply wished the League of Nations would quit "nagging" him about the Manchurian bloodshed.[10]

And if the Japanese government was deeply divided over the invasion, so, on a smaller scale, was the American. Castle was strongly pro-Japanese. Born in Hawaii in 1879 to one of the islands' leading families, he had served as chief of the State Department's Western European Affairs desk, then as assistant secretary of state, before his close friend, the President, named him special ambassador to Japan during the 1930 London Naval Conference. Castle saw the Japanese as the only hope for order in Asia. China was "totally unreliable," but a nation "where there are immense American interests." Westerners could thus never give up extraterritorial rights until "a modern and honest judicial system" appeared in the distant future. In 1930, Castle could not conceive that Americans would "go to war over the open door, nor over Japanese annexation of Manchuria." Fortunately, he added, "Japan has no intention of annexing Manchuria." When the Kwantung Army proved that prophecy wrong, Castle wanted "to keep out of it altogether," in part because "we ought not to risk losing our one useful friend in the Orient. How I wish," he signed, "the damned unnecessary thing had not happened."[11]

Castle represented the Theodore Roosevelt–Elihu Root strain of U.S. policy that saw Japan as a force for order. Stanley Hornbeck, the State Department's reigning Asian expert after 1928, represented the Willard Straight–Paul Reinsch strain that believed cooperation with China offered the great opportunity, and Japan posed the great danger. Indeed, Hornbeck, after being Colorado's first Rhodes Scholar, in 1911 received his doctorate under Reinsch's direction at the University of Wisconsin. He taught in China, witnessed firsthand the clashes with Japan over Chinese questions at Versailles in 1919, then occupied lesser State Department posts until becoming head of the Far Eastern Division in 1928. Hornbeck's views of Asia shaped U.S. policy until the attack on Pearl Harbor.

Those views had at their core a central contradiction that continually undermined U.S. policy from the 1840s until the Communist conquest of 1949: a commitment to exploring the potentially tremendous China market through the open-door policy, but believing that since "the question of the peace of the Far East lies with China," that country had to be strong. If, of course, China was strong, it would (as Chiang repeatedly demonstrated) move to shut the open door and threaten Japan. Hornbeck resolved this contradiction no better than did other U.S. officials. Nor was he any more willing to go to war over China than was Castle. He admitted that Chiang's nationalism veered "toward violence of utterance and action" against Japanese property. He even had to "ruefully agree" with Castle that perhaps Japan's control of Manchuria was to be preferred. It was Hornbeck's—and American foreign policy's—tragedy that in the end he tried to reconcile these contradictions by believing that Japan would become hopelessly mired in China, and that it was in the U.S. interest to allow this to occur. Japan would then be so vulnerable that it could not attack the United States. Such a conclusion was not only proven to be totally wrong; it assumed that the Chinese people whom he admired and vowed to protect would patiently endure years of horror.[12]

Split between their pro-Japanese and pro-Chinese views, Castle and Hornbeck nevertheless agreed about Secretary of State Stimson. "He is a man of small intellectual caliber who is in a place too big for him," Castle believed in late 1929. Castle, a Harvard graduate of 1900 who proudly wore his "Naughty Nought" sweater into old age, never approved of Stimson surrounding himself with advisers from his alma mater, Yale. In late 1931, Castle concluded that Stimson disliked him because "I did not go to Yale, am not a rich New Yorker, and above all, was not appointed by him." For his part, Stimson recorded in his memoirs (in the third person, as befitting a gentleman of his generation) that accepting Castle just because he was a Hoover protégé was a bad "mistake which Stimson often regretted," in part because Castle "did not share Stimson's basic attitude."[13]

The causes of the State Department's paralysis during the early Manchurian crisis, however, went deeper than personality. Stimson liked Shidehara personally and wanted to put no pressure on Japan that might embarrass the foreign minister or "arouse all the national spirit of Japan behind their military people." Having served as U.S. Governor-General of the Philippines, Stimson thought, "I know something about the attitude of mind of those peoples" in the Orient. (This was an interesting comment especially because it was not until four months later that Stimson discovered—to his great surprise—that the Japanese navy had long fought the army's plans to attack Manchuria.) He told the cabinet that Western treatymaking "no more fit the three great races of Russia, Japan, and China, who are meeting in Manchuria," than "a stove pipe hat would fit an African savage." The Secretary of State's racism earlier led him to tell a for once receptive Castle that, on the extraterritorial issue, "he did not want to be driven by China, that after all the White races in the Orient had got to stand more or less together." Such views led Stimson to conclude in September and early October 1931 that China needed disciplining and Japan could administer it. Then, too, many Americans—especially Stimson—were highly sensitive about condemning Japan for policing its unruly neighborhood when the United States had recently sent troops into Nicaragua, Haiti, the Dominican Republic, and Panama.[14]

Hoover certainly agreed with Stimson's reasoning. "Neither our obligation to China, nor our own interest, nor our dignity requires us to go to war" over Manchuria, he told his cabinet. Another time he suggested that "it would not be a bad thing if Mr. Jap should go into Manchuria, for with two thorns in his side—China and the Bolsheviks—he would have enough to keep him busy for awhile." If, in other words, Japan wanted to drive back revolutionary forces in China and the Soviet Union, Hoover totally sympathized. U.S. public opinion was, as usual, divided. Washington officials paid little attention to it or to the divided business community. The highly respected journalist Walter Lippmann reflected the confusion when he wrote in late September 1931 that no one could "determine the 'aggressor' " in Manchuria any more than one could "determine who first jostled each other in a crowded subway train."[15]

Within a month, that view radically changed. Japanese planes bombed Chinchow, an administrative capital close to the Great Wall and distant from the original attack at Mukden. Stimson, finally understanding the gravity of the crisis if still backing and filling in his responses, embarked on a four-step progression in U.S. policy whose climax in 1932 set that policy for the remainder of the 1930s. In the first stage, he tried to work through the League of Nations to enforce the 1928 Kellogg-Briand Pact that outlawed war. A U.S. representative even sat in on the League's deliberations. This approach, however, lasted less than a week. Stimson had the uneasy feeling that the organization was trying to pass the responsibility to the United States. He insisted that "we must not take the baby off the lap of the League." Stimson remained torn between his belief that "a firm stand" had to be taken against Japan, and, as he confidentially told reporters, that Japan was "our buffer against the unknown powers" of China and the Soviet Union. The State Department felt better on October 22 when the *New York Times* published a shrewdly crafted statement signed by Japanese Finance Minister Inoue with the title "Inouye Says Japan Is Eager to Retire." Inoue's statement calmed both the money markets and the State Department. But only temporarily, for it had been written secretly by a frightened Thomas Lamont while Inoue's days—both in the finance ministry and on earth—were numbered.[16]

The failure of Stimson's flirtation with the League, combined with Japan's drive toward Chinchow, set off a second U.S. initiative: an attempt to impose economic sanctions. Lippmann, who had downplayed Japan's aggression, drastically changed his tone in October. The Japanese were intent not merely on quelling "local disorders," but executing "a carefully prepared and far-reaching plan" to control South Manchuria. The columnist warned that if the other eight signatories of the Nine-Power Treaty did not act to save China, their influence in the "whole Oriental world" would disappear. Japan would meanwhile set a "revolutionary precedent" that could rapidly spread. This fear, later called the "domino theory" of American foreign policy, began to dominate Washington officials' thinking. South Manchuria might be closed off by force and few U.S. interests affected, they reasoned, but if Japanese troops moved to the Great Wall and beyond into northern China itself, a century of the open-door policy would be at stake. Stimson now believed that Japan was "in the hands of virtually mad dogs," with its army "running amok." When, however, he and Hornbeck suggested that the League impose an embargo on Japan, and that the United States quietly cooperate, Castle and Hoover would have none of it. Japan would rightly take the embargo as an act of war, Castle argued. Tokyo would then be justified in blockading Chinese ports—leaving the United States the most unpleasant options of surrendering all rights in China or declaring outright war on the Japanese. Whichever option was chosen, Castle warned, "If there is anything left of the stock market that little would disappear. . . . The [American cotton growers in the] South would not willingly see the sick man [the U.S. economy] murdered in his bed. . . . The world is not inclined to take another material kick in the face to maintain the sanctity of treaties which it is not convinced have been violated."[17]

On December 10, 1931, the Wakatsuki cabinet fell, the victim of the worsening depression and the Kwantung Army. With it fell Shidehara and Inoue. As Saionji noted, "From the beginning to the end, the government was made a complete fool of by the Army." The deposed ministers were replaced by the rival Seiyukai Party and its leader, Inukai Tsuyoshi, who had moved up after Tanaka's death. Close to the military, Inukai shared its doubts about the value of constitutional politics. His new Secretary of War, General Araki Sadao, was known as the "darling of the young officers." In November, Shidehara had stopped the drive on Chinchow only through the direct intervention of the young Showa Emperor. Now Inukai reversed that position. Japanese troops took Chinchow, and, despite U.S. warnings, drove into Jehol, which was beyond the Great Wall.

A stunned Stimson then moved his policy to a third level. On January 7, 1932, he announced, with Hoover's approval, that the United States

would not "recognize any treaty or agreement" between China and
Japan that impaired the rights of Americans—especially those rights in
the Nine-Power Treaty guaranteeing the open door. Stimson believed
non-recognition had teeth because it discouraged U.S. bankers from
sending credits for Japan to use in Manchuria. Tokyo officials were
surprised, but made little response. This Stimson non-recognition doctrine, as it came to be known, was ultimately accepted by Franklin D.
Roosevelt after he was elected in 1932. It did not slow the Kwantung
Army—especially after Stimson was publicly isolated for nearly two
months because no other nation, notably not even Great Britain,
expressed support for his doctrine until March 1932.[18]

By then the world had been shaken by Japan's bombing and shelling
of Shanghai. Relations in that cosmopolitan city had spun downward
after Chinese effectively boycotted Japanese goods. Shooting erupted,
the large International Settlement (including sixteen hundred Americans) was endangered, and on January 24, 1932, Japan landed eighteen
hundred troops to restore order. Tokyo officials and the Kwantung Army
disliked the diversion, especially since they feared possible retaliation
by Western powers. On January 28, Japanese planes bombed the Chapei section of Shanghai, a killing of civilians that horrified much of the
world and anticipated the mass bombings of populations a decade later.
Hoover, at Stimson's urgent request, sent reinforcements for the thirteen hundred U.S. Marines stationed at Shanghai. Otherwise nothing
else could be done. Hornbeck noted to Stimson that "the havoc of modern warfare" had spread over non-participants. Stimson wrote on the
margin of this memo: "Civilization itself will collapse."[19]

But no one could devise an effective response. Business journals did
not want to threaten Japan. Remedies such as economic sanctions, one
paper argued, were "more to be dreaded than the disease." But the
journals did insist on preserving the open door to China. When Finance
Minister Inoue was murdered on February 9, 1932, Lamont, despite the
killing of his friend, was soon helping the Japanese government set
up a propaganda bureau in the United States. Stimson, and especially
Hoover, did not want to confront Japan or even open up arms sales to
China. The Secretary of State did, however, phone British Foreign Minister Sir John Simon to ask for a common approach to uphold the open-
door principles in the Nine-Power Treaty: "Japan is much more afraid
of a Union between you and us," Stimson accurately noted, "than she
is of the whole League." Sir John tried to explain away the bombardment of Shanghai, then refused to act with a Hoover administration
whose internationalism and willpower he doubted. Lippmann publicly

wrote that Simon was not weak, but simply represented "a Tory imperialist government which at bottom sympathized with Japanese action in Manchuria." Indeed, Japanese officials calculated that they and the British could, as they had since at least 1902, work in a common imperialist club to exploit China. Tokyo officials also noted the strength of U.S.–Japan economic ties, compared with those of the United States and China, and believed Hoover would not act against them. They were correct: the President told Stimson he "would fight for the continental United States as far as anybody, but he would not fight for Asia."[20]

Amid these disheartening events, Stimson moved to the fourth and final level of his response. On February 23, 1932, he sent a public letter to Senator William Borah, chair of the Foreign Relations Committee. The Secretary of State used the letter, most of which was written by Hornbeck, to announce that if Japan violated the Nine-Power Treaty, the United States would not be bound by the Washington Conference's Five-Power Treaty. In other words, if Japan continued to violate the open-door principles, the United States would begin rebuilding its Navy. The effect on the Japanese was not dramatic. They began pulling out of Shanghai in March, but did so because they wanted to focus on North China, not because of Stimson's pressure. His was largely a "policy of bluff," as Stimson himself later phrased it.[21]

In February, the Seiyukai Party and the Inukai government won a landslide election victory, but it was meaningless. The military, not electoral politics, moved the nation's policies. The military's power became vividly clear on May 15 when several army and navy officers, in midday, gunned down seventy-five-year-old Prime Minister Inukai in front of his daughter-in-law and grandchild. One brave Japanese editorial writer saw the act as the ultimate breakdown of the society: it was "more . . . a massacre than an assassination, and more . . . a preparatory movement for revolution than . . . a massacre." *New York Times* correspondent Hugh Byas later noted that "a significant trinity had fallen—banker [Inoue], capitalist [Baron Dan Takuma], politician [Inukai], each victim the highest representative of a class," each gunned down, Byas charged, so a pure Japan of "soldiers and patriots" could be returned to the Emperor.[22]

Inukai's killing removed the last important semblance of civilian government in Japan until after World War II. He was replaced by Admiral Saito Makoto, while Uchida Yasuya became foreign minister, and Araki Sadao, the fervent militarist, remained minister of war. Handsome, known as a bon vivant while married to the daughter of a millionaire, and formerly head of the South Manchurian Railway, Uchida, before he left power in late 1933, went far in destroying the foreign ministry's influence and enhancing the army's power. As foreign minister during 1918–21, he had told the U.S. ambassador that China seemed destined to have foreign dynastic rulers: "Tarter, Mongol, Manchu emperors. Why not a Japanese Emperor?" U.S. officials recalled and widely circulated the story in 1932. By August, the Saito-Uchida cabinet decided it would woo Americans "by an appropriate allocation [sic] of the open door," but nevertheless defined the United States as "the greatest obstacle" to Japan's plans in Manchuria and Mongolia. Certainly that obstacle was not the League of Nations.[23]

Throughout 1932 a League Commission, led by A. G. R. Lytton of Great Britain, investigated the Manchurian episode. On December 10, 1932, the Lytton Report, in a remarkably even-handed assessment of the crisis, seemed to blame Chinese nationalism and disorder as much as Japanese militarism. But it refused to recognize Japan's regime in Manchuria (now renamed Manchukuo by Tokyo), and its Japanese-imposed head, Henry Pu-yi, as a front for the militarists. The report asked for the protection of Japanese rights, but demanded the restoration of China's territorial and administrative integrity. Stimson and Hornbeck called the report a "magnificent achievement." Japan called it an insult to Manchukuo and in March 1933 walked out of the League. Not that much of an alternative existed: the Kwantung Army's advance into North China made any negotiations with the League ludicrous.[24]

As he was leaving office in 1933, Stimson wrote that four years earlier he and Hoover believed the world would remain at peace because of "definite economic and evolutionary facts." Instead, of course, the economics collapsed and evolution transformed into devolution. "In Japan," Stimson wrote his mentor Elihu Root in late 1931, "the cause of Mr. Hyde against Mr. Jekyll has in large measure been victorious, and my efforts on behalf of the latter without much seeming result." Then and later, Stimson placed much of the blame on Hoover, Castle, and Simon for Mr. Hyde's victories. But given the Secretary of State's fear of Chinese nationalism, hatred of the Soviet Union (which was the only power in a position to move against Japan), and reluctance even to aid China militarily, Stimson exemplified—and was not an exception to—the dilemmas of U.S. policy in 1931–32. Hoover and Stimson, as well as Lamont, believed that American-style capitalism, duly embodied in its political dimension by the Washington treaties, could undergird U.S.–Japan cooperation. By 1932, that capitalist system seemed to be in a freefall ("depression has degenerated into a panic," Castle recorded in his diary, "and nobody seems to have the slightest idea as to the way out"). The new U.S. ambassador to Tokyo, Joseph Grew, could write Stimson in 1932 that "It is very unlikely that the Mitsuis or Sumitomos [*zaibatsu*] would allow their immense foreign . . . interests to be endangered by a super-reactionary movement." Grew should have known; he was a highly experienced diplomat, and though he did not learn to speak Japanese during the next nine years he was stationed in Japan, his wife Alice spoke it fluently—and she was Commodore Perry's granddaughter as well. But as Grew told the new U.S. President, Franklin D. Roosevelt, Japan was "menacing" because of its spirit—"a spirit which perhaps has not been equalled since . . . the Mongol hordes followed Genghis Khan in his conquest of Asia." For FDR and Asia, it was not a happy historical analogy.[25]

Takahashi, Hull, and the Race Between Trade and Politics Toward War

Certainly imperialism seemed to be a profitable enterprise for Japan by the mid-1930s, even as the Western industrial powers continued to slog in depression. Its unemployment numbered 500,000, one-tenth that of Germany and one-twentieth of the United States. By 1935, national income was climbing to historic levels, although many rural and fishing villages continued to suffer. The volume of Japanese exports in 1936 broke all previous records. Much to Tokyo officials' dismay, imports persistently exceeded those exports, but that was one reason why the Japanese people enjoyed an ever higher standard of living during the 1930s—and no doubt a major reason why they supported the army's passion for combining expansionism with an emphasis on traditional values. That combination seemed to be both reassuring and rewarding.[26]

To the horror of U.S. officials, Japan was moving ahead economically because it was pulling in politically—that is, it was centralizing policymaking and creating a tightly managed yen bloc encompassing Formosa, Korea, Manchuria, and North China, with Tokyo at the center. The guiding hand was that of Takahashi Korekiyo, finance minister from late 1931 until 1936. A close reader of John Maynard Keynes's work, the seventy-eight-year-old Takahashi began in 1932 by inflating prices with low discount rates and massive government deficits. He meanwhile protected balance of payments by ignoring the gold standard and allowing flexible exchange rates. In the trade centering on the yen bloc, exports shot up from 24 percent to 55 percent of all trade between

1929 and 1938, while imports doubled, to 41 percent. Despite the falling silk trade after 1929, the United States remained Japan's number-one overseas customer (and Japan was the third-best trading partner of Americans). The long-term prospects of the U.S. market were uncertain, however, especially after Stimson and Hornbeck hinted at imposing economic sanctions on Japan. Takahashi's measures were administered by "the new bureaucrats," as the press called them, who were alienated from 1920s-style market capitalism after the 1927–31 crashes, and who worked with the military to mobilize the economy. Much as in post-1951 Japan later, the bureaucrats brought considerable order out of the economic chaos. But they did so by further weakening a rudderless ministry that could not devise tactics to deal with the new bureaucrats or the military.[27]

The great private companies, the *zaibatsu,* led by two giants, Mitsubishi and Mitsui, had to adjust to the military-bureaucratic demands for a return to traditional values and unquestioned patriotism. The *zaibatsu,* however, never lost control of their own destiny. They cooperated with and profited from the imperialism. In their supposed *tenko* (conversion), the *zaibatsu* actually did not have far to go. By 1931–33, private business was under a cloud. Mitsui, led by Baron Dan Takuma, had made a huge profit in currency speculation that drove down the yen's value. He paid for this speculation with his life at the hand of an enraged assassin in 1932. Mitsui and its hundred or so companies then did a *tenko,* set up a patriotic foundation, sold shares to the public, and worked closely with the military. Mitsubishi did much the same under its slogan "To foster harmony and to revere the spirit of harmony"—and thus to serve the state. By the mid-1930s, Japan had, relatively, the highest military budgets in the world (43 percent of the overall national budget, compared with 18 percent in the United States), and *zaibatsu* profits rose as the nation went on a war footing. Mitsubishi's Heavy Industry division increased 150 percent between 1932 and 1936 because it made ships, airplanes, and tanks. The Nissan group's revenues increased nearly thirty times between 1931 and 1934, largely because of a Nissan-government partnership to accelerate industrialization in Manchuria. The military, with its strong anti-capitalist sentiment, tried as late as 1940 with "a new economic order" to bring the *zaibatsu* fully under state control, but it never fully succeeded—nor, given the *zaibatsu's* cooperation, did it need total control to accelerate growth. Under Finance Minister Takahashi's reign of 1931 to 1936, what was good for the militarizing state was good for the *zaibatsu.*

In United States, meanwhile, the new President, Franklin D. Roosevelt, was trying to limit the damage inflicted by the Japanese invasion of Manchuria and, more important, the post-1929 economic crash. He approached the Asian crisis by taking over Stimson's two policies: the non-recognition doctrine, and the warning that if Japan violated the Nine-Power Treaty, the United States would no longer be bound by the naval limits in the Five-Power Treaty. On a dark, cold, rainy early January morning at Roosevelt's home in Hyde Park, New York, the newly elected President warmed Stimson by saying that "he fully approved of our policy in the Far East; that his only possible criticism was that we did not begin it earlier." FDR, as on so many occasions, told in detail how he personally knew Asia well because his grandfather had been involved in the China trade. "He said," Stimson noted, "that it was his belief that Japan would ultimately fail through economic pressure," and that China would prevail against this attack as it had against so many others over the centuries. As for Japan's militarism and the murdering of "liberal leaders," Stimson saw these as only "a temporary reversion by Japan to the old position of a feudal, military autocracy." FDR agreed.[28]

On May 31, 1933, Japan and China signed a truce, but by now the Kwantung Army controlled Manchuria (or Manchukuo) to the Great Wall, and its influence reached well into North China. The Chinese remained bitterly divided between Nationalists and Communists. The State Department also gathered evidence to show that Japan, contrary to its Washington Conference pledges, was fortifying its mandated Pacific islands. At a private meeting of the New York Council on Foreign Relations, Japan's former delegate to the League, Matsuoka Yosuke, told the movers and shakers of New York and Washington that "China needs reorganization" and that "Force, and only force, can bring such a project to fruition." "The spread of Communism in China," he warned, "is a cause of anxiety to Japan." Matsuoka said he knew Americans disliked Japan's expansion. But the two nations were close trading partners, and Tokyo did not intend to close the open door to China: "You could cripple our industries by retaliatory measures. I think your heads are with us in spite of your prejudice. I think your hearts are with China in spite of your common sense."[29]

Matsuoka's pairing of American racial and economic attitudes was neat, but Roosevelt's first approach to Japan had less to do with economic retaliation, and much more to do (as he had indicated to Stimson) with aiding China. The President announced he would build up the Navy to treaty strength, then set aside nearly a quarter-billion dollars for "public work" of this kind. More directly, he helped China—despite the State Department's warning that the country was immersed in chaotic, multiple revolutions. The aid took various forms: a $50 million credit from the Reconstruction Finance Corporation for wheat and cotton exports to China; U.S. airplanes and pilots (including the famed speed flyer Major Jimmy Doolittle) helping—and in many ways being— the Chinese air force; allowing Curtiss-Wright Corporation to build a $5 million airplane factory at Hangchow; and pushing a subsidiary of the U.S. government-subsidized Pan American Airways to take over parts of China's civil aviation. Japan's response in 1934 was blunt. Foreign Office spokesman Amau Eiji issued a statement that emphasized Japan's "special position" in China, and—with specific reference to China's new airplanes and military advisers—warned that Japan would sternly oppose "any attempt on the part of China to avail herself of the influence of any other country in order to resist Japan."[30]

This "Amau statement" caused a sensation in the West, although the State Department made no direct public response. The statement was actually based on diplomatic instructions by the new foreign minister, Hirota Koki, to Japan's minister in China. Hirota, facing rising Chinese nationalism on the mainland and unrest at home, vowed to complete Japan's "mission in East Asia" despite opposition from other powers. In May 1934, Hirota had even tried to undercut U.S. policy by proposing that the Pacific region be divided into American and Japanese spheres of influence. He was Japan's central foreign policy figure between 1933 and 1937, and while often vacillating, his commitment to the "mission" in China was so intense that in 1946 he was executed by the Allies as a war criminal for crimes against Chinese civilians. Hirota and Amau's fear that Americans were helping China was of course well founded. Roosevelt refused to become directly involved by mediating the war, as the Chinese begged him to do, but—in a typical Rooseveltian maneuver—he moved so indirectly that as one admirer later noted, it could have broken a snake's back. Such U.S. publications as *News-Week, Literary Digest,* the *New York Times,* and especially *The New Republic* detailed in early 1934 how U.S. planes and advisers flowed to help Chiang Kai-shek's regime. *News-Week* drew the lesson: China now had a good air force, and its "powerful fleet of planes equipped with incendiary bombs might do terrific damage to Japanese cities, practically all of which are at least 50 percent of wooden construction."[31]

The more the Japanese tried to extend their hold in North China, the less secure they became. In 1932, they had tried to justify their aggression by floating the idea of a Japanese Monroe Doctrine for Asia. Viscount Kaneko declared in a widely noted article that in 1905, Theodore Roosevelt, in the intimacy of the President's study at Sagamore

Hill, had strongly advised such a doctrine because "Japan is the only nation in Asia which understands the principles and methods of western civilization." But the President had warned Kaneko that Japan must "observe the American policy of the 'open door' . . . in China." Since TR had used U.S. troops freely in the Caribbean region to enforce his version of the Monroe Doctrine, the implications for Japan's actions of 1931–32 were obvious. U.S. observers, however, were having no part of it. The original Monroe Doctrine aimed to maintain the political status quo in the Americas, Hornbeck told Secretary of State Cordell Hull, but Japan's version "is aimed at altering the economic *status quo* in the Orient in favor of Japan." Hornbeck had put his finger on the catalyst in the intensifying U.S.-Japan clash.[32]

The American refusal to blow air into Tokyo's trial balloon of a Japanese Monroe Doctrine seemed to be underlined in November 1933 when Roosevelt formally recognized the Soviet Union. Apparently no records of the talks between the President and Foreign Minister Maxim Litvinov that led to recognition were kept. The Soviets and their leader, Joseph Stalin, however, clearly wanted the Americans to help them in (as the Soviets phrased it) "breaking that country [Japan] as between the two arms of a nutcracker." Stalin preferred a U.S.-Japan-Soviet non-aggression pact as the nutcracker. FDR, however, had no intention of making such a direct intervention in Asia, nor did he want to exchange his indirect anti-Japanese policy for a blunt public position. Certainly the Japanese were afraid by late 1933 of being surrounded by the two large powers, but Hornbeck and others reassured Japan that the United States did not view recognition of the Soviets as an anti-Japanese act. When the Soviets discovered the U.S. reluctance to work with Stalin directly against Japan, Washington-Moscow relations quickly cooled to the freezing point. Stalin then turned in January 1935 to protect himself (a tactic he used with Hitler to greater public attention four years later) by stunning the West and formally dealing with Manchukuo. He even sold northern Manchuria's central railway to Manchukuo.[33]

If, as Stalin discovered, U.S. officials intended their political ties to be minimal, their economic ties were to be expanded. This dichotomy, of course, had been in the American tradition since at least 1801, when President Thomas Jefferson vowed "no entangling alliances," but did all he could to accelerate U.S. exports. In the 1930s, political obligations were to be minimal, in part so economic marketplaces could be maximized. Marketplaces were not to be bound by politics, but opened through competition and an absence of political restraints. This historic U.S. policy slammed up against Japan's determination to integrate Manchukuo and as much of North China as possible into its own system. Roosevelt, and especially his Secretary of State, Cordell Hull, saw two great dangers in the Japanese course: not only did it prevent Americans from having equal access to important Asian markets amid economic depression; but only the American approach could prevent the creation of warring political blocs and instead lay the foundation for long-term world peace.

In 1934, the chance for such economic remedies seemed still to exist. U.S. officials, led by Hornbeck, a skeptical Roosevelt, and an enthusiastic Hull, enticed Congress to pass the Reciprocal Trade Act (RTA), and to supplement it with a governmental Export-Import Bank. The bank was truly historic because it brought the U.S. government's financial support directly into the marketplace to replace the bankers—who had for two centuries financed the nation's exports until they destroyed themselves in the late 1920s. Hull was the central figure in these new economic policies. An avowed disciple of Woodrow Wilson's freer-trade internationalism, the former Tennessee congressman had a fanatic's faith that closed trading blocs (the kind the Japanese, Germans, and even the British were constructing) led to political blocs, and that those in turn created friction that invariably flamed into war. No one understood Hull better than Dean Acheson, his assistant secretary of state between 1940 and 1944. "His hatreds were implacable," Acheson recalled, and he usually "got" his enemy. The handsome sixty-three-year-old Tennessean, "with almost fanatical single-mindedness," as Acheson phrased it, turned all of his considerable passion to obtaining " 'mutually beneficial reciprocal trade agreements to reduce tariffs' on a basis of equal application to all nations."[34]

Hull's RTA of 1934 would remain the foundation of U.S. trade policy sixty years later at the twentieth century's close. In the mid-1930s, however, his deliberate economic approach faced a wall of opposition in Asia. Prominent Americans who had lost confidence in the Japanese believed that wall would never be scaled. Thomas Lamont not only began turning against Japan but worked to push the British to oppose "a military clique" in Tokyo that acted much like "young German Nazis." In 1934, as well, the 1924 best-seller *The Great Pacific War,* by Hector C. Bywater, appeared in a second edition. Bywater's profoundly gloomy prophecy—that American naval weakness in the Pacific combined with clashing U.S.-Japan interests equaled war—not surprisingly mirrored the U.S. Navy Department's pessimism. Then came one of the more disastrous legislative measures in the history of American diplomacy, the Silver Purchase Act of 1934. Passed at the demand of western silver interests that were led by the chair of the Senate Foreign Relations Committee, Key Pittman of Nevada, the act drove up silver prices until silver from China—whose currency was based on that metal—flooded into world markets. The already disorganized Chinese economy turned even more chaotic. In a particularly bloody irony, silver smuggled from China to Japan was used by the Kwantung Army to finance its rape of China.[35]

In 1935, Hull's plans received another heavy blow when Japan's objections led the other four nations to end the 1922 Five-Power Treaty's limitations on naval construction. It died because the United States refused repeated demands from Tokyo for a more favorable ratio in warships. Hornbeck led the opposition to any compromise with the Japanese. He was beginning to believe that if the alternatives were either to accept the continued Japanese penetration of North China in 1935 or explicitly surrender the open-door principles, he would prefer to accept Japan's invasion—for, Hornbeck concluded, despite all their victories, the Japanese had become mired in an indecisive struggle that was draining their strength. Over time, U.S. principles would be vindicated. Other leaders also refused to give up hope over the long term. "The one point that should be kept constantly in mind by American business is trade opportunity, in China," declared the business executives belonging to the National Foreign Trade Council in 1935. "It is a field which now offers, perhaps more surely than any other, the greatest promise of expanding trade." If, of course, there was time.[36]

Top Japanese officials agreed with part of Hornbeck's assessment: faced with a dangerously unpredictable China and an economy demanding more and more raw materials, they were running out of time. In 1936, splits within the army over policy toward China became explosive when Finance Minister Takahashi tried to cut back rapidly rising governmental expenditures by reducing the rate of the military budget's increase.

On February 26, several hundred young army officers occupied government buildings, murdered Takahashi and three other high officials, then cut off Tokyo's communications with the outside world. They claimed to be dedicated to purifying Japan by restoring the Emperor's full powers. They intended to do this, the rebels maintained, by attacking the *zaibatsu* and civilian politicians who had corrupted the society (and also, of course, had tried to cut back the military increase in the budget). After several days, the Emperor's opposition and an Imperial Guard of fifteen thousand loyal soldiers put down the rebellion. But the "2/26" events' effects rippled on. In the chaotic aftermath of the aborted coup, one army group, the "control" faction that included Tojo Hideki, became dominant. This "control" group wanted to move quickly to prepare Japan for possible wider (not only Asian) war by mobilizing the people and the economy. Because of the "2/26" events, the military gained an even heavier hand over terrorized civilian politicians and the foreign ministry. The militant nationalism received justification from a group of intellectuals who founded the Showa Kenkyukai Association in late 1936. Although Kenkyukai initially included liberals, it fell into the hands of ultranationalists who vowed in the name of the Emperor to free Asia from Western influences and place it under the "guidance" of traditional Japanese values. The "Western concept of freedom" was to be replaced by the "Eastern concept of morality."[37]

The "2/26" developments also sharpened the fight between army and navy leaders over the specific direction of Japan's expansion. The navy, dependent on oil, wanted to place greatest emphasis on Southeast Asia and less on North China. The army, more ideological and intent on systematic control of Asia's economy, intended to build a "new China." In August 1936, the members of the cabinet of Hirota Koki—formerly foreign minister, now prime minister—tried to reconcile their differences with a document entitled "Fundamentals of National Policy." The document's "Three Principles" undergirded Japan's future expansion. The principles were not modest. They included driving out the "tyrannical" Western powers from East Asia, developing cordial relations with other Asian peoples, and developing a powerful economic bloc with China that could be extended into Southeast Asia. The Japanese people were to be mobilized for these missions with "sound thoughts." The United States was seen as a long-term problem, so the navy was given additional resources for a buildup.[38]

The immediate danger, however, lurked in North Asia: the Soviet Union. In September 1936, Hirota and the military nearly pulled a dramatic coup by negotiating an anti-Comintern pact with Chiang Kai-shek. If they had succeeded, the Soviets would have been further isolated, the Chinese split off from the Soviets, and Chiang made more dependent on Japan. But Chiang refused to bite. On November 25, 1936, Japan instead signed the Anti-Comintern Pact with Germany. Publicly, the agreement seemed bland. Secretly, it provided that if the Soviet Union attacked or threatened either Germany or Japan, the other nation would consult to determine how to "preserve their common interest." But Americans as well as the Soviets paid a price for this pact: the Japanese military's success in obtaining the treaty struck a body blow at the foreign ministry's hope to maintain some links with the Americans and British as it had done in the 1920s. Thus, out of long historical themes—assassinations at home, ambitions in China, and the further weakening of U.S.-Japan relations—emerged the beginnings of the Axis alliance.[39]

Wars and Actors

The 1936 alliance began a five-year era in which Japan moved from weakness to weakness and the United States from weakness to strength. The Japanese tried to overcome their weakness. The Americans often seemed to try to overcome their strength. Overall, the 1937–41 years were the most instructive in the post-1853 relationship. They not only vividly demonstrated Japan's dependence on that relationship, but how each time the Japanese tried to use diplomacy or military force in Asia to break the dependence, the dependence only tightened. The relationship resembled a slipknot in which the more Japan struggled against it, the tighter it became—until, finally, the Japanese Empire strangled.

In late 1936, that empire seemed to be on the move to new conquests in North China and to gains in the industrial complex developed by the *zaibatsu*. Appearances deceived. Theorists such as Yamada Seitaro warned that the military campaigns distorted the economy while failing to improve the enormous rural population whose living conditions lagged a century or more behind. The glow of the export economy that had appeared since 1932 hid the economic cancers—massive internal imbalances, dependence on the United States for everything from oil to machine tools to export markets—that ate away at Japan. Meanwhile, China seemed to be growing stronger. In December 1936 at Sian, Chiang had been captured, and nearly executed, by dissident generals who wanted to end the civil war against the Communists so they could focus fully on killing Japanese. Chiang escaped. A "united front" of Nationalists and Communists briefly formed. The Chinese began to move north against the Japanese invaders. Meanwhile, with the help of British financial experts, the Chinese economy dramatically improved.[40]

In June 1937, Prince Konoe Fumimaro rode into power as prime minister on the hopes of the senior politicians and the Emperor that he could fashion a settlement in China. "To some extent carried along by forces which were beyond his comprehension," as the historian Ian

Nish has observed, Konoe was to be a pivotal, and sad, figure. He seemed, one diplomat noted, to be a "shy squirrel sheltered in the deep forests." The protégé of the last *genro*, Saionji, who was instrumental in making him prime minister, Konoe had been born in 1891 to one of Japan's most prestigious families. He had flirted with socialism while studying at Kyoto University, and even translated Oscar Wilde's *The Soul of Man Under Socialism* into Japanese, until in the 1930s he was attracted to Fascist thinkers. A more consistent theme in his life was a bitter view of the West for its selfishness and racism, which he had encountered at Paris in 1919. Nor did he ever forgive the United States for its failure to avert economic disaster in 1929. But he sent his son to America for his college education, and while visiting him in 1934, Konoe was astounded by the anti-Japanese feeling. In a speech the following year, he declared that Colonel Edward House's approach during World War I had been correct: the "monopolization" of world resources by the Americans and British had to end, and an "international new deal" instituted to help have-nots such as Japan take care of their growing populations.[41]

Konoe took over the government in 1937 amid rumors that Japan's North China Army was about to deal with Chiang on its own terms. The prime minister tried to short-circuit the move, but on July 7, 1937, Chinese and Japanese forces clashed at the Marco Polo Bridge south of Peking. The military convinced him that the incident was only the tip end of a Chinese offensive, perhaps supported by the Soviets, that required a tough response. Konoe allowed reinforcements to be sent, fighting escalated, and Japan and China were soon enmeshed in all-out war. Ishiwara, who had done much to trigger the Manchurian invasion in 1931, now warned that Japan had taken the wrong turn. He and his colleagues wanted Konoe to concentrate on building a long-term economic powerhouse in Manchukuo that could give Japan the assured base for future empire. Instead, Ishiwara warned, China threatened to become for Japan "what Spain was for Napoleon," that is, "an endless bog." A year later, Japan had captured Chiang's capital of Nanking and installed its own puppet government. But the fighting only intensified. Chiang refused to discuss peace terms, conflicts between Soviet and Japanese troops erupted along the Manchurian border, and war demands were destroying Japan's vital export industries. The "bog" turned out to be quicksand.[42]

Roosevelt responded to the 1937 invasion with a range of actions, few of them effective and some of them embarrassing. He was playing a weak hand, and all of his low cards were showing. In mid-1937, just as the war recommenced, the U.S. economy spun into the sharpest decline in its history. FDR's attempt to balance the budget, along with overspending, created a crash of profits and stock prices. The New Deal had failed utterly in its attempts to find a peacetime solution for the 1929–33 collapse of the system. Roosevelt also failed to gain control of foreign policy. In 1935, Congress began to pass a series of Neutrality Acts that—in an attempt to prevent a replay of the process that sucked Americans into World War I—rigidly controlled and sometimes prohibited trade with belligerents. When the Sino-Japanese conflict intensified in late summer 1937, Roosevelt skirted the dilemma by refusing to recognize that war existed. He thus did not have to recognize that the Neutrality Acts applied. Americans continued to sell arms to China (some $9 million worth over the next year), and to send vast amounts of oil and raw materials to Japan.[43]

When non-interventionists demanded that the President acknowledge a war existed and that U.S. goods not fuel the conflict, FDR weathered the storm. Nevertheless, his first public response to the 1937 conflict was merely a pious statement by Hull that condemned the use of force and neglected even to mention Japan. The administration was divided. One faction, led by Hornbeck and Secretary of the Treasury Henry Morgenthau, wanted to protect U.S. interests in China through a military and economic buildup that, they assumed, would force Japan to back down. Hornbeck and Morgenthau did not believe that the Japanese had the wherewithal, or the nerve, to confront the United States. Opposed were Hull and Ambassador Grew in Tokyo who warned that sanctions could lead to war and, at the least, undercut relative moderates such as Konoe and Saionji who were trying to rein in the militarists. Hull, with his ear to the ground of Capitol Hill, also feared that any aggressive action could unloose the fury of congressional "isolationists" who would further tie his and Roosevelt's hands.[44]

In August and September 1937, Japanese planes badly wounded the British ambassador to China and bombed civilians in Nanking. Such killing of civilians still aroused condemnation in the West. The British approached FDR with the idea of jointly imposing economic sanctions, an idea U.S. officials quickly mistrusted because of its source (were the British again trying to push the United States into protecting their colonies while they appeased both Japan and Hitler?). The President instead decided to speak out on October 5, in a Chicago speech given in the shadow of the Chicago Tribune Building, where the nation's most powerful "isolationist" newspaper was published. Condemning the "international lawlessness" in China, he urged that the "90 percent who want to live in peace under law" use "positive endeavors to preserve peace." He suggested that an attempt be made to "quarantine the patients" against the "disease" of aggression. A stunned Hull, who had not known about these words, feared the anti-interventionists' outrage would paralyze U.S. policy. Some loud opposition to the United States joining any such quarantine was indeed heard in the Senate, but the general response was more favorable than Roosevelt had expected. In any event, the President might well have decided he no longer needed the "isolationists' " votes for domestic programs, so he could defy them in foreign policy.[45]

If so, Roosevelt's bluff was quickly called. The League of Nations had been waiting since 1932 for the United States to take such a lead. Now the League asked the Americans to meet with other powers in Brussels during November 1937 to explore the President's suggestion of a "quarantine." The Soviets arrived ready to accept any help from the West. They had been involved in repeated clashes with Japanese troops along the Manchurian border. Japan, however, refused to attend. And the Western powers, especially the Americans, refused to take China seriously; they even lectured the Chinese delegation to correct the conditions (that is, aggressive nationalism) that had led to the war. The Brussels Conference taught a number of lessons: the other powers and the United States could not cooperate to stop Japan; the Americans did not yet see the Chinese as so important as to be worth a war; and now the younger Roosevelt had reversed the earlier Roosevelt's famous dictum about speaking softly and carrying a big stick. About this time, FDR shook hands with Orson Welles and told him that since America had two great actors, it was a fine thing they now had met. At Brussels, the Soviets and Chinese, among others, had demanded to see one actor's script and found the relevant pages blank.[46]

VII

The Slipknot: Part 2
. . . to Pearl Harbor

Tightening the Knot

IN DECEMBER 1937, and during early 1938, Japan rewrote the plot. Before those months, the United States had feared Japan's invasion of China because of the threat to the open door. U.S. officials nevertheless did little, in part because Tokyo leaders signaled Washington that they understood the importance of U.S. interests in the region and wanted no confrontations with Americans. Japan even hired Ralph Townsend, a former U.S. consul in China, as a propagandist to convince Americans that Japan was "fighting the white man's battle" against Chinese nationalism.

Then, on December 12, 1937, Japanese planes sank the U.S. gunboat *Panay,* on the Yangtze River close to Nanking where the ship was to help evacuate foreigners. Three Americans and an Italian citizen died, many were wounded, and some of the victims were machine-gunned in the water. U.S. diplomats were on the vessel, as was a Fox Movietone cameraman and several journalists. Two Standard Oil ships were sunk at the same time. They contained hundreds of Chinese just evacuated from Nanking, many of whom died, although the exact number has never been known. All the vessels were clearly marked. Anti-interventionists responded to the fear of war by proposing the so-called Ludlow Amendment to the Constitution. It would have required a nation-wide referendum before the country could go to battle, unless it was actually invaded. Roosevelt had to launch an all-out lobbying effort before the House narrowly killed the amendment, 209 to 188. Amid the debate came news of the Japanese "rape" of Nanking. Japan's troops massacred at least 155,000 Chinese civilians (China later put the figure at 300,000). The *New York Times* reported that especially after newspaper reporters left the city, "atrocities of all kinds reached an unprintable crescendo."[1]

Tokyo quickly moved to deflate the crisis by effusively apologizing for the sinking of the *Panay,* paying all of the U.S. demand for $2.2 million in reparations, and promising to control the rampaging troops in Nanking. At the same time, the Japanese government effectively closed much of the Yangtze River trade to Standard Oil and turned the commerce into a Japanese monopoly. The open-door policy was not following the Japanese flag. Nevertheless, with the apparent settlement of the *Panay,* U.S. opinion, as measured by editorials in leading newspapers, grew more friendly to Japan and less supportive of China in early 1938.

Roosevelt did not follow that trend. To his Dutchess County neighbor, Secretary of the Treasury Henry Morgenthau, the President speculated that all-out government spending was the only way to keep the economy together until he left office in 1941. "He wants to shoot the whole works as far as spending is concerned," Morgenthau concluded after one conversation, "and . . . he is really scared to death." FDR thus worked with Congress to pass the Naval Act of 1938, which authorized the spending of $1.1 billion over ten years to build a "Navy second to none." The bill marked the first time the U.S. Fleet went above the treaty limits set in 1922 and 1930. Congress, moreover, doubled aircraft strength by authorizing the building of three thousand warplanes. The fleet would not quickly catch up with Japan, which had begun its own program, nor did military planners think the western Pacific could be defended. But these ships, and the beginning (and highly inadequate) buildup of bases such as Guam, signaled that Roosevelt's Pacific policies had begun moving down a new path.[2]

The President secretly sounded out the British about joint blockade plans, only to have a "douche of cold water," as one U.S. official put it, poured on the plans by Prime Minister Neville Chamberlain—who disliked FDR personally, thought the New Deal quite weird economically, and believed the Americans most undependable diplomatically. On May 28 and June 4, 1938, Japanese planes killed a total of 1,500 civilians and wounded 2,600 more in indiscriminate bombings of Canton. Roosevelt responded by allowing stepped-up military aid to China, while asking U.S. manufacturers not to sell aircraft or parts to Japan. This "moral embargo" was also a departure, but the pressure was not all "moral." The State Department announced that export licences for such items would be difficult to obtain. These goods were essentially cut off by late summer 1938. FDR received strong public support from the American Committee for Non-Participation in Japanese Aggression, an active, well-financed group led by former missionaries in China. On the other side were exporters determined to hold on to Asian, especially Japanese, markets. Their exports to Japan during the 1930s actually peaked in 1937. One business journal condemned the "quarantine" speech, but congratulated FDR for not being militaristic after the *Panay* attack.[3]

In 1938, Roosevelt ignored these business voices to cut further certain kinds of trade. After suffering eleven years of war aimed at creating a more self-sufficient Japan, the militarists instead found their economy more vulnerable than ever to the U.S. sanctions. Nawa Toichi, a leading Marxist scholar, warned that Japan was trapped: the more it produced militarily, the less it had to sell to the West, and thus the fewer goods it could import from the West—above all, oil and machine tools— needed for the nation's industrialization and future self-sufficiency. The war in China, he observed, only worsened the crisis. Army officials reached the same conclusion. Not only was Japan growing more dependent on goods from the United States but military manpower was spread thin. Half of the available troops were embroiled in China. That statistic was increasingly ominous because it meant the army was vulnerable in northern Manchuria, where it was clashing with the Soviets.[4]

Nor were military officers pleased that *zaibatsu* profits fattened even as the manpower needs and the economic self-sufficiency plans suffered. Strengthened by intermarriage (especially between the Mitsui and Mitsubishi combines), the giant companies were monopolizing foreign trade. The economy as a whole might be precariously weak to support expanded war in China, but Mitsui Life Insurance Company was headed toward an 862 percent profit in 1939. Efforts by the military to bring the *zaibatsu* under tighter control continually failed. One foreign ministry official captured the dilemma by declaring that Japan's attempt to find resources by exploiting China resembled "an octopus eating its own tentacles." When Foreign Minister Ugaki tried to stop the cannibalizing by approaching the Chinese for talks, he received no response. In August 1938, the army resumed its own search for a solution by attacking Hankow. Two months later, Hull vigorously protested the growing threats to U.S. interests in Asia.[5]

Out of the growing crises, and in response to Hull, came Prince
Konoe's declaration of November 3, 1938, that Japan sought a "New
Order" in East Asia. In the pronouncement, and in separate notes to
Hull, Konoe declared that Chiang Kai-shek no longer spoke for China;
that Japan would reconstruct China on its own; and that a "tripartite
relationship of . . . Japan, Manchukuo, and China" would "create a new
culture and realize a close economic cohesion throughout East Asia."
Outside interference was not to be tolerated. Open-door principles
were irrelevant in China as they now were—Konoe pointedly noted—
in much of the world. Such views were not new. Konoe had been making many of these arguments since he had turned bitter over Anglo-
American policies at Paris in 1919. What was new was Japan's deepening economic and political problems—the kind that forced it to pay for
its trade imbalances by shipping abroad nearly half its gold reserves by
late 1937. The Konoe government believed that the potential economic
catastrophe could only be avoided by creating a new regime in North
China and Manchuria that systematically exploited the region for
Japan's interest. But he also left open the possibility that everything
to the south in China was to remain open for American and British
interests.[6]

If Konoe hoped this last provision might appease the Americans, he
was wrong. In April 1939, FDR shifted more of the U.S. Fleet to the
Pacific so British ships could remain in European waters. The move was
interpreted in editorials as an American guarantee of British holdings in
the Pacific. The President did not discourage such speculation. (The
speculation was not entirely correct. In mid-1939, Japan threatened
British interests at Tientsin. The United States simply looked the other
way and the Chamberlain government, immersed in preparations for
war in Europe, had to cut a deal with the Japanese.) When Roosevelt
asked for further reductions in U.S. commerce with Japan, Thomas
Lamont, U.S. Steel, and Alcoa were among those who broke off pend-
ing deals. Alcoa's action blocked much of Japan's aluminum supply.[7]

In early July 1939, Japanese planes bombed Chiang's capital of
Chungking and U.S. citizens in China were mistreated by Japan's soldiers. Republican Arthur H. Vandenberg of Michigan proposed on July
8 that Roosevelt give the formal six-month notice required to end the
1911 U.S.-Japan trade treaty. A leading non-interventionist, Vandenberg
wanted neither to help nor fight the Japanese, but his proposal received
support from those who did want to draw the line. For once the 1911
treaty was terminated, the U.S. government would be free to impose
economic sanctions. Congress never voted on Vandenberg's resolution,
nor did it have to: on July 26, 1939, Hull told Japan the treaty was to

end the following January. Watching this from outside the government, William Castle warned that "These pin pricks" would drive Japan into Hitler's arms and bring on a Pacific war. FDR's intention was no doubt just the opposite: increasingly preoccupied with the European crisis, he hoped to make Japan understand how vulnerable it was to U.S. pressure. Once it understood, Japan would back away from "new orders" in Asia and allow the President to concentrate on Europe. After all, Japanese dependence on the United States seemed to deepen as the war with China dragged on.[8]

China indeed resembled quicksand, and the more Japan fought, the deeper it became mired—and the more it needed U.S. goods. Konoe's inability to escape the quicksand destroyed his ministry in January 1939. His successor, Baron Hiranuma Kiichiro, tried to plot an escape by following a complex, high-stakes approach of strengthening Tokyo's relations with both the Axis and the Anglo-Saxon powers, while—in classic triangular diplomacy—trying to play one side off against the other. Japan, however, not only lacked the power and imagination to play such a high-stakes game but was pitted against two players whose cynicism exceeded all others: Hitler and Stalin. On August 23, 1939, the world, especially Japan, was stunned by the Nazi-Soviet pact that freed Hitler and Stalin to divide Eastern Europe. Germany's invasion of Poland a week later began World War II in Europe.[9]

Japanese officials could hardly believe it. Thinking that Hitler was an ally, they discovered instead he had made peace with their potential enemy, and had done so without the courtesy of even asking for their opinion beforehand. ("After all," Saionji told a friend, "Japan is being treated by Germany and Italy like a small Balkan nation, isn't it?" And if Germany and Italy win, "we must realize that Japan will be even more under their thumb than now.") Hiranuma's government soon fell. Tokyo officials could only declare neutrality in the European conflict. They then quickly approached the Soviets to settle their border disputes, which had produced heavy casualties by mid-1939. At Nomonhan, between Mongolia and Manchuria, Japan indeed suffered its greatest military defeat in forty years. The borders were never fixed, but the fighting did stop. The peace pleased Stalin because it allowed him to turn toward Europe; it pleased both Berlin and Tokyo because Japan's military could turn south to threaten British, French, and Dutch colonies, while extracting vital oil and raw materials from them.[10]

The Co-Prosperity Sphere

Out of these disasters in mid-1939 came a plan, drawn up largely by senior and middle-level army staff officers, that called for a Japanese-controlled bloc to exploit Southeast Asia's raw materials and markets. This objective became known as the "co-prosperity sphere." European influences were to be replaced in the "sphere" by Asian power, although Japanese officials never drew up a specific plan of how this was all to be accomplished. The term stated an ambition, not a detailed process. The phrase was another attempt to persuade Asians that Japan's control of their resources would work to their mutual benefit.

Japan's involvement in the region had deep roots. As early as the seventeenth century, Japanese saw themselves, rather than a corrupt China, as the model and the center for much of Asia. Between 1923 and 1939, about 10 percent of Japan's exports, 9 percent of its imports (including about half its iron ore), and 6 percent of its overseas investment were involved in Southeast Asia. These transactions centered on the Dutch colony of Indonesia, the British colony of Malaya, and the American colony of the Philippines. Less important was the French colony of Indochina. Watching Japan closely, the British War Cabinet of Winston Churchill decided that "the Japanese, who are a prudent people" and "fully occupied" in China, would not "embark upon such a mad enterprise" as seizing vital points such as British-controlled Singapore.[11]

U.S. officials were not as sanguine. Any hope they had about Japanese prudence largely disappeared in May–June 1940 when Hitler quickly seized France and the Netherlands, then stood poised to invade Great Britain. As their spring military offensive in China cost tens of thousands of casualties, Japanese leaders looked for economic relief to the southern Pacific. They warned the European colonies to stop sending war materiel to the Chinese. Military planners, afraid, as the historian Hosoya Chihiro has noted, of "missing the bus" provided by the Nazi *Blitzkreig*, accelerated plans for a southern advance. Both they and civilian officials, however, hoped they somehow could exploit the colonies without further alienating the United States.[12]

Such hope was an illusion. As Europe fell to the Axis in the summer of 1940, Roosevelt, even in the midst of a precedent-shattering campaign for a third presidential term, beefed up the Pacific Fleet, worked with Congress to pass bills that vastly increased the Air Force, and narrowly pushed the nation's first peacetime conscription act through the legislature. On the same day in July 1940 that he prepared a message to Congress asking for a $4 billion increase for the military, the Senate confirmed his choice for Secretary of War: seventy-three-year-old Henry Stimson, now an outspoken interventionist with bitter memories of dealing with Japan in 1931–32. FDR also signed the National Defense Action Act in July 1940, which gave him the power to cut off the export of goods he deemed necessary for the U.S. defense effort. With this ingenious measure, the President stopped the sale of some forty items (including aircraft and machine tools), while claiming they were needed at home and that Japan was not being discriminated against. He did not stop scrap metals and oil, the items Japan most needed.[13]

As Ambassador Grew commented in July, the U.S. economic policy was now a "sword of Damocles" hanging over the Japanese. Finding no escape from the war in China, that same month the Emperor again turned to Prince Konoe to form a government. Konoe, despite reservations of the Emperor and close advisers, appointed Matsuoka Yosuke as his foreign minister, and the dour, tough, dominant member of the army's "control" faction, Tojo Hideki, minister of war. Born in 1880, Matsuoka knew Americans and their language well from his degree at the University of Oregon. Unlike Kaneko, Katsura, and others who had studied in the United States, Matsuoka's judgment about Americans did not match his experience. His judgment was shaped more by his serving as a top executive of the South Manchurian Railroad Company in the 1920s and 1930s, and by his growing dislike of Japan's political parties. It was also molded by a hot temper, great vanity, and a ceaseless need for public acclaim—the kind he received in Tokyo during 1933 when he dramatically led the Japanese delegation out of the League of Nations. By 1940, Matsuoka was a loud voice urging that Japan fully support the Axis powers, in part so the Japanese could more effectively exploit the crumbling colonial empires in Southeast Asia.[14]

The first mention of the soon-to-be-famous "Greater East Asia Co-Prosperity Sphere" appeared in a press release from Matsuoka on August 1, 1940. The Associated Press noted that heretofore the term had been "East Asia," meaning northern China, but now "Greater" was added, to allude—as Matsuoka declared directly at a press conference—to the colonies, especially Indochina and Indonesia. Japan intended to expand not only its military power but its language and culture to create an Asian common meeting ground at the expense of the European colonials. During a celebration at New York's Astor Hotel of the 2,600th anniversary of Japan's founding, leading non-interventionist and Roosevelt-hater Hamilton Fish (R: NY) noted the new Japanese "Monroe Doctrine," then excused it with the remark, "What's sauce for the goose is sauce for the gander." This, however, was going to be quite a gander. In a secret paper of July 30, Matsuoka defined Japan's future sphere as including Indochina, Thailand, Malaya, Borneo, the Netherlands East Indies, Burma, India, Australia, and New Zealand.[15]

Everything Hull had tried to achieve since he had entered the State Department was aimed precisely at destroying such regional blocs and Japan's (or any non-American) "Monroe Doctrine." Roosevelt, with less passion, agreed. Fearing that Japanese and German military-based cartels were dividing up and organizing these blocs, FDR declared in 1940 that the United States could not live "as a lone island in a world dominated by force." The State Department and the New York Council on Foreign Relations conducted studies strongly supporting Hull's view that such blocs, run by Fascist governments, could strangle American capitalism. U.S. business understood the danger. In its 1939 and 1940 annual meetings, the national Chamber of Commerce asked that "Every possible effort . . . be made to develop and maintain trading and business opportunities for Americans in China equal to those of any other nation, in accordance with traditional American policy." The "drastic and unfair" restrictions found in parts of China, the chamber declared, called out for U.S. government actions. Interestingly, this business voice did not necessarily want Chinese control restored; it wanted law and order, not revolution, and open, not closed, doors.[16]

In September 1940, all these views were put to the test when Tokyo signed a pact with the Nazi puppet, Vichy France, that allowed Japanese troops into northern Indochina. China was again the target: the Indochinese bases enabled Japan to tighten pressure on the Chinese. But the Japanese had also moved into colonial territory. From Washington's perspective, the stakes had significantly risen because both the British and the Americans were receiving vital materials, such as rubber, from this region. On September 26, the slipknot tightened again when Roosevelt banned the export of scrap iron and scrap steel on which Japan depended. The next day, Matsuoka moved to escape the trap. The *New York Times* four-column headline read: JAPAN JOINS AXIS ALLIANCE SEEN AIMED AT U.S. The Axis partners of Germany, Japan, and Italy pledged to work with each other to create a "new order" whose terms in Europe would be decided by Germany and Italy, and in "Greater East Asia" (whose boundaries were left undefined) by Japan. The Japanese were also to be the final arbiter of what the "open door" in China meant. Of special note, the signatories promised to help one another, even militarily, if one was "attacked by a Power not at present involved in the current struggles"—that is, by the Americans or Soviets.[17]

In Tokyo, a stunned Grew, who had believed war was avoidable, said that with the Axis pact, "I saw the constructive work of eight years swept away as if by a typhoon, earthquake, and tidal wave combined." Matsuoka and Konoe hoped the pact would scare Americans from a confrontation with Japan. A leading Tokyo newspaper, *Asahi,* warned that if Washington's policy grew tougher, "inevitably" a "catastrophe" would result. And U.S. opinion did divide. Eleanor Roosevelt led the pressure on her husband to retaliate by cutting off oil. FDR refused; he believed that such a cut-off would drive the Japanese south in force. Business voices agreed with his decision although for other reasons: "If we don't sell to Japan, the British and Dutch will," as an oil executive phrased his justification for supplying the Japanese military machine.[18]

In one area, the Axis pact did transform U.S.-Japan relations. The ranking interventionist organization, the Committee to Defend America by Aiding the Allies, led by the famed Kansas newspaper editor William Allen White, for the first time linked aid to Great Britain with aid to China. Americans, most of whom knew little about how FDR was turning up the pressure on Japan, began to see the possibility of a two-front war. Roosevelt neutralized such fears during his successful run for a third term in 1940 by announcing that "your boys are not going to be sent into any foreign wars." His Republican opponent, Wendell Willkie of Indiana, who had patriotically supported FDR's increased aid to the British and Chinese, privately exploded over Roosevelt's remark: "That hypocritical son of a bitch! This is going to beat me."[19]

Roosevelt won. Matsuoka and Konoe fared much worse. They lost their bet that the Axis alliance would scare the United States away from a confrontation now certain to climax in a two-ocean war. On this pivotal point, Japan's naval officers, who had consistently warned that any Axis alliance would create a U.S.-British phalanx against them, were proven correct, and the Japanese army—which wanted the alliance to frighten the Soviets—wrong. For his part, Matsuoka was naive enough to believe he might use the United States to force China into a Japanese-dictated peace. Once the war in China ended, then (according to a secret policy statement of July 27 dictated by the military and approved by Konoe) Japan could strike south, seize oil facilities, and break its dependence on the United States. Thus Matsuoka and the other drafters saw the Axis alliance not as leading to war with the United States, but the opposite—a device to frighten Americans away from war as Japan finally realized its Asian objectives. Konoe, Saionji, and the Emperor had grave doubts. They feared the United States would not back down and the Japanese were thus moving headlong toward war.

Konoe bitterly blamed the military for his troubles, but he had made a major contribution to their cause by destroying the remaining political parties in July 1940 because, he claimed, they were too liberal and prevented the uniting of the state. Konoe urged Japanese to dedicate themselves to *kokutai* (the national weal) by pledging obedience directly to the Emperor. The military, who constitutionally enjoyed privileged access to the Emperor, certainly did not object. Within four months, the confused Konoe regretted what he had done both in regard to destroying the party system and, to a lesser extent, signing the Axis pact. But at least that pact might be salvaged by using it to pressure the Soviets into an agreement—one that would free Japan from its northern concerns, allow it to concentrate forces to the south, and settle a range of issues, including Soviet aid to China and opening Russian economic resources to Japan.[20]

Perhaps, Tokyo officials reasoned, a deal with Moscow could also send an effective warning to Roosevelt not to challenge Japan—a "double-strategic point of view," as Hosoya has characterized Matsuoka's approach to checking the Soviets and Americans simultaneously. It also, of course, was aimed primarily at obtaining resources and freedom of maneuver so that the war with China could somehow be ended. In early 1941, the army argued for a quick strike south against the British and French colonies, then a return of the forces to northern China before the Soviets could respond. This could be accomplished, army planners believed, without drawing Americans into the war. The navy vigorously disagreed and finally convinced the army that an attack against the European colonies would automatically trigger a war with the United States. Such a conflict could be waged for two years before shortages, especially of oil, would slow the Japanese war machine. The military thus required a large, immediate buildup to win a quick war, and it had to be assured that the Soviets would behave while it was occupied in the South Pacific.[21]

Matsuoka, again naively, believed his plans were finally coming together. In March and April 1941, he traveled to Europe for talks with Hitler and Stalin. Headstrong and self-centered, Matsuoka paid little attention to German hints of plans to attack the Soviet Union. The Germans paid little attention to his hints that he hoped to expand the Axis pact to include Stalin. On April 13, Matsuoka and the Soviet leader signed the neutrality treaty with Japan that Stalin had long wanted. To last for five years, the pact obligated the two nations to pledge that if one were attacked, the other would "observe strict neutrality throughout the entire duration of the conflict." In an instant, the Soviets had their hands free to face Hitler—although Stalin, always mistrustful, kept large troop contingents close to Manchuria until he was certain that Japan was moving south. For their part, the Japanese military could strike the European colonies and Japan's northern flank would be secure.[22]

Americans were shocked. Not only were the Soviets neutralized, but Stalin gave a body blow to the Chinese. He had been sending more military aid than had any other government to help China. But the Soviets secretly told Chiang they intended to keep the aid flowing and encouraged him to continue killing Japanese. Roosevelt quickly moved to help by quietly allowing U.S. airmen to resign from the service to form a "volunteer" air force in China. Thus the famed Flying Tigers were born. The President also stepped up other types of aid, and, at Chiang's request, dispatched a U.S. political adviser—Owen Lattimore, a distinguished scholar of Asia from The Johns Hopkins University.[23]

If Americans were surprised by the neutrality pact, however, the British were elated. For a year, Prime Minister Winston Churchill and his foreign minister, Anthony Eden, had been trying to bring Roosevelt into the war. Frustrated, Churchill undertook an appeasement policy toward Japan during those moments in 1940–41 when he feared the United States would remain on the sidelines and the British might face Japan alone in Asia. Eden also worried that Matsuoka—who "is in an abnormal frame of mind"—aimed to parlay the neutrality pact into another deal with Washington that would neutralize the United States in the Pacific theater. After April 1941, however, Churchill and Eden had many fewer fears that Americans would manage to stay out of the war. By June, the President sent China bombers that had the range to attack "Japanese industrial areas," and—as Chief of the Military Staff George Marshall put it later that year—"set the paper cities of Japan on fire."[24]

Meanwhile, throughout April and May 1941, Hull and Japanese Ambassador Nomura Kichisaburo exchanged drafts and ideas that usually hit dead ends when the Secretary of State demanded that Japan must leave China, swear off military conquest, and pledge itself unalterably to the open door. Nomura worsened an already highly sensitive process by misrepresenting Hull's views back to Tokyo. In one message, the ambassador even indicated the Americans were prepared to recognize Manchukuo. Nomura, despite his long personal friendship with

Roosevelt, begun during their World War I days in Washington, was not the best choice for the post. A professional naval officer with little diplomatic experience, the sixty-four-year-old ambassador provided a case study of how Japan's diplomacy deteriorated when military personnel moved into pivotal overseas embassies after the mid-1930s. Nomura himself declared publicly in late 1940 that "I am not meant to be an ambassador," for a sailor on land was "quite hopeless . . . like a stranded boat."[25]

Japan's central problem in June 1941, however, was not Nomura. It was Matsuoka's diplomacy. On June 21, it came crashing down when German armies invaded the Soviet Union. The foreign minister admitted to the cabinet that he had miscalculated, then shocked his listeners, and revealed his own mercurial behavior, by proposing that Japan make the most of it and also attack the Soviets—despite the neutrality pact he had personally signed with Stalin two months before. One cabinet member, not believing his ears, asked Matsuoka to repeat what he said, which he did. Pro-Axis to the end, Matsuoka wanted to grant Germany's new request that Japan attack the Soviets from the east. After a week of intense discussion, he was overruled. The military knew Russian troops enjoyed a two to one advantage in the north. Konoe feared that Roosevelt, who had immediately begun sending aid to the Soviets, would retaliate against Japan. In any case, preparations were under way for the occupation of the remainder of French Indochina. That occupation, the army and navy believed, would bring no significant U.S. response. The move was needed economically (Japan faced rationing and threats of unrest), and strategically (Indochina could be a springboard for assaults on its mineral-rich neighbors). On July 2, 1941, the Imperial Conference approved occupying southern Indochina. Matsuoka, in the words of the historian Ian Nish, "was discarded like a spent shot." Disgraced, he never again held a diplomatic position and was judged too mentally unbalanced to stand trial in 1946 for war crimes.[26]

The Attempt to Cut the Knot: Pearl Harbor

U.S. intelligence kept Roosevelt well informed of Japan's movements south. In September 1940, Japanese codes had been broken, and the intercepts—codenamed MAGIC—allowed U.S. officials to listen in on the many secret Japanese diplomatic and, after the Pearl Harbor attack, the military messages. MAGIC was actually masses of raw data which the ill-coordinated American intelligence offices never learned to sort

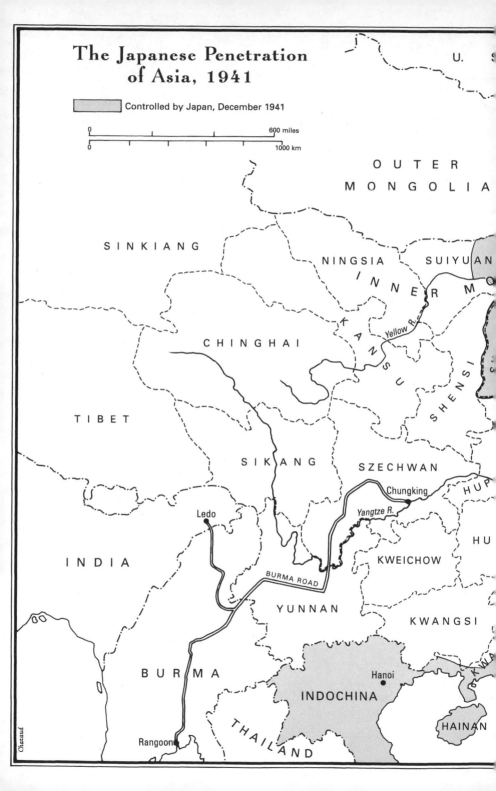

The Japanese Penetration of Asia, 1941

Controlled by Japan, December 1941

0   600 miles

0   1000 km

U. S

OUTER
MONGOLIA

SINKIANG

NINGSIA   SUIYUAN

INNER M

KANSU

Yellow R.

CHINGHAI

SHENSI

TIBET

SIKANG

SZECHWAN

Chungking

HUP

Yangtze R.

Ledo

HU

INDIA

KWEICHOW

BURMA ROAD

YUNNAN

KWANGSI

Hanoi

BURMA

THAILAND

INDOCHINA

HAINAN

Rangoon

Chazaud

R.

U. S.

Sakhalin

HEILUNGKIANG

Amur R.

S.

S.

R.

Nomonham

Harbin

KIRIN

MANCHURIA

LIAONING

Vladivostok

HAHAR

JEHOL

ULIA

Kalgan

Mukden

Peking

KOREA

HOPEH

Tientsin

Seoul

Tokyo

Yellow R.

SHANTUNG

Tsingtao

Hiroshima

JAPAN

KIANGSU

Nagasaki

ANHWEI

Nanking

Shanghai

ankow

Yangtze R.

CHEKIANG

KIANGSI

(Ryukyu Islands)

FUKIEN

Loochoo Is.

Amoy

FORMOSA
(TAIWAN)

NG

anton

Hong Kong

Shanghai

Yangtze R.

Airfield

International
Settlement

Chapei

Whanpoa R.
(Huangpu R.)

The Bund

French
Concession

0   3 miles

0   5 km

out and digest until after the war began, but it did keep Roosevelt and Hull apprised of Japanese intentions, at least until several days before the Pearl Harbor attack.

On July 18, 1941, FDR told the cabinet that Indochina would probably be occupied in two to three days. When asked what he planned to do, he shocked some members by giving a lecture which concluded the United States should do little, and especially not shut off oil, because then Japan would attack the Dutch East Indies' rich petroleum stores. Such an attack would mean war in the Pacific. After some debate, the cabinet decided to freeze Japanese assets in the United States. Roosevelt also agreed to cut off high-grade aviation gasoline.[27]

Much more than that fuel was cut, however. The freeze order was to be carried out by Assistant Secretary of State Dean Acheson, a prominent Washington lawyer, conservative Democrat, and after 1939, an outspoken interventionist whom FDR had appointed to the department in February 1941. Faced with having to make specific decisions about selling fuel to visiting Japanese ships, Acheson interpreted the order so strictly that a virtual embargo on oil was suddenly slapped on Japan. The embargo did not become apparent until after early August. Meanwhile, back in Tokyo, military planners led by ambitious, middle-level army officers had concluded that FDR's freeze order meant they would be unable to wage war for more than two years unless South Pacific resources were seized. Their forces moved into southern Indochina on July 27–28, again after a deal with the Vichy French. When Roosevelt finally found out about Acheson's interpretation, the President apparently believed he could not countermand the oil cut-off without appearing to give in to Japan's aggression. "Dean Acheson telephoned me in great triumph," Secretary of the Interior and fellow hard-liner Harold Ickes recorded in his diary of August 1. "No crude oil at all can be imported [sic] for Japan from our Pacific Coast. . . . Moreover, we will take no more of Japan's silk."[28]

The United States had been supplying 60 percent of Japan's oil. When the supply stopped, Roosevelt's warning about the probable results made him a prophet. In November 1941, Acheson told Hull that "the freezing controls had brought a great stillness over trade and financial relations" between the two countries. The prophet, however, was reluctant to trumpet his wisdom. When asked earlier, at a press conference on July 29, about "export control in relation to the Far East," the President replied, "I don't think there is any news on it." The leading anti-interventionist group, America First, nevertheless understood the consequences. While condemning Japan's aggression, it also criticized

FDR's freeze as "not in the interest of democracy or even of ourselves but in the interest of Britain's indefensible empire in the East." Other critics argued that it was all an "Asiatic question," not involving Americans. One senator made fun of a supposed Japanese threat by announcing that Tokyo "will outfit . . . soldiers with snowshoes, so they can climb over the [Rocky] mountains . . . and get at us." The American First group could grab headlines, but it, like most Americans, thought U.S. involvement more likely in Europe than in Asia, so it concentrated on European affairs.[29]

Americans did not want to know the truth about the imminence of such a war, and Roosevelt had no compulsion to tell it. He knew, probably from the time of the collapse of the Hull-Nomura talks in May–June 1941, certainly from the crisis over Indochina in late July, that Americans and Japanese were accelerating down the road to war. (In midsummer, Tokyo even ordered the disbanding of Japan's professional baseball league. The St. Louis–based *Sporting News* condemned the Japanese as ingrates and claimed the game's virtues never "penetrated their yellow skin.")

By July, Hull, as he was prone to say, thought everything was going "hellward." He told Stimson that the time for "appeasement" of Japan had passed. The time for a "firm policy" had arrived. The move into southern Indochina proved that Japan was trying to surround—not leave—China. FDR and his advisers consequently not only imposed the freeze, but after late July extended large lend-lease shipments to China, ordered more aircraft for the Flying Tigers and for U.S. bases in the Philippines, and set up a Far Eastern Command under General Douglas MacArthur—who had retired in 1937, served the Philippine government until 1941, and was now being called back by Roosevelt to head U.S. forces.[30]

FDR grew reticent as well when he met Winston Churchill at their Atlantic Conference off the coast of Newfoundland in August 1941. Churchill wanted him to give a virtual either-or warning to Japan: Either leave Southeast Asia or face "a war between the United States and Japan." The President refused. FDR said he was ready to press Germany in the North Atlantic, but he would not yet further squeeze Japan, largely because his military planners needed time to build up forces in the Pacific. The farthest he would go was to tell Ambassador Nomura on August 17, after returning from Newfoundland, that if Japan took another step in using force, the United States would immediately take "any and all steps" necessary to protect its "rights and interests . . . safety and security." Nomura reported these words to Tokyo. Of equal importance, he told his superiors in September (in a message U.S. and British intelligence intercepted) that at the highest levels the Americans had not only determined to cut off oil for Japan but aimed at "an economic stoppage over the whole field."[31]

That message was read in a Japan whose military grew in power while the economy threatened to sink from critical to chaotic. For a year, sugar, gasoline, rubber, and cotton had been rationed. As exports to overseas civilian markets dropped, so too did capital needed for imports, even for imports of the raw materials that went into steel. Konoe tried to bring some order in August 1941 by setting up government-authorized "control associations" to oversee supply and production. The zaibatsu, however, managed to capture the associations, conditions little changed, and the military again found it could not adequately control production. The economy increasingly resembled, as Ambassador Grew privately described it in May, "a mass of heterogeneous forces pulling in all directions." On September 6, Konoe's government decided to give the United States one more chance for an economic and diplomatic settlement. If nothing came of it, Japan was to prepare for war in late October.[32]

Konoe moved to circumvent the military and break the logjam by dealing directly with Roosevelt at a summit meeting, perhaps in Honolulu. Grew, still hoping for the best, argued that the United States had the leverage to obtain and guarantee a settlement. He knew, as his private secretary later phrased it, that "Every time a taxi went around the corner Japan had less oil." Grew was joined in his optimism by Eugene Dooman, a longtime expert on Japan and the ambassador's top adviser. Born of Episcopal missionary parents in Japan fifty years earlier, Dooman had been intimately involved in handling Manchurian and arms-limitation problems before joining Grew in Tokyo during 1936. Fluent in Japanese, sure of his own judgments, Dooman was especially proud of knowing the best and least known Tokyo restaurants. He and Grew thoroughly sympathized with Konoe's last-ditch effort, even as they realized that Japan's probable terms—troop withdrawal from Indochina only after a settlement in China, recognition of Japan's special position in Indochina, and restoration of normal U.S.-Japanese trade—were impossible for Roosevelt to accept. But at least these terms could provide a starting point for give-and-take. In a "Dear Frank" letter of September 22, 1941, Grew told the President that Konoe "sees the handwriting on the wall and realizes Japan has nothing to hope for" from the Axis alliance. He "will go as far as possible, without incurring open rebellion in Japan." Grew ended with the warning that it was "highly unlikely that this chance will come again," or that any other official could control the "military extremists . . . in their ignorance of international affairs and economic laws."[33]

Grew and Dooman lost the argument to the two leading China hands, Stanley Hornbeck and Joseph Ballantine, who advised Hull in Washington. Born in 1890 to missionary parents serving in India, Ballantine graduated from Amherst, joined the Foreign Service, then served in Japan but spent much of his time in China before his friend, Hull, brought him back to head the Far Eastern Division in 1941. Ballantine and Hornbeck believed that the central point could not be compromised: Japanese withdrawal from China. Only after that pullback could all else—Indochina, the Axis alliance, restoration of trade—be more easily settled. Ballantine especially worried that a deal with Konoe would resemble the Lansing-Ishii agreement of 1918—that is, a U.S. recognition of Japan's paramount position, this time in China, in return for merely a temporary peace. He also warned that if Americans were pulled in as a mediator between China and Japan, as Konoe might try to do, they could find themselves serving as a mere shield for further Japanese aggression. Finally, Ballantine doubted whether Konoe, after he returned home, could force the military to support any agreement that FDR could accept.[34]

Hornbeck went further. He argued that the United States not only could not, but need not, compromise on the pivotal question of China. The war had already left Japan so "half-beaten" and "substantially exhausted" that Tokyo "has no intention of making war on the United States." Hornbeck even argued that if Konoe offered to withdraw immediately from China, the United States should think twice about agreeing (at least until there was a complete change of government in Tokyo), because it was the China morass that limited Japan's ability to cause problems elsewhere. Of special note, Hornbeck and Ballantine argued that the prospect of a summit would have a "detrimental" effect on China, and might even lead—as the U.S. Embassy in Chungking was warning—to Chinese-Japanese peace talks if Chiang thought the Americans were considering "a 'regional detente' with Japan." Hornbeck apparently floated a remarkable proposal that any summit should include Chiang, a *ménage à trois* which neither the embattled Konoe nor the secretive Roosevelt showed any interest in joining.[35]

On September 25, 1941, Nomura handed Hull Japan's proposals for a settlement. It was the last such paper the Japanese gave the United States before they decided they had to go to war. Protesting that it shared the American desire for "peace in the world," Konoe's government downplayed the 1940 Axis pact: if the United States entered the European War, Japan "would decide" its course "entirely independently" in interpreting its obligations under the pact. The paper then moved to the core of the crisis: the United States was to act as a peacemaker in China and work for peace along Japanese lines. Americans could not resort to other "measures"—that is, send aid to Chiang Kai-shek. Sino-Japanese trade would be carried on peacefully "in conformity with the principle of non-discrimination." The United States would "without delay" resume "normal trade" with Japan. Once an "equitable peace" existed in the Pacific area, Japanese troops would withdraw from Indochina, and Americans would "alleviate" their "military measures" in the region—a reference to the military buildup in the Philippines. On September 29, Grew cabled Hull to beg him to take the proposals seriously, and not demand that Japan meet U.S. preconditions (especially on China) before Roosevelt would agree to meet. If preconditions were demanded, Grew warned, Konoe would fall and be replaced with "a military dictatorship which will lack either the disposition or the temperament to avoid colliding head-on with the United States."[36]

On October 2, in his hotel apartment, Hull responded by reading the riot act to an already disheartened, fatigued, and pessimistic Nomura. Hull said there had to be a "meeting of the minds" before any summit. He handed the ambassador a statement which demanded Japan agree to four principles that elaborated the open-door policy: respect for territorial integrity, non-interference in other nations' internal affairs, the principle of "equality of commercial opportunity," and change in the Pacific region only through peaceful means. More explicitly, "The withdrawal of Japanese troops from China and French Indochina would be most helpful in making known . . . Japan's peaceful intentions." Nomura read the statement, then replied that "the only point on which he anticipated difficulty in . . . reaching an agreement" was the U.S. demand that Japanese troops leave China. If that were required before Japan realized its aims in China—the protection of Manchukuo, obtaining economic resources, forcing Chiang to behave and cooperate with Japanese interests—then the Konoe government would collapse.[37]

The China hands, Hornbeck and Ballantine, had won the debate against the Japan hands, Grew and Dooman. Roosevelt would not go to a summit until Konoe accepted the preconditions. In mid-October, Hull unloaded his worries on a top Japanese official: "The Japanese invasion had resulted in the establishment of many monopolies in China and many special privileges and benefits . . . which probably accounts for the main desire of Japan to keep troops in China." This point was made more colorfully on October 13 when Undersecretary of State Sumner Welles jousted with the Japanese Embassy's second-in-command, Wakasugi Kaname. Why, Wakasugi asked, could not the two nations reach an "understanding" on all other "fundamental" points "and leave the China question in abeyance"? "I said," Welles recorded, ". . . this question was very much like asking whether the play of 'Hamlet' could be given on the stage without the character of Hamlet. The Minister laughed loudly and said he fully understood my point."[38]

So did the Tokyo government, although it was not laughing. Konoe, who had just celebrated his fiftieth birthday, convened a cabinet meeting on October 14. The war minister, General Tojo Hideki, noted that the early October deadline for the war-or-peace decision had passed. He demanded a decision to mobilize troops. When objections were raised that diplomacy required more time, Tojo exploded. He warned that any withdrawal of troops would be a condemnation of all Japan's efforts in China, and would also threaten Manchukuo, perhaps even Korea. Either mobilization had to be authorized or the army must stop its war preparations. The navy, which had long fought the army over war objectives, went along in what one Japanese historian has called "group think"—even though the navy had no master plan to fight a long-term war. Japanese troops in China, Tojo emphasized, were "the heart of the matter," and after too many concessions to the United States, Japan must not surrender the "heart."[39]

Two days later, Konoe resigned. Tojo became prime minister. Born in 1884, the son of a samurai who became a lieutenant general, Tojo had been educated by the army, posted early to Germany, and earned notoriety as a commander in the Kwantung Army. The powerful force in the army's "control faction" that demanded full mobilization of the society for all-out war, he urged close cooperation with Germany. The new prime minister was driven by long-held, bitter resentment against the United States for its hostility toward Japan on such issues as China, immigration, shipbuilding ratios, and trade. Highly intelligent (his nickname was "Razor Brain"), Tojo was also characterized by one of his best biographers as "churlish," "naive and aggressive," a by-the-book soldier, a simple person of great discipline—and with great hatred, especially toward the West, which he believed was led by the United States in its determination to dominate East Asia. Despite this background, the State Department's Far East Division told FDR that Tojo was "a Konoy [sic] adherent and a 'moderate.' "[40]

To call Tojo a "moderate" was a case study of situational ethics applied to diplomatic terminology. Japan's leadership, indeed the entire context of Asian politics, had moved so far toward militarism that a leading proponent of mobilization and hatred of the West could be defined as "moderate." The bankruptcy of Japanese politics was better explained by Konoe when, through an aide, he secretly informed Grew about Tojo's assuming power: "It would be impossible at the present time to form a civilian Cabinet with a liberal tinge." "There is in Japan no civilian of adequate eminence to take over the office of Prime Minister. . . . Consequently the succeeding Cabinet must be composed primarily of military men." They were now the only Japanese "capable of bringing about the downfall of the government."[41]

Chiang Kai-shek, the pivotal point for both U.S. and Japanese diplomacy, was another example of relative terminology. A militarist, tied to some of the most corrupt and criminal elements in China, anti-Western, even anti-capitalist as Americans understood the term, Chiang was a highly unlikely ally of the Western democracies. But then so was Joseph Stalin in 1941. The need for Chiang's cooperation, even while disdaining his revolutionary background, fascist beliefs, and anti-Western attitude, explains why U.S. officials, and especially Hornbeck, seemed to care less about ending the war in China than using that war to squeeze Japan until it transformed its own government and paid obedience to Hull's (and John Hay's) larger principles.

Throughout the 1930s, Americans grew enamored of heroic Chinese peasants, standing steadfastly against the Japanese invaders, as portrayed through the best-selling novels of Pearl Buck, the widely acclaimed film *The Good Earth* based on Buck's romantic perception of China, and the millions of copies of *Life* and *Time* magazines that were published each week by Henry Luce, born in China of American missionary parents. But these views of China did not shape U.S. policy after 1937. If they had, Americans would have been fighting in Asia long before December 1941.

U.S. policy was driven, rather, by Hull and Hornbeck's growing anger that Japan intended to use military force to cordon off large parts of Asia to obtain economic self-sufficiency—the open door and Pan-Asian ideology be damned. By October 1941, the differences among U.S. officials were not over whether, but how, to stop Japan. Hornbeck persuaded many, including Hull and FDR, that the slipknot would continually tighten as the Japanese struggled against it. Japan would not try to cut that knot (that is, declare war), because it knew it could not defeat the United States. Sooner or later, Hornbeck concluded, the slipknot would choke off the militarists. Grew was not persuaded. On November 3, 1941, he told Hull there were those who believed the militarists would collapse "shortly . . . from the depletion and the eventual exhaustion of Japan's financial and economic resources." But those who believed this, the ambassador warned, "unconsciously" assumed "that a dominant consideration would be Japan's retention of the capitalistic system." Grew emphasized that Japan would not soon collapse precisely because it did not have a capitalist system as Americans understood the term. Despite continual economic crisis and the depletion of "Japan's national resources," the economy worked sufficiently to make Japan resistant to U.S. economic strangulation—and to allow Japan to go to a war with the United States that "may come with dangerous and dramatic suddenness."[42]

The last, sad, meaningless discussion of these points occurred between November 20 and 27. It was mere shadow-boxing. The main event was scheduled to begin in two weeks. But the events of late November summarized why the final bout was to be held. On November 20, Nomura handed Hull Japan's final offer. It differed little from previous proposals. Nomura, however, was now accompanied by Kurusu Saburo, a fifty-five-year-old professional diplomat who, as a young man, had served in Chicago and New York as a consul (and, most unusual for a Japanese official, had married an American woman). In 1940, as ambassador to Germany, he had negotiated the Axis pact in Berlin. Tojo had dispatched him to help the worn-out Nomura and string along discussions until Japan was ready to attack. Kurusu and Hull soon began arguing over China. Kurusu dismissed the Nine-Power Treaty and its open-door provisions as "twenty years old and . . . outmoded." Hull shot back that Japanese militarism in China was "not unlike Hitler's methods."[43]

On November 26, the Secretary of State gave Nomura and Kurusu the last (as it turned out) set of U.S. proposals. The offer, Hull stressed, was only "tentative." It hinged on the American insistence that Japan had to accept the open door and "withdraw all military, naval, air, and police forces from China and Indochina" before the United States would allow trade and oil to flow again.

Kurusu blasted the document. "The Washington Conference treaties," he declared, "had given the wrong idea to China," and "China had taken advantage of them to flaunt Japan's rights." The proposals, he concluded, were "tantamount to meaning the end." Which they were. Hull had actually considered offering Japan a three-month deal in which Japan would receive oil if it reduced its troops in Indochina. The War Department, desperately in need of time to build up the Pacific forces, supported the idea. But Chiang Kai-shek had, in Hull's exasperated words, "sent numerous hysterical cable messages to different Cabinet officers" and killed the proposal. Both the Chinese and the British wanted Americans in the war sooner, not later.[44]

On December 1, an Imperial Conference in which the Emperor participated gave final approval for the military strike on Hawaii. The attack had been thoroughly discussed and agreed upon a month before by the real decision-making body, the Liaison Conference, which had been created in November 1940 to bring together the most important cabinet members and the Military Chiefs of the General Staff. The Emperor was now expected to approve, not change the earlier decision. At that earlier meeting on November 1, the mood had not been triumphant. Tojo and Foreign Minister Togo Shigenori invoked Japan's sneak attack on the Russian fleet in 1904 as the kind of success that could occur. Togo recalled that thirty-seven years earlier the army's vice chief of staff had viewed the prospects for victory as only "fifty-fifty," but Japan triumphed. Tojo declared to the doubters, "You have to plunge into war if there is some chance, however slight, of winning victory." On November 21, Japanese officials' hope swelled slightly when Hitler secretly assured them that if they went to war against the United States, so would Germany. Nevertheless, that same day, MAGIC and Signals Intelligence (SIGINT—the British counterpart to MAGIC) intercepted a Japanese Foreign Office instruction to its diplomats emphasizing that Japan now aimed at "the complete expulsion of British and American military and naval strength in CHINA." Then came the admission of weakness: in dealing with China, the Japanese must "avoid exhaustion" so "we have enough war potential to face up to a lengthy world war."[45]

The problem at the center of Japanese policy was that if Japan did not go to war, it would collapse internally and lose everything it had shed blood for (Manchukuo, parts of China, Indochina) quite soon; if it did go to war, it could lose everything later—unless the United States was forced to make peace before Americans could gear up their tremendous industrial and military potential. The one U.S. official who best understood the fundamental Japanese weakness was Hornbeck, and he had the misfortune to say one week before the attack on Pearl Harbor that given its problems Japan would not go to war soon.[46]

As for Roosevelt, he was still, as he told Secretary of the Treasury Morgenthau in May 1941, "waiting to be pushed into this situation." Morgenthau correctly observed that FDR did not want to "lead us into war." In early November, the President asked his cabinet whether the public would support him if he used naval power to stop Japan's southward advance, or did he need some "incident"? Unanimously, the cabinet told him he had public support and no incident was needed. Roosevelt made no response. At this time, 73 percent of Americans polled believed the U.S. Fleet could defeat the Japanese navy, and only 3 percent disagreed. Racism shaped such a view. Secretary of the Interior Ickes, for example, had dismissed the threat of a sneak attack a year earlier when he wrote in his diary, "It seems to be pretty well understood now that the Japanese are naturally poor airmen."[47]

If Roosevelt did little to lead, or to prepare Americans for war publicly, he did much more quietly. If he was "'waiting to be pushed,'" he put himself and the nation into the position to be shoved easily into war. By autumn 1941, the United States was sending troops to Iceland, extending a protectorate over Greenland, freezing Japanese assets, cutting off Japan's oil, pledging an American response if Japanese troops attacked the Dutch East Indies (Indonesia) or British colonies, and secretly convoying goods sent to the British through German submarine-infested waters. When the America First Committee tried to pull the United States back, the President not only criticized it publicly. He secretly ordered the FBI to wiretap anti-interventionists' phones and suggested that the Justice Department start a grand jury investigation of America First.[48]

On November 25, 1941, FDR and his top advisers, including Hull, Stimson, and the chiefs of the military services, stated the issue precisely. "The question was how we should maneuver them [the Japanese] into the position of firing the first shot without allowing too much danger to ourselves," Stimson recorded. "It was a difficult proposition." The difficulty came from their knowledge that a large Japanese naval force with five infantry divisions on board was steaming south, possibly to attack Dutch or British holdings. Roosevelt told the British that a Japanese attack would bring U.S. "armed support." He apparently planned to tell the world of this policy on December 8. MAGIC intercepts also told U.S. officials that the Tojo government had decided war with the United States "may happen sooner than expected," and it would occur in the "South"—not in the "North," that is, not against the Soviets. By December 6, Washington officials believed the Japanese force intended to strike the Kra Isthmus, the narrow, highly strategic portion of the Malay Peninsula. Although warnings about possible war had been sent to Hawaii as early as November 27, FDR and his military chiefs did not believe those islands would be initially attacked.[49]

Admiral Yamamoto Isoroku, however, was making last-minute preparations for a naval and air force attack on Pearl Harbor. Yamamoto remains one of the most fascinating of twentieth-century Japanese lead-crs. Born into a large family in 1884, adopted in 1916 by the Yamamoto family, which needed a male heir, he graduated from one of the Naval Academy's most distinguished classes. The five·foot three, 125-pound officer was a hero in the 1904–05 war, in which he lost two fingers and suffered wounds over his body when an overheated gun blew up. Shimbashi's geisha district, which he knew intimately, greeted him as "Eighty sen," because a geisha's regular charge for a manicure of ten fingers was 100 sen, or one yen. Posted to the United States in 1919, he studied English at Harvard and read widely in American history ("I like Lincoln. . . . [H]e's great not just as an American, but as a human being"). Yamamoto came to love American football, once going out of his way to see the Iowa-Northwestern game in Chicago. His passion, however, seemed to be gambling, which he had probably learned during a visit to Monaco. Legend had it that he won so much money in a Monaco casino one time that he was forbidden to return. When he came back to the United States as naval attaché from 1926 to 1928, and again when he traveled by train across the country in 1934 en route to the London Naval Conference, he devoted much time to playing mah-jong and cards, especially poker.

His closest staff officer recalled that Yamamoto "had a gambler's heart." He demonstrated such a heart when he bet during the interwar years that the future of the Japanese navy and, indeed, global security, depended on airpower. As an instructor at Japan's Naval Staff College in the 1920s he stunned students by emphasizing that the fleet's future rested on having enough oil and airplanes. As commander of the Kasumigaura Aviation Corps that gave birth to the Naval Air Force after 1930, he devised the basic training for pilots flying over the oceans. After being promoted to vice admiral in 1934, Yamamoto worked with the navy leaders who opposed ties with the Axis. Although unsuccessful in cutting those ties, he became commander in chief of the navy in 1939. He quickly understood that Japan could no longer "adjust our relations with America through diplomacy." If war—which he opposed—did come, he believed Japan had to destroy the U.S. Pacific Fleet or be destroyed itself. War planners in Tokyo said that an attack on Hawaii could not be successful. In early spring 1940, Yamamoto decided it could succeed, if it employed enough airpower. In the United States he had learned, among other things, to love football, speak his mind ("Only an asshole would say anything like that" was sometimes heard), and admire the potential of American power. He predicted accurately that the next war would be won by repeatedly conquering islands, building airfields, then bombing heavily before moving on to conquer the next stretch of ocean. The United States could do this, but "Do you think that kind of thing is possible with Japan's present industrial capacity?" When, however, his pessimism was overruled by Tojo (for whom he had little respect), Yamamoto nevertheless took his ultimate gamble.[50]

On November 25, the fleet, which included six aircraft carriers, left a secret rendezvous point in the Kuriles to sail—without radio contact, without dumping garbage or oil cans that could leave a trail, without lights at night—toward Hawaii. U.S. intelligence had no idea where the fleet was located. Because of MAGIC, U.S. officials did know on December 6 that Japan planned a major step. A thirteen-part intercept of a message sent from Tokyo to Nomura was in front of the President that Saturday night. Tokyo delayed in sending the crucial fourteenth part, that ordered a break-off in diplomatic relations, but U.S. intelligence officers were decoding the last section at 5:30 A.M. Washington time, or about eight hours before the attack was to begin. These officers could not, however, locate Army Chief of Staff General George Marshall (who was taking his usual Sunday morning horseback ride) or other cabinet officers until about 10:00 A.M. An hour later, Marshall finished reading the dispatch and sent a warning to the military in Hawaii, but by radio rather than by the scrambler phone on his desk which, he feared, the Japanese had been intercepting. The radio message reached San Francisco. Because of bad weather over the Pacific, it then went by Western Union telegram to Honolulu. Two hours after Yamamoto's first bombs fell from the sky, a young Japanese-American messenger handed Marshall's warning to military authorities in Hawaii.[51]

In minutes the 183 Japanese planes and submarines killed 2,500 Americans, destroyed 152 of 230 U.S. planes, sank five of the six best battleships in the Pacific Fleet, and damaged a dozen other vessels. An hour later a second attack destroyed additional ships and aircraft. The destruction of the Pacific Fleet was avoided only because three aircraft carriers and their escort vessels were at sea, and—due to a rare planning error by Yamamoto—the planes missed fuel and repair facilities in Hawaii. (All but two of the battleships were reclaimed, repaired, and fighting by 1944.) Japan had violated international law by not declaring war before the attack began. More to the point for Hull, Nomura and Kurusu did not hand him the note breaking off relations until after he knew the attack had begun. The two Japanese had been instructed to deliver the note at 1:00 P.M. Washington time, but because of delays in decoding, the paper was not ready until nearly 2:00 P.M. By then the attack had been under way for forty minutes. Hull had already read the message through courtesy of MAGIC. He glanced at the paper, then declared that "In all my fifty years of public service I have never seen a document . . . more crowded with infamous falsehoods . . . on a scale so huge that I never imagined until today that any Government on this planet was capable of uttering them." Nomura and Kurusu left without any response.[52]

While Hull exploded, other U.S. and Allied officials were relieved. Stimson recorded that when he heard of the attack, "my first feeling was of relief that the indecision was over and that a crisis had come in a way which would unite all our people." Prime Minister Winston Churchill, who had been urging full U.S. involvement, was equally direct when he phoned FDR: "This certainly simplifies things."[53]

Perhaps the major argument that day in Washington occurred over Roosevelt's war message to Congress. Stimson wanted FDR to blame Hitler and have Congress declare war against Germany. Hull sought personal vindication by asking that the message spell out in detail the negotiations that had led to the tragedy. Roosevelt overruled both and decided to send the short message that began: "Yesterday, December 7, 1941—a date which will live in infamy—the United States of America was suddenly and deliberately attacked by . . . the Empire of Japan." Admitting only that the damage at Pearl Harbor was "severe," he added that Japan had also attacked Malaya, Hong Kong, Guam, the Philippines, Wake Island, and Midway Island. The Senate and House passed the war resolution with only one negative vote (Representative Jeannette Rankin, a pacifist from Montana who had also voted against going to war in 1917). Stimson's (and FDR's) concern about Germany was removed when Hitler declared war against the United States on December 11.[54]

The Japanese declaration of war had a quite different opening: "WE, by grace of heaven, Emperor of Japan, seated on the Throne of a line unbroken for ages eternal, enjoin upon ye, Our loyal and brave subjects. . . ." The Emperor's declaration focused on the Chinese, who, "recklessly courting trouble," had "compelled Our Empire to take up arms." The Americans and British, "eager for the realization of their inordinate ambition to dominate the Orient," had supported China and were "inducing other countries" to join them in a policy against a peaceful Japan that "endanger[s] the very existence of Our Nation." It was a succinct statement of how Japan read the historical record quite differently than did Hull, although both versions centered on China.[55]

Those readings of history merited close attention. As a distinguished historian of Japan, John Whitney Hall, phrased it, "For if we accept, as we must, the fact that Japan did not attack the United States out of sheer madness, then it becomes possible to imagine situations in which other nations rationally driven to extremities might find peaceful coexistence with the United States impossible or at least unbearable."[56]

The Japanese had taken this course, as Admiral Yamamoto exemplified, with few illusions. A week earlier the Emperor had met with nine former prime ministers, not one of whom urged war. Most warned against fighting the United States for, as one said, such "ideals" as an Asian Co-prosperity sphere. Upon hearing of the Pearl Harbor attack, the recent prime minister, Prince Konoe, supposedly said, "It is a terrible thing. . . . I know that a tragic defeat awaits us at the end." Nor, in the first hours of fighting, as the United States suffered the greatest military disasters in its history, did American leaders have illusions about what lay ahead. A stunning example occurred late on December 8, when an aide phoned Stimson with the dramatic news that "an enemy fleet was thought to be approaching San Francisco." The Secretary of War thanked the aide for the information, "but suggested that I didn't know anything that I could do to prevent it." Stimson instead went to bed. He was soon aroused by a call that declared the report was false alarm. The war that climaxed nearly ninety years of relations between the United States and Japan was going to be long and bloody.[57]

VIII

World War II: The Clash Over Two Visions

Tenno versus the "Laws of the Machine"

IN 1961, as he looked back over the sweep of U.S.-Japanese relations, Assistant Secretary of State Walter McConaughy sorrowed over the tragic climax of December 1941. "One of fate's bitterest ironies," McConaughy declared, "was that America should find itself at war with Japan without really knowing who the Japanese were."[1]

The same comment, of course, could be made about the Japanese understanding of Americans in 1941. Each people had too often seen the other through the distorted lenses of racism and parochial national interests. But on the central issue, each understood the other quite well. For their part, Japanese officials were determined to protect their society's traditional values by breaking its long dependence on the West (and increasingly on the United States) through the creation of a "new order" in Asia that centered on China and was defined and controlled by Japan. U.S. officials were equally determined to protect their society's political-economic system by entering an open door to Asian resources, especially China's, and—in a further giant step—integrating this open Asia into a world free of totalitarian-controlled economies. That determination intensified as the U.S. gross national product (the sum of all goods and services Americans produced) amazingly doubled to $200 billion between 1940 and 1945. This fantastic increase not only finally overpowered Japan but made vivid the American need for an open, workable, global postwar marketplace.

These differences in outlooks and objectives led to war between Americans and Japanese. The differences also explained why the two sides differed fundamentally in their wartime objectives, and why the tragedy had to be fought not to a compromise peace, but to a blood-filled unconditional surrender that was so traumatic for both sides that they bitterly argued over it even a half century later.

Americans called the conflict a world war. The Japanese, however, termed it the Pacific or Great East Asian War. Asians, from Tokyo's perspective, were to be freed of Western imperialism so they could be released from the West's seeming addiction to virtually no-holds-barred marketplace competition. Instead, Asians were to be integrated into a "Greater East Asia Co-Prosperity Sphere." That vision had deep roots in Japanese history. But it was also a deeply divided vision, with one voice telling Japanese they should believe they had many common and equal interests with other Asians, and the other—increasingly predomi-nant—voice assuring the Japanese that their narrow, militant national-ism was to lead, and if necessary subjugate, other Asians. As late as World War I, Japanese emperors were identified on documents as *Kotei,* a term that was used for other, even Western, emperors as well. In December 1941, however, Emperor Hirohito's declaration of war was signed *Tenno*—the only such divine sovereign in the world allowed to be associated with saving Asia through the ancient Japanese Imperial Way. As war began, Prime Minister Tojo Hideki disdainfully dismissed those who held to the "old idea that Japan should deal with all countries as equals." He set up an East Asian ministry whose job was to plan, then usher in, a Japanese-led Asia.[2]

Washington officials, on the other hand, saw Asia as only one piece of a global puzzle, and not necessarily the most important piece. In the short run, they believed, Hitler, not Tojo, posed the greater danger because Germans controlled the greater military machine. The United States made no plans for an East Asian ministry, but instead drew up extensive blueprints for an indivisible world that would prosper in a new era. Americans did not think small.

The absolute need for such incredible worldwide vision was well stated by Will Clayton, a Texan who headed the world's largest cotton brokerage house, and then joined Roosevelt as the State Department's top economic official. In early 1941, Clayton traced the catastrophes of the 1930s "back to the Industrial Revolution . . . over a century and a half ago." For then the "basic, unchangeable laws of the machine" began generating growth and progress, but also "production and more production" that demanded "free movement . . . throughout the world." Hitler (and, Clayton could have added, the Japanese) tried to deny "this law" by creating centralized, compartmentalized economic blocs that placed "severe strain on our traditional way of life." Those blocs had to be destroyed, free markets globalized. Then, as Henry Luce (the founder of *Time, Life,* and *Fortune* magazines) wrote in widely read editorials of mid-1941, the world could enjoy an "American Century." The scope of this "Century" was boundless: the United States had "to be responsible for the world environment in which she lives." The New Deal, Luce continued, had failed to "make American democracy work" on a mere national basis. It thus had to work "in terms of a vital international economy and . . . international moral order." The famous publisher told Americans to think big: "For example, we think of Asia as being worth only a few hundred millions [of dollars] a year to us. Actually, in the decades to come Asia will be worth to us exactly zero—or else it will be worth to us four, five, ten billions of dollars a year. And the latter are the terms we must think in, or else confess a pitiful impotence." The myth of the great Asian market, then, could finally be changed into reality—if that market became part of a *global* "great American century."[3]

Later, during the fateful summer of 1941, Roosevelt had moved to create such a century by demanding that Prime Minister Winston Churchill agree to the universal principles of the Atlantic Charter—principles, such as open and equal access to markets, that were preeminently American and certainly not associated with British colonialism. During early 1943, in an incisive and prophetic analysis, Britain Foreign Office officials agreed that the United States would try to control much of Asia's trade, but not through a narrow approach: those "trade relations will be conditioned by the post-war world situation and by the degree to which the principles in the Atlantic Charter supersede tendencies toward economic regionalism." The same idea was stated more publicly that year by Wendell Willkie, the Wall Street lawyer from Indiana who had run a surprisingly strong race against FDR in 1940. The title of his book *One World* was also the thesis for a work that sold 3 million copies within a year.[4]

Americans believed they had to hurry to achieve this one world. Admiral William D. Leahy, Roosevelt's personal military chief of staff, noted in his diary in September 1942 that the war in the Pacific must be accelerated at any cost: "if Japan is allowed sufficient time to consolidate its gains in Asia and induce the Asiatic people to accept Japanese control[,] the future of America in the Pacific will be hazardous at least." Racism permeated both sides in the war and fueled the hatreds and brutalities in that conflict to a greater degree than in Europe. Perhaps, however, no aspect of that racism was more important than the U.S. fear that unless Japan was not merely beaten but destroyed to the point of unconditional surrender, Americans would face an Asian phalanx. Leahy talked with Roosevelt's diplomatic troubleshooter, General Patrick J. Hurley, in 1942, then agreed with Hurley's view that unless Japan suffered defeat, "in the near future that nation will succeed in combining most of the Asiatic peoples against the Whites." Few, however, approached the apocalyptic vision of Herbert Hoover, whom many powerful Republicans still considered the "Chief":

When the Japanese take Burma, China and organize the forces of the discontent in India [the former President wrote a Tulsa newspaper owner in early 1942], we are looking in the face of something new. . . . The white man has kept control of Asiatics by dividing parts of them each against the other . . . and generally establishing an arrogant superiority. Universally, the white man is hated by the Chinese, Malayan, Indian and Japanese alike. . . . Unless [Japanese] leadership is destroyed, the Western Hemisphere is going to confront this mass across the Pacific. Unless they are defeated, they will demand entry and equality in emigration . . . and there will be in twenty-five years an Asiatic flood into South America that will make the Nazis look like pikers. . . . And we will have to go through with it until we have destroyed [Japan]. That may take a million American lives and eight or ten years, but it will have to be done.[5]

In the end, of course, Japan could not mobilize Asians into the 1 billion potential enemies (as Roosevelt once phrased the number) because the Japanese believed in, and paraded, their own racial superiority. That they did so was not surprising. They had long thought of themselves as a unique and superior people (and believed they had the military, political, and cultural accomplishments as evidence). Their ascendancy to world power between 1860 and 1920 occurred during the heyday of supposedly scientific racism in the West, a pseudo-science the Japanese studied closely because they and other Asians were so often the victims of it. In the 1930s and 1940s, however, the Japanese racism that drove the great war effort was based not on science but on history. The source of Japan's greatness and ultimate victory, according to novelists, cartoonists, journalists, and government propagandists, was the Emperor, whose origins went back 2,600 years to Emperor Jimmu, a direct descendant of the Sun Goddess. No other people could claim such a lineage. Other races "were filthy and impure," the Orwellian-named Thought Bureau of the Ministry of Education declared in 1937. American liberalism and so-called individualism were especially filthy, some leading Japanese publicists preached, because such terms only disguised the rich exploiting the poor, the destruction of community, and the "ugly plutocracy" of the Jews. One cartoonist considered the English language so dirty that he portrayed Americans speaking into garbage cans. Thus to racial theorists such as those in the so-called Kyoto School, the Japanese were fighting a "holy war." Such historically based racism led the "yellow" and "colored" races in Asia, as well as the "liberals" in America—to borrow widely used Japanese terms—to fight to the death against Japan.[6]

To break a century-long dependency on the West and realize a 26-century-long claim to uniqueness, 1,140,429 Japanese were killed in action between 1937 and 1945, 485,000 against U.S. forces. Another 240,000 were missing in action. Some 953,000 Japanese civilians died, 668,000 from Allied air raids on the home islands. If Americans with their greater population had been killed in proportion, about 4 million would have died or been missing in action. Instead, out of the 16.3 million who served in the U.S. forces (Japan's peak strength was about half the number of the U.S. forces at peak strength), 405,399 were killed in the wars of the Pacific and European theaters, as they defended the principles that were to give meaning to Luce's American Century.[7]

California Goes to War: The Relocation Camps, and Hollywood

In 1942, the dream of an American Century seemed to face extinction. The first months of the war ranked among the worst in American history. The effects of the Pearl Harbor attack turned out to be so devastating that President Roosevelt refused to reveal the damage publicly. The Japanese unleashed quick, triumphant invasions throughout the southwest Pacific that took apart colonial empires the Europeans and Americans had assembled over the past century. Describing the Pacific situation in early 1942 as "very grave," Roosevelt feared that Japan was moving into such a dominant position that it would be "most difficult to eject her."[8]

The military crisis intensified the century-long racism. The result was summarized later in the conflict by the famous U.S. war correspondent Ernie Pyle: "In Europe we felt that our enemies, horrible and deadly as they were, were still people. But out here [in the Pacific] I soon gathered that the Japanese were looked upon as something subhuman or repulsive; the way some people feel about cockroaches or mice." More broadly, U.S. State Department officials were convinced that "democratic institutions are incompatible with the Japanese philosophy." Such beliefs, and the military crisis, not only shaped U.S. actions west of Hawaii but dramatically changed the lives of 80,000 U.S. citizens in California. These Americans had been born to Japanese families who had arrived before the 1924 Exclusion Act; such older Japanese (or *Issei*) were thus ineligible for U.S. citizenship. The *Issei* were nevertheless rounded up with the younger, U.S. citizens (*Nissei*—whose average age was just nineteen), and nearly 120,000 placed in "relocation camps" as a national security measure in early 1942. These "concentration camps," as government documents called them, marked the most flagrant breaking of civil rights in the country during the war.[9]

The camps resulted from a combination of fear, racism, intense political pressures, and judgments by usually balanced officials who became unbalanced during the early 1942 crises. The Japanese Americans in California were largely highly successful farmers who provided much of the food for the state's stunning growth during the post-1920 years. They had been unjustly attacked for driving whites off the land. These farmers were easy targets for racists who had been working Western politics since the late nineteenth century. In 1942, the socioeconomic competition that fueled the racism was easily disguised beneath the rhetoric of national security. On January 25, 1942, a government report declared that Japanese Americans in Hawaii had been involved in "subversive activities"—an unsubstantiated charge that triggered an avalanche of letters on Washington demanding the rounding up of the supposed subversives. As the *Los Angeles Times* editorialized, "A viper is nevertheless a viper wherever the egg is hatched—so a Japanese-American, born of Japanese parents, grows up to be a Japanese, not an American."[10]

Officials, especially elected politicians, needed little prodding. Earl Warren, California Attorney General in 1942 (and later a distinguished Chief Justice of the U.S. Supreme Court), observed that "some of our airplane factories in this State are entirely surrounded by Japanese land ownership or occupancy," then warned that Americans lived in a "fool's paradise" if they did not believe that "the enemy" had planned "a wave of sabotage." Americans knew and understood "Germans and Italians. . . . But when we deal with the Japanese we are in an entirely different field and we cannot form any opinion that we believe to be sound." Not for the first, or last, time, Japanese and Japanese Americans were seen to be the mysterious and unknowable. Those who spoke out for the Japanese community tried to explain, as one observed, that "we can't help being Japanese in features." But "My mother left Japan over 30 years ago," and that nation "is not the Japan of today." She had instilled in her children "courtesy, loyalty to the State and country in which we are, obedience to parents." If those traits happened to be part of Japanese culture, no reason existed to be "ashamed" of them.[11]

Warren's arguments, however, easily carried the day. As late as February 10, 1942, Secretary of War Henry Stimson worried that rounding up suspects because of their " 'racial characteristic' " could "make a tremendous hole in our constitutional system." Attorney General Francis Biddle agreed and refused to have anything to do with a forced evacuation of U.S. citizens. Stimson's top assistant, former Wall Street lawyer John McCloy, disagreed: "If it is a question of the safety of the country," then "why the Constitution is just a scrap of paper to me." Biddle finally bent when Stimson was swayed by McCloy and Warren's views. On February 19, FDR signed Executive Order 9066, which gave Stimson power to define military areas "from which any or all persons may be excluded." The military commander on the west coast, General John L. DeWitt, quickly placed nearly 120,000 Japanese Americans behind barbed wire in ten concentration camps that were located from California to Arkansas—sites where "no one had lived before and no one has lived since," in historian Roger Daniels's words.[12]

DeWitt was well suited to endure the job. As early as 1923, he had planned a similar operation in Hawaii if war erupted with Japan; in 1941, 1,400 Japanese were duly interned on the islands. The number was no larger, in part, because Japanese labor was necessary for Hawaii's economic survival. On the mainland, the camps were placed next to Indian reservations; whites wanted no one with Japanese features nearby. The sites were policed by armed guards and dogs. A U.S. immigration official caught the historical moment when he declared, "This is our time to get things done that we have been trying to get done for a quarter of a century." In two cases of 1943 and 1944, the U.S. Supreme Court declared Roosevelt, Stimson, and DeWitt's work constitutional. In a third, and unfortunately late case of December 1944, the Justices ruled that a loyal U.S. citizen could not be interned without specific charges.[13]

In 1943, the Secretary of War told the President that because U.S. forces were now winning the war, justification for the camps had disappeared. Roosevelt, however, refused to end the incarceration until after he safely won reelection in November 1944. By then, Stimson had ordered the drafting of young *Nissei* men. Some resisted; 263 were convicted for trying to avoid service. But 3,600 entered the war, mostly in the 442nd Regimental Combat Team—a segregated Japanese-American force that fought in Europe and became the U.S. Army's most decorated unit. *Nissei* soldiers were among the first to liberate, and experience the horrors of, the Dachau concentration camp. Other Japanese Americans, however, suffered little change. Some 2,500 were taken to Seabrook, New Jersey, where they worked in vegetable processing. They remained to form a community that continued to flourish a half century later. These people recalled that they had traveled east in railway cars with shades drawn so midwesterners would not think they were being invaded, or would not try to attack the travelers because a local citizen had lost a relative in the bitter Pacific fighting. The Japanese-American experience, unfortunately, was not unique. The Canadian government also relocated 21,900 persons of Japanese extraction—17,000 of whom were Canadian citizens—even though the nation's highest-ranking military officer testified they posed no threat. These people were not allowed to find new homes until 1949.[14]

In the United States, not until 1952 could all Japanese finally become naturalized citizens. Not until 1981 did a presidential commission finally conclude that the camps were "not justified by military necessity. . . . The broad historical causes which shaped these decisions were race prejudice, war hysteria, and a failure of political leadership." Not until 1988 did survivors finally receive some compensation ($20,000 each) for their suffering. The money was given over violent objections from an aged John McCloy. It is notable that the 264,000 German aliens never suffered such treatment between 1941 and 1945. Even twenty-six U.S. Fascist leaders were initially indicted, but Washington authorities moved to dismiss their case. Most striking was the comparable treatment of Chinese. In 1943, the U.S. government actually repealed the 1882 Exclusion Act so Chinese could become naturalized U.S. citizens. The difference was not just that China was an ally and Japan was an enemy, but that an active Chinese lobby, located on the east coast, aligned with humanitarian groups to take advantage of the crisis. No such lobby appeared for Japanese Americans.[15]

Hollywood films both captured and intensified this particular racism, which was summarized by General DeWitt's belief that "A Jap's a Jap— it makes no difference whether he is an American citizen or not." The films especially grasped the insight of Samuel Eliot Morison, noted historian and a rear admiral (so appointed because of his naval histories), who declared, "We were back to primitive days of fighting Indians on the American frontier; no holds barred and no quarter." In Hollywood, Pacific jungles replaced the western wilderness, and lawless Japanese assumed the roles of lawless Native Americans. To ensure that audiences could tell good Chinese from evil Japanese, Henry Luce's *Time* magazine published an article, "How to Tell Your Friends from Japs." (Japanese, for example, walked like "a conqueror," while Chinese walked easily and relaxed.) If you knew one, moreover, you knew them all: famous filmmaker Frank Capra's *Know Your Enemy—Japan* told audiences that Japanese were merely "photographic prints of the same negative." *Destination Tokyo* dramatized cultural differences: "The Japs don't understand the love we have for our women," said debonair Cary Grant, who played the leading role. "They don't even have a word for it in their language."[16]

Notably, the government's overseer of propaganda, the Office of War Information (OWI), tried to tone down Hollywood's treatment of Japanese. OWI feared these films hurt the war effort by intensifying American racism. The fears were well founded. Public opinion polls showed that a significantly higher number of African Americans than white Americans believed they would be treated better by Japanese invaders than by German soldiers. Elijah Mohammed, who later led the Black Muslims, was jailed because he insisted on declaring that he favored Japan so American black people could be freed by another colored people. And, of course, the ramifications of the racial confrontation stretched well beyond the supposed American melting pot. OWI and other observers understood that a historic turn was being taken on a global scale; they warned that Americans had to reset their cultural compasses to navigate the turn. Pearl Buck proclaimed that racial awakening in Asia had to be accompanied by an end to racial discrimination at home—if for no other reason than to undercut Japan's racial propaganda in both places. Walter Lippmann declared in early 1942 that Western nations must reverse course: they "must now do what hitherto they lacked the imagination to do . . . putting away the 'white man's burden' and purging themselves of the taint of an obsolete and obviously unworkable white man's imperialism."[17]

Americans thus confronted a two-front military struggle. They also, like their enemies, faced a further challenge: reexamining deeply rooted stereotypes and prejudices that threatened to weaken the war effort at home and destroy the war's objectives abroad.

The Failure of the Japanese Machine

In 1942–43, neither Japan nor the United States enjoyed the luxury of having the time to consider long-term perspectives. For Americans, the war threatened to turn from being critical to becoming a catastrophe. In 1942, a Japanese general in Southeast Asia caught both the racism and the urgency of his nation's plans when he told his troops, "With one blow you will annihilate the blue-eyed enemy [the Americans and British], and their black slaves [the colonized Asians]." Hong Kong, Malaya, the Netherlands East Indies (now Indonesia), Singapore, and Burma soon fell. Then came quick victories against tough U.S. resistance on Guam and Wake Island that opened the Solomons, even Australia and New Zealand, to conquest. General Tojo Hideki's government planned to cordon off Asia with a military fence stretching from the Aleutians to Burma (perhaps India), with the fence protected by outlying sentries at Guam, Wake, and, if all went well, the Solomons and, to the north, Midway. Behind this iron and steel barrier, Japan could force the Americans and British to discuss peace on Tojo's terms.[18]

A seemingly decisive and, for Americans, humiliating conflict was fought in the Philippines, a critical hinge in the fence. The U.S. commander, General Douglas MacArthur, was an already famous son of the U.S. general who had quelled the Filipino insurrection against the United States between 1899 and 1902. Douglas had been first in his 1903 West Point class, distinguished himself fighting against Mexicans in 1914 and Germans in 1918, was a general at age thirty-eight, and Army chief of staff in 1930 at age fifty. He went to the Philippines to organize the islands' military, then stayed on as commander of Filipino troops after he retired from U.S. service in 1937. As war approached in July 1941, Roosevelt reappointed him commander of U.S. forces in the Far East.

FDR ordered MacArthur to prepare a large force of the new B-17 bombers to frighten off, or, if war occurred, to kill, Japanese. MacArthur disliked the order, in part because he mistrusted the Air Force, in part because he did not want his beloved Philippines made a prime target for Japanese air attacks. Although he had at least a ten-hour advanced alert of Japan's invasion, MacArthur left the B-17s on the open runways.

Enemy planes easily destroyed half the U.S. long-range bomber force in the region on December 8. When Japanese ground forces invaded, MacArthur's ego and romanticism overcame his judgment. Instead of retreating to the fortress at Bataan peninsula and fighting a drawn-out battle that might stall Japan's advance, he threw 150,000 troops at the invaders' 43,000 men, was overwhelmed, and lost the supplies and munitions necessary for holding out on Bataan. Somehow Americans and Filipinos fought on until April, when the survivors were captured and taken on the horrors of the "Bataan Death March." MacArthur had long since left, on Roosevelt's orders, with the highly publicized promise that "I shall return."[19]

Allied forces also retreated in Burma. The U.S. commander, General Joseph ("Vinegar Joe") Stilwell, caught how Americans felt throughout the Pacific theater: "We got a hell of a beating . . . and it is humiliating as hell." A Japanese seaplane, launched from a submarine, even dropped incendiary bombs on Oregon in September 1942 to try (unsuccessfully) to ignite forest fires. Bombs attached to balloons later launched from Japan did kill an Oregon family, and similar devices landed as far south as Texas. FDR and the Democrats paid a price for these disasters when they suffered massive defeat in the 1942 congressional elections. The New Deal was dead, to be replaced by "Dr. Win the War," as FDR himself phrased it. But amid this shift, the President never changed his decision to place a higher military priority on Europe than on the Pacific. "It is of the utmost importance that we appreciate that defeat of Japan does not defeat Germany," he instructed U.S. diplomats in July 1942, but the "defeat of Germany means the defeat of Japan, probably without firing a shot or losing a life."[20]

Despite this Europe-first policy, U.S. power mushroomed so dramatically that by late 1942 the Army and Air Force had about the same number of troops (350,000) in the Pacific as in Europe. The Navy actually placed the majority of its power to the West, including four critical Air Force carrier task forces. On April 18, 1942, a dramatic breakthrough occurred when Lieutenant Colonel James H. Doolittle led sixteen B-25 bombers off the carrier *Hornet* to bomb Tokyo. (The successful takeoffs in heavy seas with the ships rising and falling some 50 feet were remarkable feats in themselves.) The raid became a catastrophe for some of the airmen. Out of fuel before they could land on Chinese bases, eight were captured by Japanese; three were executed in October, an event FDR carefully kept hidden from the public for six months. Hollywood's highly popular *Thirty Seconds Over Tokyo,* however, dramatized the crews' bravery, the courageous Chinese help, and Japan's vulnerability.

The most important result of the raid was Tojo's decision to respond by concentrating Japanese forces to destroy the U.S. Fleet and its carriers, rather than continuing the assault toward Australia.[21]

This decision turned out to be one of the most disastrous of many disastrous decisions Tokyo officials made during the war. Once again the brilliant gambler, Admiral Yamamoto Isoroku, was brought in to devise a plan to destroy the U.S. Fleet. Yamamoto launched a decoy invasion of the Aleutians to draw off part of the U.S. forces, then struck at Midway Island (south of Hawaii) to destroy or bottle up the rest of the American ships. After that, he hoped, Roosevelt would want to discuss peace terms. But in a first engagement northeast of Australia on May 3–8, 1942, two U.S. carrier task forces handed Japan its initial military setback. This Battle of the Coral Sea was the first naval engagement in which opposing ships never saw each other; it was entirely conducted by air strikes. Yamamoto's belief that airpower could decide wars, and his fear that given time America's latent power could destroy Japan, were both coming true. He did not know that the U.S. naval commander, Admiral Chester Nimitz, had the immeasurable advantage of being able to read some Japanese military codes. FDR was pouring a half-billion dollars annually into the supersecret Communication Intelligence (COMINT), and by mid-1942 its intercepts led Nimitz to rate its value as equivalent to an entire U.S. fleet. COMINT located the doomed Japanese ships in the Coral Sea engagement.[22]

COMINT also tracked Yamamoto's ships as they approached Midway, where the turning point of the Pacific War occurred. Between June 3 and 5, 1942, Nimitz ignored the decoy Aleutian invasion to concentrate his forces at Midway. Informed by COMINT, on June 4 and 5 his planes caught Japanese aircraft refueling on the carriers—the same four carriers that had carried out the Pearl Harbor attack—and sank many of the planes along with the four carriers. The Japanese made enormous errors, not least when they divided their naval forces among the Coral Sea, Aleutian, and Midway theaters, then allowed Nimitz to trap the slowest fleet that was tied to the invasion forces headed for Midway. The back of Japanese naval power was broken, although massive, bloody battles lay ahead.[23]

The U.S. counterattack ran along two tracks. The first was MacArthur's infantry-led drive in the southwest Pacific that targeted the Philippines and islands to the north close enough to Japan for air strikes. The second was Nimitz's navy-led assault through the central Pacific that moved toward Japan along the paths charted by the thirty-five-year-old (but often updated), War Plan ORANGE. In August 1942, another

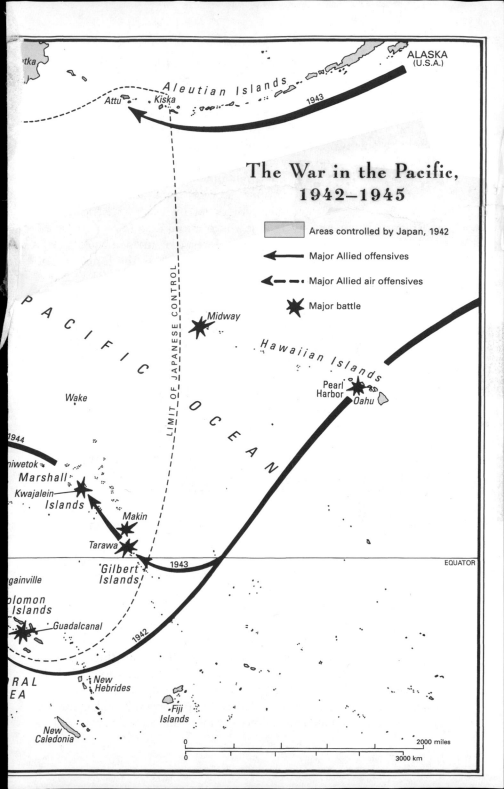

tka

ALASKA
(U.S.A.)

A l e u t i a n   I s l a n d s

1943

Attu Kiska

The War in the Pacific,
1942–1945

Areas controlled by Japan, 1942

Major Allied offensives

Major Allied air offensives

Major battle

P A C I F I C

Midway

H a w a i i a n   I s l a n d s

Wake

Pearl
Harbor
Oahu

LIMIT OF JAPANESE CONTROL

O C E A N

1944

niwetok

Marshall

Kwajalein

Islands

Makin

Tarawa

Gilbert
Islands

1943

EQUATOR

gainville

olomon
Islands

Guadalcanal

1942

New
Hebrides

Fiji
Islands

RAL
EA

New
Caledonia

0   2000 miles

0   3000 km

decisive victory began with the invasion of Guadalcanal in the Solomon Islands southeast of New Zealand. But a half-year of the bitterest fighting lay ahead, including seven naval engagements in which Yamamoto destroyed twenty-four warships and killed ten thousand U.S. sailors in Admiral William F. ("Bull") Halsey's fleet. Halsey ended this engagement with only two carriers, but also with Guadalcanal. Yamamoto lost twenty-four ships and thirty thousand of his forces, including some of his best pilots. On April 18, 1943, Yamamoto was in the Solomons when U.S. planes, tipped off by COMINT, took off from Guadalcanal to "get Yamamoto." They located and shot down his plane. His death was crushing to Japanese morale, but Tokyo authorities never considered changing the codes that COMINT read almost like an open book.[24]

As early as December 1942, Tojo had to admit to the Emperor that the Allies were taking the offensive. By then as well, Prince Konoe had formed a small, conservative, secret group to plot how to stop a Soviet occupation, and maintain internal order, should Japan lose the war. These Japanese leaders were confirming Churchill's words to Roosevelt just after December 7, 1941: "The resources of Japan are a wasting factor. The country has been long overstrained by its wasteful war in China. They were at their maximum strength on the day of the Pearl Harbor attack." In 1942–43, the Americans alone produced nearly twice as many planes (one every five minutes) as the combined Axis plants. The United States was on its way to spending $288 billion directly on the war between 1941 and 1945, while Japan could find only $41.2 billion (which was even less than China's $49 billion). As the large Japanese warships settled to the bottom of the Pacific and survivors were worried over oil supplies, Admiral Halsey replaced his losses in 1942 with three new fleet carrier task forces, and added five more in 1943. He also enjoyed easy access to the world's leading oil producer, the United States.

Japanese decision-making meanwhile became more confused as the new U.S. knot—this one in the form of arms—began tightening as early as May 1942. Tojo's cabinet had to give special priority to obtaining steel, airplane gasoline, and machine tools—all of which Japan had once largely obtained from the United States. Japanese economic planning was poor, as was their ability to mount an effective air defense system (a weakness Doolittle's raiders exploited), and their decision making in rebuilding their air force. They received insignificant help from Germany, despite Hitler's promises about cooperation. In the end, Tojo and Hitler fought separate wars while Roosevelt and Churchill masterfully coordinated their forces. Stalin was not always a willing

Allied partner, but by mid-1943 his army had destroyed 300,000 Germans at Stalingrad alone, taken the offensive, and made clear to the depressed Japanese that Hitler was not only becoming a loser, but that their historic enemy in Moscow might soon be able to extend powerful armies into East Asia. Although Japanese forces were already badly overstretched, Tokyo officials nevertheless held thirteen to fifteen divisions in Manchuria just to keep an eye on the Soviet Union and, mostly, sit on their hands. This error in decision making, together with the twenty-five and more divisions tied down in the bottomless morass of the China war, ruined Japan's ability to confront ever-increasing U.S. and British forces. In September 1943, the Emperor approved a decision to forget about the Co-Prosperity Sphere and to pull back the main defensive line. In stark contrast to such belt-tightening, the United States built a ship whose sole task was to produce 5,100 gallons of ice cream per hour for Americans in the South Pacific.[25]

The Japanese did not, however, lose their fanatical devotion to the Emperor's cause. Americans first encountered that fanaticism in May 1943 on the Aleutian island of Attu when 2,500 Japanese virtually committed suicide in fighting to the last man against 12,000 U.S. soldiers. Attu became famous for Japanese self-destruction, especially after *Time* magazine ran the story (later reprinted in *Reader's Digest*) with a title, "Perhaps They Are Human," and the answer, essentially, that the Japanese were not. Fanaticism, however, could take different forms. At Guadalcanal, U.S. Marines began to collect Japanese skulls as trophies, make necklaces from the teeth, and set about "pickling" the ears. *Life* magazine's "Picture of the Week" in May 1944 showed a Phoenix, Arizona, woman staring at a Japanese skull on which her boyfriend in the Pacific had written a thank-you note. Tokyo propagandists blasted the picture as comparable to the treatment Indians, Chinese, Filipinos, and African Americans had long suffered at American hands. A Pennsylvania congressman gave Roosevelt a letter-opener supposedly carved from a Japanese armbone, then apologized for giving "so small a part of the Japanese anatomy." This time an uproar occurred in the United States (led by Roman Catholic and Protestant church leaders), as well as in Japan. No such incidents were recorded as U.S. forces fought in the European theater.[26]

Japanese fanaticism on the battlefield slowed down the inexorable Allied advance after late 1942, but Tokyo's policies in the former colonial areas of Southwest Asia proved disastrously weak in mobilizing that region for the war. The historian Theodore Friend notes that the Japanese liked to tell the fable of Momotaro (or "Peach Boy"), who went south to fight demons and won with only the help of his dog, a monkey, and a pheasant, then returned home with wealth piled into a wagon pulled by the animals. Japanese (like Americans) loved stories about the small defeating the mighty. They also liked to think that the natives (or, in this fable, the animals) sided with them against the devil. A leading Japanese general told Southeast Asians that the slogan *hakko ichiu* ("Everyone under one roof") also meant "All nations are brothers." At first, the peoples to the south did look to the Japanese as "brothers" who would help free them from the white colonials. In one sense, that indeed was how it worked out: early Japanese victories destroyed the remains of colonial legitimacy, and the ensuing occupation became a hothouse for native independence movements that matured and triumphed after 1945. But contrary to *hakko ichiu,* Southeast Asian and Japanese cultures were quite different, and the differences widened as Japan treated the region's peoples as racially inferior. For example, the leading Burmese nationalist, Ba Maw, after first siding with the Japanese military, soon concluded that "few people were mentally so race-bound . . . and in consequence so totally incapable of understanding others or of making themselves understood by others." In French Indochina, the exploitation and skewing of the economy was deadly: at least a million people died of starvation in northern Vietnam during 1944–45.[27]

Expecting cooperation, Southeast Asians instead found that Japan expected them to sacrifice wholly for Tokyo's war plans. A case study occurred in the Philippines, an American colony since 1898. The United States had promised independence, but many Filipinos were nevertheless willing to work with Japan in 1942. When local Philippine leaders moved too slowly for its liking, Tokyo dispatched military officers to take command. They stopped all political activity. Their inability to obtain investment and shipping slashed invaluable Philippine iron ore shipments to Japan to only 10 percent of pre-1941 amounts. Because Tokyo dictated that its colony of Formosa was to be the empire's sugar producer, the rich Filipino cane fields were diverted to making liquid fuel or planted in cotton for Japan's needs. Such changes occurred not through consultation, but by orders that often began, "You are hereby informed. . . ." As unrest spread and economic activity declined, the Japanese promised to work with independence movements. They even announced principles that were the counterpart of the Allies' Atlantic Charter. But actions spoke louder than words, and as the war continued, Japan tried to govern and exploit the Philippines as if the islands resembled the Manchukuo of the 1930s. When Americans returned in

1944–45, most Filipinos welcomed them as liberators and even "brothers."[28]

"We Are Being Played for Suckers": The Enemy Begins to Replace the Friend in U.S. Postwar Planning

American diplomatic plans during most of the war revolved around hopes for China, much as Japanese plans for Asia had historically revolved around the Chinese. Roosevelt and his closest advisers professed faith that with Japan's destruction, China would emerge as their closest ally in the region. Indeed, as FDR phrased it, Chiang Kai-shek and his people were to join the United States, Great Britain, and the Soviet Union as one of the world's "four policemen." Roosevelt did not at all intend to turn Asia over to Chiang. He mused that Americans were to keep the peace in the western hemisphere, and "the United States and China would be charged with keeping the peace in the Far East." It was, of course, to be Chiang's China. The Communists of Mao Tse-tung (Mao Zedong), expanding their influence from their northern strongholds, were not to be trusted as policemen. If it all worked out, the President candidly remarked in private, China could be used "as a useful counterpoise to the Soviet Union." He had no doubt but that Chiang would line up with him against Stalin and also against Churchill, who mistrusted China and blasted the Chinese leader as the American "faggot vote." British officials suspected, with good reason, that the Americans intended to replace them as the major foreign economic power in China (a transition well on the way to apparent completion by 1943). Washington officials, their sense of mission and survival magnified by war, intended to westernize China so it would not "take the wrong path—like the Japs," in the words of a top London diplomat.[29]

More immediately, Roosevelt wanted to encourage Chiang to continue fighting Japan, for China was also the centerpiece of U.S. military plans for Asia. As the U.S. Navy and Marines under the direction of Nimitz drove across the central Pacific, and MacArthur's armies cut their way from Australia northward toward the Philippines, air bases in China were to be launching pads for reducing Japan's cities and industries to rubble. China, along with India, was also to be a hub from which Burma, Hong Kong, and other occupied regions were to be liberated. Not the least important of those regions was French Indochina (Vietnam, Laos, and Cambodia), for FDR believed in 1943 he had Chiang's agreement to replace bad French colonialism with good, cooperative Sino-U.S. supervision after the war. (Roosevelt held no hope that the Vietnamese and their neighbors were ready for immediate independence.) The Japanese understood the U.S. plans for China, and countered with their own. These revolved in part around their puppet government of Wang Ching-wei at Nanking. Tokyo officials announced grandiose projects in December 1942 and mid-1943 to work with and strengthen these particular Chinese groups. Japan even offered to surrender its concessions in China, if the war worked out properly. As fearful of the Communists as was the United States, the Japanese repeatedly urged Chiang to discuss peace terms before Mao's forces got out of hand.[30]

Both the Japanese and the Americans once again discovered that neither could shape China's politics. The moment of truth for FDR's China dreams finally came on the battlefields during 1943–44. Chiang's determination to keep his armies intact for a future showdown with the Communists led him to turn away as the Japanese launched offensives in both Burma and China. General Stilwell, fully frustrated by Chiang's refusal to fight, explained the Burma disaster by telling a reporter, "We are allied to an ignorant, illiterate peasant son of a bitch called Chiang Kai-shek." As planes from U.S. bases in China were prepared for bombing their home islands, the Japanese prepared offensives to destroy the airfields. American pilots flew one of the world's most dangerous routes from India across the Himalayas into China to supply the massive force of seven hundred B-29 bombers on these bases. Navigating through some of the globe's worst storms, in planes loaded with twice the weight for which they were designed, the airmen looked down along a route pockmarked by crashes. The transport planes themselves were so new and dangerous that they unexpectedly blew up: "We always flew with the bomb bay doors open to let the gas fumes escape," one airman recalled. Chiang meanwhile flatly defied FDR's requests to do his part by committing Chinese troops (supplied and often trained by Americans) to help the forces in Burma or defend the bases in China. He calculated that Roosevelt had no alternative but to help him, at whatever cost to the United States, and that Americans would willingly continue to die to supply air bases in China. Chiang could thus leave fighting the Japanese to the U.S. Air Force while he prepared for the more important war against the Communists.[31]

By May 1944, FDR told his cabinet he was "greatly concerned" about

the "outlook" in China, and hoped that Chiang "must realize this and
could not let America down after America had pinned such faith and
hope on China as a World Power." Japan then launched a major offensive to destroy the air bases in Southeast China and to link up with
Japanese troops in French Indochina. In August, FDR begged Chiang
to allow Stilwell to take command of Chinese forces so the bases could
be saved. Stilwell recorded that "I handed this bundle of paprika to the
Peanut [Chiang]. . . . The harpoon hit the little bugger right in the solar
plexus. . . . It was a clean hit, but beyond turning green and losing the
power of speech, he did not bat an eye." Within a month, however,
Stilwell and Roosevelt both blinked. Chiang forced FDR to recall the
general. As the President did so he began as well crossing off China as
a potential postwar policeman.[32]

The growing view of Chiang's KMT (Nationalist) Party was expressed
by Life magazine reporter Theodore White: it was "dominated by a corrupt political clique that combines some of the worst features of Tammany Hall and the Spanish Inquisition." "We are being played for
suckers" by the Chinese, White warned. Such pro-Chinese voices as
Pearl Buck, a British official chuckled, were being quieted: "An American once listed the two recent national disasters as Pearl Buck and Pearl
Harbour." The State Department bluntly told Roosevelt that "Chinese
military resistance is disintegrating." The military disaster most preoccupied FDR's advisers, but their growing pessimism about postwar
China was also intensified by fascist, anti-U.S. policies in the economic
and social realms. A detailed British analysis of American business
opinion in late 1944 concluded: "For the American enterprise system
seeking new fields of activity the economic nationalism of the [KMT]
extremists was hardly preferable to Communism." A near-perfect metaphor for U.S. policy occurred in early 1945 when FDR sent the vain,
pompous General Patrick Hurley to China on an important mission.
Hurley insisted on shipping over a huge Cadillac for his own use. The
auto ran three weeks, broke down, and Hurley could not find the necessary parts in China.[33]

Resembling the Cadillac, a broken-down China policy was becoming
less relevant for U.S. planners. MacArthur, and especially Nimitz,
seized the bases necessary for sustained air attacks against Japan. Nim-
itz's amphibious forces overcame Japanese suicide attacks to take
Tarawa in the Gilbert Islands during bloody fighting in November 1943.
The admiral accelerated his schedule to jump 2,000 miles and seize
Kwajalein and Eniwetok islands, a daring move that cut off powerful
Japanese bases in the Marshall Islands. Those bases were then bombed

into submission during the remaining months of the war. In mid-1944, U.S. forces leaped another 1,000 miles west to take the Marianas and seize vital air strips. The triumph did not come cheaply. As the invasion forces hit Saipan, the Japanese Fleet gathered itself for one last effort in the Philippine Sea. With near-perfect intelligence, effective new radar, talented pilots and sailors, and fifteen aircraft carriers, the American ships and planes destroyed the Japanese flotilla (including three carriers), and brought down nearly five hundred enemy aircraft. "The Great Marianas Turkey Shoot," as it was quickly labeled, finished off Japan's once-proud naval air force that Yamamoto had inspired. Seizing the now-vulnerable Tinian and Guam bases, Nimitz's troops prepared extensive airfields in the Marianas.[34]

Saipan, little more than twelve miles long and six miles wide, meanwhile became the scene of terrible losses for the 2nd and 4th Marine divisions, who took two thousand casualties in moving the beachhead one thousand yards the first day. The Americans were astonished by fanaticism of Japanese who had held the island since seizing it from Germany in 1914. Told by Tokyo that Americans would rape, roast babies, and skin adults alive, many civilians blew themselves up with grenades or jumped off high cliffs—where families pushed their children off first and then followed, often running backwards so they would not see the final step. At the end of the 24-day battle, 29,500 of the 31,600 Japanese troops had died, while 3,225 Americans perished and 13,400 more were wounded or missing. But the lethal B-29 bombers, each holding 10 tons of bombs, now had their bases. "Our war was lost with the loss of Saipan," Vice Admiral Miwa Shigeyoshi later said, for the Americans "could cut off our shipping and attack our homeland."[35]

Nimitz's forces moved farther in eight months than had MacArthur's in two years. When the general tried to take the island of Papua to regain the offensive, he had to regroup after his troops suffered one of the war's highest casualty rates. Australian troops took most of the casualties, although MacArthur systematically froze Australian officers out of his decision making. The general was nevertheless determined to drive on toward the Philippines. With the help of the Army's codebreakers in the ULTRA program (who made a major breakthrough in January 1944 when Japanese codebooks were captured), MacArthur could plot precisely the enemy's main forces. MacArthur's main problem was to overcome Roosevelt's reluctance to spend American lives on what was becoming an unimportant strategic objective—MacArthur's beloved Philippines—when compared with Nimitz's (or European) operations. The general allegedly threatened that if the Philippines were bypassed, he would take his case to the American people just as FDR prepared to run for a fourth term. Whatever the political background, on October 20, 1944, MacArthur sent his Sixth Army into Leyte and, wading ashore, uttered his famous "I have returned." (To ensure proper coverage, the general repeated the performance for cameras three more times.)[36]

On October 23–25, the Seventh Fleet and Admiral Halsey's aircraft carriers from the Third Fleet destroyed four carriers, three battleships, and five hundred planes at the Battle of Leyte Gulf. Again, the cost was high. The Americans lost two small carriers and three destroyers in history's largest naval battle. Even then, the Japanese were not giving up. Between October 25 and 28 off Leyte, the first *kamikaze* suicide planes scored direct hits on U.S. ships. With most of their well-trained pilots killed, the Japanese surprised Nimitz by creating this "Divine Wind Special Attack Corps," which needed little special training for their suicide missions.

MacArthur had bragged that since only poor commanders suffered heavy losses, he would take the major Philippine island of Luzon, and the capital, Manila, at low cost in lives. But the battle for Manila between February 3 and March 3, 1945, was one of the war's bloodiest. About 200,000 Japanese died in ferocious fighting. More than 100,000 Filipinos were killed by U.S. shelling and, especially, indiscriminate Japanese brutality. A captured Japanese document instructed soldiers to destroy suspect Filipinos, but waste little ammunition. This led to forcing Filipinos (men, women, and children) inside houses, burning down the house, then bayoneting any who tried to escape. Vicky Quarino, the daughter of a later Philippine president, recalled seeing her mother and sister killed by Japanese gunfire, then watching a Japanese soldier toss her two-year-old sister into the air and spear her on his bayonet. Americans suffered 47,000 casualties and nearly twice that number of non-battle casualties—a remarkably high figure that would have raised embarrassing questions about MacArthur's tactics if the information had been made public. Manila probably suffered more damage during the war than any Allied city except Warsaw.[37]

Using Saipan's bases, the U.S. Air Force began bombing Japan systematically in November 1944. The raids had little effect until a veteran of the European air wars, Major General Curtis E. LeMay, was given command. The cigar-chomping LeMay discovered that the planes were trying to drop heavy-explosive bombs from 25,000 feet where the newly discovered jet stream often blew the planes off course. He quickly ordered his pilots instead to release incendiaries and napalm from 5,000 feet on Japan's wood-constructed cities. The resulting fires, whipped into infernos by high winds, began to incinerate the cities. The bombers were helped by an earthquake and tidal wave that struck Japan on December 7, 1944—a coincidence that led FDR to tell Churchill that "Even the Almighty is helping."[38]

But the pilots of the "Divine Wind" also believed the supernatural was on their side. Throughout January 1945, the suicide planes sank ships and inflicted over one thousand casualties off the Philippines until Japan ran out of aircraft (not out of pilots). Worse lay ahead. U.S. forces invading Iwo Jima on February 19, 1945, found themselves in the bloodiest campaign in Marine Corps history. During five weeks of brutal fighting, 6,821 Marines died and nearly 20,000 were wounded, as they employed flamethrowers and dynamite to kill nearly all the 21,000 Japanese who fought from caves on the eight-square-mile island of rock and black sand. Americans, however, now held a strategic air base just seven hundred miles from Tokyo. With LeMay working his crews to exhaustion, U.S. planes burned down major Japanese cities. The night of March 9–10, 1945, some 300 B-29s killed at least 84,000 in a single raid on Tokyo. The raid targeted one of the world's most densely populated areas where more than 135,000 people per square mile lived. Flames turned so hot that water boiled in canals, while glass liquefied and ran in the street. Apparently ten U.S. bombers were destroyed by the updrafts of the heat.[39]

But even as the U.S. offensive accelerated toward the home islands, the Japanese were humiliating Chinese forces and their American supporters. The effect in Washington was direct and historic. In February 1942, FDR had established an Advisory Committee on Postwar Foreign Policy, under Secretary of State Hull, whose subcommittees on Japan were dominated by such old China hands as Stanley Hornbeck. As Hornbeck phrased it, "It will be possible for us to get along without Japan in the postwar world," and, again, "It would be quite possible for us to let the Japanese nation disappear." Or so the China hands wanted to believe. They were supported by many Republicans who had been anti-interventionist in the late 1930s and now took out their frustrations by vowing to outdo others in revenging Pearl Harbor and carrying out the supposed historic American mission in China. Ambassador Lord Halifax told London officials that Washington gossips believed "The Administration is fighting the Axis—the Republican Party is fighting Japan."[40]

By 1943, these China hands on the advisory committee found themselves losing ground to Japan hands. Seldom numbering more than eight or ten, this Japan faction was a tight-knit, experienced group led by Joseph Ballantine, Eugene Dooman, Hugh Borton of Columbia University, and other knowledgeable scholars including George Blakeslee of Clark University. By 1944, the group was dominated by former ambassador Joseph Grew. As rising concern over postwar China gripped Washington in 1944, this faction carefully, systematically, and quietly laid plans for reviving a defeated Japan. They were immensely helped by Chiang's corrupt, uncooperative regime and by Admiral Nimitz's conquests, which by late 1944 had largely removed the U.S. need for China's air bases.[41]

The Japan hands' deliberations did not shape FDR's decisions at the November 1943 Cairo Conference when he met with Chiang and Winston Churchill. But Roosevelt's actions at Cairo gave invaluable help to the Japan hands. To the world's surprise (and, to a certain extent, each other's), the leaders announced the Allies would fight until Japan and Germany surrendered unconditionally. Roosevelt did not aim the policy primarily at the Japanese and Germans. He hoped instead to reassure a restless Joseph Stalin, who was becoming prickly as Soviet troops sacrificed millions of lives while Roosevelt and Churchill stalled in opening a second front in Western Europe. The announcement nevertheless promised to strip Japan of Manchuria, Formosa, Korea, and the Pacific islands seized from Germany in 1914. As Hugh Borton later observed, FDR's decision at Cairo settled vital postwar territorial issues in the Pacific and allowed the Japan hands to concentrate on central political issues. The decision also unilaterally established a postwar policy of utmost importance: Japan would not be allowed to live by exploiting its old colonial Asian empire, but would have to integrate itself within a much larger, U.S.-dominated economic system.[42] ·

By May 1943, the Japan hands had developed a paper that discussed all sides of the emotionally explosive question of whether to keep the Emperor as an institution after the war. The paper did not explicitly take a position, but it was clear where the writers' sympathies lay—so clear that Assistant Secretary of State Dean Acheson, who wanted to eliminate the Emperor, attacked the document. Such formidable opposition did not slow the Japan hands. In October 1943, Borton circulated a paper that set out many of the essential points that were to govern actual postwar policy toward Japan. First, he recommended thorough constitutional changes that included retaining an emperor with limited powers; destroying possible military control by making the cabinet responsible to the legislature (Diet), while giving the Diet control of the budget; and removing the military from other spheres of political decision making. Second, Borton proposed a U.S.-style bill of rights. Third, U.S. authorities, he suggested, should try not to impose these fundamental changes by force or fiat, but use education and economic pressures to convince the Japanese they should institute the changes themselves. As light a hand as possible was to be used—a remarkable suggestion given the racism and bloodshed that drenched Japanese and American memories. These proposals were also startling when compared with plans for a defeated Germany, where Allied authorities planned radical change for Hitler's former Reich; FDR even talked loosely of mass castration and forcing Germans to obtain their food from soup kitchens.[43]

In 1944, Hull set up a higher-level planning group, the Postwar Programs Committee. The Japan hands, with the savvy Grew leading the way, were ready to impose their ideas on the new committee. A February 1944 paper by Borton again examined the Emperor question from various sides, but favored retention. After all, Borton argued, if the Atlantic Charter's self-determination principles were to be taken seriously, the Japanese would clearly determine to keep the Emperor. Borton added that retention would also allow the Emperor's (rather than the suicidal military's) agreement to a surrender. The Japan hands emphasized that the Emperor could be a force for postwar "stability and reform" in a highly uncertain country. Everyone agreed, however, that the Emperor was no longer to be considered divine or superior to other rulers. The Japan hands further agreed that Japan must be stripped of all military forces. If some units were later deemed necessary, their officers were to be cut off from all political decision making. Unconditional surrender, the Japan hands concluded, was not to mean annihilation. Japan was to be rebuilt and reformed, not torn apart and humiliated. Finally, all this was to occur in a united Japan undivided by occupying armies or different administrations. The United States was to run the show. The similarity of these plans to the actual policies applied to postwar Japan is extraordinary.[44]

So, too, is the wartime economic planning. An influential secret paper came from Robert Fearey, once Grew's personal secretary in Japan, now in 1944 a State Department official. With the fall of the imperial empire, Fearey argued, Japan's tragic mentality about the need for forming, exploiting, and—especially—expanding economic blocs could be destroyed. In its place could be an enlightened policy that gave Japan "access to world resources on a par with other nations," remove a need for colonial empires, and lead the Japanese to find their raw materials and markets in a global marketplace formed by multilateral relationships. The success of political reforms, Fearey believed, depended in the long run on the success of economic reforms. U.S. officials sought to recreate the Japan of the 1920s—the Japan of Shidehara, of Thomas Lamont's banking friends, of a nation integrated into a U.S.-created system. Only this time there was to be no military alternative, and policies were to be rooted in the State Department's long-held views rather than in Wall Street's short-term profit seeking.[45]

The Japan hands thus had a coherent set of postwar plans in place by the autumn of 1944 when Chiang defied FDR and as U.S. Ambassador W. Averell Harriman in Moscow warned the President about Soviet postwar ambitions in Asia. "Unless we take issue with the present policy" of Stalin, Harriman warned, "there is every indication the Soviet Union will become a world bully wherever their interests are involved. This policy will reach into China and the Pacific as well when they can turn their attention in that direction." FDR understood the danger as he prepared for summit talks at the Soviet Crimean port of Yalta in February 1945. He apparently did not study the Japan hands' papers, but most of his deals at Yalta did not undo their core plans. Without consulting Chiang, Roosevelt cut deals with Stalin in which the dictator recognized China's sovereignty in Manchuria and promised Sino-Soviet friendship talks. In what became known as the "Yalta system," FDR's major goal was less to make the Chinese a U.S.-led world policeman than shrewdly pushing Chiang and Stalin together so the Chinese Communists would be isolated. Roosevelt gratefully gave Stalin the southern half of Sakhalin (the island Japan had seized from Russia in 1905), the Kurile Islands off the Siberian coast, control of the Chinese ports of Port Arthur and Dairen, recognition of Stalin's dominance in Outer Mongolia, and de facto power over the Chinese Eastern Railway. In return, Stalin uttered the words FDR especially wanted to hear: a promise to enter the war against Japan once the European conflict ended.[46]

Truman and the Destruction of the Yalta System

Roosevelt now admitted that one of his policemen had quit on him. "Three generations of education and training would be required before China could become a serious factor," he remarked in early 1945. While, however, he improvised tactics, FDR did not surrender his strategic vision. In 1944 he had warned that "world business, after the war, must be expanded on a basis of nondiscrimination and of freedom from excessive barriers and restraints." The policemen were to ensure that such barriers came down. In the Pacific, the number of police was down to three, and perhaps two: Roosevelt fervently believed that Churchill only wanted to recreate the British colonial empire. "All they want is Singapore back," FDR said with disgust. He had once worked to replace the French colonials in Indochina, perhaps with Chinese influence. In early 1945, however, when Japan destroyed the remnants of the pro-Axis French regime and took over direct control of Indochina, Roosevelt agreed to avert his eyes while French and British troops moved to liberate the region. Dealing with the British had nevertheless become so distasteful to U.S. officials that they went along with Congress's desire to cut off all lend-lease aid to Great Britain after victory was won in Europe, except the very minimum needed to carry on the fight against Japan. Washington also later decided that neither independent French nor Dutch troops should be allowed to join in the final battles against Japan. In Asia, Washington policymakers seemed perilously close to trying to create an American Century single-handedly.[47]

U.S. power, FDR and his advisers decreed, was to be greatly strengthened after the war by taking over an array of Pacific bases. Notably, the Japan hands agreed that the United States should hold former Japanese islands as part of a network for both security and postwar commercial air travel—a form of travel that promised to be the new frontier of postwar commerce. Just before his death in April 1945, FDR supported the idea of U.S. trusteeships, under United Nations supervision, over the islands on which American bases would be built. In reality, as Roosevelt probably realized, this policy led to the Territory of the Pacific Islands (Carolines, Marianas, and Marshalls) coming under de facto U.S. control while conveniently being called a UN trusteeship. By mid-1945, U.S. officials also intended to take over Okinawa and the adjoining Ryukyus, with their Japanese inhabitants, because of the islands' strategic importance.[48]

Okinawa became a delicate question, partly because of its vital location, partly because Japan had controlled it, partly because the conquest of the island during the spring of 1945 had been unusually costly and brutal even by the Pacific War's blood-soaked standards—"an Asian *Gotterdämmerung*," as historians later called this three-month battle for an area less than half the size of Rhode Island. Fighting only 360 miles from their home islands, *kamikaze* killed 5,000 American sailors while destroying or disabling 28 ships. (In all throughout the war, 1,228 *kamikaze* pilots lost their lives while sinking 34 U.S. ships and damaging 288 others.) Japanese troops killed 10,000 Americans in two Army and two Marine divisions, wounding 30,000 more before being annihilated while suffering more than 100,000 dead. Both of the top U.S. and Japanese commanders were killed, as was the famed war reporter Ernie Pyle, victim of a sniper's bullet. At least 100,000 Okinawans died. U.S. planes caught the giant 72,000-ton battleship *Yamato*—built in the 1930s in open violation of the 1922 Washington naval agreements—en route to Okinawa and sank it along with three thousand of its crew in the largest single loss of life in naval history. By April 7, 1945, U.S. planes were using Okinawa bases to bomb Japan. Later that month, Nimitz's new blockade of Japan claimed its first victim when Tokyo had to close the port of Nagoya.[49]

On June 18, 1945, plans for the invasion of Japan (codenamed OLYM-PIC) received final approval. Doubts, however, were already rising over whether U.S. troops would ever have to storm the home islands. U.S. warships tightened the blockade until the Japanese tanker fleet and merchant marine were virtually paralyzed. Bombing became so intense that Washington officials began to see it as a laboratory study. The raids gave "us a chance to find out whether air power can bring a nation to its knees or not," as Robert Lovett of the War Department phrased it. Lovett and the Air Force assured Stimson (whose old-time morality and gentlemanly concern about civilian casualties were not shared by most other officials) that pilots dropped their bombs on military targets. By August 1945, however, the planes had destroyed most of 67 cities, killed 300,000, wounded some 400,000, while losing 437 bombers, mostly due to mechanical failures. (In comparison, more than 3,000 bombers were lost over European targets.) Stimson worried about getting "the reputation of outdoing Hitler in atrocities." Few other officials shared the Secretary of War's concern. But the publisher Oswald Garrison Villard bitterly wrote that "What was criminal in Coventry, Rotterdam, Warsaw, and London has now become heroic first in Dresden and now in Tokyo."[50]

Given the tightening air and sea noose, the central question became how many Allied (mainly American) lives would be lost in an invasion of the home islands—or whether an invasion was even necessary. The Joint Chiefs of Staff's plans projected a November 1 landing on Kyushu, the southernmost of the islands, then using the area as an air base from which to pound the rest of the country, and finally—if Japan still held out—to invade the Tokyo plain on March 1, 1946. The struggle over these plans between the Navy (which wanted to tighten the blockade) and Army (which thought only infantry could end the war) was intense. Less intense was the argument over possible costs. Americans had lost more lives in just the January–to–June 1945 Pacific battles than during the previous three years in that theater. In June 1945, President Harry Truman feared another Okinawa "from one end of Japan to the other." Twenty years later, he recalled his fear that as many as 750,000 American casualties, with 250,000 killed, might have occurred. In mid-1945, however, the top strategic planners concluded that with 767,000 troops used in the planned November 1 invasion of Kyushu, there would be 31,000 casualties in the first month, with about 25,000 dead. The March 1, 1946, invasion would cost another 15,000 to 21,000 American dead. The lower estimates were horrific enough. The War Department began planning for possible gas warfare in November; knowledge gleaned from ULTRA intercepts indicated Japanese fears that they could not deal with gas. According to General Marshall's later recollection, as many as nine atomic bombs were to be readied for use to reduce casualties.[51]

By midsummer 1945, however, another, and as it turned out more real and more ominous danger appeared to haunt Washington. Within twenty-four hours after FDR died in April, President Truman told Secretary of State Edward Stettinius "that we must stand up to the Russians at this point and that we must not be easy with them." Truman said this while knowing little, if anything, about the actual state of U.S.-USSR relations, and knowing virtually nothing about the deals Roosevelt, Churchill, and Stalin had cut at summit meetings. The new President spoke partly out of his deeply rooted anti-Soviet feelings, and mostly out of a personal insecurity that understandably marked his early months in office. Stettinius accurately told Truman that "a very tough exchange of wires between Stalin and the President" about European questions had occurred just before FDR died. But at Yalta, Roosevelt and Stalin had worked out an agreement on Asia. As an informed Russian scholar later noted, Stalin saw himself as "an heir" of the tsars who had scores to settle with Japan, and he was willing to obtain revenge (and some valuable territory) while subordinating the interests of Mao, whose growing power and peasant-based communism aroused deep suspicion in Moscow.[52]

The Yalta arrangements fit U.S. interests—as long as Truman believed he needed Soviet help to defeat Japan. By May 1945, that belief was disappearing along with the cold weather in Washington. Japan was obviously on the ropes. The Joint Chiefs of Staff decided that an "early Russian entry into the war . . . is no longer necessary." In a June 18 meeting, Admiral Ernest J. King, the Navy's top uniformed official, said flatly that the Russians were "not indispensable" and need not be begged "to come in." In a May note to Grew, however, Stimson warned that the issue was perhaps moot since the Soviets were going to enter the war anyway—"on their own military and political basis with little regard to any political action taken by the United States." Nor could they be kept out, "unless we choose to use force." Stimson considered reopening the Yalta decisions, but decided that not "much good will come of a rediscussion at this time." The powerful, fervently anti-Communist Secretary of the Navy, James Forrestal, agreed with Stimson.[53]

Truman rejected Stimson and Forrestal's advice. He was determined to dismantle the Yalta agreements. But first he had to find out what they were. Truman did this, he thought, by appointing James F. Byrnes to replace the handsome, inconsequential Stettinius as Secretary of State. Byrnes had been at Yalta with FDR before returning to help sell the agreements to Congress while parading his supposed inside knowledge. The South Carolinian was an insider: a former Supreme Court Justice, known as an "assistant President" to FDR, and confident that he had the vice presidency in 1944 until FDR and Democratic bosses picked Truman. So now the real President turned to this admired political fixer in the belief that "it's the only way I can be sure of knowing what went on at Yalta." In reality, Byrnes knew only a small part of what went on at Yalta. FDR, typically, had used Byrnes for his own purposes, then shunted him aside when the President met secretly with Stalin. Truman and Byrnes, for example, were not pleased in late May 1945 to learn that Stalin had told Harriman that the Soviets expected to share in the Japanese occupation. At Yalta, FDR had apparently never made clear the U.S. intention to keep Japan as a single occupation zone under an American commander.[54]

Truman not only intended to clarify that point, but at the upcoming summit (planned for Potsdam, Germany) to establish the open-door policy in Manchuria and elsewhere in the region. He received a strong push from Herbert Hoover, whom FDR had refused to invite to the White House but who was soon welcomed by the new President. The Russians "were Asiatics" and so "did not have the reverence for agreements that was current among Western nations," Hoover told Truman without irony. Hoover urged that the Soviets be kept out, Japan demilitarized, Manchuria returned to China, and Korea and Formosa kept under Japanese control. The Japan hands were certainly not willing to go that far. Above all, they wanted to kill the colonial empire so that the Japanese would have to be integrated into an American-led global system.

They did share Hoover's belief that Japan—not China—should serve as Washington's Asian hub. By mid-1945, moreover, they were riding high as their leader, Joseph Grew, ran the State Department while, in the much-used phrase, "Byrnes roams." The Japan hands' main objectives were now to keep the occupation wholly under U.S. control and to ensure that the Emperor be preserved to "prevent chaos." If the "emperorship" was pulled down, they warned, "the Japanese themselves would take it right back as soon as our backs were turned, and we cannot very well occupy Japan permanently." General Marshall and the Joint Chiefs agreed because, as they told Truman, the military feared that only the Emperor could convince fanatical Japanese in "outlying areas as well as in Japan proper" to surrender peacefully. When, however, Truman broadcast a message to the Japanese on the day Germany surrendered (May 9, 1945), he refused to modify "unconditional surrender" with Grew's pet phrase that the Japanese should determine "their future political structure." Truman was apparently fearful of U.S. political repercussions if he implied the Emperor could remain. Byrnes regularly reinforced those fears.[55]

The President understood that to pick apart the Yalta system, prevent Stalin from seizing valuable territory, guarantee the open door in Asia, and build the Japan he and Grew's friends wanted required more military and diplomatic leverage than even he possessed in June 1945. But great hope materialized on April 25, when Stimson briefed him for the first time about the atomic bomb. The President learned that a bomb would be available during the summer; that the Americans and British monopolized the necessary materials; and that the Soviets were spying on the project.

In May 1945, the secret eight-person Interim Committee of scientists and officials headed by Stimson (who had established it to discuss the possible use of the weapon) argued heatedly. With some dissent, the committee agreed that the bomb should not only be employed against a military target, but in an area where "the greatest psychological effect against Japan" could be registered, and also so the weapon's importance would "be internationally recognized." Stimson finally "agreed that the most desirable target would be a vital war plant employing a large number of workers and closely surrounded by workers' houses." In other words, civilians were to be targeted. The Interim Committee quickly rejected a mere demonstration; it feared, among other reasons, that the device might malfunction or the Japanese observers might not be sufficiently impressed. On May 28, Truman agreed to meet Stalin and Churchill at Potsdam in mid-July. On June 6, the Interim Committee recommended to the President that the bomb be dropped as soon as possible on a Japanese city. Stimson overruled an angry Brigadier General Leslie Groves, who headed the Manhattan Project that was building the weapon, by removing the ancient city of Kyoto from the target list. Although full of industry, Kyoto had once been the Emperor's home. Stimson wanted no "bitterness" that "might make it impossible during the long postwar period to reconcile the Japanese to us in that area [of Eastern Asia] rather than the Russians."[56]

Forrestal questioned using the bomb at all. The Secretary of the Navy represented his service's belief that its blockade and airpower could force Japan to its knees without either an invasion or an atomic bombing. Forrestal's objections went much further. Really, he asked, do "we want to Morgenthau those islands—do we want to destroy the whole industrial potential" (as former Secretary of the Treasury Henry Morgenthau had wanted to reduce Germany to a pastoral economy). The Soviets, Forrestal believed, posed the real danger. The pivotal question was "should it be China or Japan" that Americans should use as a "counterweight." Believing that the Japanese were the best bet, he wanted their postwar economy to recover quickly. Forrestal later lamented that so "little thought" was given to the larger "relationships" that had to pivot around Japan and Germany if Asia and Europe were to be orderly, healthy, and non-Communist.[57]

Truman and especially Stimson shared Forrestal's anguish, but unlike him, they saw the bomb as the answer. For them, the immediate problem was to keep the Soviets as far away from the home islands as possible. The atomic bomb was the only weapon in Truman's arsenal that could both end the war quickly and impress Stalin with overwhelming U.S. power in East Asia. In June, Stimson even worried that Japan was already so bombed out that, as he told Truman, "the new weapon would not have a fair background to show its strength." The President "laughed and said he understood." In that same conversation, Stimson urged Truman to postpone the Potsdam Conference "until the first bomb had been successfully laid on Japan." Then "quid pro quos" could be obtained from Stalin, including the settlement of the "Polish, Rumanian, Yugoslavian, and Manchurian problems."[58]

Truman decided to go ahead with the conference. When it opened just outside the rubble that had once been the city of Berlin, on July 17, 1945, the President—an avid poker player—knew he held two aces. The first was the successful test of an atomic device in the New Mexico desert the day before. The power of the explosion stunned observing scientists. "I am sure," said one, "that at the end of the world—in the last millisecond of the earth's existence—the last man will see what we saw." Truman received the news in code: "Baby satisfactorily born." He was, Stimson noted, "tremendously pepped up" by the message.

Churchill even called Truman "a changed man." The President believed he now held what Stimson had termed "your master card in your hand." But Truman had another ace: Tokyo, he knew from U.S. intelligence intercepts, had asked the Soviets to mediate a peace by modifying the unconditional surrender terms. The President also knew that Stalin had coldly turned aside the initiative. The dictator could obtain much more from the powerful United States than from a devastated Japan, especially if Truman kept his part of the Yalta arrangements.[59]

Stalin personally called on the 17th, Truman recorded. "He'll be in the Jap War on August 15th. Fini Japs when that comes about. . . . I can deal with Stalin. He is honest—but smart as hell." The President thus realized how close Japan was to surrender, even without the dropping of an atomic bomb. The dictator indicated he remained pledged to entering the war, but added that he had not yet been able to make a deal with Chiang's regime.[60]

Truman used that opening to begin dismantling the Yalta system. FDR had promised Stalin control of Dairen; Truman instead followed a State Department briefing paper's advice by successfully pushing the dictator to recognize the open-door principle in that vital commercial entranceway. The President bragged to Stimson he had "clinched the Open Door in Manchuria." The next morning when Stimson told Truman the details of the atomic test, "The President again repeated that he was confident of sustaining the Open Door policy," Stimson recorded. Having learned about the device's incredible power, Truman and Byrnes then turned against the Soviet entry into the Asian conflict. The President concluded the "Japs will fold up before Russia comes in. I am sure they will when Manhattan appears over their homeland." The bomb was not only to end the war but make the Yalta agreements on Asia irrelevant. Stalin understood the thrust of the policy, and when Truman finally told him about the bomb on July 24 (without mentioning it was an atomic device), the dictator, to the President's dismay, was passive—a pose shaped by his knowledge from spies about the Manhattan Project, but also by the realization (as a later Russian historian phrased it) that in a game with these kinds of stakes, a poker face was necessary.[61]

The "Double Shock"—and the End

On July 25, Truman gave the order for the new bomb to be used against Japan. The next day, the Big Three powers issued the Potsdam Declaration demanding "the unconditional surrender of all Japanese armed forces" before the islands suffered utter devastation. It said nothing specifically about the new weapon, nor did it mention the Emperor's future. Stimson wanted to assure the "Japanese on the continuance of their dynasty," but Byrnes outmaneuvered him. This sequence of events was important. Contrary to Truman's later claims, he secretly ordered the bomb to be dropped *before* he knew that the Japanese had not accepted the Potsdam ultimatum. He could, of course, have canceled the order. But the sequence, as well as other evidence, suggests that the President was concerned less with Japan's ultimate surrender— which, as he repeatedly noted, was imminent—than with ensuring that the surrender occurred as early as possible and preferably before the Red Army could forcefully redeem the promises made at Yalta. An alternative might have been not to use the bomb, but instead to tighten the blockade, step up air attacks, and perhaps invade Kyushu. Such an alternative, however, would certainly result in Soviet troops moving far into Manchuria, Korea, and, perhaps, in the final stage into Japan itself.[62]

The Japanese continued to approach the Soviets for help while urgently discussing in Tokyo the need to maintain the Emperor. U.S. intelligence kept Truman fully appraised of these external approaches and internal Japanese discussions. On August 6, the Air Force prepared to deliver the first atomic bomb. Colonel Paul W. Tibbets, pilot of the *Enola Gay* that was to drop the bomb, learned from the advance weather plane that conditions over the target city of Hiroshima were good. At 8:15 A.M., from 31,000 feet, the 9,000-pound bomb was released. Its detonation was timed forty-three seconds later so the blast would have the largest possible radius above ground.

When the weather plane had turned back, Hiroshima authorities sounded an all-clear signal. Thus tens of thousands, in this city of a half-million souls, were on their way to work or school. The center of the explosion, within one-millionth of a second, rose to 5,400 degrees Fahrenheit. A light appeared 3,000 times brighter than the sun. A fireball formed. Out of the fireball emanated thermal radiation that accounted for fully one-third of the bomb's energy. The radiation instantly scorched humans, trees, houses. As the air heated and rushed upward, cold air flowed in to ignite a firestorm that by 11:00 A.M., three hours after the bombing, was burning more than 50 feet per second. Between 11:00 A.M. and 3:00 P.M., a whirlwind whipped the flames to their peak until more than eight square miles were virtually in cinders. Black, muddy rain, full of radioactive fallout, began to drop. It was so sticky that people thought it was oil. The rain was cold. People shivered even as the fires spread. Fourteen-year-old Takahashi Akihiro was so badly burned that he jumped into the river, where he watched corpses float by. Estimates run that 80,000 to 100,000 died immediately, including 12 captured, imprisoned U.S. Navy fliers. An estimated 40,000 later died of atomic-bomb illness—radiation that destroyed the healthy cells and the immune system. Kuboura Hirota noted that "people walked like ghosts. They wanted to drink and they were crying and calling for their family and they lay down and couldn't get up and they died."[63]

Truman learned of the blast while en route home on his ship from Potsdam. Angry that the radio station he was listening to made only a simple announcement of the event before returning to its regular program, he told friends, "This is the greatest day in history." In a public announcement, Truman declared that "the force from which the sun draws its power has been loosed against those who brought war to the Far East." U.S. officials did not know exactly what had happened because of the "impenetrable cloud of dust and smoke" (as the War Department put it) above the city. For the next twenty-four hours, the Japanese, including a badly shaken emperor and fanatical army leaders who announced they were prepared to fight to the last man, continued to hope that somehow the Soviets would help so the surrender would not be unconditional. Tokyo officials knew quite well that U.S. and USSR global views were diverging, and they hoped to exploit the growing gap. On August 7, Foreign Minister Molotov finally agreed to meet the Japanese ambassador, Sato Naotake. To Sato's stunned surprise, Molotov handed him a declaration of war effective the next day against the Russians' historic rival.[64]

As the Red Army began overrunning the Kwantung Army on August 9, a B-29, nicknamed "Bock's Car," and carrying an atomic bomb, veered away from Kokura after a weather plane radioed that heavy clouds shrouded this primary target. The aircraft flew to the backup target, Nagasaki, and dropped its lethal cargo at 11:02 A.M. Because of clouds the bomb was dropped by radar. The weapon, made from plutonium, had a total energy greater than the Hiroshima bomb, but as a result of topography, the blast effect was less. It instantly destroyed four square miles. A violent fire developed about two hours after the explosion. Estimates placed the number killed by the blast and radiation at about seventy thousand. In a letter to the U.S. Federal Council of Churches of Christ, Truman declared, "When you have to deal with a beast you have to treat him as a beast. It is most regrettable but nevertheless true."[65]

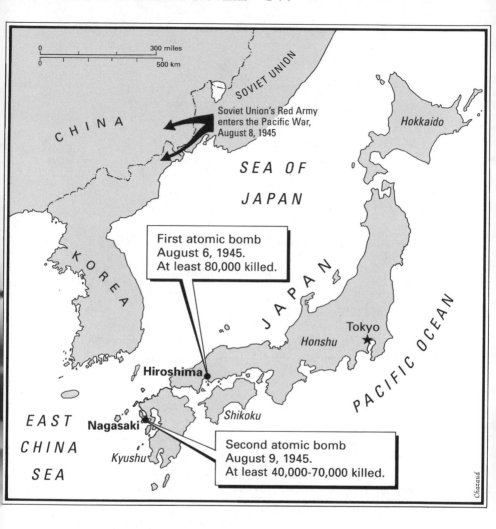

First atomic bomb
August 6, 1945.
At least 80,000 killed.

Soviet Union's Red Army
enters the Pacific War,
August 8, 1945

Second atomic bomb
August 9, 1945.
At least 40,000-70,000 killed.

The President, however, now had another immediate problem (it is "to our interest," he told the cabinet, "that the Russians not push too far into Manchuria") to complicate the first (obtaining Japan's surrender unconditionally). His fear of the Soviets did not diminish when, on August 10, Molotov encouraged the Americans to reject the Japanese surrender offer of that day, then pressed Ambassador Harriman for a Soviet role in the Japanese occupation—a request Harriman quickly called "absolutely inadmissible." When Molotov dangled the hint that U.S. cooperation in Japan might indicate how cooperative the Soviet army would be in Eastern Europe, the ambassador refused to bite. Stalin, intent on creating at least a buffer state in Manchuria, dismantled industrial facilities in the region for shipment westward. He secretly ordered Chinese and Korean Communists to prepare "to construct the Northeast" after the Red Army was finished looting. Equally revealing was Stalin's comment when he opened talks with Chiang Kai-shek's regime about postwar Asia: "In the past, Russia wanted an alliance with Japan in order to break up China. Now we want an alliance with China to curb Japan." Even after the second atomic bomb, Stalin believed the Japanese would quickly rebuild and "war may come in 10, 15, 20 years." Most revealing of all was a Red Army officer's ominous remark about the atomic bomb, a remark quickly relayed to Truman: "A revolutionary technical discovery; nevertheless we shall hold Manchuria."[66]

Stalin even parachuted troops into Port Arthur and Dairen to ensure quick control of those prizes. Truman's fears were not misplaced. Soviet documents released in the 1990s showed Stalin preparing to invade northern Japan itself about August 25. The central question for Truman was whether he could obtain Japan's surrender before the Red Army reached the home islands. It was a question the President and Byrnes mishandled during the ninety-six hours after Tokyo Radio announced on August 10 that Japan was ready to surrender if the Emperor's prerogatives were not prejudiced. During those hours of August 10 to 14, moreover, the Japanese suffered some of the war's heaviest air and sea bombardment.[67]

As early as April 1943, Emperor Hirohito had understood that the war was going badly and peace was advisable. The year before he had appeared in uniform, riding a white horse, while reviewing the troops as the supreme commander—a picture Allied propagandists constantly ran in newspapers and movie newsreels. Hirohito had even once openly congratulated Hitler for German victories, a mistake the Emperor never again made. But if he had deep reservations about continuing the war in 1943, he believed he could not intervene effectively until Prime Minister Tojo was removed. Tojo's dedication to fighting the war to victory, or to a blazing Armageddon, was total. Even with his immense political power (he held several cabinet posts, including army minister), however, Tojo could not bring order and efficiency out of the continual fighting between the army and navy. (Tojo later claimed the navy did not tell him about the dimensions of the Midway disaster until a month after it occurred.) Of perhaps equal importance, Hirohito feared that given the service rivalry, faltering war effort, and Tojo's growing responsibilities, the general was an obvious target for assassination. If such violence erupted, it could rapidly spread. Under intense pressure from

Prince Konoe and the shrewd, powerful Kido Koichi (of royal blood and Lord Keeper of the Privy Seal since 1940), Hirohito reluctantly agreed to replace Tojo with General Koiso Kuniaki. Koiso's appointment, the advisers argued, would short-circuit the service rivalry and also possible pro-Tojo revolts within the army.[68]

But Koiso's ineffectiveness accelerated Japan's military decline. Nor could he damp down the army-navy infighting. On February 14, 1945, Konoe handed his close friend, the Emperor, a memorial that urgently requested approaching the Americans and British before the army tried to make a deal with the Soviets that could bring Japan under Communist rule. Konoe warned that "What we need to fear," far more than defeat, is the Communist revolution that will follow it." Chinese Communists, he knew, were working with Japanese prisoners to form alliances with other Japanese Communists in Moscow, Korea, and Taiwan. Fearing that "the majority of young soldiers seem to believe that Communism and Japan's Sacred National Polity are by no means incompatible . . . ," Konoe added ingeniously that "I have heard there are even members of the Imperial Family who are showing some interest in this view," as were soldiers from especially the lower classes. The Emperor was not yet ready to act on these warnings, but Konoe's fears were not imaginary. Since the February 26, 1936, army revolt, the anti-Soviet military faction had been nearly destroyed, while the "control faction," once led by Tojo, had dominated policy with its plans to create an empire to the south while cooperating with the Soviets in the north.[69]

Konoe's approach to the Americans and British, however, had a price: retaining the Emperor as an institution. Konoe, resembling Kido and the other elder statesmen, viewed the Emperor as a last bastion against revolution, anarchy, and indeed the disintegration of what they saw as a 2,600-year-old Japanese state. Konoe's appeal went nowhere in early 1945 because the military hierarchy was determined to use the remaining 2.5 million soldiers and 4 million reservists to wage a fanatical resistance until Truman would have to settle for a less than unconditional surrender. By late July, however, the military's determination was being undermined. Admiral Suzuki Kantaro, prime minister since April, had been told by Kido and other elders to keep the military in line while peace talks were worked out.[70]

This assignment proved to be difficult, even suicidal, for Suzuki and his war minister, General Anami Korechika, who was to play a heroic, tragic role in the decisive August moments. Truman had rejected Stimson's plea that the Emperor be protected. The President instead went along with Byrnes, who feared the political "crucifixion" of Truman if he compromised unconditional surrender. Byrnes was forcefully joined by former Secretary of State Hull, still nursing his fury over his 1941 talks with the Japanese. Hull contemptuously condemned Stimson's suggestion as "appeasement of Japan." The absence of any mention of the Japanese throne in the U.S. response split the Tokyo government: the Foreign Office, led by Foreign Minister Togo Shigenori, believed the Potsdam Declaration opened possibilities for useful negotiations. But the supreme command disdained any terms that did not directly preserve the Emperor. The cabinet finally decided to compromise and *mokatsu* the Declaration—that is, take no notice of it until the Soviets were again approached for help. But in one of the war's great mistakes, *mokatsu* appeared in newspapers and even in a Suzuki press conference as meaning the Japanese intended to ignore the Potsdam announcement. In Washington, "ignore" was quickly interpreted, even by Stimson, as "reject."[71]

The dropping of the atomic bombs and the onslaught of massive Soviet armies followed. This "double shock," as a Japanese historian later termed it, forced the Emperor to intervene on August 9–10 and formulate a surrender offer. On August 10, the Suzuki government offered to accept "the terms . . . in the joint declaration" of Potsdam, "with the understanding that the said declaration does not comprise any demand which prejudices the prerogatives of His Majesty as a Sovereign Ruler." As Robert J. C. Butow wrote in his classic analysis of these August events, "If the Allies meant to wipe out, in one stroke, an imperial institution tenaciously rooted in the mind and soul of every true Japanese . . . if they sought to deny to His Majesty's subjects the very polity upon which they rested their claims to being Japanese," then those favoring peace would join the military fanatics and there would be no peace.[72]

The ball was now in Truman's court. Byrnes urged no compromise. Stimson grew angry. The Secretary of War had probably suffered a small heart attack on August 8, but he continued to push his argument—especially damning the "uninformed agitation against the Emperor in this country mostly by people who know no more about Japan than has been given them by Gilbert and Sullivan's 'Mikado.'" At a historic White House meeting on August 10, Leahy and Forrestal supported Stimson's demand that the Japanese offer should be immediately accepted. Only the Emperor, he told Truman, could convince Japanese fanatics to surrender and thus "save us from a score of Iwo Jimas and Okinawas." The Secretary of War had earlier told his top aides he "felt it was of great importance to get the homeland into our hands before the Russians" arrived to "help rule it." Byrnes meanwhile was trapped by his own myopia: he agreed with Stimson about stopping the Russians, but was driven by fears that Truman would be "crucified" (perhaps along with himself) if unconditional surrender were modified to save the hated Emperor. A master domestic "fixer," the Secretary of State had little talent for conceptualizing foreign policy. He could, however, convince an insecure president that he had the pulse of the American people. Forrestal suggested a compromise: Reiterate the Potsdam principles but leave open the future of the Emperor's position. Byrnes added a phrase to protect Truman: the Emperor and the Japanese government would be "subject to the Supreme Commander of the Allied powers" occupying the home islands. Stimson agreed, and emphasized that the word "Commander" was "singular in order to exclude any condominium such as we have in Poland." The reply also included the Potsdam Declaration's line that Japan's future government "shall . . . be established by the freely expressed will of the Japanese people."[73]

In Tokyo, hard-liners read this last phrase once again as an American ploy to undercut imperial institutions. Between August 11 and 14 a vicious political struggle erupted between, on the one hand, Foreign Minister Togo and Lord Keeper of the Privy Seal Kido, who wanted to accept the U.S. response; and, on the other, General Anami and the military, who feared that surrender would forever destroy *kokutai*, the revered national polity. Togo and Kido barely prevented the military from adding extraordinary new conditions to the peace terms: no occupation or disarmament of Japan. The originator of the *kamikaze* attacks, Vice Chief of the Naval General Staff Onishi, tried to convince his superiors that "If we are prepared to sacrifice 20,000,000 Japanese lives in a special attack *[kamikaze]* effort, victory shall be ours!"[74]

Meanwhile, Allied planes and ships delivered some of the most devastating attacks of the entire war. Stimson and Forrestal urged that the attacks be stopped because they were unneeded, politically unwise, and immoral. Truman did decide not to drop more atomic bombs, at least for a while, because it was "too horrible," especially killing "all those kids." But he refused to stop the massive conventional attacks. On August 10, U.S. and British battleships stood offshore and lobbed huge shells that destroyed much of the steel mill city of Kamaishi. On August 13, as Soviet troops moved through Sakhalin, 1,600 U.S. aircraft bombed Tokyo, although the city was already so ruined that the planes, to use Churchill's later phrase, mainly made the rubble bounce. On August 14, giant B-29s and other aircraft decimated six other targets, killed several thousand people, and laid on three of the raids after Japanese radio had accepted the surrender terms. The most important air strike, however, occurred late on August 13 when leaflets were dropped on Japan that revealed the Allied demands and the Tokyo government's acceptance note of August 10. The military, whose power and fury seemed to be intensifying in the secret discussions, was suddenly undercut. But the supreme command's anger nevertheless remained great enough that Kido worried the military might seize the government.[75]

Kido urgently asked his close friend since childhood, the Emperor, to convene an Imperial Conference and end the war. On August 14, Hirohito intervened. The military, which since the 1860s had vindicated—usually with much hypocrisy—its actions by invoking the Emperor's name, now was trapped. Elements in the army invaded the palace to try to find and destroy the Emperor's recording of the radio broadcast accepting peace terms, but not before Kido thought it wise to flush a number of important documents down the toilet. The invaders were stopped by loyal troops. Other army officers, however, burned down Prime Minister Suzuki's house. Kido received urgent reports that units were marching on Tokyo to demand the war's continuation.[76]

At this point, General Anami earned his place in history. An outspoken opponent of peace, he could have spearheaded a military takeover. He also could have exercised the military's post-1870s power of paralyzing the government by resigning his post, thus destroying Suzuki's cabinet and forcing the formation of a new government that the military could dominate. Anami took neither course. He and the chief of Japan's navy, Toyoda Soemu ("the admiral without a fleet," as Butow later called him), wanted to continue fighting but would not contradict the Emperor. Threats of a military uprising continued until the end of August. Nevertheless, obedience to the Emperor, as Stimson had foreseen, stopped them. Early on the morning of August 15, after drinking much sake ("When you drink *sake,* you bleed more profusely," the general had remarked), Anami sat on the floor of his home, faced the Imperial Palace, and committed suicide by first splitting open his abdomen, then slashing his neck.[77]

Later that day, an astonished Japanese people heard the Emperor announcing on the radio his Imperial Rescript on the End of the War. He never used the word "surrender," nor did he mention the possibility of an occupation. He recalled that they had gone to war "out of Our sincere desire to ensure Japan's self-preservation and the stabilization of East Asia," not out of "territorial aggrandizement." To continue, however, "would lead to the total extinction of human civilization." He saluted Japan's military and offered "deepest . . . regret" to its Asian allies, but offered not a syllable of regret to the tens of millions of other Asians and non-Asians who had died in the flames of warfare since 1931. Nor did he express regret for Japan's brutal treatment of Western prisoners, three-quarters of whom died in inhumane captivity. The effect of the speech on the Japanese was electric. As the later Nobel Prizewinner for Literature, Oe Kenzaburo, recalled of the August day when he was not yet a teenager:

> The adults sat around their radios and cried. The children gathered outside in the dusty road and whispered their bewilderment. We were most confused and disappointed by the fact that the Emperor had spoken in a *human* voice, no different from any adult's. . . . How could we believe that an august presence of such awful power had become an ordinary human being on a designated summer day?[78]

Japan was beaten, but it seemed the Japanese were not repentant. Truman was of course delighted that Konoe's great objective of dealing only with the Anglo-Saxon powers, while preventing any military-Communist takeover, had been realized. General MacArthur alone presided over the Japanese surrender signed by the diplomat Shigemitsu Mamoru on board the USS *Missouri* on September 2. The U.S. flag flying above the main mast was the same that flew above the capital on December 7, 1941. To make the message clear, Commodore Perry's flag of 1853, with its thirty-one stars, was draped over the *Missouri*'s rear turret. At the climactic point of the ceremony, Theodore White recalled forty years later, as "MacArthur intoned 'These proceedings are now closed,' we heard a drone and looked up. It is difficult to recall now, after years of floundering and blunder, how very good we were in those days, with what precision we ordered things. Four hundred B-29s had taken off from Guam and Saipan hours before to arrive over the Missouri at this precise moment of climax. They stretched across the rim of the horizon."[79]

On August 30, the first U.S. occupation forces had landed in Japan without opposition. Several days later, *New York Times* reporter W. H. Lawrence reached Hiroshima. Although a correspondent with much experience on European and Pacific battlefields, he reported that "I have never looked upon such scenes of death and destruction." Lawrence walked "through streets where the stench of death still pervades," where survivors, "wearing gauze patches over their mouths, still probe among the ruins for bodies or possessions." Japanese doctors told him that "persons who had been only slightly injured on the day of the blast lost 86 percent of their white blood corpuscles, developed temperatures of 104 degree Fahrenheit, their hair began to drop out, they lost their appetites, vomited blood and finally died"—at a continuing rate of about one hundred each day.[80]

Many informed analysts later wondered whether the suffering and the delay in ending the war had been a great, unnecessary error. John Emmerson, a distinguished Foreign Service officer and among the most respected of the Japan hands, concluded that some assurances regarding the Emperor would have ended the war earlier, and certainly "the dropping of the second bomb on Nagasaki was senseless." Many scholars who have closely studied the evidence agree that while the inexperienced, insecure Truman was understandably torn between the political fears of Byrnes and the strategic recommendations of Stimson, the President's delay in accepting the retention of a carefully circumscribed emperor, and the Japanese military's use of the unconditional surrender ultimatum to demand war to the last soldier, caused needless suffering and the "senseless" laying on of the second atomic bomb. (Not until twenty-five years after the war ended did Washington officials allow a film shot of Nagasaki after the bombing to be shown to American audiences, so worried were these officials about charges of immorality and needless brutality.) Truman's and his advisers' growing concern over Stalin's advancing armies, and in Japan Hirohito's great risk taking, finally led to an end of the bloodletting.[81]

The United States had triumphed in the war in Asia. The Pacific, acknowledged an envious British diplomat, was "an American lake." Truman alone held the secret to history's most destructive weapon (this "Frankenstein," as it was already known). But somehow, while standing at the peak of an "American Century," the United States had lost its historic foreign policy objective: an orderly Asia open to U.S. investment, trade, and principles. For China, as Truman knew, was veering toward chaos and possibly communism. Southeast Asia seemed to be condemned to outdated colonialism or explosive nationalism. Korea, by agreement between U.S. and Soviet occupiers, was divided into North and South. Only Japan remained, tenuously, open. And the future of this devastated, confused, atomic-scarred country was, to say the least, highly uncertain. Equally uncertain was whether U.S. officials could now realize their vision for Asia: turning the Japanese from a rabidly nationalist people who envisioned Asian empire into an outward-looking, democratic people who would form the Asian hub of an open, global, multilateral system.[82]

IX

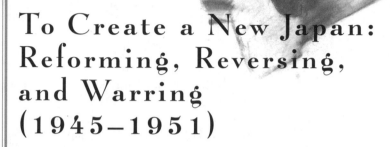

To Create a New Japan: Reforming, Reversing, and Warring (1945–1951)

"Give Me Bread or Give Me Bullets"

THE UNITED STATES began the post–World War II era as the superpower with sole possession of the atomic bomb's secrets; as an economic powerhouse (controlling half the world's entire industrial production) that intended to create an open, equitable global market; and as a triumphant democracy that meant to democratize and demilitarize Japan. Within just six years, this supposed American Century was already transformed. Stalin's dictatorship exploded its own atomic bomb. The world's two largest nations, the Soviet Union and China, forged a Communist alliance aimed at destroying capitalism. And in Japan, embattled U.S. officials pushed not democratization and demilitarization, but an economic and military buildup for fighting a hot war in Asia, a Cold War globally.

Certainly it had all seemed to start happily. With uncontested sway over the earth's great oceans, Washington officials could agree with the popular song, "To Be Specific, It's Our Pacific." Secretary of the Navy James Forrestal told the Truman cabinet in mid-1946 that "China is now our Eastern frontier." Not that all was perfect. A devastated Japan faced starvation. China was dividing between Nationalists and Communists. Manchuria, long a prime target of the open-door policy, fell under the Red Army's boots. The great Asian empires of the British, French, and Dutch had been undermined by Japanese occupation and began toppling to militant nationalists. Wartime agreements that assumed a united Korea, and a Taiwan linked with China, were simply washing away. But the United States seemed to have the power to make these things right, or at least acceptable.[1]

In the post-1945 years, as in the post-1918 era, American dreams were to be ruined by Russians and revolutionaries. During September 1945, just two months after he bragged that he had "clinched" the open door in Manchuria, President Harry Truman learned from U.S. intelligence that the Red Army was "carrying out a program of scientific looting" in that region, while "indiscriminately killing Chinese and Japanese." Stalin was ransacking the Far East (as well as Eastern Europe) for rapid rebuilding of a war-devastated Russia. General George Marshall, the U.S. manager of victory in World War II, warned that if Chiang Kai-shek could not be rescued, "There would follow the tragic consequences of a divided China and of a probable Russian resumption of power in Manchuria, the combined effect . . . resulting in the defeat or loss of the major purpose of our war in the Pacific." Trying to avert this catastrophe, Truman ordered 110,000 U.S. troops into China to help Chiang obtain strategic areas as the Japanese departed. The President then sent Marshall on a mission to reconcile Chiang with the Communists, while somehow keeping Chiang in the driver's seat. But nothing worked, especially as rampant inflation and corruption wrecked the Chinese economy.[2]

The Yalta framework for the Far East lay in ruins. "I think . . . that the main explanation for the American tendency to withdraw from China," British Foreign Office official J. C. Donnelly wrote acutely to his colleagues in November 1945, "is that the Americans now regard Japan and the formerly Japanese bases which they held as their bulwark in the Pacific. . . . Thus, tragic and paradoxical as it may seem, it is likely that the defeated Japanese will profit from American protection, while the supposedly victorious Chinese will be left to the tender mercies of the Communists whether native or Russian."[3]

Washington policymakers believed they faced stark, alarming alternatives. As U.S. trade expert Henry Grady warned, "The capitalistic system is essentially an international system. If it cannot function internationally, it will break down completely." Such views intensified as

U.S. industrial production declined 30 percent in 1945–46. Unemployment shot upward, and public opinion polls revealed growing fear of another 1929 crash.[4]

Truman and his advisers fully understood the need for rapid reconstruction and a functioning international economy. The base of the postwar system was to be the Bretton Woods framework established by the United States and its Allies at the New Hampshire resort in 1944. This system was not going to be Wilsonian—that is, it was not to follow Woodrow Wilson and other Progressives' hopes that international economic policy could be left to the private bankers (such as Thomas Lamont and Kajiwara Nakaji of the 1920s). Those bankers had self-destructed after 1929. Governments were now to play the central role, not only by establishing principles and institutions but by providing crucial funds. In 1945, those funds lay almost entirely in the United States. Thus, if the British, French, or Japanese wanted to reconstruct their societies, they had to accept U.S. principles laid out in the Bretton Woods system. Those three nations did accept the rules, for the most part. Stalin did not. Byrnes sorrowfully but accurately told Truman's cabinet in early 1946 that "the only place where money has not influenced national policy is Russia."[5]

Thus by 1946, U.S. officials had to work with a partially open world, that is, with those areas not occupied by Soviet troops. In Asia, this meant Truman faced the immense job of keeping Stalin's power at bay while creating a functioning system before the new nationalist forces swung their economies sharply to the left. The key to Asia was becoming Japan. Yet the Japanese, as the U.S. paper on "Postsurrender Policy" stated in 1945, were to be "completely disarmed and demilitarized." Their society was to be reformed fundamentally as "feudal and authoritarian tendencies" were modified. Their economy was to be stripped down, the "large industrial and banking combinations" dissolved. In late 1945, U.S. authorities wrecked and dropped into the oceans cyclotrons the Japanese had developed for creating atomic energy. American scientists loudly condemned this destruction, but Secretary of War Robert Patterson excused it by saying that for the Japanese to keep cyclotrons would be "like giving Al Capone a pistol."[6]

In late 1945 the rebuilding job seemed foreboding, even highly distasteful. After all, in early 1945 Japanese had systematically executed downed U.S. airmen. On August 12, 1945, eight airmen had been shot, and on August 15—even as the Emperor accepted surrender terms—eight more. In printing news of the surrender, Japan's leading newspaper, *Asahi*, reiterated the "superiority of our race," a theme picked up by other publications. Obviously centuries of beliefs were not going to be suddenly thrown into reverse.[7]

Fortunately for the American occupiers, however, Japan's view of them, at least, was changing. As the historian Homma Nagayo later observed, the biggest change in this view had occurred between 1941 and 1945. Once seen as inferior enemies, the Americans had dealt Japan its first military defeat in modern times with a power never imagined. The victors then acted not as classic loot-and-pillage conquerors, but as people with whom Japanese civilians could work. As a later foreign minister, Fujiyama Aiichiro, remembered about 1945–46, "many industrialists uncorked their champagne bottles and toasted the coming of a new industrialist era." These Japanese well knew, moreover, that their country was loathed throughout Asia; their only possible friend in the world was the United States. The importance of American help rose as 3 million Japanese soldiers and civilians returned to live off a virtually destroyed economy. A disastrous harvest in 1945–46 produced only 60 percent of the war years' level. Starvation loomed. During his first week as head of the occupation, a stunned General MacArthur told Washington, "Give me bread or give me bullets." On September 17, 1945, a devastating typhoon struck. It especially ravaged Hiroshima, which already lacked hospitals, medicine, policemen, firemen, and food. The United States needed the Japanese to right the Asian world. The Japanese needed the United States to survive.[8]

The two nations shared another overriding objective: keeping Japan united and not, as in Germany, allowing a divided country to emerge. After a trip to Japan, Patterson told the cabinet the Japanese were "extremely apprehensive of Russian occupation." They greatly preferred American occupiers. U.S. Allies insisted on some role, so Byrnes agreed to set up a Far Eastern Commission (FEC) of eleven nations, and an Allied Council of the Big Three plus China. The Soviets complained, accurately, that they were treated "like a piece of extra furniture." (Or like the Flying Dutchman: MacArthur amused himself by keeping the Soviet representatives' plane circling for long periods above Tokyo before allowing it to land.) The British later called the FEC, again accurately, "a useless body." Truman turned a deaf ear.[9]

He placed the occupation solely in MacArthur's hands. The President did not do so happily. "Mr. Prima Donna, Brass Hat, Five Star MacArthur" was "worse than the Cabots and the Lodges," Truman wrote in June 1945, for "they at least talked with one another before they told God what to do. Mac tells God right off." The new President marveled that the United States could produce a Lee and an Eisenhower, "and at the same time produce Custers . . . and MacArthurs." Truman sent along George Atcheson, a veteran diplomat and Far East expert, to be political adviser. But MacArthur ignored, then largely coopted, Atcheson before the diplomat died tragically in a 1947 airplane crash.[10]

In September 1945, MacArthur landed, virtually unprotected, at a *kamikaze* training base outside Yokohama while stories circulated that fanatics were gunning for him. In what Churchill called the bravest of "all the amazing deeds in the war," the general rode in a car down streets lined with thirty thousand Japanese troops. His car unfortunately broke down, and the supreme commander had to wait on the road fifteen minutes while Japanese civilians stared at the spectacle. MacArthur nevertheless successfully set the tone. He publicly considered himself an unparalleled expert on "the Asian mind" (although he admitted privately that "even after fifty years living among these people I still do not understand them"). He did understand that under the right conditions the Japanese would cooperate. He also understood and played to the centuries-old Shogun tradition, even setting up his offices across from the moat surrounding the Emperor's palace while conducting himself imperially. The distinguished scholar of Japan (and British diplomat) George Sansom wrote after a talk with the general that MacArthur expressed his views so "they appear to have a kind of absolute validity, an almost superhuman righteousness." He "is not always strictly truthful." His "great trouble is vanity," Sansom concluded. Japanese were not novices at dealing with foreigners with those characteristics. The Japanese also heard (and Truman understandably was concerned about) the rumors that MacArthur was well on his way to the 1948 Republican presidential nomination.[11]

The general moved rapidly. He had 400,000 U.S. troops to maintain order, but he helped the Japanese military save some face by asking it to disarm its own troops. He even brought Japanese officers into the occupation's bureaucracy as the U.S. military took over hundreds of acres to set up fruitful listening posts close to Soviet and Chinese borders. Of greatest significance, MacArthur quickly disposed of the Emperor question. On September 18, 1945, a powerful Georgia Democrat, Richard Russell, introduced a Senate resolution demanding that Hirohito be tried as a war criminal. Russell was in tune with most Americans, but not with the Japan hands or MacArthur. The general told Washington that "no specific and tangible evidence" linked the Emperor to war crimes. Moreover, "His indictment will unquestionably cause a tremendous convulsion" that could transform the "hope" of democracy into a regime "along communistic lines." MacArthur knew how to hit the right buttons in Washington. Taking what he modestly called the "greatest gamble in history," the general prevailed.

A breakthrough came on September 27 when the Emperor, dressed in cutaway and top hat, was driven to the U.S. Embassy, where he met MacArthur, dressed in khaki with an open neck. The Emperor nervously accepted a cigarette offered by the general, although Hirohito did not smoke. A quickly famous photo showed the tall general towering over the Emperor as both stared at the camera. (Japanese officials, finding the photo disrespectful to the Emperor, tried to stop its publication. They were overruled immediately by the Americans. A leading Japanese literary figure, Takami Jun, concluded he could now write anything: "Since I was born, this is my first experience with freedom.") The meeting went well. MacArthur was moved "to the very marrow of my bones." For the next six years, the two men would work together with mutual admiration. Of course, by absolving the Emperor of war crimes, the general also helped make it possible for Japanese who wished to escape their own past.[12]

MacArthur meanwhile brought in an American Quaker, Elizabeth Gray Vining, to teach Crown Prince (and after 1989, Emperor) Akihito. The British, whom the general unceremoniously pushed out of this particular school picture, were again left furious and frustrated. The new relationship was neatly defined some years later when an irreverent Senator William Fulbright (D: AR) quizzed diplomat John Foster Dulles behind closed doors:

> *The Chairman [Tom Connally, D: TX]:* You say the Emperor calls on MacArthur but MacArthur never calls on him?
> *Mr. Dulles:* That is right. . . .
> *Senator Fulbright:* Does that prove, you say, the Emperor is no longer regarded as God?
> *Mr. Dulles:* Yes.
> *Senator Fulbright:* What does it prove about MacArthur?
> *Mr. Dulles:* . . . I evoke my constitutional privilege.[13]

The First Occupation (1945–47)

The British occupying Japan quickly discovered they were playing second fiddle in a one-man band. But the band needed an audience. As the audience, the Japanese at first overestimated their own influence.

They were bitter when they learned of a two-part deal concocted by Byrnes in December 1945. The Soviets supported a U.S. takeover of the strategic, once Japanese-controlled Micronesian Islands. In return, the Americans supported de facto Soviet control of the Kuriles and South Sakhalin on Japan's northern doorstep. The Japanese had earlier been stunned in September 1945 when MacArthur's office ordered their media not to publish news on atomic bomb victims or damage. They were further shocked when MacArthur publicly repudiated the cabinet led by Prince Higashikuni Naruhiko (the Emperor's cousin), which Konoe and his friends had carefully put together in August to maintain order, work with MacArthur, and keep power in their own conservative hands. MacArthur ignored the cabinet and ordered the restoration of civil liberties. The government resigned. Shattered, about to be tried as a war criminal, and convinced that communism would soon rule his beloved nation, the fifty-four-year-old Konoe committed suicide by swallowing potassium cyanide. A cabinet led by Shidehara followed; it remained in power until May 1946. Not even his care in obtaining MacArthur's approval at every step could protect this ghost from the 1920s. Shidehara's unfortunate public statement that Chinese treatment of Japan in the early 1930s, not Japanese militarism, had triggered the war, fit neither the historical record nor U.S. sensibilities.[14]

Yoshida Shigeru became premier (and foreign minister) in May 1946. This new leader of the Liberal Party was to be the central Japanese figure in the occupation and beyond. Already sixty-eight years old when he first grasped power in 1946, Yoshida had been the fifth son born to a samurai and a woman who was probably a geisha. Graduation from prestigious Tokyo University; diplomatic service in Washington, London, and Tientsin, among other posts; and marriage to the daughter of a powerful diplomat gave him the leverage needed to become vice minister of foreign affairs under Tanaka in 1928, then ambassador to Great Britain. As his link with Tanaka indicated, Yoshida strongly favored a Japanese empire in North China, much as he supported annexing Korea and intervening in Siberia. But he feared the militarist governments of the 1930s as a terrible aberration in the nation's history, and, in a neat calculation of potential power, during that decade favored ties with the Americans and British rather than the Germans. In 1944-45 he worked closely with Konoe to stop the war (and was arrested for forty days as a result).[15]

This background explained why Yoshida was available for the occupation's needs. Moreover, he envisioned restoring the historic, now shattered *kokutai* (national polity) whose aura and significance went well beyond a national state. To realize this vision, he ran the Liberal Party and later the nation with an iron fist.

Throughout the occupation, Yoshida shrewdly exploited splits among U.S. policymakers. In Washington, State, Treasury, and military departments vigorously disagreed with one another over the pace and timing of reforms. They even fought bitterly within their own departments. In the State Department, for example, one group wanted Japan shunted off to the United Nations' authority, another pleaded that the Japanese be won over with an early end to the occupation, while some officials wanted to stay indefinitely to ensure the Japanese remained peaceful democrats. Such divisions, and Washington's preoccupations with Cold War crises elsewhere, gave both MacArthur's headquarters and Japanese politicians extensive freedom of action. Yet SCAP (Supreme Command of Allied Powers) itself was divided, most notably between two of MacArthur's top officers. Major General Courtney Whitney (of Government Section) believed that Japan could only be saved by "a sharp swing to the left." Major General Charles A. Willoughby (G-2 Intelligence) saw "leftists and fellow travelers" everywhere.[16]

MacArthur initially leaned toward Whitney's view. Konoe and later Yoshida might have feared an army-Communist takeover, but in October 1945, MacArthur made the small, six hundred-member Communist Party legal for the first time since it had organized in 1922. Grass-roots democracy was encouraged by massive decentralization of power, most notably in the police forces. Tokyo officials had destroyed independent labor unions in mid-1940, but three laws passed between December 1945 and March 1947 gave labor the right to organize, bargain collectively, strike, and enjoy such welfare measures as health insurance. Union membership shot up from zero in August 1945 to 6.75 million three years later. MacArthur backtracked, however, when threatened with crippling strikes which, he concluded, were led by Communist-controlled unions. In February 1947, he outlawed a planned general strike. In 1948, he decreed that government employees could neither strike nor bargain collectively. Yoshida and the Liberal Party had been deeply suspicious of, if not outright hostile to, the early reforms, but they were delighted with MacArthur's later rulings.[17]

On SCAP's instructions, in October 1945 the government ordered the release of nearly a million political prisoners in jails and concentration camps. Some were quickly replaced by one thousand officials whom MacArthur arrested and brought before a war crimes tribunal. Seven were sentenced to death, including Tōjō Hideki, two commanders of the Kwantung Army, and the military commanders in China and the Philippines. Eighteen (including Marquis Kido, Hirohito's closest adviser) received lengthy jail terms. A storm of controversy arose. Many Americans and Russians demanded that more Japanese be executed. Some thought the trials a sham, the convictions prearranged, the punishment a dangerous precedent. Winston Churchill told Forrestal that it was "stupid" to hang "prominent people" when the Allies needed Japanese cooperation; "both Roosevelt and himself would have been executed if the Allies had lost the war," the former British leader observed. The acerbic journalist H. L. Mencken noted that MacArthur had executed General Homma Masaharu, "the man who beat him in a fair fight on Bataan," who was, Mencken charged, tied to war crimes by flimsy evidence. Purges removing 200,000 Japanese from government, business, and academia similarly generated controversy. Some critics warned that this number was only half those purged in Germany. Others believed the roundup destroyed both innocent lives and a bureaucracy needed to make the country function.[18]

Despised by Yoshida, the purge policy was soon reversed. But other reforms proved more durable. In 1940, the still feudal rural system had forced 70 percent of farmers to rent their land. Many Allied officials believed that the rich, large landholders had formed the backbone of the 1930s militarism. Yoshida, as a good conservative, disliked redistribution of property in principle. But—also as a good conservative—he believed the feudal structures had to be dismantled if Japan were to become competitive and potential revolution averted. The hotly debated Owner-Farmer Establishment Law of 1946 bought some 4 million acres and sold it cheaply to 2 million farmers. The rampant inflation in 1947–50 then destroyed much of the debate (and, of course, the value of the compensation hoped for by the former landholders). The historian Richard Barnet estimates that an acre cost about a carton of black-market cigarettes (which became the common currency in both postwar Japan and Germany). Tenantry dropped to 8 percent. The new landholders became a bulwark of Yoshida's conservative coalition that dominated the political scene until the 1990s.[19]

On paper, the reforms affecting women were just as dramatic. Before 1945, Japanese women had few rights; for example, they, but not men, could be convicted of adultery. Exploitation went far beyond the absence of rights. When U.S. troops arrived in August 1945, Tokyo authorities sought to please the occupiers—and protect women of the upper classes—by setting up groups of "special prostitutes" from lower classes who personally pledged before the Imperial Palace to sacrifice themselves for *kokutai*. Determined to change the rigid family system that Americans blamed for much of Japan's militarism and fascism, SCAP quickly gave women the right to vote, hold property, enjoy higher education, enter the government, and even join the police. MacArthur decriminalized adultery and outlawed contract marriage, which had virtually enslaved wives. These and other reforms were notably pushed by American women in SCAP, and by Japanese female reformers. When in 1946 women ran for office for the first time in Japan's history, thirty-eight out of eighty female candidates won Diet seats, despite determined male opposition. The leading vote-getter was Kato Shizue, known as "the Margaret Sanger of Japan." The changes proved real, but most Japanese men (and the top British occupation official in Japan) still fought the reforms.[20]

Similar obstacles stalled many educational reforms. The attempt to decentralize authority, while denationalizing and democratizing textbooks, proved to be a contradiction. Local, conservative authorities dug in their heels against rethinking Japan's recent past. They fought a mere five-day school week, or appointing women school principals. Even "Shogun" MacArthur's fiat only traveled so far in postwar Japan.

From the start, MacArthur focused on radically revising the Meiji Constitution. On October 11, 1945, he publicly outlined his principles for a new document. If implemented, these principles would have gone far in creating a democratic, open-market Japan. First drafts borrowed core ideas from the U.S. Constitution: the individual was paramount, government was restricted, and the new document ordered that the government "shall not" infringe on individual rights. The military was never again to enjoy a veto over cabinet government. All suppression of freedom of thought, speech, and religion was to end. Women were to be emancipated through the franchise, labor protected by unionization. Schools had to be liberalized. The thought police and "secret inquisition" which had long held Japanese "in constant fear" were to end. And "democratization of Japanese economic institutions" was to occur so that "monopolistic industrial controls" could be revised, a wider distribution of income "and ownership of the means of production and trade" developed, and "full employment" enjoyed. The American "Shogun" seemed to have discovered the writing style of Karl Marx.[21]

MacArthur knew that any constitution lasting after American "bayonets" departed would have to appear to be a Japanese-originated and written document. Under the loose supervision of Whitney's Government Section, a committee led by State Minister Matsumoto Joji drafted a new constitution. Yoshida's influence permeated the document. Whitney warned MacArthur it fell far short of U.S. desires. It changed the Meiji Constitution too little, and, above all, scarcely touched the Emperor's pre-1945 powers. MacArthur concluded extensive tutoring was needed. He instructed Whitney to suggest a model constitution to the Matsumoto-Yoshida group.

Whitney's outline stripped the Emperor of claims to divinity, while the Constitution and the people's "basic will" limited his powers. Apparently Colonel Charles Kades, a former New Deal lawyer now under Whitney, made the pivotal change when he replaced MacArthur's wording that the "Emperor is at the head of the state" to a mere "symbol of the state." The draft further declared that "war as a sovereign right of the nation is abolished" and "no Japanese Army, Navy, or Air Force will ever be authorized and no rights of belligerency will ever be conferred upon any Japanese force." This central point—perhaps suggested by the Emperor himself—was the seed of the later, famous Article IX. Whitney decreed that "the feudal system of Japan will cease." Whitney handed his draft to Yoshida and Matsumoto with the advice that their earlier language was "totally unacceptable." The two Japanese were stunned. Their shock did not lessen when Whitney gave them some fatherly advice: "It is better [as the recipients recorded his words] if the Japanese conservatives moved far to the left."[22]

Whitney stressed that he and MacArthur cared about the principles; the Japanese could deal with the exact wording. Matsumoto quickly warned that foreign principles transplanted in different societies resembled "roses of the West, [which] when cultivated in Japan, lose their fragrance totally." The power given "the masses" and the Diet's power over the Emperor were " 'revolutionary' in a way." Whitney refused to bargain. Unless the cabinet accepted the principles in forty-eight hours, MacArthur would "take the constitution to the people directly" and make it a "live issue" in the forthcoming election. After more stalling and talks, Matsumoto accepted the principles.[23]

Within two days in early March 1946, his group, working with Whitney's Japanese-speaking staff, wrote a fresh draft. After further rewriting by the Privy Council, the Emperor—by his exclusive power under the Meiji Constitution—sent it to the Diet for ratification. Again changes were made that undermined U.S. wishes. The Diet, for example, struck out a provision giving aliens equal protection rights. Yoshida and his colleagues finally accepted the document with its extensive protection of human rights only after those provisions were restricted, and, above all, after the Emperor was not only explicitly retained but, by being separated from formal authority, even more protected. The Emperor became, in the historian John Dower's words, "more transcendent than ever." Other changes occurred when, as Inoue Kyoko has argued, the document was translated from English to Japanese. For example, Americans thought they guaranteed women's rights with the phrase "equality of the sexes." Many Japanese, however, interpreted the phrase to mean equal in carrying out their respective, traditional roles within the family. The document, issued in the Emperor's name, was made public in November 1946 and became law on May 3, 1947.

The renunciation of war in Article IX especially triggered U.S.-Japanese clashes over at least the next half century. The Japan hands' papers had discussed demilitarization only in broad terms. MacArthur, Whitney's staff, and perhaps the Emperor and Shidehara drew up the specific wording. Yoshida and soon-to-be Socialist Prime Minister Katayama Tetsu approved the clause. Both men understood that all fears of Japanese military resurrection had to be destroyed if Japan were to obtain the help needed from the United States and Asian neighbors with long memories. But a powerful member of the Diet, Ashida Hitoshi, wrote Article IX so that it finally read:

> Aspiring sincerely to an international peace based on justice and order, the Japanese people forever renounce war as a sovereign right of the nation and the threat of use of force as means of settling international disputes.
>
> In order to accomplish the aim of the preceding paragraph, land, sea and air forces, as well as other war potential, will never be maintained.

Ashida's final phrasing has produced wildly different interpretations. Do these phrases, for example, allow Japan to create a defense force that can not only protect the home islands but participate, say, in United Nations' missions? Charles Kades, of Whitney's staff, worked closely with Ashida and later claimed Japan could do both—that is, create the force and send it abroad within a UN contingent. Over the years, many, especially in Japan, disputed Kades's interpretation. Notably, at the time British officials paid Article IX scant attention because they thought it was of little importance.[24]

MacArthur's determination to decentralize political functions (in good U.S. federal tradition) under the 1947 Local Autonomy Law, and to apply U.S. antitrust measures to strangle the *zaibatsu*, also excited passions. Unhappily for the general, these struggles were rapidly settled. By 1949, Yoshida's second government was ignoring the 1947 law and recentralizing powers. Why? Largely because the local areas never received adequate power to tax and raise revenue.

The anti-*zaibatsu* measures suffered even quicker death. The 466 commercial banks of 1935 had merged into 186 by 1941 and only 53 in 1945. These financial giants had powered the industrial *zaibatsu*. SCAP's antitrust analyst, Eleanor Hadley, believed that the Mitsui *zaibatsu* alone was equivalent to U.S. Steel, General Motors, Standard Oil of New York, Alcoa, Douglas Aircraft, DuPont, Allis Chalmers, Westinghouse, AT&T, RCA, IBM, Dole Pineapple, National City Bank, Woolworth Stores, and Statler Hotels—among others. A few U.S. (and of course, all Soviet) officials wanted to solve the problem simply by dismantling Japan's industrial plant and shipping it off to the victors as reparations for Japanese warmaking. MacArthur and the Japan hands in Washington decapitated such plans. These officials instead tried to apply U.S. antitrust principles to decentralize and democratize the economy. Nearly everyone nevertheless agreed with one expert on Japan who concluded, "Unless the business and financial structure in Japan is radically transformed, all other changes will be rendered nugatory." MacArthur ordered banks to stand alone, thus destroying the golden links between finance and industry. SCAP closed or radically altered the old institutions, such as the Yokohama Specie Bank, that had financed the nation's colonialism. In early 1947, SCAP ordered the breakup of the most powerful *zaibatsu,* including Mitsui and Mitsubishi.[25]

Having attacked the old industrial-banking system, MacArthur now found himself governing a people who had too little food, too much inflation (prices shot up more than twelve times between early 1946 and 1949), and virtually no exports. Of immense importance, MacArthur decided to exclude foreign investors from the country. He went to great lengths to ensure that all contacts between the outside world and the Japanese economy went only through his office. The general disdained the Wilsonian theory of open-markets-openly-arrived-at. Yoshida happily agreed; resembling the Meiji leaders after 1868, he and his colleagues intended to keep the economy wholly in Japanese hands. (Yoshida was married to the granddaughter of the great Meiji nationalist, Okubo Toshimichi.) They looked to internal savings (equivalent in the late 1940s to drawing water from a stone), and some borrowing from abroad, but in any case wanted no long-term foreign ownership.[26]

By early 1947, such intense nationalism, SCAP's economic policies, and the growing turn of U.S. resources to waging Cold War in Europe had triggered a frightening crisis. Japan was on the brink of chaos. It

looked into the abyss just as the Chinese Communists took the offensive against the Nationalists, and as Truman—ever the good poker
player—prepared to fold his bet on Chiang Kai-shek, whom he now
termed "the wrong horse."

At this very moment (March 1947), MacArthur astonished Washington by declaring the occupation a rousing success. He urged that a
peace treaty be signed. Japan could then follow its own destiny and, of
course, American occupiers would go home. The general seemed to be
reacting not to what he saw in Japan, but what he thought he saw across
the Pacific—a demand that he return to enter the 1948 presidential
race. In Washington, Truman's advisers concluded the time had come
once again to make Japan aware of the outside world. They also
intended to deal with the American "Shogun."[27]

The Second Occupation (1947–50): The Americans

By early 1947, only eighteen months after the United States emerged
from the war as the strongest power in world history, Stalin's armies
controlled most of the nations in Eastern Europe. The Middle East,
under pressure from both Soviet demands and a growing Arab-Israeli
clash, was at flashpoint. Hull's dream of an open world was punctured
by fears of the "outlines of three worlds of trade," as the State Department confidentially called it in September 1946—Russian, American,
and British—with the possibility there would be " 'little trade and less
peace.' " In Asia, despite MacArthur's cheerleading, the two hubs of
U.S. policy—China and Japan—were collapsing.[28]

By default, Japan was becoming the pivotal redoubt for U.S. policy.
Washington officials had wished for considerable time to democratize
and rebuild Japan. By early 1947, time had run out. "Japan is facing
desperate economic conditions wherein lie grave dangers to the accomplishment of our objectives," George Atcheson told Truman from Tokyo
on January 3, 1947. "The Japanese economy is bankrupt. . . ." But this
bankruptcy was only one of a number of crises. A similar economic
crisis struck Western Europe, where Americans figured they would
have to spend at least $12 billion or confront the danger of the entire
region swinging sharply leftward and inward. Another crisis, the collapse of China, could destroy U.S. interests in Asia. This crisis was
succinctly stated by State Department officials on March 12, 1947: a
new, "positive economic program" must quickly "create a viable Japa-

nese economy," one "self-sustaining" by 1950. The program simultaneously had to deal with the regional crisis by permitting Japan to help
"the economic recovery of the Far East, which is desperately in need of
the products of the Japanese industry." Conveniently for the historian,
this document was written on the same day (March 12, 1947) that Truman dramatically appeared before a joint session of Congress to
announce the Truman Doctrine: the world was now divided between
the free and enslaved peoples, the President proclaimed, and unless a
penny-pinching Republican Congress gave him $400 million immedi-
ately to help Greece and Turkey, the Middle East might join the
enslaved camp while the Mediterranean and Western Europe would lie
open to Communist pressures. Suddenly, half the globe stretching from
the Mediterranean east to the Pacific seemed to be sliding away from
Western capitalism.[29]

The crises were related. If the United States hoped to save the Japanese, it could only do so by making them more self-sufficient (because
U.S. resources were headed toward more immediate threats in Europe).
Then a new, democratic Japan had to play its old role as the economic
center of the region, thus saving the remainder of Asia from the fate
fast enveloping China. On the surface, the ironies were rich. After the
Americans had supported Japan against Russia for decades, they had
switched in World War II to supporting the Soviets against Japan. Now
in 1947–48 they switched back to rebuild Japan—so it could gain a kind
of economic interdependence with the Asians it had long sought and
the Americans had tried to prevent. One U.S. policy objective remained
consistent: keeping Asia open to American interests while integrating
the region within an open, global, capitalist framework. If that objective
required opposing Japan, so be it. If the objective required rebuilding
Japan and reintegrating it with Asia, so be it. Japanese culture was
interesting and strong, but it was also viewed as malleable. It could be
put into the service of the American worldview. Japan was less an end
in itself than the means, in Washington's eyes, for achieving the larger
regional and global purposes of U.S. foreign policy.

Truman's new Secretary of State, the much-idolized George Marshall, caught this relationship in part on January 29, 1947. He ordered
Undersecretary of State Dean Acheson to plan "a definite government
of South Korea and *connect up* its economy with that of Japan." The
forty-year colonial bonds between Korea and Japan lay broken. Korea
itself lay loosely divided between Communist and capitalist halves.
Marshall moved to restore the interdependence with economic rather
than political ties. Soon a $600 million grant-in-aid was being prepared

for South Korea. If the approach worked, if capitalism proved to be more dynamic and integrative than communism, then a partially capitalist Asia could become an all-capitalist Asia—perhaps without war and with a new, U.S.-organized Japan at its center.[30]

This breathtaking approach was spelled out in calm, undramatic words by Acheson in his soon-to-be-famous speech at Cleveland, Mississippi, on May 8, 1947. Because of the war's horrible destruction, Acheson began, many nations needed U.S. goods. But they were going bankrupt paying for them. If financing was not arranged, U.S. exports— now four times greater than before the war and representing one month's work for every American man and woman—would drop. To solve the crisis, Germany and Japan, "those two great workshops . . . upon which the ultimate recovery of the two continents so largely depends," required quick rebuilding. Only in Acheson's last paragraphs did the Stalinist threat enter the picture. The immediate danger was not a Soviet invasion but an economic catastrophe.[31]

The Japanese "workshop" lay in shambles. Official food rations hovered around the 1,000-calories-per-day level. Runaway inflation made food impossibly expensive. U.S. officials now prepared to reverse the anti-*zaibatsu* program and rapidly raise industrial production.

In September 1947, with U.S. Cold War policies accelerating in Europe and Latin America, Undersecretary of the Army William H. Draper returned from Japan to condemn SCAP's antitrust policies. In March 1948, Draper (who had been a Wall Street investment banker, then chief U.S. economic adviser in Germany) publicly envisioned only three alternatives: "we can continue feeding the Japanese, we can withdraw aid and let them starve, or we can help supply industrial raw materials to pump-prime Japan's industry and put the nation on its own feet." The implications were not small: "Japan needs raw materials from the rest of Asia. . . . We foresee the revival of the old trade, not necessarily a new trade." Indeed, he told a congressional committee that Japan was now to be the "focal point in the whole recovery of the East from the effects of the war." Draper's boss, Secretary of the Army Kenneth C. Royall, underlined the central problem in a January 1948 speech. Japan had to be demilitarized, but also economically self-supporting: "With this increasing economic approach there has arisen an inevitable area of conflict," Royall worried, because those who ran "Japan's war machine . . . were often the ablest and most successful business leaders."[32]

In March 1948, it fell to George Kennan, head of the State Department's Policy Planning Staff, to beard the lion, MacArthur, in his den.

Kennan's ideas were shaping U.S. Cold War policies. His "Long Tele-gram" of February 1946 from Moscow, where he had been Ambassador Averell Harriman's chief adviser, had set out the historical and ideologi-cal reasoning for containing Soviet power. Back in Washington, the forty-three-year-old Wisconsin native was named by Marshall to head the new Policy Planning Staff. Kennan, who deeply mistrusted mercu-rial public and congressional opinion, also disliked the President's hyperbole and militant call to action in the Truman Doctrine speech. He preferred a focused, systematic, economic and political buildup of Allies, a buildup especially of what he called "the two greatest industrial complexes of East and West," Japan and West Germany, that would immunize them and their regions against communism.[33]

Having been a prime architect for the rebuilding of Western Europe, Kennan turned to deal with the other "complex." He understood in May 1947 that China's crisis "was to heighten greatly the importance of what might now happen in Japan." Instead of leaving Japan, as MacArthur wanted, Kennan believed the United States had to remain and build up the country. "Our primary goal," Kennan said as he cut to the core of U.S. policy, was to ensure that Americans would "never again be threat-ened by the militarization against us of the complete industrial [Far East] area as . . . [occurred] during the second world war."[34]

Kennan was not in awe of MacArthur (he had, after all, dealt with Stalin for many years in Moscow). What might Kennan have thought when, in their first talks in Tokyo, MacArthur dropped such nuggets as that the men who ran the *zaibatsu* were well gotten rid of because "they were the counterparts of the most effete New York club men"; or that a peace treaty demilitarizing Japan could include the Soviets because "when the Russians put their signature to something clear and explicit, they will remain faithful to their word"?[35]

Kennan thought not. No peace treaty should now be sought, he advised Marshall, because the United States must maintain full control to transform occupation policy. Anyway, he "would not trust Russian good faith" in any demilitarization treaty. An internal crackdown was needed to stop Japanese Communists from "penetrating Japanese soci-ety and seizing its key positions." Threats of extracting reparations from Japan's industry to indemnify Asian war victims had virtually paralyzed the nation's planning, so reparations had to be drastically cut—if not completely stopped. The problems of fully reviving the economy "still lie [in] the reluctance of other Far Eastern nations to accept Japanese goods."[36]

Kennan's recommendations became the core of NSC-13/2, an early paper of the newly created, powerful National Security Council (made up of the secretaries of State, Defense, and Treasury, the Central Intelligence Agency director, and presided over by the President). This October 7, 1948, document marked the official turn of policy toward Japan. There would be no peace treaty until Japan's security was assured, partly by U.S. naval bases in huge facilities south of Tokyo and on Okinawa, partly by an expanded, "centrally directed" Japanese police. No new reforms for democratization or deconcentration were planned. Purges were sharply reduced. Then a section of the paper placed policy toward Japan in the mainstream of U.S. policies since the 1840s and 1890s: Japanese economic recovery, second in importance "only to U.S. security interests," was to be realized by (1) cutting "away existing obstacles to the revival of Japanese foreign trade," (2) accelerating "private enterprise," (3) warning the Japanese they must "raise production and . . . maintain high export levels through hard work" (that is, no more strikes), and (4) attacking inflation through balanced budgets. A CIA research report of May 1948 was specific: Japan's recovery required the trade of Northeast Asia. If the Chinese collapse made that trade unreachable, commerce with Southeast Asia and the Philippines had to be substituted.[37]

No major announcement was made of this major turn. But MacArthur was neither fooled nor pleased. Not wanting to carry out NSC-13/2, he worked with other occupying powers to block it. He believed the growing conflict was "between a system of free competitive enterprise . . . and a socialism in private hands." The general told the British early in 1948 that the new Washington policy was the brainchild of "the big Wall Street combines," which wanted to control the rebuilt *zaibatsu*. MacArthur "spoke most bitterly," as the top British official in Japan, Sir Alvery Gascoigne, recorded it, about " 'tycoons' (Forrestal, Royall, Averell Harriman, Draper were all named) who were . . . anti-purge and anti-economic centralization. They were against these measures because they thought they would conflict with their own business interests." The general vowed to continue "trust-busting." But he was outgunned, especially after a devastating loss in the Wisconsin Republican primary eliminated him from the presidential race. Of some 325 companies that he had hoped to dismantle, all but 19 survived virtually intact. Kades, fearing remilitarization, political polarization, and, as he phrased it, the end of the "New Deal coalition" in Japan, quit MacArthur's staff and returned to Washington.[38]

In mid-1948, the State Department's tracking of public opinion surprisingly showed Americans strongly in favor of reconstructing Japan economically (65 percent approved, 35 percent disapproved), despite loud opposition from Asian nations and, especially, the Australians. Some 81 percent of Americans polled agreed that U.S. occupation troops should remain in Japan rather than be brought home, and 68 percent wanted to maintain troops in South Korea. Marshall used these numbers to accelerate the new policies—especially, as he told British Ambassador Sir Oliver Franks in July 1948, since Truman, to whom he was utterly devoted, would probably lose to the Republicans in the 1948 election and the winners would radically cut back overseas spending. Also accelerating the new policy was the American Council on Japan, or, as it became known, the "Japan Lobby." Led by old Japan hands Joseph Grew, William Castle, Joseph W. Ballantine, and Eugene Dooman, as well as by *Newsweek* foreign editor Henry Kern (who organized the Council), the outspokenly anti-Communist group pressured the administration and Congress to allow a Japanese economic buildup under Japanese control. The Council also urged smashing unions and Communist organizations. Neither Kennan nor other U.S. officials needed convincing. The Dooman-led group did not reverse the 1945–46 policy (it was being reversed anyway), but after 1949 it did seal U.S.-Japanese business links while taking in good profits in shipping, fishing, insurance, pearls, coal, and other areas.[39]

The Second Occupation (1947–50): Japanese, Americans, and Chinese

"The original simple problem, 'How can we hold down Japan?' " wrote a fearful, perceptive *Sunday Chronicle* of London editor in August 1948, "has been replaced by the complex proposition, 'How can we hold up Japan?' . . . It is as though the hero and villain of a Japanese *kabuki* play had exchanged roles. This [new] role has naturally been accepted by the Japanese leaders with eager hands."[40]

With the appearance of those leaders, and his own surprising triumph in the 1948 presidential election, Truman's policies rode a streak of good fortune. A year earlier the Japanese conservatives had split, and for the only time between 1945 and 1993, a Socialist became prime minister. That coalition fell apart and was replaced by a Democratic Party–Socialist coalition led by the career diplomat—and shaper of Article IX—Ashida Hitoshi. The new premier was much friendlier to the left and to anti-*zaibatsu* programs than, say, Yoshida. According to a Japanese scholar of his diaries, Ashida believed that "capitalism" was the "bud" that would replace the old, pre-1945 system with the blooms of the new. If Ashida had survived, the United States—after a century of effort—mighty finally have made headway toward the historic goal of an open Japan. Within months, however, Ashida's coalition was ripped by scandal. In October 1948, Yoshida regained the premiership. The next year Yoshida won a rousing electoral triumph that reunified the Conservatives and set himself off on an uninterrupted five years of power.[41]

The seventy-year-old Yoshida largely agreed with the Kennan-Draper policies of NSC-13/2. (Time would solve any disagreements. "Whatever harm was done through the Occupation forces not listening to what I had to say," the old man later wrote, "could be remedied after we had regained our independence.") But Yoshida sharply broke with the Americans in his determination to restore ties with China. He seemed unconcerned whether Communists or Nationalists sat in Beijing. To his mind they all came out of a superior Chinese culture. His foreign policies had long rested on three legs: China; dislike and mistrust of the Soviets; and fervent pro-British principles, in part because he had valued the Anglo-Japanese alliance that targeted Russia. The British, he regretted, were collapsing as a world power. They were, however, being replaced by their offspring, whom he had once seen as bumbling and naive. But the Americans at least had long mistrusted Russians. Holding strong racial feelings, Yoshida disdained Asians other than Chinese, and most everyone else save some British and a few post-1945 North Americans.[42]

One of those favored Americans, Detroit banker Joseph M. Dodge, reached Tokyo in early 1949 as MacArthur's senior adviser to jump-start the Kennan-Draper economic plan. Yoshida quickly fought Dodge's insistence on removing government as rapidly as possible from the marketplace. Dodge's demand for instant balanced budgets might slash inflation, but also impose austerity—and, in Yoshida's eyes, probably cause massive riots. A powerful Japanese planning board complained that Dodge's demands resembled asking "a juggler to take out a rabbit before the audience while furnishing him with a top-hat which has room only for containing a rat." Yoshida, Dodge later claimed, "sabotaged" his plan for getting Japan on its feet by opening the country fully to market forces.[43]

That charge was not wholly true. Yoshida happily helped Dodge and the SCAP conservatives kill the anti-*zaibatsu* program. The Japanese leader, of course, was also delighted when Truman's new Secretary of State, Dean Acheson, effectively halted Japan's payment of reparations to nations victimized in World War II. Japan had already paid about $3 billion from its former colonial assets. Those resources were now to be used for Japan's rebuilding, not, say, for the Soviet Union's or Australia's. Yoshida helped set up a unitary foreign exchange rate—an undervalued rate of 360 yen to the dollar—that gave Japanese exports a huge advantage. The rate also made export prices more predictable and ended the interesting practice of pricing goods from Sears, Roebuck catalogues.[44]

Yoshida took the Kennan-Draper policy to mean that he could allow some convicted war criminals out of jail. (He would have appointed two of them to his cabinet, but MacArthur stopped him.) Japanese officials simultaneously began a "red purge" of the liberal left that soon claimed about one thousand university and school faculty. For some Japanese, the purge smacked of prewar militarist purges that avowedly targeted Communists, but usually hit liberals. Not only was the Communist Party attacked, but 5,500 unions with some 880,000 members were squeezed out of existence. Surviving unions assumed characteristics valued by the newly resurrected *zaibatsu*. As Igarashi Takeshi has argued, Yoshida set out to win two Cold Wars: against the Soviets who were a threat from abroad, and against groups he considered a threat at home. The two wars were intimately related in his mind, as they were in Kennan's, Draper's, and Acheson's.[45]

One of Yoshida's striking accomplishments was putting in place a highly trained bureaucracy that, as the historian Takemae Eiji aptly puts it, rose out of the war's ashes like the mythical phoenix. The bureaucracy began to shape the economy as Yoshida's government, but not always Dodge, wanted. This right arm of government thus embarked on a long, successful life marked by bitter clashes with the United States. But U.S. economic reforms ironically helped strengthen this bureaucracy. SCAP's sweeping economic directives, for example, depended on Japanese officials for implementation. The 1949 Foreign Exchange and Foreign Trade Control Law, proposed by SCAP and passed by the Diet, allowed for export, import, and exchange controls to be operated by the government. The 1950 Law Concerning Foreign Investment was immediately used by the government. Four giant U.S. banks, for example, had moved into Japan to serve military personnel, and American Express began to handle travelers' needs. The Ministry of Finance then called a halt. The "bamboo curtain" dropped. Exchange and trade controls became sophisticated protectionism to shield nascent industries from New York capital. Under MacArthur's beneficent gaze, economic controls and the bureaucracy grew evermore effective.[46]

In October–December 1949, Yoshida's two Cold Wars melded when

Truman accepted NSC-48/2, "The Position of the United States with Respect to Asia." The document was drawn up amid crisis. In September, Truman announced that the Soviets had exploded an atomic device. Americans no longer alone held the secret to ultimate destructive power. During early October, Mao's Communist forces claimed control of all China. In Europe, the Marshall Plan was not doing its job. Europeans could not revive their economies quickly enough to produce dollars to buy vital American goods. Truman privately feared an economic crisis of enormous proportions.[47]

U.S. and Japanese economies were not immune. When their economy slumped in 1949, Americans feared they were entering their usual postwar depression. Stalin's propagandists crowed to other "proletariat" that with China gone red, capitalism would soon be paralyzed, then overwhelmed by revolution. In early 1950, U.S. production revived, but Washington officials remained fearful. In closed-door testimony to the Senate Foreign Relations Committee, Secretary of State Acheson made a remarkable admission. "Even if there were no Russia, even if there were no communism," the Secretary of State declared, "we would have very grave problems in trying to exist and strengthen those parts of the free world which have been so badly shaken by the war and its consequences." Japan faced special danger, Acheson publicly noted that month: the Japanese had lost their historic markets and sources of raw materials, and "other countries" did not want to help them recover.[48]

The danger, then, had less to do with the Soviet military than with preventing the global breakdown of capitalism. In this poisoned atmosphere, U.S. policymakers drafted and refined NSC-48/2. The historian Bruce Cumings has noted that an early, unsigned August 1949 draft outlined the desired policy principles: that "economic life of the modern world is geared to expansion"; that such exporting should occur in a world of liberal trading policies; and that such policies must center around "reciprocal exchange and mutual advantage." John Hay and Woodrow Wilson would have applauded. Yoshida and the new Japanese finance ministry, however, had considerable reservation about the "reciprocal exchange" phrase.[49]

The final draft of NSC-48 revealed how these principles were to be realized: by encouraging the creation of "regional associations of non-Communist states of the various Asian areas." Such associations could help the United States ensure security. They could also accelerate economic recovery by reviving trade and capital movement "along multilateral, non-discriminatory lines." The General Agreement on Tariffs and

Trade, formed in 1947 to batter down tariff walls around the world, was to be applied to Japan. At long last, the Japanese were to be integrated into an open, global—and reciprocal—trade complex. Communist China, of course, threatened to be a nightmare among these dreams. Washington officials concluded, however, that as long as they held the "off-shore islands" of Japan, Okinawa, and the Philippines, U.S. security was assured. Recognition of China could be delayed.[50]

NSC-48/2 was a giant stride in the evolution of U.S. policy. The first steps, democratizing and rebuilding Japan by solely U.S. means, had proven insufficient. Hence the second step, taken by Kennan, Draper, and Dodge, to push Japan toward self-sufficiency—in other words, to work with Yoshida and the resurrected *zaibatsu*. But that step also fell short. Western and Japanese economic crises combined with the spread of revolution in Asia to form an explosive mixture. In late 1949, U.S. officials diluted the mixture by creating regional associations revolving around Japan and India. Such associations could institutionalize multilateralism and create a rising tide of security and development.

But the tide did not rise in early 1950. Japan's all-important exports grew sluggishly. The country meanwhile suffered a terrible trade imbalance with the United States. America took only 12 percent of Japan's exports in 1947, but sold it 92 percent of its imports. Before the war, Asia, and especially the colonial empire of Korea, Formosa, and Manchuria, had accounted for 53 percent of Japanese imports and 64 percent of exports; regional trade in 1947, by contrast, amounted to only 6 percent of Japan's imports and an incredibly low 4.3 percent of its exports. To top it off, Japan's birth rate exploded at twice the expected numbers.[51]

Thus in 1949 and early 1950, U.S. officials swallowed hard, and, while keeping a wary eye on Republicans determined to punish those "who lost China," quietly allowed Japan to open trade with the Chinese Communists. The State Department overcame ardent opposition from the Pentagon and the newly created Central Intelligence Agency. Both warned that trade could build up China and open Japan to Communist infection. The State Department countered that the trade would open China to non-Russian influence, more likely make the Chinese dependent on Japan than vice versa, and—of special importance—provide Japan a healthy profit to help take it off the U.S. dole. China, which had lost millions of people during its long war with Japan, outspokenly opposed the rapid American rebuilding of the nation. But the Beijing government needed help, and its supposed new friend, the Soviet Union, was providing precious little. Chinese officials moved to set up barter deals (their coal and salt for Japan's machinery and medicines). Yoshida was ready to rush in: "I don't care whether China is red or green. China is a natural market, and it has become necessary for Japan to think about markets." He received support from intellectuals, such as Takeuchi Yoshimi, who feared the values and culture of American occupiers, and insisted that the Japanese again use Chinese civilization as their guide to a better society. Private Japanese business groups, quickly organized to exploit China, were encouraged by SCAP. From a postwar low of $7.2 million in 1946, Sino-Japanese trade jumped to nearly $80 million in 1950. Japan enjoyed a slightly favorable balance.[52]

It soon became clear that China would not deliver the jolt needed by a declining Japanese economy. In March 1950, Kennan spilled out his anguish when he privately lamented that "we had made perhaps unavoidably a great strategic mistake by letting the war end in the complete destruction of German and Japanese strength." The Japanese, Kennan believed, were "in as good a bargaining position as they were in the 1920s and 1930s" to "do business with China, but we will have to get off their necks first." One other possibility for Japan's salvation loomed that Kennan did not then discuss: linking the Japanese to the markets and resources of Southeast Asia.[53]

By early 1950, the United States was already enmeshed in Vietnam, or French Indochina as it was known in the West. The dilemma began in early 1945 when Franklin D. Roosevelt at first opposed, then finally acquiesced in, a joint British-French colonial reoccupation of Indochina. The Europeans even used Japanese soldiers "to reconquer the little people we promised to liberate," MacArthur bitterly complained at the time. "It is the most ignoble kind of betrayal" and it "makes my blood boil." Vietnamese nationalists, urged by the U.S. intelligence personnel, asked Truman for support. The President never answered. When the Vietnamese responded in September with an uprising that killed over one hundred Westerners, including a U.S. intelligence officer (the first American victim of the thirty-year war), the revolution commenced. By 1949–50, Acheson was committing the United States to help the French because he needed France's cooperation in building Western European defenses. But another, more comprehensive motive also drove U.S. policy. By at least mid-1949, Kennan and Deputy Undersecretary of State Dean Rusk (who had served as a military officer in Southeast Asia at the close of the war) had concluded that Japan's economic survival depended on Southeast Asian trade.[54]

Acheson slowly came around to accept the inevitable. He was pushed by Rusk, who argued that the region's rice was necessary to feed Japan's population, and by Ambassador-at-large Philip Jessup, who visited Asia in early 1950 and became convinced that three prizes could be collected in one move. Since the United States could not send needed technicians to help Southeast Asia, Jessup reasoned, "Japan would be required to fill the gap. This would help to promote Japanese trade and to placate any anti-Japanese sentiments which might still be abroad." Privately, Acheson now saw "the American interest in the great underbelly of Asia as depending on two pillars, India and Japan." On March 29, 1950, Jessup and Acheson gave a remarkable summary of this policy behind closed doors to the Senate Foreign Relations Committee. Jessup applauded the suddenly mushrooming Japan trade with Southeast Asia (rice for locomotives with Thailand, for example). Acheson essentially admitted the United States was already trapped in the region in an effort to contain Chinese influence. He had pushed the French to be more enlightened in dealing with Asians, the Secretary of State observed, but "we" must "not press the French to the point where they say, 'All right, take over the damned country. We don't want it,' and put their soldiers on ships and send them back to France." When a senator worried that "we are very much in the position of those who were opposed to helping the American colonies" in 1776, Acheson made no direct response. By late May 1950, a month before the Korean War erupted, a forty-two-person U.S. aid mission set up shop in Saigon to disperse $23.5 million in economic help to buttress the French position.[55]

One Asian prime minister joked that the best approach to economic development was to attack the Americans, then let them occupy your country. By early 1950, however, Acheson's policy was stumbling on the realities of Vietnamese resistance and Japanese stagnation. A young professor of Far East languages, Edwin O. Reischauer, had visited Japan the year before and the State Department circulated his "penetrating" analysis. His report warned that the Japanese, once in awe of the occupation, "see it today as a conglomeration of persons having conflicting views and widely varying abilities. . . . Even General MacArthur has lost his aura of sanctity." It was time to "get off their necks," as Kennan had phrased it, and sign a peace treaty.[56]

Bureaucratic warfare erupted in Washington. Acheson later said that four groups fought a peace treaty: the Communists, the Pentagon, former Allies, and Japan. "Of these the Communists," he thought, "gave the least trouble." The State Department wanted the treaty to undercut anti-U.S. sentiment in Japan. Yoshida could then go off on his own, within certain limits of course. But the Pentagon wanted nothing to threaten its network of bases in Japan and Okinawa that formed the cornerstone of the entire U.S. security structure in Asia. The central question thus became clear: Which U.S. controls and bases should remain after a peace treaty went into effect? The State Department rightly feared that such demands would rekindle the Japanese memory of the hated 1853 to 1899 treaties.[57]

Yoshida did not make it easy for Acheson. In December 1949, his government announced the 1945 Yalta agreements to be non-binding on Japan. In other words, the Japanese reasserted their legal claims to the Kuriles and South Sakhalin, and also to the Bonins, Okinawa, and Iwo Jima, where U.S. officials intended to retain bases. Yoshida, moreover, feared that many Japanese army officers favored communism (or, as the phrase went, that they were "Red Fascists"). He consequently frowned on U.S. requests for a Japanese military buildup that would ease the burden of American taxpayers. In reality, since 1946 Japan had built a thirty-five-ship force of minesweepers, and since 1947 a coastguard to protect fishing rights. Yoshida wanted this navy to grow no further. By early 1950, his reluctance to rearm led the Truman administration to decide it must have long-term bases around Japan. After all, as a report to Congress phrased it, Japan did act as the "West coast" of the United States. The view of Japan as the key to a far western frontier seemed branded on American minds.[58]

In February 1950, Americans were shocked when the two great Communist powers signed a Treaty of Friendship and Mutual Assistance. Article I specifically targeted Japan and the United States: the Soviets and Chinese vowed "to adopt all necessary measures" to stop "the resumption of aggression . . . on the part of Japan or any other state that may collaborate with Japan directly or indirectly in acts of aggression." If either signatory was attacked by Japan or any allied state, the other signatory would immediately give "assistance by all means at its disposal." Japan was thus threatened with another atomic attack. The United States thus faced a possible war with the Soviets if it went to war with China.

A month earlier (January 1950), Acheson had anticipated such dangers by announcing that Japan fell within the defense perimeter which Americans would defend alone if necessary. The Secretary of State realized, however, that the United States was overstretched: Truman, obsessed with balancing the government's books, was forcing the military to defend much of Europe and parts of Asia on a $13 billion budget. In February to April 1950, Acheson and Paul Nitze (who had replaced Kennan as head of Policy Planning) secretly drew up NSC-68, a blueprint for fighting the post-1950 Cold War. The document aimed at nothing less than destroying the Soviet Union. It planned to accomplish this by quadrupling the military budget and creating global "situations of strength," as Acheson liked to call them. One of those situations was to be Japan.[59]

In April 1950, Truman appointed the chief Republican foreign policy voice, John Foster Dulles, as Acheson's special adviser. Dulles was specifically charged with negotiating a Japanese peace treaty. In late April 1950, Yoshida sent a delegation led by his intimate adviser, Ikeda Hayato, to Washington—ostensibly to discuss economic issues, in reality to tell U.S. officials that Japan was ready to negotiate a bilateral treaty allowing U.S. bases on Okinawa and the Bonins. Yoshida feared both the Sino-Soviet alliance and the sudden upsurge of Communist Party strength in Japan. He also realized that a treaty was the price the Japanese must pay Washington for their independence. When Dulles flew to Tokyo in June to work out the details, however, the canny Yoshida refused to be explicit about U.S. bases. The prime minister would not play his high cards until the stakes were clearly on the table. Dulles was "flabbergasted" and angered. He intensified the pressure. By June 22 (three days before the Korean War unexpectedly exploded), Dulles was not only demanding bases but a limited rearming of Japan. The rearming was proposed over MacArthur's fervent objections.[60]

Dulles's negotiations bogged down. U.S. officials, however, would not retreat from their new, grand design of NSC-68 and Japan's pivotal role in it. While Acheson awaited the proper moment to accelerate the military budget and rearm Japan, the CIA helped Japanese trading companies return to Southeast Asia. It also secretly dispatched Japanese military officers to advise Chiang Kai-shek as he planned to overthrow the Communists on the mainland. Assistant Secretary of State Dean Rusk later observed, "Our general attitude in those days was that it was important for the United States to have control of every wave in the Pacific Ocean." On June 25, 1950, the Korean War suddenly broke out. The conflict "prove[d] our thesis," Acheson later remarked, and thus made possible the realization of NSC-68's vast plans to control those and other ocean waves. Or, as he and his assistants concluded, "Korea came along and saved us."[61]

Korea: The War for Japan— "A Gift of the Gods"

The 1949 to 1953 years resembled a historical meat grinder: one Cold War went in and out came another, somewhat similar in ingredients, but quite changed in form. Faced with the Korean War, which was quickly seen as a tremendous, if unexpected, opportunity, the United States hurriedly built positions of strength that incorporated Japan, Taiwan, the southwest Pacific, and South Korea. Since 1853, the United States had hoped to lock an open Japan into a vast, liberalized trading system while using the islands as a partner in protecting U.S. interests in Asia. The war suddenly allowed an acceleration of these plans.

Even these historical earthquakes, however, were not enough to open Japan's economic system as U.S. officials had long hoped. Japan's "collectivist feeling," Dulles's top assistant (and later U.S. Ambassador to Japan), John Allison, privately lamented to a Senate committee in 1951, "is one of the problems you cannot get away from." Nor did the earthquakes close the long arguments between Washington and Tokyo over China. To the contrary, as China became a focal point of American hatred, it became a target of Japanese economic ambitions. The century-old themes that had shaped American-Japanese relations changed and intensified rather than melted away.[62]

The war climaxed five years of civil conflict between Communist North Korea and the capitalist South. The two had been quickly and artificially divided along the 38th parallel in 1945 for purposes of delineating Soviet and U.S. occupation zones. Between 1947 and 1949, both Soviet and U.S. troops began withdrawing from their respective zones. By June 1950, the southern regime of the aged Syngman Rhee was corrupt and stumbling. Deeply mistrustful of Rhee, Truman had reduced U.S. troop presence but not the commitment to protect South Korea. As Acheson had declared in a January speech, Americans would do so with the aid of the United Nations.

The North's drive across the 38th parallel on June 25 was only one of many crossings made by both Koreas during recent months. This particular invasion, however, was more massive and successful. As revealed in Soviet archives opened after 1989, the attack had been planned by North Korean dictator Kim Il-sung for a year and cleared in personal conversations by Joseph Stalin. The Soviet ruler, however, wanted Kim to get help from the Chinese Communists. He also emphasized that, while Kim could employ Soviet equipment and advisers, if the invasion went sour the Koreans were on their own. Stalin was not going to fight World War III with the United States over South Korea. Nevertheless, the Russians and Japanese had been enemies for centuries. The ancient hatreds felt by Koreans for Japanese had been fueled to white heat by a half century of Tokyo's rule. Now, as Dulles intensified his mission, Japan was to be rebuilt and used as a long-term, well-anchored aircraft carrier for U.S. forces. Stalin and Kim agreed that the chance to neu-tralize such dangers was worth the risks of invasion. The two Commu-nist leaders did not foresee, however, that Truman would quickly mobilize United Nations support and commit U.S. forces to fight the invasion.

North Korean forces knifed through the peninsula, but they were finally stopped in mid-July by MacArthur's United Nations forces (which were actually more than 90 percent American). Washington officials, led by Kennan, Dulles, and CIA analysts, had no doubt: an ultimate Communist target was the U.S. position in Japan. Then and later, Kennan believed the U.S. buildup in Japan was a central reason for the invasion. Dulles told Acheson that "it is probable that one of the purposes of the Korean attack was to break up United States planning of a peace treaty for Japan," which, in Dulles's mind, made such plan-ning even more urgent. In a nationwide CBS Radio speech, Dulles declared that if the Soviets held Korea as well as Sakhalin, "Japan would be between the upper and lower jaws of the Russian bear." Within hours after the invasion, CIA analysts told U.S. officials that "Soviet military domination of all Korea" could turn Japan away from "future alignment with the U.S.," and lead to "neutralizing the usefulness of Japan as an American base."[64]

Acheson seized this golden opportunity to push ahead not only in Japan but globally. Truman finally, reluctantly, agreed to set NSC-68 plans in motion and bust the budget limits on a massive military buildup. The draft was reinstated so the army could quickly rise from 630,000 to over a million soldiers. U.S. policies toward defeated Nation-alist Chinese on Taiwan were changing from withdrawal to commit-ment even before the war; immediately after the invasion, Truman stationed U.S. forces around Taiwan to protect Chiang's remnants and began to view the island as a vital "free-world" outpost. Of special worry to Stalin, Acheson planned to arm West Germany. In perspective, few American decisions of these days were more significant than Acheson ordering the first major U.S. military mission to French Indochina.

Truman made an equally important decision on September 11, 1950, when, urged on by Acheson and Rusk, he ordered MacArthur to take his successful counteroffensive north of the 38th and into North Korea itself. Four days later, MacArthur pulled off a stunning, near-impossible invasion back of Communist lines in Inchon. Only recently has it been learned—thanks to the work of Bruce Cumings and Jon Halliday—that Japanese military units secretly played a vital role in the drive north-ward. In October, Japanese minesweepers cleared Wonsan Harbor. This operation reintroduced Japan's military presence to other Asians just five years after the end of World War II. In the opinion of the admiral who commanded the minesweepers, it also helped persuade U.S. officials to give Japan independence in 1951.[65]

Because of open-ended instructions, and a belief in his own invincibility, MacArthur drove toward the Yalu River separating Korea from China. At first tentatively in October, then with human-wave attacks in November, the Chinese intervened to inflict on the United States some of the worst military defeats in its history. The Communists nearly drove the U.S.-UN forces to the sea before bloody fighting in 1951 began to produce a stalemate.

MacArthur, for all his disastrous decisions, provocatively summarized the crisis when he remarked that "At one fell blow, everything that had been so laboriously built up since the days of John Hay [in 1898–1905] was lost." In late December, the frightened general secretly asked Truman for permission to drop atomic bombs on twenty-six targets to stop the Chinese advance. Truman turned down the request, although a month earlier the President himself had publicly refused to rule out the use of such weapons. In April 1951, Truman did order nine atomic bombs to Okinawa for possible use against Chinese or Russians, but after second thoughts, stopped the task force at Guam. The historian Roger Dingman argues that while Truman did not come close to ordering nuclear weapons to be dropped, sending the bombs had a striking political effect: it helped convince the military Joint Chiefs that the President was finally committed to fighting the war, and so made possible their support of Truman in April when he fired MacArthur and recalled him home after the general publicly criticized administration policies in Asia. The stakes in Asia had suddenly skyrocketed. As a joint State-Defense team told Acheson during late 1950, "America without Asia will have been reduced to the Western Hemisphere and a precarious foothold on the western fringe of the Eurasian continent. Success [in Korea] will vindicate [and] give added meaning to America and the American way of life."[66]

Yoshida and many other Japanese were, to understate, more relaxed about the war. The premier declared in early 1951, "We do not have slightest expectation that the Communist countries will invade Japan." (Nor should the Japanese, given the U.S. military commitment in the region.) Since 1953, Japanese scholars have paid little attention to the conflict relative to their work on other post-1945 events. As Dingman phrased it, for Japanese with any sense of history, "the Korean War becomes simply another Korean War." Where Americans saw a historic crisis, Japanese saw an unfortunate but welcome opportunity—"a gift of the gods," as Yoshida later called the war.[67]

Yoshida used the conflict not only to obtain Japan's political independence and to ease its dependence on Americans. Since 1947 he had secretly developed an intelligence organization, the Cabinet Research Office (still in existence a half century later), that emphasized Soviet affairs but did little at the outset in studying the United States. The Tokyo government could thus obtain its own, usually calmer, views of Soviet intentions instead of wholly relying on U.S. intelligence. The CIA worked with the Japanese, notably when the agency served Yoshida's purposes. During the Korean War, for example, Japan's conservatives needed money and the United States needed tungsten, used to harden steel. As the late Howard Schonberger revealed in his unpublished history of the affair, the CIA and the Japan hands, led by Dooman, worked out a secret deal: for $10 million, the Pentagon bought tungsten hoarded by former Japanese military officers. Much of the money then went to the conservatives' political causes (after, that is, the Dooman group apparently skimmed off more than $2 million in profit). Using the well-known political fixer, Kodama Yoshio, as a broker, the CIA began more than a decade-long funneling of money to conservative factions.[68]

Yoshida's government and the Americans also enjoyed mutual benefits when MacArthur demanded that a Police Reserve of 75,000 men be created, and that the Maritime Safety Force be expanded by 8,500. These groups were to do internal policing once done by U.S. troops now in Korea. Washington officials, as Allison said, wanted a centralized police force that could efficiently put down "extremist elements" who might "take the law into their own hands," as they had in the "old Japanese police state." Yoshida quieted critics who feared rearming by appointing as head of the Police Reserve a person with no military experience. Over time it did develop into a capable military unit. In 1950–54, however, his long-held fear of army officers who seemed to be susceptible to communism, and his determination not to waste resources on a military while U.S. protection was in sight (and Communist invaders were not), led him to build up the civilian economy, not military budgets.[69]

Yoshida also used the Korean crisis to complete his roundup of Communist suspects and the restoring of rights to some seventy thousand former military and wartime officials. Stalin inadvertently helped him in early January 1951 by ordering Japanese Communists to shift tactics and violently oppose U.S. defense policies. Yoshida could joke to a U.S.

reporter, "You Americans are very difficult. We had all the Communists in jail when you occupied the country in 1945. Then you told us to release them. Now you ask us to find them and put them in jail again. A very cumbersome process." He was, however, most happy to cooperate. Japan seemed to be in step with Truman's Cold War policies. Hollywood began to reflect this perception. In 1951, just six years after Hiroshima and Nagasaki, the film *Go for Broke* portrayed the World War II exploits of the 442nd Regimental Combat Team of Japanese-American volunteers. Racism seemed in abeyance as Van Johnson, playing the Anglo commanding officer, learned as much from his troops about honor and courage as they did from him.[70]

The moment seemed perfect for Dulles to write a peace treaty. He and Acheson devised a shrewd strategy. They knew the Soviets opposed any U.S. bases in Japan, the Pentagon demanded such bases, and Allies (especially Australia, New Zealand, and Great Britain) feared a resurgence of Japanese militarism. So Dulles and Acheson made separate agreements to deal with these problems. They drafted a treaty giving Japan its independence that most other parties, perhaps even the Soviets, could sign. They then wrote a separate bilateral agreement between Japan and the United States to guarantee the bases and assure the Pentagon of long-term control of Okinawa and the Bonin Islands. Dulles meanwhile flew thousands of miles to pacify Australia and New Zealand's fears of Japanese militarism. (He "practically invented shuttle diplomacy," wrote Roger Buckley.) Dulles devised the ANZUS pact guaranteeing Australia and New Zealand's security. Dulles privately told the Senate that any Russian attack on the Australians and New Zealanders "seems . . . very remote," but "they had the hot breath of Japan's aggression blowing right on them" in the early 1940s, and fear remained. The British bitterly protested being excluded from a deal that released Japan for a major export offensive on British markets in Asia. At one point, Dulles departed London with the angry pronouncement that the Japanese peace treaty was going to be signed, whether or not the British decided to be one of the signers.[71]

Charles Evans Hughes's work at the 1921–22 Washington Conference was now being completed. Hughes had broken the backbone of British power in the Far East by destroying the Anglo-Japanese alliance and giving Japan's fleet supremacy in the western Pacific. Dulles and Acheson essentially announced that the British Empire was finished in the region (outside of a few remaining economic outposts such as Hong Kong and Singapore). American power, working with London's former Asian partner, would take over.

Dulles's real frustrations, however, were not with the British or the Communist powers. They were with the Pentagon and Yoshida. The Pentagon finally came around because of the bases' guarantee and, as well, because the Secretary of Defense in 1950–51 was George Marshall, former Secretary of State and a close ally of Acheson's. Marshall understood the urgency of signing a peace treaty before a frustrated Japan turned anti-American. Whenever a deadlock did appear, Truman invariably came down on the State Department's side. Trusting Acheson completely, the President had the interesting idea that foreign policy should be decided in the place where it was best understood.

Yoshida was tougher than even the Pentagon. He was determined to create an "autonomous Japan," to use the historian Hirano Ken'ichiro's phrase. Japan's security might remain dependent on U.S. forces, but this same dependence was to be used to free up resources Japan needed to become economically autonomous. Above all, Yoshida did not want his country to be sucked into the Korean War, expensive rearming, or a U.S.-controlled anti-Communist alliance system. He and his advisers agreed that a security treaty had to be separate from a peace treaty, and there was to be no rearming. Yoshida's famous nickname, "One Man," indicated his willingness to stand alone and act dictatorially, but it perhaps also revealed his determination that Japan would stand alone as much as possible just six years after a crushing defeat.[72]

On January 25, 1951, Dulles arrived in Tokyo for decisive talks. His entourage included Allison, Pentagon officials, and John D. Rockefeller III, whose family had long been generous in developing Japanese medical and philanthropic cultural activities. Dulles wanted Rockefeller to restart U.S.-Japan cultural exchanges.

In the first talks on January 29 the chief stumbling blocks emerged as Dulles and Yoshida maneuvered for advantage. First, the premier asked for a restoration of laws promoting the "family system"—a code phrase referring to prewar educational controls and the traditional role of women. Dulles made no response. Second, Yoshida emphasized the "long term necessity of trading with China." He argued that Japanese businessmen were "the best fifth column" to break down communism. Dulles warned that Japan could expect "restrictions" on any trade with China. Third, Yoshida, to Dulles's displeasure, objected to quick rearming—in part because "Japanese militarists who had now gone 'underground'" might resurface to seize the government. Rearming would also impose "a severe strain" just as "Japan was beginning to get its feet on the ground financially."[73]

In talks over the next week, a fourth problem appeared: the United

The Results of the 1945–1951
U.S.-Japan Peace Treaty Negotiations

U. S. S. R.

Sakhalin

Ⓐ

Kuril Is.

CHINA

KOREA

JAPAN

■ Claims and titles renounced by Japan

Ⓐ Ceded to Russia

Ⓑ Concurrence by Japan in any U.S. proposal for a U.S. trusteeship under the United Nations

Ⓒ Claims and titles renounced by Japan: Japanese acceptance of United Nations decision of April 1947 establishing a U.S. trusteeship

Ryukyu Is.

Bonin Is.

Ⓑ

Volcano Is.

FORMOSA
(TAIWAN)

Wake Is.

PHILIPPINE
ISLANDS

Mariana
Islands

Guam

Ⓒ

Eniwetok   Bikini

Yap

Marshall Is.

Truk Is.

Kwajalein

Caroline Islands

Chazaud

States insisted on retaining bases in Okinawa and the Bonins, while a disappointed Yoshida asked for the return of those islands. In the end, Dulles both pleased the Pentagon and gave an important sop to Yoshida by holding the bases but recognizing Japan's "residual sovereignty" in the islands, a phrase finally incorporated in the 1951 treaty. A fifth problem, Japanese reparations to countries it had invaded after 1931, was settled when Dulles proposed a formula that committed Japan to pay, but a limited amount and—in an especially imaginative stroke—tied to Japanese exports so the funds would ultimately be spent in Japan itself. Yoshida, needless to say, saw "no difficulties" with this arrangement. He must have appreciated how the reparations could now be used to penetrate the very markets that Japan had failed to seize or hold militarily not long before.[74]

The main obstacle was rearmament. In a decisive meeting of MacArthur, Yoshida, and Dulles, the general came down hard against rearming and suggested instead that Japan become the productive arsenal of military goods and weapons for its allies in the region. Yoshida seconded that view by observing that given Asians' memories of 1940 to 1945, any Japanese threat to rearm would short-circuit the necessary economic offensive. In the Diet he continued to ridicule any threat of a Communist invasion. And, as was revealed a quarter century later, Yoshida had a fallback position: on February 3, 1951, he secretly agreed to creating limited ground forces, but only after U.S. and Japanese negotiators went through a highly complicated labyrinth of consultation procedures that he had carefully devised.[75]

Dulles surrendered. A compromise was reached. In a bilateral security pact, the United States retained bases in Japan and Okinawa. The Americans gave a vague promise to defend Japan (a signal they expected the Japanese to rearm soon to defend themselves). After Truman's massive response in Korea, however, no sane person doubted how U.S. forces would react if Japan were attacked. American forces were also allowed, under the treaty, to put down riots and disturbances at the request of the Tokyo government. Again, this provision was so loosely drawn that for the rest of the 1950s the Japanese complained that the United States could use force whenever it desired within Japan. Yoshida successfully demanded that the rights of the U.S. troops in Japan be handled separately, and quietly, in an executive agreement (that is, in a form not requiring legislative debate), so Japanese opinion would not be upset. Dulles thus obtained the peace treaty and bases, but only with a blurred, complicated commitment from Yoshida to rearm. "The Oriental mind," Dulles told a Chinese friend in 1951, "particularly that of the Japanese, was always more devious than the Occidental mind."[76]

In September 1951, fifty-four nations, not including mainland China or India, met to discuss and sign the peace treaty. The British diplomat R. H. Scott gave his friends in London a private, firsthand account of how the conference illustrated American power and a new technological revolution:

It took place in the San Francisco Opera House, an enormous theatre, seating I suppose a couple thousand, with Acheson and Secre-
tariat on the platform. The orchestra pit was roofed over and what
the Americans call a "podium" was placed on it from which the
speakers addressed the conference. There were no desks or tables
and we all sat in the ordinary theatre seats. The delegates themselves
occupied (in alphabetical order) the first six rows of the orchestra
stalls and the whole of San Francisco and indeed most of California
queued up to occupy the other seats. . . . There were also very strong
contingents of press men, radio men, radio commentators and television operators. Acheson made one or two half-hearted attempts to
prevent the spectators from taking part but [anti-Communist orators]
found it very easy to draw rounds of cheers from the galleries. . . . It
was by coincidence the first occasion on which the Americans had
coast to coast television, so the television audience was colossal. . . .
[Our] row was frequently raked by the cameras because they could
present to their audience in one line the U.S.A., the U.K. and the
U.S.S.R., and I believe that 45 million people had the pleasure of
seeing me pick my nose.[77]

Acheson, suffering from ptomaine poisoning, dragged himself to the
podium to act as chair so he and his allies could enforce the rules of
procedure. The rules prevented any Soviet bloc amendments. When,
for example, the Soviet delegate proposed that Communist China be
invited, Acheson simply ruled him out of order. After the United States
and its allies (especially those from Latin America) rammed the treaty
through, it was signed by Japan, the United States, and forty-seven
other countries, but not by the Soviets, Poles, or Czechs. The treaty was
supplemented by the U.S.-Japan security treaty, and later by separate
Japanese peace treaties with the Republic of China (on Taiwan) in
1952.[78]

The peace and security treaties now came before the U.S. Senate for
ratification. Dulles had earlier opened secret testimony to the Senate
by giving an almost exclusively economic explanation for the pacts. If
the United States did not move quickly, he warned, the Japanese could
join the Communist bloc because they needed both "vast raw material
resources" from Manchuria and their "natural market, that is the big
China Market." The Soviets, he added, sat on Japan's doorstep; they
occupied Sakhalin and the Kurile Islands. Dulles's was an honest but
not necessarily wise approach. Many senators, rabidly committed to
protecting Taiwan and overthrowing Communist China, noted that Yos-

hida—like Dulles—had emphasized Japan's possible links with China. Before, and even for some months during the Korean War, Japanese-Chinese trade grew. At the San Francisco Conference, Yoshida told receptive British officials that "the future of Japan could not be separated from the future of China." He wondered whether "Japan's role would be to 'democratize' China"—words that echoed his remarks to Dulles in late January.[79]

Yoshida could balance his remarks with others, such as his condemning the 1950 Sino-Soviet alliance as a gun aimed at Japan. But William Knowland (R: CA), a leader of the Senate's so-called China Lobby, was not reassured. He obtained the support of fifty-six senators to warn that they might vote against the peace treaty unless the Japanese unequivocally agreed to support the Republic of China on Taiwan and oppose mainland China. Dulles, accompanied by two senators, dutifully flew back to Tokyo in December 1951. They asked Yoshida to sign a statement that would appease Knowland. The Americans carried a potent threat: earlier in the year, Congress had passed the Battle Act that cut off aid to nations trading with Communists. Japan's survival depended on that aid. On December 24, the prime minister reluctantly signed a so-called Yoshida letter. The letter's phrase that Japan had "no intention to conclude a bilateral treaty with the Communist regime of China" gave the senators satisfaction. Great Britain, which had recognized mainland China and desperately wanted to steer Japanese trade toward China and away from British markets in Southeast Asia, blasted the letter. Too bad, Dulles told the British through a letter to Acheson: given Japan's dependence on Americans, "it is inconceivable that . . . Japan should pursue foreign policies which cut across those of the United States." In 1957, Yoshida recorded in his memoirs that such dependence was unfortunate: the "British and Japanese" best understood China, he wrote, while the Americans did not "truly" know the Chinese and thus adopted policies that "have been almost a total failure." Not surprisingly, historians later discovered that the "Yoshida letter" was written by Dulles.[80]

By 1951, the debate over the direction of Japan's trade was passionate, all-consuming politically, and at the heart of the U.S.-Japanese relationship. The Korean War's immense impact on Japan's economy intensified the debate. Between 1950 and 1952, special U.S. military procurements suddenly accounted for 70 percent of Japan's exports. A once war-devastated economy that had survived on aid and narrow markets suddenly became infused with capital. Four months after the war began, the nation's industrial production reached postwar highs (actually 106 percent of the 1934 to 1936 base). Employment soared. The large annual trade deficit began to be more than covered by U.S. military spending in Japan. Later, Japanese and other experts downplayed the war's positive effects because its shock distorted the economy and provided only a little of Japan's overall capital investment between 1950 and 1953. But such criticisms turned out to be much less important than, as a British businessman in Tokyo observed, the "unexpected windfall in hard currency" that enabled the Japanese "to re-equip and modernize their plants, to expand in an amazing way"—while keeping out foreign capital and its influence.[81]

The Korean War was to the rebuilding of Japan as the Marshall Plan was for rebuilding Western Europe. The long-term effects were terrific. Two of them were to shape American, as well as Japanese, lives for the rest of the century. First, Japan's most powerful business association (the *keidanren*, or Federation of Economic Organizations) and the government decided to work closely with the United States in importing and developing dual-use technology. Such technology could be used for U.S. and others' military needs while giving Japan an edge in exploiting civilian markets. For example, a struggling Mitsui factory making specialized steel products suddenly generated vast amounts of capital by becoming the nation's leading commercial arms producer. The seedbed of the Japanese economic "miracle" of the 1960s and 1970s was being planted.[82]

The second long-term effect of the wartime buildup was an accelerated interest by Tokyo, and especially Washington, in Southeast Asia. In 1945, John Emmerson had found that he was to help run the U.S. occupation from an office in Tokyo occupied by a Mitsui executive. As Emmerson moved into the office, the Japanese pointed to a map showing his country's "Co-Prosperity Sphere" in East Asia. "We tried," the Mitsui official observed. "See what you can do with it!" Emmerson later noted that "at that moment the whole burden of American Foreign Policy in Asia hit me in the stomach." This historic step of restoring Japan's relationship with the region was not taken without impassioned debate. At a private Council on Foreign Relations meeting in New York City on October 23, 1950, Japan hand Eugene Dooman flatly told Dulles that any attempt to keep Japan out of Communist China's market "will be self-defeating." Perhaps, Dulles responded, but a Japanese-Chinese relationship could harm vital U.S. relations with Tokyo. He believed that "amicable relations" meant "finding new trade outlets for the Japanese." And crucial outlets, as he had specified earlier in the meeting, lay "in the underdeveloped areas of Southeast Asia." Dooman lost the argument, at least in the short run, after Yoshida seemed to agree in public with Dulles. The idea that Japan depended on Chinese trade was mere Communist propaganda, Yoshida told the Diet in October 1951; instead, "Japan intended to cooperate in developing natural resources in the Southeast Asian countries."[83]

There was, unfortunately, a problem. The Viet Minh revolt against French colonialism continued to tear up parts of Southeast Asia. "The biggest Viet Minh appeal," a State Department official observed, "is . . . land, education, and a chance to shoot French. It is difficult to match that platform." The attempt nevertheless had to be made. Among top U.S. officials, the conventional wisdom developed that without Southeast Asia Japan could not be orderly and cooperative, and without that kind of Japan there could be no effective U.S. policy in an inflamed Far East. A leading Japanese scholar of the occupation later put a different spin on it. The post-1947 policies, Takemae Eiji believed, created an emphasis on materialism that was only a "mischievous reform" and lacked an "ethos of democracy." This point seemed to be driven home in early 1952 when Yoshida tried to pass an anti-subversive law that reminded many Japanese of the McCarthyism then infecting American politics. In the "Bloody May Day" riots that erupted, U.S. military vehicles were attacked and fourteen hundred people, including several Americans, injured.[84]

After six years of occupation, then, some trouble brewed, but Japan's economy, thanks to the Korean War, was reviving. No one, however, not even MacArthur, could assume that Americans had created an open, liberalized Japan. Indeed, no knowledgeable observer could conclude that the primary U.S. aim had been to democratize Japan. The highest objectives were, first, to use Japan as the hub of an open, multilateral capitalism in Asia; second, to contain communism; and third, to reassure neighbors by keeping Japan orderly and controlled. American economic policies and the containment of communism, as Acheson's close adviser, Paul Nitze, later noted, "were viewed as being one and the same thing." China and Vietnam, however, were about to challenge such assumptions about U.S.-Japan relations.[85]

X

The 1950s:
The Pivotal Decade

"Japan . . . Has a Unique Capacity for Good or Evil"

IN THE United States, massive military spending characterized the post-1950 years of the Korean War and implementation of NSC-68. These expenditures replaced the spending on civilian social needs that had driven the political economy between 1865 and 1939. In Japan, on the other hand, a rebuilding of industry-for-export replaced the military demands of 1868 to 1945 as a driving force. Americans and Japanese seemed to have switched places. These economic differences between the two nations led to repeated clashes in the post-1950 years. Americans, for example, defined China as a military danger. Japanese defined it as an economic opportunity.

The root cause of the growing clash, however, was the U.S. intention to keep Japan dependent, and Japan's determination to be economically independent. In 1952, the country still had a long way to go. As a British diplomat in Tokyo recalled, "many people were still homeless, sleeping rough, under railway viaducts or in the shells of buildings awaiting repair or demolition." With this as background, Joseph Dodge bluntly told Japanese officials of the Ministry of International Trade and Industry (MITI) that "Japan can be independent politically but dependent economically." He spoke to an increasingly powerful agency, which was setting out precisely to destroy such dependence. John Foster Dulles was even more direct. He remarked to British officials that the 1951 security arrangements actually "amounted to a voluntary continuation of the Occupation." Some U.S. officials did realize that such dependence could eat away the entire relationship unless it was modified. Bitter debates over the peace settlement, after all, had already splintered Japanese politics. Some groups accepted the deal as a necessary evil, others accepted the peace treaty but deplored any ties to unpredictable U.S. military policies, and still others condemned it all. Many wanted the freedom to resume Japan's historic destiny of Pan-Asianism. Japanese thus grew nervous in 1952 when Republican presidential candidate Dwight Eisenhower promised that in the future he would have Asian soldiers (not Americans) fighting Asians for the sake of U.S. interests.[1]

In 1952, Senator Everett Dirksen (R: IL) stated the obvious but enveloped it in traditional racist terms: "Every ethnic argument is on my side when I say they [the Japanese] are Asiatics and they will be Asiatics." John Allison, Dulles's top adviser on Japan and soon U.S. ambassador to Tokyo, warned the State Department in mid-1952 that the Japanese continued to believe their "distinctive culture" vastly superior to the American. They "have generally been prone to regard Americans as shallow, materialistic, and lacking in cultural values."

Allison then pinpointed three sources of past and future clashes: specifically, Japanese intellectuals follow what they believe to be "a logically ordered, universalistic" philosophy "influenced by Hegelian and neo-Hegelian" systems. They find little of interest in "the more eclectic philosophical system of America." More generally, the Japanese "emphasis upon socially-oriented values is in marked contrast with the individually-oriented values" of Americans. Perhaps above all, the Japanese are haunted by "a sense of vulnerability to external attack and a continuing search for national security." They are "beset by confusion and conflict," Allison emphasized, because they know they need U.S. protection, but fear the resulting "impact on sovereignty." The future ambassador warned, in other words, that each nation had yet to understand the swift, often dangerous undercurrents that drove the other nation's history.[2]

Dulles told MacArthur in March 1951 that "the United States and Japan are the only significant source of power in the Pacific." But it was also true, he informed a French audience in mid-1952, that Japan "has a unique capacity for good or evil." After all, Dulles announced, "the Japanese people have historically been susceptible to militarism." If their "ability to produce modern types of precision weapons" should ever be used by "the Soviet Communist program of world conquest," then, as "Stalin has said . . . the Soviet Union would be 'invincible.'" Americans and Japanese had often clashed during the previous century because their relationship was so central to each nation's progress. Now, as Dulles saw it, the relationship was also central to the "free world's" very survival.[3]

A relationship could not be much more important than that, so when Eisenhower and Dulles took power in January 1953, they quickly moved to strengthen the links so Communist power could be further contained in Asia. Their main thrusts came in the military and economic arenas. As a military strategist, Eisenhower had no American peer, and he knew it. The former general, however, was much less confident about the American economy. He had run for the presidency in part by hammering home to voters how the Democrats' spending threatened to destroy the nation through inflation and then bankruptcy. The Texas-born and Kansas-raised leader believed he had a sure intuition about judging when and how much defense spending could be cut to save the economy without jeopardizing U.S. security. He worried often about the republic's fate once a president took office who accepted the Pentagon's argument for ever more defense spending. An economy dependent on the military budget, Eisenhower flatly told his cabinet, "would either drive us to war—or into some form of dictatorial government." He set about cutting Truman's $52 billion military budget to $34 billion by the mid-1950s. Eisenhower meanwhile increased the one thousand nuclear weapons in 1953 by some eighteen times over the next eight years. Containment would be achieved cheaply through the threat of "massive retaliation"—the ability to "retaliate, instantly, by means and at places of our own choosing," as Dulles phrased it in 1954. It was implied, moreover, that the awesome weapons would be used first, if necessary, and not simply as a last resort.[4]

The Japanese had experienced such weapons firsthand. They were, understandably, profoundly disturbed by the Eisenhower strategy. Tokyo officials, led by Prime Minister Yoshida, were equally disturbed by another result of the cost cutting. As fewer American troops came to guard the ramparts of freedom, other nations' soldiers were expected to step up to the ramparts. In a public speech of 1953, the new U.S. Vice President, Richard M. Nixon, told seven hundred Japanese leaders that Americans had "made a mistake in 1946" by placing Article IX in Japan's Constitution. Washington wanted Japan to rearm. During the height of the Korean War, Yoshida had increased the Police Reserve from 75,000 to 110,000, and rechristened it a "Self-Defense Force." The prime minis-

ter, however, was reluctant to go farther. He seemed obsessed by the
fear that Americans wanted Japanese troops to be used in Korea and
elsewhere. Yoshida's fears grew more intense after the Socialists (who
opposed any rearming) picked up surprising strength in elections of
1952 and 1953. His own conservative coalition meanwhile fragmented as
the Liberal Party came under the increasing influence of old, aggressive
nationalist leaders.[5]

For Yoshida, therefore, the Eisenhower-Nixon policies could hardly
have come at a worse moment. In May 1954, he tried to find a middle
ground through two laws that transformed the nation's defense policies
by setting up a functioning Defense Agency. This landmark legislation
was also shaped by Americans bearing gifts. In March 1954, the United
States had offered a mutual security agreement that provided $150 mil-
lion in military equipment, and another $100 million in agricultural
goods and U.S. purchases of Japanese products. In immediate need of
dollars to pay for food and raw material imports, Japan agreed to the
deal. U.S. military payments between 1952 and 1956 were equivalent to
paying for a critical one-quarter of Japan's commodity imports. In
return, Yoshida bit his lip and built up the postwar Japanese military,
but in 1950, 1954, and 1956 (when another government was in power),
laws were carefully written to guarantee civilian control.[6]

The U.S. military aid also had another far-reaching effect: the money
went through Japan's Ministry of Finance and thus bolstered its already
growing power. This ministry guided Japan's "economic miracle." Ironically, it was U.S. policy after 1946 to work with the Ministry of Finance
(so Japan's economy could be accelerated), while largely ignoring the
Foreign Ministry (so Japan's foreign policies would be largely shaped in
Washington). British Ambassador to Japan Sir Esler Dening reported
home in 1955 that U.S. officials were making a "mistake" to favor the
finance ministry "in what may be called the Whitehall of Tokyo for use
as a PX [military post exchange, or supermarket], while the Japanese
Foreign Office still languishes squalidly in part of a commercial building
without amenities or security." Dening warned that Americans asked
too much from Japan, "and the parallel of Egypt comes to mind." The
Egyptian military had just ousted British rule after nearly a century of
London-directed colonialism.[7]

American attempts to reshape Japan did not stop at favoring the
Ministry of Finance over the foreign ministry. They also included U.S.
impacts on Japanese culture. The Korean War, for example, increased
the number of uniformed Americans in Japan some two and a half
times, to 250,000. They brought with them English-language radio and

other services that blanketed much of urban Japan. This was part of a large U.S. cultural offensive. During 1950 to 1956, about three thousand Japanese students studied in the United States, the first wave of a flood to follow. Many of these—numbering about 250 per year—belonged to the Fulbright Scholar program, which was extended to Japan in 1953. The first major positions for the study of American history were established. Inspired by the work of Charles Beard, and working especially with Professor Merrill Jensen of the University of Wisconsin, Japanese scholars—notably at the Kyoto Seminars—focused on Jensen's specialty, the American Revolutionary era. The focus had a purpose: to suggest that 1930s militarism had brought down Japan because the nation had not gone through the bourgeois revolution and mass democratization unleashed in eighteenth-century America. In Tokyo, International Christian University was built to demonstrate U.S. encouragement of Christianity. A new generation of Japanese students studied democracy and social change in quite a new, and American, context. Some Japanese scholars even argued that U.S. occupation policies had brought about the needed "bourgeois revolution," so Japan could now peacefully and profitably adjust to the postwar world.[8]

The Rockefeller Foundation, active in Japan long before the war, returned to become a hub for the new exchanges. Its driving force was Dr. Charles Burton Fahs, who had studied in Japan during the 1930s, then helped spy on his former hosts between 1941 and 1945 as a member of the Office of Strategic Services (the forerunner of the CIA). After joining the Rockefeller Foundation in 1946, he wrote a confidential report emphasizing dismay at MacArthur and SCAP's attempts to impose U.S. textbooks and educational principles on the Japanese—an imposition Fahs believed was doomed to failure once the Americans departed. He advised that SCAP prohibition of travel be lifted, then with Rockefeller money began in 1949 to send selected young Japanese and Korean journalists and broadcasters to Columbia University for training. SCAP officials selected the participants while constantly worrying that the visitors would learn the bad manners of U.S. journalists and return to be "annoying to General MacArthur." Some did shape Japan's media after 1952. When Dulles visited in early 1951, his fellow traveler, John D. Rockefeller III, strengthened the Rockefeller Foundation's work, and also helped create the highly influential International House of Japan, where experts from around the globe were hosted at conferences by Japanese over the next four decades.[9]

Popular culture soon reflected the new relationship. The best-selling author James Michener (who knew Japan well and had married a Japanese woman) wrote *The Bridges at Toko-ri* (in which Japanese and Americans learn about each other as persons rather than wartime stereotypes) and *Sayonara*. When published in *Life* magazine during 1953, *Sayonara* immediately reached an audience of 5 million. Perhaps most popular of all were the *Godzilla* movies made in Japan, which became smash hits in the United States, where audiences who watched monsters attacking Japanese cities were usually ignorant that *Godzilla* was replaying the U.S. bombings of those cities during the war.[10]

Deming, Dulles, and the Great Choice: China or Vietnam?

Then there was W. Edwards Deming. Born in 1900, trained in industrial management, Deming had worked in the U.S. government, before teaching his new philosophy of business management at New York University and Columbia University. His theory viewed production not as bit parts but as "a total system," in his phrase. This system required full cooperation (not competition) among all persons in a firm to produce the best (not necessarily the most) products. Deming demanded that a company's policies begin not with the top management's views, but with the customer's wants. He believed these wants to be, above all, products of dependable quality. Trained in statistical and mathematical theory, Deming devised within his system statistically based quality controls to secure customer satisfaction. The Union of Japanese Scientists and Engineers that brought him to Japan in 1950 understood the importance of his work. His first eight-day seminar was attended by over two hundred Japanese engineers, including top corporate officials. Deming emphasized the need to find export markets, and stressed that profitable, long-term markets required quality products. In 1951, Japan began awarding the highly coveted Deming Prize to industries that produced superior goods.[11]

Deming's immense popularity among Japanese ironically worsened U.S.-Japan clashes. He enjoyed little popularity in his own country until after 1970, when the Japanese "economic miracle" forced embattled U.S. firms to listen to him. Born in Iowa, raised in Wyoming, Deming learned from his late-frontier experience the importance of cooperation where everyone, as he liked to say, could be in a "win-win" situation. U.S. companies, however, stressed competition. If one did not win, one lost in a so-called zero-sum game. These companies were riding the crest of world power because, they believed, of a tradition of vigorous

American competition. They seemed assured of an infinite market driven by pent-up wartime demand and the rapid expansion of military purchases. To meet the demand, American executives stressed mass production that relied on Frederick Taylor's time-and-motion studies of the early 1900s, which ruthlessly broke down the production process to emphasize and put pressure on the individual unit.

Deming condemned Taylorism. He believed it stressed quantity over quality and also failed to see the individual as a key part of an entire system. He damned the merit rating systems for pitting employee against employee. Of special importance, Deming emphasized long-term objectives ("What will we be doing a year from now, five years from now, ten years from now?"), an approach the Japanese quickly embraced. Most U.S. producers, conversely, were fixated on quarterly or semi-annual profit reports. Americans did not bother with an equivalent of the Deming Prize until the 1980s (the Malcolm Baldridge Prize), when quality Japanese goods were outselling many U.S. products in the global marketplace.

In one of history's neater coincidences, Deming's theories arrived in Japan just as the Korean War began. As the conflict's demands helped Japan rebuild its industrial complex, Deming's procedures gave the complex maximum efficiency. In both senses, the war, as Yoshida termed it, was "a gift of the gods." On July 7, 1950—a dozen days after fighting erupted and as Deming's first seminars were starting in Japan—Dulles told Secretary of State Dean Acheson that the Japanese remained "a confused and uncertain people." Dulles, echoing business representatives he had consulted, was "pessimistic about Japan's economic prospects unless it could trade with the Asiatic continent" (read: Communist China and Southeast Asia), because Japanese goods were of such "poor quality" that even nearby South Korea preferred buying expensive U.S. rather than cheaper Japanese machines.[12]

In an amazingly short time, one part of Dulles's fear evaporated. In August 1951, the *New York Times* reported that Japan was already competing less "on the basis of cheap labor and unreliable products" than with quality and precision work. The once-powerful textile industry, for example, was reorganizing itself along these new lines. Of special note, an optical lens producer, Nippon Kogaku K. K., was meticulously producing extraordinary "Nikon" lenses. Regardless of the large demand, the company and its fifteen hundred workers refused to make more than five hundred cameras per month. Reporters noted that through the assistance of the U.S. government, Japanese firms were also working with Lowell O. Mellen, a management expert from Cleveland,

Ohio, to put Deming's theories into practice by bringing foremen on the factory floor into management decisions. Thus the company saved money with the suggestions and exemplified what the *Times* termed the new "political democracy" in Japan. With such innovations as guaranteed lifetime employment, wage scales based on seniority and loyalty, and integration of labor and management, productivity took off.[13]

Fahs, Deming, and Mellen helped lay foundation stones for the later "economic miracle." But the Japanese themselves never lost sight of their true goal—not to create the military force that Nixon and Dulles begged for, but to create, in Hirano Ken'ichiro's phrase, an "autonomous Japan." Above all, government worked to ensure that business had access to Japanese capital. There was to be no begging from foreigners. Repeatedly in the early 1950s, U.S. Ambassador John Allison bitterly protested. Tokyo officials claimed to welcome foreign money, then imposed "restrictions in screening investments." He could not see why the Japanese were so difficult—especially given "Japan's foreign exchange difficulties." In March 1954, Allison reported that three U.S. corporations—Coca-Cola, Schaeffer Pen, and Studebaker automobiles—had been stopped from investing. He could not understand it. The Japanese only "consider the proposals as subterfuges by the American companies to obtain a foothold in the economy. After the facade and rationalizations are stripped away, the basic reason . . . is clearly exposed, fear of competition." MITI, moreover, feared Studebaker was only the camel's nose inside the tent; the ministry would then not be able to prevent other foreign auto firms from entering. Allison had trouble accepting such "rationalizations," as he called them. The ambassador could, of course, have referred to Meiji Japan. This blossoming U.S.-Japanese clash had deep, tough, historical roots. No amount of free trade chemicals seemed to destroy it.[14]

The Japanese were determined to control their own society, which meant controlling investment. The government-sponsored Development Bank of 1951 provided funds (at low interest) for industry. Tax reforms accelerated industrial productivity. The Ministry of Finance shrewdly used subsidies, import quotas, controls over foreign capital—and other weapons more associated with nineteenth-century mercantilism than post-1945 U.S. economic policy. The government set up an Export-Import Bank, based on the U.S. model that dated from 1934, to help finance overseas sales. Tokyo officials also allowed concentration of resources; by 1955, both Mitsui and Mitsubishi, nearly broken up in the late 1940s, were largely rebuilt. Unlike the old *zaibatsu* that had generated its own capital, however, the new *zaibatsu* depended on a concentrated banking system that worked intimately with the finance ministry or MITI. During the 1950s, about 80 percent of new capital came not from within firms, nor from stock issues, but from banks closely watched over by the government. The banks increasingly obtained their capital from savings accounts. In 1947, the Japanese had consumed 100 percent of their income to rebuild wartorn lives. By 1955, they were saving at the prewar level of about 9 percent, and soon that number doubled to reach nearly twice the prewar rate.[15]

The bureaucracy-business teams also employed technology transfers as alternatives to foreign investment. Austin automobile helped Nissan, RCA cooperated with NEC, DuPont aided Toyo Rayon in chemicals. Many U.S. companies sold their technology secrets because Japan's market seemed too small to be worth developing. Other firms, as Motorola, moved in because Eisenhower told the electronics giant that it had "to do business with Japan," even if Japanese goods were inferior, because "that country must become economically strong." Motorola taught its Japanese counterparts very well indeed about electronics (although forty years later Motorola continued to believe that its own products remained unfairly shut out of Japan's domestic market). The Tokyo bureaucracy also set out to break Japan's dependence on foreign oil companies. By 1958, the nation's initial economic takeoff in steel and synthetic fibers already made it the world's seventh-largest oil consumer. MITI bought oil for these firms, used preferences and regulations to favor new local refiners, and strongly backed Japanese companies' movement into Iranian oil in 1953 and Soviet oil during the detente years of 1955–56. Much of that oil was used for satisfying "a technology lust," as one Tokyo official put it. Americans were also happily helping to quench that lust by sharing their cutting-edge technology in such fields as rocketry, machine tools, and nuclear reactors for peaceful use. Dulles's pessimism in 1950 about Japan's economic prospects was beginning to appear ridiculous.[16]

Dulles's second concern, however—the continuing Japanese need for markets on the Asian continent—was not ridiculous. Indeed, the economic miracle elevated this concern to the center of the U.S.-Japanese relationship. If Japan did not sell in Asia, it had to sell in the Americas. Between 1953 and 1956, its exports to the United States doubled to $5.5 million—enough for some American producers to demand that this Asian ally look elsewhere for markets. As Eisenhower and Dulles took office in early 1953, the question could be sharply posed: Should Japan seek its needed markets and raw materials in Communist China or a revolutionary Southeast Asia? Without the adjectives before the two regions, the question resembled the debate that tormented U.S.-Japan relations down to December 7, 1941. But adjectives now seemed to make the difference: with China in Communist hands, the answer had to be Southeast Asia.

China remained a vast glowering ghost hovering over the U.S.-Japan relationship. Washington officials seemed determined to keep Japanese and Chinese divided. This determination was due in part to the Taiwan Lobby in Congress. In part it was due to the containment policy. ("I'm a little old-fashioned," the new, brash Secretary of Defense, Charles E. Wilson, told Eisenhower. "I don't like selling firearms to the Indians.") In part, the determination came from Joseph Dodge's belief that "Japan can be independent politically, but dependent economically." Access to China could lessen such dependency considerably—which was why Yoshida, and his successors, urged Japanese business leaders to move into the bottomless mainland markets. Yoshida believed U.S. policy toward China was doomed to failure; but, at least publicly, he had to go along with it.[17]

In June 1952, Japanese business people signed a trade agreement with China. They and the government explained it was only a private deal, thus not in violation of the "Yoshida letter," which involved only official relations. The Truman administration was not persuaded. In July, U.S. officials requested that Japan join COCOM (the Coordinating Committee of the U.S. allies, sitting in Paris, that limited and closely watched over trade with the Soviets), and CHINCOM (the equivalent oversight of trade with the Chinese). Two months later, U.S. officials forced Yoshida to accept a secret agreement imposing even harsher restraints on Japan in its China trade than other CHINCOM members had accepted. Being unfairly singled out, the Japanese "national obsession with [China] trade," as the historian Sayuri Shimizu has called it, only intensified. Three more private Sino-Japanese trade agreements followed in 1952–53. From a tiny base, their mutual trade jumped 120 percent in 1953 and another 75 percent in 1954. In a late 1953 deal between the suave Chinese Foreign Minister Chou En-lai (Zhou Enlai) and a Japanese delegation, both cultural and economic exchanges were promised.[18]

Japan's ignoring the spirit of CHINCOM's restrictions pleased some of its allies, especially the British, who also saw China as a potential economic saviour and who wanted Japanese diverted from Britain's Asian markets. But it triggered vigorous discussion in the Eisenhower administration. Dulles and Dodge (who headed the Council on Foreign Economic Policy) wanted to sever Sino-Japanese ties. Dulles argued that

China could be split apart from the Soviets, but only if "maximum pressure" was applied, not by enticing the Chinese with Japanese or Western goods. Eisenhower, with a broader view, strongly disagreed. "If we don't assist Japan, gentlemen, Japan is going Communist," he told congressional leaders in June 1954. "Then instead of the Pacific being an American lake, believe me it is going to be a Communist lake. If we do not let them trade with Red China, with Southeast Asia, then we are going to be in for trouble." Indirect support came from his deeply conservative Secretary of the Treasury, George Humphrey. This former steel executive urged that "Japanese business . . . be spread throughout the world and not concentrated only in American markets," for "American industry could not compete with the intricate, delicate hand labor of Japan," and the imports "would cause great unemployment here."

As Nikita Khrushchev (Stalin's successor) unleashed a detente policy during 1954 to 1956 to win Asian hearts with aid and cooperation, Eisenhower's fear about losing "the great industrial potential of Japan" intensified. The struggle in Asia was, he believed, "an economic one." This view deepened his conviction that, within limits, Japanese-Chinese trade had to be tolerated; otherwise, "where was Japan to get the iron and coal which it formerly got from Manchuria and North China?" Eisenhower could wax so eloquent about Japan's trading needs that Humphrey once quipped that perhaps Americans had defeated "the two wrong nations in the last war." "You don't mean that," Eisenhower quickly interjected, "you mean we licked these two nations too thoroughly." Special presidential assistant Robert Cutler picked up that clue to ask the National Security Council whether it wished to "look to the restoration of Japan's colonial empire." No, Eisenhower responded. That seemed to be going too far.[19]

In 1954, the President quietly loosened some U.S.-imposed bonds on Sino-Japanese trade. But not even Eisenhower meant to open up the torrent of trade Japan needed with the Chinese to right its unfavorable trade balance (especially with Americans). Such unwillingness left Southeast Asia as the remaining hope.[20]

As early as 1951, U.S. policy to integrate the Japanese and Southeast Asian economies had moved so rapidly that it produced an astonishing and prophetic document. The author was George Clutton, a British diplomat who reported from the embassy in Tokyo to the Foreign Office in a long memorandum of October 2, 1951. Clutton's analysis first brilliantly constructed a historical context:

> It would . . . probably not be wrong to say that from the time of
> Commodore Perry's landing, Japan's national ambition has been to

achieve for herself the position, not of a great Asiatic power, but of a great maritime world power, and to be treated as an equal with the "Western" and world powers, specifically the United States, Britain and France. . . . It is even possible that, had other things been equal, Japan's history in the Meiji era might have been gradually to dissociate herself more and more from Asia. Unfortunately other things were not equal. Japan's ambition to become a world power made it impossible (and this was the real paradox and Japan's dilemma), for her to ignore Asia. . . .

Clutton destroyed the popular idea that Japan (with its seapower, imperial ambitions, and home islands) was the "Great Britain of the Pacific." At the same time, he put his finger on the needs and dependence that historically propelled Japanese policies:

Unlike her fellow islanders in the Great Britain of the 19th century, she did not have the capital, the resources or the national strength to dispense with the continent to which she was adjacent. . . . Thus in her pre-war pretensions to leadership in Asia, Japan exploited her geographical position not because of common ties . . . but because in order to achieve her aspirations and justify her inclusion among the Great Powers, she required the political and economic support of the Asian land-mass. . . .

Japan, Clutton noted with delicious irony, had lost a horrible war but gained its great objective of the 1930s: to eliminate most Western power from Asia. In 1951, however, that achievement forced the new Asian nations to beg for help from the Communist bloc—or from Japan, supported by the Americans. The ironies, and the demands of postwar capitalism, were stunning:

. . . requests have already come from at least some of the Asiatic countries for Japanese technicians. What Japan once attempted to make these countries accept by force, is now being asked as a favour. . . . [A]s time goes by and the memory of the Japanese Occupation dims, we must certainly be prepared to see Japan exploit the real, if indirect contribution she made to their liberation. . . .

Such exploitation would, again with nice irony, now be made possible by the conqueror's capital. Japan failed in the 1930s because it lacked capital, so had to resort to force. Such use of force "is no longer necessary." The Americans and other Westerners were supplying capital through a variety of government programs—Point Four technology, economic and military aid—and also by creating "a framework of international cooperation into which Japan can . . . fit herself . . . and into which, it seems clear it is United States policy to fit her." Clutton continued:

> Though [the] Co-Prosperity [approach of the 1930s] may change its name, and probably some of its more detestable features, it still remains from Japan's point of view a sound conception, one prerequisite of which, the elimination of paramount Western influence in Asia, has been established. . . . The old, Co-Prosperity Sphere is open under favourable conditions to Japanese economic penetration and Japan's security is now guaranteed by the greatest military and naval power in the world.[21]

Japan would find its natural source of markets and raw materials in Asia. Or, in other words, Clutton's analysis implied that a war over Vietnam for the sake of Japan's recovery was unneeded and irrelevant. He clearly saw that Asia's future would not be determined by U.S. military force, but by the force of capitalism working through Japan. Asia's only alternative was developmental help from the Communist bloc, and while such help was possible, Clutton understood it could be overpowered by the peaceful, steady sweep of Japanese commerce southward.

Unfortunately, Eisenhower and Dulles did not share Clutton's conclusions. They believed that only military victory in Southeast Asia could save the region for Japan and Western-style capitalism. A series of Japanese governments, beginning with Yoshida's, pointedly disagreed. Oddly, a British Foreign Office analyst and Japanese governments placed greater confidence in the power of capitalism than did the Americans who shaped much of that capitalism.

The fervent belief that massive military expenditures were necessary had been built into NSC-68. U.S. officials quickly played Southeast Asian variations on the NSC-68 themes. The NSC-124 series of policy papers in 1952 was the Truman-Acheson legacy to Eisenhower that justified U.S. commitments in Indochina. French colonial forces were headed off the cliff, NSC-124 feared. They somehow had to be stopped, for if "any of the countries of Southeast Asia" were lost "as a consequence of overt or covert Chinese Communist aggression," it would bring down "the rest of Southeast Asia and India," and, "in the longer term . . . the Middle East." Obviously, Japan would be a falling domino:

"The loss of these rice exporting areas would impose a two-fold pressure on Japan by removing simultaneously a source of food and a potential field for Japanese export development." Either all Southeast Asia remained open for Japanese exploitation, or it was "dubious that Japan could refrain from reaching an accommodation with the Communist bloc." Truman and Acheson were consequently ready to "continue and increase [U.S.] military and economic assistance programs for Indochina."[22]

Eisenhower and Dulles intensified this commitment as the French stumbled toward their decisive defeat at the hands of Ho Chi Minh's forces at Dienbienphu in mid-1954. "Indochina is the key to Southeast Asia, upon the resources of which Japan is largely dependent," Dulles told the French in 1952. He was not in any mood to await the working out of capitalist development in the region. The Secretary of State instead anticipated using "massive retaliation," that is, the possible use of nuclear weapons. As Eisenhower emphasized, he had no intention of fighting a conventional war against major Communist aggression. There were to be no more frustrating, expensive Koreas.[23]

U.S. policy had thus moved in just six short years after 1948 from the need to rebuild Japan, to the belief that Southeast Asia was essential for that rebuilding, to public hints that nuclear strikes might be necessary. As Eisenhower explained in a soon-to-be-famous press conference of April 7, 1954, the highest stakes were on the table:

> You have a row of dominoes set up, you knock over the first one, and what will happen to the last one is a certainty that it will go over very rapidly. . . .
>
> It turns the so-called island defensive chain of Japan, Formosa, of the Philippines. . . .
>
> It takes away, in its economic aspects, that region that Japan must have as a trading area or Japan, in turn, will have only one place to go—that is, toward the Communist areas in order to live.
>
> So the possible consequences of the loss are just incalculable to the free world.[24]

Over the next month, Eisenhower approached, then backed away from, the use of U.S. forces, even nuclear weapons, to save the French at Dienbienphu. He knew he lacked the support of Congress, of the British, and, especially, of "local Asiatic peoples" to intervene. France made peace with Ho Chi Minh's forces, agreeing in the process to divide—temporarily—Vietnam north and south until nationwide elections could be held, presumably in 1955. Eisenhower refused to go along with any elections (which would have resulted, as the President later noted, in Ho's certain victory). The United States replaced the French in the South and constructed a Southeast Asian Treaty Organization (SEATO) that was to prop back up any falling "dominoes."[25]

The Japanese watched all this with wonder and dismay. Wanting (to understate considerably) no military role in SEATO, Tokyo never joined. Yoshida could feel vindicated in keeping the Japanese military too small to be of use for Americans. "The test of strength in fighting communism lies as much, if not more, in the political and economic fields as in the military," a Japanese position paper concluded in later 1954. As the United States moved to militarize the region, Japan signed agreements with Burma, and reaffirmed deals with Indonesia, in which Tokyo paid over $1 billion in "reparations." This money was then used to finance Japanese investments and exports to these nations, while they in turn sold food and raw materials to Japan. The Japanese steel, shipbuilding, automobile, and electrical businesses handsomely profited. Japan began lucrative long-term relationships with Southeast Asia even as U.S. officials worried how to keep the "dominoes" erect in the capitalist camp.[26]

A New Cold War

The Southeast Asian crises of 1954 symbolized, in hindsight, a major transition in the Cold War. A prophetic article in *BusinessWeek* of October 16, 1954, observed that "Asia [not Europe] is the front now—and the West is shaping new ways to counter a new partnership between Russia and Red China." Between 1954 and 1958, moreover, the Soviets successfully launched rockets that demonstrated they were not only ahead of the United States in this technology but had the capacity to hit Western Europe—or Japan—with nuclear-tipped missiles. Neither of the two superpowers, however, could stop an ominous splintering of its own bloc. In 1956, the Soviets had to send in tanks to maintain their hold on Poland and Hungary. But they could do nothing to repair the damage caused by arguments with China over military and nuclear weapons policies. By 1957–58, the vaunted Sino-Soviet bloc was splitting apart. In 1959, Cuba's Fidel Castro successfully imposed an anti-U.S. revolution ninety miles from Florida. The rise of the smaller powers (Dulles and Eisenhower called it "the tyranny of the weak") was tormenting both blocs.[27]

For the United States and Japan, the new era began tragically on

March 1, 1954, when a Japanese fishing boat, ironically named *Lucky Dragon,* unwittingly sailed close to the Marshall Islands' test site of a U.S. atomic bomb explosion. Captain Tsutsui Isao later reported that "about 90 minutes after the blast snow-white ashes began falling all around the ship. The ashes continued showering the ship for two hours." Three days later, blisters appeared on the crew members' skins. Tsutsui headed home, where the news created fear that the Japanese had long been eating fish that was radioactive. Street demonstrations erupted along with anti-American rhetoric. As crew members began to die from the blast's aftereffects, U.S. officials (who at first actually believed that Communists had deliberately sailed the boat into the blast area to embarrass the United States) issued an apology. After bitter exchanges and countercharges, Eisenhower offered, and Japan accepted, a $2 million indemnity.

The "conclusions" drawn from the tragedy "are unpleasant, some even ominous," Ambassador John Allison told Washington. The Japanese government had nearly broken down in handling the episode. Unable to get its story straight, Yoshida's government suffered a political revolt from within and stinging anti-U.S. criticism from without. Allison warned that the position of "neutralists, pacifists, feminists and professional anti-Americans . . . had been strengthened." The "government and the people cracked," the ambassador wrote. Allison and his readers in Washington (which included Eisenhower) thus turned a Japanese tragedy into a tragedy as well for U.S. plans for Japan.[28]

Allison was bitter. The best U.S. efforts had too little dulled the historic clash between the two countries. Japanese always took but never gave, the ambassador complained. They neither put their own political house in order nor opened their economic house to the self-invited American visitors. "Japan does not consider itself an ally or partner with the United States," he wrote in 1954, "but rather a nation which for the time being is being forced by circumstances to cooperate with the United States and which intends . . . to wring out of this relationship every possible advantage at minimum cost." That view, of course, did not match Japan's. The Japanese felt "the U.S. had no real benevolence toward Japan," Allison recorded powerful Finance Minister Ikeda Hayato declaring in 1954—otherwise how could Americans have made such mistakes as trying to impose school reforms and political-economic decentralization policies on Japan after 1945?

Eisenhower and Dulles recognized the growing strain. They tried to help by ushering Japan into the membership of two all-important, Western-dominated organizations, the General Agreement on Tariffs and Trade (GATT) in 1955, and—after four vetoes from the Soviets—the

United Nations in 1956. Eisenhower also looked the other way as Japanese signed private trade agreements with Communist China. These deals ostensibly did not involve the Tokyo government, but, in fact, during 1955 they led to the exchange of trade representatives who to American eyes uncomfortably resembled diplomatic corps.[29]

This aggressive China policy was pushed by Premier Hatoyama Ichiro, a conservative who had ended Yoshida's six-year reign. Yoshida had fallen in December 1954 amid ringing scandals involving his government, shipping companies, and investment firms. Hatoyama united enough of the Progressive Party and Liberal Party with his new Democratic Party to form a government, but only with votes as well from Socialists who opposed any alliance with the Americans. An early 1955 national election led to a united, impressive Socialist Party. Frightened conservative businessmen and political leaders finally forced the Liberals and Democrats to merge in a conservative coalition in late 1955. The resulting Liberal Democratic Party (LDP) formed a conservative party of bitterly divided factions, but its powerbrokers would periodically piece the factions together to rule Japan imperiously for the next thirty-eight years. The "1955 setup," as Japanese political analysts later termed it, was made up of shrewd politicians, talented bureaucrats, and rich business groups (led by the *keidanren,* or Federation of Economic Organizations, which regularly swamped the LDP with money to keep it in power). It created the semblance of a stable two-party political system, albeit one of a smaller left versus a powerhouse right.[30]

As the new premier, Hatoyama seemed a transitional figure, a seventy-two-year-old partially paralyzed from a stroke of three years earlier. His two years in power nevertheless became pivotal for Japanese relations with the Communist bloc. Hatoyama named as his foreign minister Shigemitsu Mamoru, already sixty-five, and having lost a leg in 1932 when a Korean nationalist tossed a bomb. Shigemitsu had signed the surrender documents for Japan in 1945, then served time in jail as a Class A war criminal. Unlike Hatoyama, Shigemitsu was neither popular nor a good politician. He seemed "ruthless, cold, and unapproachable," in a British diplomat's phrase. The two new leaders agreed on the need to widen trade with China and open political relations with the Soviet Union. They accomplished the former in 1955, the latter in 1956. Shigemitsu, who when young had been a consul in Portland, Oregon, before serving in China and the Soviet Union, knew English well, mistrusted Americans greatly, supported rearming enthusiastically, and feared dependence on the United States totally. His views and the time seemed well matched.[31]

The Japanese economy meanwhile picked up speed in 1956 when it equaled its highest prewar level of production. As Allison and other U.S. officials worried about Japan's economic policies, the real gross national product shot up an average of 7 percent yearly between 1953 and 1958. One reason: its industrialists learned how to substitute home-made goods (such as rayon and wood pulp) for imports (such as cotton and foreign-grown wood). Meanwhile, the U.S. industrial machine suddenly sputtered through a series of recessions. Its gross national product rose at less than half the rate of Japan's, or the Soviets'. By 1957, the U.S. Treasury's gold supply (which undergirded the dollar as the international economy's cornerstone) began to be sucked out of the country by overseas military commitments, U.S. investors moving billions of dollars into a unifying Europe, and a declining merchandise trade balance. No group worried more about this growing dilemma than Eisenhower's cabinet. One member warned in 1958 about "pricing ourselves out of world markets." Dulles privately told Senate leaders that this dilemma loomed just as the newly emerging nations threatened to go to the Communists for help if the West could not provide enough.[32]

As Japan's economy accelerated, its politics grew more complex and independent of U.S. pressure. Dulles and Shigemitsu—neither known as "Mr. Warmth"—clashed repeatedly over the U.S. determination to move, unannounced, nuclear weapons and nuclear-powered ships into Japanese bases. When Shigemitsu told a greatly annoyed Dulles in 1955 that the 1952 security treaty should be renegotiated, the Secretary of State shot back, yes, when the Japanese were willing to pay for their own military to defend the home islands and to help the United States abroad.[33]

At the April 1955 Bandung, Indonesia, Conference of mostly non-aligned nations, Japan gently separated itself from U.S. policies in Southeast Asia. Dulles, who once labeled neutralism as "immoral," was not pleased. Nor was the highly influential, hawkish journalist Joseph Alsop. Visiting Tokyo in 1955, Alsop announced that the United States had blown its great opportunity in 1954 by not saving the French and destroying Vietnam's Communist forces. For, he emphasized, "Every Japanese businessman, without exception [,] regards Southeast Asia as Japan's most promising future trading area." Now they had lost trust in Washington: "Anti-Americanism here can be expected to become uncontrollable" as Japan turns neutral. "Asia is a seamless web," Alsop preached. "If the web is too badly torn anywhere, it will unravel everywhere. And it is tearing now."[34]

U.S.-Japan cooperation on Chinese questions certainly seemed to be unraveling. As Americans vigorously dueled with China to protect Taiwan, the Japanese worked to increase trade with both China and Taiwan. An analysis forwarded by Dulles to the President bluntly warned that many Japanese believed " 'Communist China' is almost a contradiction in terms; that Chinese can never be 'Communist.' " Dulles obviously thought this view weird. He considered equally weird the "professional" Japanese diplomats, who, the report noted, "believe that Peiping can be split from Moscow by peaceful means." The Eisenhower administration decided, in Dulles's phrase, to let Japan "go it alone." Perhaps Clarence Randall, the new chair of the Council of Foreign Economic Policy after July 1956, was right. A rabid believer in open markets, Randall convinced the sympathetic President that letting Japan trade in roughly half the goods listed on the embargo statutes would improve U.S.-Japanese relations and perhaps wean China away from Communist bloc products. Randall won this compromise victory over angry opposition from the Defense Department and the passionately pro-Taiwan assistant secretary of state, Walter Robertson, who feared any contact with China.[35]

The Soviets were now warmly courting Japan and the new Asian nations. In June 1955, Soviet leader Nikita Khrushchev proposed talks to make (finally) a peace treaty with Japan. It was not lost on U.S. officials that Khrushchev took this initiative after his scientists successfully tested a 1,500-mile missile that could be targeted on the Japanese. The initiative collapsed when Japan demanded that the Soviets surrender their hold on the Kurile Islands north of Hokkaido. With their continued control of the Kuriles and Sakhalin, the Soviets had a strategic grip on the region and its rich fishing grounds on which many Japanese depended. Ambassador Allison feared that "Japan is on the verge of slowly slipping away from us." A secret report to Eisenhower's National Security Council agreed: "Japan's tendency to drift away is due to decreasing economic, military, and diplomatic dependence on the United States and to the growth of national pride and spirit of independence." One conclusion starkly stood out: "The major U.S. objective—a firm alliance in the Pacific—is not being achieved."[36]

The Explosion Over the Security Pact (1957–60)

U.S. officials feared the worst, and their fears soon seemed to be justified. In December 1956, Hatoyama retired, only to be replaced by Ishibashi Tanzan, a bon vivant, seventy-two-year-old economist keen to lead the rush into China's market. When he lasted as prime minister for only two months, Washington breathed more easily—especially since he was replaced by his foreign minister, the smooth, powerful political broker, Kishi Nobusuke. Kishi was more pro-American, yet during his reign Japan and the United States endured their worst crisis since 1945.

The crisis revolved around the renewal of the 1952 security treaty. According to the pact's provisions, it had to be renewed by 1960. Kishi seemed nicely positioned to do this job. Born in 1896 of a well-connected Choshu sake brewer, he had been raised by the powerful Sato family of Choshu, and thus moved easily in the clan that shaped Meiji Japan. An early and ardent admirer of German literature and philosophy, Kishi read Hegel and Nietzsche in the original. A graduate of prestigious Tokyo University, where he was influenced by ardent nationalists, he concluded that Russian communism and Western capitalism were twin evils threatening the heart of Japan. These views developed while he rose rapidly through the bureaucracy. In 1941, he became Tojo's minister of commerce and industry. Kishi helped overthrow Tojo in 1944 after a series of Japanese military defeats, but continued to be a pivotal economic planner for the doomed war effort. MacArthur's officials labeled Kishi a Class A war criminal. He spent three and a half years in prison before being depurged in 1952.[37]

Entering politics with gusto, and running a major steel trading company with efficiency, Kishi worked to overthrow the occupation reforms that limited the *zaibatsu*, liberalized education, and restricted rearmament. The head of Japan's 3 million-member labor unions condemned Kishi as a "guardian of the monopolists." The new premier's economic views, his hatred of the Soviets, and (unlike Yoshida and Hatoyama) his fear of getting too close to China—not to mention his love of golf—made him welcome in Eisenhower's Washington. U.S. officials liked Kishi's idea that since Asian communism had ended Japan's manifest destiny on the mainland, the Japanese had to turn toward non-Communist Southeast Asia. These officials seemed blind to the determination of the Kishi faction to use tight, powerful governmental controls to guide and accelerate the Japanese economic machine. Kishi, it became clear, was moving to undermine many of the occupation's democratic reforms so that Japan could be more efficient, economically competitive—and independent of the United States. He even floated the idea of restoring the Emperor as "Head of State," although without the former claims to divinity. For the Eisenhower administration and many other Cold War warriors, however, such reactionary politics were of less interest than was Kishi's anti-communism and his willingness to ram a renewed security treaty through the Diet.[38]

Just two months after obtaining power, Kishi handed Ambassador Douglas MacArthur II (the general's nephew) a tough paper. It criticized Japan's subordination to the United States under the 1952 pact, expressed disappointment over U.S. policies to restrict trade with China, and indicated Okinawa should now return to Japanese control. He implied that Japan dissented from any American attempt to use military force to overthrow communism. Kishi indeed wanted a new understanding on the entire issue of security. Clearly, his supposed pro-American attitudes were well under control. His offensive received support when a U.S. soldier, Sergeant William S. Girard of Ottawa-LaSalle, Illinois, shot a forty-six-year-old Japanese woman as she was picking up casings of exploded shells so she could sell them. U.S. officials asked that Girard be tried by Americans. Tokyo officials, claiming they had allowed Americans to dictate the penalties for 97 percent of the 14,000 "off-duty" crimes committed by U.S. soldiers between 1953 and 1957, demanded that Girard face a Japanese court. Americans' anti-Japanese feeling now shot upward. But Eisenhower and Dulles sided with the Japanese: the President privately "said that Girard would receive an easier trial in Japanese court than in a [U.S.] court martial, [and] said that he could not understand a public that makes a hero out of a 'man who shoots a woman in the back at 25 yards as she is running away.'" As Eisenhower expected, the Japanese court released Girard on a suspended three-year sentence.[39]

Kishi's demands and the uproar over the Girard case only partly explained the growing tensions. Japanese officials worried when Eisenhower, as part of his cheaper, nuclear-centered New Look defense policy, reduced U.S. troops in Japan from 210,000 in 1953 to 77,000 in 1957 (and 48,000 by 1960). More than half the remaining personnel were in the Air Force. This ratio signaled to the Japanese that in any new conflict, the United States intended to fight a nuclear war from local bases. They thus felt even more threatened by possible annihilation without consultation. U.S. officers were meanwhile working so assiduously to develop Japanese air and naval forces that English, not Japanese, was the Japanese air force's operational language. Yet how could this air force and navy be used? Such lack of clarity, and lack of confidence in future U.S. intentions, led elder statesman Yoshida to favor an independent Japanese deterrent. Kishi then told a cabinet committee that "there would be nothing against using nuclear weapons if they were within the limits of self-defense" (as, presumably Article IX of the Constitution allowed). With this remark as background, Kishi visited the United States in June 1957 to tell Eisenhower directly: since U.S. forces in Japan were "subject to the unilateral determination of the United States, we would like to have this subject to consultation with the Japanese side."[40]

Many U.S. officials, preoccupied with a global, complex Cold War, were in no hurry to renegotiate the treaty with a subordinate Japan. If the Japanese were worried, they were to stop grumbling and spend more on their own military. Moreover, the first whiffs of Japanese exploitation of U.S. markets hung in the air. By 1956–58 American textile interests demanded protection against cheap Japanese imports. State Department officials thought the demands absurd, given the Americans' domination of both their domestic and international markets. But influential southern congressmen, and complaints from American producers and fishermen, drowned out State Department views. Eisenhower sharply disliked and feared using protectionist measures against an ally such as Japan. He pressed Kishi to act. The Japanese reluctantly (and in violation of the GATT principles to which they had agreed in 1955) reduced their exports of textiles, tuna, and electrical goods to the United States. Then Europeans demanded and received similar concessions.[41]

Kishi had little choice. Japan, as Ambassador MacArthur phrased it, had to "trade to live." The long-hoped-for China market was disappearing amid the political and economic chaos of the "Great Leap Forward" of 1956–58—Mao's disastrous attempt to infuse renewed revolutionary vigor into China's sagging production. In 1958, U.S.-Chinese forces almost clashed over the small Taiwan-controlled islands off the mainland. The climactic event occurred at a Nagasaki trade fair that same year. Two young Japanese nationalists tore down the Communist Chinese flag. The resulting crisis led Beijing to cancel trade with Japan. Noting that the security pact was being discussed, China accused Japan of being a shield for U.S. militarism as Americans pitted "Asians against Asians." After all, Beijing pointed out, Kishi had been intimately involved in warring against Asians in 1941. The Chinese further accused the premier of being the frontman for capitalist imperialism in Southeast Asia. Perhaps worst of all, in the Communists' eyes, during 1957 Kishi had moved to reinforce rapidly growing Japanese interests by visiting Taiwan—that most sensitive of all Chinese concerns.[42]

Kishi's room for maneuver was rapidly shrinking by late 1958. The shrinking continued that year because of extraordinary political skulduggery that accompanied a national election. In the supposedly messy

U.S. political system, Eisenhower kept a firm hand on foreign policy, while in the supposedly orderly Japanese system, the prime minister found himself cobbling together policies to try to stay a step ahead of his party's fractious leaders. The Communists and the Socialist left wing lost ground in the 1958 vote, largely because they were discredited by their fondness for a now-stumbling, hostile China. These losses allowed LDP leaders the freedom to neglect the left and go after each other. Kishi temporarily quieted his major rival, Ikeda Hayato, with a cabinet appointment. But the prime minister believed he could only save his government with a new, improved security treaty. He needed to remove long-held Japanese complaints about American domination. Then he could happily climax his long, checkered, and not always exalted career among Japanese voters.[43]

U.S. officials soon learned about Kishi's insecurity—and about the "mother's milk" of Japanese as well as American politics. His younger brother, Sato Eisaku, secretly met in a Tokyo hotel room on July 25, 1958, with S. S. Carpenter, first secretary of the American Embassy. The Soviets and Chinese were funding Japanese leftists, Sato lamented. The nation's business community had nearly emptied its pockets to ensure the recent LDP electoral win. Could Washington "supply financial funds to aid the Conservative forces in this constant struggle against Communism?" Usually this turned on the money spigots: Americans gave generously to anti-Communist causes. But the embassy had seen this request coming. For a year Sato had been suggesting such gifts. U.S. officials in the embassy saw little reason to risk being discovered dropping secret funds into the maelstrom of Japan's personal politics. The CIA, however, suffered no such compunction. "We financed them," was the flat statement years later of Alfred C. Ulmer, Jr., the CIA's Far East operations officer. The financing was probably unnecessary, given the Japanese business communities donations, although the information obtained by CIA moles in the LDP and Socialist Party did prove useful.[44]

Kishi was running scared, and the United States seized the advantage. In October 1958, it gave him a new draft treaty little changed from the 1952 pact. The draft did explicitly promise the U.S. defense of Japan (which few thinking persons doubted would occur in any event). In return, Americans were to be able to use bases in Japan to defend the Pacific region. At no time did polls indicate that a majority of Japanese wanted U.S. military bases on the home islands, and in 1958 only 7 percent wanted the all-important bases in Okinawa to remain. A Tokyo District Court actually declared the 1952 treaty unconstitutional. The

Supreme Court overturned that ruling, but notably refused to say whether or not the nation's "Self-Defense Forces" were legal under the 1947 Constitution. As Kishi was buffeted at home, Dulles—whom the prime minister called "the man who best understood Japan"—died of cancer in May 1959.[45]

As the new Secretary of State, Christian Herter, and the Japanese pushed ahead on the treaty talks, opposition solidified in Japan. A core group was *Zengakuren,* or the Federation of Students Self-Government Associations, whose 222,000 members in 1948 (about 70 percent of the nation's college students) had begun planning strikes for educational reform. In the mid-1950s, *Zengakuren* was turning toward international, especially anti-American, causes. British experts on Japan ascribed this turn to a rebellion against U.S. teachers and influences in the schools. The analysts also believed that Japanese students, who felt "lost" after the humiliation of the 1945 surrender, sought refuge in "pleasure," or "Christianity," or, more commonly, leftist politics. *Zengakuren,* ironically, was influenced by American left liberals, most notably C. Wright Mills, whose "power elite" theory helped critics explain the pro-Cold War characteristics of both the U.S. and Japanese elites. By 1958, *Zengakuren* members had joined large labor organizations to conduct street protests against Kishi's policies.[46]

In January 1960, the embattled Kishi flew to Washington to sign the new treaty. He assured Eisenhower that the LDP control of the Diet meant cooperation with the Americans and "left-wing opposition" could be discounted. But Kishi's own foreign minister, Fujiyama Aiichiro, had learned that the prime minister was not, as he thought, going to retire and give him the premiership, but pass it on to Fujiyama's rival, Ikeda Hayato. The foreign minister then set about undercutting his prime minister by telling Americans that Kishi's days in power were numbered. Despite such backbiting, on January 19, Kishi and Herter signed the new treaty in the White House East Room—the same room where one hundred years before, President James Buchanan had welcomed Japan's first diplomatic mission to the United States. It had been a more eventful century than Buchanan or the Japanese visitors could have imagined.[47]

The 1960 treaty, unlike the old, explicitly committed the United States to defend Japan, and to consult with the Japanese before putting forces into action under the pact's provisions. Also unlike the 1952 arrangement, the treaty had a definite ten-year duration. Either party could then give notice to end the agreement. Article VI granted Japanese bases to U.S. forces. Kishi, it turned out, had not obtained many concessions. For example, the United States no longer had the explicit right to intervene to put down upheavals inside Japan, but U.S. forces could actually do so under the disguise of protecting what both Articles IV and VI called "the security of Japan . . . and security in the Far East."

Japanese critics quickly zeroed in on "the Far East" phrase: did it mean they were obligated to help the Americans fight a war against China over Taiwan? In the Diet on February 26, 1960, Kishi gave in to U.S. views by defining the "Far East" provision as including "primarily the region north of the Philippines inclusive, as well as Japan and its surrounding area, including the Republic of Korea [South Korea], and the area under the control of the Republic of China [Taiwan]." But that was not all. In 1981, U.S. expert on Japan (and former Ambassador to Tokyo) Edwin Reischauer revealed that a secret verbal agreement in 1960 had given the United States the right to move nuclear weapons freely in and out of Japan. If that understanding had leaked in 1960, Kishi could have quickly been forced to give up power.[48]

U.S. Assistant Secretary of State Graham Parsons privately bragged to the British that the treaty gave Washington everything it wanted. The Soviets publicly warned that the pact could pull the Japanese directly into the line of fire in a nuclear war, adding that Moscow had no intention of returning the northern islands until "all foreign armies" left Japan. Kishi, embattled on all sides, determined to push ahead. In February 1960, he ordered debate to begin in the Diet. Socialists, the largest minority, tried unsuccessfully to stall or kill debate. Opponents of the treaty then brutally equated Kishi's action with his signing of the war declaration in December 1941 that had nearly destroyed Japan. On May 7, in the middle of this uproar, the Soviets shot down a U.S. U-2 spy plane that had been photographing Russian facilities. Eisenhower lied that it was a weather plane, only to have a gleeful Khrushchev produce the pilot and evidence of the plane's spy mission. Not only had the United States been caught flagrantly spying and lying, but it became known that some U-2 planes were stationed in Japan.[49]

The United States stood humiliated just as Kishi moved to force the treaty through the Diet on May 19–20. Yoshida and a few other conservatives, who disliked the treaty for bending too far to U.S. wishes, boycotted these sessions. When Socialists with other opposition members tried to stop voting by sitting in the aisles, Kishi ordered five hundred policemen to remove them. Rioters, led by students in *Zengakuren,* attacked Kishi's home; they also prevented him from leaving the Diet building. Violent protests in the streets replaced parliamentary debates. Some 6 million people went out on strike. U.S. and Japanese officials realized to their horror that Eisenhower was scheduled to fly into Tokyo on June 20 to help Kishi celebrate ratification. As late as June 8, Fujiyama answered worried queries from Washington by emphasizing that the visit had to go forward or Kishi would be humiliated.[50]

But two days later, Eisenhower's press secretary, James Hagerty, arrived in Tokyo to survey the situation. His car was surrounded and nearly toppled by thousands of protesters. After eighty minutes of terror, he escaped to advise Eisenhower to cancel the visit. On June 15, protesters led by labor and *Zengakuren* invaded the Diet grounds to fight police. A student was trampled to death as 482 students and 536 police were injured. British observers noted "the unusual violence on both sides." On June 19, the upper house, the House of Councilors, automatically ratified the treaty. It was automatic because the Constitution provided that a treaty passed by the lower house became law if the Councilors did not act, and Socialist protesters prevented the upper house from convening. On June 22, the largest mass protest in the nation's history erupted as 6.2 million went on strike. Their concern was no longer merely the treaty, but the growing fear that Kishi—who had systematically tried to slash the rights of workers and civil servants since 1947—might try to use the military and police to impose a despotic regime.

Fujiyama and Ambassador MacArthur finally exchanged ratifications at the foreign minister's residence in a secret meeting, but only after Fujiyama arranged an alternative flight plan with neighbors: if protesters stormed the house, MacArthur was to escape by climbing over fences and across adjacent gardens. In the historian John Welfield's phrase, "Japan showed every indication of emerging as America's Hungary"—a reference to the other superpower's use of military force during 1956 to keep a rebellious people in the Soviet bloc. The ratification did not stop the violence. On July 14, Kishi was stabbed in his residence by a right-wing fanatic. The prime minister escaped with minor injuries. In October, a young nationalist killed the Socialist Party leader, Asanuma Inejiro (who had helped organize the mass protests), and did so in full view of television cameras.[51]

New York Times columnist James Reston concluded that the pact had been put into force, but "at best the United States had lost face, at worst it had lost Japan." Such losses, however, did not occur. Japan instead seemed to forget about the treaty. Explaining why Reston misjudged explains as well why a different Japan emerged after 1960. The explanation begins with the July 11, 1960, announcement by Fujiyama that the U-2 planes, the "Black Jets" hated by many Japanese, were leaving the country because their "weather observation mission has been completed." On July 19, Ikeda Hayato replaced the wounded, disgraced Kishi as head of the LDP and thus as prime minister.[52]

Ikeda made a historic contribution: he helped change the mind-set of Japanese politics by taking it off the Cold War and placing it on economic growth. This sixty-year-old son of a rice brewer in Hiroshima had been educated at Kyoto University and law school, then rose rapidly in the finance bureaucracy. As Japan militarized in the 1930s, he came down with a rare skin disease whose care both forced him into seclusion and killed his wife who exhausted herself caring for him. Finally searching for cures at Buddhist temples, he met a distant relative, Mitsue, was miraculously cured, married Mitsue, and named their first child after his first wife. With little involvement in 1930s Japanese politics, Ikeda therefore escaped the postwar purges. As a protégé of Yoshida, he resumed his climb to the powerful post of finance minister. He was, as Aruga Tadashi has observed, the first of the new political generation whose members rose to power after 1945. Ikeda demonstrated some new thinking by appointing the first woman to a Japanese cabinet, Welfare Minister Nakayama Masa. Certainly Beijing officials considered Ikeda to be a fresh breeze. The Chinese applauded the "Japanese people" for being "victorious" over Kishi and "Imperialist America." "The days when Japan accepts U.S. policies peacefully," China announced, "are over."[53]

U.S. officials agreed with neither Reston's nor the Chinese assessment of the situation in late 1960. Washington did not fundamentally reformulate Asian policy in part because it believed its policies had triumphed in 1960. Refusing to take seriously the Soviet attempt to thaw the Cold War, growing more obsessive about China, and refusing to restructure military budgets to give relief to a slipping economy, the new Kennedy administration instead honed old policies, especially by spending more money on them. Eisenhower had shown some understanding that rethinking was necessary. He privately related how he had reflected on President William McKinley's 1901 speech, "delivered the day before he was shot," which urged "freer trade" and warned that "isolation is no longer possible or desirable.' " Eisenhower's reading of McKinley's speech suggests why he, along with a few others such as Clarence Randall, were capable of rethinking and so tolerated increasing Sino-Japanese trade. As enlightened capitalists, they believed in the interdependence and demonstration of capitalism's power that such trade produced.[54]

The post-1951 era in U.S.-Japan relations had begun with Joseph

Dodge declaring that "Japan can be independent politically but dependent economically." Dulles meanwhile claimed that the security relationship was the continuation of the occupation by other means. The 1950s ended with massive protests against that security relationship—and with Ikeda's determination to end economic dependence. The decade also ended with continued friction between the all-out U.S. support of Chiang on Taiwan and by the LDP powerbrokers, who yearned to try again to profit from mainland China. The Tokyo government of the 1950s thus formed links in a long line of Japanese ruling parties who tried to lessen their nation's insecurity, strengthen its different capitalism, and, as the astute British diplomat George Clutton wrote in 1951, redefine its necessary role in Asia.

On the American side, no one had better anticipated the stark alternatives facing U.S. officials than did John Allison in a memorandum to the Secretary of State in early January 1952. After summarizing extensive CIA analyses of the situation, Allison concluded:

> China is the heart of the whole U.S. policy toward Asia and what we do or don't do with respect to China will vitally affect our policy toward Japan and Southeast Asia. There is considerable agitation in Japan to resume its relations, particularly economic, with the mainland of China . . . [and] over a long-term period it will be almost impossible to prevent Japan having once again the close relationship with China that has been true throughout its history. Through United States economic and military assistance and through United States help in increasing Japan's economic opportunities in Southeast Asia, dependence on the mainland of China may be kept at a minimum for a short time. However, it is not believed that this can go on for much more than five years at the maximum. Sooner or later Japan will have to deal with the mainland of China and it is to be the interest of the United States to see to it that within the approximately five-year period available conditions in China are so changed that Japan may resume its close relationship with that area without it being a security threat to this country.
>
> The importance of China to Southeast Asia is obvious. . . . In view of the alarming reports recently received from Southeast Asia concerning the possibility of Chinese Communist intervention in Indochina, the urgency of action is apparent.[55]

But neither U.S. direct pressure nor an attempt to drive a "wedge" between the Soviets and Chinese—nor even the threat of possible nuclear war over the offshore islands—had "so changed" China by 1960 that it was safe for Japan to "resume its close relationship." If salvation for Japan were not to be found in a converted China, then, Clutton and Allison predicted, salvation for Japan—and, indeed, for historic U.S. interests in Asia—had to be found in a resurrected Southeast Asia. U.S. officials set about arranging the resurrection.

XI

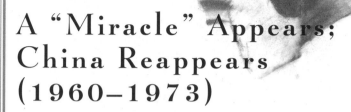

A "Miracle" Appears;
China Reappears
(1960–1973)

The "Miracle" of Ikeda—and Other
"Merchants of Transistors"

IKEDA HAYATO and Dwight Eisenhower—so different in background and politics—shared one notable characteristic: both were known for using words badly. Seen in the 1950s by many as confused, preferring golf over work, and a master of bad syntax, Eisenhower fully controlled his government and sometimes deliberately used the bad syntax to confuse or dull the message for his own advantage. Ikeda had a nickname: *hogen koji,* or "one whose tongue slips." He won the nickname in the early 1950s when, as a finance official, Ikeda told the Diet that the new concentration of Japanese industry might extract a price: "It cannot be helped if five or ten medium and small entrepreneurs go into bankruptcies and hang themselves" (as, indeed, several had already done).[1]

Critics similarly thought Ikeda's tongue slipped in 1960 when he astonishingly committed Japan to doubling its income within a single decade. Again, Ikeda only spoke from conviction. He understood from his experience as head of MITI in 1959–60 that such a goal was achievable and—of special importance—necessary. After the bloodshed and seemingly constant rioting of early 1960, thenation needed to focus on more constructive pursuits. Rapidly rising income could, and did, take the wind from the political sails of the Japanese left wing. Such a program, moreover, could give the nation the kind of leverage in world affairs it had not enjoyed since the 1930s—only this time the leverage would be economic, not military, and this time others (especially Americans and Asians) would be dependent on Japanese, not vice versa. Ikeda even had the imagination to view Japan as one of the "three pillars" of the "free world," along with the United States and Western Europe. But as this "three-pillar" statement indicated, the premier's emphasis on economics misled: his program to quiet the country, decimate the left, and diminish Japan's dependence required working closely with the United States politically. Japan needed military protection to free up resources for industry rather than for an armed forces' budget. It would also avoid bitter internal debates over militarization. And American markets for Japan's industrial goods were most welcome.[2]

Ikeda's economic scheme succeeded astoundingly, but, at the same time, slowly ate away at the ties between Japan and the United States. The two nations clashed over China, then over China and Vietnam, and finally, climactically, over the "Nixon shocks" that marked the terminus of the post-1945 U.S.-Japan relationship. Waves of production from the Japanese economic "miracle" finally washed away most of the foundations of both the post-1945 relationship and Japan's political structure. By 1964, Japanese gross national product had risen to sixth place globally; in another three years it flew past France, Great Britain, and Germany to settle into third place just back of the two superpowers.

With the LDP's success, the left splintered. China played a pivotal role in causing the splintering: its alienation from the Soviets created ruptures between pro-Chinese and pro-Soviet factions in Japan's Socialist and Communist parties. The CIA poured in more money just to ensure the left's demise. One CIA official later said that paying off LDP leaders "is the heart of darkness and I'm not comfortable talking about it, because it worked." Others, however, did talk. The U.S. ambassador to Japan between 1966 and 1969 (and longtime Japanese hand), U. Alexis Johnson, recalled that "the principle [of funneling money secretly to the LDP] was certainly acceptable to me. We were financing a party on our side." But given local resources, the LDP did not need the CIA funds, and the Agency obtained greater cost efficiency by infiltrating the Socialist Party, youth groups, and labor organizations throughout the 1960s. The CIA–State Department covert activities were a waste of money.[3]

For Ikeda had things in hand. The conservatives' power rose along with his income-doubling plan. He successfully pushed to recentralize control over education, and to fill the youth with traditional nationalist values and ethics—instead of the "wishy-washy social science course instituted by the Americans," as a British observer condescendingly called it. When he returned from a European trip in 1962, the premier went first to bow to the Emperor, then paid homage at the Yasukuni Shrine to the war dead that was linked to the nation's pre-1945 military deeds. His visit to the shrine angered Americans, and other Asians, while gratifying Japanese nationalists. Ikeda was forced by cancer to give up his post in 1964, but by then he had shredded the left (and much of the center). The political vacuum began to be filled by *Komeito,* or "Clean Government Party." Komeito was spawned by Buddhists whose goals included neutralism, more help to small businesses, and more aid to those dispossessed by the "miracle." In its first election of 1967, it won twenty-five Diet seats, and within a decade it became Japan's third-largest party. But the LDP rolled on.[4]

The irony lay here: as the CIA-helped LDP increased its power, it not only grew more corrupt but increasingly clashed with the United States. This clash revolved as usual around China. It also centered on the never-ending question of how to deal with an aggressive Japanese capitalism that refused to play by American ground rules. Certainly Japan's own ground rules seemed productive; its growth rate averaged nearly 10 percent annually over a fifteen-year era that spanned the 1960s—the highest real growth rate ever recorded over such a span by a leading economic power. Japan won full membership in such crucial international groups as the Organization for Economic Cooperation and Development in 1964. (OECD had been formed to expedite free trade, but Japan was able to negotiate a series of reservations that allowed it to maintain trade barriers.) The auto industry, producing a half-million vehicles in 1960, quadrupled to 2.2 million in 1966, then increased 50 percent again to replace Germany as the world's number-two maker by the 1970s. The globe's largest shipbuilding industry had order books double the size of its three closest rivals. By 1966, the United States had sold Japan $2.4 billion worth of goods during the year and bought $2.9 billion. An unfavorable trade balance had set in for Americans.[5]

In 1967, French President Charles de Gaulle denigrated the Japanese prime minister as a mere "merchant of transistors." Uncharacteristically, de Gaulle missed the point. The Japanese government indeed saw its role as selling shiploads of better transistors, among other products, because such sales realized the larger goal Japan had long sought: economic security that would produce political autonomy that would lead to domestic order (or *wa,* as the Meiji generation had phrased it). De Gaulle sought glory for France by building a nuclear force, playing balance-of-power politics to the hilt, and checking U.S. global power. Ikeda and his successors realized not mere glory but security for Japan by escaping the endless costs of a nuclear force, playing their economic cards to the hilt, and reluctantly cooperating with (or often politely and quietly sidestepping) U.S. Cold War policies. De Gaulle lost power in 1969. Ikeda's LDP successors held power for nearly another quarter century.

The "merchants of transistors" had a labor-management relationship in the 1960s that looked oddly different from the American. Japanese stressed—especially in the largest exporting firms—lifetime employment that ensured stability, company unions that ensured predictability, wages based on seniority that ensured an end to ruinous worker competition, and (as W. Edwards Deming's techniques demanded) a maximum of cooperation. An end-of-the-year bonus system secured the workers' interest in the company profit and spread risk to workers as well as owners. The "transistor salesmen" also kept governmental expenditures low, especially for welfare and the military.[6]

The Japanese government instead created neo-mercantilistic policies (taxes, industrial regulations, control over imports) that favored new industries (electronics, steel, autos, and synthetics), and deemphasized old (as coal). It encouraged successful firms, such as Nissan, Toyota, Hitachi, New Japan Steel, to merge with others in their sector to form world-competitive enterprises. A great "science city" was planned north of Tokyo where a collective of 52,000 scientists and engineers could turn out, and adapt, the latest technology. These developments were overseen by a highly trained, elite bureaucracy. Insulated against political firestorms, it nevertheless produced the prime ministers (such as Ikeda, from both the Ministry of Finance and MITI) who presided over Japan for twenty of the years between 1955 and 1980. The bureaucracy, then and later, excelled in information collection, especially from such leading competitors as the United States.[7]

Nowhere, however, was the government more successful, and more un-American, than in controlling capital, the "miracle's" lifeblood. After 1945, Japanese businesses depended utterly on bank loans. That dependence enabled Tokyo bureaucrats to shape industrialization by turning on the banks' money supply for certain companies and denying others. The government did this by employing several wrenches. Its Reconstruction Finance Bank was the prime source of capital from 1945 into the 1950s, especially after New York City capital was largely excluded. Then the government created the Japan Development Bank to favor cutting-edge export industries. The Bank of Japan became both an investor and a referee in the economy. The United States embraced the private marketplace, or slow-moving governmental fiscal and taxing policies, to develop competitive businesses. Japan used ruthless, efficient, and unusually well-informed bureaucratic decision making to implement its decisions effectively: by creating low-interest loans for Japanese businesses through control of the capital supply.

Thus American firms depended on the stock markets for capital, and were often held hostage by their short-term profit objectives. Japanese companies took the long-term view encouraged by MITI and the finance ministry. By the mid-1960s, the state provided nearly 30 percent of gross domestic capital formation (or about twice the percentage found on the American side). Above all, the government accumulated capital at home through a variety of weapons to accelerate the Japanese people's already strong habits of saving. MITI and the finance ministry sought Japan's salvation through exporting technology, not, as in the United States, through a society (or global military force) based on increasing consumption.[8]

By 1966, a surprised *U.S. News & World Report* observed that Japan, lying in ruins just twenty years before, had become one of the few nations exporting more capital than it imported. Most of this investment went to secure raw materials and mineral resources. Japan targeted Brazil, where masses of Japanese had emigrated, and Canada. This historic shift in the yen's power occurred as the John F. Kennedy and Lyndon B. Johnson administrations worked feverishly to shore up U.S. credit. Dollars flowed out for war in Southeast Asia, global military commitments, private investments in a unifying Europe—and a growing unfavorable trade balance with Japan. U.S. officials demanded that Japanese open their markets, including capital markets. By 1970, of the two hundred largest American corporations, seventy-eight were operating in Japan. But to exist they largely had to work closely with Japanese firms—an arrangement that helped channel U.S. technology and capital into Japan under tight Japanese control. After intense U.S. pressure was applied, Tokyo announced in 1967 that seventeen types of business would finally be opened to 100 percent American ownership. The announcement meant little because the businesses included steel, shipbuilding, and motorcycles, where Japanese dominance was overwhelming. Earlier, the authorities had made the mistake of allowing in several U.S. food companies; the Americans soon held 80 percent of the instant coffee market. Tokyo bureaucrats would not repeat that error. As one Japanese official declared: "Most Japanese businessmen don't want to make the same mistake that European businessmen did—turning over most of their businesses to American business."[9]

Americans might have better tolerated Japan's economic success had it not had two glaring characteristics: sudden triumph just as the United States headed into the nightmare of the Vietnam War, and a focus on selling to Chinese (and even Vietnamese) whom Americans opposed in that war. A rapid buildup of U.S. troops in Vietnam occurred during 1965. That year was also a watershed for the U.S.-Japan trade relationship: before then, the Americans enjoyed a favorable balance. Afterwards, Japan's favorable balance grew to $1.5 billion in 1969 (out of $9 billion two-way trade), then $3.2 billion in 1971. Honda and Yamaha first sold motorcycles in the United States during 1960; by 1966, they accounted for 85 percent of all motorcycles bought by Americans. The story was quickly, if less dramatically, repeated in autos and electronics. North American markets were taking 36 percent of Japan's exports—a figure like that of the 1920s when Japanese prosperity rested on those markets. By 1972, a top Japanese diplomat warned that "a trade imbalance of this magnitude cannot simply continue without creating serious difficulties in the bilateral economic relationship"—and, he might have added, also in the political. Japan's exports remained low-priced too, while American prices suffered from Vietnam War–stoked inflation.[10]

The American trade wound was deepened by the Japanese determination to sell to Communists and other Asians alike. Trilateral trade among Japan, the Asian continent, and the United States (with Japan the pivot for most of the trade) grew so fast that experts predicted a "Pacific trading bloc." It would include Australia (which now had Japan as its largest trading partner), and even Peru and Chile. U.S. officials feared the bloc might also include the Soviet Union, for Japan signed consular and air-traffic agreements with Moscow while planning to increase trade and joint ventures for opening Siberia's mind-boggling mineral resources. Clearly, a powerful LDP faction led by Miki Takeo was urging the development of Soviet and Asian trade as an alternative to dependence on the U.S. market. Thus in Burma, Japan's goods were becoming so prominent that people ran to catch the "hino" rather than the "bus." Japan was Taiwan's leading trade partner (the United States was second), and although the balance was overwhelmingly in Tokyo's favor, U.S. officials showed little concern.[11]

They were more exercised, however, with the so-called L-T deals (named after the negotiators' initials) that supposedly private Japanese signed with China in 1962. In these arrangements, the parties agreed that "politics and economies are inseparable." The U.S. "imperialists' open intervention" into Sino-Japanese relations was condemned. In January 1963, Ikeda told a press conference that Japan was ready to act "independently from beginning to end" on China trade, although he emphasized the 1962 deals were agreed to by non-governmental groups. Bilateral Sino-Japanese trade then jumped from $136 million in 1963 to $560 million in 1969. In a break with the past, Tokyo officials supplied credit arrangements for some of that trade. Japan, becoming China's number-one trading partner, was "looking 10 or 20 years ahead," *The Times* of London declared, "when the Chinese economy should have changed radically."[12]

Americans meanwhile died in Asia, supposedly to contain China's expansionism. Anti-war and civil rights protests created chaos on college campuses and in major urban areas. The U.S. economy overheated, was wracked by inflation, and became less competitive. Between 1971 and 1973, the U.S.-devised international economic system put into place after World War II came to an end.

This apocalyptic climax gradually hove into view throughout the 1960s. The American economy boomed along toward a gross national product that moved from $23 billion in 1947 to $900 billion in 1969 (Japan's was barely 10 percent of that, or $91.1 billion in 1968). But overall increases in agricultural productivity hid a frightening decline in annual industrial productivity from a 3.6 percent increase early in the 1960s to only 1.5 percent by 1966–70. This decline was doubly ominous, for imports (notably from Japan) increased their share of the American market during the 1960s by a whopping 50 percent. Dollars flowed out to pay for these imports just as the Vietnam War's budgets rose dramatically. The head of Mitsui believed in 1967 that Japanese profited from between $500 million and $4 billion every year for producing items to be used in fighting that war.[13]

U.S. officials moved to stanch the financial bleeding by trying to regulate (that is, tax) investment capital moving overseas. That approach was doomed to failure, not least because American officials and investors soon discovered that if they could not invest abroad, others, including Japanese, happily stepped in. Washington officials also moved to retilt the international marketplace toward their interest by initiating the so-called Kennedy Round of tariff cuts that by 1969 did, indeed, reduce tariffs by as much as 60 percent in some parts of the world. But quotas and "voluntary restraints" replaced tariffs as barriers to increased world trade. President Kennedy had personally worked out an arrangement with Tokyo that limited U.S. imports of some Japanese textiles.

In May 1969, the CIA reported that Japan was providing too little help for the embattled American economy: "informal administrative means," as the Agency nicely termed Tokyo's bureaucracy, effectively barred most U.S. capital and goods. Meanwhile, the CIA warned, the Japanese effectively exploited ties with U.S. firms—even computer giant IBM—to obtain cutting-edge technology and then "effectively shut out" those firms from the Japanese market. Undersecretary of State U. Alexis Johnson could proudly announce in 1963 that because of astounding successes since 1945 in U.S.-Japan trade, the Japanese had become a "model" and "source of modern technology" for other Asians. "The Far East," Johnson declared, "from our vantage point is more correctly called the 'Far West,'" or, even better, the "'Near West.'" Other Americans, however, began to wonder whether, in the racial stereotypes of their western movies, the Japanese were going to play the friendlies or the hostiles in this "Near West."[14]

Kennedy, Ikeda, and the Illusion of "Equal Partnership"

The new administration in Washington had no doubt about who was to play the cavalry. As the British journalist Louis Heren recalled, "When I arrived in Washington just before the inauguration of John Kennedy, the mood of the city could only be described as euphoria." A new generation, Kennedy announced in his inaugural, was taking leadership to fight the Cold War more effectively, and reform society more dramatically. The new President, a veteran of the Pacific War, had been decorated "involuntarily," as he phrased it. The Japanese destroyed his torpedo boat and forced him bravely to rescue his crew. U.S.-Japan relations, however, seemed to be recovering well from the memories of the early 1940s and the riots of early 1960. In September 1960, Prince Akihito, heir to the throne, and Princess Michiko took the political risk of visiting Hawaii to help celebrate the centennial of the 1860 Japanese mission. They dropped a lei on the USS *Arizona* memorial at Pearl Harbor. A British diplomat, marveling at the visit's success, privately admitted, "I can't see ourselves permitting such a visit under similar circumstances."[15]

In late 1961, the first meeting of the U.S.-Japan Joint Committee on

Scientific Cooperation took place. So did the initial convening of the U.S.-Japan Cultural and Educational Cooperation committee. Harvard expert-on-Japan Edwin Reischauer and others preached that as Japan finally modernized, it would become more like the United States. The British evaluation of the relationship, however, was not kind: "It must . . . be comforting for the Americans to have a country and a people with whom they can indulge in mutual admiration."[16]

The two cultures might have appeared to be converging, but foreign policies do not always follow culture. In their first meeting in 1961, Kennedy pressed Ikeda to play a larger international role. The prime minister lamented that Japan first needed better command of the English language. U.S. officials then proposed sending one hundred Peace Corps volunteers to help Japanese learn English. Japan's Ministry of Education quickly objected that the new Peace Corps was for under-developed nations; its appearance in the home islands would be taken as an insult. Instead, the Japanese began to demand what they called "equal partnership," by which they seemed to mean more economic access while America bore the responsibility for maintaining Asian security.[17]

Kennedy appointed Reischauer as U.S. ambassador to Tokyo. Reischauer, in a widely noted 1960 essay, had criticized the "broken dialogue" between the two nations, especially between Americans and the Japanese left. He and his Japanese-born wife, Haru, did much to repair that break over the next six years—not least after he was seriously wounded when stabbed by an unbalanced young Japanese in 1964. Reischauer was intent on using modernization theory (essentially that Japan was following U.S. development) as a weapon against Marxist theories of development that were popular in important Japanese intel-lectual circles. The ambassador, however, grew frustrated that few top U.S. officials wished to visit Japan. Attorney General Robert Kennedy was an exception. The President's brother scored a triumph during a 1962 trip when he effectively debated Japanese protesters.

The young President meanwhile fretted over declining U.S. competi-tiveness in the world marketplace. His reading of history concluded that great empires of the past had been destroyed by enemies who nibbled away at the empire's most exposed frontier. In the case of nei-ther the economic nor security problems, Kennedy privately com-plained, could he pull fresh, effective ideas from a stagnating American liberalism. Louis Heren later caught the moment: the 1930s New Deal "initiatives had run their course by the sixties. . . . The United States had also turned its back on the examples of social reform prevalent in northern Europe, and the intellectual isolationism was to say the least stultifying."[18]

Kennedy's "New Frontier" threatened to become little more than the old frontier studded with Hollywood glitter. Confronting U.S. trade imbalances and edgy Asian security, the President and his advisers came up with variations of policies from the late 1940s and 1950s: preaching open markets and practicing containment. On the pivotal trade problem, a secret State Department analysis of March 1962 defined the dilemma. Its logic, to a point, was impeccable: "We see Japan as our principal ally in East Asia, our second largest world trading partner, the host for important forward U.S. military facilities, and a source of technical skill and capital contributing to the economic development of South and South East Asia." But Japan's cooperation with Washington, and its "continued control by moderate elements," as well as its ability to be helpful in Asia, depended "primarily on the maintenance of a high level of economic activity which, in turn, depends to an unusual extent upon access to world markets." These tough-minded officials quickly saw the opportunity: "This dependence on trade . . . provides the United States with very considerable leverage in Japan." That assumption, of course, had also been shared by Thomas Lamont, Charles Evans Hughes, Cordell Hull, and Stanley Hornbeck. Their policies toward Japan now formed a thin layer in the ashheap of history.[19]

The New Frontiersmen found themselves trapped between two tectonic plates of the post-1945 era: on one side the traditional U.S. trade surplus, which had paid bills for expensive, far-flung military containment, was shifting into deficits; on the other side, the Japanese economy, whose devastation and slow recovery had given Americans a powerful leverage over Tokyo's policies, was beginning to accelerate. Between 1958 and 1971, the United States became a more normal economic power while Japan became a more-than-normal economic power.

Caught in these historic transitions, and light on new ideas, the State Department echoed the 1930s by asking Japan to help in the "alleviation of the United States balance of payments problem" through "trade liberalization." Americans would in turn further open their own markets to Japanese goods—unless, of course, U.S. restraints on Japanese imports were "absolutely essential." Japan was meanwhile urged to find outlets in Asia (although not China) and Western Europe. In 1962, Undersecretary of Defense Roswell Gilpatrick demanded that the Japanese were now in a position to help by paying more of the costs of U.S. bases in the home islands and Okinawa. In reality, Gilpatrick realized that Japan could not pay those costs without an eviscerating public debate in which the left could blast pro-American conservatives. Gilpatrick touched upon, then quickly backed away from, the idea that money could be saved by reducing or restructuring the U.S. base complex in Japan. For Reischauer, the very thought that Gilpatrick could float such an idea was abhorrent. As the ambassador lectured W. Averell Harriman (the assistant secretary of state for Far Eastern affairs) in late 1962: "The primary role of our bases in Japan, I feel, is to help insure that this country [Japan] does not fall or gravitate into Communist hands or into a neutralist position." But the Pentagon "seems to be judging them solely on their secondary value as bases for the defense of other areas in the Far East."[20]

The 169 U.S. bases had 45,000 American military personnel, 54,600 dependents, 3,300 American civilians, and nearly 70,000 Japanese employees. That such force might be in Japan primarily to shape internal Japanese politics rather than provide for Asian security had, of course, also crossed many Japanese minds. Such ideas helped trigger the 1960 riots. Moreover, the secret State Department analysis noted in 1962, "The Japanese are haunted by the fear of involvement in another nuclear war." If the "conservatives" tried to "flout these fears," the price would be high for both the LDP and U.S. policy.[21]

Supporting U.S. policy, LDP politicians understood, could be politically equivalent to eating the great delicacy of blowfish: perhaps rewarding, but one mistake could be fatal. Mishandling the issue of U.S. bases could be the one mistake. Another could be handling the growing U.S. pressure from domestic manufacturers (especially textiles) to force Japanese export reduction "voluntarily." These pressures built as Kennedy preached the need for more liberal trade and adherence to the "Kennedy Round" of tariff talks. The secret State Department policy statement of March 1962 was blunt. Essential to U.S. policy was "the continuation in power of a moderate, Western-oriented conservative government."

Such laudable objectives excused the CIA's covert funding of the LDP in 1955. In February 1961, a CIA official and a representative of the top-secret National Security Agency briefed Kennedy's national security adviser, McGeorge Bundy; Secretary of State Dean Rusk; and Rusk's adviser on Asia, Roger Hilsman. The CIA operation had begun under Eisenhower, the two briefers explained, because Communist nations were helping the left wing. The assistance simply paralleled CIA activities in Italy, France, and Greece to block the left. Hilsman suggested the operation might now be stopped. The CIA agent replied that perhaps it should never have started, but if it were suddenly stopped now, the LDP would be furious. U.S.-Japan relations would suffer. The briefer suggested the money-passing be stopped gradually, and "after 30 years nobody will notice this." (Thirty-three years later the revelation of the operation become a much-discussed page-one story in the *New York Times*.) Money continued to flow through the 1960s, apparently $2 million to $10 million per year. It was usually passed in Hawaii, where LDP couriers flew "to do you know what" *(reino mono)*, as one future prime minister, Ohira Masayoshi, called it. While paying off the right, the CIA and other U.S. officials also infiltrated the Japanese left, especially the giant trade union *Sohyo*. The goal was to split and weaken these groups, or win them over to the fervent anti-Communist policies of the American labor movement. These operations were overseen by a Special Group (SG), chaired by the President's national security adviser. It met in Room 40 of the Old Executive Office Building next to the White House, and thus was known as "the 40 Committee." The SG guided the most important U.S. covert operations in Japan and elsewhere into the Nixon-Kissinger era of the 1970s.[22]

Above all, Kennedy demanded help from Japanese (as well as from highly reluctant Europeans) to contain, if not drive back, China's power. After the world approached nuclear war during the Cuban missile crisis of October 1962, Kennedy concluded that the Soviet leaders had learned their lesson about the dangers of challenging the United States. But, he also concluded, China had not learned those hard lessons. During a joint U.S.-Japan economic meeting in Washington two months after the missile crisis, the President took the highly unusual step of lecturing the Japanese in public. "The rise of the Communist power in China combined with an expansionist, Stalinist philosophy," Kennedy began, had led to the need for containing China. Japan must help contain this menace, "which is in its essence today a believer not only in class struggle but also in the international class struggle of a Third World War." Foreign Minister Ohira's response notably emphasized instead the need to develop trade.[23]

Japan clearly wanted trade, not confrontation. The 1962 L-T agreement, increasing private trade between China and Japan, anticipated the future. In February 1963, Ikeda was reminded by a Diet member about Kennedy's condemnation of China and the prime minister's own earlier declaration that he would "not allow any foreign intervention in Sino-Japanese relations. Is he still of the same mind?" Ikeda replied, "Japan will cooperate in checking the expansion of communism, but Sino-Japanese trade is, I believe, another question." Then came announcements that China would receive credits to pay for purchases from Japan. Assistant Secretary of State Harriman warned that the United States could not approve such arrangements. By April 1963, nevertheless, reports circulated that Mitsubishi and several other huge Japanese firms had set up dummy companies to open business with China. The dummies were especially useful, the report noted, in allowing their U.S. branches to profess that the firms were not directly involved in the China market. In October of that year, the largest Japanese trade fair in China's history occurred in Beijing.[24]

In truth, Kennedy's policies were sinking. U.S. officials knew that Japan's trade with China was domestically popular and increasingly necessary for Japan's long-term prosperity (especially if Americans continued to insist on the Japanese "voluntarily" cutting back exports to the United States). Moreover, U.S. policies—by Washington officials' own admission—depended utterly on close links with Ikeda and LDP leaders who wanted to move into China. In July 1962, Ikeda had to restructure his cabinet after an internal party crisis brought pro-Chinese factions, led by Miki Takeo, to power. The pro-U.S. group, headed by Kishi Nobusuke, Sato Eisaku, and Fukuda Takeo, received a temporary setback. Americans wanted to embrace the LDP, but the object of their affections suffered from a deeply split personality. Washington's alternative pressure point was to work through the foreign ministry, but it lacked the clout of the finance ministry or MITI. The CIA therefore penetrated the latter bureaucracies while the foreign ministry remained a willing but weak ally.[25]

The Kennedyites, then, wanted Japan to become fully involved in South and Southeast Asia, as well as in Taiwan, but not in nearby China. *The Times* of London underlined the paradox: "With distant Asian countries, alien to her own civilization, Japan can thus deal with ease and freedom. With those neighbors with whom she shares much in culture and outlook relations are more complex." U.S. pressures only accelerated Japan's "strong desire for neutralism." Or, as the British ambassador in Tokyo told his superiors in 1963, "The Japanese can neither love the Americans nor endure being loved by them" because Americans could not bring themselves to see that Japan was now a sovereign nation.[26]

No U.S. official was more determined to use Japan (and any other available nation) to contain China than Secretary of State Dean Rusk. Rabidly anti-Communist, Rusk harbored bitter memories of how the Chinese invasion of Korea in late 1950 had threatened and humiliated the U.S. position in Asia when he was a top State Department official. He fed Kennedy's fixation on China. In December 1962, Rusk told Foreign Minister Ohira that the Sino-Soviet split meant not an easing of pressure, but perhaps "serious consequences in South East Asia." China could be more aggressive once freed of Moscow's restraint. When Ohira tried to respond that the problem in the region was "poverty combined with nationalist sentiment," Rusk would have none of it: he "saw little evidence that trade with the Communist countries led to the promotion of peace."[27] Thus grew a quiet but ominous clash between Japan and the United States. Determined to contain and discipline China, Kennedy increased U.S. military personnel in South Vietnam from 600 to 16,000. Two months before his own assassination in November 1963, he secretly agreed to the Vietnamese military's overthrow of the Ngo Dinh Diem regime—the act by "the young president, in his zeal," General William Westmoreland later observed, that "morally locked us in Vietnam." The Japanese meanwhile opened wider trade and cultural exchanges with Beijing. In South Vietnam, they contributed handsomely to U.S. development projects and created highly profitable trade links, but they wanted nothing to do with Kennedy's military escalation. Tokyo even cultivated trade with Communist North Vietnam through "private" trade associations. As U.S. attacks on the North intensified in 1964–65, Japanese agents and Vietnamese Communists worked out complex channels through third-country carriers to continue a trade that was vital for the North. Given the extent of U.S. power and the diverging interests of Japan, as the historian Kono Yasuko later observed, chances were evaporating of realizing a truly "equal partnership" between Tokyo and Washington.[28]

Johnson, Sato, and Vietnam

In one 1964 spectacular, the Japanese tried to demonstrate that they were worthy of being equal partners and had come to terms with their crushing defeat of 1945. This sports-crazy people hosted the Olympic Games with a dedication bordering on frenzy. Even the sixty-three-year-old Emperor Hirohito stood stiffly at attention for several hours as ninety-four national teams paraded by. Hirohito stunned many critics by giving the First Class Order of the Rising Sun, the highest honor a foreigner can receive from Japan, to General Curtis LeMay—the architect of the firebombing that destroyed hundreds of thousands of Japanese, and the highest U.S. Air Force officer involved in the field operation that dropped the two atomic bombs in 1945. LeMay was honored—on December 7, 1964, no less—for developing Japan's postwar defense system. Protests erupted over the award. The Japanese government ignored them.[29]

Any hope that such spectaculars would lead to a more equal partnership with the United States, however, disappeared as the new President, Lyndon B. Johnson, escalated the war in Vietnam. The Japanese wanted to avoid a war that made little sense, and even uncomfortably reminded them of their own earlier quagmire on the Asian mainland. Of greater importance, they fundamentally disagreed with the U.S. determination to teach China a lesson by warring on Vietnam. In 1965, China became Japan's fourth-largest trading partner (after the Americans, Australians, and Canadians).[30]

As the war accelerated, so did three disagreements between Americans and Japanese: the return of Okinawa; trade with China; and the removal of U.S. discriminations against imports from Japan while Japanese discriminations against U.S. exports (and capital) remained in place. The vitality of these disagreements is stunning, especially since they surged during the premiership of Sato Eisaku, probably the most pro-American of all postwar Japanese prime ministers.[31]

Sato held power longer than any of those leaders—from November 9, 1964, just as Lyndon Johnson celebrated his landslide election victory, to July 7, 1972, as Richard Nixon prepared to celebrate a similar triumph. Born March 27, 1901, in southern Honshu, he was upper-class bred and educated. Becoming a power in the railway ministry, he strongly supported the war effort, but endured terrifying personal experiences when his wife and children barely escaped the firebombing of Tokyo, only to be bombed again in Osaka. His nephew died at Hiroshima on August 6, 1945. Although suspected of being a war criminal, he was never tried, due to lack of evidence. Sato accrued power rapidly during the occupation as Yoshida's cabinet secretary. Other than Yoshida, Sato's chief sponsor was his brother, Kishi Nobusuke, ruined in 1960 by his handling of the U.S. security treaty. The brothers had different names because each had been adopted by their wives' families, as is frequently done in Japan when a woman has no brother to pass down the family name.

"Ruggedly handsome and large for a Japanese," according to U.S. Ambassador U. Alexis Johnson, Sato "had a master politician's easy, friendly manner." He also had a master politician's ability to scheme and find common ground. As head of the powerful Ministry of Finance under his brother's premiership, and also as close adviser to his intimate friend Ikeda, Sato took a tough line against the left and headed one of the most pro-American factions of the LDP. His intimacy with Ikeda did not prevent him from unsuccessfully trying to dethrone the prime minister in 1963. "Friendship should not be permitted to interfere with a person's decision when it has any bearing on his course of action in public life," Sato declared in a sentence that deserved close study in Washington. In 1964, when Ikeda developed throat cancer, Sato finally climbed to the top rung. Of special note, Sato was extraordinarily well connected through marriage to both powerful political factions and rich corporations. He epitomized *keibatsu,* whose characters mean "clique-out-of-bedroom." Resembling other Japanese leaders, he combined an intense devotion to both technology and tradition: he loved and critically studied cinema, for example, while he was also renowned as an expert on the ancient, highly ritualistic tea ceremony.[32]

Lyndon Johnson was too restless to sit through many films, and certainly knew nothing of tea ceremonies. (The tall Texan once told friends that he only enjoyed "whiskey, sunshine, and sex.") But he harbored hopes for a profitable relationship with Japan because he appreciated Sato's pro-U.S. beliefs. In personal meetings he got along well with the prime minister. As Sato observed, however, personal friendship did not necessarily resolve the deeply rooted, substantive differences.[33]

"The key issue on Sato's mind," LBJ was told in early 1965, "is *Communist China.*" But there was no meeting of minds about China. Rusk had lectured Japanese cabinet members in 1964 on the evils of trade with China (and was even harsher in questioning Japan's recent deal to buy sugar from Castro's Cuba). Foreign Minister Ohira played down the trade, but pointedly reminded Rusk that "it is still fresh in our memory" that China not long ago took 20 percent of Japan's exports. The threat magnified on October 16, 1964, when the Chinese exploded an atomic device equal to the weapon that destroyed Hiroshima. By mid-1966, they exploded a bomb ten times larger than the first. The next year they triggered their first hydrogen bomb. In the short term, China's new arsenal made U.S. protection more important to Japan. In the long run, however, Sato believed Japan needed the capability for similar weapons. He refused to sign a non-proliferation agreement, despite intense U.S. pressure. Professor Robert Scalapino of the University of California–Berkeley accurately predicted in 1967 that Japan would develop space and peaceful nuclear power technologies that could be easily converted to military use "on the quickest, easiest and cheapest basis, should the necessity arise." In December 1967, Sato issued his soon-to-be-famous "Three Nonnuclear Principles": Japan

ABOVE. *Hiroshima, August 1945, at ground zero.* (UN/DPI Photos)

RIGHT. *General Douglas MacArthur and Emperor Hirohito, September 1945. For a number of reasons, this photo symbolized a transformation in Japan, as well as in Japanese-U.S. relations.* (AP/Wide World Photos)

ABOVE. President Lyndon B. Johnson, with Ladybird Johnson, greets Prime Minister Sato Eisaku in January 1965 to begin difficult talks on Vietnam and trade. (LBJ Library Collection)

BELOW. President Lyndon B. Johnson and U.S. Ambassador to Japan Edwin Reischauer. Johnson came to mistrust Reischauer because of the ambassador's long commitment to bringing Americans and Japanese closer together. (LBJ Library Collection)

Prime Minister Sato Eisaku's dour look, not the smiles of the President, Mrs. Sato, and Mrs. Nixon, reveals the tough give-and-take on Okinawa and textiles that marked the November 1969 watershed negotiations. (Nixon Library Collection)

Pomp and circumstance in Alaska, September 1971, as President Richard Nixon welcomes Emperor Hirohito. But not even the seventy-year-old Emperor's first visit out of Japan could reverse the downward spiral of U.S.-Japan relations. (Nixon Library Collection)

ABOVE. *Prime Minister Nakasone Yasuhiro flaunts Japan's technology as he presents a miniature television set to President and Nancy Reagan, April 1989. (Reagan Library Collection)*

BELOW. *At their tough 1995 talks, U.S. trade representative Mickey Kantor and Japan's trade minister (and future prime minister) Hashimoto Ryutaro playfully parried with a Japanese fencing sword—a sport in which Hashimoto notably excelled. (AFP Photos)*

would not possess, manufacture, or allow nuclear weapons to enter the country. The development of peaceful nuclear power, along the lines Scalapino foresaw, nevertheless accelerated.[34]

How to respond to China's nuclear program generated heated disagreement between Tokyo and Washington. So did the question of how to respond to China's role in the Vietnam War. Throughout 1964, U.S. officials assumed the Chinese were back of the Vietnamese revolutionary forces led by Ho Chi Minh. If the Viet Minh prevailed, the entire region would fall under Communist control like collapsing dominoes. In July 1964, Secretary of Defense Robert McNamara asked Japan's top defense official, Fukuda Takeo, to estimate the effect on the Japanese "if the U.S. lost South Vietnam." Fukuda coolly replied that the "left" would probably strengthen and protest more vigorously against American bases, while "Japan would lose trading opportunities in [Southeast Asia]." Fukuda was having no part of the U.S. fear about China pushing over the dominoes: he believed that the Chinese cared more about their "domestic build-up" than "improving their military forces." To make his dissent from U.S. policies clear, Fukuda added that "it was difficult to maintain control of such an area [as Vietnam] solely through military means."[35]

Johnson, Rusk, and McNamara, however, put much of their faith in military means. After replacing the slain Kennedy in November 1963, Johnson came under constant pressure from the late President's closest advisers—especially McGeorge Bundy, Rusk, and McNamara—to escalate U.S. military involvement in Vietnam rapidly lest the divided, corrupt Saigon governments collapse. McNamara, former "whiz kid" president of Ford Motor Company, believed his Pentagon could manage the war and kill enough of the enemy with legendary American efficiency—all the while building a new nation in South Vietnam. In 1964, Johnson beat back these pressures except for one fateful moment. As LBJ began his election campaign against Republican hard-liner Senator Barry Goldwater of Arizona, McNamara urgently reported during the first week of August 1964 that U.S. ships off the Vietnamese coast had twice been the victim of unprovoked attacks. It later emerged that American vessels were actually engaged in a covert operation against North Vietnam. The circumstances of the first attack were muddy. The second attack probably did not occur. But Johnson seized on the opportunity to show his toughness. He bombed the North and obtained from Congress the Gulf of Tonkin resolution that, as he interpreted it, gave him a blank check in responding to North Vietnam.[36]

In Tokyo, the foreign ministry carefully declared that Johnson's response was justified under the right to self-defense, then even more carefully added, "There is no way to ascertain for sure" exactly what had occurred in the Gulf of Tonkin. When Socialists asked whether the presence of U.S. bases might draw Japan into the war, the government—then and forever after—anesthetized most Japanese by responding that Americans were responsibly acting under the terms of the duly ratified 1960 treaty. The response did not, however, anesthetize protesters who greeted the U.S. nuclear submarine, *Sea Dragon,* when it visited Sasebo in late 1964.[37]

Between February and July 1965, a reluctant Johnson crossed his own Rubicon. He launched a systematic bombing campaign and dispatched some 120,000 troops in an escalation that by 1968 had reached 550,000 soldiers. He took these historic steps for many reasons. As South Vietnam's governments grew weaker, and northern infiltration and influence grew, he believed he had to honor the commitment to Southeast Asia. Bundy, Rusk, and McNamara, among others, pressured him to do so. He also truly wanted to help the Vietnamese develop, much as his cherished New Deal of the 1930s had helped his native Texas develop. An earlier British Foreign Office analysis of Johnson concluded that he was "relatively inexperienced" in foreign affairs, but "has firm ideas about the pre-excellence of the American Way of Life, and tends to regard it as the only possible form of democracy." This paper also accurately predicted he would want "to devote most of his time and effort to domestic affairs." LBJ's beloved Great Society program to help minorities, children, poor, and the elderly came first. But Johnson believed he could not push controversial domestic legislation through Congress if he "lost" Vietnam—much as Harry Truman, to his great political cost, had "lost" China. Johnson realized, moreover, his incredible power: with a telephone call to McNamara he could send hundreds of thousands of personnel halfway around the globe via the world's most powerful navy and air force.[38]

Above all—and always—there was China. Only now China played a slightly different role. Before the 1960s, U.S. officials had worried that the Japanese would grow dependent on the China market if Southeast Asia (and North American) markets were not open to them. Now those officials became obsessed with the fear that failure in Vietnam would be viewed as a Chinese triumph. Japan, along with much of Asia, would then move leftward. As White House aide Michael Forrestal noted, the 1965 escalation by Johnson was necessary to "delay China swallowing Southeast Asia until (a) she develops better table manners and (b) the food is somewhat more indigestible."[39]

U.S. officials seemed beside themselves that Japan ignored such danger. At their January 1965 summit, the President expressed his "grave concern that Communist China's militant policies and expansionist pressures against its neighbors endanger the peace of Asia." Sato commented only that Japan intended "to continue to promote private contact" with China. Later, at a press conference, Sato dealt with Vietnam by remarking that Asian problems could often be solved not by the West's "rational approach" but required the patience and understanding of the "Asian mind." Relations were not helped when LBJ began his bombing campaign and escalation of troop strength without briefing Sato. The President had informed others, including New Zealand. Japan made gestures. It sent 11,645 radios to the South Vietnamese so they could hear their government's decrees (and programs from Japan), and also gave medical supplies. Tokyo secretly dispatched twenty-eight landing craft, flying the Stars and Stripes and manned by Japanese wearing U.S. uniforms, to help move supplies along the Vietnamese coast. These crews suffered dead and wounded.[40]

But Johnson wanted far more from Japan. Rusk blamed Ambassador Reischauer for being too pro-Japanese, for not educating Japan about the great danger, for assuming that the two nations were converging in their interests while, in reality, the Japanese were going off on their own. As Reischauer lay in serious condition after he was stabbed in 1964, neither Johnson nor Rusk sent him a personal note. In mid-1966, Reischauer was finally replaced by the hawkish U. Alexis Johnson. Tokyo, however, only now differed with two Johnsons instead of one over China and Vietnam.

The President was trapped. He meant to escalate U.S. power until the North Vietnamese broke and allowed the South's to exist. But to his surprise, the northerners sacrificed themselves in large numbers while moving south in even larger numbers. The other claw of the trap then snapped: if his escalation went too far—if, as he put it, he turned to "rape rather than seduction—. . . Chinese reaction might be instant and total." Johnson's strategy in Vietnam was neither cowardly nor confused, but quite rational; it was gradual and restrained because he rightly feared any repeat of the Korean War tragedy when the Chinese massively entered. Extensive bombing of the North's ports, moreover, might not only threaten sensitive Chinese interests. With only one-third of North Vietnam's shipping arriving from Communist countries, the other two-thirds came chiefly from British, Japanese, Norwegian, and Greek ships—that is, from American allies. When a *New York Times* correspondent asked Johnson in late 1965 whether he was trying to save face in Vietnam, the President replied, "I'm not trying to save my face. I'm trying to save my ass."[41]

Americans and Japanese did agree on some issues between 1965 and 1968. One was that Japan was profiting handsomely from the war. Only the amounts were in dispute. In a thorough analysis of its effect on Japan, Thomas Havens estimated that, in all, the war brought at least an extra $1 billion per year to Japanese firms between 1966 and 1976. A U.S. Treasury estimate of late 1967 reached the same figure. Bank of Japan figures were lower because they left out hard-to-calculate monies spent by U.S. soldiers resting in Japan. Only 7 to 8 percent of Japan's annual exports, this war-generated trade was nevertheless a godsend for small companies. U.S. soldiers used Japanese-made tents, watches, cameras, generators, Jeeps, and toilet paper. They "drank Kirin beer, chewed Lotte gum," as Havens observed, while "some of the injured received transfusions of Japanese blood, and those who died were sent home in polyethylene body bags made in Japan." The Sato government used some profits to buy military goods, especially high-technology weapons and aircraft from Americans. Meanwhile, Japan's trade with both North and South Vietnam grew. By 1970, war-devastated South Vietnam overflowed with Japanese radios, televisions, trucks, and motorcycles. Newsweek quoted a MITI official in 1966: "Japan is nicely involved in the Vietnam War, no matter how you look at it. We are enjoying our own escalation."[42]

Tokyo and Washington officials also agreed about war protesters. In the United States, protests focused on civil rights as well. Urban riots ripped through the United States during 1964–65; by late 1965, thirty-four had died during an uprising in the southern California ghetto of Watts. Protesters were joined by anti-war groups in a number of cities, including Washington, D.C. Reverend Martin Luther King, Jr., winner of the Nobel Prize for Peace, began to argue that his plea for non-violent, fundamental change in race relations was impossible until Americans quit warring on Asians. By 1967–68, riots had spread to many cities, including Detroit, where forty-three died. FBI director J. Edgar Hoover lamented that in 1967 alone, thirty thousand Americans had illegally avoided the military draft.

Japan's powerful mass-circulation newspapers reported all this. They featured U.S. brutalities in Vietnam. But Japanese society was not immune. Led by the widely read novelists Oda Makoto and Oe Kenza-buro (the latter the 1994 recipient of the Nobel Prize for Literature), a massive anti-war movement, Beheiren, or Citizens' Federation for Peace in Vietnam, spread. It targeted the Japanese bureaucracy and the American policies. An anti-Marxist who had lived in Europe and the United States, Oda made *Beheiren* part of a worldwide protest network. Among other activities, it helped U.S. military personnel in Japan disappear so they would not have to go to Vietnam. The Japanese protests were usually more polite and respectful of lives and property than were the American, but their effect was powerful: when Johnson hinted he would like to visit Japan, Tokyo officials quickly replied that it was "inconceivable."[43]

Johnson and Sato also largely agreed on policy in a surprising but pivotal region: Indonesia. With its 132 million people on 3,000 islands spread over 580,000 square miles, Indonesia had long been a huge, rich (notably in oil), and strategic nation. Its durable president, Sukarno, was known internationally for his political skills and womanizing. When leftists tried to seize power in late September 1965, they were destroyed by the army's commander, Suharto. The military then killed at least 250,000 actual and suspected Communists. The CIA and U.S. Embassy allegedly helped Suharto pick out the victims. Johnson was convinced that a dangerous shift toward a pro-China position had been stopped just in time. The Japanese, who quietly had become the largest source of aid for Sukarno's regime, were much less convinced. But as Washington pressed them to help Suharto, Tokyo officials pumped in $30 million of credits. Japan indeed became so active that in 1966 the State Department concluded that "Japanese interests" aimed to push out "American interests with regard to oil concessions in Indonesia."[44]

As the Indonesian episode revealed, Sato was determined to increase Japan's presence in Southeast Asia as the United States demanded, but in his own way. Thus in 1966, his government joined the Asian and Pacific Council (ASPAC), an anti-Communist alliance designed to expedite economic exchanges. Sato soon mistrusted ASPAC for being too anti-Chinese, too militant. ASPAC became defunct in the 1970s. More congenial for the Japanese was the Association of Southeast Asian Nations (ASEAN), established in 1967 by Indonesia, Malaysia, the Philippines, Singapore, and Thailand. Its purpose was twofold—to accelerate economic interchange, but to keep uninvited great powers (including China and the United States) out of Southeast Asian affairs. ASEAN was helped by the new Asian Development Bank (ADB). Japan gave the ADB $200 million of its first $1 billion in capital.

Absorbed in Vietnam, U.S. officials missed the importance of ASPAC and especially ASEAN. For the first time, Southeast Asian nations were creating institutions to develop their region cooperatively while excluding unwanted outside involvement. Japan was at the center of these movements. The Acheson-Dulles policy of integrating the Southeast Asian–Japanese economies was succeeding. But such success no longer enraptured American observers. Their soldiers were dying as Japanese and Southeast Asians stood apart and profited. In 1967, U.S. News & World Report raised bad memories by declaring that Japan was developing a "New idea for [a] 'Co-Prosperity Sphere.'. "[45]

By late 1967, Sato's attempted goodwill trip to South Vietnam, and his friendship with Johnson, merely disguised what James Reston had earlier identified in the New York Times as Japan's "slowly diverging path away from American policy." One step in the path involved the Ryukyus (Okinawa especially) and the Bonin Islands. Sato probably went as far as he did with Johnson on Vietnam, Indonesia, and trade issues in the hope that Japan would in turn regain the Ryukyus and Bonins. But the President, more specifically his top military advisers, had little interest in helping the prime minister. Okinawa bases were indispensable for warring on North Vietnam; U.S. license plates on the island called Okinawa the "Keystone of the Pacific." Sato joined Socialists in condemning the island's use by huge B-52 aircraft that carpet-bombed parts of Vietnam. A secret U.S. government analysis in late 1967 concluded that returning Okinawa to Japan's control would, surprisingly, have little effect on waging conventional war, as long as the air bases could be used. Those conclusions naturally ran into intense opposition from the military. The President tried to make the best of it by signing an executive order in 1968 that returned the Bonins to Japan. The Okinawa issue was left to fester.[46]

That festering, however, was minor compared with the crisis that blindsided U.S.-Japan relations after the North Vietnamese launched their surprise Tet (New Year) Offensive in late January 1968. The Communists suffered devastating losses (probably thirty thousand killed), but, astonishingly, penetrated Saigon, even the grounds of the U.S. Embassy. The shock of Tet turned important media figures (such as Walter Cronkite of CBS News) against the war. Powerful informal advisers to Johnson reversed themselves to warn him that, in Dean Acheson's words, we "can no longer do [the] job we set out to do."[47]

The Tet catastrophe began the year from hell. The largest Japanese newspapers, led by Asahi Shimbun, had for months headlined stories about American ignorance of Asia and U.S. soldiers committing brutal crimes against Vietnamese, especially women. Then the huge U.S. nuclear aircraft carrier Enterprise docked at Sasebo naval base. Massive protests tied up the area around Sasebo and Nagasaki. The U.S. nuclear submarine Swordfish was next, and questionably, charged with leaking radioactive materials into Japanese waters. As tensions rose, a U.S. fighter plane taking off from its air base crashed into a building of Kyushu University, only yards from a Japanese nuclear research laboratory. Miraculously, no one was injured—except Sato and his pro-American political reputation. In April, Martin Luther King, Jr., was murdered in Memphis. Two months later, Robert Kennedy was gunned down in Los Angeles. But perhaps most shocking for Sato was Johnson's announcement of March 31 that he would not run for reelection in 1968. Done without informing the prime minister, the President's dramatic broadcast put Sato, as Ambassador Johnson phrased it, "under heavy attack in both press and Diet for having too closely tied [Japan] to a highly unpredictable [United States]."[48]

Sato realized he had lost the second battle of Okinawa. He now declared that he had always doubted U.S. policies in Vietnam. Nakasone Yasuhiro and Miki predicted the end of American hegemony and the consequent welcome rise of Chinese cooperation. Washington retaliated in kind. Ambassador Johnson used blunt language when Foreign Minister Miki invited him to a hidden hotel room for talks—always a sign that the Japanese had serious business in mind. Johnson wasted no time on politeness. "The biggest threat to Japanese-U.S. relations," the ambassador began, "was feeling on part of US that after sacrificing thousands of lives and billions of dollars in defense of areas of East Asia, an area which is at least of equal interest to Japan, we not only did not get any understanding from Japan but received criticism and harassment on essentially minor matters." It was time for Japan to bear "a responsibility commensurate with its growing power rather than continuing to seek to be treated by the US [as] a minor and weak country." Johnson became specific: Tokyo had to cooperate more with the American military while dismantling "protectionist measures" that produced a "large and growing trade gap" in Japan's favor. Miki "took this in good spirit," Johnson reported. Sato, however, showed more interest in keeping his fractious coalition together so he could win the election—which he did, despite a 38 percent increase in his opposition's vote over the 1966 ballotting.[49]

Thus the year from hell ended with Sato's guarded win and Richard Nixon's narrow victory over Hubert Humphrey in the U.S. presidential campaign. Nixon celebrated his triumph on election night by returning to his New York apartment, cooking bacon and eggs, and listening to his favorite record: Richard Rodgers's *Victory at Sea*, which celebrated the U.S. defeat of Japan and Germany in World War II. The year from hell was about to turn into a decade from hell for U.S.-Japan relations.[50]

Nixon and Sato—or "Trading with the Enemy"

Sato moved to start his relationship with Nixon on the right foot by firing Foreign Minister Miki and appointing Aichi Kiichi. Miki's coolness toward U.S. policies and warmth for Chinese were not appropriate for the political weather in Washington. (More to the point, Miki unwisely ran against Sato inside the LDP for the top job and lost by a two to one margin.) But Aichi did nothing to dam up the growing anti-American feelings. By 1969, only 12 percent of Japanese polled felt better because of the U.S. "nuclear umbrella," while 67 percent feared the relationship could drag them into a war. Two-thirds of those asked favored improved or normal diplomatic relations with China. Washington's return of thirty-two base sites did little to reassure the Japanese, perhaps because ninety-eight U.S. installations remained in Japan. In October 1969, *Beheiren* got out nearly a half-million anti-establishment protesters. Violence erupted during more than 2,400 street battles with police, although not one fatality occurred. The next month, Sato, amid more demonstrations, flew off for his first meeting with President Nixon.[51]

The Japanese saw Nixon as a loose cannon. As early as 1953, he had declared that Article IX was a mistake and Japan should rearm. A trip through Asia produced a widely noted 1967 essay that argued the United States must avoid the traps of future Vietnams by allowing Asians to defend themselves. He believed the great danger was China, at least "until China changes." "We have now to reach out westward [sic] to the East, and to fashion the sinews of a Pacific community." Japan, Nixon added, would play a pivotal role in fashioning those "sinews" when it began limited rearmament. These comments frightened many Japanese, as did his emphasis on the need to "Vietnamize" the war—a view Asians took to mean that they were to fight other Asians for U.S. objectives.[52]

To realize these and other foreign policy visions, the new President appointed Henry Kissinger of Harvard University as NSC adviser and his closest foreign policy confidant. Kissinger shared Nixon's ideas as well as his obsession for secrecy and control. The former professor later admitted, "When I first came into office, there was no major country I understood less than Japan." Kissinger, whose ego was as great as Nixon's was insecure, noted that "The hardest thing for us to grasp was that the extraordinary Japanese decisions were produced by leaders who prided themselves on their anonymous style. . . . A Japanese leader does not announce a decision; he evokes it."Kissinger soon belittled Japan's fixation on mere internal economic development ("little Sony sales-men," he privately called Japanese). American destiny, he believed, was instead shaped by the vast landed "frontier" that had become trans-formed into an "emotional commitment" for Americans to care for the "well-being of all mankind." Kissinger's formulation of the two diverse manifest destinies demonstrated once again how top officials could view Japan's historic "frontiers" in Asian markets clashing with Ameri-cans' conceptions of their global "frontiers." If misunderstanding existed, however, it seemed to go in both directions. The German-born NSC adviser (whose immediate family had barely escaped the Holo-caust) privately complained that "Every time the Japanese Ambassador has me to lunch he serves me Weiner Schnitzel."[53]

Sato and the Nixon-Kissinger team nevertheless shared several important beliefs. They agreed, for example, that "The greatest need of the contemporary international system is an agreed concept of order," as Kissinger phrased it. (He even professed to believe that for a statesman, "justice and disorder" was less preferable than "injustice and order.") In 1969–70, such order had to start at home. Several Japanese cities were tied up by protests. Anti-war demonstrations grew so large in American cities, especially Washington, that Nixon secretly ordered three hun-dred troops to hide in the White House and the neighboring Executive Office Building in case he needed protection.[54]

The President moved to restore order in mid-1969 by announcing his "Nixon Doctrine," and later—with more effect—deciding to end the military draft. The Nixon Doctrine, issued at Guam and later elabo-rated, declared that the United States would maintain its treaty com-mitments and continue to provide a "shield" if friends were threatened by "nuclear power." In other cases it would furnish military and eco-nomic aid while letting the threatened nation defend itself. To Japa-nese, the doctrine confirmed fears that the U.S. President wanted Asians to fight Asians, and that he expected Japan to move to the front of the fight. These fears heightened as rumors spread that Nixon and Kissinger were privately encouraging the development of Japanese nuclear weapons. Both Kissinger and the Pentagon publicly denied such remarks, but close aides later testified, as one phrased it, that "Henry believed it was good to spread nuclear weapons around the world." He and Nixon apparently thought that particularly Japan and Israel would benefit the world order if they helped hold up the nuclear umbrella. The two Americans hinted as much to Sato, who came away

quite confused about U.S. policy. In reality, the Nixon Doctrine indicated not a U.S. retreat from Asia but a plan for containing Asian Communists on the cheap. U.S. treaty commitments and nuclear umbrellas
were to remain in place, but under the doctrine Japan was to be a leader
in assuming the burden.[55]

Nixon believed he held a fine carrot to entice Japanese cooperation:
Okinawa. Foreign Minister Aichi had declared 1969 to be the "year of
Okinawa." Sato's political fortunes were becoming so enmeshed with
the island's future that the new U.S. ambassador to Japan, Armin H.
Meyer, told the State Department, "As Okinawa goes, so goes Japan."
An NSC analysis informed Nixon that a winding down of the U.S.
effort in Vietnam, the advent of intercontinental missiles, and the new
Polaris submarines carrying nuclear weapons made control of Okinawa
less important. The President was prepared to hand Okinawa back if
U.S. base rights were protected and Japan would assume "an increasingly large role in Asia."[56]

As more anti-war protests erupted in Washington, the first Sato-
Nixon summit in November 1969 struck a deal. Okinawa would return
to Japanese control in 1972. As compensation, the United States
received use of the bases in language so loose that Nixon retained the
power to use them for launching nuclear attacks. Sato also agreed to
renewal of the 1960 security treaty. (His agreement averted another crisis in the relationship, but also brought out 750,000 protesters in Japan
during June 1970). The prime minister went along with a statement that
Japan considered both South Korea and Taiwan vital to its security.
Critics in Tokyo quickly blasted Sato for letting Nixon commit Japan to
wars it did not want—especially any war triggered by the unpredictable,
heartily disliked South Koreans. Finally, Sato agreed to send more aid
to Southeast Asia (which Japanese observers viewed as a wedge to open
markets for their goods), and to cut back textile exports to U.S. markets.[57]

The 1969 summit results seemed to be a major achievement for both
sides—if all the provisions were carried out. Sato enthusiastically lectured the National Press Club in Washington about the "new Pacific
Age" that was to "be created by Japan and the United States." An official
government White Paper released in Tokyo a month later noted that
Japan's economic aid to Asia, especially Southeast Asia, had tripled
since 1965 and was to double again by 1975. (Much of this money, it
turned out, was to develop Asian raw materials while integrating the
region within a large Asian bloc under Japanese, and some U.S., capital.) In February 1970, Asians and most Americans were pleased when

Sato's government signed the nuclear non-proliferation treaty. The prime minister won the Nobel Prize for Peace in 1974 for his ardent anti-nuclear stand. This was somewhat ironic, since later in 1970 Nakasone Yasuhiro's Defense Agency announced that military spending was to double by 1975. The nation's defense budgets would then approach, if not surpass, those of West Germany, France, and Great Britain. Japan, moreover, was ready to develop an air force and a fleet capable of defending other Asian nations, not just the home islands.[58]

But all was not resolved. Japan continued to trade with the North Vietnamese and promised more help once the conflict ended. The major clash—indeed, a confrontation that rocked U.S.-Japan relations—emerged from Sato's promise to cut back textile exports to the United States. The issue was of immense importance to Nixon for political, not economic, reasons: in the 1968 campaign he had pledged to southern textile-making areas, especially South Carolina, that he would protect them from cheap imports. Sato then promised to help in return for Okinawa's reversion. Okinawa reverted, but Sato never delivered on his end of the bargain. His problem was not, as claimed at the time, that something was lost in the translation when the two leaders cut the deal. Sato's problem was that Japanese textile makers and, especially, their supporters in the government bureaucracy flatly refused to go along. The prime minister could not whip them into line. The Japanese, moreover, then condemned Nixon for asking them to break the free trade rules that Washington had itself written since 1945. Nixon was beside himself with anger. His fury intensified when a powerful Democratic congressman, Wilbur Mills of Ohio, took matters into his own hands and worked out an agreement with the Japanese. Nixon coldly rejected the deal.[59]

A State Department Foreign Service officer said privately in 1971 that the White House now considered Japan an "enemy." The term probably referred to Nixon's threat that unless Japan met his demands, he would impose quotas on Japanese imports under the 1917 wartime Trading with the Enemy Act. As U.S.-Japan relations plummeted to a post-1945 low, Ambassador David Kennedy finally hammered out an agreement in October 1971. His weapon: a threat to import cheaper textiles from other Asian producers if the Japanese did not restrict their own exports. After all the agony, acrimony, and "stupidity" on both sides, as Assistant Secretary of State Philip Trezise later noted, Japan never filled most of the quotas set by Kennedy's deal.[60]

Nixon saw Japan as an "enemy." Tokyo officials and some Japanese industrialists believed that U.S. demands represented a "second coming of Commodore Perry's black ships." Internal politics and economics were replacing the old Cold War security issues as the combustible materials that could blow apart the post-1945 U.S.-Japan relationship.[61]

The Nixon Shocks

During the last four years of Nixon's presidency, a new era emerged in world affairs. Between 1971 and 1974, the once-imperial American presidency weakened, although not before Nixon reconfigured the Cold War by embarking upon detente with the Soviets and, more surprisingly, opening ties with China. During these years as well, the U.S. economy labored under war expenses, inflation, and a growing inability to compete internationally. Nixon responded by declaring economic war on some of his closest allies, including Japan.

Publicly, Japan-admiring seemed to be the order of the day. In 1971 several widely noted books applauded the Japanese "miracle," while warning about its future. Herman Kahn's *The Emerging Japanese Superstate* predicted that Japan's investment rate (twice America's), and its workers' real income (doubling about every six years), would enable it to rule the globe economically by the year 2000. Some critics damned Kahn's methodology and complained that Americans now wrote about the "miracle" with the same unthinking euphoria that "they used to write about achieving *satori* [Buddhist spiritual enlightenment] on the Hollywood freeway." Few, however, disputed Kahn's conclusions. Lauded as Prime Minister Sato's favorite "futurologist," he nevertheless feared the Japanese lacked the worldly sophistication necessary to handle onrushing political responsibilities.[62]

In early 1972, Zbigniew Brzezinski's *The Fragile Blossom* also received attention, in part because the author, a Columbia University professor, had some State Department experience and ties to the Rockefeller family. Brzezinski admired Japan's talent in adapting to technological change, but worried whether the society was too fragile to suffer the inevitable social and political consequences. Notably, leading Japanese intellectuals were not returning such admiration. Kawabata Yasunari, awarded the 1968 Nobel Prize for Literature, had broken with American—and European—influenced writers forty years earlier. He now reasserted that Japan's salvation lay in its own tradition and uniqueness, not in the traditions of overseas allies. His best-known disciple, the brilliant, flamboyant Mishima Yukio, publicly committed suicide because he professed to fear that westernization was eating away at Japanese greatness.

Richard Nixon's tolerance for intellectuals was not unlimited unless they constantly admired and flattered him. The President understood the Kahn-Brzezinski arguments, but arrived at quite different conclusions. For two years, Nixon had tried to strengthen the U.S.-Japanese alliance so Sato would move his country more fully into world affairs and cooperate in Vietnam and on trade issues. Nixon believed Japan's uniqueness was less important than its cooperation. By 1971 he had decided—as the U.S. trade deficit with the Japanese skyrocketed from $1.2 billion in 1970 to $3.2 billion—that Sato would not cooperate. Nixon's interest in the alliance, not to mention in Japan's supposed uniqueness, began to plummet.

Consequently, at Kansas City in mid-1971, the President proclaimed the emergence of "five great economic superpowers" (the United States, Soviet Union, Japan, Western Europe, China). Americans, he warned, faced a severe challenge since "economic power will be the key to other kinds of power . . . in the last third of this century." Two parts of his formulation had direct consequences for U.S.-Japan relations: first, the Chinese were no longer seen as outcasts but joined the Japanese as an Asian power to contend with; second, since Japan's "miracle" made it the great potential economic competitor, it would be dealt with as less an ally than a rival. The month before Nixon spoke, twenty-seven U.S. business leaders had told his administration that Japan was systematically treating Americans as inhabitants of an underdeveloped region. The Japanese bought only raw materials and sold profitable finished goods—meanwhile keeping their own market closed to U.S. finished goods. The Japanese already controlled "the forest products industry in Alaska," one businessman announced. Japan, another bitterly noted, "is like the golfer who is shooting in the 80s with the same 25 handicap he used when he was shooting in the 100s."[63]

These business leaders begged for "a coordinated U.S. foreign trade policy." The sense of crisis heightened when *Time* quoted a cabinet member, thought to be Secretary of Commerce Maurice Stans: "The Japanese are still fighting the war, only now instead of a shooting war it is an economic war. Their immediate intention is to try to dominate the Pacific and then perhaps the world." During the summer of 1971, Nixon opened his own counterattack by breaking the dollar from gold. He left the dollar to float (within limits), a process that aimed at lowering its value while raising the yen's. Thus U.S. exports became cheaper and Japan's more expensive. The President did not stop there. Realizing that inflation endangered both the economy and his 1972 reelection chances, he imposed temporary controls on prices and wages—then stuck a 10 percent surcharge on imports. That was a shot across Japan's bow. The surcharge especially hit Japanese (and Canadian) exporters.

In all this, Nixon happily followed the advice of Secretary of the Treasury John Connally, a former Texas governor, who viewed the international marketplace as an extension of the old Texas frontier: "[T]his cowboy knows that you can ride a good horse to death," White House aide Patrick Buchanan recorded Connally regaling a delighted Nixon, "and the world has been riding the U.S., a good horse, to death in the post-war years, and this has got to stop." Americans were hit with 30 percent of Japan's exports, Connally complained, but Europe only 5 percent, "because Europe keeps these goods out, while we take them." (With reason, Japanese soon nicknamed Connally "Typhoon," after the summer hurricanes that devastated their islands.) The President volunteered why Americans had been suckered for so long: "The goddam State Department hasn't done its job. We're changing the rules of the game." Notably, Nixon announced his new, tough policies on V-J (1945 Victory over Japan) Day, 1971.[64]

His toughness had less visible effect on the Japanese than the President had hoped. In September 1971, the CIA warned Nixon that Japan's powerful industrial and agricultural groups were working with MITI to stop any reforms. The two nations moved toward "a complete breakdown in discussions," as a Japanese official termed it. Tokyo finally agreed to revalue the yen, thus making Japanese exports more expensive. The cobbled-together agreement, however, did not save Nixon from having to devalue the floundering dollar again in 1973. Nor did it turn around Japan's growing trade surpluses. The "miracle" was moving too fast for such a turnaround. It was not the old Texas frontier after all, but more like a classic Japanese painting: "We are like a mountain climbing party at the foot of a very steep mountain whose summit is still shrouded in clouds," warned Nixon's special representative for trade, William D. Eberle.[65]

Amid this disorder came a second, greater shock. In July 1971, Nixon—an arch anti-Communist who had damned the Democrats for "losing" China in 1949—amazed the world by announcing that Kissinger had secretly flown to Beijing to arrange a visit by Nixon himself in February 1972. With one stone, the President hit three targets. Democrats, prepping for the 1972 reelections, were stunned. The Soviets, believing they could corner Nixon in bilateral talks, suddenly were trumped by his "China card." Russian-Chinese relations had approached flashpoint: heavy casualties resulted when their troops fought along their lengthy, inflammable border. Now Nixon was going to profit from their problems. Finally, Japan reeled from this Nixon shock. Since the late 1960s, its business community had quietly accelerated its movement into the China market. Sato meanwhile angled to please Nixon by keeping Tokyo-Beijing political relations cool. Japanese observers compared Sato's policy with a duck: it seemed to be placid above the water, but underneath it was paddling furiously toward China. Nixon now took aim for the duck.[66]

As recently as the month before (June 1971), Nixon and Secretary of State William Rogers had promised Sato to collaborate with him on China questions. No collaboration had occurred. Undersecretary of State U. Alexis Johnson believed that Nixon's announcement of his trip to China instantly dissipated much of the trust built with Tokyo since 1945. Kissinger's later excuse for not informing Sato was revealing: "Japanese policy was not undercut by ours, but only deprived of its desired opportunity to stay ahead of us on a road [to China] it had started traveling long before we did." In Tokyo, officials agreed they had to jump back ahead of the Americans at all costs. One high cost was paid by Sato in July 1972—he had to hand over the prime ministership to the longtime leader of the LDP's pro-Chinese, cool-toward America, faction, Tanaka Kakuei. Sato had been victimized by Nixon's shocks and his own inability to control MITI and finance ministry bureaucrats.[67]

The century-old competition between Americans and Japanese over China fully reopened. In contrast to the pre-1941 years, of course, they now dealt with a China that controlled nuclear weapons and—mostly healed from the Cultural Revolution's chaos—an effective government. Nixon agreed with China's aging leader, Mao Zedong, and the shrewd premier, Zhou Enlai, that Soviet influence must be reduced. They also agreed, after many exchanges, on recognizing Taiwan as part of China (although Taiwan itself remained fiercely independent), while allowing the Beijing government to take Taiwan's seat in the United Nations.

Japan proved to be a thorny topic in the Nixon-Chinese talks. Chou, one American visitor recorded in mid-1971, was "very agitated indeed about Japan." The Japanese had finally signed the nuclear non-proliferation treaty, but the Diet would not ratify the pact (nor did it until June 1976). The Chinese worried that Japan's growing number of nuclear facilities could turn out material for weapons. Mao and Zhou had doubtless heard stories that Nixon and Kissinger did not care if the Japanese military went nuclear. "Japan's feathers have grown on its wings and it is about to take off," Zhou told Nixon. He then changed the metaphor: "Can [the] U.S. control the 'wild horse' of Japan?" Nixon neatly turned the argument (and metaphor) around: "The United States can get out of Japanese waters, but others will still fish there. If we were to leave Japan naked and defenseless, they [sic] would have to turn to others for help or build the capability to defend themselves." Mao and Zhou came around to the President's view, not least because they understood the "others" meant the Soviets. For good measure, Nixon assured the Chinese that as the United States gradually pulled out of Taiwan, he would work to ensure the Japanese did not move in.[68]

Here was a remarkable turnabout. After twenty-three years of working to contain China, Nixon was promising China that he would contain Japan, his own closest Asian ally. Of course, the President actually had it every way: with Mao and Zhou's consent, he maintained the 1960 U.S.-Japan security treaty, which if necessary could be used to contain China. And he could depend on both the Chinese and the Japanese to help him contain the Soviets. As Nixon counted his winnings, the Soviets and Japanese counted their losses. Soviet leader Leonid Brezhnev quickly recovered enough to invite Nixon to Moscow for a summit conference in the spring of 1972. The visit paid high diplomatic and political dividends for the President. The Japanese took longer to recover, as Sato's political demise in mid-1972 indicated.

The new prime minister, Tanaka Kakuei, was a quite different type from Sato and his predecessors. Born in 1918 of a poor, failed farmer in an isolated region two hundred miles north of Tokyo, Tanaka had no university education. Self-made, he earned a fortune in the construction and real estate business during and after the war. He meanwhile married his landlady's daughter (without bothering with the usual Japanese custom of an arranged marriage by third parties). Open, convivial, outgoing, the tycoon moved into politics and rose rapidly to the head of mighty MITI, where he often thwarted Sato. With access to piles of money, Tanaka became a lordly LDP powerbroker. The Chinese, understanding Tanaka's love of trade and his growing skepticism about American dependability, clearly favored him. His first summit, however, was with the triumphant Nixon at Honolulu in late August 1972. In an informal toast, the ebullient President declared that Tanaka, a new "pitcher" with the old reliable team, "has all the pitches. He has a 'fast ball,' a 'curve,' a 'slider,' a 'knuckler,' but no 'spitball.'" Nixon's toast, the record read, "was received with friendly laughter and appreciation."[69]

If so, the Japanese had outdone even themselves in politeness. Nixon's China shock rubbed raw the relationship inside the LDP between the pro-Taiwan faction (headed by former Prime Minister Kishi) and

Tanaka's pro-PRC faction. As this infighting grew fiercer, Tanaka had to listen to Nixon lecture him at Honolulu about the unacceptable $3.5 billion trade deficit. Apparently it was then that the President successfully twisted Tanaka's arm so All-Nippon Airlines and the Japanese air force would help cut the trade deficit by buying planes from Lockheed Corporation. (In 1970, Nixon and Congress had barely saved Lockheed from bankruptcy by giving federal guarantees for loans from private banks.) The new purchases led to a scandal when evidence surfaced in the mid-1970s of bribery payments made by Lockheed to Tokyo politicians, including Tanaka.[70]

If this were not humiliating enough, Tanaka had to travel to Beijing in September 1972. The business and political communities in Tokyo demanded that he regain the initiative toward China. He was fair game for Zhou Enlai. Tanaka first had to offer public regret for Japanese treatment of China before 1945. He then had to have Foreign Minister Ohira announce that Japan's treaty with Taiwan was null and void. In return, Zhou agreed to surrender China's claims to war reparations from Japan. Finally, apparently without fully realizing its meaning, Tanaka agreed to a statement that implied a joint Sino-Japanese condemnation of "hegemony" (a Chinese euphemism for the Soviets) would be included in a peace treaty between China and Japan. Nixon had accepted a similar statement because it served his purpose of checking the Soviets, but the Japanese wanted little to do with such big-power power politics. Tanaka, unlike Nixon, had failed to play off the two Communist powers for his own nation's benefit.[71]

Tanaka had no stomach for such games. Japan's future lay neither in the Soviet market nor in mimicking Nixon and Kissinger's obsession with balance-of-power politics. It lay in securing some independence, security, and order in Japanese society by exploiting the markets of Asia. And this was being done. Americans were moving into Asia "at a snail's pace" compared with Japan, wrote correspondent James Sterba in the *New York Times.* "Japanese now do more business with Asian countries than the countries do among themselves, including China. . . . [Japan] replaced the United States as Asia's leading trading partner in 1969." Former World Bank president Eugene Black noted that "the Japanese are already invading [Southeast Asia] again, this time with businessmen."[72]

Americans had grown tired of acting as a shield for the Japanese. The Vietnam War and the Nixon shocks had shaken the relationship. Even the old, ill Mao Zedong lectured Kissinger to pay attention to the Japanese. In February 1973, Mao first uttered pleasantries ("I don't look bad, but God has sent me an invitation") and personal complaints (the United States should take in 10 million Chinese women because they "will create disasters" by having more babies in China). He then told Kissinger: "When you pass through Japan, you should perhaps talk a bit more with them. You only talked with them for one day [on the last trip] and that isn't good for their face." The chastened American agreed. But Kissinger took the offensive by declaring that Nixon "put the highest value on relations with Japan," and warning that "any attempt [by Americans and Chinese] to compete for Tokyo's allegiance could end up encouraging resurgent Japanese nationalism."[73]

For all the rhetoric, Japan no longer held pride of place in U.S. plans. China, once again, intervened. "We are now in the extraordinary situation that, with the exception of the United Kingdom," Kissinger told Nixon, "the PRC [People's Republic of China] might well be closest to us in its global perceptions." Americans again were thinking globally, while, as in the 1930s, Japan thought primarily in terms of Asia and the United States. And then there was Vietnam, a devastated ghost that haunted Americans and U.S.-Japan relations. Democratic Governor George Wallace of Alabama, planning for the 1972 presidential race, expressed the view of many Americans: "The war in Vietnam would have been over a long time ago if Japanese troops had joined us." In December 1972, Nixon tried to force a settlement with a brutal carpet-bombing of North Vietnam. Japanese condemned the bombing; the chief editorialist of the giant *Asahi* newspaper privately described Nixon's tactics as "almost identical to Nazis' atrocities at Auschwitz." When a deal was finally signed with North Vietnam during January 1973 that allowed U.S. forces to withdraw after a quarter century of warfare, Nixon invited China and the Soviets to the signing. He excluded Japan.[74]

The distinguished historian Aruga Tadashi believes that these 1972–73 events were more important for East Asia than the fall of the Berlin Wall in 1989. That assessment seems accurate. Americans and Japanese, however, never agreed on the reasons for this transformation that marked the early 1970s. Because they interpreted history differently, their differences were about to be dangerously magnified.[75]

XII

The End of an Era
(Since 1973)

The Watershed of the Cold War Era

IN 1971 HIROHITO became the first Emperor in more than two thousand years to leave the home islands. On September 27, the seventy-year-old Emperor and Empress Nagako flew to Anchorage, Alaska, where Richard and Patricia Nixon greeted them. The meeting was full of happy symbols. Noting this was the first time a Japanese emperor and an American president had met, Nixon praised the statesmanship "which spans the space between our two countries." He gave no hint of his deep anger over the space between the two because of textile and other trade and security issues. The Emperor thanked Americans for their "unstinted assistance, materially and morally," since 1945. These words were exchanged in a huge, lavishly decorated airplane hangar where five thousand people (mostly from the Anchorage Elks, Lions, and American Legion clubs) loudly applauded.[1]

That same year, *Time* magazine was less polite: "If Japan does not follow the gentlemanly rules [on trade], it is not because of simple greed but because it does not adhere to Western principles on much of anything." As *Time* implied, the two nations were headed toward a series of clashes that marked the 1971–74 era as a turning point in the partnership, and as the turning point in the Cold War era. Nixon's and Mao's transformation of the U.S.-

Chinese relationship changed American and Japanese political, economic, and diplomatic priorities.[2]

No one had foreseen the hammer blows that rocked U.S. power and global relationships in 1973–74. First came the Vietnam peace treaty, that is, the American pullout that others interpreted as a massive U.S. defeat after a quarter-century effort and fifty-eight thousand American dead. Then Congress passed the War Powers Act of 1973 over Nixon's veto. For the first time in history, Congress systematically attempted to limit the President's power to commit troops to an actual or threatened conflict. "King Richard" of the 1972 presidential triumph was becoming "Little Richard." Worse was to come. In mid-1973, Congress opened hearings to discover whether Nixon had committed a crime by trying to cover up the burglarizing of Democratic Party offices in Washington's Watergate apartment complex by a small group of highly incompetent White House agents in June 1972. By August 1974, as damning evidence piled up, Nixon decided he could avoid possible impeachment only by becoming the first U.S. chief executive to resign his office.[3]

As the ghost of Vietnam hovered, the economy stumbled, and Nixon's power disintegrated, came another potentially crushing blow. On October 6, 1973, a surprisingly effective Egyptian attack posed the Israeli state's most dangerous challenge since its creation in 1948. Israeli forces finally turned the tide of battle, but when Nixon, and newly appointed Secretary of State Henry Kissinger, supported Israel, six Arab nations retaliated by denying their oil to the United States and its allies, including Japan.

The Japanese imported almost 80 percent of their oil from the Middle East. The incredibly profligate Americans bought more than half their petroleum supplies overseas. The embargo could have been a catastrophe. Both Americans and Japanese, however, imposed controls to cut demand, while secretly buying off other producers (such as the Shah of Iran), who willingly sold oil quietly and at great profit. As gasoline prices quadrupled in the United States, inflation began to undermine the Western and the Japanese economies. In early 1974, Kissinger worked out a truce between Egypt and Israel that reduced tensions and reopened the oil tap, but economic pain lingered. So did the belief among U.S. allies, not least the Japanese, that the war exposed the limits and vulnerability of American power.

As if all this were not enough, Nixon's carefully crafted detente with the Soviets came undone. The U.S. Congress refused to extend pivotal economic help to Moscow. In 1974–75, the superpowers wrestled each other for influence in the so-called Third World, especially in Angola, the newly decolonized West African nation. It seemed the worst of times. When Nixon's sudden successor, former Vice President Gerald Ford, gave a State of the Union message in January 1975, the *New York Times* termed it "the gloomiest delivered by a President since the Depression [of] the nineteen-thirties." Ford described "millions of Americans out of work," with others' incomes being eaten away by "recession and inflation," while both the national budget deficit and trade deficit shot upward.[4]

These traumas sharpened the American-Japanese conflict. Kissinger lamented to Nixon the need somehow to create "a coherent overall political approach rather than getting bogged down in economic arm-wrestling" with Japan. But no such approach could be devised. Neither nation, moreover, could tame inflation. Prime Minister Tanaka poured gasoline on an already red-hot economy by giving money to a host of companies threatened by the Nixon shocks and textile deal. Pressure thus intensified on Japan's exporters to find even more markets abroad, especially in the United States and China. A U.S.-Japan relationship that was souring in 1971 grew even more bitter.[5]

The responses to these crises provide case studies of the differences between the two capitalisms (and governmental systems) by the 1970s. The American response came in three steps. First, in late 1973, Nixon announced a "Project Independence" based on great hope and little analysis. It tried to accelerate development of oil supply rather than reducing demand (for example, by requiring users to become energy-efficient). Second, Kissinger formed an International Energy Agency of consumer nations, including Japan, that pledged to build oil stockpiles for 60–90-day supplies in case of another emergency. Finally, Nixon and a badly divided Congress agreed on the Emergency Petroleum Allocation Act (EPAA), which extended Nixonian controls over petroleum prices and production. The emphasis was on ensuring equity of distribution, not slashing demand, except through market forces of higher prices. (Over the years, the ever cheaper dollar used to purchase overseas oil even took the force out of these market devices.) The only other major restraints were a 55-mile-an-hour speed limit on national highways (removed by the mid-1990s and little observed before), and a ruling that auto producers were to build cars averaging 27.5 miles-per-gallon by 1985.[6]

Oil company profits rocketed upward. Many Americans came to see the "crisis" as manufactured by petroleum firms for immense profits. In this political hothouse, governmental controls were badly managed. One analyst, a government official in the 1970s, later drew the conclusion that the oil crisis revealed "a large and fragmented government, responsive to claims . . . from interests of many kinds, [that is] passive or immobilized with respect to the definition of broad national objectives, and suffering from eroding legitimacy."[7]

Japan's response was quite different. The crisis actually pumped life into a MITI that had been losing its grip. The "miracle" had been making the ministry's intervention less necessary—and less welcome. One instance: in 1969 Mitsubishi revolted against MITI's favoritism to Toyota and Nissan autos to sign a shocking deal to make cars with Chrysler. The oil crisis was like oxygen to MITI.

Tanaka's first response was a massive conservation program, aimed especially at export-oriented heavy industry that depended on imported energy. A second response was a trip by MITI's top man, Nakasone Yasuhiro, to cut bilateral deals with Middle East producers and thus break free from U.S. policies in the region. Simultaneously, MITI developed alternative sources by encouraging nuclear and natural gas suppliers. The crisis forced Japan to become more active in world affairs—to undergo a "shedding of the skin," in Inada Juichi's phrase. Certainly, the Japan-China ties took new forms. Japanese imports of 80,000 tons of refined oil from China in 1973 suddenly soared to 1 million tons of crude oil in 1974 and 8 million tons in 1975. Japanese-Arab relations also took a new form. Despite a hurried trip by Kissinger to Tokyo to keep Tanaka in line, Japan took an anti-Israeli stance—and put an exclamation point on the new approach by suspending jet-fuel supplies to U.S. bases in Japan.

One Japanese response was forced by rising prices and the sudden scarcity of goods (even toilet paper) dependent on petroleum. MITI received the power to set prices for some goods and to crack heads among suppliers who violated the national interest. A final, more comprehensive response was especially important. The bureaucracy employed subsidies, outright cash grants, new regulations, and other government powers to force efficiencies on producers and—for the longer term—transform energy-consuming heavy industry (steel, textiles) into services and knowledge-based industries (electronics). Thus between 1973 and 1986 Japan's energy consumption grew only 7 percent, while gross national product roared ahead by 50 percent. The government meanwhile provided help to coal, textiles, and other heavy manufacturing to cushion the social and political shocks of this shift.[8]

Some Japanese efforts were misguided. An emphasis on nuclear power proved costly and denied Japan benefits from lower oil prices in the 1980s. Overall, the policies seemed quite out of step with some

Western views—"a mix of modern industry with feudal ideas," as a British analysis sniffed. But the "mix" produced a continuing "miracle" with domestic order. Since 1853, that combination had often not worked together.[9]

For U.S.-Japan relations, MITI's policies seemed too successful. Japan's more efficient export industries raised a $1.7 billion favorable trade balance with Americans in 1974 sixfold, to $10.4 billion by 1980. In the late 1970s, Washington demanded—and Tokyo grudgingly accepted—"voluntary" reduction of color television exports to the United States. When Tokyo refused to do the same for autos, President Jimmy Carter imposed a 25 percent tariff on Japanese light trucks that pushed many out of the U.S. market. Japan meanwhile continued to reject demands that more American agricultural products be allowed in, even as Japanese paid five times the world price for their heavily protected staple, rice. On the Cold War front, while U.S.-Soviet political relations soured, Soviet-Japanese economic ties sweetened. Steel and machinery moved from Japan to the Soviets, while cotton and forest products came back from Russia.[10]

Tanaka's economic success was not enough to save him from something approaching Nixon's fate. In December 1974, personal financial scandals forced the prime minister to resign. Allegations arose that Lockheed had handed him millions to ensure profitable aircraft contracts. "Mr. Clean," Miki Takeo, took charge. He lasted two years until December 1976, when President Ford, just defeated by Carter, and Miki both had to leave office. Only MITI's power, a worsening Cold War, and intensifying U.S.-Japan clashes seemed predictable.[11]

Needed: American Bodies, Not American Banks—Or, Japan as Number One

Senator Mike Mansfield—Senate majority leader, Asian expert, and later U.S. ambassador to Japan—began in the 1970s to emphasize that "the U.S.-Japanese relationship is the most important bilateral relationship in the world, bar none." Many travel agents agreed. By this time, about 1 million Japanese tourists arrived annually in the United States. They clung together in large groups (a Japanese travel custom dating back a thousand years when all classes traveled together to hear Buddhist teachings in various temples). Because of the language barrier and group traveling, few new bridges resulted to link the two cultures. Only about one-third as many Americans journeyed to Japan. Few more seemed driven to understand a culture that had built the world's second most powerful economy.[12]

Two Americans were trying to understand. The new President, Jimmy Carter, and his top foreign policy adviser, national security adviser Zbigniew Brzezinski, had grown deeply interested in Japan. In 1972, Brzezinski had written *The Fragile Blossom*. Then, with banker David Rockefeller, he helped found the Trilateral Commission—a group of business people and governmental leaders from the United States, Japan, and Western Europe who tried to coordinate policies for problems bedeviling these industrial nations. Carter, then a little-known governor of Georgia, became an early member. By the time of his election, however, Carter, as well Brzezinski, was shifting gears. The Trilateral Commission seemed to produce little but interesting discussions. The Cold War, moreover, was picking up speed, and Brzezinski—from an anti-Soviet Polish family—began to focus on the traditional enemy. Carter found himself caught between Brzezinski's ardent anti-Sovietism and Secretary of State Cyrus Vance's belief that cooperation with the Russians was necessary to resolve such life-and-death issues as arms control.

Carter's confusion quickly afflicted U.S.-Japan relations. In February 1977, the one-month-old administration told Tokyo that some U.S. troops were to be pulled out of South Korea, an area of extraordinary sensitivity to Japan for a thousand years. Carter believed he had to cut expenditures and reorient foreign commitments. This proved to be the wrong approach, especially given the recent U.S. withdrawal from Vietnam. Asians—above all, Japanese—were closely watching how Americans would respond to the loss. President Ford had responded in 1975 with a "doctrine": "The center of political power in the United States has shifted westward. Our Pacific interests and concerns have increased." He added that a "first premise is that American strength is basic to any stable balance of power in the Pacific." Ford emphasized the commitment by becoming the first U.S. President to visit Japan. With such assurances, Japanese business poured into South Korea, where it already enjoyed 64 percent of all foreign investment. (Americans, with 17 percent, were a distant second.) Now Carter seemed to be reversing Ford's policies. An uproar in Tokyo, Seoul, and the U.S. Congress forced Carter to retreat. The troops remained.[13]

But doubts had been sown. Japan saw U.S. military commitments as crucial. They provided Ford's "balance of power," behind which Japanese overseas investment could march. Tokyo's defense budgets could meanwhile remain low. Japan, in other words, wanted American bodies but not American banks.

Japanese banks and their *keiretsu* (networks) in big industry were mounting an all-out assault on Southeast Asian and Chinese markets as well. "Japan Inc."—the team of efficient businesses, aggressive government bureaucracy, and cooperative labor unions—appeared unstoppable. When Japan seemed to be falling behind in the semiconductor industry, pivotal in the onrushing computerization of the globe, the government ensured tax breaks and subsidies for a Research Association (including Mitsubishi, Fujitsu, NEC, and Toshiba). The association pooled research efforts between 1976 and 1979 to develop patents that brought Japan up with the U.S. computer industry. Americans were meanwhile left knocking on Japan's door, their technology either coopted or excluded.

A major exception was the considerably low-tech baseball players hired by the sports-crazy Japanese. Even this hiring, however, was reluctant. "If you ask a Japanese manager what he considers the most important ingredient of a winning team," a U.S. correspondent wrote, "he would most likely answer 'wa'" or harmony. "If you ask him how to knock a team's *wa* away, he'd probably say, 'Hire an American.'" Another U.S. success, McDonald's, was finally allowed in after bitter struggle and below-the-table resistance from Japan's food chains. The native Japanese executive who headed the nation's McDonald's enterprise nevertheless won out—in part by lightly arguing, "If we eat hamburgers for a thousand years, we will become blond, and when we become blond—we can conquer the world."[14]

The nation's economy soared as its need for lawyers sank. All of Japan had fewer lawyers than Los Angeles alone. The crime rate actually declined from the already low levels of the 1950s. In 1977, 20.8 murders struck every 100,000 people in New York City; in Tokyo, the rate was 1.7. New York's rate for robberies per 100,000 was 994; Tokyo's 3.1. In 1979, Professor Ezra F. Vogel's *Japan as Number One* explained these phenomena to become a best-seller in the United States and Japan. Vogel noted MITI's success in combining competition with government help to "create the strongest possible companies with the greatest competitive potential." He rated such traits superior to U.S. beliefs in free markets, the automatic evil of bureaucracies, and the supposed efficiencies of antitrust acts. Japanese bureaucrats made major errors (for example, in not believing initially that Sony's transistors had a future). But they had learned. Japan did pay a price, Vogel warned: "strong pressure toward conformity and consensus [is] sometimes at the expense of the deviant, the opposition, the little man, the outsider." On the other hand, Americans "do not have the confidence to carry out the will of the majority against the egoistic deviant. . . . America needs all the help it can get in moving toward group cooperation."[15]

President Carter agreed. A deeply religious man who cared about the needy as well as the larger community, the Georgian harked back to the 1930s when Democrats helped both giant corporations and society's downtrodden. In mid-1980, Carter trumpeted a three-year plan to save Detroit's auto industry against the Japanese invasion. Imports were to be reduced, environmental regulations eased for U.S. producers, and aid given to cities hurt by Japan's success. Carter's top domestic aide declared, "We consider this the first part of a national industrial policy." Chrysler's head, Lee A. Iacocca, was more explicit: "We have taken a page from Japan's book." But the next pages were not torn from that book. Chrysler nearly went bankrupt several years later until Washington saved it with a massive bailout. The entire U.S. auto industry stumbled through the 1980s while Japanese models controlled 30 percent of the American market. The United States lacked the tradition, homogeneity, and bureaucracy for an effective "national industrial policy." Indeed, six months after Carter announced his grand plan, he lost the presidency to Ronald Reagan. The triumphant former Republican California governor launched an attack on industrial policy and promised to get the government "off our backs."[16]

Meanwhile, the Japanese moved to control the burgeoning Southeast Asian and Chinese markets. In 1971, the United States held 36.4 percent of foreign investments in Southeast Asia, the Japanese 15.4 percent. Five years later, the U.S. share had sunk to 26 percent; the Japanese more than doubled, to 36.4 percent. Tokyo officials tellingly resurrected a 1930s metaphor, the "flying geese" model. In this model, the smaller geese followed the head goose, Japan, in employing technology and new processes. Thus, as Japan moved into cutting-edge, profitable electronics at home, it passed down auto and steel production to lower-waged geese, such as Taiwan and South Korea. It also targeted a new goose, Vietnam, even as the United States had tried to kill, then cage, it. The morning after Nixon had agreed to retreat from Vietnam in early 1973, the LDP headquarters in Tokyo hung a large banner: CONGRATULATIONS VIETNAM CEASE-FIRE. NEXT LET'S COOPERATE IN RECONSTRUCTION AND DEVELOPMENT. An initial $10 million in foreign aid opened the way for $216 million in trade with both North and South Vietnam by the time the Communists unified the country in 1975.

Another $16 million of aid to the victors led to a 1978 agreement that locked Vietnam into Japan's economic orbit. By now, some 60 percent of Japanese foreign aid targeted Southeast Asia—nearly all, of course, requiring purchase of Japanese goods. The Acheson-Dulles hope of using the region to ensure Japanese prosperity was being realized—at a level neither man could have foreseen.[17]

Not all was smooth sailing. Riots erupted against Japan's growing presence in Thailand, Indonesia, and China. In August 1977, Prime Minister Fukuda Takeo decisively moved to undercut the protests. The newly elected leader was one of the most powerful post-1945 political powerbrokers. Scion of a silk-farming family, a Tokyo University Law School graduate, protégé of Kishi Nobusuke, twice head of the all-powerful finance ministry, the sophisticated Fukuda led a well-financed faction of the LDP. His faction also proved to be corrupted by such finances. As early as 1952, a bribery scandal forced him to resign from the ministry. His salvation seemed to lie in the even greater corruption charges afflicting his chief LDP rival, Tanaka.

Fukuda's triumph over Tanaka's cleaner successor, Miki, in 1976, however, went beyond personal politics. Fukuda's faction was deeply interested in Southeast Asia, notably Taiwan. Its financial backers had grave doubts about normalizing relations with China if it meant signing blatant anti-Soviet provisions, as Beijing demanded. Tanaka and his faction, on the other hand, wanted to profit from Southeast Asia, but emphasized as well ties with China—especially knotting those ties before the Americans. The LDP thus divided along foreign policy, as well as personal, fault lines.[18]

In August 1977, Fukuda stroked suspicious Southeast Asians by announcing at Manila a Fukuda Doctrine. It embraced three principles: the guarantee that Japan would never again become a military power; "heart-to-heart" understandings with Southeast Asians; and full partnership with the new ASEAN (Association of Southeast Asian Nations) group. ASEAN's appearance announced this part of the globe's arrival on the world's political stage. Part of the Fukuda's Doctrine was, as *The Economist* of London called it, "a con." In 1978, for example, Fukuda publicly reserved the right to build "any type of weapon" if necessary "for self-defense purposes, even if this means nuclear or bacteriological weapons." But Japanese aid to ASEAN nations doubled during Fukuda's watch. U.S. auto executives vowed not to lose Southeast Asian markets—the fastest-growing car markets in the world. The race, however, was actually over by 1980. And Japan had won.[19]

The next race would be for the China market. That race had enormous military as well as economic implications. Carter and Brzezinski wanted to move quickly toward China. The President was again restrained by Secretary of State Vance, who placed greater value on relations with the more powerful Soviets. Brzezinski, however, outmaneuvered Vance by constantly "pestering" (Brzezinski's word) the President to send Vance to Moscow while he, the NSC adviser, worked things out in Beijing. Carter surrendered. The result was full diplomatic relations, effective January 1, 1979. The two giants furthermore pledged to cooperate against Russian imperialism and to continue cutting the links between the United States and Taiwan, which China considered part of its own country. Brzezinski was so taken with the Chinese that Carter recorded, "I told him he had been seduced." But "seduced" was hardly the word when Carter sent Brzezinski halfway around the world to propose.[20]

So the race for the China market was on—again. The Japanese had a head start of a thousand years or so, but also a bad recent track record of atrocities inflicted on tens of millions of Chinese in the 1930s and 1940s. Carter thought he could draw on a century of goodwill because of the open-door approach that aimed to keep foreign imperialists from carving up China. When, however, Carter told a group of Americans that "the people of our country had a deep and natural affection for the people of China," he was embarrassed when "most of the group laughed." The President mislearned the nature of U.S.-China relations by accepting the mistaken version of history offered by U.S. missionaries and churches. Between 1949 and 1972, moreover, U.S. presidents—epitomized by John F. Kennedy—had been the sworn enemy of Beijing. All in all, Americans and Japanese seemed roughly equal as they set to race for Chinese concessions.[21]

The concentrated firepower of the *keidenren*'s banking-industrial complex made Japan (to use Orwell's phrase) more than equal. Even as Brzezinski and the top Chinese leader, Deng Xiaoping, raised their glasses in Beijing to damn the Russians, Japanese Foreign Minister Sonoda Sunao had been secretly courting the Chinese for full diplomatic relations for nearly a year. These talks, along with U.S. interest, accelerated as Deng announced in 1978 that China would rapidly modernize with a selected infusion of capitalism—under tight Communist Party control, of course. By 1978, trade between China and Japan had exploded to $5 billion, nearly five times the 1972 figure. Chinese oil exports became of special importance to Tokyo.[22]

The rise of Ohira Masayoshi to power in late 1978 accelerated this rush to Beijing. Tanaka, always the powerbroker, had pushed Ohira to challenge and defeat a surprised Fukuda. Determined to release the Lockheed scandal's brake on his power, the aggressive sixty-year-old Tanaka collected so much money from businesses that his faction was twice the size of Fukuda's. And these businesses had strong interest in China. The victorious Ohira threw out all of Fukuda's cabinet—except Foreign Minister Sonoda, who had performed so well in Beijing. As the United States and China discussed normalizing relations, Japan actually did so by signing a Treaty of Peace and Friendship with the Chinese in late 1978. Deng's state visit to Tokyo in early 1979 was accompanied by the first major Japanese loan—some $2 billion—from the Export-Import Bank, tied entirely to Japan's exports and services. By late 1979, the Chinese had to back away from some of Japan's generous loan arrangements because they were unable to deal with the tide of money. Within the next five years, the relationship flourished until China became Japan's number-two trading partner—just behind the United States.[23]

Ohira began to discuss a "Pacific rim" strategy to integrate China and Southeast Asia's raw materials and markets into Japanese capital and technology. The idea was sometimes extended to a "Pacific Basin" that took in Canada and the United States. North Americans, however, were to provide raw materials for Japan's machines. California officials began to think that "The Japanese see California as part of their 'Pacific coprosperity sphere,' " as one phrased it. Japan's firms had invested $25 billion in the United States, one-third of it in the West where they exploited forests and fisheries for exports back to Japan. They also moved decisively into electronics, a field which California's "Silicon Valley" firms were shaping. The "question is whether we want to become a banana republic . . . ," a California electronics manufacturer declared in 1978. "If we think we are trying to balance our trade imbalance with the Japanese by selling them beef and grapefruit, we'll end up killing our industrial base." Anti-Japanese feelings rose among workers in lumber, fisheries, and electronics.[24]

These inroads, and American complaining, confirmed Japanese beliefs that the United States was in a state of decline. Japan did not openly gloat; it was too dependent on Americans for that. But it began to rethink its military as well as economic priorities. A second oil shock of 1979–80, arising from revolutionaries overthrowing Washington's close friend, the Shah of Iran, brought ineffective responses from Carter. Inflation battered American savings and investments. In late 1979 the Soviets invaded Afghanistan. The month before, Ohira declared that the "military balance" had changed; the Soviets had "caught up

. . . in some ways." He asserted during a trip to Washington that "U.S. hegemony has been relatively declining." Japan used to "just . . . follow the U.S. lead," but "Japan today is different." In a 1978 defense report, Tokyo expressed doubts that the U.S. Navy could protect Japan's sea-lanes and oil supplies. Ohira's government responded with a defense budget that jumped from $1.6 billion in 1970 to more than $10 billion in 1978, although the increase was also due to the yen's surging value and a high inflation rate.[25]

A major turn had begun in both military establishments. After equiv-ocating between Vance's and Brzezinski's conflicting advice, Carter, in just six months of 1980, jacked up the projected five-year U.S. military budget from an awesome $800 billion to an incredible $1.25 trillion. Vance finally resigned when Carter and Brzezinski insisted on using force in April 1980 to try to free fifty-three American hostages held by the Iranian revolutionaries. The attempt failed disastrously, costing American lives but not liberating the hostages. "What can the United States be thinking of?" Ohira wondered aloud. The prime minister responded with a new military policy, "Comprehensive National Secu-rity," that included more cooperation with Western militaries, to raise Japan's military profile. A July 1980 Defense Agency report noted the "termination of clear American supremacy in both military and eco-nomic spheres." The report urged building up Japan's defenses, espe-cially to secure oil supplies.[26]

Ohira died suddenly in mid-1980. He was replaced by a weaker fig-ure, Suzuki Zenko. But Ohira, Fukuda, and Tanaka had accomplished much since 1974: they buffered the miracle against Middle East crises, moved into Southeast Asia, renewed the historic tie with China, and began transforming the nation's military strategy.

Carter also surrendered power in 1980, the victim of indecisiveness and Ronald Reagan's promises to cut taxes while reinvigorating the mili-tary effort to fight the Cold War. Often confused by Carter's policies, the Japanese were not at all prepared for Ronald Reagan and George Bush's willingness to use force, or to distort the economy so more force would be available. Thus the scene was set for the clashes of the 1980s and the final stages of the Cold War.

The 1980s: From "Ron-Yasu" . . .

The 1980s opened and closed with crises in U.S.-Japan relations. The stakes were becoming ever higher. In 1980, U.S.-Asian trade surpassed

U.S.-European trade for the first time in history. The American economy, however, was devastated by a deadly inflation and 18 percent interest rates, even as its trade deficit with Japan soared toward $50 billion in 1985. The respected political analyst Walter Dean Burnham noted the growing, dangerous disillusionment with the American state: "a generalized crisis of legitimacy develops while the [economic] surplus declines." "Please Japan," a *New York Times* guest editorial pleaded in March 1981, "Return the Favor: Occupy Us."

The editorial reflected the malaise that continued under Reagan in 1981–82. Japan's concern grew as the Cold War intensified. In August 1983, Soviet jets shot down a South Korean civilian airliner flying off course and over some of Russia's most sensitive military bases in the Far East. The result was 269 dead. A U. S. Marine Corps general called limited war between Americans and Russians "an almost inevitable probability" within a generation. Such a war would probably be fought in part from U.S. bases in Japan—bases long programmed into the sights of Soviet nuclear missiles. Suzuki could not stem anti-American protests, especially after a U.S. nuclear submarine collided with and sank a Japanese merchant ship in 1981. Two Japanese lives were lost; the sub left the scene without trying to save the thirteen survivors. Reagan's handling of foreign policy did not inspire confidence in Japan. The assassination attempt on his life in March 1981 reaffirmed Japanese views that violence and disorder dangerously corrupted American society.[27]

In late 1982, the relationship showed signs of improving. Not only was the U.S. economy snapping back, but a different kind of leader took power in Tokyo. Nakasone Yasuhiro had been a powerful player in the LDP since election to the Diet in 1947 when this son of a lumber dealer was twenty-nine years old. He was such a central member of the well-oiled, Lockheed scandal–tainted Tanaka faction that critics called Nakasone's administration "Tanakasone." "Nakasone is the jockey," Tanaka immodestly explained. "I own the horse." The new prime minister, however, ran his own race—especially after 1984, when Tanaka was finally convicted for taking $1.6 million in bribes.

Between 1972 and 1974, Nakasone had led MITI, where he took the nation's first tentative steps toward trade liberalization. Unlike other top leaders, however, he had also run the Defense Agency. Nakasone criticized Sato's three "nonnuclear principles" of the 1970s, but finally opposed building nuclear arms. He also opposed further dependence on U.S. forces. Nakasone wanted a new security treaty allowing Japan to defend itself with a "truly autonomous defense." He harbored a healthy respect for U.S. power: as a World War II sailor, he had watched from a distance the nuclear obliteration of Hiroshima. But the sixty-four-year-old leader believed Japan's political and military maturity now had to equal its economic powerhouse. He also learned (by watching John Kennedy) about using the new medium to shape "television democracy." Nakasone learned so well that in 1986 he won a landslide reelection that slashed the Socialists to all-time post-1955 lows. (The desperate Socialists then became Japan's first party to choose a woman, Doi Takako, to lead it.)[28]

Nakasone moved so decisively to upgrade Japan's military that a fascinating argument erupted in Washington. The main combatants were Secretary of State George Shultz (who took office in June 1982) and Secretary of Defense Caspar Weinberger. In 1982–83, Weinberger and his military advisers wanted Nakasone to rearm quickly so Japan could—as an NSC paper phrased it in late 1982—"as soon as possible within this decade . . . assume defense of its own territory, its surrounding seas, skies, and its sea-lanes to a distance of 1,000 miles." For his part, Shultz believed Japan was "the centerpiece" of U.S. policy in Asia. But the blunt Secretary of State "exploded" (his word) when he discovered the Pentagon's plan. Shultz only wanted Japan to pay more for U.S. protection. "But the last thing America should want," this World War II Marine told Weinberger, "is the re-creation of a massive Japanese military machine." (Shultz vividly recalled the "savagery" in the Palau campaign, "when the Japanese snipers were finally talked into coming out with their hands up," only to be "hit by [American] fire from all over the beach.") While visiting the Philippines, Shultz learned that if the thousand-mile arena for the Japanese Fleet was to include their islands, "One thing was clear: the Filipinos didn't want to be included."[29]

Shultz lost the argument. During a January 1983 visit to Washington, Nakasone quickly moved to a "Ron-Yasu" relationship with Reagan. As with Nixon, baseball bridged the cultures. "You be the pitcher, I'll be the catcher," the prime minister told the President. "But once in awhile, the pitcher must listen to the catcher's good advice." Reagan accepted "Yasu's" advice that Japan should be "an unsinkable aircraft carrier putting up a tremendous bulwark of defense."[30]

Japan's military budget remained within the sacred 1 percent of gross national product. But the GNP grew so fast that the budget ranked eighth in the world in the late 1970s, and third—just behind the two superpowers—a decade later. Nakasone, moreover, breached the 1 percent limit in 1987. Most of the money went into new technology, the air force, and the navy. Authorized ground forces remained at the 1953 level—180,000—although they carried advanced weapons. With Reagan's approval, Japan for the first time since 1945 began to export military goods. With its fixation on the Soviets, China accepted the buildup and even exchanged views with senior Japanese military advisers. Some Japanese, however, bitterly condemned Nakasone. Professor Kan Hideki of Kita Kyushu University, for example, implied that the buildup smelled of the 1930s, warned that it distorted the economy, and demanded that Japan learn to say no to Washington. But Kan admitted that "the majority of Japanese are not seriously concerned about these issues."[31]

Several U.S. demands were not as warmly received. One was in the secret 1982 NSC Decision Directive on Japan. It declared the Americans should "press for . . . access to the Japanese economy for U.S. high technology firms," and "full opportunity for U.S. firms to invest in Japan in high-technology ventures." Technology, however, mostly moved one-way: westward. Another, related (and bewhiskered) demand came from Paul Wolfowitz, assistant secretary of state for East Asian and Pacific affairs: "Japan's movement toward greater liberalization of its domestic capital markets and a broader international role for the yen."[32]

. . . to Two Competing Capitalisms . . .

The two economic systems were moving toward not cooperation but full-throated competition. Nakasone told Americans that "Japan Inc. does not exist." But he personally had honed the machine as head of MITI. He also, in a tone far from "Ron-Yasu," had written in 1978 about a "new civilization" that would integrate less developed countries under Japan's guidance. During 1983, he told an audience in Hiroshima that "the Japanese have done well for . . . 2000 years because there are no foreign races" in the country. The remark—untrue—brought down criticism on Nakasone. He nevertheless stuck with a policy that excluded nearly all Asian refugees, especially those from Vietnam, even as other nations, such as the United States and Canada, took in hundreds of thousands. The Japanese had also repeatedly promised to be more cooperative on economic issues. By the mid-1980s, however, widely noted work of Ezra Vogel and Chalmers Johnson persuasively argued that the problem was not quantitative trade figures, but qualitative politics: the *keiretsu* and bureaucracy had created a very different system from the American. Nakasone and Reagan were both extroverts and politically ingenious, but the former remained the heir of the Meiji and Yoshida, the latter the descendant of Woodrow Wilson and Cordell Hull.[33]

Not that the two economies were all one thing or all another. Nakasone rightly noted that a smaller share of Japan's economy was owned by the government than was true of any other major industrial economy—including the United States. In 1986, only 19.4 percent of Japanese research and development expenditures came from the government; in the United States, it was 48.2 percent. The real difference lay in research goals. Most of the U.S. research went into the military (50.8 percent compared with 4.9 percent in Japan). The Japanese put 60 percent into industry, agriculture, energy, and infrastructure; Americans invested about 17 percent in these sectors. Nakasone also correctly observed that Japan prospered because the "bond between the large companies and their subcontractors is different [from] in the United States." And again: Japanese managers, he emphasized, planned "over a period of 20 to 30 years. . . . This is a different approach from American business." He did not add that the long view was possible in part because Japan rigidly controlled the sources of, and access to, its capital. In any case, the plan to build export powerhouses worked so well that Japanese automakers sold 29 percent of their cars at home, 71 percent abroad.[34]

Americans meanwhile publicly worshipped at the shrine of freer trade. But they also pressured Japan to slash its exports, "voluntarily," to the United States in cotton textiles (1956), steel (1968 and 1974), televisions (1977), automobiles (1981), semiconductors (1986), and machine tools (1987), among other products. During the Reagan years especially, Americans preached Adam Smith but practiced Lord Keynes. Thus when Republican budget cutters targeted governmental agencies, such as the Export-Import Bank and the Overseas Private Investment Corporation that provided cheap financing for U.S. exports and investments, the agencies were saved by massive corporate lobbying. "Corporate leaders," one analyst wrote, "have no particular interest in the withering away of the state; they simply seek a relationship with the Federal Government that will enhance corporate profits." When Reagan seemed not to understand this, corporate leaders "have come into conflict with him."[35]

Most of the time no conflict occurred. The government bailed Chrysler out of bankruptcy. It hastened the disintegration of the labor movement by breaking the Air Traffic Controllers Union. It bought political peace with huge budget deficits that maintained social programs at a level at which Americans hoped to be accustomed. It poured money into research and development through contracts paid for by the highest peacetime defense budgets in history. The money was specifically targeted. When, for example, the machine tool industry faced cheaper and better Japanese products, a decision was made at the top— by the National Security Council—to declare U.S. machine tools as "a small yet vital component of the U.S. defense base." The industry was to be integrated "more fully . . . into the defense procurement process." "During the supposedly lean Reagan years," one disillusioned Republican leader later wrote, "overall [government] spending jumped from $746 billion in the 1982 fiscal year to $1.1 trillion in the 1989 fiscal year—a 65 percent increase."[36]

The state was thus deeply involved in both economic systems. In Japan, however, involvement was usually less formal (except in handling capital); overseen by politically insulated, highly educated, and information-saturated bureaucrats; focused on specific civilian production or dual-use functions; and, by the later 1980s, so consensual that bankers and real estate developers began to resemble economic buccaneers whose swords were happily honed by MITI and finance ministry employees. In the United States, government involvement was more formal and legislated; worked through special private interest groups rather than as part of a more comprehensive policy; depended on a bureaucracy less respected and systematized; and—of overriding importance—was geared far more to winning the Cold War than to dominating international markets in selected goods.

In 1984, Reagan's personal popularity climaxed in a landslide reelection victory. In 1985, Americans not only became debtors to the world for the first time since World War I, but were piling up more debt during the Reagan years than under all the other presidents since 1789. High interest rates (needed to kill inflation) attracted vast amounts of foreign capital. Nakasone observed that the dollar became so strong that it sucked in foreign investment and trade "like a black hole absorbing stars." As the "black hole" absorbed massive imports, the strong dollar drove up the prices of U.S. exports, thus creating a historic trade deficit to accompany the historic budget deficit. By 1986, Japan was shipping $80 billion of goods and taking only $30 billion of products in its U.S. trade. Or, as one observer figured, every two days the Japanese were selling to the United States the equivalent of their entire bilateral trade in 1955.[37]

Americans had entrapped themselves. They nevertheless blamed the Japanese. Senator Robert Dole (R: KA) condemned Japanese "selfishness and myopia" for not opening their markets to American goods. Senator John Danforth (R: MO) called the Japanese "leeches." As protectionism and anger grew, the Reagan administration voiced the hope in a secret NSC paper that "the severe problem" could be solved by convincing Nakasone to open markets. Japan did open its capital markets a crack after the 1984 Yen-Dollar Agreement allowed foreign banks to begin trust-banking operations and participate in its bond markets. In 1985, foreign security firms could trade on the Tokyo Stock Exchange for the first time. But the Japanese were surrendering little and would go no further. They were not about to change thirty-five years of highly successful policies just to please Americans.[38]

Tokyo and Washington officials searched for a quick fix to remedy the growing trade crisis. Led by U.S. Secretary of the Treasury James Baker III, finance ministers of the globe's five leading economic powers met during September 1985 in the White and Gold Room of New York City's Plaza Hotel. They agreed to concert policies to lower the dollar and raise the value of other currencies, especially the yen. Japan finally agreed to reverse policy and revalue the yen only after Nakasone mediated several bitter internal arguments. The Plaza accord turned out to be the most significant financial agreement since Nixon destroyed the dollar-for-gold part of the Bretton Woods system in 1971. The yen soared almost 100 percent against the dollar, from about 250 yen in the mid-1980s to 130 yen in early 1989.[39]

Economic theory dictates that with the dollar's value sinking like a stone, U.S. goods will be cheaper to buy abroad. Thus, as their goods move overseas, Americans' trade balance will turn favorable. But accepted economic theory seemed irrelevant to the realities of Japanese trade policies. In 1986–87, the U.S. global trade deficit skyrocketed to over $160 billion; $59 billion flowed from the trade with Japan. Despite the Plaza agreement, U.S. exports to Japanese markets rose only 5.5 percent in 1986, but Japan's exports to Americans jumped 21 percent. Japanese producers, it turned out, willingly absorbed the yen's massive reevaluation in order to keep market share abroad. It also turned out that the finance ministry and MITI strongly supported the producers, especially with easy money, so market share could be retained. It further turned out that only about one-third of Japanese exports (and a mere 3 percent of imports) were accounted for in yen; the rest was largely in the declining dollar.[40]

Reagan and Baker had been blindsided by Japan. No one around Baker either knew enough about the Japanese practices or was able to convince the Treasury Secretary that the finance ministry would use every ounce of its considerable power to exploit the Plaza accord fully. The Japanese found themselves in a happy win-win situation: not only did the agreement increase their favorable trade balance, it performed miracles for their investments. As the yen ballooned in value, Japanese investors gobbled up prize manufacturing and real estate assets at seemingly bargain-basement prices. Southeast Asia, China, and the United States were special targets. The "miracle's" version of a co-prosperity sphere took shape. In 1980, American firms had about $5 billion invested directly in Southeast Asia, Japanese about $7 billion. By 1989, the Americans had doubled their holdings to $10 billion, but the Japanese more than tripled theirs to $23 billion. By 1989 as well, Japan had replaced the United States as the leading donor of foreign aid to Southeast Asia. The aid, of course, was closely tied to the region's acceptance of Japan's goods and capital.[41]

In 1989, Australia recognized the urgency for dealing with such startling developments. It took the lead in creating the Asia-Pacific Economic Cooperation (APEC) forum. "APEC was born out of fear," Funabashi Yoichi notes, "fear of a unilateralist or isolationist America, fear of the balkanization of the world into competing economic blocs." Fearing, for their part, that they were being ganged up on, Tokyo officials disliked APEC until it became clear that the United States would be allowed to join. Americans entered over bitter Southeast Asian protests and after Washington and Tokyo applied pressure. APEC became a focus for many players: Southeast Asians interested in protecting themselves against rich outsiders; Japanese investors intent on keeping the region open to the powerful yen; and Washington officials determined not to allow the world market to be divided into protectionist, anti-U.S. regions. APEC thus became a battlefield for forces that set about to reshape the world of the 1990s after the Cold War ended.[42]

The muscular yen also affected China. By 1985, Japan had become China's leading trading partner, as exports soared 40 percent alone in 1984 to reach $8.6 billion, against imports of only $5.3 billion. (Comparable Chinese figures with the United States were $3.8 billion and $2.3 billion.) Trade and yen investment climbed despite Chinese student protests against Japanese goods. The protests notably erupted after Nakasone marked the fortieth anniversary of World War II's end by visiting the Yasukuni Shrine to pay homage to Japan's war dead, including convicted war criminals. The lure of Chinese oil fields, the power of Japanese banks and *keiretsu,* and a 1988 agreement for protecting investments nevertheless helped Japan provide more than half of all development loans made to China in the late 1980s.[43]

The hyperactive yen also swarmed eastward. Through 1986, the United States received more Japanese investment ($25.3 billion) than any other nation. Indonesia ranked second, with $8.4 billion. Between 1985 and 1990, Japanese invested an incredible $650 billion abroad, with nearly half going to the United States. Tokyo investors bought such jewels as the major share of Rockefeller Center in New York City, leading Hollywood studios, and Pebble Beach, perhaps the nation's most beautiful golf course. Some observers warned of a Japanese invasion. Others, however, viewed the yen as a jumpstart for the sagging U.S. economy, especially as Japanese built Honda, Toyota, and Nissan plants to revive so-called Rust Belt, deserted midwestern manufacturing plants. A distinctly non-Rust Belt state, North Carolina, alone had sixty Japanese companies by 1989, thirty-eight of them manufacturers.[44]

A most awesome display of Japan's power occurred in October 1987. Japanese had been fueling the New York City stock market and, especially, financing the huge U.S. budget deficit by purchasing as much as 30 percent of the American government's bonds issued to cover the deficit. Then, in October, these investors grew concerned over poor U.S. trade performances and worldwide interest-rate hikes. The Japanese began pulling money from the New York Stock Exchange. The result was Black Monday: the exchange lost more than 500 points on the Dow-Jones Index, the largest absolute decline in its history. Other exchanges, including Tokyo's, quickly began sliding. The Ministry of Finance rapidly pressured Tokyo's leading security houses to prop up both their own and the New York exchanges. The crisis passed. Several studies concluded, in the words of one, that "the crash . . . started and stopped in Tokyo." Such power was less surprising when it became apparent that of the world's ten largest banks, nine—perhaps ten—were Japanese.[45]

Debates erupted over how Americans could respond to such power. U.S. elites sharply divided. A number (such as Senators Dole and Danforth) wanted to retaliate. Others (such as experts-on-Japan Chalmers Johnson, Karl van Wolferen, and Clyde Prestowitz) warned that Americans must adapt their own system to compete against a fundamentally different Japanese capitalism. Many (such as U.S. multinationals who worked hard to establish beachheads in Japan, the Rockefeller interests, and Hollywood moguls who sold properties at inflated prices) were glad to take Japanese money.

American laborers and white-collar workers similarly divided. Those who worked in competitive export industries (such as autos) agreed with Senator Dole. Those who worried about the new Asian immigration into the United States, as well as about the new competition, sought (like Johnson and Prestowitz) comprehensive political change. The tens of thousands who gained employment in Japanese-owned plants in North Carolina, Indiana, Tennessee, and New Jersey took Japanese money with few complaints.

Given these divisions, a fragmented U.S. political system could not pull itself together to work out a coordinated response. At most, flanking attacks were launched—as when Washington officials and twenty leading semiconductor firms banded together in 1987 to establish Sematech, in Austin, Texas. Sematech did basic research that within a decade gave U.S. companies a lead over Japan in this cornerstone industry. More commonly, however, Americans hoped to readjust the balance of economic power by trusting to the magic of the international marketplace—a marketplace that MITI and the *keiretsu* had long worked to fix. MITI, for instance, had set up the Japanese version of Sematech sixteen years earlier. "It used to be that we could say America should be moving into the future," Clyde Prestowitz declared in 1987. "Now we are finding out that we don't have a future."[46]

. . . to "Relations Have Not Been So Low Since 1960"

For the first time in their history, and despite the Plaza agreement, Americans in 1986 suffered a trade deficit in high-technology goods. *Forbes* showed a one-dollar bill in which George Washington's face was replaced by Mount Fuji. Kanemitsu Hideo, an economics professor at Tokyo's Sophia University, recalled that in 1955 his nation resembled a starfish trying to survive in a huge global pool dominated by Americans. In 1970, the starfish had become "a squid" stretching its long legs. In 1986, it was "a giant octopus crawling out from the pool."[47]

Many Americans seemed to think of the Japanese economy as a shark—carnivorous, primitive, never giving up even after having to retreat temporarily. Secretary of State Shultz spent a year in what he described as "a painful, tooth-pulling effort" to open sectors of Japan's markets. These MOSS (market-oriented, sector-selective) deals seemed promising when signed in 1986. In the widely noted Maekawa Report of that year, moreover, a distinguished Japanese panel told Prime Minister Nakasone that the nation's economy was not open; to compete internationally in the future, "we must totally change our economic policies and way of life." But little changed. A 1987 U.S. Treasury study complained that American investing services, probably the world's best, were "effectively frozen out" of Japan's bond market. U.S. construction firms, also among the globe's most efficient, were denied contracts for building a new airport in Osaka Bay because Japanese officials claimed only local builders understood the soil conditions. (When the airport began sinking into the sea, hurried reevaluations of the soil and structures drove its cost up 50 percent, to $15 billion.)[48]

Secretary of State Shultz, a professional economist, avoided a confrontation. The U.S.-Japan security arrangements were too important to weaken with trade disputes. Besides, Shultz concluded, if the Japanese wanted to pay "astronomical prices for goods that are cheaper elsewhere, that is more their problem than ours." He believed Americans should concentrate on producing superior goods, and—instead of depending on Japanese to finance the U.S. government debt—"increase our own savings to finance our own investment. In other words . . . if we wanted to see our real problem we should look in the mirror." Shultz followed his own advice by negotiating with Japan a Structural Impediments Initiative in 1988—each nation agreed to reform weaknesses the other nation identified. For Japan, this meant opening up; for Americans, it meant saving-for-investment and closing budget deficits, rather than more credit-card spending.[49]

Changes resulted, but neither nation was ready to go cold turkey. Seventy-four percent of Japanese polled called their nation's economic system unfair. MITI and the finance ministry nevertheless held a steady course. LDP governments resembled conservative governments in Washington and London: they jacked up consumption taxes while reducing taxes on those with high incomes. When Socialists won stunning victories in the 1989 parliamentary elections for the upper house, it was a warning shot. But the "octopus" did not change course.

Stronger reactions erupted in the United States. Books appeared with titles that identified Japan's "Threat to America," and at times even identified that threat as "war." In 1988, the U.S. Congress prepared for a trade war. It passed the Omnibus Trade measure bristling with retaliatory weapons, notably the so-called Super 301 provision that gave the President extended power to retaliate against those he considered unfair traders. The bill, in Shultz's phrase, "had Japan in its sights." When the two nations tried to cooperate in technology transfers (as cooperating in building the advanced FSX fighter plane), each attacked the other for holding back information. In 1987, Foreign Minister Abe Shintaro lamented that the U.S.-Japan trade relationship "is at its worst since the war."[50]

On both sides, racism further corrupted the relationship. An extreme form struck Rhode Island. In 1946, Victory Over Japan Day of August 14 became a legal holiday in many states. By 1975, however, every state had abolished the holiday except Rhode Island. When a state representative tried in 1985 to rename it World Peace Day, she lost overwhelmingly; her co-sponsors were called "traitor" and "Communist." In 1989, observers at legislative hearings wore American Legion and Veteran-of-Foreign-Wars paraphernalia as they swore at "Japs" and waved photos of Pearl Harbor. A woman at Brown University was attacked when she identified herself as Japanese. Another repeal attempt in 1992 suffered defeat by an even larger margin than in 1985.[51]

Clashes broke out as well over policies toward volatile regions of the globe. In 1986, the U.S. Congress condemned South Africa's *apartheid* policies by imposing tough economic sanctions. Washington officials warned others not to fill the void left by departing U.S. business. Tokyo signaled cooperation by cutting off imports of South African iron and steel. Japanese goods and business people nevertheless continued to move into South Africa; they even secretly sold a $50 million steel plant to a Pretoria company. Japan's firms were widely criticized for selling computers and Land Rovers to South African police and military. By January 1988, Japan had become the largest economic partner of the condemned South African regime.[52]

"The Cold War Is Over, the Japanese Won"

Differences over South Africa demonstrated larger differences between American and Japanese priorities (and values) in the post–Cold War world after 1989. Mikhail Gorbachev's post-1985 reforms laid bare the weaknesses within the Communist bloc. Germany stunningly reunited in 1989–90. The Soviet Union itself finally imploded and disappeared on December 25, 1991. Americans and Japanese found their world, and their relationship, under new strains. The U.S. economy stagnated. Millions of Americans discovered their jobs endangered by reduced defense budgets—and rising tides of Japanese products. In mid-1989, polls revealed that 68 percent of Americans believed Japan's economic threat was greater than the Soviet military danger.[53]

At this historic moment, Japan's political leadership began to unravel—slowly at first, then with a speed nearly as surprising as the decline of the Cold War. Nakasone's LDP had won three hundred lower house seats in the 1986 election. But his resignation in late 1987, a highly unpopular tax reform enacted by his successor, Takeshita Noboru, and stories of LDP corruption led to a surprising setback in 1989. For the first time, the LDP lost its majority in the upper House of Councilors.

Takeshita, son of a sake brewer, had risen through LDP ranks as part of Waseda University's old-boy network. He had been schooled by his powerful father-in-law, Kanemaru Shin, a top-rank LDP powerbroker. In May 1989, Kanemaru and Takeshita touched wealthy friends to raise $14.5 million in just two hours for the sake of the son-in-law's career. Observers nodded when Takeshita's cabinet filled with LDP old boys. Then the bad news began. The prime minister admitted that he, along with Nakasone and other political fixers, had received large amounts of money from Recruit Corporation (a services firm that placed temporary workers). Recruit bought politicians and some bureaucrats in the free marketplace that was elite Japanese politics. Takeshita's successor, Uno Sosuke (another son of a sake brewer), held power for all of two months before a forty-year-old former geisha testified that Uno had paid her for sex during an affair four years earlier. That women's groups played a role in forcing Uno to resign was notable in a nation where politicians had dismissed the small feminist movement.[54]

As the LDP staggered, the terminus of the Cold War tore at the party's leaders much as it tore at Republicans in the United States: anti-communism could no longer be used to hold together groups that differed on sensitive domestic issues. In 1989, Emperor Hirohito's death and the end of the sixty-three-year-long Showa era further disoriented the country's politics.

Uno's successors, Kaifu Toshiki and Miyazawa Kiichi, were struggling with this new world when, in 1990–91, Japan suddenly faced U.S. demands to join a war against Iraq. Kaifu, another link in the Waseda University old-boy chain, had years before gotten into trouble by loudly opposing U.S. occupation policies. He had, however, found a useful patron, Miki Takeo ("Mr. Clean"), who swept Kaifu to the top. Once there, Kaifu's limited political experience and lack of any foreign policy background fatally weakened him. As noted below, his mishandling of the Iraqi War further soured relations with Washington. In November 1991, seventy-two-year-old Miyazawa Kiichi took over. Miyazawa, as finance minister in 1985, had negotiated the highly profitable Plaza accord. But he had also been stained by the Recruit scandal, by associating with Kanemaru, and by a questionable visit to a hotel room where he barely escaped being killed by an attacker. In late 1992, corruption brought down the top LDP powerbroker: Kanemaru was charged with receiving as much as $50 million from contributors linked to organized crime.[55]

More a financial cesspool than a political party, the LDP split. Under the lead of Ozawa Ichiro, the Japanese Renewal Party claimed to demand real reform, including bringing the bureaucracy under control and conducting a more aggressive foreign policy. Japan had to become " 'a normal nation,' " as Ozawa phrased it in his best-selling *Blueprint for a New Japan*. Ozawa was a younger version of Kanemaru; but, faster on his feet, Ozawa escaped many of the corruption charges. In September 1993 elections, the truncated LDP lost power in the important lower house for the first time since the "1955 system" went into place. A coalition of new parties, Socialists, and Komeito (Clean Government Party) formed. The left and the coalition rejoined what remained of the LDP to insert a new prime minister. Indeed, four prime ministers moved into—and out of—office in eleven months. Japan, the historian Homma Nagayo had accurately predicted in 1991, would endure a "borderless economy and leaderless politics."[56]

That "borderless economy" bent under new strains in the post–Cold War era, as did the "leaderless politics." While prime ministers passed through political revolving doors, bureaucrats quietly made policy with even fewer domestic restraints. The head of Japan's largest supermarket chain complained that regulations had become such that "You even need approval to sell condoms in a vending machine." But the bureaucracy proved startlingly inept in handling the worst economic crisis since World War II—and, indeed, was largely responsible for it.[57]

As the yen's value soared after the 1985 Plaza agreement, the finance ministry tried to cure the pain of Japan's exporters by easing monetary restraints. Borrowing rapidly increased. Much of it bought up real estate. The value of the property, moreover, was set less by the market than by price indexes compiled by several bureaucratic agencies which established land prices to suit their own interests. The result was chaos and illusion, boom and then crash. Economist David Asher described the climax: "a speculative bubble of a magnitude greater than previously experienced anywhere in the world." This was not hyperbole. "By 1988," Asher noted, "the paper value of all Japanese property had risen to four times that of all land in the United States—a nation 25 times its size." In theory, the Imperial Palace grounds in the middle of Tokyo equaled in value all of California. (No one could test that theory because the Imperial Palace grounds were not for sale.) These lands were then used as security to purchase stocks. So the stock market soared in a trajectory reminiscent of the New York Stock Exchange in 1928. Many small firms, however, proved uncompetitive. As loans became worthless, the bubble in real estate popped, to be followed in 1990-91 by the pricking of the stock market bubble. That market plummeted 20 percent before the government began ineffectively shoring it up.[58]

Part of Japan's problem paralleled a similar adjustment forced upon the United States and areas of Western Europe in the 1980s—moving the economy from manufacturing to services and new technologies. In one sense, Japan managed this shift better than its competitors, for unemployment reached only a little over 3 percent by the early 1990s—according to official figures—while the United States suffered twice that figure. In parts of Europe, it was 12 percent. Meanwhile, Japan's trade surpluses—and American tempers—rose as the bureaucrats allowed the *keiretsu* to coordinate suppliers, producers, and bankers behind closed doors.[59]

U.S. officials shouted and threatened, but other than ineffectively reducing the discount rate to an unbelievable 0.5 percent, supposedly to stir up domestic demand, Tokyo's unelected administrators stayed true to course. And why not? The bureaucrats who actually drafted the nation's laws came from the cream of university graduates, rose through a cutthroat competitive system, and had presided over the "miracle" that uplifted their nation from bombed rubble to the globe's second-richest economy. On a per capita basis, it was probably the richest.

Their accomplishment, however, was bitterly debated in the United States. The debate revolved not only around the "miracle" but the value of "free," less regulated markets. The economist Robert J. Samuelson, for example, argued that Japan's more controlled post-1991 economy was growing at one-tenth the speed of America's open-market system. The " 'control freaks' " of Tokyo's bureaucracy "have met the 'market'—and lost," Samuelson concluded. Close observers of Japan, such as Chalmers Johnson and Clyde Prestowitz, considered such comments myopic because they confused several years of adjustment with forty years of success. Such criticism as Samuelson's also missed the administrators' long-term policies that seemed to be putting Japan into an excellent position for competition in the twenty-first century.[60]

As the Hammer and Sickle was lowered for the last time at the Kremlin, Chalmers Johnson observed: "The Cold War is over, the Japanese won." President George Bush disagreed. "By the grace of God," Bush told the nation in early 1992, "America won the Cold War" and was "the undisputed leader of the age." In truth, both Tokyo and Washington officials had been slow to comprehend the Cold War's termination and its meaning. Bush never shared a central belief of some Tokyo officials that the new world would be less violent. To the contrary, and to the Kaifu government's shock, the President had invaded Panama in late 1989 with 27,000 troops to remove an obnoxious dictator. (In the bargain, he challenged the media that had labeled him "a wimp.") Both Americans and Japanese thus believed what their own strengths led them to believe. The United States, with an unrivaled military and beleaguered economy, foresaw a world of spreading chaos unless U.S. force could be made credible. Japan, with its "miracle" and limited military, foresaw new, intensified economic competition. Then came the war with Iraq.[61]

The Gulf War: A Case Study of the Clash

The war broke out on August 1, 1990, when Iraqi armies invaded neighboring Kuwait over disputes that included territorial boundaries and petroleum pricing. Both Japan and the United States had quietly befriended Iraqi dictator Saddam Hussein during the 1980s. The Japanese were either the dominant or second-largest trading partner of Iraq during the decade (as, indeed, they had become of nearly every Middle East nation since the 1973–74 oil embargo trauma). The United States supported Saddam Hussein in his bloody, nearly decade-long war against revolutionary Iran, the nation most despised by Americans. The Reagan and Bush administrations even pumped in several billion dollars of agricultural credits so the Iraquis could purchase U.S. products, especially rice, and sent an impressive array of non-nuclear weapons to the dictator. Iraq's aggression thus caught both Tokyo and Washington officials by surprise.[62]

Those officials had talked with each other too little about these (and other) emerging problems. Between 1989 and 1993, Secretary of State James Baker visited Tokyo the same number of times he visited the capital of Kazakhstan. Bush's National Security Council was notably strong on arms control issues and notably weak in the number of officials attending to Asian developments. None of this escaped the Japanese.

The Iraqi War erupted, moreover, in the context of an especially notable American-Japanese clash. The occasion for this clash was, as usual, Chinese developments. China's post-1978 opening to capitalism had spawned an energetic movement supporting political rights and condemning Communist Party corruption. In May 1989, over a million people gathered in Beijing's Tiananmen Square demanding reform. On

June 5, 1989, party hard-liners used tanks to end the demonstrations. A massacre followed. The number of killed ran above seven hundred, but exact casualties remain unknown.

Bush soon condemned the crackdown, gave sanctuary to prominent Chinese dissidents, cut off military sales, canceled high-level U.S.-China meetings, and declared he opposed loans to China from international agencies. As American business deals in China were put on hold, Washington pressured Tokyo to follow suit and, above all, not try to fill the vacuum left by the United States. The new Uno government, in power only two days before the massacre, responded sluggishly. Two weeks after the slaughter, it finally announced a "delay" in its aid program. Japanese firms continued to do business in China, even as the government wrung its hands and asked for self-restraint so Japan would not be seen "as the kind of country that takes advantage of other people's troubles." U.S. condemnation of Tokyo's equivocation was severe.[63]

The condemnation, however, contained a dose of hypocrisy. In 1990, Americans learned that after the Tiananmen massacre, Bush sent top-level officials to discuss with Chinese leaders how to restore normal relations. Arguing that China's growing military and economic power could not be ignored, the President refused to cancel the most-favored-nation (MFN) status that gave China access to U.S. markets. He did so even though Congress had mandated that MFN should be extended only to nations with improving human rights records. When Congress moved to retaliate against China, Bush vetoed the attempt. The Japanese began to feel they were watching a lower-voltage repeat of the 1971 "Nixon shocks." They moved quickly to take the lead (and gain credit in Beijing) in easing international sanctions by releasing $6 billion of governmental credit for China. Plans for the new Emperor's trip to Beijing in 1991 remained on course. By 1993, a fresh wave of Japanese money had flooded into cheap labor Asian countries, but this time more went into China than into any Southeast Asia nation.[64]

In this context, on August 1, 1990, Saddam Hussein invaded Kuwait. Bush initially hesitated. He found it difficult suddenly to throw into reverse a decade of pro-Iraqi policies. But pushed especially by Prime Minister Margaret Thatcher of Great Britain (whose banks heavily depended on Kuwaiti billions), Bush imposed economic sanctions. He also began a military buildup in Saudi Arabia. Having finally taken the plunge, Bush demanded that Kaifu throw him a life jacket: the President personally called the prime minister to ask for money. The request hit a stone wall. The finance ministry was determined to keep governmental expenditures low. Japanese recalled, moreover, other ventures when both they and Americans had gone thousands of miles to impose their military might, only to retreat in disgrace. A large number of Japanese also believed U.S. society was so decadent that it could not effectively wage war. The 1986 *Challenger* tragedy in space, for example, seemed to exemplify American technological decline. Just before Iraq's invasion, a Tokyo foreign ministry official publicly warned that in an anarchic post–Cold War world, the United States—given its enormous budget deficits—could not prop up international order on its own. Other observers pointed out that, after all, it was not in Japan's interest to anger Saddam: about 12 percent of its oil came from Iraq. Iraq also owed Japan nearly $2.5 billion in loan repayments. MITI wanted this money, but wanted no part of any U.S. effort that hurt exports, raised oil prices, and damaged trade. Finally, within weeks of the invasion, Iraq seized 141 Japanese, stranded by the crisis, as virtual hostages. (About 103 Americans were also held.)[65]

Kaifu, if he hoped to cooperate with Bush, faced a steep mountain to climb—a mountain loaded with traps set by his own bureaucracy. He was, moreover, a weak member of a bitterly factionalized and corrupt party who was elevated to the top because he was relatively honest and presentable. But he also presided over the world's second-largest economy—and the globe's third-largest military budget. Bush expected help from such a well-endowed partner, especially since thousands of American soldiers had provided security in Japan since 1951. Now, the President implied, it was payback time.

Kaifu promised money and materiel, but by mid-September 1990 only 800 vehicles had left Japan to help 200,000 troops Bush had rushed into the Middle East. The U.S. House of Representatives condemned such cheapness. By an overwhelming vote, it demanded that Tokyo pay the entire $4.5 billion cost of maintaining American troops in Japan, rather than the 50 percent currently being paid. Kaifu tried to respond with a historic bill that would, for the first time since 1945, send Japanese troops abroad, albeit unarmed and used only for logistics and medical care. Even this proposal ran into a storm of opposition led by Socialist leader Doi Takako. She warned that armed soldiers would follow the unarmed "as surely as night follows day." Asian capitals agreed. Kaifu's support from the pro-American foreign ministry was no match for MITI and finance ministry opposition. Outspoken opponents echoed the views of Morita Akio and Ishihara Shintaro. Their best-selling *The Japan That Can Say "No"* argued it was time to teach Americans who had the power. U.S. missiles, after all, depended on Japanese-made semiconductors and guidance systems. If "Japan sold chips to the Soviet Union and stopped selling them to the U.S., this would upset the entire military balance." The moment had arrived to use Japan's technology triumphs to discipline the Americans.[66]

In early November, the Japanese struck a deal with Saddam Hussein to release many of their hostages. Americans damned the deal for breaking the anti-Iraqi front that Bush had so painstakingly built. Kaifu insisted that no concessions were given Iraq. Later that month, however, he gave up his plan to send unarmed soldiers into the war zone. More criticism cascaded down Capitol Hill. Summarizing his view of Kaifu's policies, Senator John McCain (R: AR) labeled them "contemptible tokenism." Senator Alphonse D'Amato (R: NY) claimed Tokyo's policy was again "guided by greed and avarice." Many Japanese agreed. The debate that erupted throughout Japan during the autumn of 1990 was profound. Critics of Kaifu's policies declared, in the words of one, that "The Government is behaving like a rich man whose neighbour's house is on fire. Its attitude is astonishing; here's some money, but please don't ask for any water."[67]

At Bush's insistence, Kaifu finally pried $4 billion out of the legislature. When U.S. Defense Secretary Richard Cheney refused to exclude using nuclear weapons, however, Japan's criticism of American plans again swelled. Then, to the surprise of many Japanese (and Americans), the U.S.-led coalition softened Iraqi troops with a month of bombings before launching a massive ground assault in February 1991 that liberated Kuwait. The war ended in one hundred hours. During the bombing, Washington asked Japan to pay more of the expenses for stationing U.S. soldiers in Okinawa and the home islands (the Japanese agreed), and for another $10 billion to support the war. Kaifu squeezed $9 billion from the Diet, but only on March 6—weeks after the spectacular U.S.-led victory. Even then, the prime minister suffered for cooperating with Bush. Kaifu was said to have a "Bush-button phone." He lasted until November 1991. Before departing, he did send four minesweepers to join eight other nations in clearing operations. Japanese business leaders urged this step to sweeten U.S. relations.[68]

The American triumph led some Japanese to reassess both their view of U.S. decline and the role of force. But the victory created fears as well: in mid-1991, for the first time since 1945, more Japanese viewed Americans rather than Russians as the greatest threat to Japan's security. As for the Americans, polls indicated that nearly one-third of those asked had lost respect for Japan. Some irony existed. U.S. officials, including Joint Chiefs Chairman General Colin Powell, had harbored doubts during the war. Could the nation use force effectively in the aftermath of the Vietnam tragedy? But in the end, Americans and their partners committed sons and daughters to the battlefield while Japanese politicians and bureaucrats argued over money. Bush pointedly did not invite Japan to Washington for the victory celebration. Nor did the Kuwaiti government mention the Japanese when it issued a public letter of thanks for being liberated.[69]

These 1989–92 events—the end of the Cold War, the LDP's disintegration, the bursting of the speculative bubble, the bitter arguments over the action in Tiananmen Square, the fallout from the Iraqi war—marked a major turn in Japan's postwar history and U.S.-Japan relations. Kaifu was not the only political casualty. The anti-war Socialist Party endured major losses in spring 1991 elections. Ms. Doi had to step down as leader. The victorious LDP, however, also suffered as it split in 1993. Meanwhile, the Iraqi War generated pressure that breached post-1945 defense policies. In June 1992, the Diet passed an International Peace Cooperation law that for the first time permitted Japan to participate in United Nations peacekeeping operations. (The Japanese already ranked second only to the United States in financial contributions to the United Nations.) Japanese troops moved into peacekeeping and humanitarian operations in Cambodia (where Japan's firms were aggressively exploring for oil), Mozambique, and Rwanda. It was a victory for the long-beleaguered foreign ministry. It also led to Tokyo's requests for a permanent seat (and the power of the veto) on the UN Security Council.[70]

Japan's coming to terms with its new international role did not mean it was coming to terms with the United States. The clash with the Americans instead intensified as a new president, Bill Clinton, took power early in 1993.

The 1990s: "American Policy in Asia Begins with Japan"

The conflict centered on the competition that raged between "free-market capitalism" (the United States) and "non-capitalist market economies" (the phrase used by Sakakibara Eisuke of the finance ministry to describe Japan's—and, he believed, the larger evolving Asian—system). Each system had its advocates, but both sides agreed that Asian markets held the key to a prosperous future. By 1993, Americans' two-way trade across the Pacific reached $369 billion, over 50 percent more than their transatlantic trade. Exports to Asia provided more than 2 million U.S. jobs in the embattled manufacturing sector. East Asian economies making up 4 percent of the world's gross national product in 1960 soared to 25 percent in 1991 and headed for 30 percent by the year 2000. The contest focused on the 600 million Southeast Asians and China's 1.5 billion potential customers. The diplomatic implications of the contest became clear to Clinton early in his presidency: U.S. business successfully insisted that he establish diplomatic relations with Vietnam's Communist government, largely so Americans could have some chance of competing with Japanese who had been working in Vietnam's markets since the 1960s and 1970s.[71]

Japan's movement into Southeast Asia was unrelenting. Between the mid-1980s and 1992, the percentage of its exports going to the United States dropped from 40 to 28 percent, while those to Southeast Asia rose by half, 20 to 31 percent. Simultaneously, the Japanese moved car and computer factories into the region. Japan's exports to China doubled during 1991–92 in dollar terms. *Asahi Shimbun* correspondent Funabashi Yoichi accurately described these trends as demonstrating "The Asianization of Asia."[72]

For its part, U.S. trade and investment also continued to flow into China, despite Beijing's miserable human rights record. Clinton ignored his own 1992 campaign pledges by granting China most-favored-nation status in U.S. markets. The competition for China, now the world's third-largest economy and perhaps its largest by 2020, left little alternative. As Clinton's special trade representative, Mickey Kantor, observed in 1995, "I have one job: to protect American workers and create markets for U.S. products and exports. I cannot control what China's leadership does. That is none of my business." But the United States seemed to have little choice since, in the World Bank's words, Japan was "quietly replacing the U.S. as the key partner in the development of East Asia." Such quiet replacement led to this outburst from Assistant Secretary of State Winston Lord in 1996: "One of our biggest problems in China is that our friends in Europe and Japan hold our coats while we take on the Chinese [on such issues as human rights and nuclear arms proliferation], and they gobble up the contracts."[73]

Secretary of State Warren Christopher's statement in 1995 that "American policy in Asia begins with Japan" thus seemed to have several meanings. For one, the U.S.-Japan security and economic relationships were the axis for Washington's overall approach to Asia. A second meaning seemed to be that by 1994–95, Americans—learning from the Japanese—believed that sacrificing market share for the sake of human rights was quixotic, not to mention bad business.[74]

Christopher's observation also meant that the 47,000 U.S. troops in Japan formed the linchpin of Washington's policies in Asia. U.S. Department of Defense officials viewed the troops as a guarantee of Asian stability. Other officials saw them as one of the few remaining levers the United States could effectively exert in the vast region's affairs. Asians, including the Chinese, hoped they would be a check on possible Japanese militarism. For their part, Japanese willingly paid about $5 to $7 billion annually for the U.S. contingent because it saved them billions more in military expenditures while reassuring those Asians Japan wanted as customers.

In all, Washington and Tokyo officials viewed the security arrangement as sacrosanct. They agreed that it had to be shielded against the vitriol emitted by the trade disputes. Growing animosity over trade was therefore not only a danger arising from the clash of two capitalist systems but a danger to the U.S.-Japan security relationship. Thus among the paradoxes that characterized American policy toward Japan was this one: U.S. military men and women were stationed in Japan to keep in place a system with which many American business men and women found it increasingly difficult to compete.

Since 1945, U.S. policymakers had not planned it this way. They fought wars in Asia for the sake of an open Asia. Non-tariff administrative obstacles and the *keiretsu* networks nevertheless kept Japan's market heavily protected. In 1992, President Bush led a delegation of powerful U.S. auto executives to Tokyo to demand better cooperation in trade. It did not help when Bush suddenly became ill at dinner and vomited on the Japanese prime minister. The President nevertheless succeeded in forcing Japan to pledge to buy more U.S. auto parts. The purchases, such as they were, did little to shrink the ballooning U.S. trade deficit.[75]

Initially, the Clinton administration seemed to be more realistic. The President himself read books and learned from the past. He also appointed Wall Street veterans whose firms knew Japanese techniques firsthand. Clinton undertook a three-front offensive. On one front he supported new Asian regional organizations, especially APEC, to ensure Americans would not be excluded from such important forums. (Bush initially had mistrusted APEC, in which the United States was in a white minority, and instead stressed the need for open, bilateral trade arrangements.)

Clinton's second front was notable: he began to develop a series of government–private-sector relationships avowedly aimed at competing with Japan's (and some Europeans') profitable government–private-sector linkages. In truth, of course, the United States had long followed such an industrial policy. The Export-Import Bank, the Overseas Private Investment Corporation (that provided insurance for overseas transactions), massive subsidies to farmers and corporations that sold abroad, and especially the mammoth military budget—all were government contributions to U.S. entrepreneurs. Economist John Kenneth Galbraith's observation that the American version of socialism appeared when the corporate jets descended on Washington was interesting in this context.

Clinton moved to expand this relationship. He announced a program to commit $150 million to help match Japanese and European export subsidies. Some $3 billion of loan guarantees were extended to U.S. shipbuilders. With fanfare, the President initiated a ten-year partnership between Washington and Detroit to build a "super car" that could dominate global markets. (Foreign automakers, who made 25 percent of all U.S. cars and employed 34,000 Americans, were omitted from these plans.) "Not since the days when the American Navy was sent to open up trading ports in Japan and China. . . ," David E. Sanger wrote in the *New York Times,* "has the United States made such a concerted effort to win deals for American companies."[76]

But Clinton also stumbled. Beset by political pressures and concern about the stock and bond markets, his administration feared any breakdown of trade talks with Japan—a fear Japanese bureaucrats fully exploited. His offensive on the third front was a mere replay of the old tried-and-failed tactic of talking the dollar down, and the yen up, so U.S. exports would be more competitive. That tactic had seldom reduced the trade gap for any length of time. A finance ministry researcher was quoted as saying, "The Clinton Administration was full of suckers waiting to be manipulated from the word go."[77]

The failure of this monetary approach, and the Republicans' landslide victory in the 1994 congressional elections, forced—and allowed—Clinton to change tactics. He directly assaulted Japan's regulated markets. Its political party system in chaos, its "bubble economy" punctured, Japan seemed vulnerable. As Karl van Wolferen phrased it, the Japanese had entered an "age of uncertainty" that produced "a disorientation without precedent in postwar Japan." The Japanese who had bought up valuable American properties during the 1980s (especially in Hollywood) found their investments bleeding money and themselves veering toward bankruptcy. Between 1989 and 1993, Japan's investments in the United States sank 50 percent, to less than $15 billion. At home, Japan became the first industrial country since the 1930s to suffer general price deflation. Clinton and Kantor therefore maneuvered into this battleground confident they could force Japan to open its market for autos and car parts. The 1986 deal on semiconductors, which had specified numerical targets—and ended with success for U.S. firms entering the Japanese market—provided a model.

But the Japanese government, led by former Finance Minister Hashimoto Ryutaro, refused to retreat. Tokyo's bureaucracy would not tolerate a repeat of the semiconductor experience. The nation's economic problems signaled that a "severe change" was overtaking it, "the kind of transformation that takes place once every half century," as the managing director of Japan's Industrial Bank phrased it. The trauma only made protecting the mercantilistic system that had produced the miracle more important. It was worth noting that even amid the bursting of the "bubble," Osaka's economy alone was larger than Canada's. It was also worth noting that even at the depths of the depression in late 1994, Japan continued to pour money into basic research that was, in terms of percentage of the gross national product, several times higher than U.S. research monies. The Japanese were using the economic downturn to position themselves to dominate technology markets in the twenty-first century.[78]

Hashimoto refused to bend very far to Clinton's demands. The President threatened prohibitive tariffs on Japanese luxury cars sold in the United States. (After all, R. Taggart Murphy observed, Lexus dealers probably voted Republican anyway.) A deal resulted, although not solely because of this threat. Many U.S. and Japanese experts feared that managing trade by setting numerical targets could reverse fifty years of open trade and even undermine U.S. liberal trading principles. Japanese business wanted no damage done to long-term relations. U.S. exporters, such as Boeing and agribusinesses, had begun to penetrate Japan and feared retaliation. Both sides exerted pressure for a deal. So did intelligence agencies, the State Department, and Tokyo's foreign ministry—all of whom worried that the acid seeping from the economic relationship might eat away security ties.[79]

Hashimoto succeeded in getting an agreement in which Japan gave little away. He used his achievement to propel himself into the leadership of a revamped LDP coalition. Hashimoto became the first prime minister since the 1940s who made his reputation by repeatedly and publicly bashing, rather than cooperating with, Americans. As for Clinton's mini-industrial policy, its results could only be assessed much later. Unlike the policies that shaped the miracle, the U.S. approach had no comprehensive long-term goals or sense of priorities; lacked a politically insulated and elite bureaucracy to carry out such a plan; and was constantly vulnerable to powerful interest groups of political and corporate leaders whose patience for payoffs was usually short. Japan, moreover, had created one of the most powerful, well-financed lobbies in Washington to ensure that any changes would not unduly harm its interests. A similar pro-American lobby had no chance of operating successfully in Tokyo, if for no other reason than that it could not effectively penetrate bureaucratic decision making.

Despite all the attempts to protect the security arrangements from the trade talks' bitterness, those arrangements too came under pressure. A test case arose in North and South Korea. Both had vivid memories of forty years of Japanese colonialism after 1905. Since Japan had normalized relations with the capitalist South Koreans in 1965, it had worked to preserve the peninsula's status quo. Japanese influence in the Communist North grew from curious roots: the $1 to $2 billion that 300,000 Koreans working in Japan sent annually to their relatives in the impoverished region. Much of the cash came from profits of Korean-owned Pachinko gambling parlors which, as it happened, also provided major support for Japan's Socialist Party. In 1993–94, the United States condemned North Korea's plans to build nuclear weapons plants, and for barring international inspectors from the sites. Clinton moved to impose tough economic sanctions, perhaps a blockade. Talk of military action swirled. But Clinton encountered Pachinko diplomacy. Tokyo officials feared that cutting off the flow of gambling profits might create dangerous unrest in both North Korea and Japan. The nation's largest liberal newspaper, *Asahi Shimbun,* also worried that cooperation in imposing tough sanctions would renew memories of Japanese militarism.[80]

The crisis eased when North Korea admitted international inspectors in return for massive economic help. The episode revealed how two demands whipsawed the U.S.-Japan security arrangements. Washington wanted Japan to become more involved abroad, to become, in Ozawa's phrase, a "normal country." The other demand emanated from Asian capitals and many Japanese, but also, paradoxically, from Americans too. They demanded that Japan's military be kept under tight restraints. Its advanced nuclear power and missile programs had to be minutely watched and rigidly controlled. In 1994, Prime Minister Hata Tsutomu had not eased those anxieties when he declared that "Japan has the capability to possess nuclear weapons, but has not made them." The resulting uproar forced Hata to deny that Japan had any such "capability."[81]

In 1995, the rape of a twelve-year-old girl by three U.S. servicemen on Okinawa further strained the security arrangements. Investigations revealed a string of such crimes in Okinawa and Japan. In Japanese society, rape ruined marriage prospects and brought special stigma to the woman's family and school, even when she was an innocent victim. Japanese took to the streets and legislative podiums to demand the reduction, if not removal, of U.S. bases. Washington officials feared, however, that such a retreat could unsettle other parts of Asia, while forcing themselves to rethink their entire security policy. "Security is a lot like oxygen," one Pentagon official declared in 1995. "You tend not to notice it until you begin to lose it, but once that occurs there's nothing else you'll think about."[82]

Larger questions remained. Did the post-1945 U.S.-Japan relationship already exist on a life-support system? At the end of an era, was a quite different relationship waiting to be born?

Conclusion

The Clash: The Present in Retrospect

ANY HELPFUL answer to those two questions—whether the post-1945 U.S.-Japan relationship was finally passing from the scene, and whether in the post–Cold War world a quite different relationship would replace it—required first understanding the relationship's history.

In 1852, President Millard Fillmore instructed Commodore Matthew C. Perry to deliver an unusual letter to the Japanese Emperor. "We know that the ancient laws of your imperial majesty's government do not allow of foreign trade, except with the Chinese and the Dutch," the note observed. But Fillmore implored the Emperor to allow "a free trade between" Japan and the United States. In 1989, as Secretary of State James Baker III recalled, the Bush administration took power with the "goal" of turning "Japan from an inward-looking, mercantilist economic giant to an outward-looking economic and political power with strong ties to the United States." If only these two documents formed the record of U.S.-Japan relations, observers would conclude that little changed between Americans and Japanese during 136 years.[1]

In reality, few relationships have been as eventful. Yet Fillmore's and Baker's words reveal fundamental themes that have shaped the relationship: the United States was determined to push for an open Japan and, beyond that, an open Asia. The Japanese were determined to break free of Western constraints and exert maximum control over their foreign relations (and hence their domestic order) by closing the door to foreign goods and capital. At historic turning points (1910–15, 1918–22, 1931–45, the 1970s), the conflict between the two approaches centered on China.

In the 1990s, U.S. officials insisted on policies that, with rare exceptions, their predecessors had been thumping for over 140 years: a fairfield-and-no-favor (in John Hay's words) for developing the bottomless markets of Asia; and a political approach in which a Western power (before World War I Great Britain; afterwards, the United States) was to be the senior, Japan the junior, partner. The heyday of that dual policy occurred in the 1920s. But the relationship broke apart when its central link, the dollar, disintegrated after 1929. The Japanese vowed never to be so dependent again, and—ironically with General Douglas MacArthur's help in the late 1940s—they rigidly controlled their own capital flows. A 1947 internal Ministry of Finance analysis concluded that since Japanese ownership of "basic industries" was "essential for the independence of the Japanese economy . . . we must be vigilant in order to prevent foreign capital from gaining control of company management."[2]

The post-1951 clashes should not have surprised. By the 1960s, Japan had recovered spectacularly from the war. Japanese, like Americans, were shaped by their history as they vigorously pursued independence. An elite bureaucracy, which a century earlier applied the ethic of the samurai to the Meiji era, was reconstituted in the late 1940s with the U.S. occupation officials' blessing to rebuild the economy and generate exports. These administrators dominated economic and foreign policy. The economy was shaped by the *keiretsu,* the corporate families that informally linked powerful banks and industries. The *keiretsu*'s control over capital allowed the Japanese both to plan longer-term and go far in realizing their long-sought goal of economic autonomy. Japan's policies focused on Asia before World War II; on the United States after that war; and, again, increasingly on a very different Asia in the post-1973 era.

The United States meanwhile created a weaker central state whose bureaucracy was more maligned than systematically empowered. In the late nineteenth century, Americans had enacted a series of protectionist, mercantilist measures (including steep tariffs and huge if selective subsidies). These policies produced the highest savings rate in recent U.S. history and an economic miracle that made Americans the globe's premier economic power by the early twentieth century. Because they had such power to compete, Americans were determined to open up

international trade and capital flows. They believed that liberal economic policies best allowed the world marketplace to generate and distribute wealth. At home, competition was to be the rule; not *keiretsu*
informal family and corporate networks but antitrust laws were to be
. the guideposts. If capital depended on swirling markets rather than
steady savings, this was all right: quarterly reports were a welcome regular check on producers—and, as well, encouraged Americans to switch
swiftly to stay on the cutting edge of ever-changing technology.

U.S. officials thought globally. Japan, like the rest of Asia, was to
be integrated into worldwide policies. When Tokyo tried to close off
neighboring regions, as in 1904–15 or in the 1930s, conflict with the
United States accelerated. After 1989, a central question became
whether Asian regional groups (such as ASEAN and APEC) presaged
a fresh conflict. The new East Asian Economic Caucus was described
by *The Economist* as "an Asian-only version of APEC invented to
exclude America." Japan meanwhile wondered during the 1990s
whether NAFTA (the North American Free Trade Agreement, comprised of the United States, Canada, and Mexico) was a Washington-
directed attempt to exclude Japanese exporters from the richest western
hemisphere markets. Americans replied that NAFTA had been in the
works for at least eighty years, and that their market remained the
world's most open. The United States viewed Japan's complaints about
NAFTA or U.S. attempts to protect domestic producers as the height
of hypocrisy. For their part, Japanese saw NAFTA and massive U.S.
help to industry as examples of American practices not following American preaching.[3]

As James Baker's plaintive hopes of 1989 intimated, the United
States had been trying, it seemed forever, to turn Japan outward. When
Japan obliged—as in 1905, 1915–20, or 1931–45—it did so for its own
reasons. The results were not happy. After 1945, nevertheless, Americans gave it another try—not least because, as a top U.S. Japan hand
observed, the Far East had long since become the American "Far West,"
or, more accurately, "Near West." Tokyo was the hub of U.S. plans to
integrate that Near West into a larger world trading system. By 1993, the
hub functioned so well that Japanese trade and investment dominated
Southeast Asia and flowed into China. The Japanese enjoyed a per
capita income of $31,450, compared with $24,135 in the United States.
Of the 500 largest firms around the globe, 151 were American, 149 Japanese.[4]

As this book has argued, the causes of the U.S.-Japan clashes have
deep historical roots. The roots might be controlled. They will not be

eradicated. The two different kinds of capitalism create clashes on the cultural level as well. An increasingly powerful finance ministry official, Sakakibara Eisuke, declared in the 1990s that Japan was a non-capitalist, market-based economy, while the United States was a capitalist, market-based economy. He added that he and some of his new nationalist colleagues intended to make the differences between the two systems even greater.[5]

When the Berlin Wall collapsed in 1989, "it was as if the curtain fell on the 1980s," as one foreign ministry official, Kuriyama Takakazu, wrote in 1990. But the curtain did not fall on the fundamental causes of the post-1951 clashes between Americans and Japanese. As Kuriyama himself prophesied, "particularistic nationalisms" contained by the Cold War burst out after 1989 to destabilize world affairs. Because of the relative decline of their power, Americans could no longer "sustain the international order . . . alone." Kuriyama (who would serve as a popular ambassador to the United States between 1992 and 1995) hoped for a reprise of the 1922 Washington Conference–type cooperation— this time with a happy ending. But he worried that because of the deep-seated differences between the two capitalisms, strains would nevertheless intensify. Widely noted American experts on Japan, including Chalmers Johnson, James Fallows, Clyde Prestowitz, and R. Taggart Murphy, largely agreed with Kuriyama's conclusions.[6]

That much of the conflict is due to centuries-old cultural differences is apparent. Other causes, however, are too often lost. There is little culturally based about U.S. free trade, "one-world" policies after 1945. Until the early twentieth century, U.S. economic policies were shaped more by mercantilist tariffs and heavy governmental involvement than by any belief in free trade. In Japan, post-1945 industrial and social cooperation contrasted sharply with the explosive struggles that pockmarked pre-1945 years—struggles that at times ended in violence and assassinations. The lauded lifetime employment of the "miracle" did not exist before World War II because, in part, factory employees were often young women who worked briefly (and very cheaply) before marriage, while labor organizations were smashed.

In the United States, freer trade and related economic policies after World War II thus arose from a determination not to repeat the errors of the 1930s. (Or as President Harry Truman phrased it in 1947, "We can't go through the thirties again.") They also resulted from Americans' once-in-a-millennia opportunity of uncontested hegemony in the capitalist world to benefit from open-market policies. Japanese officials similarly learned from and adapted to their history. They concluded that the quest for order and independence that had ended so horribly in 1945 could be better achieved by suppressing the military and emphasizing the nation's talent for industrial organization. Yoshida's approach replaced Yamagata's. *Keiretsu* replaced colonialism. By the 1980s, Japanese governmental leadership bent to U.S. demands for fewer restrictions, but successful policies died slowly. As the historian Carol Gluck has observed, opening Japan's heavily protected rice market, for example, proceeded "kernel by kernel."[7]

Indeed, after fifty years of peace and frequent cooperation, Americans and Japanese too often bashed each other with a fervor unknown, say, in U.S.-German relations. The Japanese perspective on Americans, concluded the *Washington Post*'s correspondent in Tokyo, T. R. Reid, seemed to be that

> You can kill your parents while they're eating ice cream in front of the TV. You can ravage your wife. You can maim your husband. You can pull out a gun big enough to kill a grizzly bear and blow the life out of an innocent 16-year-old foreign exchange student who rings your door on Halloween. You can do any of those things and then find an American jury that will let you get away with it.

All of these actual events had been featured on U.S. and Japanese television. By 1995, Sakakibara Eisuke, head of the finance ministry's international bureau, publicly claimed that any American attempt to "reform" Japanese capitalism, given the violent nature of U.S. society, "is nothing but an act of barbarism against our own cultural values."[8]

To help protect their cultural values, Japanese resurrected heroes from their past. Saigo Takamori, who had led a samurai rebellion against Western modernization in the 1870s, was glorified in a series of books that sold 8.4 million copies. Even Lafcadio Hearn's work enjoyed a revival because his love for traditional Japan made him, in the words of one Japanese author, "the most eloquent and truthful interpreter of the Japanese mind."[9]

Thus the culture of the past was refurbished to defend the miracle of the present against American-style modernization of the future. But, of course, both sides manipulated the past. In 1995, as nations commemorated the fiftieth anniversary of the end of World War II, several episodes revealed the power of that past.

In the United States, an unwillingness to confront the past occurred at the Smithsonian's Air and Space Museum in Washington, D.C., the world's most heavily attended museum. The Smithsonian Institution

planned an exhibit on the dropping of the two atomic bombs in 1945
and how they shaped the war's conclusion. Leading scholars painstakingly wrote multiple drafts of a 400-plus-page analysis to provide a context for the exhibit. The text, however, included Japanese perspectives.
The exhibit further displayed such horrors as artifacts of those killed in
the Hiroshima blast. The texts posed sharp questions about whether
dropping the bombs was necessary—questions based on wide-ranging
scholarship and new documentation.

These historical accounts ignited a firestorm of criticism from veterans' groups and their friends in Congress. They refused to accept the
new scholarship, rejected the Japanese perspective, attacked "revisionism," and threatened to slash the Smithsonian's budget. The chastened
museum disavowed the scholarship; the Air and Space Museum's director resigned. The fiftieth anniversary was marked by an exhibit of the
bare fuselage of the *Enola Gay,* without any accompanying text. A
widely respected historian of the Pacific War, Ronald Spector, recalled
that when he was director of Naval History and was pressured to give
the official U.S. Navy slant to past events, he replied, "We don't have
government approved history in this country. If you want government
approved history you ought to move to Russia." After the Smithsonian
episode, Spector concluded that "it appears they can just stay in Washington." Obviously, he added, many Americans had decided that some
events were "too significant to be left to the historians."[10]

The Smithsonian Institution's solution to the controversy, wrote a
U.S. journalist who knew Japan well, was "a classically Japanese solution." Japan, highly adept at avoiding its World War II record, placed
interesting military relics in museums, but with little explanation as to
why they had been deployed in the 1930s and 1940s. At a particularly
trashy level, fantasy novels refought the war and sometimes ended with
Japanese troops liberating California, or General Douglas MacArthur
being prosecuted for war crimes. These best-sellers (sometimes in numbers above 100,000 copies) found an audience among young people who
had no memory of war, but knew it largely through school texts carefully
cleansed of stories about Japanese atrocities. (By the 1990s, some of
these texts had finally been made more truthful.) Several museums and
television networks did present honest history. NHK network's documentary graphically recounted the suffering of Korean women forced
to act as "comfort women," or sex slaves, to the Japanese army in the
1940s. Such perspectives were unfortunately not reflected at the top
political level. Several Japanese cabinet members justified the nation's
war record. A minister of justice denied the 1937 slaughter of more than

150,000 Chinese in Nanking by his nation's troops. These officials were finally forced to resign by the resulting outcry in Japan and abroad.[11]

American admirers of the legendary filmmaker Akira Kurosawa sounded a similar outcry in 1991. Since the 1950s, Kurosawa had redefined filmmaking with, among other pictures, *Rashomon, Seven Samurai,* and *Ikiru* (which brilliantly attacked Japan's bureaucrats). *Rhapsody in August,* however, commemorated the Pearl Harbor attack's fiftieth anniversary by having actor Richard Gere—in the unlikely role of a Japanese American—go to Nagasaki and tearfully apologize for the atomic bomb of August 9, 1945. While blaming Americans for Japanese suffering, the film never mentioned Japan's rape of China, treatment of U.S. prisoners, or the Pearl Harbor attack itself. The two bombs seemed to have been dropped on Japan only out of American brutality. Kurosawa was surprised and shocked when Westerners blasted the film.[12]

Angry with such manipulation of the past, Americans wanted the Japanese government to explore why one of every twenty-five U.S. prisoners of war in German camps died, but one of every three perished in Japanese prisons—often horribly (as by decapitation). Ian Buruma's widely noted *The Wages of Guilt* detailed how Germany tried to reconcile with its past while Japan had not, and how that difference helped explain why their neighbors had come to trust the Germans more than the Japanese. In mid-1995, when members of the Diet proposed passing a resolution of apology for wartime aggression and atrocities, 70 percent of the LDP members banded together with other opponents to kill the measure. (The acrimony, one American journalist noted, resembled what might happen if "Democrats and Republicans in the U.S. House of Representatives" tried "to write a joint declaration about the U.S. role in the Vietnam War.") After considerable hand-wringing, in August 1995 Japan's first Socialist prime minister in nearly forty years, Murayama Tomiichi, cut through the bitter debate. He offered, for the first time by any top Japanese official, an "apology" for the suffering and devastation Japan had inflicted during the war. He especially offered a "heartfelt apology" to other Asians. His contrition was probably also a Socialist warning against Japanese involvement in any future conflict resembling the Gulf War. Even so, Murayama's cabinet unanimously approved his apology. Then many of the ministers made a pilgrimage to the Yasukuni Shrine to honor the Japanese soldiers who died in battle— including some six thousand *kamikaze* pilots who in their "tragic bravery" (as a plaque at the shrine reads) "struck terror into their [American] foes."[13]

Notably, in the 1990s neither Japanese nor Americans found it necessary to mark China's role, and suffering, in the war. Chinese officials were absent from the commemorations. The century-long struggle between the two nations over China was ignored—just as that struggle quickened in the 1990s within a quite different China.[14]

"For the last 100 years, our focus in foreign affairs has been on America," a top Japanese official observed in 1996. "From now on, it will have to be China." By the year 2010 or 2020, China could be the world's largest economy. Some 55 million overseas Chinese supply much of the capital and expertise for this phenomenon, but U.S. and Japanese investors also battle for the vast market. Matsushita, the giant electronics firm, employed 18,000 in 32 Chinese operations, part of a massive Japanese move into Asia to exploit cheap labor and vast markets. World-leading U.S. computer and service industries, such as Microsoft, IBM, and American Express, meanwhile expanded in China. Three characteristics of the Japanese approach set it off from the American. First, the Japanese understood the need to cooperate with Chinese family networks to obtain preference in the market. Such kinship undergirded the pre-1945 *zaibatsu* and postwar *keiretsu* that shaped Japan's unique economy. Second, as the 1989 Tiananmen Square tragedy revealed, Japan joined its Asian neighbors, not Americans, in viewing human rights abuses as internal matters that should not be allowed to interrupt trade and investment. Democracy and accountability, many Asian nations believed, were not necessary prerequisites to capitalist development, but could get in its way. Nor were West Europeans about to challenge such beliefs in China. U.S. automakers thought in 1995 they had the inside track to build new plants in China, only to see the rich contracts go to a German firm whose government protested little about Chinese human rights abuses. Finally, Japan, unlike the United States, expanded foreign aid and tied it closely to purchases of Japanese goods. Foreign aid became a flying wedge for Japan's entry into China and Southeast Asia, while the U.S. Congress ruthlessly cut aid until the nation ranked last among industrial nations on a per capita basis. Americans saw foreign aid as security protection, so in the post–Cold War slashed it. Japanese saw the aid as economic, so after 1989 consistently expanded it.[15]

The potential fissure in Sino-Japanese relations was China's major military buildup and territorial claims in the 1990s. Other Asians, including Japanese, approached flashpoint with Beijing over China's claims to rich oil fields in the East China Sea and South China Sea. Tokyo officials also grew concerned as Russia profitably sold technology to China as part of an apparently developing long-term military relationship. Trapped between a fear of China and a fear of building up its own military, Japan reluctantly solidified security ties with the United States in 1995–96. While slightly reducing its own forces, Tokyo pledged to continue paying 70 percent of U.S. military costs in Japan. It also quietly reinterpreted the treaty so U.S. forces could use Japanese bases for operations as distant as the Persian Gulf—and Japan would, for the first time, supply weapons parts and logistical support.

No one knew, however, how the Japanese would react if shooting erupted between Americans and Chinese. A senior U.S. official noted in 1996 that containment worked against the Soviets because "we had a large number of good allies." Against China, though, "we'd have not a single ally in Asia to help us carry it out. You'd cause great strains with Japan, Korea, and all of Southeast Asia, let alone Australia." Nishihara Masashi, a leading Japanese defense analyst, concurred. Japan alone could not handle the Chinese or protect vital sealanes, Nishihara believed, so it needed the United States; "but the problem is, the Japanese Government does not want to talk about the C-word [China] or the K-word [Korea]."[16]

Crises will continue to test whether Americans and Japanese have learned from their history. The historian Yamamoto Mitsuru notes that "A basic and deep process of adjustment" was forced on the relationship after the Cold War's end; but both nations continue "to use old words for new problems." For Americans, the test will be whether they can accept an Asia for and by Asians in which the United States will have a relatively declining role both economically and, despite strong Pentagon objections, militarily. The probable answer is that Americans will not accept such a situation. Two hundred years of history and especially the sense of being the post-1989 global superpower make such an acceptance most unlikely. Asian markets offer too many profits; a growing defense budget for an already all-powerful U.S. military is too tempting. For the Japanese, one test will be whether they have learned, finally, to view other Asians differently than they have historically, and whether they can maintain institutional safeguards on their own military. Another test will be how Japan can maintain its social and political order against the typhoon of new technologies and foreign financial power that threatens to engulf that centuries-old order. In neither the American nor Japanese case, then, does the historical record promise an easy new relationship to replace the old. "One should realize," *Asahi Shimbun* editorialized in 1993, "that the Japan-U.S. relationship has entered an era of genuine competition in which any attempt at equivocation simply will not do."[17]

History therefore promises continued clashes. But learning from that past can offer better understanding between these two peoples, and—if they are lucky—can lead to the understanding that the clashes must be accepted, managed, limited. Certainly their causes, so deeply anchored in history, cannot be safely extinguished. For the primary cause of those earlier clashes—the century-old rivalry to decide which system was to lead in developing Asian and especially Chinese markets—will continue to shape both United States and Japanese domestic and foreign policies in the twenty-first century.

Notes

THE following abbreviations have been used for archival, manuscript, and selected periodical materials

Acheson Papers	Papers of Dean Acheson, Harry S. Truman Library, Independence, Missouri
Adams Papers	Papers of Henry Adams, Houghton Library, Harvard University
AHR	*American Historical Review*
Baker Papers	Papers of Newton D. Baker, Herbert Hoover Library, West Branch, Iowa
Barker Papers	Papers of Wharton Barker, Library of Congress
Bartlett, *Record*	Ruhl J. Bartlett, ed., *The Record of American Diplomacy. Documents and Readings in the History of American Foreign Relations,* 4th edition enlarged (New York, 1964)
Beasley, *Documents*	W. G. Beasley, ed., *Select Documents on Japanese Foreign Policy, 1853–1868* (London, 1955)
Bourne, *Documents*	Kenneth Bourne and D. Cameron Watt, *British Documents on Foreign Affairs—Reports and Papers from the Foreign Office Confidential Print. Series E. Asia* (Frederick, MD, 1989)
Butler, *Documents*	Rohan Butler, ed., *Documents on British Foreign Policy, 1919–1939. 1st Series* (London, 1946–)
Castle Diaries	Diaries of William Castle, Houghton Library, Harvard University

Castle Papers	Papers of William Castle, Herbert Hoover Library, West Branch, Iowa
CIA Reports	CIA Research Reports: Japan, Korea, and the Security of Asia, 1946–1976 (Frederick, MD, 1976)
Cabot Papers	Papers of John Moors Cabot, Fletcher School, Tufts University
CJ	Contemporary Japan (Tokyo, 1932–70)
Cortelyou Papers	Papers of George B. Cortelyou, Library of Congress
CFR	Council on Foreign Relations, New York City
Daniels, Cabinet	Josephus Daniels, The Cabinet Diaries of Josephus Daniels, 1913–1921, ed. E. David Cronon (Lincoln, NE, 1963)
Davis Papers	Papers of Norman Davis, Library of Congress
DDQ	Declassified Documents Quarterly Catalogue (Washington, DC, 1975–)
DH	Diplomatic History
Dickman Papers	Papers of Major-General John T. Dickman, Notre Dame University
Dulles Papers	Papers of John Foster Dulles, Princeton University
Eisenhower Library	Dwight D. Eisenhower Library, Abilene, Kansas
FRUS	U.S. Department of State, Foreign Relations of the United States (Washington, DC, 1861–), followed by year and, if necessary, volume
FRUS: Japan	U.S. Department of State, Foreign Relations of the United States: Japan, 1931–1941, 2 vols. (Washington, DC, 1943)
FRUS: Lansing	U.S. Department of State, Foreign Relations of the United States: The Lansing Papers, 1914–1920. 2 vols. (Washington, DC, 1940)
FRUS: Paris	U.S. Department of State, Foreign Relations of the United States: Paris Peace Conference. 1919, 13 vols. (Washington, DC, 1942–47)
Gage Papers	Papers of Lyman Gage, Library of Congress
Gaimusho, Komura	Gaimusho [Japanese Foreign Ministry], Komura Gaikoshi [The Diplomacy of Komura] (Tokyo, 1953)
Gaimusho, Nippon	Gaimusho [Japanese Foreign Ministry], Nippon Gaiko Nenpyo Narabimi Shuyo Bunsho [Japanese Foreign Relations Chronicle and Documents], Vol. I (Tokyo, 1965)
Goldberg, Documents	Harold J. Goldberg, ed., Documents of Soviet-American Relations (Gulf Breeze, FL, 1993–)
Grew Papers	Papers of Joseph C. Grew, Houghton Library, Harvard University

Hara Takashi	*Hara Takashi Nikki [Diaries of Hara Takashi]*, Vol. 8 (Tokyo, 1950)
Harriman Papers	Papers of W. Averell Harriman, Library of Congress
Hay Papers	Papers of John Hay, Library of Congress
Henderson Papers	Papers of Loy Henderson, Library of Congress
Hoover Library	Herbert Hoover Library, West Branch, Iowa
Hoover Papers	Papers of Herbert Hoover, Herbert Hoover Library, West Branch, Iowa
Hopkins Papers	Papers of Harry Hopkins, Franklin D. Roosevelt Library, Hyde Park, New York
Hosoya, "Documents"	Chihiro Hosoya, ed., "Japanese Documents on the Siberian Intervention, 1917–1922. Part 1, November, 1917–January, 1919," *Hitotsubashi Journal of Law and Politics*, 1 (April 1960): 30–53.
House Papers	Papers of Edward Mandel House, Yale University
IHR	*International History Review*
JACS	*Journal of American and Canadian Studies* (Tokyo, 1988–)
JAEAR	*Journal of American–East Asian Relations* (Chicago, 1992)
JAH	*Journal of American History* (Bloomington, IN, 1964–)
JAS	*Journal of Asian Studies* (Ann Arbor, MI, 1941–)
JJAS	*Japanese Journal of American Studies* (Tokyo, 1981–)
JJS	*Journal of Japanese Studies* (Seattle, WA, 1974–)
JMJS	*Journal of Modern Japanese Studies* (Tokyo, 1977–)—in Japanese
Kennedy Library	John F. Kennedy Library, Columbia Point, Boston
Kimball, *Corresp.*	Warren F. Kimball, ed., *Churchill and Roosevelt: The Complete Correspondence*, 3 vols. (Princeton, 1984)
Lansing Diaries	Robert Lansing Diaries, Library of Congress
LBJ Library	Lyndon Baines Johnson Library, Austin, Texas
Leahy Diaries	Admiral William E. Leahy Diaries, Harry S. Truman Library, Independence, Missouri
Link, *Council*	Arthur S. Link, ed. and translator, *The Deliberations of the Council of Four (March 24–June 28, 1919). Notes of the Official Interpreter Paul Mantoux*, 2 vols. (Princeton, 1992)
Link, *Wilson Papers*	Arthur S. Link, ed., *The Papers of Woodrow Wilson*, 68 vols. (Princeton, 1966–93)
Maki, *Documents*	John M. Maki, ed., *Conflict and Tension in the Far East, Key Documents, 1894–1960* (Seattle, WA, 1960)

McKinley Papers | Papers of William McKinley, Library of Congress

Moore Papers | Papers of R. Walton Moore, Franklin D. Roosevelt Library, Hyde Park, New York

Moore, J. B., Papers | Papers of John Bassett Moore, Library of Congress

Morgenthau Diaries | Henry Morgenthau, Jr., Presidential Diaries, Franklin D. Roosevelt Library, Hyde Park, New York

NA, RG 59 | National Archives, Washington, DC, Record Group 59

NYT-GCI | *New York Times, Great Contemporary Issues. Japan* (New York, 1974)

Olney Papers | Papers of Richard Olney, Library of Congress

PHR | *Pacific Historical Review* (Berkeley, 1932–)

Princeton Seminars | Princeton Seminars, Papers of Dean Acheson, Harry S. Truman Library, Independence, Missouri

POQ | *Public Opinion Quarterly* (New York, 1937–)

PRO | Public Record Office, Kew, United Kingdom

PSQ | *Political Science Quarterly*

Rockhill Papers | Papers of William W. Rockhill, Houghton Library, Harvard University

Roosevelt Library | Franklin D. Roosevelt Library, Hyde Park, New York

Roosevelt, *Letters* | Theodore Roosevelt, *Letters,* selected and edited by Elting E. Morison, 8 vols. (Cambridge, MA, 1951–54)

Roosevelt Papers | Papers of Theodore Roosevelt, Library of Congress

Root Papers | Papers of Elihu Root, Library of Congress

Saionji Memoirs | Harada Kumuo, *The Saionji-Harada Memoirs (1931–1940)* U.S. Army, Civil Intelligence Section Special Report (Tokyo, 1946–47)

Senate FRC, *Executive* | United States Congress, Senate, Foreign Relations Committee, *Executive Sessions of the Senate Foreign Relations Committee (Historical Series)* (Washington, DC, 1976–)

Seward Papers | Papers of William Seward, University of Rochester

Signals Intelligence | Great Britain, Public Record Office, "Signals Intelligence Passed to the Prime Minister, Messages and Correspondences (ENIGMA Messages)," HW 1, Kew, United Kingdom

Stettinius Papers | Papers of Edward R. Stettinius, University of Virginia

Stimson Diary | Henry Stimson Diary, Yale University

Straight Papers | Papers of Willard Straight, Cornell University

Taft Papers | Papers of William Howard Taft, Library of Congress (microfilm)

Truman Library   Harry S. Truman Library, Independence, Missouri

Webster, *Papers*   Daniel Webster, *The Papers of Daniel Webster. Series 3*, ed.
                             Kenneth E. Shewmaker (Hanover, MA, 1974–89)

Preface

1. Records of Groups, 97 (1964/1965), Dec. 7, 1964, CFR.
2. E. Herbert Norman, *Japan's Emergence as a Modern State: Political and Economic Problems of the Meiji Period* (New York, 1940).
3. Quoted in Michael H. Armacost, *Friends or Rivals? The Insider's Account of U.S.-Japan Relations* (New York, 1996), p. 27.
4. Seymour Hersh, *The Price of Power; Kissinger in the Nixon White House* (New York, 1983), p. 382.
5. A provocative analysis of the three-cornered U.S.-Japan-China relationship by the mid-1990s, and the important role of Southeast Asia as a fourth player, is Chalmers Johnson, "Nationalism and the Market: China as a Superpower," *JPRI Working Paper no.* 22 (July 1996), esp. pp. 5–13. A useful overview is Richard Halloran, "The Rising East," *Foreign Policy*, 102 (Spring 1996): 3–21.
6. Armacost, *Friends or Rivals?*, pp. 65–67, 80.
7. Faulkner is quoted and analyzed in Michael Kammen, *Salvages and Biases* (Ithaca, NY, 1990), p. 175.

Chapter I

1. Alexis de Tocqueville, *Democracy in America*, 2 vols. (New York, 1948), II, 292–295. As noted earlier, "Americans" is used as a synonym for U.S. citizens, for purposes of succinctness and variation.
2. Ibid., 421–424.
3. William Neumann, "Determinism, Destiny, and Myth in the American Image of China," in *Issues and Conflicts*, ed. George L. Anderson (Lawrence, KA, 1959), pp. 1–22; Samuel Eliot Morison, *The Maritime History of Massachusetts, 1783–1860* (Boston, 1941), pp. 328–329; William Neumann, "Religion, Morality, and Freedom: The Ideological Background of the Perry Expedition," *PHR*, 23 (August 1954): 247–258.
4. This paragraph is especially indebted to John Emmerson and Harrison M. Holland, *Eagle and the Rising Sun* (Reading, MA, 1988), pp. 5, 19, 22–23, 32–33.
5. Tocqueville, *Democracy*, II, 243; Walt Whitman, *The Gathering of the Forces*, 2 vols. (New York, 1920), I, 32–33.
6. A helpful analysis is Charles Sellers, *The Market Revolution* (New York, 1991), esp. pp. 3–102 and 364–395 on the "market's cultural conquest"; see also Marvin Meyers, *The Jacksonian Persuasion* (Stanford, 1957), which outlines the acquisition-for-ascent theme, and Louis B. Hartz, *The Liberal Tradition in America* (New York, 1955), which made the classic (and much-debated) case that without feudal restraints Americans were born free.
7. See esp. Emmerson and Holland, *Eagle*, p. 30.
8. T. J. Pempel, *Policy and Politics in Japan* (Philadelphia, 1982), pp. 3–7; Emmerson and Holland, *Eagle*, p. 33.
9. Emmerson and Holland, *Eagle*, pp. 34–35.
10. Beasley, *Documents*, p. 3; William H. Lockwood, *Japanese Economic Development, 1868–1938* (Princeton, 1954), p. 4 note; W. G. Beasley, *Japanese Imperialism, 1894–1945* (New

York, 1991); Ronald P. Toby, "Contesting the Centre: International Sources of Japanese National Identity," *IHR*, 7 (August 1985): 347–363.

11. Paul Akamatsu, *Meiji 1868* (New York, 1972), pp. 35–36, 441.

12. Beasley, *Documents*, p. 4; W. G. Beasley, "The Foreign Threat and the Opening of the Ports," in Marius B. Jansen, ed., *The Cambridge History of Japan*. Vol. 5. *The Nineteenth Century* (New York, 1989), p. 262; Beasley, *Japanese Imperialism*, p. 22.

13. Walter A. McDougall, *Let the Sea Make a Noise* (New York, 1993), pp. 270–275. Neumann, "Religion," p. 251; Emmerson and Holland, *Eagle*, p. 41; Julius W. Pratt, "The Ideology of American Expansion," in *Essays in Honor of William E. Dodd*, ed. Avery Craven (Chicago, 1935), pp. 342–343.

14. Ohashi Kenzaburo, *Melville and Melville Studies in Japan* (Westport, CT, 1993), esp. pp. 221–243; Charles Olson, *Call Me Ishmael* (San Francisco, 1947).

15. Beasley, *Japanese Imperialism*, p. 22: Beasley, "The Foreign Threat," p. 268; "whole Oriental trade" quote in Merle Curti, *The Growth of American Thought* (New York, 1942), p. 663.

16. Webster, *Papers*, II, 244; Kenneth E. Shewmaker, "Daniel Webster and the Politics of Foreign Policy," *JAH*, 63 (September 1976): 314.

17. Webster, *Papers*, II, 253–254, 289–293.

18. Ibid., 289–291.

19. Ibid., 256–258, 290.

20. Akamatsu, *Meiji*, pp. 92–93; U.S. Congress, *Senate Executive Document 751*, 33d Cong., 2nd Sess. (Washington, D.C., 1854?), pp. 53–55; Ian Buruma, "Japan: In The Spirit World," *New York Review of Books*, June 6, 1996, pp. 31–35.

21. Akamatsu, *Meiji*, pp. 88–89, 94–100.

22. Wallace Gagne, "Technology and Political Interdependence: Canada, Japan, and the United States," *JACS*, 9 (Spring 1992): 48–49; Bartlett, *Record*, pp. 272–273.

23. *New York Times*, July 11, 1854, in *NYT-GCI*, p. 2; Akamatsu, *Meiji*, pp. 100–101.

24. *New York Times*, July 11, 1854, in *NYT-GCI*, p. 2; Emily Hahn, "A Yankee Barbarian at the Shogun's Court," *American Heritage*, 15 (June 1964): 62–63.

25. Aruga Tadashi, "Editor's Introduction: Japanese Interpretations of the American Revolution," *JJAS*, 2 (1985): 5–7, 8–9; Professor Aruga to author, February 5, 1996: John Whitney Hall, "East, Southeast, and South Asia," in Michael Kammen, ed., *The Past Before Us* (Ithaca, NY, 1980), p. 170; Marius Jansen, Introduction to Jansen, ed., *The Nineteenth Century*, pp. 14, 16; Neumann, "Religion," p. 252.

26. Victor Koschmann, *The Mito Ideology* (Berkeley, 1987), pp. 56–64; Beasley, *Japanese Imperialism*, p. 29.

27. Koschmann, *Mito*, pp. 30–32; Hall, "East," pp. 166–167; Lockwood, *Economic Development*, pp. 5–8; Emmerson and Holland, *Eagle*, pp. 36–37.

28. W. G. Beasley, in his *Japanese Imperialism*, notes the need for a study of the effect of the West's trade and diplomacy on Japanese administrative structure at this time.

29. Michael A. Barnhart, *Japan and the World Since 1868* (London, 1995), p. 7; Aruga, "Editor's Introduction," pp. 9–11.

30. Hahn, "Yankee," pp. 63, 89–90.

31. This and the previous paragraph are drawn from Townsend Harris, *The Complete Journal of Townsend Harris*, ed. Mario E. Consenza, 2nd rev. ed. (Garden City, NY, 1959), pp. 9, 206, 209–210, 227, 252; Hahn, "Yankee," p. 90.

32. Hahn, "Yankee," pp. 90–93.

33. Harris, *Complete Journal*, p. 330.

34. Ibid., pp. 325, 347, 351–352; Akamatsu, *Meiji*, pp. 105–106; Beasley, *Japanese Imperialism*, pp. 28–29; Hahn, "Yankee," p. 94.

35. Harris, *Complete Journal*, pp. 436–437; Hahn, "Yankee," pp. 94–95.

36. Harris, *Complete Journal*, pp. 475, 485–487, 550; Robert J. Smith, *Japanese Society* (Cambridge, UK, 1983), p. 57.

37. Text is in Beasley, *Documents*, pp. 183–189, esp. p. 185; Payson J. Treat, *Diplomatic Relations Between the United States and Japan, 1853–1895*, 2 vols. (Stanford, 1932), I, 48–63, 85; Beasley, *Japanese Imperialism*, p. 24.

38. "Imperial Court to Hotta Masayoshi, 3 May, 1858," in Beasley, *Documents*, pp. 180–181; Akamatsu, *Meiji*, pp. 110–112; Koschmann, *Mito*, pp. 141–143, 149–151.

39. "Imperial Court to Manabe Akikatsu, 2 February 1859," in Beasley, *Documents*, pp. 41–52, 193–194; Beasley, "Foreign Threat," pp. 282–283; Koschmann, *Mito*, pp. 150–151.

40. Masao Miyoshi, *As We Saw Them* (Berkeley, 1960), pp. 3, 13, 21–33; *New York Times*, June 18, 1860, June 27, 1860, Nov. 18, 1858, all in *NYT-GCI*, pp. 3–4.

41. *New York Times*, June 27, 1860, p. 2; a brief context is in Justin Kaplan, *Walt Whitman* (New York, 1980), pp. 256–257; Miyoshi, *As We Saw Them*, pp. 66–75.

42. Hallie M. McPherson, "The Interest of William McKendree Gwin in the Purchase of Alaska, 1854–1861," *PHR*, 3 (no. 1, 1934): 29–38; Lloyd C. Gardner, Walter F. LaFeber, and Thomas J. McCormick, *The Creation of the American Empire* (Chicago, 1976), chapter 11.

43. Fukuzawa Yukichi, soon to be Japan's leading intellectual, recalled that in the 1860s, "any person who showed . . . any favor towards admitting foreigners into Japan—indeed, any person who had any interest in foreign affairs—was liable to be set upon by the unrelenting *ronin*." Yukichi Fukuzawa, *The Autobiography of Yukichi Fukuzawa*, revised and translated by Eiichi Kiyooka (New York, 1966), p. 122; Akamatsu, *Meiji*, pp. 143–144; Treat, *Diplomatic*, I, 105–106; Hahn, "Yankee," p. 96.

44. Beasley, "Foreign Threat," pp. 286–287.

45. Treat, *Diplomatic*, I, 171–182, has a good overview.

46. Ibid., 185–200.

47. William H. Seward, *The Works of William H. Seward*, ed. George E. Baker, 5 vols. (Boston, 1884), III, 618; ibid., V, 246; Frederick H. Stutz, "William Henry Seward, Expansionist," Unpublished master's thesis, Cornell University, 1937, p. 26; Ernest N. Paolino, *The Foundations of the American Empire* (Ithaca, NY, 1973), pp. 170–173.

48. Seward to Burlingame, March 6, 1862, Instructions, China, NA, RG 59; Paolino, *Foundations*, pp. 172–174.

49. *FRUS, 1864*, III, 594; Paolino, *Foundations*, pp. 172–173. The argument is spelled out in detail, with specific reference to Seward, by Walter LaFeber, *The American Search for Opportunity, 1865–1913*, in Warren Cohen, ed., *The Cambridge History of American Foreign Relations* (New York, 1993), chapters 1–2.

50. Paolino, *Foundations*, pp. 174–175, 184–186; Treat, *Diplomatic*, I, 201–237; Beasley, *Japanese Imperialism*, p. 20.

51. *New York Times*, Nov. 27, 1864, in *NYT-GCI*, p. 5; Paolino, *Foundations*, pp. 186–187; Seward W. Livermore, "American Naval-Base Policy in the Far East, 1850–1914," *PHR*, 13 (June 1944): 114; Hilary Conroy, *The Japanese Seizure of Korea, 1868–1910* (Philadelphia, 1960), p. 107.

52. Beasley, *Japanese Imperialism*, pp. 24–25.

53. Koschmann, *Mito*, pp. 1–2, 170–171; Ian Hill Nish, *Japanese Foreign Policy, 1869–1942* (London, 1977), p. 10; Theda Skocpol, *States and Social Revolutions* (Cambridge, UK, 1979), p. 169.

54. Smith, *Japanese Society*, pp. 15, 17, 31–32.

55. Ibid., pp. 18–21; *New York Times*, July 5, 1868, in *NYT-GCI*, p. 6; John Whitney Hall, "Reflections on a Centennial," *JAS*, 27 (August 1968): 713.

56. Quoted in Smith, *Japanese Society*, pp. 134–135; Beasley, *Japanese Imperialism*, p. 14; Byron K. Marshall, "The Late Meiji Debate Over Social Policy," in Harry Wray and Hilary Conroy, eds., *Japan Examined* (Honolulu, 1983), pp. 160–162.

Chapter II

1. Robert Smith, *Japanese Society* (Cambridge, UK, 1983), pp. 4, 108.
2. The argument here is that industrial development and the resulting disorder in both societies led Japan and the United States to follow an imperialist path in the 1890s and after. A consensus exists on the belief that both were imperialistic, especially during the post-1882 era. The Japanese side is succinctly stated by Bonnie B. Oh in Harry Wray and Hilary Conroy, eds., *Japan Examined* (Honolulu, 1983), pp. 122–123, where the author writes that "imperialism [is] being defined here as extension of control over alien peoples and territories either by conquest or by economic and cultural penetration." The process is well described on the U.S. side in Thomas Schoonover, *Dollars Over Dominion* (Baton Rouge, LA, 1978), pp. xiii–xiv.
3. Alfred D. Chandler, Jr., with the assistance of Takashi Hikino, *Scale and Scope* (Cambridge, MA, 1990), esp. pp. 62–63; Stuart Bruchey, *Enterprise* (Cambridge, MA, 1990), pp. 337–349, although the handling of foreign policy is highly questionable. Gresham and other officials are discussed in this context, and with further citations in Walter LaFeber, *The New Empire* (Ithaca, NY, 1963), pp. 136–149, 197–283, 376–406; "Olney on the Labor Revolution," June 20, 1894, Olney Papers; Samuel Gompers, *Seventy Years*, 2 vols. (London, 1925), II, 3.
4. G. P. Sansom, *The Western World and Japan* (New York, 1950), p. 317. An important overview of the policies and their consequences is Michael A. Barnhart, *Japan and the World Since 1868* (London, 1995), pp. 9–10.
5. Kazushi Ohkawa and Henry Rosovsky, "A Century of Japanese Economic Growth," in William W. Lockwood, ed., *The State and Economic Enterprise in Japan* (Princeton, 1969), pp. 53–64; Michael A. Barnhart, *Japan Prepares for Total War* (Ithaca, NY, 1987), p. 22.
6. Aruga Tadashi, "Editor's Introduction: Japanese Interpretations of the American Revolution," *JJAS*, 2 (1985): 16–17; Smith, *Japanese Society*, p. 114; Akira Iriye, "Japan's Drive to Great Power Status," in Marius B. Jansen, ed., *The Cambridge History of Japan. Vol. 5. The Nineteenth Century* (Cambridge, UK, 1989), pp. 729, 731.
7. W. G. Beasley, "Foreign Threats," in Jansen, ed., *The Nineteenth Century*, p. 300; Smith, *Japanese Society*, p. 108;
8. Fukuzawa Yukichi, *Fukuzawa Yukichi's An Outline of a Theory of Civilization*, translated by David A. Dilworth and G. Cameron Hurst (Tokyo, 1973), esp. pp. 20–22 on Sino-Japanese cultural differences, and pp. 42–43 on early America and Japan; Yukichi Fukuzawa, *The Autobiography of Yukichi Fukuzawa*, revised and translated by Eiichi Kiyooka (New York, 1966), pp. 214–216; Aruga, "Editor's Introduction," pp. 11–13; Shumpei Okamoto, *The Japanese Oligarchy and the Russo-Japanese War* (New York, 1970), p. 47; a revisionist critique of Fukuzawa is Earl H. Kinmonth, "Fukuzawa Reconsidered: *Gakumon no susume* and Its Audience," *JAS*, 37 (August 1978): esp. 677–684, 695–696.
9. *New York Times,* Oct. 17, 1871, in *NYT-GCI*, p. 7; *New York Times,* Dec. 15, 1871, in ibid., p. 8; Sansom, *Western World and Japan*, pp. 385–386.
10. Marlene J. Mayo, "Western Education of Kume Kunitake, 1871–76," *Monumenta Nipponica. Studies in Japanese Culture*, 28 (Spring 1973): 3–67 is important on the mission; Ian Nish, *Japanese Foreign Policy, 1869–1942* (London, 1977), pp. 10–12, 18, 20.
11. "Tomomi Iwakura . . . Introduction by George Akita," in U.S. Capitol Historical Society, *Foreign Visitors to Congress: Speeches and History*, 2 vols. (Milwood, NY, 1989), I, 15, 17.
12. Mayo, "Western Education of Kume," pp. 19–23.
13. Ibid., pp. 27–28; Aruga, "Editor's Introduction," pp. 19–20.
14. Mayo, "Western Education of Kume," pp. 41–61.
15. Nish, *Japanese Foreign Policy*, p. 21; Chitoshi Yanaga, "The First Japanese Embassy to the United States," *PHR*, 9 (June 1940): 138.

16. Smith, *Japanese Society*, pp. 24–25; T. J. Pempel, *Policy and Politics in Japan* (Philadelphia, 1982), p. 33; Nish, *Japanese Foreign Policy*, pp. 28–29.

17. Tyler Dennett, *Americans in Eastern Asia* (New York, 1922), pp. 512–520; Nish, *Japanese Foreign Policy*, pp. 30–31.

18. Smith, *Japanese Society*, pp. 30–31.

19. Brainerd Dyer, *The Public Career of William M. Evarts* (Berkeley, 1933), pp. 235–236.

20. Emily Rosenberg, *Spreading the American Dream* (New York, 1982), p. 19; Robert W. Rydell, *All the World's a Fair* (Chicago, 1985), pp. 29–30.

21. Hilary Conroy, *The Japanese Seizure of Korea: 1868–1910* (Philadelphia, 1960), pp. 28–36, 47–48; Iriye, "Japan's Drive," pp. 739–740, 745.

22. Conroy, *Japanese Seizure*, pp. 18–19, 51.

23. Ibid., pp. 36–38, 55–58; Jonathan Spence, *The Search for Modern China* (New York, 1990), p. 220.

24. Iriye, "Japan's Drive," p. 746; Conroy, *Japanese Seizure*, pp. 52–53.

25. C. I. Eugene Kim and Han-Kyo Kim, *Korea and the Politics of Imperialism, 1876–1910* (Berkeley, 1967), pp. 21–29; Fred Harvey Harrington, "An American View of Korean-American Relations, 1882–1905," in Yur-Bok Lee and Wayne Patterson, eds., *One Hundred Years of Korean-American Relations* (University, AL, 1986), pp. 48–49. Frederick C. Drake, *The Empire of the Seas* (Honolulu, 1984), is the standard biography of Shufeldt and emphasizes his passion for Asian and other foreign markets.

26. Payson J. Treat, *Diplomatic Relations Between the United States and Japan, 1853–1895*, 2 vols. (Stanford, 1932), II, esp. 155–159.

27. Ohkawa and Rosovsky, "A Century," pp. 65–66.

28. Ibid., p. 55; Peter Duus, *Economic Aspects of Meiji Imperialism* (Berlin, 1980), pp. 10–12; William W. Lockwood, *The Economic Development of Japan* (Princeton, 1954), pp. 14, 27; W. B. Beasley, *The Rise of Modern Japan* (New York, 1990), p. 110.

29. Theda Skocpol, *States and Social Revolution* (Cambridge, UK, 1979), pp. 103–104.

30. Oka Yoshitake, *Five Political Leaders of Modern Japan*, translated by Andrew Fraser and Patricia Murray (Tokyo, 1986), pp. 3–6.

31. Ibid., pp. 6–9, 21, 23, 36–37, 39.

32. Peter J. Katzenstein and Nobuo Okawara, *Japan's National Security* (Ithaca, NY, 1993), pp. 11–12, 16–17; W. G. Beasley, *Japanese Imperialism, 1894–1945* (New York, 1991), pp. 34–37; Roger F. Hackett, *Yamagata Aritomo in the Rise of Modern Japan, 1838–1922* (Cambridge, MA, 1971), chapters 1–3.

33. Harrington, "An American View," pp. 46–67.

34. Yur-Bok Lee, "Korean-American Diplomatic Relations, 1882–1905," in Lee and Patterson, eds., *One Hundred Years of Korean-American Relations*, pp. 12–45; Harrington, "An American View," pp. 60–61; Fred Harvey Harrington, *God, Mammon and the Japanese* (Madison, WI, 1944), pp. 1–17, 52–53, 134–135; Iriye, "Japan's Drive," p. 751; Nish, *Japanese Foreign Policy*, p. 34; Charles C. Tansill, *The Foreign Policy of Thomas F. Bayard, 1885–1897* (New York, 1940), pp. 417–449.

35. Barnhart, *Japan and the World*, pp. 13–14, esp. for legal and educational implications; Charles W. Calhoun, *Gilded Age Cato* (Lexington, KY, 1988), pp. 180–181; Nish, *Japanese Foreign Policy*, pp. 26–27.

36. Conroy, *Japanese Seizure*, pp. 208–212, 218–222; Marius Jansen, "Japanese Imperialism: Late Meiji Perspectives," in Ramon Myers and Mark Peattie, eds., *The Japanese Colonial Empire* (Princeton, 1984), pp. 61–79; Jeffrey M. Dorwart, *The Pigtail War* (Amherst, MA, 1975), p. 23.

37. Nish, *Japanese Foreign Policy*, pp. 34–37; Beasley, *Japanese Imperialism*, pp. 31–32; Dorwart, *Pigtail War*, p. 32.

38. Dorwart, *Pigtail War*, pp. 11–12, 20–21; Pauncefote to McKinley, July 10, 1894, Confiden-

tial, FO 5/2234, PRO; Lee, "Korean-American," p. 43; Jack Hammersmith, "The Sino-Japanese War, 1894–95: American Predictions Reassessed," *Asian Forum*, 4 (January–March 1972): 48–54.

39. Rydell, *All the World's a Fair*, pp. 48–49, 50–51; Dorwart, *Pigtail War*, pp. 96, 108–110; *Commercial and Financial Chronicle*, Aug. 18, 1894, 256–257; Thomas McCormick, *China Market* (Chicago, 1967), pp. 49–50; Calhoun, *Gilded Age Cato*, pp. 173–175; Akira Iriye, *From Nationalism to Internationalism* (London, 1977), p. 125.

40. Dun to Gresham, March 4, 1895, Dispatches, Japan, NA, RG 59; Beasley, *Japanese Imperialism*, pp. 61–62.

41. Dun to Gresham, May 2, 1895, Dispatches, Japan, NA, RG 59; Hugh Seton-Watson, *The Russian Empire, 1801–1917* (Oxford, 1967), pp. 582–583.

42. Harrington, "An American View," pp. 66–67; Harrington, *God, Mammon*, chapter 9.

43. Dun to Olney, Nov. 23, 1895, Dispatches, Japan, NA, RG 59; Alfred Vagts, *Deutschland und die Vereinigten Staaten in der Weltpolitik*, 2 vols. (New York, 1935), II, 960–961; Duus, "Economic Aspects," pp. 5–6; Beasley, *Japanese Imperialism*, pp. 51–52, 59–60, 74; Nish, *Japanese Foreign Policy*, pp. 41–42.

44. Edward I-Te Chen, "Japan's Decision to Annex Taiwan: A Study of Ito-Mutsu Diplomacy, 1894–95," *JAS*, 37 (November 1977): 61–72.

45. Shumpei Okamoto, *The Japanese Oligarchy and the Russo-Japanese War* (New York, 1970), pp. 49–50; Philadelphia *Press*, Dec. 12, 1905, p. 6; Lockwood, *Economic Development*, p. 19; Dorwart, *Pigtail War*, p. 113. See also William Elroy Curtis, *The Yankees of the East: Sketches of Modern Japan*, 2 vols. (New York, 1896).

46. *Public Opinion*, Nov. 14, 1895, pp. 627–628; Jonathan Cott, *Wandering Ghost: The Odyssey of Lafcadio Hearn* (New York, 1991), pp. xiii–xiv.

47. William A. Russ, Jr., *The Hawaiian Revolution (1893–1894)* (Selinsgrove, PA, 1959), pp. 30–32; Tansill, *Thomas F. Bayard*, p. 361.

48. Gary Okihiro, *Cane Fires* (Philadelphia, 1991); pp. 25–57; Cleveland quoted in LaFeber, *New Empire*, p. 54.

49. Okihiro, *Cane Fires*, esp. p. 42; Wiltse to Tracy, Jan. 18, 1893, Naval Records, Area 9 file, box 19, National Archives.

50. Homer E. Socolofsky and Allen B. Spetter, *The Presidency of Benjamin Harrison* (Lawrence, KA, 1987), pp. 200–206; Okihiro, *Cane Fires*, p. 57; the *New York World* quote is in *Public Opinion*, Feb. 11, 1893, pp. 439–441, Feb. 4, 1893, pp. 415–417.

51. Russ, *Hawaiian Revolution*, pp. 34–35; Belknap to Herbert, March 17, 1893, Naval Records, Area 9 file, box 9, National Archives; Hilary Conroy, *Japanese Expansion into Hawaii, 1868–1898* (San Francisco, 1973), pp. 140, 146.

52. Conroy, *Japanese Expansion into Hawaii*, pp. 179–180; Sylvester K. Stevens, *American Expansion in Hawaii, 1842–1898* (Harrisburg, PA, 1945), pp. 282–284; LaFeber, *New Empire*, pp. 329–332.

53. Theodore Roosevelt, *Letters of Theodore Roosevelt*, ed. Elting E. Morison, 6 vols. (Cambridge, MA, 1951), I, 601; Dun to Sherman, June 21, 1897, Dispatches, Japan, NA, RG 59; Long to Commanding Officer, USS *Oregon*, Naval Records, Confidential Correspondence, vol. 2, National Archives; State Department to Sewall, July 10, 1897, Naval Records, Area 9 file, box 30, July 1–15 folder, National Archives; McNair to Long, Aug. 3, 1897, Naval Records, Area 10 file, box 15, August folder, for the attack on U.S. sailors, National Archives.

54. Nathan Miller, *Theodore Roosevelt, A Life* (New York, 1992), pp. 257–259.

55. Mahan to Roosevelt, May 1, 1897, Roosevelt to Goodrich, May 28, 1897, Roosevelt Papers; Roosevelt, *Letters*, I, 695; Alfred T. Mahan, *The Interest of America in Sea Power* (Boston, 1897), p. 162.

56. Diary-Memoranda, May 1894, Moore Papers; J. M. Devine to Wharton Barker, Dec. 16,

1895, box 14, Barker Papers, on Japanese invasion of America; Statement of Phoenix Silk Manufacturing Company in U.S. Congress, House, *House Report* 2263, 54th Cong., 1st Sess. (Washington, DC, 1896), p. 368.

57. This account of 1896–98 is told in more detail, with note references, in Walter LaFeber, *The American Search for Opportunity, 1865–1913*, in Warren Cohen, ed. *The Cambridge History of American Foreign Relations* (New York, 1993), pp. 126–145.

58. Nish, *Japanese Foreign Policy*, pp. 51–52; Charles S. Campbell, Jr., *Anglo-American Understanding, 1898–1903* (Baltimore, 1957), pp. 17–18.

59. *Chattanooga Tradesman*, Dec. 15, 1897, p. 59; McCormick, *China Market*, pp. 75–76; Robert Beisner, *From the Old Diplomacy to the New, 1865–1900* (Arlington Heights, IL, 1986), p. 84; Julius W. Pratt, *Expansionists of 1898* (Baltimore, 1936), p. 281 has missionary quote; Dennett, *Americans*, pp. 580–581; William Neumann, "Determinism, Destiny, and Myth in the American Image of China," in George L. Anderson, ed., *Issues and Conflicts* (Lawrence, KA, 1959), p. 10 for trade statistics.

60. McCormick, *China Market*, pp. 153–154; *New York Tribune*, March 18, 1898, p. 6; Pauncefote to Salisbury, March 17, 1898, FO 5/2361, PRO.

61. Roosevelt to Dewey, Feb. 25, 1898, Naval Records, Ciphers Sent, no. 1, 1888–98, National Archives; Joseph Fry, "Imperialism, American Style, 1890–1916," in Gordon Martel, ed., *American Foreign Relations Reconsidered* (London, 1994), p. 60; Ernest Samuels, *Henry Adams* (New York, 1989), p. 323; McCormick, *China Market*, pp. 164–165.

62. Cortelyou diary, June 8, 1898, container 59, Cortelyou Papers; Pratt, *Expansionists of 1898*, pp. 323–325.

63. Emily Rosenberg, *Spreading*, p. 43; Campbell, *Anglo-American*, p. 162; Mahan to Col. John Sterling, Dec. 23, 1898, Mahan Papers; McCormick, *China Market*, pp. 186–187.

64. On Mahan and others on sea versus land powers, especially useful are Alfred Thayer Mahan, *The Influence of Sea Power Upon History, 1660–1783* (Boston, 1890), pp. 324, 416; Mahan, *Interest of America*, pp. 220–222; Vagts, *Deutschland*, II, 608–615, 961–968.

65. William Elliot Griffis in *New York Times*, July 30, 1905, p. 8; Gaimushu, *Komura*, esp. chapters 4–5.

66. Adee to McKinley, Sept. 28, 1898, with enclosure, container 57, Cortelyou Papers; James K. Eyre, Jr., "Japan and the American Acquisition of the Philippines," *PHR*, 11 (March 1942): 55–71.

67. Barbara Schaaf, ed., *Finley Peter Dunne: Mr. Dooley, Wise and Funny* (New York, 1988), p. 217.

68. *The China and Japan Sporting Register* (Shanghai, 1877); Allen Guttmann, *Games and Empires* (New York, 1994), pp. 75–77.

69. *Public Opinion*, Aug. 20, 1896, p. 245; Sept. 24, 1896, pp. 405–406.

Chapter III

1. Ernest Samuels, *Henry Adams* (New York, 1989), p. 326.

2. For this and the previous paragraph, see Thomas McCormick, *China Market* (Chicago, 1967), pp. 34–37, 131; Akira Iriye, *Pacific Estrangement* (Cambridge, MA, 1972), p. 123; Warren Cohen, *America's Response to China* (New York, 1980), pp. 81–82; Julius Pratt, *Expansionists of 1898* (Baltimore, 1936), p. 287 on missionaries; Alfred Vagts, *Deutschland und die Vereinigten Staaten in der Weltpolitik*, 2 vols. (New York, 1935), II, 1046; Emily Rosenberg, *Spreading the American Dream* (New York, 1982), pp. 16–17, 18; Charles S. Campbell, *The Transformation of American Foreign Relations, 1865–1900* (New York, 1976), pp. 327–32.

3. McCormick, *China Market*, pp. 231–232; David Healy, *U.S. Expansionism* (Madison, WI,

1970), p. 166; Brooks Adams, "The Spanish War and the Equilibrium of the World," *Forum,* 25 (August 1898): 641–651.

4. Ian Nish, *Japanese Foreign Policy, 1869–1942* (London, 1977), p. 48.

5 Sugihara Kaoru, "Japan as an Engine of the Asian International Economy, c. 1880 1936," *Japan Forum,* II (April 1990): 129–131; Peter Duus, *The Abacus and the Sword* (Berkeley, 1995), pp. 245–247, 434–435; Peter Duus, *Economic Aspects of Meiji Imperialism* (Berlin, 1980), pp. 7–8; W. G. Beasley, *Japanese Imperialism, 1894–1945* (New York, 1991), pp. 127–128; Baron Albert d'Anethan, *The d'Anethan Dispatches from Japan, 1894–1910,* selected, translated, and edited by George Alexander Lensen (Tokyo, 1967), p. 107; Nish, *Japanese Foreign Policy,* pp. 54–56.

6. Jonathan Spence, *The Search for Modern China* (New York, 1990), pp. 231–233.

7. McCormick, *China Market,* pp. 233–237; Theodore Roosevelt, *Letters of Theodore Roosevelt,* ed. Elting E. Morison, 8 vols. (Cambridge, MA, 1952), II, 934; Walter LaFeber, "John Hay," in *Encyclopedia of American Biography,* ed. John A. Garraty (New York, 1974).

8. Ueda Toshio, "The Latter Half of the Meiji Era," in *Japan-American Relations in the Meiji-Taisho Era,* ed. Kamikawa Hikomatsu, translated by Kimura Michiko (Tokyo, 1958), pp. 178–188.

9. Conger to Secretary of State, May 29, 1900, McKinley Papers.

10. Michael A. Barnhart, *Japan and the World Since 1868* (London, 1995), pp. 29–31 for a succinct analysis of the Japanese debates and number of troops sent; Nish, *Japanese Foreign Policy,* pp. 52–53; Roosevelt, *Letters,* II, 1423; III, 6.

11. H. C. Lodge to Rockhill, July 16, 1900, Rockhill Papers; McCormick, *China Market,* pp. 156–164; A. J. P. Taylor, *The Struggle for Mastery in Europe* (Oxford, 1971), pp. 391–392.

12. Democratic Party, *Democratic Campaign Book, Presidential Election 1900* (Chicago, 1900), pp. 324–325, italics in the original; Finley Peter Dunne, *Mr. Dooley: Now and Forever,* ed. Louis Filler (Stanford, 1954), p. 137.

13. Pierce to Secretary of State, Aug. 30, 1900, McKinley Papers; Hay to Adee, Sept. 14, 1900, McKinley Papers; McCormick, *China Market,* pp. 161–175.

14. Beasley, *Japanese Imperialism* p. 135.

15. d'Anethan, *d'Anethan Dispatches,* pp. 146–157; Inoue Kiyoshi, *Nihon teikoki shugi no kesei* [The Formation of Japanese Imperialism] (Tokyo, 1968), p. 318 for Japan's relative economic weakness in 1900.

16. d'Anethan, *d'Anethan Dispatches,* p. 126.

17. Oka Yoshitake, *Five Political Leaders of Modern Japan,* translated by Andrew Fraser and Patricia Murray (Tokyo, 1986), pp. 29–30; Shumpei Okamoto, *The Japanese Oligarchy and the Russo-Japanese War* (New York, 1970), pp. 19–20; Nish, *Japanese Foreign Policy,* pp. 62–63.

18. Okamoto, *Oligarchy,* pp. 22–23; Peter Duus, Introduction to Duus, ed., *Cambridge Modern History.* Vol. 6. *Japan in the Twentieth Century* (New York, 1988), pp. 39–40.

19. Okamoto, *Oligarchy* pp. 25–26, 32; Nish, *Japanese Foreign Policy,* p. 60.

20. Beasley, *Japanese Imperialism,* pp. 82–83; Nish, *Japanese Foreign Policy,* p. 82.

21. Nish, *Japanese Foreign Policy,* pp. 65–66; Beasley, *Japanese Imperialism,* pp. 76–77; the Komura interview is in *New York Times,* Feb. 28, 1904, p. 7; the point on the lack of economic motives before 1904 is made by one of Japan's best-known and controversial historians, Inoue Kiyoshi, *Nihon teikoku shugi no kesei,* which sees the war as the turning point leading to Japan's later economic-driven imperialism.

22. Gaimusho, *Komura,* especially early sections of chapter 8 on Komura's British and U.S. policies; Nish, *Japanese Foreign Policy,* p. 68, on background of British alliance; Hugh Seton-Watson, *The Russian Empire, 1801–1917* (Oxford, 1967), pp. 580–588.

23. Beasley, *Japanese Imperialism,* p. 79; Nish, *Japanese Foreign Policy,* pp. 70–71; Paul Varg, *The Making of a Myth* (East Lansing, MI, 1968), pp. 51–55.

24. This and the previous paragraph are based on Okamoto, *Oligarchy,* pp. 43, 91–93, 97;

Marius Jansen, "Japanese Imperialism: Late Meiji Perspectives," in Ramon H. Myers and Mark R. Peattie, eds., *The Japanese Colonial Empire, 1895–1905* (Princeton, 1984), pp. 65–66. I am indebted to Professor Robert Smith's translation of parts of Kiyozawa Manshi, *Bukkyo to shinkaron* [Buddhism and Evolutionary Theory], reprinted in *Kiyozawa Manshi Zenshu* [The Collected Works of Kiyozawa Manshi] (Kyoto, 1953), pp. 101–118 for some of the material on evolutionary theory in Japan. Akira Iriye, *China and Japan in the Global Setting* (Cambridge, MA, 1992), p. 26; Hilary Conroy, *The Japanese Seizure of Korea* (Philadelphia, 1960), pp. 328–329.

25. Okamoto, *Oligarchy*, pp. 38–39, 96; d'Anethan, *d'Anethan Dispatches*, pp. 176–177; Gaimusho, *Komura*, chapter 8 for the Komura-Hay relationship; Duus, *Abacus and the Sword*, pp. 188–189, 427–428.

26. Okamoto, *Oligarchy*, pp. 101–102; Robert W. Rydell, *All the World's a Fair* (Chicago, 1985), pp. 180–181, 200; Eleanor Tupper and George E. McReynolds, *Japan in American Public Opinion* (New York, 1937), pp. 4–5.

27. George Queen, "The United States and the Material Advance in Russia, 1881–1906," Unpublished Ph.D. dissertation, University of Illinois, 1942, pp. 169–170, 226; J. H. Wilson to Rockhill, June 30, 1904, Rockhill Papers; Akira Iriye, *From Nationalism to Internationalism* (London, 1977), p. 289; Henry Adams to Elizabeth Cameron, Jan. 10, 1904, in Henry Adams, *Letters of Henry Adams (1892–1918)*, ed. Worthington C. Ford (Boston, 1938), pp. 409–410; Duus, *Abacus and the Sword*, pp. 436–437.

28. Roosevelt, *Letters*, IV, 832–833; John Morton Blum, *The Republican Roosevelt* (Cambridge, MA, 1954), pp. 26–29; Brooks Adams to Rockhill, May 28, 1903, Rockhill Papers; Stephen Gwynn, ed., *The Letters and Friendships of Cecil Spring-Rice*, 2 vols. (London, 1929), I, 231; Nathan Miller, *Theodore Roosevelt* (New York, 1992), p. 443; Thomas G. Dyer, *Theodore Roosevelt and the Idea of Race* (Baton Rouge, LA, 1980), is standard and especially important regarding Lamarckianism.

29. Roosevelt, *Letters*, IV, 700–701; ibid., 829–832.

30. Ibid., 701; Okamoto, *Oligarchy*, p. 105; Bruce Lincoln, *In War's Dark Shadow* (New York, 1983), p. 268.

31. Grosvenor Jones to Hoover, Aug. 7, 1926, Commerce, Office Files, box 130, Hoover Library; Gary Dean Best, "Financing a Foreign War: Jacob H. Schiff and Japan, 1904–05," *American Jewish Historical Quarterly*, 61 (June 1972): 313–324, esp. pp. 313–315, 322.

32. Gaimusho, *Komura*, chapter 8, part 5, on Komura and Roosevelt; Okamoto, *Oligarchy*, pp. 108–109; Walter A. McDougall, *Let The Sea Make a Noise* (New York, 1993), pp. 448–456.

33. Roosevelt, *Letters*, IV, 1201–1203; Okamoto, *Oligarchy*, p. 119; Lincoln, *In War's Dark Shadow*, p. 268.

34. Roosevelt, *Letters*, IV, 1230–1231, 1233–1234.

35. Beasley, *Japanese Imperialism*, pp. 83–84; Nish, *Japanese Foreign Policy*, pp. 72–73; Okamoto, *Oligarchy*, pp. 117–118, 121–122, 148.

36. Okamoto, *Oligarchy*, pp. 144, 150; Miller, *Roosevelt*, p. 446.

37. Okamoto, *Oligarchy*, pp. 117–118; Nish, *Japanese Foreign Policy*, p. 75.

38. Jansen, "Japanese Imperialism," p. 74; Okamoto, *Oligarchy*, pp. 167, 184, 218–221; d'Anethan, *d'Anethan Dispatches*, pp. 211–212.

39. Gaimusho, *Komura*, chapter 5, parts 6–8; Roosevelt, *Letters*, IV, 1079–1080; Tupper and McReynolds, *Japan*, p. 14.

40. C. I. Eugene Kim and Han-kyo Kim, *Korea and the Politics of Imperialism, 1876–1910* (Berkeley, 1967), pp. 114–118; Michael H. Hunt, *Frontier Defense and the Open Door* (New Haven, 1973), pp. 144–145; Fred H. Harrington, "An American View of Korean-American Relations, 1881–1905," in Yur-bok Lee and Wayne Patterson, eds., *One Hundred Years of Korean-American Relations* (University, AL, 1986), p. 62; John Gilbert Reid, ed., "Taft's Telegram to Root, July 29, 1905," *PHR*, 9 (March 1940): 66–70; Walter LaFeber,

"Mission to Tokyo," *Constitution*, 6 (Fall 1994), for an overview; John Edward Wilz, "Did the United States Betray Korea in 1905?" *PHR*, 54 (August 1985): 243–270; Taft to H. H. Taft, July 31, 1905, Taft Papers.

41. Gaimusho, *Komura*, chapter 8, parts 8–9; Beasley, *Japanese Imperialism*, pp. 91–94; Viscount Kaneko, "Japan's Monroe Doctrine," *Peiping Chronicle*, Sept. 7, 1932, p. 6, and Sept. 8, 1932, p. 6, where Kaneko tells how Komura supposedly stopped Harriman.

42. For this and the previous paragraph, see Jansen, "Japanese Imperialism," p. 68 on Ito's background; Gaimusho, *Nippon gaiko nenpyo narabini shuyo bunsho* [Japanese Foreign Relations Chronicle and Major Documents], Vol. I (Tokyo, 1965), 261–269; Oka, *Five Political Leaders*, p. 30; Beasley, *Japanese Imperialism*, pp. 97–98; Duus, *Economic Aspects*, pp. 1–5.

43. Oka, *Five Political Leaders*, p. 41.

44. Dunne, *Mr. Dooley*, pp. 290, 297–298.

45. Teruko Kachi, *The Treaty of 1911* (New York, 1988); Tupper and McReynolds, *Japan*, pp. 21, 18–19; Philip C. Jessup, *Elihu Root*, 2 vols. (New York, 1938), II, 16–17.

46. Kachi, *1911*, pp. 162–164; Tupper and McReynolds, *Japan*, p. 24; Miller, *Roosevelt*, p. 479; Paul Gordon Lauren, *Power and Prejudice* (Boulder, CO, 1988), p. 57.

47. John Milton Cooper, Jr., *The Warrior and the Priest* (Cambridge, MA, 1983), pp. 111–112; Roosevelt, *Letters*, IV, 1205; Kimura Masato, "The Opening of the Panama Canal and Japanese-American Relations" (in Japanese), *JMJS*, 16 (1989): 39–44.

48. Cooper, *Warrior*, p. 112; James Chace and Caleb Carr, *America Invulnerable* (New York, 1988), pp. 138–140.

49. d'Anethan, *d'Anethan Dispatches*, pp. 234–235; Tupper and McReynolds, *Japan*, p. 40; James Miller, *War Plan Orange* (Annapolis, MD, 1995), pp. 89–90.

50. Peter Duus, "The Takeoff Point of Japanese Imperialism," in Harry Wray and Hilary Conroy, eds., *Japan Examined* (Honolulu, 1983), pp. 156–157; Sandra Caruthers Thomson (Taylor), "Meiji Japan Through Missionary Eyes; The American Protestant Experience," *Journal of Religious History*, 7 (June 1973): esp. 253–259; Warren F. Kuehl, *Seeking World Order* (Nashville, TN, 1969), p. 106; G. B. Sansom, *The Western World and Japan* (New York, 1950), p. 391 on link between treaty revision and missionaries.

51. The scholar quoted is Peter Duus, "Takeoff Point of Japanese Imperialism," pp. 156–157; Gaimusho, *Komura*, chapter 10; Jansen, "Japanese Imperialism," p. 69.

52. Kamikawa Hikomatsu, ed., *Japan-American Diplomatic Relations in the Meiji-Taisho Era*, translated by Kimura Michiko (Tokyo, 1958), pp. 270–272; Jessup, *Root*, II, 24–43.

53. Henry F. Pringle, *Theodore Roosevelt* (New York, 1931), p. 382.

54. Maj. Gen. John T. Dickman to his brother, Jan. 30, 1910, Dickman Papers; Chace and Carr, *America Invulnerable*, p. 141.

55. This argument is outlined, with further citations, in Walter LaFeber, *The American Search for Opportunity, 1865–1913*, in Warren I. Cohen, ed., *The Cambridge History of American Foreign Relations* (New York, 1993), pp. 206–208, 228–229.

56. Stuart Bruchey, *Enterprise* (Cambridge, MA, 1989), p. 388 for Taft quote on support; Henry F. Pringle, *The Life and Times of William Howard Taft*, 2 vols. (New York, 1939), II, 678–683.

57. William H. Lockwood, *The Economic Development of Japan* (Princeton, 1954), pp. 22–23; Duus, "Takeoff Point," p. 155; Shinobu Seizaburo, *Nichiro Sensoshi no Kenkyu* [A Study of the Historiography of the Russo-Japanese War], revised ed. (Tokyo, 1972), esp. p. xix on the Japanese dilemma of capital exports, and throughout for the 1907 turn; Sansom, *Western World*, pp. 503–504.

58. Inoue, *Nihon teikoku shugi no keisei*, esp. p. 158, 322, 341 on the turning point.

59. Nish, *Japanese Foreign Policy*, pp. 6–7; Lockwood, *Economic Development*, pp. 35–36; Duus, "Takeoff Point," pp. 155–156.

60. Gaimusho, *Nippon gaiko nenpyo narabini shuyo bunsho*, pp. 305–308 for the 1908 document on the cabinet debate.
61. Ibid., esp. p. 309; Beasley, *Japanese Imperialism*, pp. 98–99.
62. Tupper and McReynolds, *Japan*, pp. 13, 17, 82–83, 88; Iriye, *From Nationalism*, p. 224.
63. A. Whitney Griswold, *The Far Eastern Policy of the United States* (New York, 1938), pp. 144–145, esp. for Knox's views.
64. *FRUS, 1910*, pp. 237–238, 243–245.
65. M. W. Lampson, "The Manchurian Question," in Bourne, *Documents*, Part I, series E, pp. 285–288; Kimura, "The Opening of the Panama Canal" (in Japanese), pp. 50, 60–61; William L. Neumann, *America Encounters Japan* (Baltimore, 1963), p. 131 quoting Griswold.
66. Lampson, "The Manchurian Question," pp. 287–288; Walter V. and Marie V. Scholes, *The Foreign Policies of the Taft Administration* (Columbia, MO, 1970), pp. 121–122; William D. Puleston, *Mahan* (New Haven, 1939), pp. 193–194, 201; Asada Sadao, *Ryodai Senkan no Nichi-bei kankei: Kaigun to Seisaku kettei katei* [Japanese-American Relations Between the Wars: Naval Policy and the Decision-Making Process] (Tokyo, 1993), pp. 26–36 for Japanese officers' views.
67. Duus, *Abacus and the Sword*, pp. 240–241; Nish, *Japanese Foreign Policy*, pp. 49–50; Kachi, *1911*, pp. 154–155; Miller, *War Plan Orange*, pp. 24–25.
68. Bryce to Foreign Office, Dec. 4, 1912, FO 371, 45 / 53529 / 12, PRO.
69. Sansom, *Western World*, pp. 307–308.

Chapter IV

1. William W. Lockwood, *The Economic Development of Japan* (Princeton, 1954), pp. 31, 33; Peter Duus, Introduction to Duus, ed., *The Cambridge History of Japan*. Vol. 6. *The Twentieth Century* (Cambridge, UK, 1988), p. 26; Sherman Cochran, "Japan's Capture of China's Market for Imported Cotton Textiles Before World War I," Institute of Economics, *The Second Conference of Modern Chinese Economic History, January 5–7, 1989* (Taipei, 1989), pp. 809–838.
2. Kimura Masato, "The Opening of the Panama Canal and Japanese-American Relations" (in Japanese), *Journal of Modern Japanese Studies*, 11 (1989), esp. 45–46, 50–55; Asada Sadao, *Ryodai Senkan no Nichi-Bei kankei* [Japanese-American Relations Between the Wars] (Tokyo, 1993), pp. 28–36; Lockwood, *Economic Development*, pp. 36–37; Roger Dingman, *Power in the Pacific* (Chicago, 1976), pp. 14–16; E. Sydney Crawcour, "Industrialization and Technological Change, 1885–1920," in Duus, ed., *The Twentieth Century*, pp. 444–445.
3. Ikuhiko Hata, "Continental Expansion, 1905–1941," in Duus, ed., *The Twentieth Century*, pp. 278–279; Roger F. Hackett, *Yamagata Aritomo* (Cambridge, MA, 1971), esp. pp. 249–264.
4. Nobuya Bamba, *Japanese Diplomacy in a Dilemma* (Kyoto, 1972), pp. 49–50; Hackett, *Yamagata*, pp. 270–275, has the quote; Marius Jansen, *Japan and China* (Chicago, 1975), pp. 199–202.
5. This view of Wilson draws heavily from Martin J. Sklar's *The Corporate Reconstruction of American Capitalism, 1890–1916* (New York, 1988), esp. pp. 36–37, 390–411; Wilson's view of revolution is in "Democracy," Dec. 5, 1891, Link, *Wilson Papers*, VII, 350.
6. The quote is in Arthur S. Link, *Wilson the Diplomatist* (Baltimore, 1957), p. 7.
7. William Diamond, *The Economic Thought of Woodrow Wilson* (Baltimore, 1943), pp. 132–133.

8. Roland N. Stromberg, *Collective Security and American Foreign Policy* (New York, 1963), p. 66; Jerry Israel, *Progressivism and the Open Door* (Pittsburgh, 1971), p. 101.

9. Straight to Harry P. Davison, Oct. 28, 1911, Straight Papers; Daniel M. Crane and Thomas A. Breslin, *An Ordinary Relationship* (Miami, 1986), p. 49.

10. Daniels, *Cabinet*, pp. 7–8; Israel, *Progressivism*, p. 108.

11. Arthur S. Link, *Wilson. The New Freedom* (Princeton, 1956), pp. 285–288; Secretary of State Memorandum of Aug. 20, 1913, State Department Records Relating to the Internal Affairs of China, 1910–1929 (microcopy 329; roll 148), 893.51 / 1361–1500, NA, RG 59.

12. Kimura, "The Opening of the Panama Canal" (in Japanese), p. 53; Gaddis Smith, *The Last Years of the Monroe Doctrine, 1945–1993* (New York, 1994), pp. 26–28; William C. Widenor, *Henry Cabot Lodge and the Search for an American Foreign Policy* (Berkeley, 1980), pp. 135–136.

13. For this and the previous paragraph, see Teruko Kachi, *The Treaty of 1911* (New York, 1978), pp. 255–256; Link, *Wilson. New Freedom*, pp. 289–290; Link, *Wilson Papers*, XXIV, 351–353, 382–383.

14. Link, *Wilson Papers*, XXVII, 365; Kendrick A. Clements, *The Presidency of Woodrow Wilson* (Lawrence, KA, 1992), pp. 107–108; Eleanor Tupper and George E. McReynolds, *Japan in American Public Opinion* (New York, 1937), p. 59.

15. Daniels, *Cabinet*, pp. 52–68; Link, *Wilson. New Freedom*, pp. 293–297.

16. Link, *Wilson Papers*, XXVII, 451–452.

17. Duus, Introduction, p. 7; Akira Iriye, *China and Japan in the Global Setting* (Cambridge, MA, 1992), pp. 33–34.

18. *Chronicle Reprints. Two Japanese Statesmen. Marquis Okuma and Prince Yamagata* (Kobe, 1922), pp. 1–16; Junji Banno, "External and Internal Problems After the War," in Harry Wray and Hilary Conroy, eds., *Japan Examined* (Honolulu, 1983), pp. 167–168.

19. Ian Nish, *Japanese Foreign Policy, 1869–1942* (London, 1977), pp. 83–85.

20. Richard Storry, *Japan and the Decline of the West in Asia, 1894–1943* (New York, 1979), pp. 108–111; Dingman, *Power*, pp. 49–53.

21. Sir C. Eliot to Curzon, Aug. 17, 1922, FO 371 F2942 / 2942 / 23, PRO; Jon Halliday, *A Political History of Japanese Capitalism* (New York, 1975), p. 94; Nish, *Japanese Foreign Policy*, pp. 93–95; W. G. Beasley, *Japanese Imperialism, 1894–1945* (New York, 1991), p. 116.

22. Nish, *Japanese Foreign Policy*, pp. 106–107; Clements, *Wilson*, p. 108; Link, *Wilson. The Struggle for Neutrality, 1914–1915* (Princeton, 1960), pp. 267–270.

23. Storry, *Japan*, pp. 102–103; Beasley, *Japanese Imperialism*, pp. 104–7.

24. Nish, *Japanese Foreign Policy*, pp. 98–99; Beasley, *Japanese Imperialism*, pp. 112–113; Link, *Wilson. Struggle for Neutrality*, pp. 269–270.

25. Link, *Wilson. Struggle for Neutrality*, pp. 272–278.

26. Link, *Wilson Papers*, XXXIII, 140–141; Clements, *Presidency*, pp. 109–110; Link, *Wilson. Struggle for Neutrality*, pp. 269–285, 300–308.

27. Nish, *Japanese Foreign Policy*, pp. 99–100; Lloyd C. Gardner, *Safe for Democracy* (New York, 1984), pp. 80–83; William L. Neumann, *America Encounters Japan* (Baltimore, 1963), p. 145.

28. Link, *Wilson Papers*, XXXIII, 121–122.

29. The Japanese loan offensive is outlined in Hirano Ken'ichiro, "Nishihara shakhan kara shinshikoku shakkanda e" [From the Nishihara Loan to the Four-Power Consortium], in Hosoya Chihiro and Saito Makoto, eds., *Washinton taisei to Nichi-Bei kankei* [The Washington Treaty System and Japanese-U.S. Relations] (Tokyo, 1978), pp. 291–294; *FRUS, 1917*, pp. 135–136; *FRUS, 1918*, pp. 170–175; Foreign Office Memorandum, Nov. 23, 1920, FO 371 F2753 / 2 / 10, PRO; N. Gordon Levin, Jr., *Woodrow Wilson and World Politics* (New York, 1968), p. 21.

30. Link, *Wilson. Progressivism and Peace, 1916–1917* (Princeton, 1965), chapter 9.
31. Lansing Diaries, Feb. 4, 1917, box 2, microfilm, reel #1; Edward H. Buehrig, *Woodrow Wilson and the Balance of Power* (Bloomington, IN, 1955), pp. 137–144.
32. Dean Acheson, "The Eclipse of the State Department," *Foreign Affairs,* 40 (July 1971): 598, has Wilson's "associates" quote; Link, *Wilson. Progressivism,* pp. 265–275.
33. Viscount Kikujiro Ishii, *Diplomatic Commentaries,* translated and edited by William R. Langdon (Baltimore, 1936), pp. v, 112; *New York Times Magazine,* June 24, 1917, has interview and quotes.
34. Ishii, *Diplomatic Commentaries,* pp. 116–120; Gardner, *Safe,* pp. 217–219; Takashi Matsuda, "Woodrow Wilson's Dollar Diplomacy in the Far East," Unpublished Ph.D. dissertation, University of Wisconsin-Madison, 1979, pp. 174–175, 182.
35. *FRUS: Lansing,* II, 432–451, esp. p. 436 on "special interest" and pp. 450–451 on exchange of notes; Nish, *Japanese Foreign Policy,* pp. 115–117.
36. Straight to Frederick Moore, Nov. 10, 1917, Straight Papers; Robert Lansing, *War Memoirs of Robert Lansing* (Indianapolis, IN, 1935), pp. 303–304; *FRUS: Lansing,* II, 451–453; Gardner, *Safe,* pp. 222–224; MacMurray to Long, Sept. 20, 1918, 893.51/2013, NA, RG 59.
37. Lloyd Gardner, Walter LaFeber, and Thomas J. McCormick, *The Creation of the American Empire* (Chicago, 1976), pp. 336–337 for further citations.
38. Goldberg, *Documents,* I, 35–39; Gardner, *et al., Creation,* pp. 335–336.
39. Bamba, *Japanese Diplomacy,* pp. 38–39; Beasley, *Japanese Imperialism,* pp. 160–161; Nish, *Japanese Foreign Policy,* pp. 112–113.
40. Hosoya Chihiro, "Origins of the Siberian Intervention, 1917–1918," *Annals of Hitotsubashi Academy,* 9 (October 1958): 96–102; Hosoya, *Documents,* p. 36; Dingman, *Power,* pp. 57–59; Michael A. Barnhart, *Japan Prepares for Total War* (Ithaca, NY, 1987), p. 40 for background of the military's need for raw materials.
41. Lansing Diaries, March 18, 1918, box #2, microfilm, reel #1; Arthur Link, *Woodrow Wilson: Revolution, War, and Peace* (New York, 1979), p. 85; Bullitt to House, June 24, 1918, folder 45, House Papers.
42. Thomas J. Knock, *To End All Wars* (New York, 1992), pp. 155–156; Gardner, *Safe,* pp. 186–191; Hosoya, "Origins," pp. 105–108.
43. Hosoya, *Documents,* pp. 45–48; Hosoya, "Origins," pp. 103–105; Bamba, *Japanese Diplomacy,* pp. 38–39, for "mystic" quote; *FRUS: Paris,* II, 466, for railroad situation.
44. Hosoya, *Documents,* pp. 52–53; Bullitt to House, Jan. 30, 1919, folder 45, House Papers; Nish, *Japanese Foreign Policy,* p. 117; David S. Foglesong, *America's Secret War Against Bolshevism* (Chapel Hill, NC, 1995), pp. 147–149.
45. Link, *Wilson Papers,* XLI, 438–484; *New York Times,* Aug. 1, 1915, in NYT-GCI, p. 57.
46. Foreign Office Memorandum, Nov. 23, 1920, FO 371 F2753/2/10, PRO; Iriye, *China and Japan,* pp. 22–24.
47. Dingman, *Power,* pp. 55–56 for favorable account of Hara's background; Chalmers Johnson, *MITI and the Japanese Miracle* (Stanford, 1982), p. 91 for rice riots and causes.
48. *Hara Takashi,* pp. 317, 346, 449; *FRUS: Paris,* I, 490; Yoshitaka Oka, *Five Political Leaders of Modern Japan,* translated by Andrew Fraser and Patricia Murray (Tokyo, 1986), pp. 177–179, 192–193, 194; Nish, *Japanese Foreign Policy,* p. 119.
49. *FRUS: Paris,* I, 489, 519; Link, *Council,* I, xxii.
50. Arthur Link, *Wilson. Confusions and Crises* (Princeton, 1964), p. 33; Charles E. Neu, *The Troubled Encounter* (New York, 1975), pp. 90–91, 150–151; William Reynolds Braisted, *The United States Navy in the Pacific, 1909–1922* (Austin, TX, 1971), pp. 418–426.
51. Levin, *Wilson,* pp. 113–114; Link, *Wilson. New Freedom,* p. 69; Neu, *Troubled,* p. 92 for House quote.
52. Robert Lansing, *The Peace Negotiations* (Boston, 1921), pp. 98–99; Ronald Steel, *Walter*

Lippmann and the American Century (New York, 1980), pp. 149–150; *FRUS: Paris*, II, 520–525; ibid., XI, 21.

53. Shimazu Naoko, "The Japanese Attempt to Secure Racial Equality in 1919," *Japan Forum*, 1 (April 1989): 93–94; Link, *Wilson Papers*, LVII, 259–261; Paul Gordon Lauren, *Power and Prejudice* (Boulder, CO, 1988), pp. 82–90; Nish, *Japanese Foreign Policy*, p. 121.
54. Link, *Wilson Papers*, LVII, 261–265; Lauren, *Power*, pp. 78–79, 83, 93.
55. Link, *Council*, I, 320–321, 326; *FRUS: Paris*, V, 129–130; Lansing, *Peace Negotiations*, p. 262; Herbert C. Hoover, *The Ordeal of Woodrow Wilson* (New York, 1958), pp. 208–211.
56. Link, *Council*, I, 399–408; Knock, *To End All Wars*, pp. 249–250; Harold Nicolson, *Peacemaking, 1919* (London, 1933), p. 146.
57. Hoover, *Ordeal*, pp. 223–228; *New York Times*, Jan. 21, 1920, in *NYT-GCI*, p. 40.
58. Neumann, *America*, p. 156; Wayne Patterson and Hilary Conroy, "Duality and Dominance," in Yur-bok Lee and Wayne Patterson, eds., *One Hundred Years of Korean-American Relations* (University, AL, 1986), p. 6.
59. Widenor, *Lodge*, pp. 327–328; Root to Lodge, June 19, 1919, Root Papers.
60. Bullitt to Lansing, May 17, 1919, Lansing Papers; Daniel M. Smith, "Lansing and the Wilson Interregnum," *The Historian*, 21 (February 1959): 152–153.
61. Arno Mayer, *Politics and Diplomacy of Peacemaking* (New York, 1967), pp. 876–877; Gardner, *Safe*, p. 295.
62. Bourne is quoted in David Green, *Shaping Political Consciousness* (Ithaca, NY, 1987), p. 83.

Chapter V

1. Bourne, *Documents*, Part II, series E, III, 113.
2. Ian Nish, *Japanese Foreign Policy, 1869–1942* (London, 1977), p. 4; Herbert C. Hoover, *The Ordeal of Woodrow Wilson* (New York, 1958); Herbert Hoover, *American Individualism* (Washington, DC, 1922).
3. "Address Before American Bankers' Association, Chicago, Dec. 10, 1910," Addresses, Letters . . . AG1, vol. 5, Hoover Papers.
4. Hoover to Hughes, April 29, 1922, Secretary's Files, Hoover Papers; Robert Freeman Smith, "Thomas W. Lamont," in Thomas C. McCormick and Walter LaFeber, eds., *Behind the Throne* (essays in honor of Fred Harvey Harrington) (Madison, WI, 1993), pp. 101–102.
5. Lloyd C. Gardner, *Safe for Democracy* (New York, 1984), p. 296; Sir C. Addis to Mr. Bentinck, July 29, 1920, FO 371 F1651/2/10, PRO; Sir A. Geddes to Earl Curzon, Sept. 9, 1920, FO 371 F2180/2/10, PRO.
6. *FRUS, 1920*, I, 498–499; "Thomas W. Lamont's Visit to the Far East," March 29, 1920, in B. Alston to Earl Curzon, March 29, 1920, FO 371 F784/2/10, PRO; Hirano Ken'ichiro, "Nishihara shakhan kara shinshikoku shakhanda e" [From the Nishihara Loan to the Four-Power Consortium], in Hosoya Chihiro and Saito Makoto, eds., *Washinton taisei to Nichi-Bei kankei* [The Washington Treaty System and Japanese-U.S. Relations] (Tokyo, 1978), pp. 306–312.
7. Sir C. Addis to Bentinck, April 20, 1920, FO 371 F588/2/10, PRO; B. Alston to Earl Curzon, March 29, 1920, FO 371 F784/2/10, PRO.
8. *FRUS, 1920*, I, 537, 556; *Japan Advertiser*, May 13, 1920, pp. 1, 10, for joint statements; Carl P. Parrini, *Heir to Empire* (Pittsburgh, 1969), pp. 201–202.
9. Ron Chernow, *The House of Morgan* (New York, 1990), pp. 231–235; Warren Cohen, "Consortia," in Alexander DeConde, ed., *Encyclopedia of American Foreign Relations*, 3 vols.

(New York, 1978), I, 172–173; G. C. Allen, *A Short Economic History of Modern Japan*. 4th ed. (New York, 1981), pp. 100–106.

10. Nobuya Bamba, *Japanese Diplomacy in a Dilemma* (Kyoto, 1972), pp. 42–57, 50–51; Peter Duus, Introduction to *Cambridge History of Japan*. Vol. 6. *The Twentieth Century*, Duus, ed. (New York, 1988), p. 35; Roger Dingman, *Power in the Pacific* (Chicago, 1976), pp. 131–132.

11. Bamba, *Japanese Diplomacy*, pp. 42–51; Eguchi Kiichi, *Futatsu no taisen* [Between the Two Great Wars] (Tokyo, 1989), pp. 115–120 for theater and hairstyles; Dingman, *Power*, p. 131.

12. Dingman, *Power*, pp. 124–125; Tadashi Aruga, "Editor's Introduction," *JJAS* (2, 1985): 23–26; Duus, Introduction, p. 8.

13. Dingman, *Power*, pp. 132–133, 183; Goldberg, *Documents, I, 169–173* on exchange over Siberia; F. O. Minute, Oct. 4, 1920, on Eliot to Foreign Office, Sept. 3, 1920, FO 371 F2281 / 2281 / 23, PRO; Peter J. Katzenstein and Nobuo Okawara, *Japan's National Security* (Ithaca, NY, 1993), p. 16.

14. *Congressional Record-Senate*, Dec. 14, 1920, 66th Cong., 3d Sess., vol. 60, part 1, p. 310; Philip C. Jessup, *Elihu Root*, 2 vols. (New York, 1937), II, 446; Dingman, *Power*, p. 143; Merlo J. Pusey, *Charles Evans Hughes*, 2 vols. (New York, 1951), II, 453.

15. Walter A. McDougall, *Let the Sea Make a Noise* (New York, 1993), pp. 524–527. Dingman, *Power*, pp. 147–148; Sir C. Eliot to Foreign Office, July 29, 1922, FO 371 F2493 / 2493 / 23, PRO; Allan R. Millett and Peter Maslowski, *For the Common Defense* (New York, 1984), p. 362; Pusey, *Hughes*, p. 459.

16. "Memorandum," Neville to Hughes, June 15, 1921, in MacMurray to Hughes, June 27, 1921, 790.94 / 5, box 7112, NA, RG 59.

17. Sir C. Eliot to Foreign Office, June 29, 1922, FO 371 F2493 / 2493 / 23, PRO; Ira Klein, "Whitehall, Washington, and the Anglo-Japanese Alliance, 1919–1921," *PHR*, 46 (no. 2, 1968): 468–469, 477; Pusey, *Hughes*, II, 442; Gardner, *Safe*, p. 308, has elephant story; Dingman, *Power*, pp. 97–98, 155–156; Jessup, *Root*, II, 449–450.

18. Pusey, *Hughes*, pp. 468–473.

19. Hiroyuka Agawa, *The Reluctant Admiral: Yamamoto and the Imperial Navy*, translated by John Bester (New York, 1979), pp. 27–28; Dingman, *Power*, pp. 257, 192, 218.

20. Kato and the anti-Washington naval faction are noted in Hosoya Chihiro, "Washinton taisei no tokushitsu to henyo" [Characteristics of Changes of the Washington System] in Hosoya and Saito, eds., *Washinton taisei to Nichi-Bei kankei*, pp. 3–5; *New York Times*, Sept. 9, 1919, p. 47; ibid., March 11, 1951, p. 92; Bamba, *Japanese Diplomacy*, pp. 156–158; Castle Diaries, May 4, 1930; Morris to Lansing, Nov. 27, 1918, *FRUS: Paris*, I, 491 on Shibusawa.

21. This and the next paragraph are drawn especially from Herbert O. Yardley, *The American Black Chamber* (London, 1931), pp. 194–222; James Bamford's Introduction in Herbert O. Yardley, *The Chinese Black Chamber* (New York, 1983); and James Bamford, *The Puzzle Palace* (Boston, 1982), pp. 8, 16.

22. Japanese economic dependence on Americans at this time is stressed in Nakamura Takafusa, "Sekai keizai no naka no Nichi-Bei," [Japanese-U.S. Economic Relations in the World Economy], in Hosoya and Makoto, eds., *Washington taisei to Nichi-Bei kankei*, pp. 476–482; Pusey, *Hughes*, pp. 476–477; Agawa, *Yamamoto*, pp. 28–29; Akira Iriye, *Across the Pacific* (New York, 1967), p. 144.

23. W. G. Beasley, *Japanese Imperialism, 1894–1945* (New York, 1991), pp. 266–267; Pusey, *Hughes*, pp. 481, 499; Klein, "Whitehall," p. 482.

24. Hughes to Hoover, Sept. 27, 1921, Commerce, Official File, box 55, Hoover Papers; Jessup *Root*, II, 452, 458–459; Bartlett, *Record*, pp. 486–490.

25. Sadao Asada, "Japan's 'Special Interests' and the Washington Conference, 1921–22," *AHR*,

67 (October 1961): 63–70; James B. Crowley, *Japan's Quest for Autonomy* (Princeton, 1966), p. 29; Russell H. Fifield, "Secretary Hughes and the Shantung Question," *PHR*, 24 (no. 4, 1954): 375–385.

26. FO Minute, Oct. 18, 1920, on Geddes to FO, Oct. 14, 1920, FO 371 F2446 / 2343 / 23, PRO; "C-in-C Asiatic," to "Opnav-Washington," Feb. 14, 1921, 790.94 / 3 (1910–29), box 7112, NA, RG 59, on Japan's view of its "special interests."

27. Beasley, *Japanese Imperialism*, p. 167; Iriye, *After Imperialism*, pp. 19–20; Hirano, "Nishihara shakhan kara shinshikoku shakkanda e," p. 314, for how loans helped divide U.S. and Japan.

28. Sir C. Eliot to FO, May 25, 1922, FO 371 F2109 / 2109 / 23, PRO; Akira Iriye, "Japan's Policies Toward the United States," in James William Morley, ed., *Japan's Foreign Policy, 1868–1941* (New York, 1974), pp. 243–244; Manfred Jonas, "Isolationism," in Alexander DeConde, ed., *Encyclopedia of American Foreign Policy*, 3 vols. (New York, 1978), II, 496.

29. For this and the previous paragraph, see *FRUS, 1922*, I, 773–774; Crowley, *Japan's Quest*, p. 29; Yardley, *Chinese*, p. xvii, has White quote; Herbert O. Yardley, *The Education of a Poker Player, Including Where and How One Learns to Win* (New York, 1957).

30. Charles Evans Hughes, *The Pathway of Peace* (New York, 1925), p. 259; Roger Daniels, *Coming to America* (New York, 1990), pp. 282–283.

31. Roger Daniels and Harry H. L. Kitano, *American Racism* (Englewood Cliffs, NJ, 1970), pp. 54–55; Vernon M. Briggs, Jr., *Mass Immigration and the National Interest* (Armonk, NY, 1992), pp. 4–5.

32. Asada Sadao, *Ryodai Senkan no Nichi-Bei kankei* [Japanese-American Relations Between the Wars] (Tokyo, 1993), pp. 338–339 for "yellow peril" image at this time; Aruga Tadashi, "Hainichi mondai to Nichi-Bei kankei: Hanihara shokan o chusin ni" [The Japanese Exclusionary Policy and Japanese-U.S. Relations: The Hanihara Letter], in Iriye Akira and Aruga Tadashi, eds., *Senkanki no Nippon gaiko* [Japanese Foreign Policy During the Interwar Period] (Tokyo, 1984), pp. 65–96; Pusey, *Hughes*, pp. 512–516.

33. Izumi Hirobe, "American Attitudes Toward the Japanese Immigration Question, 1924–1931," *JAEAR*, 2 (Fall 1993): 275–280; Sandra C. Taylor, *Advocate of Understanding* (Kent, OH, 1984), is the standard biography of Gulick, especially for his work in Japan.

34. Bamba, *Japanese Diplomacy*, pp. 157, 158, 214, 119.

35. Ibid., pp. 196–198; Asada, *Ryodai Senkan no Nichi-Bei kankei*, p. 300 for Japanese attempts to understand the act; Akira Iriye, "The Failure of Economic Expansionism, 1918–1931," in Bernard Silberman and Harry Harootunian, eds., *Japan in Crisis* (Princeton, 1974), pp. 259–260; Viscount Kikujiro Ishii, *Diplomatic Commentaries*, translated and edited by William R. Langdon (Baltimore, 1936), pp. 306–307.

36. Iriye, "Failure," pp. 254–255, 259–260; Bamba, *Japanese Diplomacy*, pp. 297–298; MacVeagh to Kellogg, Aug. 2, 1926, 790.94 / 13, box 7112, NA, RG 59 on Pan-Asian fiasco; Sadako N. Ogata, *Defiance in Manchuria* (Berkeley, 1964), p. 39.

37. Gardner, *Safe*, pp. 322–323; C. F. Remer, *Foreign Investments in China* (New York, 1933), p. 274; Grosvenor Jones to Hoover, Aug. 7, 1926, Commerce, Official Files, box 230, Hoover Papers, for Rockefeller involvement.

38. Asada, *Ryodai Senkan no Nichi-Bei kankei*, pp. 343–344 on Japan-U.S. banking cooperation; FO Minute, Ashley Clarke, May 27, 1944, and enclosed memorandum by Sir J. Pratt, FO 371 F2592 / 1787 / 10, PRO; Iriye, "Japan's Policies," pp. 436–437.

39. Asada, "Japan's 'Special Interests,' " p. 62 on "Shidehara period"; Iriye, "Failure," pp. 245–247; Duus, Introduction, pp. 36–37; Bamba, *Japanese Diplomacy*, p. 52.

40. Iriye, *China and Japan*, pp. 55–56; Ogata, *Defiance*, p. 8; Nish, *Japanese Foreign Policy*, p. 155, for Shidehara quote; background on this economic perspective is in Hirano, "Nishihara jakkan kara shinshikoku jakkandan 3," pp. 309–314.

41. Hosoya, "Washinton taisei no tokushitsu to henyo," pp. 4, 6; Pauline Tompkins, *American-

Russian Relations in the Far East (New York, 1949), chapter 9, and especially p. 212; Beasley, *Japanese Imperialism,* p. 171; Iriye, "Japan's Policies," p. 438.

42. Memorandum for Hoover from Batchelder, Nov. 22, 1921, Commerce, Official File, box 170, Hoover Papers; Chernow, *House of Morgan,* pp. 234–236.

43. Hoover to Hughes, April 29, 1922, Secretary's Files, Hoover Papers; Parrini, *Heir,* pp. 194–195, 202–203; Taichiro Mitani, "Manchuria: American Capital and Japanese Special Interests in the 1920s," in Ian Nish, ed., *Some Foreign Attitudes to Republican China* (London, 1980), pp. 1–3, 6–12.

44. Gardner, *Safe,* pp. 315–317; Chernow, *House of Morgan,* pp. 236–237, 338.

45. Warren I. Cohen, *Empire Without Tears* (New York, 1987), pp. 80–81; Ogata, *Defiance,* pp. 7–8.

46. Bamba, *Japanese Diplomacy,* pp. 15, 25–26, 40; Nish, *Japanese Foreign Policy,* pp. 152–153; Ogata, *Defiance,* pp. 10–11.

47. Mitani, "Manchuria," pp. 12–24.

48. Barnhart, *Japan Prepares,* p. 51; Ogata, *Defiance,* pp. 10–13; Iriye, *China and Japan,* p. 51.

49. Ogata, *Defiance,* pp. 16–17; Beasley, *Japanese Imperialism,* pp. 187–188.

50. Nish, *Japanese Foreign Policy,* p. 164.

51. U.S. Department of Commerce, *Historical Statistics of the United States* (Washington, DC, 1961), p. 564.

52. "The Future of Our Foreign Trade," March 16, 1926, Secretary of Commerce Official File, Foreign Trade, 1926, Hoover Papers; Frank Costigliola, *Awkward Dominion* (Ithaca, NY, 1985), chapter 1; "Business Depression and Policies of Government," June 15, 1931, Public Statements, AG1, vol. 52, no. 1587, Hoover Papers; Castle Diaries, June 29 and Dec. 31, 1930.

53. Castle Diaries, May 3, 1931; "Business Depression," Hoover Papers.

54. Charles Kindleberger, *The World in Depression, 1929–1939* (Berkeley, 1973), p. 59; Sato Kazuo, "Nichi-Bei boeki to Nihon keizai no fukinkan seicho" [Japan-U.S. Trade and the Imbalance of Growth in the Japanese Economy], in Hosoya and Makoto, eds., *Washinton taisei to Nichi-Bei kankei,* pp. 502–506 for silk and cotton goods and rice; Barnhart, *Japan Prepares,* p. 65; Allen, *Economic History,* pp. 106–115 on Japanese consolidation; Beasley, *Japanese Imperialism,* pp. 236–237 on comparison of trade; Oct. 11, 1931, Saionji Memoirs for ties between New York and Japan's gold reserve crisis.

55. Kindleberger, *World,* p. 144; Allen, *Economic History,* pp. 108–109; Bamba, *Japanese Diplomacy,* p. 47; Duus, Introduction, p. 22, has Chamber of Commerce quote; ibid., pp. 23–24 on labor; Tatsunosuke Ueda, "Some Aspects of Industrial Japan," *The World Tomorrow,* 13 (November 1930): 459–460 on "warm-feeling principle."

56. Sato, "Nichi-Bei boeki to Nihon keizai no fukinkan seicho," pp. 502–510 for economic causes of rural breakdown; Duus, Introduction, p. 20, on lack of government control; *Monthly Labor Review,* 33 (August 1931): 396–399; *Current History,* 33 (December 1930): 479 has note on suicides; James T. Shotwell, "The Fateful Dilemma of Young Japan," *New York Times Magazine,* March 2, 1930, pp. 4ff; Beasley, *Japanese Imperialism,* pp. 175–176.

57. Chernow, *House of Morgan,* pp. 342–343; Castle Diaries, March 2, April 26, 1930.

58. Nish, *Japanese Foreign Policy,* pp. 165–166, 173–174; Iriye, "Japan's Policies," p. 440; Beasley, *Japanese Imperialism,* p. 173.

59. Asada, *Ryodai senkan no Nichi-Bei kankei,* p. 179 for Japanese divisions over 1930 talks; Millett and Maslowsky, *Common Defense,* p. 373; Nish, *Japanese Foreign Policy,* pp. 166–170; Castle Diaries, May 31, 1930, Feb. 15, 1930 (for Shidehara quote).

60. Castle Diaries, Jan. 31, 1930, on Japanese fear of U.S. war over China; Castle to Stimson, Jan. 31, 1930, Foreign Affairs-China, 1930, box 1-G / 847, Hoover Papers; Iriye, "Japan's Policies," p. 441 has Ishiwara quote; Ogata, *Defiance,* pp. 28–29; *New York Times,* June

6, 1930, p. 6 has Inoue quote; *Current History,* 33 (December 1930): 480 for Hamaguchi quote.
61. Ogata, *Defiance,* p. 29; Castle Diaries, March 4, 1931; *New York Times,* Dec. 11, 1930, p. 7; ibid., March 13, 1931, p. 1.

Chapter VI

1. John G. Roberts, *Mitsui. Three Centuries of Japanese Business,* 2nd ed. (New York, 1989), p. 259; Justus D. Doenecke, *The Diplomacy of Frustration: The Manchurian Crisis of 1931–1933 as Revealed in the Papers of Stanley K. Hornbeck* (Stanford, 1981), p. 7; Michael A. Barnhart, *Japan Prepares for Total War* (Ithaca, NY, 1987), pp. 28–29; W. G. Beasley, *Japanese Imperialism, 1894–1945* (New York, 1991), pp. 188–190.
2. Peter Katzenstein and Nobuo Okawara, *Japan's National Security* (Ithaca, NY, 1993), p. 19; Chalmers Johnson, *MITI and the Japanese Miracle* (Stanford, 1981), pp. 93–94, 98–104, 112–115.
3. Richard J. Samuels, *"Rich Nation, Strong Army"; National Security and the Technological Transformation of Japan* (Ithaca, NY, 1994), pp. 93–99; Barnhart, *Japan Prepares,* pp. 24–25.
4. Katzenstein and Okawara, *Japan's National Security,* pp. 13–15; Robert J. Smith, *Japanese Society* (Cambridge, UK, 1983), pp. 129–130; Ian Nish, *Japanese Foreign Policy, 1869–1942* (London, 1977), p. 255.
5. Peter Duus, Introduction to Duus, ed., *Cambridge History of Japan.* Vol. 6. *The Twentieth Century* (Cambridge, UK, 1988), pp. 15–16, has the 1930 quote; Akira Iriye, "The Failure of Economic Expansionism," in Bernard Silberman and Harry Harootunian, eds., *Japan in Crisis* (Princeton, 1974), p. 265; Sadako N. Ogata, *Defiance in Manchuria* (Berkeley, 1964), pp. 35–36 has Matsuoka quote.
6. Hiroyuki Agawa, *The Reluctant Admiral: Yamamoto and the Imperial Navy,* translated by John Bester (Tokyo, 1979), p. 4; Ogata, *Defiance,* pp. 44–45; July 13, 1931, Saionji Memoirs, esp. pp. 5–10; Beasley, *Japanese Imperialism,* p. 182; Doenecke, *Diplomacy of Frustration,* pp. 9–10; Barnhart, *Japan Prepares for War,* p. 29.
7. Ogata, *Defiance,* pp. 17–19, 42–43; July 13, 1931, Saionji Memoirs; "Imperial Japanese Army in Manchuria, 1894–1945," in U.S. Army, *Japan, War in Asia and the Pacific* (New York, 1980), pp. 66–67; Doenecke, *Diplomacy of Frustration,* p. 9.
8. Ogata, *Defiance,* pp. 45–49; Sept. 23, 1931, Saionji Memoirs; Beasley, *Japanese Imperialism,* pp. 192–193.
9. Sept. 23, 1931, Saionji Memoirs, esp. p. 74; Barnhart, *Japan Prepares,* pp. 32–33; Ogata, *Defiance,* pp. 42, 63–67, 76.
10. Castle Diaries, Aug. 24 and Sept. 9, 1931; Doenecke, *Diplomacy of Frustration,* pp. 3–4; Ogata, *Defiance,* p. 72.
11. *New York Times,* Oct. 14, 1963, p. A29; Castle Diaries, June 29, 1930; ibid., Jan. 12, March 8, 1931, and Jan. 24, 1930, on discussion with Nelson Johnson; ibid., Sept. 29, 1931, wishing it had not happened, Oct. 6, 1931. Castle to Johnson, Oct. 13, 1930, Castle Papers—China, Hoover Papers.
12. Doenecke, *Diplomacy of Frustration,* pp. 10–16.
13. *Washington Post,* Oct. 14, 1962, p. B2 for Castle's obituary; Castle Diaries, Sept. 7, 1929, Dec. 31, 1931; Doenecke, *Diplomacy of Frustration,* p. 11; Henry L. Stimson and McGeorge Bundy, *On Active Service in Peace and War* (New York, 1947), p. 192.
14. Elting E. Morison, *Turmoil and Tradition: The Life and Times of Henry L. Stimson* (Boston, 1960), pp. 373–374; Sept. 22, 1931, and Jan. 8, 1932, Stimson Diary; Doenecke, *Diplomacy of Frustration,* p. 15; Castle Diaries, Dec. 27, 1930, for Stimson on "White races"; "Memorandum of Transatlantic Telephone Conversation Between Secretary Stimson,

Norman Davis, and Hugh Wilson," Sept. 23, 1931, Presidential Papers, Foreign Affairs, Far East (Japanese Incident), Hoover Papers.

15. Doenecke, *Diplomacy of Frustration,* pp. 13–14; Walter Lippmann, *Interpretations, 1931–1932* (New York, 1932), pp. 187–189.

16. Ogata, *Defiance,* p. 87; Doenecke, *Diplomacy of Frustration,* pp. 16–17; Castle Diaries, Oct. 10, 1931; Ron Chernow, *The House of Morgan* (New York, 1990), pp. 339–340.

17. Lippmann, *Interpretations,* pp. 191–192; "Transatlantic Telephone Conversation between Secretary Stimson and General Dawes, Paris, Nov. 19, 1931, 11:00," in Presidential Papers, Foreign Affairs, Far East (Japanese Incident), Hoover Papers; Doenecke, *Diplomacy of Frustration,* pp. 20–23; Castle Diaries, Dec. 7, 1931, on blockade.

18. Barnhart, *Japan Prepares,* p. 65; Castle Diaries, Dec. 23, 1931, on cable to Tokyo; Oct. 2, 1931, Saionji Memoirs; Nish, *Japanese Foreign Policy,* p. 180; Ogata, *Defiance,* p. 138; Doenecke, *Diplomacy of Frustration,* pp. 24–25.

19. Doenecke, *Diplomacy of Frustration,* p. 26; Lippmann, *Interpretations,* p. 200; Hornbeck to Stimson, Feb. 7, 1933, on Feb. 6 memorandum in Lot File 244, General Records of the . . . Far Eastern Division, 1932–1941, box 2, NA, RG 59.

20. Armin Rappaport, *Henry L. Stimson and Japan, 1931–1933* (Chicago, 1963), pp. 148–149 on business support; Doenecke, *Diplomacy of Frustration,* pp. 28–30; Chernow, *House of Morgan,* p. 343; "Memorandum of Transatlantic Telephone Conversation," between Stimson and Simon, Feb. 13, 1932, Presidential Papers, Foreign Affairs, Far East (Japanese Incident), Hoover Papers, on Japan fearing both; Lippmann, *Interpretations,* pp. 224–225; Stimson, *Active Service,* pp. 243–244, has Hoover quote; Hornbeck's view of British problem is in "Manchuria Situation. . . ." Feb. 17, 1921, folder January–February 1932, box 453, Hornbeck Papers, Hoover Institution Stanford, California. I am indebted to Anne Foster for this Hornbeck document.

21. Stimson, *Active Service,* pp. 246–256.

22. Ogata, *Defiance,* pp. 145–146, 152–154; Hugh Byas, *Government by Assassination* (New York 1942), pp. 24–30.

23. Ogata, *Defiance,* pp. 156–161; Nish, *Japanese Foreign Policy,* pp. 175–176; Attachment in Hamilton to Castle, June 13, 1932, F / HS 790.94 / 29 box 4396, NA, RG 59, has Uchida quote; see also Akira Iriye, "The Failure of Military Expansionism," in James Morley, ed., *Dilemmas of Growth in Prewar Japan* (Princeton, 1971), p. 445.

24. Ogata, *Defiance,* pp. 159–161, 173–174; Nish, "The Showa Emperor and the End of the Manchurian Crisis," *Japan Forum,* 1 (October 1989): 266–268.

25. Henry L. Stimson, "Bases of American Foreign Policy During the Past Four Years," *Foreign Affairs,* 11 (April 1933): 383; Stimson to Root, Dec 14, 1931, Presidential Papers, Foreign Affairs, Far East (Japanese Incident), Hoover Papers; Stimson to Lippmann, May 26, 1932, Baker Papers; Castle Diaries, Dec. 14, 1931; Grew to Stimson, Sept. 23, 1932, F/ HS 790.94/31, box 4396, NA, RG 59; Ogata, *Defiance,* p. 132 on Kwantung Army; Grew to Hull, May 11, 1933, enclosed in Hull to the President, May 27, 1933, PSF: Japan, Roosevelt Library.

26. Akira Iriye, *China and Japan in the Global Setting* (Cambridge, MA, 1992), pp. 68–69.

27. Charles P. Kindleberger, *The World in Depression, 1929–1939* (Berkeley, 1973), pp. 166–167; Duus, Introduction, pp. 41–42 on the "new bureaucrats"; Barnhart, *Japan Prepares for War,* p. 67; John W. Masland, "Commercial Influence Upon American Far Eastern Policy, 1937–1941," *PHR,* 11 (September 1942): 282.

28. Jan. 9, 1933, Stimson Diary.

29. Matsuoka speech at Council on Foreign Relations, March 27, 1933, Record of Meetings, vol. V (7/33–6/35), CFR.

30. "China-Economic Matters," May 2, 1933, Lot File 244, General Records of the Far Eastern Division, 1932–1941, box 1, NA, RG 59; *News-Week,* April 28, 1934, pp. 7–8; *New York Times,* April 21, 1934, p. 8.

31. Nish, *Japanese Foreign Policy*, pp. 197, 210 on Hirota; Iriye, *China and Japan*, p. 77; Beasley, *Japanese Imperialism*, p. 197; Herbert Feis, *1933: Characters in Crisis* (Boston, 1966), pp. 299–300; *New York Times*, April 29, 1934, section 8, p. 1; *New Republic*, May 2, 1934, p. 323 esp; ibid., May 16, 1934, p. 14; *News-Week*, April 28, 1934, pp. 7–8; an alternative view of the Amau statement is Inoue Toshikazu, *Kiki no naka no kyocho gaiko: Nitchu senso ni itaru taigai seisaku no kesei to tenkai* [A Conciliatory Foreign Policy in the Midst of Crisis: The Formation and Development of Japanese Foreign Policy Until the Sino-Japanese War] (Tokyo, 1993), pp. 118–129.

32. *The Peiping Chronicle*, Sept. 7, 1932, p. 6, has Kaneko's article; Hornbeck to Hull, Jan. 27, 1934, with attachment, 790 94/65 box 4396, NA, RG 59; George H. Blakeslee, "The Japanese Monroe Doctrine," *Foreign Affairs*, 11 (July 1933): 680.

33. "Summary of the Morning Newspapers . . . Nov. 7, 1933," box 18, Russian file, Moore Papers; Pauline Tompkins, *American-Russian Relations in the Far East* (New York, 1949), chapter 12 for discussion of the "nutcracker"; Hornbeck to Hull, Oct. 28, 1933, and Hornbeck to Phillips, Oct. 31, 1933, 711.6./333, NA, RG 59, on reassuring Japan; Feis, *1933*, pp. 329–330; Nish, *Japanese Foreign Policy*, p. 195.

34. Dean Acheson, *Present at the Creation* (New York, 1969), pp. 9–10.

35. Chernow, *House of Morgan*, p. 345, on Lamont; Allan R. Millett and Peter Maslowski, *For the Common Defense* (New York, 1984), p. 377; Warren Cohen, *America's Response to China* (New York, 1980), pp. 139–140; Barnhart, *Japan Prepares*, pp. 41–42, 66, 116, esp. good on silver purchases.

36. Agawa, *Yamamoto*, pp. 33–35; Inoue, *Kiki no naka no kyocho gaiko*, pp. 172–176; Barnhart, *Japan Prepares*, pp. 61–62, 116–117; Cohen, *America's Response*, p. 136; Masland, "Commercial," p. 234 for the National Foreign Trade Council quote.

37. *New York Times*, Feb. 26, 1936, in *NYT-GCI*, pp. 206–207; Duus, Introduction, p. 37; Nish, *Japanese Foreign Policy*, pp. 221–222; Beasley, *Japanese Imperialism*, pp. 180–181, 204–205.

38. Beasley, *Japanese Imperialism*, pp. 201–203.

39. Inoue, *Kiki no naka no kyocho gaiko*, pp. 269, 273–274; Nish, *Japanese Foreign Policy*, pp. 214–215, 228–229.

40. Duus, Introduction, p. 16; Iriye, *China and Japan*, p. 68.

41. Yoshitake Oka, *Konoe Fumimaro*, translated by Shumpei Okamoto and Patricia Murray (Tokyo, 1983), pp. 3–9, 16–19, 29–38; Nish, *Japanese Foreign Policy*, pp. 218–219, has good sketch; John K. Emmerson, *The Japanese Thread* (New York, 1978), pp. 104–105.

42. Barnhart, *Japan Prepares*, pp. 28–83, 84–89, 91, 118.

43. David Green, *Shaping Political Consciousness* (Ithaca, NY, 1987), p. 144. Wayne Cole, *Roosevelt and the Isolationists, 1932–1945* (Lincoln, NE, 1983), pp. 242–243; Barnhart, *Japan Prepares*, pp. 119–120.

44. Barnhart, *Japan Prepares*, p. 121; Cole, *Roosevelt*, p. 244.

45. Bartlett, *Record*, pp. 577–580; Cole, *Roosevelt*, pp. 243–244; Barnhart, *Japan Prepares*, p. 125.

46. "4th Meeting, Brussels Conf." box 5, Meetings, Nov. 1937, Davis Papers; Barnhart, *Japan Prepares*, p. 124; Lloyd C. Gardner, *Economic Aspects of New Deal Diplomacy* (Madison, WI, 1963), pp. 95–96; Richard J. Barnet, *The Rockets' Red Glare* (New York, 1990), has FDR-Welles quote, p. 218.

Chapter VII

1. Irvine H. Anderson, Jr., *The Standard-Vacuum Oil Company and United States East Asian Policy, 1933–1941* (Princeton, 1975), pp. 107–109; *New York Times*, Dec. 13, 1937, and Dec.

19, 1937, in *NYT-GCI*, pp. 109–110; *New York Times,* May 13, 1994, for recent figures; Richard J. Barnet, *The Rockets' Red Glare* (New York, 1990), p. 201, on Townsend; Wayne S. Cole, *Roosevelt and the Isolationists, 1932–1945* (Lincoln, NE, 1983), p. 252.

2. Waldo Heinrichs, *Threshold of War* (New York, 1988), pp. 8–9 for the 1938 shift; Anderson, *Standard-Vacuum,* pp. 110–111; Quincy Wright and Carl J. Nelson, "American Attitudes Toward Japan and China, 1937–38," *POQ,* 3 (January 1939): 47–49; Conversation, Jan. 16, 1938, Presidential Diaries, book #1, Morgenthau Diaries; ibid., April 1, 1938, book #1, on FDR panicking: Allan R. Millett and Peter Maslowski, *For the Common Defense* (New York: 1984), pp. 387–388, 394.

3. Cole, *Roosevelt,* pp. 248–249; John W. Masland, "Commercial Influence Upon American Far Eastern Policy, 1937–1941," *PHR,* 11 (September 1942): 290; Akira Iriye, *China and Japan in the Global Setting* (Cambridge, MA, 1992), pp. 162–163; Mira Wilkins, "The Role of U.S. Business," in Dorothy Borg and Shumpei Okamoto, eds., *Pearl Harbor as History* (New York, 1973), pp. 348–349.

4. Kaoru Sugihara, "Japan as an Engine of the Asian International Economy, 1880–1936," *Japan Forum,* 2 (April 1990): 140.

5. Richard J. Barnet, *The Alliance* (New York, 1983), p. 84 on Mitsui; Michael A. Barnhart, *Japan Prepares for Total War* (Ithaca, NY, 1987), pp. 101, 112–113, has octopus quote; Memorandum by Hornbeck, Sept. 28, 1938, 790.94/85, box 4396, NA, RG 59, has a more sanguine view of Japan's position in China.

6. Maki, *Documents,* pp. 78–79; Barnhart, *Japan Prepares,* pp. 109–113, 131–132.

7. C. A. MacDonald, *The United States, Britain and Appeasement, 1936–1939* (New York, 1981), pp. x, 148–150; Barnhart, *Japan Prepares,* pp. 133–134; Conversation, June 19, 1939, book #1, Morgenthau Diaries.

8. Hosoya Chihiro, *Ryo taisenkan no Nihon gaiko, 1914–1945* [Japanese Foreign Policy in the Period Between the Two World Wars] (Tokyo, 1988), pp. 283–284 for Japan's view of commercial treaty revocation; Cole, *Roosevelt,* pp. 347–352.

9. Aruga Tadashi, "Japanese Scholarship in the History of U.S.-East Asian Relations," Manuscript in author's possession (1993), pp. 21–22.

10. Hosoya, *Ryo taisenkan no Nihon gaiko,* pp. 195–198; Yohitake Oka, *Five Political Leaders of Modern Japan,* translated by Andrew Fraser and Patricia Murray (Tokyo, 1986), p. 219; Ian Nish, *Japanese Foreign Policy, 1869–1942* (London, 1977), pp. 231–232, for USSR clashes.

11. Ronald P. Toby, "Contesting the Centre," *IHR,* 7 (August 1985): 354–356 for seventeenth-century background; W. G. Beasley, *Japanese Imperialism, 1894–1945* (New York, 1991), pp. 223–225, 233, 244; Martin Gilbert, *The Churchill War Papers.* Vol. I. *At the Admiralty* (New York, 1993), p. 401.

12. Hosoya, *Ryo taisenkan no Nihon gaiko,* pp. 283–286.

13. Allan R. Millett and Peter Maslowski, *For the Common Defense* (New York, 1984), pp. 395–397; Barnhart, *Japan Prepares,* pp. 186–188; July 9, 1940, Stimson Diary.

14. Anderson, *Standard-Vacuum,* frontispiece, has Grew "sword of Damocles" quote; Oka Yoshitake, *Konoe Fumimaro* (Tokyo, 1983), pp. 97–98; Nish, *Japanese Foreign Policy,* pp. 235–236.

15. *New York Times,* Aug. 2, 1940, in *NYT-GCI,* p. 113; *New York Times,* June 30, 1940, in ibid., p. 32, for Fish quotes; Takemae Eiji, *Senryo sengoshi* [Occupation and Postwar Policy] (Tokyo, 1980), pp. 322–325 for cultural expansion; Beasley, *Japanese Imperialism,* pp. 226–227.

16. Melvyn P. Leffler, *The Specter of Communism* (New York, 1994), chapter 1; Masland, "Commercial," pp. 292–294.

17. *New York Times,* Sept. 28, 1940, in *NYT-GCI,* pp. 114–115.

18. Grew to Franklin Mott Gunther, Feb. 24, 1941, Letters, vol. 111–112, Grew Papers; *New*

York Times, Oct. 12, 1940, p. 6 for "catastrophe" quote; Hosoya, *Ryo taisenkan no Nihon gaiko,* pp. 291–292 for Matsuoka-Konoe views of U.S.; Masland, "Commercial," pp. 288 289, 298.

19. Cole, *Roosevelt,* p. 355, Warren I. Cohen, *America's Response to China* (New York, 1980), p. 150 on the White Committee; Robert A. Divine, *Foreign Policy and U.S. Presidential Elections, 1940–1948* (New York, 1974), pp. 82–83.

20. Oka, *Konoe,* pp. 94–105.

21. Hosoya, *Ryo taisenkan no Nihon gaiko,* pp. 204–206; Barnhart, *Japan Prepares,* pp. 198–200.

22. Maki, *Documents,* p. 95; Nish, *Japanese Foreign Policy,* pp. 241–242.

23. James McGregor Burns, *Roosevelt, Soldier of Freedom* (New York, 1970), p. 83.

24. Eden to Halifax, May 21, 1941, in Grew to Hornbeck, May 26, 1941, vol. 111–112, Grew Papers; Kimball, *Corresp.,* I, 136; Conrad C. Crane, *Bombs, Cities, and Civilians* (Lawrence, KA, 1993), p. 126 on sending bombers.

25. Barnhart, *Japan Prepares,* pp. 222–224; R. J. C. Butow, "Marching Off to War on the Wrong Foot," *PHR* (February 1994): 67.

26. Robert J. C. Butow, *Tojo and the Coming of the War* (Stanford, 1961), pp. 212–219; Barnhart, *Japan Prepares,* p. 238 on economic situation; Nish, *Japanese Foreign Policy,* pp. 239–245, 249.

27. "After Cabinet," July 18, 1941, book #4, Morgenthau Diaries.

28. Heinrichs, *Threshold,* pp. 20–21; Barnhart, *Japan Prepares,* pp. 227–228, 232, 239–240; Dean Acheson, *Present at the Creation* (New York, 1969), pp. 25–27; Hosoya Chihiro, "Japan's Decision for War in 1941," *Hitotsubashi Journal of Law and Politics,* 5 (April 1967): 28–29 on middle-level officers' response; Harold Ickes, *The Secret Diary of Harold Ickes.* 3 vols. (New York, 1953), III, 591–592.

29. Hosoya, *Ryo taisenkan no Nihon gaiko,* pp. 290, 292–294; Acheson, *Present at the Creation,* p. 27; Richard W. Steele, *Propaganda in an Open Society* (Westport, CT, 1985), p. 124 on FDR reticence; Justus D. Doenecke and John E. Wilz, *From Isolation to War, 1931–1941,* 2nd ed. (Arlington Heights, IL, 1991), pp. 122–123 for Rocky Mountain quote; Cole, *Roosevelt,* pp. 490–491, 493.

30. Millett and Maslowski, *Common Defense,* pp. 298–299; for baseball, Allen Guttmann, *Games and Empires* (New York, 1994), pp. 78–79.

31. Kimball, *Corresp.,* I, 229; Cole, *Roosevelt,* p. 490; Japanese Ambassador, Washington to Foreign Ministry, Tokyo, Sept. 19, 1941, in "C" to Prime Minister, Sept. 19, 1941, Signals Intelligence.

32. Barnhart, *Japan Prepares,* p. 170; Chalmers Johnson, *MITI and the Japanese Miracle* (Stanford, 1982), pp. 153–154; Grew to Castle, May 8, 1941, Letters, vol. 111–112, Grew Papers; Akira Iriye, *Power and Culture* (Cambridge, MA, 1981), pp. 29, 32.

33. Grew to Dr. James A. B. Scherer, July 24, 1941, Letters, vol. 111–112, Grew Papers; Grew to FDR, Sept. 22, 1941, ibid.; Robert A. Fearey, "My Year with Ambassador Joseph C. Grew, 1941–1942," *JAEAR,* 1 (Spring 1992): 99–105; Oka, *Konoe,* pp. 143–145.

34. Mitani Taichiro, "Senzen senchuki Nichi-Bei kankei ni okeru sin-Nichiha gaikakan no yakuwari; J. Barantain to E. Douman ni tsuite" [The Role of the Pro-Japanese American Diplomats in U.S.-Japan Relations, Before and During the Pacific War: Joseph Ballantine and Eugene Dooman], *Gaiko Forum,* 36–39 (September–December 1991): 83–86 for background.

35. James Fetzer, "Stanley K. Hornbeck and Japanese Aggression, 1941," *SHAFR Newsletter,* 24 (March 1993): 34–38; Memorandum of Conversation, Sept. 29, 1941, and enclosures, Lot File 244, General Records of the . . . Far Eastern Division, 1932–1941, box 2, NA, RG 59; Memorandum by Ballantine, Sept. 25, 1941, with comments by Hornbeck, ibid.; Schmidt of Far Eastern Division to Hull, Oct. 21, 1941, ibid.; State Department draft to Hirohito, Oct. 16, 1941, ibid., with last document containing the Chiang reference.

36. *FRUS: Japan,* II, 637–640.

37. Ibid., 645–661.

38. Ibid., 688; Memorandum of Conversation, Oct. 13, 1941, Lot File 244, General Records of the . . . Far Eastern Division, box 3, NA, RG 59; also in *FRUS: Japan,* II, 685 for Hamlet reference.

39. Oka, *Konoe,* pp. 155–159; Asada Sadao, *Ryodai Senkan no Nichi-Bei kankei: Kaigun to Seisaku kettei katei* [Japanese-American Relations Between the Wars: Naval Policy and the Decision-Making Process] (Tokyo, 1993), pp. 249–256, esp. p. 248 for "group think."

40. Butow, *Tojo,* pp. 6–11, 22–27, 280, 295–296; Doenecke and Wilz, *Isolation,* p. 129; "Memorandum for the President," drafted by Far Eastern Division, Oct. 17, 1941, Lot File, 244, box 3, NA, RG 59, has the "moderate" reference for Tojo.

41. *FRUS: Japan,* II, 690.

42. Ibid., 701–704.

43. Ibid., 753–756; Jonathan Utley, "The United States Enters World War II," in *Modern American Diplomacy,* ed. John M. Carroll and George C. Herring (Wilmington, DE, 1986), pp. 102–103; Schmidt to Ballantine, Nov. 4, 1941, Lot File 244, box 3, NA, RG 59, on Kurusu.

44. *FRUS: Japan,* II, 764–770; *FRUS, 1941,* IV, 685; Nov. 27, 1941, Stimson Diary; Usui Katsumi, "Nichi-Bei kaisen to Chugoku" [The Pacific War in China] in Hosoya Chihiro, *et al.,* eds., *Taiheiyo Senso* [The Pacific War] (Tokyo, 1993), pp. 51–67; Barnhart, *Japan Prepares,* p. 23.

45. Hosoya, "Japan's Decision," pp. 11–12, 15–16; Marquis Kido, *The Diary of Marquis Kido, 1931–1945* (Tokyo, 1983), pp. 310, 320–321; Nish, *Japanese Foreign Policy,* p. 246; Foreign Minister, Tokyo to Japanese Consul-General, Hong Kong, in circular letter, Nov. 21, 1941, in "C" to Prime Minister, Nov. 21, 1941, Signals Intelligence; Peter Duus, Introduction to Duus, ed., *The Cambridge History of Japan.* Vol. 6. *The Twentieth Century* (Cambridge, UK, 1988), p. 27 on Japan's dilemma.

46. Barnhart, *Japan Prepares,* pp. 270–271.

47. Conversation of May 17, 1941, book #4, Morgenthau Diaries; Steele, *Propaganda,* pp. 122–124; Ron Chernow, *The House of Morgan* (New York, 1990), p. 466; Ickes, *Secret Diary,* III, 387.

48. Justus D. Doenecke, "American Isolationism, 1939–1941," *Journal of Libertarian Studies,* 6 (Summer–Fall 1982): 211; Stephen C. Craft, "Deterring Aggression," *SHAFR Newsletter,* 24 (March 1993): 27–28; Doenecke and Wilz, *Isolationism,* p. 145 for FDR to Grew; British War Cabinet Minutes, Aug. 19, 1941, CAB 65, 84 (41), PRO; Cole, *Roosevelt,* pp. 12–13, 488–489.

49. Doenecke and Wilz, *Isolationism,* pp. 151–152 on FDR and Southeast Asia; Nov. 25, 1941, Stimson Diary; Japanese Foreign Minister to Japanese Ambassador, Berlin, Dec. 2, 1941, in "C" to Prime Minister, Dec. 2, 1941, Signals Intelligence; an excellent discussion is R. J. C. Butow's review of Gordon Prange's *At Dawn We Slept* in *JJS,* 9 (Summer 1983): 413–416.

50. Agawa, *Yamamoto,* pp. 1–2, 6–9, 21–24, 70–75, 127; Asada, *Ryodai Senkan no Nichi-Bei kankei,* pp. 247–248 on Yamamoto and army-navy differences; Gordon W. Prange, *At Dawn We Slept* (New York, 1982), pp. 9–15.

51. David Kahn, "U.S. Views of Germany and Japan in 1941," in Ernest R. May, ed., *Knowing One's Enemies* (Princeton, 1984), pp. 496–501 on intelligence foul-up; Butow, "Marching," pp. 76–78, for the lack of villains or conspiracies; Prange, *At Dawn,* pp. ix–x, 712–723, 727–736; Henry Clausen and Bruce Lee, *Pearl Harbor: Final Judgment* (New York, 1992), an extended argument on the chronology of the intercepts.

52. Harry S. Truman Library, "World War II Continued at the Library," *Whistlestop,* 21 (no. 2, 1993): 7; Millett and Maslowski, *Common Defence,* p. 401; *FRUS: Japan,* II, 787.

53. Dec. 7, 1941, Stimson Diary; Kimball, *Corresp.,* I, 281, for Churchill.

54. *FRUS: Japan*, II, 793–795.
55. Maki, *Documents*, pp. 104–105; Barnhart, *Japan Prepares*, p. 272, a good statement of these readings.
56. John Whitney Hall, "Japanese History in World Perspective," in Charles F. Delzell, ed., *The Future of History* (Nashville, TN, 1977), p. 185; a slightly different view that places some emphasis on irrationality is Hosoya, *Ryo taisenkan no Nihon gaiko*, pp. 293–294.
57. Oka, *Konoe*, p. 161; Marquis Kido, *Diary*, pp. 320–321; Dec. 8, 1941, Stimson Diary.

Chapter VIII

1. Walter McConaughy to Japan-American Society, Oct. 2, 1961, "State Department Press Release," FO 371 FJ103145/13, PRO.
2. Miwa Kimitada, *Japanese Policies and Concepts for a Regional Order in Asia, 1938–1940*, Sophia University, Institute of International Studies, 1983, pp. 1–23; Akira Iriye, *Power and Culture* (Cambridge, MA, 1981), pp. 64–66, 70; Michael A. Barnhart, *Japan Prepares for Total War* (Ithaca, NY, 1987), p. 9.
3. Jonathan G. Utley, "The United States Enters World War II," in John M. Carroll and George C. Herring, eds., *Modern American Diplomacy* (Wilmington, DE, 1986), p. 99 for Clayton; Henry Luce, *The American Century* (New York, 1941), pp. 16–19.
4. Hudson to Ashley Clarke, Feb. 10, 1943, FO 371 F877/877/61, PRO; Wendell L. Willkie, *One World* (New York, 1943).
5. Sept. 20, 1942, Leahy Diaries; Oct. 2, 1942, ibid.; Akira Iriye, *Power and Culture* (Cambridge, MA, 1981), pp. 72–73; Hoover to R. L. Jones, Feb. 18, 1942, Post-Presidential Individual: Lloyd-Jones, Hoover Papers.
6. John W. Dower, *War Without Mercy* (New York, 1986), pp. 203–247, esp. pp. 204, 217, 221, 225, 227, 229.
7. Allan R. Millett and Peter Maslowski, *For the Common Defense* (New York, 1984), p. 408; Robert Goralski, *World War II Almanac: 1931–1945* (New York, 1981), pp. 424–429 tables.
8. Richard J. Barnet, *The Rockets' Red Glare* (New York, 1990), p. 224; Kimball, *Corresp.*, I, 390.
9. Dower, *War Without Mercy*, p. 78 has Pyle's quote; Iriye, *Power and Culture*, p. 37; Roger Daniels, *Prisoners Without Trial* (New York, 1993), pp. 16, 78–80.
10. Daniels, *Prisoners Without Trial*, pp. 17–18, 28; Daizaburo Yui, "From Exclusion to Integration," *Hitotsubashi Journal of Social Studies*, 24 (December 1992): 56–57; Gary Y. Okihiro, *Margins and Mainstreams* (Seattle, WA, 1994), p. 169 has the "viper" quote.
11. Richard Polenberg, ed., *America at War* (New York, 1968), pp. 98–102, 103–107.
12. Richard Polenberg, *One Nation Divisible* (New York, 1980), pp. 78–81, 84; Daniels, *Prisoners Without Trial*, pp. 40–41, 47–48; Okihiro, *Margins*, p. 137; Ronald Takaki, *A Different Mirror* (Boston, 1993), pp. 378–380.
13. Paul Gorden Lauren, *Power and Prejudice* (Boulder, CO, 1988), pp. 132–133 has Dewitt and immigration official quotes; Sandra Taylor, *Jewel of the Desert* (Berkeley, 1993) is a major case study of internment.
14. Geoffrey S. Smith, "Doing Justice," *Public Historian*, VI (Summer 1984): 83–97; Daniels, *Prisoners Without Trial*, p. 64; Takaki, *Different Mirror*, pp. 376–377; *New York Times*, July 20, 1994, p. B1.
15. Daniels, *Prisoners Without Trial*, pp. 3–4, 88; Takaki, *Different Mirror*, pp. 400–402; Barnet, *Rockets' Red Glare*, pp. 230–231; Yui, "From Exclusion to Integration," pp. 55–68.
16. *New York Times*, July 20, 1994, p. B1; Clayton R. Koppes and Gregory D. Black, *Hollywood Goes to War* (Berkeley, 1990), pp. 60, 250–253; Polenberg, *One Nation*, pp. 51–52; *Boston Globe*, Aug. 1, 1993, pp. B21, B25, a fascinating analysis by Jon Haber and John Galligan.

17. Koppes and Black, *Hollywood*, p. 248; Polenberg, *One Nation Divisible*, pp. 69–70; Iriye, *Power and Culture*, p. 76; Lauren, *Power and Prejudice*, pp. 13, 201 for Lippmann quote.

18. Theodore Friend, *The Blue-Eyed Enemy* (Princeton, 1988), p. 279; Millett and Maslowski, *Common Defense*, pp. 401–402; Paul Kennedy, *Strategy and Diplomacy, 1870–1945* (London, 1983), pp. 184–185.

19. Stanley L. Falk, "Douglas MacArthur and the War Against Japan," in William M. Leary, ed., *We Shall Return!* (Lexington, KY, 1988), pp. 2, 4, 58; *Washington Post*, Dec. 5, 1993, pp. C1–C5.

20. Millett and Maslowski, *Common Defense*, p. 401; Conrad C. Crane, *Bombs, Cities and Civilians* (Lawrence, KA, 1993), p. 122; Barnet, *Rockets' Red Glare*, p. 219 on 1942 elections; "Memorandum for General Marshall. . . ." from "Commander in Chief," July 15, 1942, PSF, container 3, Hopkins Papers.

21. Lt. Gen. H. H. Arnold to Roosevelt, *May 3, 1942*, PSF, Japan, FDR Library; Millett and Maslowski, *Common Defense*, p. 420; Koppes and Black, *Hollywood*, pp. 266–267.

22. Kennedy, *Strategy*, pp. 186–188; James Bamford, *The Puzzle Palace* (Boston, 1982), pp. 43–44 on COMINT.

23. Kimball, *Corresp.*, I, 507; Kennedy, *Strategy*, pp. 187–188.

24. The best, and critical, account on the two-track strategy, and how service rivalry shaped it, is Ronald H. Spector, *Eagle Against the Sun* (New York, 1985); Goralski, *World War II Almanac*, p. 263; Millett and Maslowski, *Common Defense*, pp. 407, 422.

25. For this and the previous paragraph, see John Welfield, *Empire in Eclipse* (London, 1988), p. 31 for Konoye group; Kimball, *Corresp.*, I, 305; David Halberstam, *The Next Century* (New York, 1991), pp. 58–59; Goralski, *World War II Almanac*, pp. 382, 421 has spending figures and ice cream story; Thomas Havens review of Ben-Ami Shillony, *Politics and Culture in Wartime Japan*, in *JJS*, 9 (Winter 1983): 185–186; Kennedy, *Strategy*, pp. 181–182 on Japan's decision making, and pp. 183–192; Barnhart, *Japan Prepares*, p. 197 on raw materials; Ian Nish, *Japanese Foreign Policy, 1869–1942* (London, 1977), p. 247 on Axis cooperation.

26. Dower, *War Without Mercy*, p. 231; James J. Weingartner, "Trophies of War," *Pacific Historical Review*, 61 (February 1992): 56–65.

27. Friend, *Blue-Eyed Enemy*, pp. 59–61, 281; W. G. Beasley, *Japanese Imperialism, 1894–1945* (New York, 1991), p. 245; Thomas R. Havens, *Fire Across the Sea* (Princeton, 1986), p. 15 on starvation in northern Vietnam.

28. Beasley, *Japanese Imperialism*, pp. 240–243, 248–249; Iriye, *Power and Culture*, p. 119, on Atlantic Charter comparison; Friend, *Blue-Eyed Enemy*, pp. 100–101, 260.

29. "President's Conversation at Luncheon," Nov. 13, 1942, PSF: United Nations, box 102, FDR Library; "Memorandum—Hopkins, Eden Visit," March 27, 1943, box 138, Hopkins Papers; Strang Foreign Office Minute, March 29, 1943, FO 371 F1878 / 25 / 10, PRO, especially for Butler comments on China; also Butler Minute on Clauson to Ashley Clarke, Oct. 25, 1943, FO 371 F5611 / 74 / 10, PRO.

30. "Joint Chiefs of Staff Strategic Plan for the Defeat of Japan," May 8, 1943, JCS 287 / 1, FDR Library; Report of talk from Dominions Office to Canada, etc., Jan. 12, 1944, FO 371 F118 / 66 / 61, PRO; Iriye, *Power and Culture*, pp. 44–45 for Japanese approach to China, also pp. 98–100, 109.

31. May 2, 1943, Leahy Diaries; E. J. Kahn, Jr., profile on Stilwell in *New Yorker*, April 8, 1972, p. 64; Millett and Maslowski, *Common Defense*, p. 434; *Washington Post*, Dec. 8, 1993, on dangers of flying the "Hump"; FDR to Admiral Brown, enclosure, Dec. 4, 1944, Map Room, Naval Aide, China, FDR Library.

32. Stettinius to Grew, May 24, 1944, Division of Far Eastern Affairs, box 217, Stettinius Papers; FDR to Chiang, Aug. 21, 1944, enclosed in Marshall to FDR, Aug. 18, 1944, Map Room, FDR Library; Jonathan Spence, *To Change China* (New York, 1980), pp. 263–264

has Stilwell quote; FDR to Admiral Brown, enclosure, Dec. 4, 1944, Map Room, Naval Aide, China, FDR Library.

33. *Life*, May 1, 1944, pp. 101–103, has White quote; "Special Information for the President," from Stettinius, Nov. 27, 1944, PSF: State Department, FDR Library; Gore-Booth to Far Eastern Department, Sept. 18, 1944, FO 371 F4552 / 357 / 10, PRO, for Pearl Buck allusion; FO Research Department, Oct. 9, 1944, FO 371 AN334 / 20 / 45, PRO, has survey of U.S. business reaction; Seymour to Sterndale Bennett, May 17, 1945, FO 371 F3172 / 127 / G61, PRO, for Hurley story.

34. Millett and Maslowski, *Common Defense*, pp. 442–444; Falk, "MacArthur," p. 15; Kennedy, *Strategy*, pp. 189–190.

35. William Branigan wrote a superb retrospective on Saipan in the *Washington Post*, June 15, 1994, pp. A27–A28; Millett and Maslowski, *Common Defense*, pp. 443–444.

36. Falk, "MacArthur," p. 10; John Ray Skates, *The Invasion of Japan* (Columbia, SC, 1994), p. 135; Kimball, *Corresp.*, III, 191–193 for MacArthur's alleged threat; Millett and Maslowski, *Common Defense*, pp. 444–445; Paolo E. Coletta review of Edward J. Drea's *MacArthur's Ultra Codebreaking* in *Pacific Historical Review*, 63 (February 1994): 118–119; Goralski, *World War II Almanac*, pp. 353–354.

37. *Washington Post*, Oct. 27, 1994, p. A34; Falk, "MacArthur," p. 19; Millett and Maslowski, *Common Defense*, p. 461; Spector, *Eagle Against the Sun*, pp. 416–417 compares Manila and Warsaw.

38. Kimball, *Corresp.*, III, 448–449.

39. Millett and Maslowski, *Common Defense*, pp. 457–462, is the major source for this and the preceding paragraph; Crane, *Bombs*, p. 132.

40. Akira Iriye, "Continuities in U.S.-Japan Relations, 1941–49," in Akira Iriye and Yonosuke Nagai, eds., *The Origins of the Cold War in Asia* (New York, 1977), pp. 380–382; Halifax to Foreign Office, Feb. 22, 1943, FO 371 F1317 / 1317 / 61, PRO.

41. Robert E. Ward, "Presurrender Planning," in Robert E. Ward and Sakamoto Yoshikazu, eds., *Democratizing Japan* (Honolulu, 1987), pp. 36–37; Mitani Taichiro, "Senzen senchuki Nichi-Bei kankei ni okeru sin-Nichiha gaikakan no yakuwari: J. Barantain to E. Douman ni tsuite" [The Role of the Pro-Japanese American Diplomats in U.S.-Japanese Relations, Before and During the Pacific War: Joseph Ballantine and Eugene Dooman], *Gaiko Forum*, 36–39 (September–December 1991): 67–69.

42. Hugh Borton, *American Presurrender Planning for Postwar Japan* (New York, 1967), pp. 12–13.

43. Mitani, "Senzen senchuki Nichi-Bei," pp. 69–71; Ward, "Presurrender," pp. 3–4, 9, 19–20.

44. Borton, *Planning*, pp. 15–17; Iriye, "Continuities," p. 386; Gabriel Kolko, *The Politics of War* (New York, 1968), p. 544 on Grew group; Ward, "Presurrender," pp. 7, 23–24.

45. Iriye, *Power and Culture*, pp. 126–127; Kolko, *Politics of War*, pp. 544–545.

46. Harriman to Hopkins, Sept. 10, 1944, Harriman file, Hopkins Papers; Borton, *Planning*, pp. 13, 30; Diane Shaver Clemens, *Yalta* (New York, 1970), p. 245 for FDR; *The Economist*, Aug. 26, 1944, pp. 267–268, received special Foreign Office attention.

47. Kimball, *Corresp.*, III, 524, on FDR and China; Lloyd C. Gardner, *Economic Aspects of New Deal Diplomacy* (Madison, WI, 1964), p. 310 quotes FDR; "Memorandum for the Secretary's Files," Quebec, Sept. 15, 1944, Morgenthau Diaries, book #6; Oct. 24, 1944, Leahy Diaries; J. C. Sterndale Bennett to War Cabinet Chiefs of Staff Committee, March 3, 1945, C.O.S. (45) 143 (O) CAB80.92, PRO, has summary of Indochina events; *FRUS, 1945, Berlin*, I, 939.

48. U.S. Congress, House, Committee on Armed Services, *United States–Vietnam Relations, 1945–1947*, 12 vols. (Washington, DC, 1971), I, A19–A20; "Record," vol. VI, April 8–14, 1945, Stettinius Papers for FDR's last words; Ernest Llewellyn Woodward, *British Foreign Policy in the Second World War* (London, 1962), pp. 534–535.

49. Millett and Maslowski, *Common Defense,* pp. 463–464; Goralski, *World War II Almanac,* pp. 392–394, 396, 400, 409.

50. Crane, *Bombs,* pp. 118–119 for Lovett quote, p. 120, pp. 133–136 for Stimson; Millett and Maslowski, *Common Defense,* p. 456; Grew to Frederic W. H. Stott, March 31, 1945, Letters, Grew Papers.

51. Harry S. Truman, *Where the Buck Stops,* ed. Margaret Truman (New York, 1989), pp. 205–206 for 1965 speech; Louis Morton, "Analysis of Decision," in Kent Roberts Greenfield, ed., *Command Decisions* (Washington, DC, 1960), pp. 394–396; Skates, *Invasion,* pp. 96–97, on gas warfare, pp. 237–238, p. 243 on Marshall; Barton J. Bernstein, "A Postwar Myth: 500,000 U.S. Lives Saved," *Bulletin of Atomic Scientists,* 42 (June–July 1986): 38–40; Barton J. Bernstein, "The Atomic Bombings Reconsidered," *Foreign Affairs,* 74 (January–February 1995): 149.

52. Private calendar notes, March 13, 1945, box 224, Stettinius Papers; Konstantin Pleshakov, "Taiheiyo Stalin no ketsudan" [The Pacific War: Stalin's Choices] in Hosoya Chihiro, *et al.,* eds., *Taiheiyo senso* [The Pacific War] (Tokyo, 1993), pp. 184–190.

53. Iriye, "Continuities," p. 392; Morton, "Decision," p. 396; *FRUS, 1945,* VII, 864–878.

54. Robert L. Messer, *The End of an Alliance* (Chapel Hill, NC, 1982), pp. 16–23, 51–70, 79–80; Borton, *Planning,* p. 24; Bernstein, "Atomic Bombings Reconsidered," pp. 142–146.

55. For this and the previous paragraph, see Memo from Hoover-Truman meeting, May 24, 1945, Post-Presidential Individual: Truman, Hoover Papers; Mitani, "Senzen senchuki Nichi-Bei," pp. 71–80 on Japan hands; Borton, *Planning,* pp. 21, 29; Kolko, *Politics of War,* p. 457; Skates, *Invasion,* p. 239 on Marshall; Grew to Randall Gould, April 14, 1945, Grew Papers; Grew to Judge Samuel I. Rosenman, June 16, 1945, Grew Papers.

56. For this and the previous paragraph, see Gregg Herken, *The Winning Weapon* (Princeton, 1988), pp. 13–14; Iokibe Makoto, *Nichi-Bei senso to sengo Nihon* [U.S.-Japan War and Postwar Japan] (Osaka, 1989), pp. 112–120 on Stimson and Kyoto; Martin Sherwin, *A World Destroyed* (New York, 1987), pp. 202–203, 229–231; July 24, 1945, Stimson Diary.

57. Townsend Hoopes and Douglas Brinkley, *Driven Patriot* (New York, 1992), pp. 208–209, 212.

58. June 6, 1945, Stimson Diary.

59. *New York Times,* Dec. 12, 1983, p. 18E; Herken, *Winning Weapon,* pp. 17–19; Messer, *End of an Alliance,* pp. 102–103; Pleshakov, "Taiheiyo Stalin no ketsudan," pp. 191–193.

60. Harry Truman, *Off the Record,* ed. Robert H. Ferrell (New York, 1980), p. 53; Melvyn Leffler, *A Preponderance of Power* (Stanford, 1992), p. 83.

61. July 17, 1945, Stimson Diary; Pleshakov, "Taiheiyo Stalin no ketsudan," pp. 195–198; Leffler, *Preponderance of Power,* pp. 83–89; Messer, *End of an Alliance,* pp. 103–104.

62. July 24, 1945, Stimson Diary; Barton J. Bernstein, "Research Note," *DH,* 16 (Winter 1992): 163–173 discusses alternatives and Truman's inaccurate recollection; Borton, *Planning,* p. 26.

63. OSS to State, "Source Unknown to JA," July 31, 1945, Lot Files 56D 225, 56D256, Records of the Bureau of Far Eastern Affairs, 1945–1953, NA, RG 59; Committee for the Compilation of Materials on Damage Caused by the Atomic Bombs in Hiroshima and Nagasaki, *Hiroshima and Nagasaki* (New York, 1981), pp. 11–21, 87–92; Sherwin, *World Destroyed,* p. 232 on U.S. prisoners; Donna R. Casella, "Rebirth and Reassessment," *Journal of American and Canadian Studies,* 4 (Autumn 1989): 133–138; Godfrey Hodgson, *The Colonel* (New York, 1990), pp. 337–338.

64. *New York Times,* Aug. 7, 1945 in *NYT-GCI,* pp. 133–135; Kai Bird, *The Chairman* (New York, 1992), p. 259; Barnet, *Rockets' Red Glare,* p. 265.

65. Committee for Compilation of Materials, *Hiroshima and Nagasaki,* pp. 27, 55–56, 115; Weingartner, "Trophies," has Truman on "a beast."

66. Herken, *Winning Weapon,* p. 21; Aug. 8, 1945, Leahy Diaries; Kolko, *Politics of War,* pp.

598–599, on Stalin and Japan; Sergei N. Goncharov, *et al.*, *Uncertain Partners* (Stanford, 1993), pp. 3, 9–10 for Stalin's policy; "Memorandum for the President," Aug. 11, 1945, Lot File 53D 444, NA, RG 59.

67. Letter to Editor from Robert Cowley, *New York Times*, Feb. 2, 1995, p. 16, on new Soviet documents.

68. Stephen S. Large, *Emperor Hirohito and Showa Japan* (London, 1992), pp. 117–119.

69. Yoshitake Oka, *Konoe Fumimaro* (Tokyo, 1983), pp. 171–174, which paraphrases the memorial; Iriye, *Power and Culture*, pp. 220–222; Welfield, *Empire*, pp. 32–35; Kolko, *Politics of War*, pp. 550–551.

70. James W. Morley, "The First Seven Weeks," *Japan Interpreter*, 6 (no. 2, 1970): 152–154 is important on Konoe; Kennedy, *Strategy*, pp. 193–194.

71. Robert J. C. Butow, *Japan's Decision to Surrender* (Stanford, 1954), pp. 140–149, and 243–244 for Potsdam Declaration text.

72. Butow, *Japan's Decision*, pp. 141, 243; Hata Ikuhiko, *Nihon saigunbi* [The Historical Record: Japan's Rearmament] (Tokyo, 1976), p. 17 has "double shock."

73. Hodgson, *The Colonel*, p. 338; Aug. 10, 1945, Stimson Diary; James Forrestal, *The Forrestal Diaries*, ed. Walter Millis (New York, 1951), p. 83; Barton J. Bernstein, "The Perils and Politics of Surrender," *PHR*, 46 (February 1977): 6–7; the U.S. reply is in Butow, *Japan's Decision*, p. 245; also David Robertson, *Sly and Able: A Political Biography of James F. Byrnes* (New York, 1994), pp. 434–437.

74. Butow, *Japan's Decision*, pp. 192–205; Iokibe, *Nichi-Bei senso to sengo Nihon*, pp. 115–124.

75. Bernstein, "Perils and Politics," pp. 9–17; Goralski, *World War II Almanac*, pp. 416–417.

76. Marquis Kido Koichi, *The Diary of Marquis Kido, 1931–1945* (Frederick, MD, 1984), pp. 448–450.

77. Butow, *Japan's Decision*, pp. 206–209, 218–220; Large, *Emperor Hirohito*, pp. 124–129.

78. Iokibe, *Nichi-Bei senso to sengo Nihon*, p. 125; rescript in Maki, *Documents*, pp. 123–124; a good review essay on prisoner treatment is Stanley L. Falk, "Prisoners of Japan," *JAEAR*, 4 (Fall 1995), esp. pp. 279–281; Oe Kenzaburo, *A Personal Matter* (New York, 1968), pp. vii–viii.

79. Theodore White, "The Danger from Japan," *New York Times Magazine*, July 28, 1985, pp. 19–21.

80. *New York Times*, Sept. 5, 1945, in *NYT-GCI*, pp. 142–143; Robertson, *Sly and Able*, pp. 434–437.

81. John K. Emmerson, *The Japanese Thread* (New York, 1978), p. 240; Bernstein, "Atomic Bombings Reconsidered," pp. 135–152; Sherwin, *World Destroyed*, chapters 8–9; Gar Alperovitz, *The Decision to Use the Atomic Bomb* (New York, 1995), esp. pp. 610–612 on the Nagasaki film, and pp. 629–670; important essays from *DH* collected in *Hiroshima in History and Memory*, ed. Michael L. Hogan (New York, 1996); and Ian Buruma's "The War Over the Bomb," *New York Review of Books*, Sept. 21, 1995, esp. p. 34 on Nagasaki.

82. Balfour to Foreign Office, Aug. 25, 1945, FO 371 AN2597 / 4 / 45, PRO; Barnet, *Rockets' Red Glare*, p. 264; William H. McNeill, *America, Britain, and Russia* (New York, 1953), p. 640 for a good overview of the Asian situation in late 1945.

Chapter IX

1. Christopher Thorne, *Allies of a Kind* (New York, 1978), pp. 688–690 for succinct overview; John Dower, *Japan in War and Peace* (New York, 1993), p. 163; "Cabinet Meeting, Friday, Aug. 2, 1946," in Notes on Cabinet Meetings, 1945–1946, by Matthew Connelly, HST Library, for Forrestal; Peter Duus, Introduction to Duus, ed., *The Cambridge History of Japan*. Vol. 6. *The Twentieth Century* (Cambridge, UK, 1988), p. 11.

2. Donovan, "Memorandum for the President," Sept. 17, 1945, OSS Memoranda for the President, Donovan Chronological File, box 15, HST Library; *FRUS, 1945*, II, 60, for mistrust of Soviets; Tang Tsou, *America's Failure in China, 1941–1950*, 2 vols. (Garden City, NY, 1955–56), II, 81; Sakamoto Yoshikazu, "The International Context of the Occupation of Japan," in Robert E. Ward and Sakamoto Yoshikazu, eds., *Democratizing Japan* (Honolulu, 1987), pp. 56–57.

3. Akira Iriye, "Continuities in U.S.-Japanese Relations, 1941–49," in Akira Iriye and Yonosuke Nagai, eds., *The Origins of the Cold War in Asia* (New York, 1977), p. 399; J. C. Donnelly Minute on Halifax to Foreign Office, Nov. 10, 1945, FO 371 AN3447 / 4 / 45, PRO.

4. Lloyd Gardner, *Economic Aspects of New Deal Diplomacy* (Madison, WI, 1964), pp. 308, 344; Lloyd Gardner, *Architects of Illusion* (Chicago, 1970), is important for the early fears of depression.

5. Thorne, *Allies of a Kind*, p. 675; "Cabinet Meeting, Friday, April 19, 1946," in Notes on Cabinet Meetings, 1945–1946, by Matthew Connelly, HST Library.

6. Maki, *Documents*, pp. 125–132 for initial U.S. post-surrender policy; "Cabinet Meeting, Friday, Oct. 26, 1945," in Notes on Cabinet Meetings, 1945–1946, by Matthew Connelly, HST Library.

7. John Dower, *War Without Mercy* (New York, 1986), pp. 300–301.

8. Homma Nagayo, *Utsuriyuku Amerika* [The Changing America] (Tokyo, 1991), pp. 243–244; Jacques Hersh, *The USA and the Rise of East Asia Since 1945* (London, 1993), for Aiichiro quote; Ronald McGlothlen, *Controlling the Waves* (New York, 1993), pp. 25, 56, on food crisis; Richard Barnet, *The Alliance* (New York, 1983), p. 64 for MacArthur quote, p. 67 for repatriation; G. C. Allen, *A Short Economic History of Modern Japan* (London, 1981), pp. 187–188.

9. Watanabe Akio, Preface to Watanabe, ed., *Sengo Nihon no taigai seisaku* [Postwar Japanese Foreign Policy] (Tokyo, 1985), pp. 2–3; "Cabinet Meeting, Friday, Feb. 1, 1946," in Notes on Cabinet Meetings, 1945–1946, by Matthew Connelly, HST Library; Barnet, *Alliance*, p. 63; FO Minute by Johnston, June 1, 1951, FO 371 FJ1027 / 1, PRO, on "useless body"; James Forrestal, *The Forrestal Diaries*, ed. Walter Millis (New York, 1951), p. 104; Melvyn Leffler, *A Preponderance of Power* (Stanford, 1992), pp. 90–91.

10. Harry Truman, *Off the Record,* ed. Robert H. Ferrell (New York, 1980), p. 47; Leahy to MacArthur, Oct. 2, 1945, RG 10, VIP Correspondence, Douglas MacArthur Library, Norfolk, VA.

11. Iokibe Makoto, *Nichi-Bei senso to sengo Nihon* [Japanese-American Relations in Postwar Japan] (Osaka, 1989), pp. 141–150 for a comparison of MacArthur and Perry; John K. Fairbank, "Digging Out Doug," *New York Review of Books,* Oct. 12, 1978, p. 16; Barnet, *Alliance*, pp. 62–64; Mitani Taichiro, "Senzen senchuki Nichi-Bei kankei ni okeru sin-Nichiha gaikokan no yakuwari: J. Barantain to E. Douman ni tsuite" [The Role of Pro-Japanese American Diplomats in Japanese-U.S. Relations, Before and During the Pacific War: Joseph Ballantine and Eugene Dooman], *Gaiko Forum,* 36–39 (September 1991–December 1991), esp. pp. 85–91 on Shogun allusion; *New York Times,* Sept. 8, 1945, in *NYT-GCI*, p. 148 on the breakdown; Sansom is quoted in Sir A. Gascoigne to Scott, Jan. 22, 1951, FO 371 FJ1019 / 3, PRO; Sir A. Gascoigne to Foreign Office, Feb. 6, 1951, FO 371, FJ1019 / 5 recalling Harriman saying MacArthur was a front-runner for 1948.

12. This and the previous paragraph are based on Robert E. Ward, "Presurrender Planning," in Robert E. Ward and Sakamoto Yoshikazu, eds., *Democratizing Japan* (Honolulu, 1987), pp. 11–16; Hugh Borton, *American Presurrender Planning for Postwar Japan* (New York, 1967), p. 27; Dower, *Japan in War and Peace*, pp. 166–167 on Japanese military; Akira Iriye, *The Cold War in Asia* (Englewood Cliffs, NJ, 1974), pp. 124–126; Igarashi Takashi, "Senso to senryo, (1941–1951)" [War and Occupation], in Hosoya Chihiro, ed., *Nichi-Bei*

kankei tsushi [Japan-U.S. Relations] (Tokyo, 1995), pp. 164–175 for photo story and Takami Jun quote; Stephen S. Large, *Emperor Hirohito and Showa Japan* (London, 1992), pp. 134–144, esp. on Hirohito as war criminal; Dower, *War Without Mercy*, p. 307.

13. Sir A. Gascoigne to Bevin, Feb. 6, 1951, FO 371 FJ1019 / 5, PRO, for Vining; U.S. Congress, Senate, *Executive Sessions of the Senate Foreign Relations Committee (Historical Series)*, vol. III, part 1 (Washington, DC, 1976), p. 290.

14. Kimitada Miwa, "Japan's Northern Territories," *Journal of American and Canadian Studies*, 6 (Autumn 1990): 6–7 on Byrnes deal; Committee for the Compilation of Materials on Damage Caused by the Atomic Bombs in Hiroshima and Nagasaki, *Hiroshima and Nagasaki* (New York, 1981), p. 12 on censorship; James W. Morley, "The First Seven Weeks," *Japan Interpreter*, 6 (no. 2, 1970): 151–164; Yoshitake Oka, *Konoe Fumimaro* (Tokyo, 1983), pp. 182–198; Kyoko Inoue, *MacArthur's Japanese Constitution* (Chicago, 1991), p. 7; *New York Times*, Oct. 5, 1945, p. A1; ibid., Oct. 10, 1945, p. A4 on Shidehara.

15. This and the following paragraph are especially drawn from Dower, *Japan in War and Peace*, pp. 211–212; Barnet, *Alliance*, pp. 76–78.

16. Major General Courtney Whitney, *MacArthur* (New York, 1956), pp. 263–311; Major General Charles A. Willoughby and John Chamberlain, *MacArthur, 1941–1951* (New York, 1954), p. 323; Barnet, *Alliance*, p. 69.

17. Dower, *Japan in War and Peace*, p. 166; Allen, *Short Economic History*, p. 219; Barnet, *Alliance*, pp. 67, 80–81; Justin Williams, Sr., "A Forum," and John Dower and Howard Schonberger, "A Rejoinder," *PHR*, 57 (May 1988): 188–189.

18. Eto Jun, *Mo hitotsu no sengoshi* [Another Postwar History] (Tokyo, 1978), pp. 474–476; Forrestal, *Forrestal Diaries*, p. 524; Barnet, *Alliance*, pp. 65, 70–71; *New York Times*, Nov. 12, 1948, in *NYT-GCI*, pp. 168–169.

19. Gascoigne to Bevin, Feb. 6, 1951, FO 371 FJ1019 / 5, PRO; Allen, *Short Economic History*, p. 222; Barnet, *Alliance*, pp. 74–75.

20. Susan J. Pharr, "The Politics of Women's Rights," in Ward and Sakamoto, eds., *Democratizing Japan*, pp. 222–224, 240–248; Dower, *War Without Mercy*, p. 308; Barnet, *Alliance*, p. 72; *New York Times*, April 13, 1946, in *NYT-GCI*, p. 159 on Kato Shizue; Gascoigne to Bevin, Feb. 6, 1951, FO 371 FJ1019 / 5, PRO; Carol Gluck, "Entangling Illusions," in Warren I. Cohen, ed., *New Frontiers in American–East-Asian Relations* (New York, 1983), pp. 192–193; Robert J. Smith, "The Sources and Proponents of 'Tradition' and 'Modernity' in Japanese Law," *Journal of Legal Pluralism and Unofficial Law*, 33 (1993): 231–237.

21. Inoue, *MacArthur's Japanese Constitution*, pp. 75–77, 266–270; a good summary by a central participant is Charles L. Kades, "The American Role in Revising Japan's Imperial Constitution," *PSQ*, 104 (Summer 1989): 217–220.

22. Kades, "American Role," pp. 225–230; Kyodo News Service, Japan Economic Newswire, May 2, 1992, p. 2 for Kades's use of "symbol." I am indebted to Professor Robert Smith for the Kyodo document.

23. This and the following paragraphs are based on Kades, "American Role," pp. 232–236; Dower, *Japan in War and Peace*, pp. 219, 228–229; Inoue, *MacArthur's Japanese Constitution*, pp. 230–262, 269–270 for the remarkable debate.

24. Kades, "American Role," pp. 236–238; Ward, "Presurrender," pp. 33–34; C. P. Scott Minute, April 16, 1951, on Gascoigne to Bevin, Feb. 6, 1951, FO 371 FJ1019, PRO.

25. W. Miles Fletcher, "Taiheiyo senso. . . ." [Economic Impact of the Pacific War on Japan], in Hosoya Chihiro, *et al.*, eds., *Taiheiyo senso* [The Pacific War] (Tokyo, 1993), pp. 381–383; Barnet, *Alliance*, p. 83 quotes Hadley, also p. 84; Geoffrey Gorer, "The Special Case of Japan," *POQ*, 7 (Winter 1943): 574; Allen, *Short Economic History*, p. 204; Yutaka Kosai, "Postwar Japanese Economy, 1945–1973," in Duus, ed., *The Twentieth Century*, pp. 496–497.

26. Allen, *Short Economic History*, p. 189; Leon Hollerman, "International Economic Con-

trols in Occupied Japan," *JAS,* 38 (no. 4, 1979): 710; Wallace Gagne, "Technology and Political Interdependence: Canada, Japan, and the United States," *JACS,* 9 (Spring 1992): 50.

27. Igarashi Takashi, "MacArthur's Proposal for an Early Peace with Japan and the Redirection of the Occupation," in Aruga Tadashi, ed., *United States Policy Toward East Asia, 1945–1950,* a volume of *JJAS,* I (1981), pp. 67–83, 86; *New York Times,* May 25, 1947, p. A25; ibid., June 2, 1947, p. A3.

28. U.S. Department of State, *Fortnightly Survey of American Opinion on International Affairs,* Sept. 4, 1946, pp. 2–3 on trade blocs; "Cabinet Meeting, Friday, Aug. 2, 1946," in Notes on Cabinet Meetings, 1945–1946, by Matthew Connelly, HST Library; Forrestal, *Forrestal Diaries,* pp. 179, 190; Daily Staff Summary, Feb. 5, 1947, Lot Files, NA, RG 59; Robert Divine, *Foreign Policy and U.S. Presidential Elections, 1940–1948* (New York, 1974), pp. 223, 245, 270.

29. *FRUS, 1947,* VI, 159, 184; Osborn to Clayton, with copy to Harriman, July 11, 1947, "Public Service, Secretary of Commerce . . . Japan," Harriman Papers.

30. Bruce Cumings, "Japan's Position in the World System," in Andrew Gordon, ed., *Postwar Japan as History* (Berkeley, 1993), p. 39 for Marshall quote in which italics are Marshall's emphasis; Minute by E. Dening, March 26, 1947, FO 371, UN2001 / 1754 / 78, PRO; Yoshikazu, "International Context," pp. 58–60.

31. Joseph M. Jones, *The Fifteen Weeks* (New York, 1955), has the Cleveland speech text; *Fortune* (February 1950): 67.

32. *Nippon Times,* March 28, 1948, in "Political . . . Tokyo," March 31, 1948, FO 371 F5396 / 662 / 23, PRO, for Draper; Hersh, *USA and Rise of East Asia,* p. 19; Vidya Prakash Dutt, ed., *East Asia . . . 1947–1950* (London, 1958), pp. 631–637 for Royall speech text.

33. Kennan's view is in his *Memoirs, 1925–1950* (Boston, 1967), pp. 271–368; an important and different view is Lloyd Gardner's analysis of Kennan in *Architects of Illusion* (Chicago, 1970), pp. 270–300.

34. Kennan, *Memoirs,* pp. 368–382; Leffler, *Preponderance,* p. 253.

35. Leffler, *Preponderance,* pp. 382, 389; *FRUS, 1948,* VI, 697, 712.

36. FRUS, 1948, VI, 712–794.

37. Ibid., 858–862; "CIA Research Reports: Japan-Korea, Security of Asia, 1946–1976," reel 2, Fletcher School Library, Tufts University.

38. Yoshikazu, "International Context," p. 63 on MacArthur opposition; Hersh, *USA and Rise of East Asia,* p. 16 on MacArthur and socialism; Williams, *et al.,* "Forum," pp. 212–213 for Schonberger analysis; Gascoigne to Dening, Jan. 10, 1948, FO 371 F1287 / 661 / 23, PRO; Gascoigne to Foreign Office, April 7, 1948, FO 371 F5237 / 662 / 23, PRO; Barnet, *Alliance,* p. 86; Hata Ikuhiko, *Shiroku: Nihon saigunbi* [The Historical Record: Japan's Rearmament] (Tokyo, 1976), p. 106 for Kades.

39. U.S. Department of State, *Monthly Survey of American Opinion* (July 1948): 9; Franks to Foreign Office, July 15, 1948, FO 371 F9870 / 662 / 23, PRO; Howard B. Schonberger, *Aftermath of War* (Kent, OH, 1989), esp. pp. 143–151; Williams, *et al.,* "Forum," p. 216 for Schonberger on Dooman.

40. *Sunday Chronicle* (London) clipping by Hughes in Tokyo, Aug. 15, 1948, in "Extract," Aug. 15, 1948, FO 371 F11450 / 662 / 23, PRO.

41. Shindo Eiichi, "Ashida Hitoshi and Postwar Reform" (in Japanese), *International Relations,* 85 (May 1987), esp. p. 62; *New York Times,* Oct. 7, 1948, p. A17; Oct. 15, 1948, p. A10.

42. John W. Dower, *Empire and Aftermath* (Cambridge, MA, 1988), pp. 36–38, 136–170, 400–401; John Welfield, *An Empire in Eclipse* (London, 1988), pp. 38–39; Barnet, *Alliance,* p. 79.

43. Dower, *Empire and Aftermath,* pp. 274, 422–423.

44. *FRUS, 1949*, VII, 640–642, 716–720 for Acheson and reparations; Hollerman, "International Economic Controls," p. 718 for Sears, Roebuck reference.

45. Williams, *et al.*, "Forum," p. 205 for Dower overview, also pp. 217–218 on purges; *New York Times*, Oct. 14, 1949, in *NYT-GCI*, p. 179; ibid., Oct. 22, 1949, p. 173; Barnet, *Alliance*, p. 81; Yoshikazu, "International Context," on purge and intellectuals; Igarashi Takeshi, "Reisen to kowa" [Cold War and Peace], in Watanabe, *Sengo Nihon no taigai seisaku*, pp. 48–60.

46. Takemae Eiji, *Senryo sengoshi* [Occupation and Postwar Japanese History] (Tokyo, 1980), pp. 56–57; Duus, Introduction, pp. 42–43; Ron Chernow, *The House of Morgan* (New York, 1990), p. 551 on banks; Hollerman, "International Economic Controls," pp. 716–719.

47. The 1949–50 crisis, especially as viewed by Truman and his advisers, is discussed, with citations, in Walter LaFeber, "NATO and the Korean War: A Context," in Lawrence S. Kaplan, ed., *American Historians and the Atlantic Alliance* (Kent, OH, 1991), pp. 33–51.

48. Minute by P. A. Wilkinson, Jan. 10, 1950, on Kelly to Bevin, Dec. 12, 1949, FO 371 N10789 / 1024 / 38, PRO, for overview of U.S. troubles; Frederick C. Barghoorn, *The Soviet Image of the United States* (Port Washington, NY, 1969), pp. 133–135; U.S. Congress, Senate, *Executive Sessions of the Senate Foreign Relations Committee (Historical Series), 1949–1950*, I, 108; Dean Acheson, *Crisis in Asia* (Washington, DC, 1950), p. 117.

49. Barnet, *Alliance*, p. 94; Cumings, "Japan's Position in the World System," pp. 43–44.

50. *FRUS, 1949*, VIII, 1210–1220.

51. McGlothlen, *Controlling the Waves*, pp. 24, 75–76, 134; Akira Iriye, *China and Japan in the Global Setting* (Cambridge, MA, 1992), pp. 94–95.

52. An important account is Nancy Bernkopf Tucker, "American Policy Toward Sino-Japanese Trade in the Postwar Years," *DH*, 8 (Summer 1984): 183–208; Welfield, *Empire*, p. 41; Iriye, *China and Japan*, pp. 98–99.

53. "Regional Conference of U.S. Chiefs of Mission. Rio de Janeiro, Brazil," March 8, 1950, Records of Inter- and Intra-Departmental Committees: Inter-American Economic Affairs Committee, 1945–1950, NA, RG 353, esp. pp. 44, 88, 90.

54. Chester Cooper, *The Lost Crusade* (New York, 1970), pp. 49–50; McGlothlen, *Controlling the Waves*, pp. 189–191; Gascoigne to Foreign Office, Jan. 18, 1950, FO 371 FJ1022 / 1, PRO.

55. U.S. Congress, *Executive Sessions, 1949–1950*, I, 267–269, 278; UK Consulate General to Foreign Office, June 1, 1950, FO 371 / F11345 / 3, PRO, on U.S. aid mission.

56. Iokibe Makoto, *Nichi-Bei senso to sengo Nihon* [U.S.-Japan War and Postwar Japan] (Osaka, 1989), p. 2–6; *FRUS, 1949*, VII, 663.

57. Dean Acheson, *Present at the Creation* (New York, 1969), pp. 428–429, 434–435; "Premature" and other Pentagon objections are in "Memorandum of Conversation" of State and Defense officials, April 24, 1950, Acheson Papers; Sept. 22, 1948, Leahy Diaries; Welfield, *Empire*, p. 30; Roger Buckley, *U.S.-Japan Alliance Diplomacy, 1945–1990* (Cambridge, UK, 1992), pp. 36–37.

58. *New York Times*, Dec. 23, 1949, in *NYT-GCI*, p. 180, on Yalta; Welfield, *Empire*, pp. 69–70; Dower, *Japan in War and Peace*, p. 182.

59. Sergei N. Goncharov, *et al.*, *Uncertain Partners* (Stanford, 1993), p. 260 for Communist pact; *FRUS 1950*, I, 234–272 for NSC-68 and background; Princeton Seminars, Oct. 10–11, 1953, Acheson Papers.

60. Sato, *Ohira*, pp. 133–134; Ronald W. Pruessen, *John Foster Dulles* (New York, 1982), pp. 448–452; Welfield, *Empire*, pp. 29, 46; Dower, *Japan in War and Peace*, pp. 174–175; Chihiro Hosoya, "Japan's Response to U.S. Policy on the Japanese Peace Treaty," *Hitotsubashi Journal of Law and Politics*, 10 (December 1981), esp. p. 18.

61. Dower, *Japan in War and Peace*, p. 185; McGlothlen, *Controlling the Waves*, p. 21 for Rusk; Princeton Seminars, July 8–9, 1953, Acheson Papers; ibid., Oct. 10–11, 1953, for "Korea . . . saved us."

62. U.S. Congress, *Executive Sessions of the Senate Foreign Relations Committee (Historical Series), 1951*, Vol. III, Part 1 (Washington, DC, 1976), 290.

63. A classic account, with an emphasis on the long civil war, is Bruce Cumings, *The Origins of the Korean War*, 2 vols. (Princeton, 1981, 1990), especially first two chapters of vol. II; the new documents are analyzed in the *Los Angeles Times* and the *New York Times* of July 21, 1994, and I am indebted to Milton Leitenberg for calling them to my attention; John W. Garver, "Polemics, Paradigms," *JAEAR*, 3 (Spring 1994): 27–28; Roger Dingman, "Korea at Forty-plus," *JAEAR*, 1 (Spring 1992): 139.

64. Buckley, *U.S.-Japan Alliance*, p. 37; McGlothlen, *Controlling the Waves*, p. 80; U.S. Department of State, *Korea (Preliminary Version). An Intelligence Estimate . . . June 25, 1950*, OACST-"P File," State Department, Office of Intelligence Research Intelligence Estimate #7, NA, RG 319, p. 5; I am indebted to David Langbart for calling this document to my attention.

65. Forrest C. Pogue, *George C. Marshall*, 4 vols. (New York, 1963–87), IV, 452; Glenn D. Paige, *The Korean Decision* (New York, 1968), pp. 132–133, 164; U.S. Department of State, *Monthly Survey of American Opinion* (September 1950): 3–4; Gaddis Smith, *Dean Acheson* (New York, 1972), p. 172; Jon Halliday and Bruce Cumings, *Korea* (New York, 1988), pp. 115, 165.

66. Thomas J. Christensen, "Threats, Assurances, and the Last Chance for Peace," *International Security*, 17 (Summer 1992): 128–131, footnote; Thorne, *Allies of a Kind*, pp. 691–692 for Hay reference; Nov. 30, 1950, Diary entry, box 17, Papers of Eban A. Ayers, HST Library; Richard J. Barnet, *The Rockets' Red Glare* (New York, 1990), p. 314; Roger Dingman, "Atomic Diplomacy. . . ," *International Security*, 13 (Winter 1988–89): 72–75, 89; Lloyd Gardner, *Approaching Vietnam* (New York, 1988), chapter 3 for quote and its context.

67. Roger Dingman, "The Dagger and the Gift: The Impact of the Korean War Upon Japan," *JAEAR*, 2 (Spring 1993): 30–31; Dower, *Empire and Aftermath*, pp. 389–391.

68. Welfield, *Empire*, pp. 70–71; the CIA operation is outlined by Tim Weiner, Stephen Engelberg, and James Sterngold in the *New York Times*, Oct. 9, 1994, p. A14.

69. Welfield, *Empire*, pp. 72, 76–77; Dingman, "Dagger," p. 37; Chancery Tokyo to Far Eastern Department, July 26, 1950, FO 371 FJ1193, PRO; *New York Times*, July 8, 1950, in *NYT-GCI*, p. 183; Allison to Rusk, July 10, 1950, in "Special Assistant Subject File . . . Japanese Treaty June 1950," Harriman Papers.

70. Goncharov, *et al.*, *Uncertain Partners*, p. 89; Frank Gibney, "The First Three Months of War," *JAEAR*, 2 (Spring 1993): 106 for Yoshida quote; *New York Times*, June 20, 1951, in *NYT-GCI*, p. 184, *Boston Globe*, Aug. 1, 1993, pp. B21, B25 on the film.

71. "Notes for letter to General MacArthur," undated, probably late November 1950, Conference Dossiers, UN-Formosa, Dulles Papers; Pruessen, *Dulles*, pp. 468–477; the U.S. approach is also outlined in Acheson, *Present at the Creation*, pp. 432–435, 544–545; Buckley, *U.S.-Japan Alliance*, p. 35; Dulles's quote is in U.S. Congress, Senate, 82nd Cong., 1st Sess., *Executive Sessions . . . (Historical Series), 1951*, Vol. III, part 1, 292–293; *FRUS, 1951*, VI, 831 has British fears of Japanese exports; Marks, *Power and Peace*, p. 136 for Dulles warning the British.

72. Hosoya, "Japan's Response," pp. 16–17; Hirano Ken'ichiro, "Sengo Nihon gaiko ni okeru 〈Bunka〉" [Postwar Japanese Foreign Policy in Relation to "Culture"] in Watanabe, ed., *Sengo Nihon no taigai seisaku*; Welfield, *Empire*, p. 48; Hosoya, "Japan's Response," pp. 18–19; Dower, *Japan in War and Peace*, p. 208.

73. Hosoya, "Japan's Response," pp. 20–21; *FRUS, 1951*, VI, 827–829; Ishii Osamu, "Nichi-Bei . . . 1952–1969" [The Japan-U.S. Partnership, 1952–1969], in Hosoya, ed., *Nichi-Bei kankei tsushi*, p. 223 on Rockefeller.

74. Hosoya, "Japan's Response," pp. 26–27; Carol Gluck, "Entangling Illusions," in Cohen, ed., *New Frontiers*, pp. 169–236; "Notes on Conversations . . . Feb. 7, 1951," by Dulles,

Lot File 56D225, 56D256, Records of the Bureau of Far Eastern Affairs, 1945–1953, box 1, NA, RG 59.

75. Hosoya, "Japan's Response," pp. 21–25; Barnet, *Alliance*, p. 91; Dower, *Japan in War and Peace*, p. 190; Dower, "Peace and Democracy," p. 23; Igarashi Takeshi, "Peace-Making and Party Politics," *JJS*, 11 (no. 2, 1985): 323–356 for analysis of how parties and treaty negotiations intersected.

76. Hosoya, "Japan's Response," pp. 23, 26; Dower, *War Without Mercy*, p. 310 has the Dulles quote; *Maki, Documents*, pp. 132–147 for peace treaty, esp. p. 135 on bases.

77. F.O. Minute by R. H. Scott, Sept. 26, 1951, FO 371 FJ1027 / 5, PRO.

78. Acheson, *Present at the Creation*, pp. 545–47.

79. U.S. Congress, Senate, *Executive Sessions . . . (Historical Series) 1951*, Vol. III, Part 1: 260–261; Yashuhara Yoko, "Japan, Communist China, and Export Control in Asia, 1948–1952," *DH*, 10 (Winter 1986): 75–89; F.O. Minute by R. H. Scott, Sept. 26, 1951, FO 371 FJ1027 / 5, PRO.

80. *FRUS, 1951*, VI, 1464–1470; Dower, *Japan in War and Peace*, p. 234; Dower, *Empire and Aftermath*, pp. 400–414.

81. *New York Times*, Jan. 3, 1951, in *NYT-GCI*, p. 183; Kotaro Suzumura and Mashahiro Okuno-Fujiwara, *Industrial Policy in Japan* (Canberra, 1987), pp. 10–11; Yamamoto, "Cold War," pp. 412–413; Richard J. Samuels, *"Rich Nation, Strong Army"* (Ithaca, NY, 1994), pp. 133–134; W. E. Smith to R. H. Scott, March 22, 1951, FO 371 FJ1019 / 6, PRO, for British view; I am indebted to Milton Leitenberg for statistics and other material in this paragraph.

82. Samuels, *"Rich Nation,"* pp. 136–143.

83. Pruessen, *Dulles*, p. 478; Council on Foreign Relations Study Group Reports, Oct. 23, 1950, meeting, Conference Dossiers, draft of Japanese Peace Treaty, Dulles Papers; Yoshida is paraphrased by Dening in Sir E. Dening to Foreign Office, Oct. 19, 1951, FO 371 FJ1027 / 9, PRO; John K. Emmerson, *The Japanese Thread* (New York, 1978), p. 256.

84. Frank Costigliola, *France and the United States* (New York, 1992), chapter 3 has the State Department official's quote and an excellent discussion; Sir A. Gascoigne to Scott, Jan. 22, 1951, FO 371 FJ1019 / 3, PRO; Takemae Eiji, *Senryo sengoshi*, pp. 53–54.

85. Igarashi, "Peace-Making and Party Politics," pp. 354–355; McGlothlen, *Controlling the Waves*, p. 203 for Nitze quote.

Chapter X

1. John Welfield, *An Empire in Eclipse* (London, 1988), pp. 54–55; Roger Buckley, *U.S.-Japan Alliance Diplomacy, 1945–1990* (Cambridge, UK, 1992), p. 78; *FRUS, 1955–1957*, XXIII, 86–87.

2. Sydney Giffard, *Japan Among the Powers, 1890–1990* (New Haven, 1994), p. 147 on internal conditions; Buckley, *U.S.-Japan Alliance*, p. 74; John Dower, *War Without Mercy* (New York, 1986), p. 310 has Dirksen quote; Allison to J. E. MacDonald, Exec. Sec., Panel "D"—Japan, Psychological Strategy Board, May 27, 1952, p. 14 in Lot File 56D225, 56D256, Records of Bureau of Far Eastern Affairs, 1945–1953, NA, RG 49.

3. "Far Eastern Problems. Address by John Foster Dulles Before French National Political Science Institute, Paris, May 5, 1952," Primary Correspondence, 1916–1952, box 33, Eisenhower Library.

4. The themes are well explored in Lloyd Gardner, *A Covenant with Power* (New York, 1984), esp. pp. 50–52; Robert Divine, *Eisenhower and the Cold War* (New York, 1981), esp. pp. 33–39; and David Alan Rosenberg, "The Origins of Overkill. . . ," *International Security*, 7 (Spring 1983): 27.

5. *New York Times,* Nov. 19, 1953, in *NYT-GCI,* p. 214 for Nixon quote; Douglas H. Mendel, Jr., "Japanese Views of the American Alliance," *PSQ,* 23 (Fall 1959): 9; Welfield, *Empire,* pp. 79, 84, 103.

6. W. G. Beasley, *The Rise of Modern Japan* (New York, 1990), p. 226; Welfield, *Empire,* pp. 61, 82; George C. Allen, *A Short Economic History of Modern Japan* (London, 1981), p. 190.

7. Peter J. Katzenstein and Nobuo Okawara, *Japan's National Security* (Ithaca, NY, 1993), pp. 7–8; Dening to Macmillan, Oct. 3, 1955, FO 371 FJ10345 / 33, PRO.

8. Ishii Osamu, "Nichi-Bei paatonashippu e no dotei, 1952–1969" [The Road to Japan-U.S. Partnership, 1952–1969], in Hosoya Chihiro, ed., *Nichi-Bei kankei tsushi* [Japan-U.S. Relations] (Tokyo, 1995), pp. 221–223; an argument that 1945–51 was a "bourgeois revolution" is in Oishi's essay in Tokyo Daigaku, Shakai Kagaku Kenkyujo (Tokyo University, Social Science Institute), *Sengo kaikaku* [Postwar Reform], 8 vols. (Tokyo, 1974), I, 92–97; Roger Dingman, "The Dagger and the Gift: The Impact of the Korean War on Japan," *JAEAR,* 2 (Spring 1993): 50–52; Aruga Tadashi, "Editor's Introduction," *JJAS,* 2 (1985): 26–29.

9. Dingman, "Dagger," pp. 51–52; Reiko Maekawa, "The Rockefeller Foundation and Cultural Politics in Postwar Japan," *Research Reports from the Rockefeller Archive Center* (Spring 1993): 10–12.

10. *Boston Globe,* Aug. 1, 1993, pp. B21, B25; Dingman, "Dagger," p. 52 on Michener; Michael Schaller, "Altered States," in Diane B. Kunz, ed., *The Diplomacy of the Crucial Decade* (New York, 1994), p. 254 for the *Godzilla* interpretation.

11. *Washington Post,* Dec. 23, 1993, p. A23; John Dower, *Japan in War and Peace* (New York, 1993), p. 206; "W. Edwards Deming: The Prophet of Quality," CC-M Productions, Public Broadcasting System, Nov. 30, 1994; Rafael Aguayo, *Dr. Deming* (New York, 1991).

12. Dulles "summary report" of July 7, 1950, P. C. Jessup files, Lot File 53D211, box 1, NA, RG 59, for which I am indebted to Professor Frank Costigliola; Dower, *Japan in War and Peace,* p. 193.

13. *New York Times,* Aug. 26, 1951, in *NYT-GCI,* p. 185; ibid., Sept. 23, 1951, p. 185; Peter Duus, Introduction to Duus, ed., *The Cambridge History of Japan.* Vol. 6. *The Twentieth Century* (Cambridge, UK, 1988), p. 24.

14. *FRUS, 1952–1954,* XIV, 1623–1627; ibid., 1682–1684.

15. Hirano Ken'ichiro, "Sengo Nihon gaiko ni okeru ⟨Bunka⟩" [Postwar Japanese Foreign Policy in Relation to "Culture"], in Watanabe Akio, ed., *Sengo Nihon no taigai seisaku* [Postwar Japanese Foreign Policy] (Tokyo, 1985), pp. 343–348; Allen, *Short Economic History,* pp. 204–205; Beasley, *Rise,* pp. 245–246; Yutaka Kosai, "The Postwar Japanese Economy, 1945–1973," in Duus, ed., *The Twentieth Century,* pp. 507–508, 513–515.

16. Kosai, "Postwar Japanese Economy," pp. 520–521; Welfield, *Empire,* pp. 96–97; Richard J. Samuels, *"Rich Nation, Strong Army"* (Ithaca, NY, 1994), pp. 142–153 for dual-use technology; *Washington Post,* July 18, 1993, p. H1 for Eisenhower and Motorola.

17. Emmet John Hughes, *The Ordeal of Power* (New York, 1963), p. 76; John Dower, "Peace and Democracy in Two Systems," in Andrew Gordon, ed., *Postwar Japan as History* (Berkeley, 1993), p. 12.

18. *FRUS, 1952–1954,* I, 885, 918–919 for COCOM deal; Sayuri Shimizu, "A Bothersome Triangle . . . 1952–1958" (1992), Manuscript in author's possession; Akira Iriye, *China and Japan in the Global Setting* (Cambridge, MA, 1992), pp. 103–104; Nancy Bernkopf Tucker, "American Policy . . . ," *DH,* 8 (Summer 1982): 208 notes trade figures; Ishii Ahira, "Or Taiwan or Pekin," in Watanabe, ed., *Sengo Nihon no taigai seisaku,* pp. 80–84 on 1953–54 meetings.

19. The quotations in these two paragraphs can be found in *FRUS, 1952–1954,* XII, 1011–1012, esp. p. 396, for Eisenhower; also in *FRUS, 1952–1954,* V, 1808–1810; James C. Hagerty,

The Diary of James C. Hagerty, Robert H. Ferrell ed. (Bloomington, IN, 1983), pp. 70, 111, 141, 167; Dower, "Peace and Democracy in Two Systems," p. 51 on restoring Japan's empire.

20. *FRUS, 1952–1954*, I, 1250–1252 on CHINCOM loosening; MM139 (28), April 16, 1953, Minutes of Meetings of National Security Council, supplement III (microfilm) (Bethesda, MD, 1995).

21. George Clutton to Foreign Office, Oct. 2, 1951, FO 371 FJ1027 / 6, PRO.

22. *FRUS, 1952–1954*, XIII, 82–89.

23. Press conference in New Delhi, May 22, 1953, Dulles Papers; Douglas Kinnard, *The Secretary of Defense* (Lexington, KY, 1980), p. 69 for use of nuclear weapons; *The Pentagon Papers, Senator Gravel Edition*, 4 vols. (Boston, 1971), I, 83–84 for NSC-124 / 2.

24. U.S. Government, *Public Papers of the Presidents . . . Eisenhower, 1954* (Washington, DC, 1958), pp. 382–383; "Far Eastern Problems. Address by . . . Dulles."

25. Eisenhower to Gen. Alfred M. Gruenther, April 26, 1954, Diary Series, box 5, Eisenhower Library; Lloyd Gardner, *Approaching Vietnam* (New York, 1988), esp. ch. 6 analyzes debates shaping SEATO; George C. Herring and Richard H. Immerman, "Eisenhower, Dulles, and Dienbienphu," *JAH*, 71 (September 1984): 352–353, 356–357. Divine, *Eisenhower and Cold War*, esp. p. 51.

26. Allison to J. E. MacDonald, Exec. Secretary, Panel "D"-Japan, Psychological Strategy Board, May 27, 1952, Lot Files 56 D225, 56 D256, Record of Bureau of Far Eastern Affairs, box 1, NA, RG 59; John Dower, *Empire and Aftermath* (Cambridge, MA, 1988), pp. 472–473 for position paper; Welfield, *Empire*, p. 95.

27. *BusinessWeek*, Oct. 16, 1954, pp. 25–26; "Memorandum of Luncheon Conversation with the President," March 15, 1954, White House Memoranda Series, box 1, Papers of John Foster Dulles, Eisenhower Library; Yamakage Susumu, "Ajia Taiheiyo to Nihon" [Asia, Japan, and the Pacific], in Watanabe, ed., *Sengo Nihon no taigai seisaku*, pp. 151–153 for analysis of 1950s splintering.

28. Hagerty, *Diary*, p. 40 for Communist allegations; *New York Times*, March 16, 1954, in *NYT-GCI*, p. 213; *FRUS, 1952–1954*, XIV, 1643–1648 for Allison's May 20, 1954, report.

29. For this and the previous paragraph, see the good analysis by Stuart Auerbach, "How the U.S. Built Japan Inc.," *Washington Post National Weekly Edition*, July 26–Aug. 1, 1993, p. 21; Shimizu, "Bothersome Triangle," pp. 9–11.

30. Dening to Eden, Jan. 19, 1955, FO 371 FJ1011 / 1, PRO; Beasley, *Rise*, p. 230; Karel van Wolferen, "Japan's Non-Revolution," *Foreign Affairs*, 7 (September–October 1993): 55.

31. "Biographic Report" by Department of State, Aug. 22, 1955, in FO 371 FJ1012 / 3 PRO; *New York Times*, Dec. 10, 1954, p. A1.

32. Allen, *Short Economic History*, pp. 191–192, 231; Walt W. Rostow, *The Diffusion of Power* (New York, 1972), pp. 60–61; "Minutes of Cabinet Meeting, April 20, 1956," pp. 1–2, Cabinet Meetings of President Eisenhower, Eisenhower Library; U.S. Congress, Senate, *Executive Sessions of the Senate Foreign Relations Committee (Historical Series)* (Washington, DC, 1980), Vol. X, pp. 2–3.

33. *FRUS, 1955–1957*, XIII, 128–129; *FRUS, 1955–1957*, IX, 30–31 on defense purchases; R. H. Scott to Macmillan, Sept. 3, 1955, FO 371 FJ10345 / 23, PRO, for Dulles's annoyance; Scott to Foreign Office, Sept. 9, 1955, FO 371 FJ10345 / 25, PRO.

34. Welfield, *Empire*, p. 94; clipping from the *Washington Post*, May 4, 1955, in FO 371 FJ10345 / 17, PRO, on Alsop in Tokyo.

35. Burton Kaufman, "Eisenhower's Foreign Economic Policy with Respect to Asia," in Warren Cohen and Akira Iriye, eds., *The Great Powers in East Asia, 1953–1960* (New York, 1990), pp. 110–112; Qing Simei, "The Eisenhower Administration . . . ," in ibid., pp. 121–124; Iriye, *China and Japan*, p. 107; Shimizu, "Bothersome Triangle," pp. 6–9; Buckley, *U.S.-Japan Alliance*, pp. 70, 196; McHugh to John Keswick, July 30, 1955, Papers of Col. James McHugh, Cornell University.

36. Momose Hiroshi, "Futatsu no taisei no aida de" [Interaction Between Two Systems], in Watanabe, ed., *Sengo Nihon no taigai seisaku*, pp. 91–96; *FRUS, 1955–1957*, XIX, 154–157 on missile's effects; Sato Seizaburo, *et al., Postwar Politician: The Life of . . . Ohira* (Tokyo, 1990), p. 315; Buckley, *U.S.-Japan Alliance*, p. 75 for Allison quote, and p. 76 for Dulles; "Progress Report on U.S. Policy Toward Japan," NSC-5516, by Operations Coordinating Board, Feb. 6, 1957, *Documents of the NSC*, 6th supplement (microfilm), reel (Bethesda, MD).

37. This and the following paragraph on Kishi are drawn especially from U.S. Department of State Biographical Report, Aug. 22, 1955, FO 371 FJ1012 / 3, PRO; and Welfield, *Empire*, pp. 116–122.

38. Ishikawa Tadao, Nakajima Mineo, and Ikei Masaru, eds., *Sengo shiryo Nit-Chu kankei* [Postwar Documents in Japanese-Chinese Relations] (Tokyo, 1970), p. viii on Kishi and China; *New York Times*, Feb. 25, 1957, p. A7 for labor unions quote; March 9, 1957, p. A6 on the Emperor; *FRUS, 1955–1957*, XXIII, 518–520, and also note references in #37 above.

39. Pre-press conference briefing, July 17, 1957, Eisenhower Diaries, reel 13 (microfilm), frame 00590, original in Eisenhower Library; Frederick W. Marks III, *Power and Peace* (Westport, CT, 1993), p. 225.

40. Welfield, *Empire*, pp. 110–111, 152, 257; "Memorandum of Conversation, June 19, 1957," Kishi Call on President, *Declassified Documents*, 003463 (microfiche).

41. Welfield, *Empire*, p. 90; Buckley, *U.S.-Japan Alliance*, pp. 83–84.

42. Ishikawa, *et al., Sengo shiryo*, esp. pp. ix–x, 105–106 on the Chinese reaction; Operations Coordinating Board, "Progress Report on Japan (NSC-5516 / 1, approved April 9, 1955)," Sept. 25, 1957, esp. p. 4, copy in author's possession; Hiwatari Yunu, "U.S.-Japanese Relations in the Late 1950s: Kishi's Southeast Asian Policy" (in Japanese), *JMJS*, 11 (1989): 211–212.

43. Lascelles to Foreign Office, May 29, 1958, FO 371 FJ1017 / 8, PRO, for election analysis; Buckley, *U.S.-Japan Alliance*, pp. 80–89.

44. "Memorandum of Conversation," July 25, 1958, of Sato and S. S. Carpenter, in Douglas MacArthur II to "Jeff" and J. Graham Parsons, RM / R Files, 794.00 / 7-2958, NA, RG 59. I am greatly indebted to David Langbart for noting this document. *New York Times*, Oct. 9, 1994, p. 14 analysis by Tim Weiner.

45. Mendel, "Japanese Views of the American Alliance," p. 341; Marks, *Power and Peace*, p. 128 for the Kishi quote.

46. Chancery, Tokyo to Foreign office, July 23, 1951, FO 371 FJ1019 / 19, PRO; *Asahi Journal*, "Zengakuren's Thought and Action," Dec. 20, 1959, Summaries of Selected Japanese Magazines, Jan. 18, 1960, issued by translation services branch, American Embassy, Tokyo, copy in author's possession.

47. "Memorandum of Conversation: Japanese Domestic Political Situation," Eisenhower and Kishi, Jan. 19, 1960, Eisenhower Diaries, reel 24 (microfilm), frame 00452, Eisenhower Library; de la Mare to Peter Dalton, Feb. 5, 1960, FO 371 FJ10345 / 18, PRO.

48. Maki, *Documents*, pp. 220–225 for treaty and accompanying documents; Morland to Foreign Office, Jan. 29, 1960, FO 371 FJ10345 / 13, PRO; Chancery Tokyo to Far Eastern Department, Feb. 29, 1960, FO 371 FJ10345 / 24, PRO, for Kishi statement analysis; Welfield, *Empire*, p. 143–145.

49. Parsons to Caccia quoted in Caccia to Foreign Office, Jan. 13, 1960, FO 371 FJ10345 / 6, PRO; Reilly to Foreign Office, Jan. 28, 1960, FO 371 FJ10345 / 12, PRO; Buckley, *U.S.-Japan Alliance*, pp. 92–94.

50. MacArthur to Secretary of State, May 26, 1960, *Declassified Documents*, 00869 (microfiche); Welfield, *Empire*, p. 138.

51. This and the previous paragraph on the Japanese reaction are based on *New York Times*, July 14, May 27, June 16, and June 17, 1960, and also June 19, 1962, all in *NYT-GCI*, pp.

271–281; Morland to Foreign Office, June 17, 1960, FO 371 FJ101345/60, PRO, on June 15 riots; Thomas R. H. Havens, *Fire Across the Sea* (Princeton, 1987), p. 10, Welfield, *Empire*, p. 138.

52. Caccia to Foreign Office, June 18, 1960, FO 371 FJ10345/57, PRO, quotes Reston; Chancery Tokyo to Foreign Office, July 15, 1960, FO 371 FJ10345/69, PRO; Welfield, *Empire*, p. 140, on right-wing assassination attempts.

53. *New York Times*, July 19, 1960, p. A14; Aruga, "Japanese Scholarship," p. 40; Ishikawa, *et al., Sengo shiryo*, entry for July 2, 1960, is Chinese commentary on Kishi's retirement.

54. Eisenhower to Swede Hazlett, Aug. 3, 1956, Ann Whitman File—Hazlett, Eisenhower Library.

55. Mr. Allison to the Secretary, Jan. 3, 1952, p. 3, copy in author's possession; I am indebted to David Langbart for pointing out this document, which was declassified on Sept. 12, 1995.

Chapter XI

1. *New York Times*, July 19, 1960, p. A14.

2. Thomas R. H. Havens, *Fire Across the Sea* (Princeton, 1987), p. 20; John Welfield, *An Empire in Eclipse* (London, 1988), pp. 170–171; Akira Iriye, *China and Japan in the Global Setting* (Cambridge, MA, 1992), p. 118.

3. Tim Weiner story in *New York Times*, Oct. 9, 1994, p. 14; and Kazumoto Ono, "Shin shogen: CIA tai nichi himitsu kosaku no zenbunsho" [New Testimony: Documents on Covert CIA Operations in Japan], *Bungei Shunju* (December 1994): 144–156.

4. Sir O. Morland to Far Eastern Department, Jan. 23, 1963, FO 371 FJ2041/1, PRO; Sir O. Morland to Foreign Office, Jan. 7, 1963, FO 371 FJ1011/1, PRO; W. G. Beasley, *The Rise of Modern Japan* (New York, 1990), pp. 234–235.

5. *BusinessWeek*, Aug. 19, 1967, p. 94; William R. Nester, *Japan and the Third World* (New York, 1992), pp. 13–14 on OECD reservations; G. C. Allen, *A Short Economic History of Modern Japan* (London, 1981), p. 212; *New Scientist Japanese Supplement*, Nov. 16, 1967, pp. 8–9; William S. Borden, *The Pacific Alliance* (Madison, WI, 1984), pp. ix, 3–17, 37–41, 218–222; *New York Times*, July 6, 1967, in *NYT-GCI*, p. 308.

6. Kosai Yutaka, "The Postwar Japanese Economy, 1945–1973," in Peter Duus, ed., *The Cambridge History of Japan. Vol. 6. The Twentieth Century* (Cambridge, UK, 1988), p. 530; Allen, *Short Economic History*, p. 225; Jacques Hersh, *The USA and the Rise of East Asia Since 1945* (London, 1993), p. 32.

7. *Wall Street Journal*, Nov. 11, 1966, p. 22; Suzumara Kitaro and Masahiro Okuno-Fujiwara, *Industrial Policy in Japan* (Canberra, 1987), pp. 11–12, 15–16; Beasley, *Rise*, pp. 230–232; *New Scientist Japanese Supplement*, Nov. 16, 1967, p. 1 for the "science city."

8. Kitaro and Okuno-Fujiwara, *Industrial Policy in Japan*, pp. 14–15; Allen, *Short Economic History*, pp. 226–227.

9. *U.S. News & World Report*, July 24, 1967, p. 90; Peter Duus, Introduction to Duus, ed., *The Twentieth Century*, pp. 29–30 on raw material investment; Yatuka, "Postwar Japanese Economy," p. 528; *New York Times*, Jan. 19, 1968, p. 56; *Far Eastern Economic Review*, May 21, 1970, p. 74; Ron Chernow, *The House of Morgan* (New York, 1990), pp. 552–554; *BusinessWeek*, Sept. 6, 1969, pp. 124–125, for the Japanese official's quote; ibid., Aug. 19, 1967, p. 106.

10. *New York Times*, June 10, 1968, p. 71; Michael Schaller, "Altered States: U.S. and Japan . . . ," in Diane Kunz, ed., *The Diplomacy of the Crucial Decade* (New York, 1994), pp. 259–260; Seymour Broadbridge and Martin Collick, "Japan's International Policies," *Inter-*

national Affairs, 44 (April 1968): 249; Kunio Moraoka, *Japanese Security and the United States. Adelphi Papers* (London, 1973), p. 9.

11. Broadbridge and Collick, "Japan's International Policies," pp. 240–253 on the Pacific Basin Economic Community; Peter Drysdale, "Japan, Australia, and Pacific Economic Integration," *Australia's Neighbors,* 4th series, nos. 50–51 (November–December 1967), pp. 6–9; Mike Mansfield, *The Rim of Asia* (Washington, DC, 1967), p. 5; *BusinessWeek,* Aug. 19, 1967, p. 93 on "hino"; *New York Times,* Jan. 19, 1968, p. 65 on Taiwan; Garvey to Foreign Office, Jan. 1, 1963, FO 371 FJ113110 / 1, PRO.

12. Hsinhua press report, Jan. 19, 1963, in FO 371 FJ113110 / 2, PRO, for Ikeda quote; Garvey to Foreign Office, Oct. 8, 1963, FO 371 FJ113110 / 21, PRO, on credit deals; Iriye, *China and Japan,* pp. 116–117; *The Times* "Press Cutting," FO 371 FJ113110 / 8, PRO.

13. *New York Times,* Jan. 11, 1981, p. 18; Lewis Beman, "How to Tell Where the U.S. Is Competitive," *Fortune,* 86 (July 1972): 54–55; *New York Times,* July 6, 1967, in *NYT-GCI,* p. 308.

14. CIA, *Intelligence Memorandum. Japan: The Effectiveness of Informal Import and Investment Controls* (Washington, DC, 1969), National Security Archive, no. 73714; *New York Times,* Nov. 26, 1967, p. F14; Philip H. Trezise to Editor, *Foreign Affairs,* 72 (September–October, 1993): 188; Ledward to Far Eastern Department, April 3, 1963, FO 371 FJ113145 / 2, PRO, for Johnson speech.

15. Louis Heren, *No Hail, No Farewell* (New York, 1970), p. 118; Hindle to Earl of Home, Sept. 26, 1960, FO 371 FJ10345 / 77, PRO.

16. Laura E. Hein, "Free-Floating Anxieties on the Pacific: Japan and the West Revisited," *DH,* 20 (Summer 1996): 414–419; Ledward to de la Mare, Oct. 11, 1961, FO 371 FJ103145 / 15, PRO.

17. Trench to de la Mare, Nov. 17, 1961, FO 371 FJ103145 / 18, PRO; Kono Yasuko, " 'Sengo no owati,' " [The End of the Postwar Era], in Watanabe Akio, ed., *Sengo Nihon no taigai seisaku* [Postwar Japanese Foreign Policy] (Tokyo, 1985), pp. 187–190 for the "equal partnership" theme; Schaller, "Altered States," pp. 261–262.

18. Sir H. Carcia to FO, July 1, 1961, FO 371 FJ1031458 / 8, PRO; Heren, *No Hail,* pp. 118–119.

19. U.S. Department of State, "Japan. Department of State Guidelines for Policy and Operations . . . March 1962," pp. 1, 9, National Security Archives, no. 74095 (hereafter cited as Department of State, "Japan, March 1962").

20. "Memorandum for the President" from Roswell Gilpatrick, Feb. 7, 8, 1963, National Security Archive, no. 71594; Reischauer to Harriman, Oct. 22, 1962, FE 5790 / 102.20 / 8-22-62, NA, RG 59.

21. For this and the following paragraph, see *Wall Street Journal,* Sept. 13, 1962; Denson to Foreign Office, Sept. 13, 1962, FO 371 FJ103145 / 15, PRO, for U.S. bases; Department of State, "Japan, March 1962," p. 4; British Embassy in Tokyo to London, April 19, 1963, FO 371 FJ13145 / 3, PRO.

22. This paragraph is based especially on the reporting of Kazumoto Ono, "Shin shogen." Professor Michael Schaller to author, Feb. 2, 1995, has specific annual amounts.

23. Greenhill to Foreign Office, Dec. 20, 1962, FO 371 FJ113145 / 16, PRO, has Kennedy's speech and describes the meeting.

24. Tokyo Embassy to Foreign Office, Feb. 5, 1963, FO 371 FJ113110 / 4, PRO, on Ikeda and China; C. G. Harris to Foreign Office, March 9, 1963, FO 371 FJ113110 / 6, PRO.

25. Welfield, *Empire,* pp. 174–178, 182; Kazumoto, "Shin shogen," pp. 153–156, alluding to CIA penetration of ministries.

26. Editorial page of *The Times* (London), Oct. 21, 1961; Morland to Foreign Office, Jan. 7, 1963, FO 371 FJ1011 / 1, PRO.

27. Report in Ledward to de la Mare, Feb. 1, 1963, FO 371 FJ103145 / 2, PRO.

28. Larry Berman, "From Intervention to Disengagement," in Ariel Levite, Bruce Jentleson, and Larry Berman, eds., *Foreign Military Intervention* (New York, 1992), pp. 30-31 for Westmoreland quote; Havens, *Fire*, pp. 18–19; Kono, " 'Sengo no owati,' " pp. 194–195.

29. *New York Times*, Oct. 11, 1964, in *NYT-GCI*, p. 325; *New York Times*, Dec. 7, 1964, p. 5 for Lemay; I am indebted to Kathryn Comerford for finding this episode.

30. Schaller, "Altered States," p. 272.

31. For U.S. bitterness over Japan's capital control, an NSC briefing book for Johnson is instructive: "Visit of Prime Minister Sato, January 11–14, 1965. Background Paper. Japanese Restrictions on Direct Foreign Investment," National Security Archive, no. 73330.

32. *New York Times*, Nov. 9, 1964, p. A1; John K. Emmerson, *The Japanese Thread* (New York, 1978), pp. 384–385 on Sato; Welfield, *Empire*, p. 129; U. Alexis Johnson, *The Right Hand of Power* (Englewood Cliffs, NJ, 1984), pp. 463–464.

33. George E. Reedy, *Lyndon Johnson, A Memoir* (New York, 1982), p. 36; "Memorandum for Mr. Bundy," Jan. 7, 1965, National Security Archive, no. 73346.

34. "Memorandum for Mr. Bundy," Jan. 7, 1967, National Security Archive, no. 73346; "Record of Third meeting of Joint U.S.-Japan Committee on Trade and Economic Affairs. Tokyo. January 27, 1964. IV . . . ," National Security Archive, no. 73309; Jonathan Spence, *To Change China* (New York, 1980), pp. 286–287; Reischauer to Office of the Secretary of State, telegram, Feb. 24, 1966, National Security Archive, no. 73406, for non-proliferation treaty; Scalapino is quoted in *Los Angeles Times*, Nov. 14, 1967.

35. *FRUS, 1964–1968*, I, 486–487, 916–918; "Memorandum of Conversation, Subject: Visit of Mr. Fukuda," July 11, 1964, National Security Archive, no. 73028; "Memorandum of Conversation. Subject: United States-Japan Relations and Policy Problems in Asia," Jan. 13, 1965, National Security Archive, no. 73217.

36. George Kahin, *Intervention* (New York, 1986), emphasizes the pressures on Johnson from his advisers.

37. Havens, *Fire*, pp. 21–23.

38. Berman, "From Intervention," pp. 32–33; FO Minute by J. L. N. O'Laughlin, Dec. 2, 1963, FO 371 AU1012 / 5, PRO; Johnson's motives and the context are analyzed in Lloyd C. Gardner, *Pay Any Price* (Chicago, 1995), which stresses the New Deal background.

39. Forrestal quote is in William Chafe, *The Unfinished Journey* (New York, 1986), p. 281.

40. For this and the following paragraph, see *New York Times*, Jan. 14, 1965, in *NYT-GCI*, pp. 327–328; Havens, *Fire*, pp. 25–28, 89–90 on Japan's response; *The Economist*, Oct. 22, 1966, p. 359; Schaller, "Altered States," pp. 262–263.

41. Allen S. Whiting, *The Chinese Calculus of Deterrence* (Ann Arbor, MI, 1975), pp. 170–172, 182; Dean Rusk Oral History, LBJ Library, on the Chinese; Kahin, *Intervention*, p. 338 for Japan–North Vietnam; James Reston, *Deadline* (New York, 1991), p. 321 for LBJ quote.

42. Havens, *Fire*, pp. 87, 94–97, 103–104; Johnson, *Right Hand*, p. 451; "Economic Benefits to Japan Traceable to the Vietnam Conflict," Nov. 9, 1967, Sneider to Jorden, National Security Archive, no. 73575; *Newsweek*, Aug. 15, 1966, pp. 68–69.

43. *New York Times*, Dec. 31, 1967, p. 3 for Japan's nationalism; Havens, *Fire*, pp. 32–35, 56–60, 71, 114; Welfield, *Empire*, pp. 228–229.

44. The important analysis of Indonesia at this time is George and Audrey Kahin, *Subversion as Foreign Policy* (New York, 1995); *New York Times*, July 12, 1990, p. A13 for U.S. involvement; *The Economist*, April 2, 1966, p. 76; Rusk to U.S. Ambassador, "Eyes Only . . . ," May 12, 1966, National Security Archive, no. 73415; U.S. Embassy, Japan, to Department of State, Dec. 7, 1966, "Secretary–Sato Conversation: Indonesia," National Security Archive, no. 73431; Johnson, *Right Hand*, p. 482.

45. Richard Halloran, *Japan: Images and Realities* (New York, 1969), pp. 192–193; Havens, *Fire*, p. 114; *U.S. News & World Report*, July 24, 1967, pp. 90–93.

46. *New York Times*, Jan. 15, 1965, p. 42; Nicholas Evan Sarantakes, "Continuity Through Change . . . ," *JAEAR*, 3 (Spring 1994): 37, 46; Havens, *Fire*, pp. 87–88, 124; Welfield, *Empire*, pp. 226–227; "Memorandum for Mr. Walt W. Rostow," from Benjamin H. Read, Oct. 13, 1967, National Security Archive, no. 73517.

47. "Memo for Mr. Rostow," from Dick Moose, Feb. 8, 1968, NSC file, Subject file, Press Appointments, LBJ Library, for media response; Harry McPherson Oral History, tape #5, pp. 5–6, LBJ Library, on White House view of Tet; Acheson's words, in LBJ's handwriting, are shown in Walter LaFeber, *The American Age* (New York, 1994), p. 619.

48. U.S. Department of State, "Growing Severity of Japanese Press on U.S.-Related Issues," Nov. 9, 1967, National Security Archive, no. 73576; Welfield, *Empire*, p. 234; Johnson, *Right Hand*, p. 491 on riots; Johnson to Bundy, April 4, 1968, National Security Archive, no. 73623, for Japanese surprise and Sato's dilemma; Havens, *Fire*, pp. 144–145, 175.

49. Welfield, *Empire*, pp. 236–239; Johnson, *Right Hand*, p. 444; Johnson to Secretary of State, Aug. 21, 1968, National Security Archive, no. 73671, for Johnson-Miki conversation.

50. Richard Nixon, *RN* (New York, 1978), p. 335.

51. Johnson, *Right Hand*, p. 509 on Sato-Miki; Havens, *Fire*, pp. 163, 189–191 on cutbacks and riots.

52. Richard M. Nixon, "Asia after Viet Nam," *Foreign Affairs*, 46 (October 1967): 111–125.

53. Henry Kissinger, *Years of Upheaval* (Boston, 1982), p. 735; Henry Kissinger, *White House Years* (Boston, 1979), p. 324; John Dower, *Japan in War and Peace* (New York, 1993), p. 323 on "little Sony salesmen"; Henry Kissinger, *American Foreign Policy. Expanded Edition* (New York, 1974), pp. 182–183; Johnson, *Right Hand*, p. 521.

54. Kissinger, *American Foreign Policy*, p. 57; John Stoessinger, *Henry Kissinger* (New York, 1976), pp. 12–14.

55. Kissinger, *White House Years*, pp. 224–225; Seymour Hersh, *The Price of Power* (New York, 1983), pp. 148, 281; Hersh, *USA*, pp. 40–41; Leslie H. Brown, *American Security Policy in Asia. Adelphi Papers* (London, 1977), pp. 6, 8.

56. "National Security Decision Memorandum 13," May 28, 1969, signed by Kissinger, outlines U.S. negotiating position on Okinawa, copy in author's possession; Sarantakes, "Continuity Through Change," pp. 46–47; Welfield, *Empire*, pp. 243–244; Takemae Eiji, *Senryo sengoshi* [Occupation and Postwar Japanese History] (Tokyo, 1980), pp. 53–55 for Okinawa's internal conditions.

57. Text of agreement is joint communiqué, Nov. 21, 1969, *U.S. Foreign Policy, 1969–1970* (Washington, DC, 1971), pp. 503–505; Kissinger, *White House Years*, pp. 334–335; Havens, *Fire*, pp. 192–193.

58. Havens, *Fire*, pp. 91–92, 151–152, 199; Gabriel Kolko, "Oiling the Escalator," *The New Republic*, March 13, 1971, on Southeast Asia link; *Christian Science Monitor*, Dec. 1, 1969, p. 21 on White Paper; *Christian Science Monitor*, March 31, 1970, p. 7 on air force; Meyer to Department of State, March 15, 1971, National Security Archive, no. 73994, on nuclear weapons.

59. Johnson, *Right Hand*, pp. 549–550 on context; Havens, *Fire*, p. 222 on Communist trade; *Christian Science Monitor*, Nov. 24, 1969, p. 11; Sato, *Ohira*, pp. 254–255; "Memorandum for the President's Files," March 11, 1971, National Security Archive, no. 71710, for Mills; I. M. Destler, Haruhiro Fukui, and Hideo Sato, *The Textile Wrangle* (Ithaca, NY, 1979), esp. p. 320.

60. Kissinger, *White House Years*, pp. 340, 359; Destler, *et al.*, *Textile Wrangle*, p. 320.

61. Sato, *Ohira*, p. 250 for Perry reference.

62. Herman Kahn, *The Emerging Japanese Superstate* (Englewood Cliffs, NJ, 1970); criticial reviews are in *The Economist*, June 26, 1971, p. 59; and by Henry Rosovsky in *Science*, Feb. 5, 1971, p. 467.

63. *Public Papers of the Presidents . . . Nixon . . . 1971* (Washington, DC, 1972), pp. 806–812;

"Summary of Discussion . . . Eighth Japan-U.S. Businessmen's Conference," June 18, 1971, National Security Archive, no. 74108 has the business leaders' quotes; Robert E. Osgood, *et al., Retreat from Empire?* (Baltimore, 1973), p. 229 for trade.

64. This and the previous paragraph are based on "Summary of Discussion, Government-Business Debriefing Session"; "Opening Remarks of William P. Rogers at 8th Meeting of Joint U.S.-Japan Committee on Trade and Economic Affairs," Sept. 9, 1971, National Security Archive, no. 74117; "Memorandum for the President's File," Nov. 16, 1971, National Security Archive, no. 71698, for Connally-Nixon exchange; Destler, *et al., Textile Wrangle*, p. 27 has the Stans quote from *Time*; Bruce Cumings, "Japan's Position in the World System," in Andrew Gordon, ed., *Postwar Japanese History* (Berkeley, 1993), p. 55.

65. CIA, "Intelligence Memorandum. Japan's Eight-Point Economic Program: Progress and Prospects," September 1971, National Security Archive, no. 73718; "Memorandum for the Secretary," by Harold B. Scott, Dec. 14, 1971, National Security Archive, no. 74118; Tadashi Kawata, "The Rise and Fall of Economic Hegemony and Policy Change," *Journal of American and Canadian Studies*, 5 (Spring 1990): 24: *New York Times*, April 24, 1972, p. 53 for Eberle quote.

66. Tanaka Akihito, "Bei, Chu, So no aida de" [Inside the United States, China, and the Soviet Union], in Watanabe Akio, ed., *Sengo Nihon no taigai sesaku* [Postwar Japanese Foreign Policy] (Tokyo, 1985), pp. 228–231 for the duck analogy; "Memo for the President's File," April 8, 1971, National Security Archive, no. 71701; Ogata Sadako, *Normalization with China* (Berkeley, 1988), pp. 18–21 on Sino-Soviet clash.

67. Ogata, *Normalization*, p. 37 on Nixon-Rogers promise; Johnson, *Right Hand*, pp. 501, 553–554; Kissinger, *White House Years*, pp. 761–762; Havens, *Fire*, pp. 227–228 for Sato's unpopularity.

68. Hersh, *Price of Power*, p. 382 on Zhou's fears; Nixon's handwritten personal notes, "China Visit," Feb. 15, 1972, National Security Archive, no. 74177; Welfield, *Empire*, pp. 252–253; Nixon, *RN*, p. 567 on "others . . . defend themselves"; Ogata, *Normalization*, pp. 33–35.

69. *New York Times*, July 6, 1972, p. A1 on Tanaka; Ogata, *Normalization*, pp. 46–47; "Memorandum for the President's File," Aug. 31, 1972, by Ron Ziegler, National Security Archive, no. 71666, for toast.

70. *New York Times*, March 22, 1970, p. 4 on LDP split; Tad Szulc, *The Illusion of Peace* (New York, 1978), pp. 616–617 on Lockheed.

71. Iriye, *China and Japan*, pp. 124–125; Beasley, *Rise*, pp. 241–242; Ogata, *Normalization*, pp. 54–55 on Tanaka; Havens, *Fire*, p. 228.

72. Sterba story in *New York Times*, Aug. 28, 1972, p. 14; *Japan Times*, March 1, 1970, p. 3 has Eugene Black quote.

73. "Memorandum of Conversation," by Kissinger, Feb. 17, 1973, National Security Archive, no. 71723; "Memorandum for: The President," from Kissinger, March 2, 1973, National Security Archive, no. 71717.

74. "Memorandum for: The President," from Kissinger, Feb. 27, 1973, National Security Archive, no. 71724; Havens, *Fire*, pp. 92, 226, 232; George Herring, *America's Longest War* (New York, 1986), esp. pp. 250–256.

75. Aruga Tadashi, "Japanese Scholarship in the History of U.S.-East Asian Relations" (1993), pp. 42–43, in author's possession.

Chapter XII

1. *New York Times*, Sept. 28, 1971, in *NYT-GCI*, p. 395; Robert J. Smith, *Japanese Society* (Cambridge, UK, 1983), p. 21.

2. Yamamoto Mitsuru, *Fumo no gensetsu: Kokkai toben no naka no Nichi-Bei kankei* [The

Barren Discourse: The Diet's Response to the Japan-U.S. Relationship] (Tokyo, 1992), esp. pp. 15–20 on the 1970s as a major break; I. M. Destler, Harukiro Fukui, and Hideo Sato, *The Textile Wrangle* (Ithaca, NY, 1979), p. 27 has quote.

3. These 1972–74 events and their importance as a watershed, with leading scholarly analyses of them, are discussed in Walter LaFeber, "From *Detente* to the Gulf," in Gordon Martel, ed., *American Foreign Relations Reconsidered, 1890–1993* (London, 1994), pp. 147–151.

4. *New York Times*, Jan. 16, 1975, p. 1.

5. Destler, *et al., Textile Wrangle*, pp. 313–315, 320; "Memorandum," Kissinger to Nixon, Feb. 27, 1973, National Security Archive, no. 73724: Chalmers Johnson, *MITI and the Japanese Miracle* (Stanford, 1982), pp. 292–296.

6. Franklin Tugwell, *The Energy Crisis and the American Political Economy* (Stanford, 1988), pp. 98–112.

7. Ibid., pp. 113, 212–213.

8. This and the previous paragraph on the Japanese response are based on John Welfield, *Empire in Eclipse* (London, 1988), pp. 344–346; Johnson, *MITI*, pp. 286–288, 297–300; F. C. Perkins, "A Dynamic Analysis of Japanese Energy Policies," *Energy Policy*, 22 (July 1994): 595–597, 606; and Inada Juichi, "Hattentojokoku to Nihon" [Developing Countries and Japan], in Watanabe Akio, ed., *Sengo Nihon no taigai seisaku* [Postwar Japanese Foreign Policy] (Tokyo, 1985), pp. 313–314.

9. *The Economist*, July 9, 1994, p. 17.

10. George C. Allen, *A Short Economic History of Modern Japan* (London, 1981), pp. 223–224; Welfield, *Empire*, pp. 330–331, 338.

11. Ono Kazumoto, "Shiu shogen: CIA tai nichi himitsu kosaku no zenbunsho" [New Testimony: Documents on Covert CIA Operations in Japan], *Bungei Shunju* (January 1995): 5.

12. Masao Miyoshi, *As We Saw Them* (Berkeley, 1979), pp. 183–185; Ezra F. Vogel, "Japanese-American Relations After the Cold War," in Aspen Strategy Group, *Harness the Rising Sun* (Lanham, MD, 1993), p. 165.

13. Background and detailed citations on Carter are provided in Walter LaFeber, "From Confusion to Cold War: The Memoirs of the Carter Administration," *DH*, 8 (Winter 1984): 1–12; Ford "doctrine" speech is in *New York Times*, Dec. 8, 1975, p. C14; Thomas R. H. Havens, *Fire Across the Sea* (Princeton, 1987), pp. 241–244; Welfield, *Empire*, p. 339; *New York Times*, Jan. 13, 1976, p. A4 on Miki views.

14. Suzumara Kitaro and Mashahiro Okuno-Fujiwara, *Industrial Policy in Japan* (Canberra, 1987), p. 21 on Research Association; Smith, *Japanese Society*, p. 50 for baseball; Miyoshi, *As We Saw Them*, p. 95 for the hamburger reference.

15. Smith, *Japanese Society*, pp. 124–125; Ezra F. Vogel, *Japan as Number One* (New York, 1979, 1980), esp. pp. 70–73, 90–91, 232–245.

16. *The Economist*, July 15, 1995, p. 87; Sadako Ogata, *Normalization with China* (Berkeley, 1988), pp. 89–99; *Washington Post*, July 10, 1980, p. B1 for Iacocca quote; William Nester, *Japan and the Third World* (New York, 1992), pp. 18, 106, 114.

17. Welfield, *Empire*, p. 346; Havens, *Fire Across the Sea*, pp. 245, 248; Jacques Hersh, *USA and the Rise of East Asia* (London, 1993), pp. 53–56; Sydney Giffard, *Japan Among the Powers, 1890–1990* (New Haven, 1994), pp. 179–180; *New York Times*, Aug. 6, 1978, p. 1.

18. *The Economist*, July 15, 1995, p. 88.

19. Richard P. Cronin, *Japan, the United States and Prospects for the Asia-Pacific Century* (New York, 1992), p. 59; Hersh, *USA*, pp. 62–63.

20. Zbigniew Brzezinski, *Power and Principle* (New York, 1982), pp. 190, 206, 214–215; Jimmy Carter, *Keeping the Faith* (New York, 1982), pp. 193–196.

21. Carter, *Keeping Faith*, p. 48.

22. Welfield, *Empire*, p. 334; *New York Times*, Nov. 9, 1976, p. A61, and July 23, 1978, p. A9.
23. *Los Angeles Times*, Nov. 28, 1978, p. I1, and Dec. 8, 1978, p. I4; Nester, *Japan and Third World*, pp. 152–153; Giffard, *Japan Among the Powers* (New Haven, 1994), pp. 179–180.
24. W. G. Beasley, *The Rise of Modern Japan* (New York, 1990), pp. 268–269; *Washington Post*, July 31, 1978, p. A1.
25. Takashi Inoguchi, *Japan's Foreign Policy in an Era of Global Change* (New York, 1993), p. 20; Ohira's interview is in *New York Times*, Nov. 23, 1979, p. A27, and also see Aug. 6, 1978, p. 1. Akira Iriye estimates that in yen, the defense budget rose from 593 billion in 1970 to 1,881 billion in 1978. During these years, the dollar dropped from 360 yen to 195 yen, and the price index spiraled upward from 577 to 1227 (1934–36 = 1); Professor Iriye to author, Feb. 17, 1996.
26. *Washington Post*, June 26, 1980, p. A31 on Carter's military budget; Seizaburo Sato, Koyama Ken-ichi, and Kumon Shumpei, *Postwar Politician, The Life of Former Minister Masayoshi Ohira*, translated by William R. Carter (Tokyo, 1990), p. 534; Yamamoto, *Fumo no genetsu*, pp. 61–67 on Carter, pp. 74–75, 99–100 on Ohira; Giffard, *Japan Among the Powers*, pp. 185–186; Cronin, *Japan, the United States*, pp. 60–61 on Defense Agency; Bruce Cumings, "Japan's Position in the World System," in Andrew Gordon, ed., *Postwar Japan as History* (Berkeley, 1993), pp. 55–56.
27. The background and quotes in this and the previous paragraph are from Inoguchi Takashi, *Kokusai kankei no seiji keizaigaku: Nihon no yakuwari to sentaku* [Economics and Politics in International Relations: Japan's Role and Choices] (Tokyo, 1985), pp. 124–130; *New York Times*, May 21, 1981, p. A6 on U.S. sub and protests; Hersh, *USA*, pp. 100–101; Walter Dean Burnham, "American Politics in the 1980s," *Dissent*, 27 (Spring 1980); Brzezinski, *Power and Principle*, p. 515; *Los Angeles Times*, July 17, 1980, pp. I14–16 on Suzuki; Robert E. Ward and Sakamoto Yoshikazu, *Democratizing Japan* (Honolulu, 1987), pp. x–xi for "Occupy Us."
28. Giffard, *Japan Among the Powers*, pp. 177–178; Kent E. Calder, *Crisis and Compensation* (Princeton, 1988), pp. 114–116; *New York Times*, Nov. 27, 1982, p. A1; *Los Angeles Times*, Nov. 25, 1982, p. I1 for Tanaka versus Fukuda; Richard J. Samuels, "*Rich Nation, Strong Army*" (Ithaca, NY, 1994), pp. 171–175; "Yasuhiro Nakasone . . . ," interviewed by Alan M. Webber, *Harvard Business Review*, 67 (March–April 1989): 93 for "television democracy."
29. "National Security Decision Directive Number 62. *National Security Decision Directive on United States-Japan Relations*," Oct. 25, 1982, National Security Archive, no. 73855; George P. Shultz, *Turmoil and Triumph* (New York, 1993), pp. 173–178, 193.
30. "Yasuhiro Nakasone," pp. 84–85 for baseball metaphor; Cumings, "Japan's Position in the World System," pp. 57–58.
31. Havens, *Fire*, p. 244; Calder, *Crisis*, pp. 416–417 on defense levels; John Dower, "Peace and Democracy in Two System," in Gordon, *Postwar Japan as History*, p. 30 on exports; Hideki Kan, "The Reagan Administration and the Expansion of the Military-Industrial Complex," *Journal of American and Canadian Studies*, 3 (Spring 1989): 68–71.
32. "National Security Decision Directive Number 62," p. 2; Paul D. Wolfowitz, "Taking Stock of U.S.-Japan Relations," June 12, 1984, *Current Policy*, no. 593, p. 4.
33. "Yasuhiro Nakasone," p. 89 for "Japan Inc."; John Dower, *War Without Mercy* (New York, 1986), p. 315; Havens, *Fire*, pp. 249–251 on Nakasone's and Japanese racial views.
34. "Yasuhiro Nakasone," pp. 89–90; Nester, *Japan and Third World*, pp. 40–41 has the percentages; Andrew Boltho, "Was Japan's Industrial Policy Successful?" *Cambridge Journal of Economics*, 9 (1985): 191–192; Inoguchi, *Japan's Foreign Policy*, p. 32.
35. Calder, *Crisis*, p. 119 has "voluntary" figures; Sidney Blumenthal, "Whose Side Is Business On, Anyway?" *New York Times Magazine*, Oct. 25, 1981, esp. p. 95 on quoted corporate view.
36. "National Security Decision Directive Number 226. *Machine Tools and National Secu-*

rity," May 21, 1986, National Security Archive, no. 73862, for machine tool decision; John R. Kasich, "Get Rid of Corporate Welfare," *New York Times,* July 9, 1995, p. E15.

37. "Yasuhiro Nakasone," p. 88; Hersh, *USA,* pp. 86–87; Hideo Kanemitsu, "Trends in U.S.-Japan Economic Relations from 1955 to 1986." *Journal of American and Canadian Studies,* 2 (Autumn 1988): 94 for 1955 comparison.

38. Yoichi Funabashi, *Managing the Dollar* (Washington, DC, 1989), p. 4; Ellen L. Frost, *For Richer, For Poorer* (New York, 1987), p. 165 for Dole and Danforth; "National Security Decision Directive Number 154, *U.S.-Japan Trade Policy Relations,"* National Security Archive, no. 73860; Mike M. Mochizuki, "Japan and the Strategic Quadrangle," in Michael Mandelbaum, ed., *The Strategic Quadrangle* (New York, 1995), p. 117 on capital markets.

39. Frost, *For Richer,* p. 13 for post-Plaza; Nester, *Japan and Third World,* p. 35; Funabashi, *Managing the Dollar,* is important throughout for internal Japanese debates.

40. Cronin, *Japan,* pp. 9–10; Calder, *Crisis,* p. 120 has figures; Nester, *Japan and Third World,* p. 35 on yen transactions.

41. R. Taggart Murphy, *The Weight of the Yen* (New York, 1995), esp. pp. 164–177; Stephen W. Bosworth, "The United States and Asia," *Foreign Affairs,* 71 (no. 1, 1991–92): 119; Nester, *Japan and Third World,* p. 19 on aid division; *New York Times,* Aug. 21, 1985, p. D2 for China figures; Beasley, *Rise,* pp. 252, 267; Giffard, *Japan,* pp. 180–182 on Japan in China.

42. Yoichi Funabashi, *Asia Pacific Fusion* (Washington, DC, 1995), pp. 105, 187–189; Cronin, *Japan,* pp. 73–74.

43. Nester, *Japan and Third World,* p. 160.

44. Ibid., p. 65; David Gelsanliter, *Jump Start: Japan Comes to the Heartland* (New York, 1990), is excellent on the effects overall; John Dower, *Japan in War and Peace* (New York, 1994), pp. 303–304.

45. *New York Times,* April 16, 1995, p. E5, and also March 10, 1989, p. D2 on 1987 crash.

46. These points are covered elsewhere in this chapter, and there is good discussion and overview in Mark Mason, *American Multinationals and Japan* (Cambridge, MA, 1992), esp. pp. 202–242, with case studies; Jean-Claude Derian, *America's Struggle for Leadership in Technology,* translated by Severen Schaeffer (New York, 1990), pp. 8, 172–173 for Sematech; Dower, *Japan in War and Peace,* pp. 303–304 has Prestowitz quote; Akio Morita and Shintaro Ishihara, *The Japan That Can Say "No"* (Washington, DC, 1989), pp. 7–11.

47. Derian, *America's Struggle,* pp. 2–5; Kanemitsu, "Trends," pp. 103–105; Dower, *Japan in War and Peace,* p. 308 for cartoon.

48. Shultz, *Turmoil and Triumph,* p. 190; Hersh, *USA,* p. 144 for Maekawa Report and after; U.S. Department of the Treasury, "The Yen / Dollar Talks: Progress to Date and Current Issues," March 1987, National Security Archive, no. 71587; *Washington Post,* Aug. 22, 1994, p. A12 for the airport; Allen Wallis, "The U.S. and Japan," April 19, 1988, *Current Policy,* no. 1072.

49. Shultz, *Turmoil and Triumph,* pp. 189–190; C. Fred Bergsten and Paula Stern, "A New Vision for United States–Japan Economic Relations," in Aspen Strategy Group, *Harness the Rising Sun,* pp. 101–102.

50. Kevin Phillips, *Boiling Point* (New York, 1993), pp. 37–40; Dower, *Japan in War and Peace,* p. 304 for Abe quote, also pp. 312–314 for books; Shultz, *Turmoil and Triumph,* p. 195; Derian, *America's Struggle,* p. 270; Kan, "Reagan Administration," pp. 69–71.

51. Steve Rabson, " 'V-J Day' in Rhode Island," *Journal of American and Canadian Studies,* 9 (Spring 1992): 1–18.

52. Nester, *Japan and Third World,* pp. 233–234, 250–251.

53. Cronin, *Japan,* p. 5.

54. Homma Nagayo, *Utsuriyuku Amerika* [Changing America] (Tokyo, 1991), pp. 282–303 for quote and discussion; *Los Angeles Times*, Aug. 9, 1989, p. I1, Oct. 12, 1991, p. A1; Oct. 21, 1987, p. I8; and June 30, 1989, p. I6; *New York Times*, May 26, 1989, p. A1; Kato Tetsuro, "Japanese Perception of the 1989 Eastern European Revolution," *Hitotsubashi Journal of Social Studies*, 23 (August 1991): 12 on 1989 election.
55. Courtney Purrington, "Tokyo's Policy Responses During the Gulf Crisis," *Asian Survey*, 31 (April 1991): 179–180.
56. Ichiro Ozawa, *Blueprint for a New Japan*, translated by Louisa Rubinfien (Tokyo, 1994), esp. pp. 91–99; Homma, *Utsuriyuku Amerika*, p. 304.
57. *Wall Street Journal*, July 16, 1993, p. A6.
58. Taggart, *Weight of the Yen*, pp. 200–202 discusses price setting; James K. Glassman, "Down and Out in Japan," *Washington Post*, Sept. 12, 1995, p. A19 quotes and analyzes Asher; *Washington Post*, Nov. 29, 1994, p. C3; *The Economist*, July 9, 1994, p. 14 of "Survey of Japan" section.
59. Milton Ezrati, "Who Controls the Yen? Just Japan." *New York Times*, July 24, 1994, p. F9; *The Economist*, Sept. 10, 1994, p. 34.
60. Robert J. Samuelson, "They Have Met the Market—and Lost," *Washington Post*, March 29, 1995, p. A23; Chalmers Johnson, *Japan: Who Governs?* (New York, 1995), esp. pp. 7–18, 21–37, 115–140, 296–323; *Washington Post*, Sept. 12, 1995, p. D12.
61. David Halberstam, *The Next Century* (New York, 1991), has Johnson quote; *New York Times*, Jan. 29, 1992, p. A16 for Bush speech; Inoguchi, *Japan's Foreign Policy*, pp. 103–104.
62. For the U.S. side, note especially Bruce Jentleson, *With Friends Like These* (New York, 1994), on the Reagan-Bush pre-August 1991 policies; Theodore Draper, "The Gulf War Reconsidered," *New York Review of Books*, Jan. 16, 1992, pp. 46–53; Gilbert Rozman, *Japan's Response to the Gorbachev Era* (Princeton, 1992), p. 277.
63. Inoguchi, *Japan's Foreign Policy*, p. 101; Kato, "Japanese Perception," pp. 5–6; Rozman, *Japan's Response*, p. 308; Larry Berman and Bruce W. Jentleson, "Bush and the Post-Cold-War World," in Colin Campbell and Bert A. Rockman, eds., *The Bush Presidency; First Appraisals* (Chatham, NJ, 1991); Cronin, *Japan*, p. 35; Nestor, *Japan and Third World*, pp. 163–164.
64. William H. Gleysteen, Jr., "Japan and Korea in U.S.-China Policy during the 1990s," in Barber B. Conable, *et al.*, eds., *United States and China Relations at a Crossroads* (Lanham, MD, 1995), p. 247; Cronin, *Japan*, p. 35; *The Economist*, May 7, 1994, pp. 75–76.
65. Inoguchi, *Japan's Foreign Policy*, p. 111; Lawrence Freedman and Efraim Karsh, *The Gulf Conflict, 1990–1991* (Princeton, 1993), pp. 81–82, 122–123, 156; *Washington Post*, July 3, 1988, p. A29; Kuriyama Takakazu, "Geikido no kyujunen dai to Nihon gaiko no shin tenkai" [Tremors in the 1990's and New Developments in Japanese Foreign Policy], *Gaiko Forum*, 12 (May 1990): 12–21 is the foreign ministry official.
66. Freedman and Karsh, *Gulf Conflict*, pp. 124–125; Nester, *Japan and Third World*, pp. 227–228; Morita and Ishihara, *The Japan That Can Say "No,"* esp. pp. 3–5.
67. Nester, *Japan and Third World*, pp. 227–231; Freedman and Karsh, *The Gulf Conflict*, p. 122 has Japanese quote.
68. Purrington, "Tokyo's Policy Responses," pp. 167–172; *Washington Post*, March 7, 1991, p. A18; Toshiki Gome, "American Public Opinion During the 'Persian Gulf Conflict' and Its Image of Japan" (in Japanese), *Journal of American and Canadian Studies*, 8 (Spring 1992): 33–52.
69. Peter Katzenstein and Nabuo Okawara, *Japan's National Security* (Ithaca, NY, 1993), pp. 1–2 for Japanese opinion; Purrington, "Tokyo's Policy Responses," pp. 169–171.
70. *The Economist*, Sept. 17, 1994, p. 364; Steven R. Weisman, "Land of the Setting Sun?", *New York Times Book Review*, Sept. 11, 1994, p. 22; Ozawa, *Blueprint*, pp. 91–99; an

important view of the UN question is Sato Kinya's column "From a Tokyo Window," *Asahi Evening News,* May 26, 1994. Especially useful is Cronin, *Japan,* pp. 70, 89–96.

71. Sato Kinya, "From a Tokyo Window," *Asahi Evening News,* Feb. 10–11, 1994; Chalmers Johnson and E. B. Keehn, "The Pentagon's Ossified Strategy," *Foreign Affairs,* 72 (July–August 1995): 112 has Sakakibara quote; Robert A. Manning and Paula Stern, "The Myth of the Pacific Community," *Foreign Affairs,* 73 (November–December 1994): 81–82.

72. *The Economist,* Jan. 30, 1993, p. 59; Yoichi Funabashi, "The Asianization of Asia," *Foreign Affairs,* 72 (November–December 1993): 75–85.

73. *New York Times,* Feb. 5, 1995, p. 12 has Kantor's quote; *Washington Post,* May 5, 1994, p. A38; *The Economist,* Feb. 20, 1993, p. 17 has World Bank quote; *New York Times,* June 12, 1996, p. A7 for Lord.

74. Warren Christopher, "America's Strategy for a Peaceful and Prosperous Asia-Pacific," July 28, 1995, in author's possession; Robert S. Ross, "The United States and China and the Stability of Southeast Asia," in Conable, *et al.,* eds., *United States and China Relations,* pp. 256–257.

75. *Washington Post,* May 11, 1995, p. A18 is a useful survey.

76. *Far Eastern Economic Review,* April 15, 1993, pp. 10–11; *New York Times,* April 5, 1995, p. A25; *Wall Street Journal,* June 21, 1995, p. A20; *Washington Post,* Oct. 7, 1993, p. D23; *New York Times,* Feb. 19, 1995, p. F1 has Sanger quote.

77. Murphy, *Weight of the Yen,* pp. 268–282.

78. *Washington Post,* Feb. 22, 1994, p. A17; Karl van Wolferen, "Japan's Non-Revolution," *Foreign Affairs,* 72 (September–October 1993): 54; *New York Times,* Oct. 16, 1994, p. E5 on Japan's investment; *Washington Post,* Sept. 30, 1995, p. H2 for "once every half century" quote; *Newsweek,* Jan. 30, 1995, p. 30; *The Economist,* Oct. 21, 1995, p. 77 for deflation.

79. Murphy, *Weight of the Yen,* p. 281; *Washington Post,* June 29, 1995, p. A32; *New York Times,* June 30, 1995, p. D5; Jim Hoagland column in *Washington Post,* July 5, 1995, p. A33.

80. Izumi Hajime, "Chikakute poi rinjin" [A Near Far Neighbor], in Watanabe Akio, ed., *Sengo Nihon no taigai seisaku: Kokusai kankei no hen ijo to Nihon no yakuwari* [Postwar Japanese Foreign Policy: The Changes in International Relations and Japan's Role] (Tokyo, 1985), pp. 179–182; *New York Times,* April 24, 1994, p. 3; *Washington Post,* Jan. 9, 1994, p. H6. A leading *Asahi* columnist, Sato Kinya, interestingly dissented from Japan's and his newspaper's position in his column, "From a Tokyo Window," *Asahi Evening News,* March 24, 1994.

81. *New York Times,* June 22, 1994, p. A10; Shultz, *Turmoil and Triumph,* p. 193.

82. *Washington Post,* Sept. 20, 1995, p. A15; Joseph S. Nye, Jr., "The Case for Deep Engagement," *Foreign Affairs,* 74 (July–August 1995): 91 for oxygen reference.

Conclusion

1. Edward M. Barrows, *The Great Commodore* (Indianapolis, IN, 1935), pp. 284–285; James A. Baker III, *The Politics of Diplomacy* (New York, 1995), p. 44.

2. R. Taggart Murphy, *The Weight of the Yen* (New York, 1995), p. 87.

3. *The Economist,* Jan. 14, 1995, p. 13.

4. "Far West" quotes are discussed in Chapter XI above; *Washington Post,* Aug. 15, 1995, p. A14.

5. Clyde Prestowitz, "Japan and the United States: Twins or Opposites?" in Aspen Strategy Group, *Harness the Rising Sun* (Lanham, MD, 1993), p. 79.

6. Kuriyama Takakazu, "Geikido no kyujyunen dai to Nihon gaiko no shin tenkai" [Tremors

in the 1990s and New Developments in Japanese Foreign Policy], *Gaiko Forum,* 12 (May 1990): 12, 15, 20–21; Miyazato Seigen, "Posuto haken jidai no Nichi-Bei kankei" [Japan-U.S. Relations in the Post-Hegemony Period, 1985–1993], in Hosoya Chihiro, ed., *Nichi-Bei kankei* [Japan-U.S. Relations] (Tokyo, 1995), pp. 264–293; James Fallows, "What Is an Economy For?" *Atlantic Monthly* (January 1994): 76–92; Chalmers Johnson, *Japan: Who Governs?* (New York, 1995), esp. chapters 3–5, 11, 15; Thomas K. McCraw and Patricia A. O'Brien, "Production and Distribution: Competition Policy and Industry Structures," in Thomas K. McCraw, ed., *America versus Japan* (Boston, 1986), pp. 79–80; Paul Krugman, "The Myth of Asia's Miracle," *Foreign Affairs,* 73 (November–December 1994): 77–78 is an opposing view.

7. Truman's reference to the 1930s is in U.S. Government, *Public Papers of the Presidents . . . Truman, 1947* (Washington, DC, 1963), pp. 167–172; Robert B. Reich, "Playing Tag with Japan," *New York Review of Books,* June 24, 1982, pp. 37–39; Carol Gluck, "Patterns of Change," *Bulletin of the American Academy of Arts and Sciences,* XLVIII (March 1995): 48–51; Ezra F. Vogel, "Japan-American Relations After the Cold War," in Aspen Strategy Group, *Harness the Rising Sun,* p. 179; Warren Christopher, "The U.S.-Japan Relationship," *Department of State Dispatch,* March 11, 1994, p. 3.

8. *Washington Post,* Feb. 6, 1994, p. C1; *New York Times,* Sept. 16, 1995, p. 31.

9. *The Economist,* Oct. 1, 1994, pp. 42–44; Jonathan Cott, *Wandering Ghost: The Odyssey of Lafcadio Hearn* (New York, 1991), pp. xvi–xvii.

10. David E. Sanger, "Coloring History," *New York Times Magazine,* July 2, 1995, pp. 30–31; John W. Dower, "How a Genuine Democracy Should Celebrate Its Past," *Chronicle of Higher Education,* June 10, 1995, pp. B1–B2; Ronald H. Spector, "Reflections on the Enola Gay Debacle," *GW Magazine* (Fall 1995): 35; I am indebted to Michael Kammen for the Spector reference.

11. For background and quote, see especially Sanger, "Coloring History," p. 30; Sato Kinya, "From a Tokyo Window" column, *Asahi Evening News,* May 12, 1994, on officials' resignations; *New York Times,* March 4, 1995, p. 5 on pulp fiction; and an important series of articles, "Hiroshima in History and Memory: A Symposium," *DH,* 19 (Spring 1995): 197–365; as well as Sadao Asada, "The Mushroom Cloud and National Psyches," in author's possession.

12. A good overview is given by T. R. Reid in the *Washington Post,* Dec. 28, 1993, p. C2.

13. *Washington Post,* March 16, 1995, p. D1 for prisoner statistics; Ian Buruma, *The Wages of Guilt* (New York, 1994), important for comparison of Japan and Germany; *New York Times,* Aug. 16, 1995, p. A3 for Japanese "apology"; T. R. Reid's overview of Japanese coverage of the war commemoration in *Washington Post,* Aug. 14, 1995, p. A13; Nicholas Kristof's story on Yasukuni Shrine in *New York Times,* July 30, 1995, pp. 8xx–9xx in Travel Section.

14. Yoichi Funabashi, "Clinton Missed Chance," *Asahi Shimbun,* Sept. 5, 1995, pp. 2–3, on China not being involved in commemorations; Kevin B. Phillips, *Boiling Point* (New York, 1993), p. 237; Ian Buruma, "Ghosts of Pearl Harbor," *New York Review of Books,* Dec. 19, 1991, p. 13.

15. Especially important are Thomas L. Friedman's columns in the *New York Times,* Feb. 28, 1996, p. A17, and March 3, 1996, p. E15; also Nicholas Kristof's report of June 16, 1996, p. E3 in the *New York Times,* and Sandra Sugawara, *Washington Post,* June 6, 1996, p. D9.

16. *New York Times,* Feb. 25, 1996, p. E5 quotes U.S. official; *New York Times,* Feb. 28, 1996, p. A17 has Nishihara quote; *The Economist,* Feb. 20, 1993, pp. 19–22 has background; *Washington Post,* April 17, 1996, p. A29, and April 19, 1996, p. A29, and *New York Times,* May 28, 1996, p. A8 on new security arrangements.

17. Yamamoto Mitsuru, *Fumo no gensetsu: Kokkai toben no naka no Nichi-Bei kankei* [The

Barren Discourse: The Diet's Response to the Japan-U.S. Relationship] (Tokyo, 1992), pp. 232–236; Peter J. Katzenstein and Nobuo Okawara, *Japan's National Security* (Ithaca, NY, 1993), pp. 6–7; *New York Times*, April 20, 1993, p. D2 quotes *Asahi Shimbun; The Economist*, Oct. 7, 1995, pp. 35–36 for succinct historical perspective on Japan's role in Asia.

Bibliography

THIS bibliography has been chosen to supplement and elaborate the book's endnotes. Items have been selected on the basis of whether they are referred to more than once in the notes, and / or whether they have been important sources for the book's overall argument.

Manuscript and archival sources, as well as some collections of published documents, are not listed in the Bibliography. Rather, for easy reference, they are listed at the beginning of the Notes section.

Acheson, Dean G. *Crisis in Asia. An Examination of U.S. Policy.* Washington, DC, 1950.
———. *Present at the Creation. My Years in the State Department.* New York, 1969.
Agawa Hiroyuki. *The Reluctant Admiral: Yamamoto and the Imperial Navy.* Translated by John Bester. Tokyo, 1979.
Aichi Kiichi. "Japan's Legacy and Destiny of Change." *Foreign Affairs,* 48 (October 1969).
Akamatsu, Paul. *Meiji 1868. Revolution and Counter-Revolution in Japan.* New York, 1973.
Allen, G. C. *A Short Economic History of Modern Japan.* New York, 1981.
Allison, John M. *Ambassador from the Prairie; or, Allison Wonderland.* Boston, 1973.
Alperovitz, Gar. *The Decision to Use the Atomic Bomb and the Architecture of an American Myth.* New York, 1995.
Anderson, Irvine H., Jr. *The Standard-Vacuum Oil Company and United States East Asian Policy, 1933–1941.* Princeton, 1975.
Anethan, Albert d'Baron. *The d'Anethan Dispatches from Japan, 1894–1910.* Selected, translated, and edited, with a historical Introduction by George Alexander Lensen. Tokyo, 1967.

Armacost, Michael H. *Friends or Rivals? The Insider's Account of U.S. Japan Relations.* New York, 1996.

Aruga Tadashi. "Editor's Introduction: Japanese Interpretations of the American Revolution." *Japanese Journal of American Studies,* 2 (1985).

———. *Japanese Scholarship in the History of U.S.-East Asian Relations.* MS in possession of author. 1993.

———. "Japanese Views of the Pacific War." *JAIR International Newsletter* (October 1992).

Asada Sadao. "Japan's 'Special Interests' and the Washington Conference, 1921–22." *American Historical Review* (October 1961).

———. "The Japanese Navy and the United States." In Dorothy Borg and Shumpei Okamoto, eds. *Pearl Harbor as History: Japanese-American Relations, 1931–1941.* New York, 1973.

———. *Ryodai senkan no Nichi-Bei kankei: kaigun to seisaku kettei katei* [Japanese-American Relations Between the Wars: Naval Policy and the Decision-Making Process]. Tokyo, 1993.

———, ed. *Japan and the World, 1853–1952: A Bibliographic Guide to Japanese Scholarship in Foreign Relations.* New York, 1989.

Asahi Shimbun. *The Pacific Rivals: A Japanese View of Japanese-American Relations.* New York, 1972.

Aspen Strategy Group. *Harness the Rising Sun: An American Strategy for Managing Japan's Rise as a Global Power.* Lanham, MD, 1993.

Baker, James A. III, with Thomas M. DeFrank. *Politics of Diplomacy. Revolution, War, and Peace, 1989–1992.* New York, 1995.

Bamba Nobuya. *Japanese Diplomacy in a Dilemma: New Light on Japan's China Policy, 1924–1929.* Kyoto, 1972.

Barnet, Richard J. *The Alliance.* New York, 1983.

———. *The Rockets' Red Glare: When America Goes to War, the Presidents and the People.* New York, 1990.

Barnhart, Michael A. "Hornbeck Was Right: The Realist Approach to American Policy Toward Japan." In Hilary Conroy and Harry Wray, eds. *Pearl Harbor Reexamined: Prologue to the Pacific War.* Honolulu, 1989.

———. *Japan and the World Since 1868.* London, 1995.

———. *Japan Prepares for Total War: The Search for Economic Security.* Ithaca, NY, 1987.

Beasley, William G. *Japanese Imperialism, 1894–1945.* New York, 1991.

———. *The Rise of Modern Japan.* New York, 1990.

———, ed. *Modern Japan.* Berkeley, 1975.

———, translator and editor. *Select Documents on Japanese Foreign Policy, 1853–1868.* London, 1955.

Beisner, Robert L. *From the Old Diplomacy to the New, 1865–1900.* 2nd edition. Arlington Heights, IL, 1986.

Bergsten, C. Fred, and Paula Stern. "A New Vision for United States–Japan Economic Relations." In Aspen Strategy Group. *Harness the Rising Sun.* Lanham, MD, 1993.

Berman, Larry. "From Intervention to Disengagement." In Ariel Levite, Bruce Jentlesen and Larry Berman, eds. *Foreign Military Interventionism: The Dynamics of Protracted Conflict.* New York, 1992.

———, and Bruce W. Jentlesen. "Bush and the Post-Cold War World." In Colin Campbell and Bert A. Rockman, eds. *The Bush Presidency: First Appraisals.* Chatham, NJ, 1996.

Bernstein, Barton J. "An Analysis of 'Two Cultures': Writing About the Making and the Using of the Atomic Bombs." *Public Historian,* 12 (Spring 1990).

———. "The Atomic Bombings Reconsidered." *Foreign Affairs,* 74 (January–February 1995).

———. "The Perils and Politics of Surrender: Ending the War with Japan and Avoiding the Third Atomic Bomb." *Pacific Historical Review,* 46 (February 1977).

———. "A Postwar Myth: 500,000 U.S. Lives Saved." *Bulletin of the Atomic Scientists*, 42 (June–July 1986).

———. "Writing, Righting, or Wronging the Historical Record: President Truman's Letter on His Atomic-Bomb Decision." *Diplomatic History*, 16 (Winter 1992).

Best, Gary Dean. "Financing a Foreign War: Jacob H. Schiff and Japan, 1904–05." *American Jewish Historical Quarterly*, 61 (June 1972).

Bird, Kai. *The Chairman, John J. McCloy and the Making of the American Establishment.* New York, 1992.

Bix, Herbert P. "The Showa Emperor's 'Monologue' and the Problem of War Responsibility." *Journal of Japanese Studies*, 18 (Summer 1992).

Boltho, Andres. "Was Japan's Industrial Policy Successful?" *Cambridge Journal of Economics*, 9 (1985).

Borden, William S. *The Pacific Alliance: United States Foreign Economic Policy and Japanese Trade Recovery, 1947–1955.* Madison, WI, 1984.

Borg, Dorothy. *The United States and the Far Eastern Crisis of 1933–1938.* Cambridge, MA, 1964.

———, and Shumpei Okamoto, eds. *Pearl Harbor as History: Japanese-American Relations, 1931–1941.* New York, 1973.

Borton, Hugh. *American Presurrender Planning for Postwar Japan.* New York, 1967.

Braisted, William Reynolds. *The United States Navy in the Pacific, 1909–1922.* Austin, TX, 1971.

Briggs, Vernon M., Jr. *Mass Immigration and the National Interest.* Armonk, NY, 1992.

Broadbridge, Seymour, and Martin Collick. "Japan's International Policies." *International Affairs*, 44 (April 1968).

Brown, Leslie H. *Adelphi Papers, 132. American Security Policy in Asia.* London, 1977.

Bruchey, Stuart. *Enterprise: The Dynamic Economy of a Free People.* Cambridge, MA, 1989.

Brzezinski, Zbigniew. *The Fragile Blossom: Crisis and Change in Japan.* New York, 1971.

———. *Power and Principle.* New York, 1982.

Buckley, Roger. *U.S.-Japan Alliance Diplomacy, 1945–1990.* New York, 1992.

Burton, David H. *Theodore Roosevelt: Confident Imperialist.* Philadelphia, 1968.

Buruma, Ian. "Ghosts of Pearl Harbor." *New York Review of Books*, Dec. 19, 1991.

———. *The Wages of Guilt: Memories of War in Germany and Japan.* New York, 1994.

Butow, Robert. *Japan's Decision to Surrender.* Stanford, 1954.

———. "Marching Off to War on the Wrong Foot: The Final Note Tokyo Did *Not* Send to Washington." *Pacific Historical Review*, 63 (February 1994).

———. *Tojo and the Coming of the War.* Stanford, 1961.

Byas, Hugh. *Government by Assassination.* New York, 1942.

Calder, Kent E. *Crisis and Compensation. Public Policy and Political Stability in Japan, 1949–1986.* Princeton, 1988.

Calleo, David. "The Political Economy of Allied Relations: The Limits of Interdependence." In Robert E. Osgood, *et al. Retreat from Europe? The First Nixon Administration.* Baltimore, 1973.

Calman, Donald. *The Nature and Origins of Japanese Imperialism: A Reinterpretation of the Great Crisis of 1873.* London, 1992.

Campbell, Charles S. Jr. *The Transformation of American Foreign Relations, 1865–1900.* New York, 1976.

Carter, Jimmy. *Keeping Faith: Memoirs of a President.* New York, 1982.

Central Intelligence Agency. *CIA Research Reports: Japan, Korea, and the Security of Asia, 1946–1976* (microfilm). Frederick, MD, 1983.

———. *Intelligence Memorandum. Japan: The Effectiveness of Informal Import and Investment Controls.* Washington, DC, May 1960.

Chace, James, and Caleb Carr. *America Invulnerable: The Quest for Absolute Security from 1821 to Star Wars.* New York, 1988.

Chandler, Alfred D., with the assistance of Takashi Hikino. *Scale and Scope: The Dynamics of Industrial Capitalism.* Cambridge, MA, 1990.

Chen, Edward I-Te. "Japan's Decision to Annex Taiwan: A Study of Ito-Matsu Diplomacy, 1894–95." *Journal of Asian Studies,* 27 (November 1977).

Chernow, Ron. *The House of Morgan: An American Banking Dynasty and the Rise of Modern Finance.* New York, 1990.

China and Japan Sporting Register, The. Shanghai, 1877.

Christensen, Thomas J. "Threats, Assurances and the Last Chance for Peace: The Lessons of Mao's Korean War Telegrams." *International Security,* 17 (Summer 1992).

Clausen, Henry, and Bruce Lee. *Pearl Harbor: Final Judgement.* New York, 1992.

Clemens, Diane Shaver. *Yalta.* New York, 1970.

Clements, Kendrick A. *The Presidency of Woodrow Wilson.* Lawrence, KA, 1992.

Cochran, Sherman. "Japan's Capture of China's Market for Imported Cotton Textiles Before World War I: The Role of the Mitsui Trading Company." *The Second Conference on Modern Chinese Economic History.* Taipei, 1989.

Cohen, Warren I. "America's New Order for East Asia: The Four Power Financial Consortium and China, 1919–1946." *East Asia Occasional Papers.* Michigan State University, 1982.

———. *America's Response to China; An Interpretive History of Sino-American Relations.* New York, 1980.

———. *The Chinese Connection: Roger S. Greene, Thomas W. Lamont, George E. Sokolsky and American-East Asian Relations.* New York, 1978.

———. "Consortia." Ed. Alexander DeConde. *Encyclopedia of American Foreign Relations.* 3 vols. New York, 1978.

———. *Empire Without Tears. America's Foreign Relations, 1921–1922.* New York, 1987.

———, ed. *New Frontiers in American East Asian Relations. Essays Presented to Dorothy Borg.* New York, 1983.

———, and Akira Iriye, eds. *The Great Powers in East Asia, 1953–1960.* New York, 1990.

Cole, Wayne S. *Roosevelt and the Isolationists, 1932–1945.* Lincoln, NE, 1983.

Coletta, Paolo E. " 'The Most Thankless Task': Bryan and the California Alien Land Legislation." *Pacific Historical Review,* 36 (May 1967).

———. *The Presidency of William Howard Taft.* Lawrence, KA, 1973.

Committee for the Completion of Materials on Damage Caused by the Atomic Bombs in Hiroshima and Nagasaki. *Hiroshima and Nakaski: The Physical, Medical and Social Effects of the Atomic Bombings.* New York, 1981.

Conroy, Hilary. *The Japanese Expansion into Hawaii, 1868–1898.* San Francisco, 1973.

———. *The Japanese Seizure of Korea: 1868–1910.* Philadelphia, 1960.

———, and Harry Wray, eds. *Pearl Harbor Reexamined: Prologue to the Pacific War.* Honolulu, 1990.

Cooling, B. Franklin. *Gray Steel and Blue Water Navy: The Formative Years of America's Military-Industrial Complex, 1881–1917.* Hamden, CT, 1979.

Cooper, Chester. *The Lost Crusade: America in Vietnam.* New York, 1970.

Costigliola, Frank. *France and the United States. The Cold Alliance Since World War II.* New York, 1992.

Cott, Jonathan. *Wandering Ghost: The Odyssey of Lafcadio Hearn.* New York, 1991.

Cowhey, Peter F. "Domestic Institutions and the Credibility of International Commitments: Japan and the U.S." *International Organization,* 47 (Spring 1993).

Craft, Stephen G. "Deterring Aggression Abroad or at Home? A Rejoinder to 'FDR's Day of Infamy.' " *SHAFR Newsletter,* 24 (March 1993).

Crane, Conrad C. *Bombs, Cities, and Civilians*. Lawrence, KA, 1993.

Cronin, Richard P. *Japan, The United States and Prospects for the Asia-Pacific Century*. New York, 1993.

Crowley, James B. *Japan's Quest for Autonomy. National Security and Foreign Policy, 1930–1938*. Princeton, 1966.

———, ed. *Modern East Asia: Essays in Interpretation*. New York, 1970.

Cumings, Bruce. "Japan's Position in the World System." In Andrew Gordon, ed. *Postwar Japan as History*. Berkeley, 1993.

———. "The Origins and Development of the Northeast Asian Political Economy: Industrial Sectors, Produce Cycles, and Political Consequences." *International Oraganization*, 38 (Winter 1984).

———. *The Origins of the Korean War*. 2 vols. Princeton, 1981–90.

Curtis, Gerald L., ed. *Japan's Foreign Policy After the Cold War: Coping with Change*. Armonk, NY, 1992.

Daniels, Roger. *Asian America: Chinese and Japanese in the United States Since 1850*. Seattle, WA, 1988.

———. *Prisoners Without Trial: Japanese Americans in World War II*. New York, 1993.

Dawson, Carl. *Lafcadio Hearn and the Vision of Japan*. Baltimore, 1992.

DeConde, Alexander. *Ethnicity, Race, and Foreign Policy. A History*. Boston, 1992.

Derian, Jean-Claude. *America's Struggle for Leadership in Technology*. Translated by Severen Schaeffer. Cambridge, MA, 1990.

Dietrich, William S. *In the Shadow of the Rising Sun: The Political Roots of American Economic Decline*. University Park, PA, 1991.

Destler, I. M., Haruhiro Fukui, and Hideo Sato. *The Textile Wrangle: Conflict in Japanese-American Relations, 1969–1971*. Ithaca, NY, 1979.

Dingman, Roger. "Atomic Diplomacy During the Korean War." *International Security*, 13 (Winter 1988–89).

———. "The Dagger and the Gift: The Impact of the Korean War on Japan." *Journal of American-East Asian Relations*, 2 (Spring 1993).

———. "Korea at Forty-plus: The Origins of the Korean War Reconsidered." *Journal of American-East Asian Relations*, 1 (Spring 1992).

———. *Power in the Pacific: The Origins of Naval Limitation, 1914–1922*. Chicago, 1976.

———. "The U.S. Navy and the Cold War: The Japan Case." In Craig L. Symonds, ed. *New Aspects of Naval History*. Annapolis, MD, 1981.

Divine, Robert A. *Eisenhower and the Cold War*. New York, 1981.

———. *Foreign Policy and U.S. Presidential Elections, 1940–1948*. New York, 1974.

Doenecke, Justus. "American Isolationism, 1939–1941." *Journal of Libertarian Studies*, 6 (Summer–Fall 1982).

———. *The Diplomacy of Frustration: The Manchurian Crisis of 1931–1933 as Revealed in the Papers of Stanley K. Hornbeck*. Stanford, 1981.

———, ed. *In Danger Undaunted: The Anti-Interventionist Movement of 1940–1941 as Revealed in Papers of the American First Committee*. Stanford, 1990.

———, and John E. Wilz. *From Isolation to War, 1931–1941*. 2nd edition. Arlington Heights, IL, 1991.

Dore, Ronald. *Taking Japan Seriously: A Confucian Perspective on Leading Economic Issues*. Stanford, 1987.

Dorwart, Jeffrey M. *The Pigtail War: American Involvement in the Sino-Japanese War of 1894–1895*. Amherst, MA, 1975.

Dower, John. *Empire and Aftermath: Yoshida Shigeru and the Japanese Experience, 1878–1954*. Cambridge, MA, 1979.

———. *Japan in War and Peace: Selected Essays*. New York, 1993.

————. "Peace and Democracy in Two Systems." In Andrew Gordon, ed. *Postwar Japan as History.* Berkeley, 1993.

————. *War Without Mercy. Race and Power in the Pacific War.* New York, 1986.

Drake, Frederick C. *The Empire of the Seas: A Biography of Rear Admiral Robert Wilson Shufeldt, USN.* Honolulu, 1984.

Draper, Theodore. "The Gulf War Reconsidered." *New York Review of Books,* Jan. 16, 1992.

Drea, Edward J. *MacArthur's ULTRA Codebreaking and the War Against Japan, 1942–1945.* Lawrence, KA, 1991.

Dudden, Arthur Power. *The American Pacific: From the Old China Trade to the Present.* New York, 1992.

Dutt, V. P. *East Asia: China, Korea, Japan, 1947–1950.* New York, 1958.

Duus, Peter. *The Abacus and the Sword. The Japanese Penetration of Korea, 1895–1910.* Berkeley, 1995.

————. *Economic Aspects of Meij Imperialism.* Berlin, 1980.

————."Economic Dimensions of Meiji Imperialism: The Case of Korea, 1895–1910." In Ramon Myers and Mark Peattie, eds. *The Japanese Colonial Empire.* Princeton, 1984.

————. "The Takeoff Point of Japanese Imperialism." In Harry Wray and Hilary Conroy, eds. *Japan Examined: Perspectives on Modern Japanese History.* Honolulu, 1983.

————, ed. *The Cambridge History of Japan.* Vol. 6. *The Twentieth Century.* Cambridge, UK, 1988.

————, Ramon H. Myers, and Mark R. Peattie, eds. *The Japanese Informal Empire in China, 1895–1937.* Princeton, 1989.

Eguchi Keiichi. *Fatatsu no taisen* [Between the Two Great Wars]. Tokyo, 1989.

Eisenhower, Dwight D. *The White House Years: Mandate for Change, 1953–1956.* Garden City, NY, 1963.

Emmerson, John K. *The Japanese Thread: A Lifetime in the U.S. Foreign Service.* New York, 1978.

————, and Harrison M. Holland. *Eagle and the Rising Sun: American and Japan in the Twentieth Century.* Reading, MA, 1988.

Emmott, Bill. *Japanophobia: The Myth of the Invincible Japanese.* New York, 1993.

Encarnation, Dennis. *Rivals Beyond Trade: America versus Japan in Global Competition.* Ithaca, NY, 1992.

Esthus, Raymond A. *Double Eagle and the Rising Sun: The Russians and Japanese at Portsmouth in 1905.* Durham, NC, 1988.

Eto Jun. *Mo hitotsu no sengoshi* [Another Postwar History]. Tokyo, 1978.

Falk, Stanley L. "Douglas MacArthur and the War Against Japan." In William M. Leary, ed. *We Shall Return: MacArthur's Commanders and the Defeat of Japan, 1942–1945.* Lexington, KY, 1988.

Fallows, James M. *Looking at the Sun: The Rise of the Near East Asian Economic and Political System.* New York, 1994.

Fearey, Robert A. "My Year with Ambassador Joseph C. Grew, 1941–1942: A Personal Account." *Journal of American-East Asian Relations,* 1 (Spring 1992).

Ferrell, Robert H. *American Diplomacy in the Great Depression: Hoover-Stimson Foreign Policy, 1929–1933.* New Haven, 1957.

Fetzer, James. "Stanley K. Hornbeck and Japanese Aggression, 1941." *SHAFR Newsletter,* 24 (March 1993).

Fifield, Russell H. "Secretary Hughes and the Shantung Question." *Pacific Historical Review,* 23 (November 1954).

Fingleton, Eamonn. "Japan's Invisible Leviathan." *Foreign Affairs,* 74 (March–April 1995).

Finn, Richard B. *Winners in Peace: MacArthur, Yoshida, and Postwar Japan.* Berkeley, 1992.

Fletcher, W. Miles. "Taiheiyo senso: No nihou keizai e no eikyo" [The Economic Impact of the Pacific War on Japan]. In Hosoya Chihiro, *et al. Taiheiyo senso* [The Pacific War]. Tokyo, 1993.

Foglesong, David S. *America's Secret War Against Bolshevism: U.S. Intervention in the Russian Civil War, 1917–1920.* Chapel Hill, NC, 1995.

Foot, Rosemary. *The Wrong War: American Policy and the Dimensions of the Korean Conflict, 1950–1953.* Ithaca, NY, 1985.

Forrestal, James. *The Forrestal Diaries.* Ed. Walter Millis. New York, 1951.

Freedman, Lawrence, and Efraim Karsh. *The Gulf Conflict 1990–1991: Diplomacy and War in the New World Order.* Princeton, 1993.

Friend, Theodore. *The Blue-Eyed Enemy: Japan Against the West in Java and Luzon, 1942–1945.* Princeton, 1988.

Frost, Ellen L. *For Richer, For Poorer: The New U.S.-Japan Relationship.* New York, 1987.

Fry, Joseph. "Imperialism, American Style, 1890–1916." In Gordon Martel, ed. *American Foreign Relations Reconsidered.* London, 1994.

———. "In Search of an Orderly World: U.S. Imperialism, 1898–1912." In John M. Carroll and George C. Herring, eds. *Modern American Diplomacy.* Wilmington, DE, 1995.

Fukuyama, Francis. "Virtue and Prosperity." *The National Interest,* 40 (Summer 1995).

Fukuzawa Yukichi. *The Autobiography of Yukichi Fukuzawa.* Revised translation by Eiichi Kiyocka. New York, 1966.

———. *Fukuzawa Yukichi's An Outline of a Theory of Civilization.* Translated by David A. Dilworth and G. Cameron Hurst. Tokyo, 1973.

Funabashi Yoichi. *Asia Pacific Fusion. Japan's Role in APEC.* Washington, DC, 1995.

———. "Japan and the New World Order." *Foreign Affairs,* 70 (Winter 1991–92).

———. *Managing the Dollar: From the Plaza to the Louvre.* Washington, DC, 1989.

Gallichio, Marc. "Recovery Through Dependency: American-Japanese Relations, 1945–1970." In Warren I. Cohen, ed. *Pacific Passage: A Study of American-East Asian Relations on the Eve of the Twenty-First Century.* New York, 1996.

Gardner, Lloyd. *Approaching Vietnam.* New York, 1988.

———. *Architects of Illusion. Men and Ideas in American Foreign Policy, 1941–1949.* Chicago, 1970.

———. *A Covenant with Power. American and World Order from Wilson to Reagan.* New York, 1984.

———. *Economic Aspects of New Deal Diplomacy.* Madison, WI, 1964.

———. *Safe for Democracy: The Anglo-American Response to Revolution, 1913–1923.* New York, 1984.

Gelsanliter, David. *Jump Start: Japan Comes to the Heartland.* New York, 1990.

Gibney, Frank. "The First Three Months of the War." *Journal of American-East Asia Relations,* 2 (Spring 1993).

———. *Japan: The Fragile Superpower.* Tokyo, 1975.

Giffard, Sydney. *Japan Among the Powers, 1890–1990.* New Haven, 1994.

Gleysteen, William H., Jr. "Japan and Korea in U.S.-China Policy During the 1990's." In Barber B. Conable, Jr., *et al.,* eds. *United States and China Relations at a Crossroads.* Lanham, MD, 1995.

Gluck, Carol. "Entangling Illusions—Japanese and American Views of the Occupation." In Warren I. Cohen, ed. *New Frontiers in American-East Asian Relations. Essays Presented to Dorothy Borg.* New York, 1983.

———. *Japan's Modern Myths: Ideology in the Late Meiji Period.* Princeton, 1985.

———. "Patterns of Change: A 'Grand Unified Theory' of Japanese History." *Bulletin of the American Academy of Arts and Sciences,* 48 (March 1995).

———, and Stephen R. Graubard, eds. *Showa: The Japan of Hirohito.* New York, 1992.

Gomi, Toshiki. "American Public Opinion During 'The Persian Gulf Conflict' and Its Image of Japan" (In Japanese). *Journal of American and Canadian Studies,* 8 (Spring 1992).

Goncharov, Sergei N., John W. Lewis, and Yue Litai. *Uneven Partners: Stalin, Mao and the Korean War.* Stanford, 1993.

Goralski, Robert. *World War II Almanac, 1931–1945.* New York, 1981.

Gordon, Andrew, ed. *Postwar Japan as History.* Berkeley, 1993.

Griswold, A. Whitney. *The Far Eastern Policy of the United States.* New York, 1938.

Guttmann, Allen. *Games and Empires: Modern Sports and Cultural Imperialism.* New York, 1994.

Hackett, Roger F. *Yamagata Aritomo in the Rise of Modern Japan, 1838–1922.* Cambridge, MA, 1971.

Hagerty, James C. *The Diary of James C. Hagerty: Eisenhower in Mid-Course, 1954–1955.* Ed. Robert H. Ferrell. Bloomington, IN, 1983.

Hahn, Emily. "A Yankee Barbarian at the Shogun's Court." *American Heritage,* 15 (June 1964).

Halberstam, David. *The Next Century.* New York, 1991.

Hall, Francis. *Japan Through American Eyes: The Journal of Francis Hall, Kanagawa and Yokohama, 1859–1866.* Ed. F. G. Notehelfer. Princeton, 1992.

Hall, John Whitney. "Japanese History in World Perspective." In Charles F. Delyell, ed. *The Future of History.* Nashville, TN, 1977.

———. "East, Southeast, and South Asia." In Michael Kammen, ed. *The Past Before Us: Contemporary Historical Writing in the United States.* Ithaca, NY, 1980.

———. "Reflections on a Centennial." *Journal of Asian Studies,* 27 (August 1968).

Halliday, Jon. *A Political History of Japanese Capitalism.* New York, 1975.

———, and Bruce Cumings, *Korea: The Unknown War.* New York, 1988.

Halloran, Richard. *Japan: Images and Realities.* New York, 1969.

Hammersmith, Jack. "The Sino-Japanese War, 1894–95: American Predictions Reassured." *Asian Forum,* 4 (no 1, 1972).

Harrington, Fred Harvey. "An American View of Korean-American Relations, 1882–1905." In Yur-Bok Lee and Wayne Patterson, eds. *One Hundred Years of Korean-American Relations, 1882–1982.* University, AL, 1986.

———. *God, Mammon, and the Japanese; Dr. Horace N. Allen and Korean-American Relations, 1884–1905.* Madison, WI, 1944.

Hart, Jeffrey A. *Rival Capitalists: International Competitiveness in the United States, Japan, and Western Europe.* Ithaca, NY, 1992.

Hata Ikuhiko. *Shiroku: Nihon saigunbi* [The Historical Record: Japan's Rearmament]. Tokyo, 1976.

Hattori Akira. "Is Japanese-Style Capitalism Counterproductive?" *International Economic Insights,* 4 (September–October 1993).

Havens, Thomas R. H. *Fire Across the Sea: The Vietnam War and Japan, 1965–1975.* Princeton, 1987.

———. *Valley of Darkness: The Japanese People and World War Two.* New York, 1978.

Hein, Laura E. "Free-Floating Anxieties on the Pacific: Japan and the West Revisited." *Diplomatic History,* 20 (Summer 1996).

Heinrichs, Waldo. *Threshold of War: Franklin D. Roosevelt and American Entry into World War II.* New York, 1988.

Heren, Louis. *No Hail, No Farewell.* New York, 1970.

Herken, Gregg. *The Winning Weapon. The Atomic Bomb in the Cold War, 1945–1950.* Princeton, 1988.

Herring, George. *America's Longest War. The United States in Vietnam, 1950–1975.* 2nd edition. New York, 1986.

Hersh, Jacques. *The USA and the Rise of East Asia Since 1945: Dilemmas of the Postwar International Political Economy.* London, 1993.

Hersh, Seymour. *The Price of Power: Kissinger in the Nixon White House.* New York, 1983.

Hideki Kan. "The Reagan Administration and the Expansion of the Military-Industrial Complex." *Journal of American and Canadian Studies,* 3 (Spring 1989).

Hideo Tanaka. "The Conflict Between Two Legal Traditions in Making the Constitution of Japan." In Robert E. Ward and Sakamoto Yoshikazu, eds. *Democaratizing Japan: The Allied Occupation.* Honolulu, 1987.

Hideo Kanemitsu. "Trends in U.S.-Japan Economic Relations from 1955 to 1986." *Journal of American and Canadian Studies,* 2 (Autumn 1988).

Hirano Ken'ichiro. "Nishihara shakhan hara Shinshikoku shakkanda e" [From the Nishihara Loan to the Four-Power Consortium]. In Hosoya Chihiro and Saito Makoto, eds. *Washinton taisei to Nichi-Bei kankei* [The Washington Treaty System and Japanese-U.S. Relations]. Tokyo, 1988.

———. "Sengo Nihon gaiko ni okeru 〈Bunkat〉" [Postwar Japanese Foreign Policy in Relation to "Culture"]. In Watanabe Akio. *Sengo Nihon no taigai sesaku: Kokusai kankei no hen yo to Nihon no yakuwari* [Postwar Japanese Foreign Policy]. Tokyo, 1985.

Hirano Kyoko. *Mr. Smith Goes to Tokyo; Japanese Cinema Under the American Occupation, 1945–1952.* Washington, DC, 1992.

Hirobe Izumi. "American Attitudes Toward the Japanese Immigration Question, 1924–1931." *Journal of American-East Asian Relations,* 2 (Fall 1993).

Hiwatari Yume. "U.S.-Japanese Relations in the Late 1950's: Kishi's Southeast Asian Policy" (in Japanese). *Journal of Modern Japanese Studies,* 11 (1989).

Hobsbawm, Eric. *The Age of Empires.* New York, 1987.

Hodgson, Godfrey. *The Colonel. The Life and Wars of Henry Stimson, 1867–1950.* New York, 1990.

Hogan, Michael L., ed. *Hiroshima in History and Memory.* New York, 1996.

Homma Nagayo. "The Peril of Revisionism." *Japan Review of International Affairs,* 2 (Spring–Summer 1990).

———. *Utsuriyuku Amerika: Gendai Nichi-Bei kankei ko* [Changing America: A Modernist Overview of Japan-U.S. Relationships]. Tokyo, 1991.

Hoopes, Townsend, and Douglas Brinkley. *Driven Patriot: The Life and Times of James Forrestal.* New York, 1992.

Hoover, Herbert. *The Ordeal of Woodrow Wilson.* New York, 1958.

Hosoya Chihiro. "Japan's Decision for War in 1941." *Hitotsubashi Journal of Law and Politics,* 5 (April 1967).

———. *Ryotaisenkan no Nihon gaiko, 1914–1945* [Japanese Foreign Policy in the Period Between the Two World Wars]. Tokyo, 1988.

———, ed. *Nichi-Bei kankei tsushi* [Japan-U.S. Relations]. Tokyo, 1995.

———, and Saito Makoto, eds. *Washington taisei to Nichi-Bei kankei* [The Washington Treaty System and Japanese-U.S. Relations]. Tokyo. 1978.

———, Homma Nagayo, Iriye Akira, and Hitano Sumio, eds. *Taiheiyo Senso* [The Pacific War]. Tokyo, 1993.

Hoyt, Edwin Palmer. *Warlord: Tojo Against the World.* Lanham, MD, 1993.

Hunt, Michael H. *Frontier Defense and the Open Door: Manchuria in Chinese-American Relations, 1895–1911.* New Haven, 1973.

———. *Ideology and U.S. Foreign Policy.* New Haven, 1987.

Ibe Hideo. *Japan Thrice-Opened: An Analysis of Relations Between Japan and the United States.* New York, 1992.

Ienaga Sahuro. *Japan's Lost War: World War II and the Japanese, 1931–1945.* New York, 1979.

Igarashi Takashi. "MacArthur's Proposal for an Early Peace with Japan and the Redirection of the Occupation." In Aruga Tadashi, ed. *Japanese Journal of American Studies,* 1 (1981).

————. "Peace-Making and Party Politics: The Formation of the Domestic Foreign-Policy System in Postwar Japan." *Journal of Japanese Studies*, 11 (no. 2, 1985)

————. "Reisen to Kowa" [Cold War and Peace]. In Watanabe Akio. *Sengo Nihon no taigai seisaki* [Postwar Japanese Foreign Policy]. Tokyo, 1985.

————. "Senso to senyo, 1941–1951" [War and Occupation]. In Hosoya Chihuro, ed. *Nichi-Bei kankei tsushi* [Japan and the United States]. Tokyo, 1995.

Inada, Juichi. "Hottentojoku to Nihon" [Developing Countries and Japan]. In Watanabe Akio, ed. *Sengo Nihon no taisai seisaku* [Postwar Japanese Foreign Policy]. Tokyo, 1985.

Inoguchi Takashi. *Japan's Foreign Policy in an Era of Global Change*. New York, 1993.

————. *Kokusai kankei no seiji keizaigaku: Nihon no yakuwari to sentaku* [Economics and Politics in International Relations: Japan's Role and Choices]. Tokyo, 1985.

Inoue, Kiyoshi. *Nihon teikoku shugi no kesei* [The Formation of Japanese Imperialism]. Tokyo, 1968.

Inoue, Kyoko. *MacArthur's Japanese Constitution. A Linguistic and Cultural Study of Its Making*. Chicago, 1991.

Inoue, Toshikazu. *Kiki no naka no kyocho gaiko: Nitchu Senso ni itaru taigai seisaku no keisei to tenkai* [A Conciliatory Foreign Policy in the Midst of Crisis: The Formation and Development of Japanese Foreign Policy Until the Sino-Japanese War]. Tokyo, 1994.

Iokibe Makoto. *Nichi-Bei senso to sengo Nihon* [The Japan-U.S. War and Postwar Japan]. Osaka, 1989.

Iriye Akira. *After Imperialism: The Search for a New Order in the Far East, 1921–1931*. Cambridge, MA, 1965.

————. *China and Japan in the Global Setting*. Cambridge, MA, 1992.

————. *The Cold War in Asia*. Englewood Cliffs, NJ, 1974.

————. "The Failure of Economic Expansionism: 1918–1931." In Bernard Silberman and Harry Harootunian, eds. *Japan in Crisis*. Princeton, 1974.

————. "The Failure of Military Expansionism." In James Morley, ed. *Dilemmas of Growth in Prewar Japan*. Princeton, 1971.

————. *From Nationalism to Internationalism: U.S. Foreign Policy to 1914*. London, 1977.

————. "Japan's Drive to Great-Power Status." In Marius Jansen, ed. *The Cambridge History of Japan*. Vol. 5. *The Nineteenth Century*. Cambridge, UK, 1989.

————. Japan's Policies Toward the United States." In James William Morley, ed. *Japan's Foreign Policy, 1868–1941. A Research Guide*. New York, 1974.

————. *The Origins of the Second World War in Asia and the Pacific*. London, 1987.

————. *Power and Culture: The Japanese-American War, 1941–1945*. Cambridge, MA, 1981.

————, ed. *Mutual Images: Essays in American-Japanese Relations*. Cambridge, MA, 1975.

————, and Warren I. Cohen, eds. *The United States and Japan in the Postwar World*. Lexington, KY, 1989.

Irokawa Daikichi. *The Age of Hirohito: In Search of Modern Japan*. Translated by Mikiso Hane and John K. Urta. New York, 1995.

————. *The Culture of the Meiji Period*. Translated and edited by Marius B. Jansen. Princeton, 1985.

Ishii Osamu. "Nichi-Bei paatonashippu e no dotei, 1952–1969" [The Road to Japan-U.S. "Partnership" 1952–1969]. In Hosoya Chihiro. *Nichi-Bei kankei tsushi* [Japan-U.S. Relations]. Tokyo, 1995.

Ishii, Viscount Kikujiro. *Diplomatic Commentaries*. Translated and edited by William R. Langdon, Baltimore, 1936.

Ishikawa Tadao, Nakajima Mineo, and Ikei Masaru, eds. *Sengo shiryo: Nit-chu kankei* [Postwar Documents in Sino-Japanese Relations]. Tokyo, 1970.

James, D. Clayton. *The Years of MacArthur*. 3 vols. Boston, 1975–85.

Jansen, Marius. *Japan and China: From War to Peace, 1894–1972.* Chicago, 1975.

———. "Japanese Imperialism: Late Meiji Perspectives." In Ramon Myers and Mark Peattie, eds. *The Japanese Colonial Empire.* Princeton, 1984.

Jentlesen, Bruce W. *With Friends Like These: Reagan, Bush, and Saddam, 1982–1990.* New York, 1994.

Jessup, Philip C. *Elihu Root.* 2 vols. New York, 1938.

Johnson, Chalmers. *Japan: Who Governs?* New York, 1995.

———. *MITI and the Japanese Miracle: The Growth of Industrial Policy, 1925–1975.* Stanford, 1982.

———, and E. B. Keehn. "The Pentagon's Ossified Strategy." *Foreign Affairs,* 74 (July–August 1995).

Johnson, Sheila, *The Japanese Through American Eyes.* Stanford, 1988.

Johnson, U. Alexis, with Jel Olivarious McAllister. *The Right Hand of Power.* Englewood Cliffs, NJ, 1984.

Kachi, Teruko. *The Treaty of 1911 and the Immigration and Alien Land Law Issue Between the United States and Japan, 1911–1913.* New York, 1978.

Kades, Charles L. "The American Role in Revising Japan's Imperial Constitution." *Political Science Quarterly,* 104 (Summer 1989).

Kahin, George McT. *Intervention: How America Became Involved in Vietnam.* New York, 1986.

———, and Audrey Kahin. *Subversion as Foreign Policy: The Secret Eisenhower and Dulles Debacle in Indonesia.* New York, 1995.

Kahn, David. "U.S. Views of Germany and Japan in 1941." In Ernest R. May, ed. *Knowing One's Enemies: Intelligence Assessment Before the Two World Wars.* Princeton, 1984.

Kahn, Herman. *The Emerging Japanese Superstate.* Englewood Cliffs, NJ, 1970.

Kajima, M. *The Diplomacy of Japan, 1894–1922.* 3 vols. Tokyo, 1976–80.

Kamikowa Hikomatsu, ed. *Japan-American Diplomatic Relations in the Meiji-Taisho Era.* Translated by Kimuro Michiko. Tokyo, 1958.

Kan Hideki. "The Reagan Administration and the Expansion of the Military-Industrial Complex." *Journal of American and Canadian Studies,* 3 (Spring 1989).

Kanemitsu Hideo. "Trends in U.S.-Japan Economic Relations from 1955 to 1986." *Journal of American and Canadian Studies,* 2 (Autumn 1988).

Kaoru Sugihara. "Japan as an Engine of the Asian International Economy, c. 1880–1936." *Japan Forum,* 2 (April 1990).

Katzenstein, Peter J., and Nobuo Okawara. *Japan's National Security; Structures, Norms, and Policy Responses in a Changing World.* Ithaca, NY, 1993.

Kaufman, Burton. "Eisenhower's Foreign Economic Policy with Respect to Asia." In Warren Cohen and Akira Iriye, eds. *The Great Powers in East Asia, 1953–1960.* New York, 1990.

Kazumoto Ono. "Shin shogen: CIA tai nichi himitsu kosaku no zenbunsho" [New Testimony: Documents on Covert CIA Operations in Japan]. *Bungei Shunju.* (December 1994).

Kennan, George. *Memoirs, 1925–1950.* Boston, 1967.

Kennedy, Paul M. *The Samoan Tangle: A Study in Anglo-German-American Relations, 1878–1900.* New York, 1974.

———. *Strategy and Diplomacy, 1870–1945: Eight Studies.* London, 1983.

Kido Koichi. *The Diary of Marquis Kido, 1931–1945: Selected Translation into English.* Frederick, MD, 1984.

Kim, C. I. Eugene, and Han-kyo Kim. *Korea and the Politics of Imperialism, 1876–1910.* Berkeley, 1967.

Kimura Masato. "The Opening of the Panama Canal and Japanese-American Relations" (in Japanese). *Journal of Modern Japanese Studies,* 11 (1989).

Kinmouth, Earl H. "Fukuzawa Reconsidered: *Gakumon no susume* and Its Audience." *Journal of Asian Studies,* 37 (August 1978).

Kissinger, Henry. *American Foreign Policy.* Expanded edition. New York, 1974.

———. *White House Years.* Boston, 1979.

———. *Years of Upheaval.* Boston, 1982.

Kitaro Suyumara and Masahiro Okuno-Fujiwara. *Industrial Policy in Japan: Overview and Evaluation.* Canberra, 1987.

Klein, Ira. "Whitehall, Washington, and the Anglo-Japanese Alliance, 1919–1921." *Pacific Historical Review,* 46 (no 2, 1968).

Knock, Thomas J. *To End All Wars: Woodrow Wilson and the Quest for a New World Order.* New York, 1992.

Kolko, Gabriel. *The Politics of War: The World and U.S. Foreign Policy, 1943–1945.* New York, 1968.

Kono Yasuko. " 'Sengo no owati' " [The End of the Postwar Era]. In Watanabe Akio, ed. *Sengo Nihon no taigai seisaku* [Postwar Japanese Foreign Policy]. Tokyo, 1985.

Koppes, Clayton R., and Gregory D. Black. *Hollywood Goes to War: How Politics, Profits and Propaganda Shaped World War II Movies.* Berkeley, 1990.

Koschmann, J. Victor. *The Mito Ideology. Discourse, Reform, and Insurrection in Late Tokugawa Japan, 1790–1864.* Berkeley, 1987.

Kosai Yutaka. "The Postwar Japanese Economy, 1945–1973." Translated by Andrew Gable. In Peter Duus, ed. *The Cambridge History of Japan.* Vol. 6. *The Twentieth Century.* Cambridge, UK, 1988.

Krasner, Stephen D. "Japan and the United States: Prospects for Stability." In Takashi Inoguchi and Daniel I. Okimoto, eds. *The Political Economy of Japan.* Vol. 2. Stanford, 1988.

Krugman, Paul. "The Myth of Asia's Miracle." *Foreign Affairs,* 73 (November–December 1994).

Kublin, Hyman. "The Evolution of Japanese Colonialism." *Comparative Studies in Society and History,* II (1959).

Kuriyama Takakazu. "Geikido no kyujunen dai to Nihon gaiko no shin tenkai" [Tremors in the 1990s and New Developments in Japanese Foreign Policy]. *Gaiko Forum,* 12 (May 1990).

Kurosawa Fumitaku. "A Prelude to Disaster: The Japanese Imperial Army's Total War Plan Before World War II." In Sophia University Institute of American and Canadian Studies. *Beginnings of the Soviet-German and the U.S.-Japanese Wars and Fifty Years After.* Tokyo, 1993.

Large, Stephen. *Emperor Hirohito and Showa Japan: A Political Biography.* New York, 1992.

Lauren, Paul Gorden. *Power and Prejudice: The Politics and Diplomacy of Racial Discrimination.* Boulder, CO, 1988.

———, and Raymond F. Wyle, eds. *Destinies Shared: U.S.-Japanese Relations.* Boulder, CO, 1989.

Leary, William M., ed. *We Shall Return! MacArthur's Commanders and the Defeat of Japan, 1942–1945.* Lexington, KY, 1988.

Lee, Yur-Bok. *Diplomatic Relations Between the United States and Korea, 1866–1887.* New York, 1970.

———, and Wayne Patterson, eds. *One Hundred Years of Korean-American Relations, 1882–1982.* University, AL, 1986.

Leffler, Melvyn P. *A Preponderance of Power. National Security, the Truman Administration, and the Cold War.* Stanford, 1992.

Levin, N. Gordon, Jr. *Woodrow Wilson World Politics: America's Response to War and Revolution.* New York, 1968.

Lockwood, William W. *The Economic Development of Japan*. Growth and Structural Change, 1868–1938. Princeton, 1954.

———. *The State and Economic Enterprise in Japan*. Princeton, 1985.

Mandel, Richard. "The Struggle for East Asia's Rimlands: Franklin D. Roosevelt, the Joint Chiefs of Staff, and U.S. Far East Policy, 1921–1945." Unpublished doctoral dissertation, Cornell University, 1990.

Mandelbaum, Michael, ed. *The Strategic Quadrangle: Russia, China, Japan and the United States in East Asia*. New York, 1995.

Manning, Robert A., and Paula Stern. "The Myth of the Pacific Community." *Foreign Affairs*, 73 (November–December 1994).

Marks, Frederick W. III. *Power and Peace: The Diplomacy of John Foster Dulles*. Westport, CT, 1993.

———. *Velvet on Iron: The Diplomacy of Theodore Roosevelt*. Lincoln, NE, 1979.

Marshall, Jonathan. *To Have and to Have Not: Southeast Asian Raw Materials and the Origins of the Pacific War*. Berkeley, 1995.

Martel, Gordon, ed. *American Foreign Relations Reconsidered, 1890–1993*. London, 1994.

Maruyama Masao. *Thought and Behavior in Modern Japanese Politics*. Ed. Ivan Morris. London, 1963.

Masland, John W. "Commercial Influence Upon American Far Eastern Policy, 1937–1941." *Pacific Historical Review*, 11 (September 1942).

Mason, Mark. *American Multinationals and Japan: The Political Economy of Japanese Capital Controls, 1899–1980*. Cambridge, MA, 1992.

Matsuda Takeshi. "Woodrow Wilson's Dollar Diplomacy in the Far East: The New Chinese Consortium, 1917–1921." Unpublished doctoral dissertation, University of Wisconsin-Madison, 1979.

May, Ernest R. ed. *Knowing One's Enemies: Intelligence Assessment Before Two World Wars*. Princeton, 1984.

Mayer, Arno J. *Politics and Diplomacy of Peacemaking: Containment and Counterrevolution at Versailles, 1918–1919*. New York, 1967.

Mayo, Marlene. "The Western Education of Kume Kunitake, 1871–76." *Monumenta Nipponica*, 28 (1973).

McCormick, Thomas. *America's Half-Century: United States Foreign Policy in the Cold War*. 2nd edition. Baltimore, 1995.

———. *China Market*. Chicago, 1967.

McCraw, Thomas K., ed. *America versus Japan*. Boston, 1986.

McDougall, Walter A. *Let the Sea Make a Noise: A History of the North Pacific from Magellan to MacArthur*. New York, 1993.

McGlothlen, Ronald. *Controlling the Waves: Dean Acheson and U.S. Foreign Policy in Asia*. New York, 1993.

McMahon, Robert J. "The Cold War in Asia: Toward a New Synthesis?" *Diplomatic History*, 12 (Summer 1988).

McNeil, Frank. *Japanese Politics: Decay or Reform?* New York, 1993.

McNelly, Theodore H. " 'Induced Revolution': The Policy and Process of Constitutional Reform in Occupied Japan." In Robert E. Ward and Sakamoto Yoshikazu, eds. *Democratizing Japan: The Allied Occupation*. Honolulu, 1987.

———. "The Renunciation of War in the Japanese Constitution." *Political Science Quarterly*, 77 (September 1962).

Mendel, Douglas H., Jr. "Japan Reviews Her American Alliance." *Public Opinion Quarterly*, 30 (Spring 1966).

———. "Japanese Views of the American Alliance." *Public Opinion Quarterly*, 23 (Fall 1959).

Messer, Robert L. *The End of an Alliance*. James F. Byrnes, Roosevelt, Truman, and the Origins of the Cold War. Chapel Hill, NC, 1982.

Miller, Edward S. *War Plan* ORANGE *The U.S. Strategy to Defeat Japan, 1897–1945*. Annapolis, MD, 1991.

Miller, Nathan. *Theodore Roosevelt: A Life*. New York, 1992.

Millett, Allan R., and Peter Maslowski. *For the Common Defense: A Military History of the United States of America*. New York, 1984.

Mitani Taichiro. "Manchuria: American Capital and Japanese Special Interests in the 1920's." In Ian Nish, ed. *Some Foreign Attitudes to Republican China*. London, 1980.

————. "Senzen senchuki Nichi-Bei kankei ni okeru sin-Nichiha gaikokan no yakuwari: J. Barantain to E. Douman ni tsuite" [The Role of the Pro-Japanese American Diplomats in U.S.-Japanese Relations, Before and During the Pacific War: Joseph Ballantine and Eugene Dooman]. In *Gaiko Forum*, 36–39 (September–December 1991).

Miwa Kimitada. *Japanese Policies and Concepts for a Regional Order in Asia, 1938–1940*. Sophia University, Institute of International Relations for Advanced Studies on Peace and Development in Asia, 1983.

Miyazoto Seigen. "Posuto haken jidai no Nichi-Bei kankei" ["Japan-U.S. Relations in the Post-Hegemony Period"]. In Hosoya Chihiro, ed. *Nichi-Bei kankei* [Japan-U.S. Relations]. Tokyo, 1995.

Miyoshi Masao. *As We Saw Them: The First Japanese Embassy to the United States (1860)*. Berkeley, 1979.

Mochizuki, Mike M. "Japan and the Strategic Quadrangle." In Michael Mandelbaum, ed. *The Strategic Quadrangle: Russia, China, Japan and the United States in East Asia*. New York, 1995.

————. "Review Essay: The Past in Japan's Future." *Foreign Affairs*, 73 (September–October 1994).

Morita Akio and Ishihara Shintaro. *The Japan That Can Say "No": The New U.S.-Japan Relations Card*. Washington, DC, 1989.

Morley, James W., ed. *Dilemmas of Growth in Prewar Japan*. Princeton, 1976.

————. "The First Seven Weeks." *Japan Interpreter*, 6 (no. 2, 1970).

Munro-Leighton, Judith. "A Post-Revisionist Scrutiny of American's Role in the Cold War in Asia, 1945–1950." *Journal of American-East Asian Relations*, 1 (Spring 1992).

Murphy, R. Taggart. *The Weight of the Yen. How Denial Imperils America's Future and Ruins an Alliance*. New York, 1995.

Nagai Yonosuke and Akira Irye, eds. *The Origins of the Cold War in Asia*. New York, 1977.

Nakamura Takafusa. "Seikai keigai no naka no Nichi-Bei" ["Japanese-U.S. Economic Problems in the World Economy"]. In Hosoya Chihiro and Saito Makoto, eds. *Washinton tasei to Nichi-Bei kankei* [The Washington Treaty System and Japanese-U.S. Relations]. Tokyo, 1978.

Nester, William R. *Japan and the Third World: Patterns, Power, Prospects*. New York, 1992.

Neu, Charles. "Higashi Ajia ni okeru Amerika gaikokan" [American Diplomats in East Asia]. In Hosoya Chihiro and Saito Makoto, eds. *Washinton taisei to Nichi-Bei kankei* [The Washington Treaty System and Japanese-U.S. Relations]. Tokyo, 1978.

————. *The Troubled Encounter: The United States and Japan*. New York, 1975.

Neumann, William L. *America Encounters Japan: From Perry to MacArthur*. Baltimore, 1963.

————. "Religion, Morality and Freedom: The Ideological Background of the Perry Expedition." *Pacific Historical Review*, 23 (August 1954).

Ninkovich, Frank A. *Modernity and Power: A History of the Domino Theory in the Twentieth Century*. Chicago, 1994.

Nish, Ian. *Alliance in Decline*. A Study in Anglo-Japanese Relations 1908–1928. London, 1972.

————. *Britain and Japan, 1600–1975*. 2 vols. London, 1977.

————. *Japanese Foreign Policy, 1869–1942. Kasumigaski to Miyakezaka*. London, 1977.

————. *The Origins of the Russo-Japanese War*. London, 1985.

————. "The Showa Emperor and the End of the Manchurian Crisis." *Japan Forum*, 1 (October 1989).

Nixon, Richard M. "Asia After Vietnam." *Foreign Affairs*, 46 (October 1967).

————. *RN: The Memoirs of Richard Nixon*. New York, 1978.

[Notter, Harley]. U.S. Department of State. *Postwar Foreign Policy Preparation, 1939–1945*. Washington, DC, 1949.

Nye, Joseph S., Jr. "The Case for Deep Engagement." *Foreign Affairs*, 74 (July–August 1995).

O'Connor, Raymond G. *Force Diplomacy: Essays, Military and Diplomatic*. Coral Gables, FL, 1972.

Ogata Sadako N. *Defiance in Manchuria. The Making of Japanese Foreign Policy, 1931–1932*. Berkeley, 1964.

————. *Normalization with China: A Comparative Study of the U.S. and Japanese Processes*. Berkeley, 1988.

Ohkawa Kazushi, and Henry Rosovsky. *Japanese Economic Growth*. Stanford, 1973.

Ohmae Kinichi. *The Borderless World: Power and Strategy in the Interlinked Economy*. New York, 1990.

Oishi Kaichiro. *Nihon teikoku shugishi* [Japan's Imperialistic History]. Tokyo, 1985.

Oka Yoshitake. *Five Political Leaders of Modern Japan. Ito Hirobumi, Okuma Shigenobu, Hara Takashi, Inukai Tsuyoshi, and Saionji Kimmochi*. Translated by Andrew Fraser and Patricia Murray. Tokyo, 1986.

————. *Konoe Fumimaro: A Political Biography*. Translated by Shumpei Okamoto and Patricia Murray. Tokyo, 1983.

Okamoto Shumpei. *The Japanese Oligarchy and the Russo-Japanese War*. New York, 1970.

Okihiro, Gary. *Cane Fires: The Anti-Japanese Movement in Hawaii, 1865–1945*. Philadelphia, 1991.

————. *Margins and Mainstreams: Asians in American History and Culture*. Seattle, WA, 1994.

————. *Whispered Silences. Japanese-Americans and World War II*. Essay by Gary Y. Okihiro. Photographs by Joan Myers. Seattle, WA, 1996.

Osgood, Robert, *et al., Retreat from Empire? The First Nixon Administration*. Baltimore, 1973.

Ozawa Ichiro. *Blueprint for a New Japan*. Introduction by John Rockefeller. Translated by Louisa Rubinfen. Edited by Eric Gower. Tokyo and New York, 1994.

Packard, George R. III. "Living with the Real Japan." *Foreign Affairs*, 46 (October 1967).

————. *Protest in Tokyo: The Security Treaty Crisis of 1960*. Princeton, 1966.

Paige, Glenn D. *The Korean Decision, June 24–30, 1950*. New York, 1968.

Paolino, Ernest N. *The Foundations of American Empire; William Henry Seward and U.S. Foreign Policy*. Ithaca, NY, 1973.

Peattie, Mark R. *Ishiwara Kanji and Japan's Confrontation with the West*. Princeton, 1975.

Pelz, Stephen E. *Race to Pearl Harbor: The Failure of the Second London Naval Conference and the Onset of World War II*. Cambridge, MA, 1974.

Pempel, T. J. *Policy and Politics in Japan. Creative Conservatism*. Philadelphia, 1982.

————. "The Tar Baby Target: 'Reform' of the Japanese Bureaucracy." In Robert E. Ward and Sakamoto Yoshikazu, eds. *Democratizing Japan: The Allied Occupation*. Honolulu, 1987.

Perkins, F. C. "A Dynamic Analysis of Japanese Energy Policies." *Energy Policy*, 22 (July 1994).

Perry, John Curtis. *Facing West: Americans and the Opening of the Pacific*. New York. 1994.

Perry, Commodore Matthew C. *The Japan Expedition 1852–1854: The Personal Journal of Commodore Matthew C. Perry.* Ed. Roger Pineau. Washington, DC, 1968.

Petillo, Carol Morris. "The Cold War in Asia." In John M. Carroll and George C. Herring, eds. *Modern American Diplomacy.* Wilmington, DE, 1986.

Pharr, Susan J. "The Politics of Women's Rights." In Robert E. Ward and Sakamoto Yoshikazu, *Democratizing Japan: The Allied Occupation.* Honolulu, 1987.

Phillips, Kevin P. *Boiling Point: Republicans, Democrats, and the Decline of Middle-Class Prosperity.* New York. 1993.

Pleshakov, Constantine V. "Taiheiyo senso: Stalin no ketsudan" [The Pacific War: Stalin's Choices]. In Hosoya Chihiro, et al., eds. *Taiheiyo senso* [The Pacific War]. Tokyo, 1993.

Pogue, Forrest C. *George C. Marshall.* 4 vols. New York, 1963–87.

Polenberg, Richard. *One Nation Divisible: Class, Race, and Ethnicity in the United States Since 1938.* New York, 1980.

———, ed. *America at War: The Home Front, 1941–1945.* Englewood Cliffs, NJ, 1968.

Prange, Gordon W., in collaboration with Donald M. Goldstein and Katherine V. Dillon. *At Dawn We Slept: The Untold Story of Pearl Harbor.* New York, 1982.

Prestowitz, Clyde. "Japan and the United States: Twins or Opposites?" In Aspen Strategy Group. *Harness the Rising Sun.* Lanham, MD, 1993.

———. *Trading Places: How We Allowed Japan to Take the Lead.* New York, 1988.

Rozman, Gilbert. *Japan's Response to the Gorbachev Era, 1985–1991: A Rising Superpower versus a Declining One.* Princeton, 1992.

Rydell, Robert W. *All the World's a Fair: Visions of Empire at American International Expositions, 1876–1916.* Chicago, 1985.

Sakaiya Taichi. *What Is Japan? Contradictions and Transformations.* New York, 1993.

Samuels, Richard J. *"Rich Nation, Strong Army": National Security and the Technological Transformation of Japan.* Ithaca, NY, 1994.

Sanger, David E. "Coloring History." *New York Times Magazine,* July 2, 1995.

Sansom, George B. *Japan: A Short Cultural History.* London, 1931.

———. *The Western World and Japan: A Study in the Interaction of European and Asiatic Cultures.* New York, 1950.

Sarantakes, Nicholas Evan. "Continuity Through Change: The Return of Okinawa and Iwo Jima, 1967–1972." *Journal of American-East Asian Relations,* 3 (Spring 1994).

Sato Kinya, "From a Tokyo Window." *Asahi Evening News.* February 10–11, March 24, May 12, and May 26, 1994.

Sato Seizaburo, Ken'ichi Koyama, and Shumpei Kumon. *Postwar Politician: The Life of Masayoshi Ohira.* Translated by William R. Carter. New York, 1990.

Scalapino, Robert A., ed. *The Foreign Policy of Modern Japan.* Berkeley, 1977.

Schaller, Michael, "Altered States: The United States and Japan During the 1960s." In Diane B. Kunz, ed. *The Diplomacy of the Crucial Decade: American Foreign Relations During the 1960s.* New York, 1994.

———. *The American Occupation of Japan: The Origins of the Cold War in Asia.* New York, 1985.

———. *Douglas MacArthur: The Far Eastern General.* New York, 1989.

———. "MacArthur's Japan: The View from Washington." *Diplomatic History,* 10 (Winter 1986).

Scheiber, Harry N., and Akio Watanabe. "Occupation Policy and Postwar Planning in Postwar Japan." In E. Aerts and A. S. Milward, eds. *Economic Planning in the Post-1945 Period.* Leuven, Belgium, 1990.

Scholes, Walter and Marie. *The Foreign Policies of the Taft Administration.* Columbia, MO, 1970.

Schonberger, Howard B. *Aftermath of War: Americans and the Remaking of Japan, 1945–1952.* Kent, OH, 1989.

Sherwin, Martin J. *A World Destroyed: Hiroshima and the Origins of the Arms Race.* New York, 1987.

Shillony, Ben-Ami. *Politics and Culture in Wartime Japan.* New York, 1981.

Shimazu Naoko. "The Japanese Attempt to Secure Racial Equality in 1919." *Japan Forum,* 1 (April 1989).

Shimizu Sayuri. "A Bothersome Triangle: The United States, Japan, and the Problem of Trade with Communist China, 1952–1958," 1992. Manuscript in author's possession.

———. "Clarence Randall and the Control of Sino-Japanese Trade." *Journal of American and Canadian Studies,* 7 (Spring 1991).

Shindo Eiichi, "Ashida Hitoshi and Postwar Reform: Between Liberalism and Conservatism" (in Japanese). *International Relations,* 85 (May 1987).

Shinobu Seizaburo and Nakayama Jiichi. *Nichi-ro senso-shi no kenkyu* [A Study of the History of the Russo-Japanese War]. Tokyo, 1972.

Shiraishi Masaya. *Japanese Relations with Vietnam: 1951–1987.* Ithaca, NY, 1990.

Shiraishi Takashi. *Japan's Trade Policies, 1945 to the Present Day.* London, 1989.

Shultz, George P. *Turmoil and Triumph. My Years as Secretary of State.* New York, 1993.

Skates, John Ray. *The Invasion of Japan: Alternative to the Bomb.* Columbia, SC, 1994.

Sklar, Martin J. *The Corporate Reconstruction of American Capitalism, 1890–1916. The Market, the Law, and Politics.* New York, 1988.

Skocpol, Theda. *States and Social Revolutions: A Comparative Analysis of France, Russia, and China.* Cambridge, UK, 1979.

Smith, Gaddis. *Dean Acheson.* New York, 1972.

———. *The Last Years of the Monroe Doctrine, 1945–1993.* New York, 1994.

Smith, Geoffrey S. "Doing Justice: Relocation and Equity in Public Policy." *The Public Historian,* 6 (Summer 1984).

———. *To Save a Nation: American Countersubversives, the New Deal, and the Coming of World War II. With a New Epilogue.* Chicago, 1992.

Smith, Robert Freeman. "Thomas W. Lamont. International Banker as Diplomat." In Thomas J. McCormick and Walter LaFeber, eds. *Behind the Throne: Servants of Power to Imperial Presidents, 1898–1968* [Essays in Honor of Fred H. Harrington]. Madison, WI, 1993.

Smith, Robert J. *Japanese Society: Tradition, Self, and the Social Order.* Cambridge, UK, 1983.

———. "The Sources and Proponents of 'Tradition' and 'Modernity' in Japanese Law." *Journal of Legal Pluralism,* 33 (1993).

Socolofsky, Homer E., and Allan B. Spetter. *The Presidency of Benjamin Harrison.* Lawrence, KS, 1987.

Somura Yasunobu. *Peri wa naze Nihon ni kita ka* [Why Perry Came to Japan]. Tokyo, 1987.

Spector, Ronald. *Eagle Against the Sun: The American War with Japan.* New York, 1985.

———. "Reflections on the Enola Gay Debacle." *GW Magazine* (Fall 1995).

Spence, Jonathan. *The Search for Modern China.* New York, 1990.

———. *To Change China.* New York, 1980.

Steele, Richard W. *Propaganda in an Open Society: The Roosevelt Administration and the Media, 1933–1941.* Westport, CT, 1985.

Stevens, Sylvester R. *American Expansion in Hawaii, 1842–1898.* Harrisburg, PA, 1945.

Stimson, Henry L., and McGeorge Bundy. *On Active Service in Peace and War.* New York, 1949.

Storry, Richard. *Japan and the Decline of the West in Asia, 1894–1943.* New York, 1979.

Suzamura Kotaro and Okuno-Fujiwara Masahiro. *Industrial Policy in Japan: Overview and*

Evaluation. Australia-Japan Research Centre. Pacific Economic Paper no. 146, April 1987.

Suzuki, Gengo. "The Impact of the Korean War on Japan: An Overview." In William Nimmo, ed. *The Occupation of Japan: The Impact of the Korean War.* Norfolk, VA, 1990.

Szulc, Tad. *The Illusion of Peace: Foreign Policy in the Nixon-Kissinger Years.* New York, 1978.

Tadashi Kawata. "The Rise and Fall of Economic Hegemony and Policy Change." *Journal of American and Canadian Studies,* 5 (Spring 1990).

Takaki, Ronald. *A Different Mirror: A History of Multicultural America.* Boston, 1993.

Takemae Eiji. *Senryo sengoshi* [Occupation and Postwar Japanese History]. Tokyo, 1980.

Tanaka Hideo. "The Conflict Between Two Legal Traditions in Making the Constitution of Japan." In Robert E. Ward and Sakamoto Yoshikazu, eds. *Democratizing Japan: The Allied Occupation.* Honolulu, 1987.

Tansill, Charles Callan. *The Foreign Policy of Thomas F. Bayard, 1885–1897.* New York, 1940.

Taylor, Sandra. *Advocate of Understanding: Sidney Gulick and the Search for Peace with Japan.* Kent, OH, 1984.

———. *Jewel of the Desert: Japanese American Internment at Topaz.* Berkeley, 1993.

Thayer, Nathaniel B. "Japanese Foreign Policy in the Nakasone Years." In Gerald L. Curtis, ed. *Japan's Foreign Policy.* Armonk, NY, 1993.

Thomson (Taylor), Sandra C. "Meiji Japan Through Missionary Eyes: The American Protestant Experience." *Journal of Religious History,* 7 (June 1973).

Thorne, Christopher. *Allies of a Kind: The United States, Great Britain and the War Against Japan, 1941–1945.* New York, 1978.

Toby, Ronald P. "Contesting the Centre: International Sources of Japanese National Identity." *International History Review,* 7 (August 1985).

Tokyo Daigaku. *Sengo kaikaku* [Postwar Reform]. Shakai Kagaku Kenkyujo [Tokyo University Social Science Institute]. Vol. 1 of 8 vols. Tokyo, 1974.

Truman, Harry S. *Memoirs.* 2 vols. Garden City, NY, 1955–56.

———. *Off the Record: The Private Papers of Harry S. Truman.* Ed. Robert H. Ferrell. New York, 1980.

———. *Where the Buck Stops. The Personal and Private Writings of Harry S. Truman.* Ed. Margaret Truman. New York, 1989.

Tsuru, Shigeto. *Japan's Capitalism: Creative Defeat and Beyond.* Cambridge, MA, 1993.

Tucker, Nancy Bernkopf. "American Policy Toward Sino-Japanese Trade in the Postwar Years." *Diplomatic History,* 8 (Summer 1994).

Tugwell, Franklin. *The Energy Crisis and the American Political Economy: Politics and Markets in the Management of Natural Resources.* Stanford, 1988.

Tupper, Eleanor, and George E. McReynolds. *Japan in American Public Opinion.* New York, 1937.

United States Capitol Historical Society. *Foreign Visitors to Congress. Speeches and History.* Ed. Mary Lee Kerr. 2 vols. Millwood, NY, 1989.

United States Congress, House, Committee on Armed Services. *United States-Vietnam Relations, 1945–1967; Study Prepared by the Department of Defense* [The Pentagon Papers]. 12 vols. Washington, DC, 1971.

United States Congress, House, Committee on Foreign Affairs. *United States–Japan Relations.* Washington, DC, 1982.

United States Department of State. *Korea (Preliminary Version). An Intelligence Estimate Prepared by the Estimates Group, Office of Intelligence Research.* June 25, 1950. OACST-"P File. Record Group 319. National Archives. Washington, DC.

Unterberger, Betty Miller. *The United States, Revolutionary Russia, and the Rise of Czechoslovakia.* Chapel Hill, NC, 1989.

Usuri Katsumi. "Nichi-Bei kaisen to chugoku" [Japan-U.S. and the War in China]. In Hosoya Chihiro, *et al.,* eds., *Takeiyo senso* [The Pacific War]. Tokyo, 1993.

Utley, Jonathan G. "Cordell Hull and the Diplomacy of Inflexibility." In Hilary Conroy and Harry Wray, eds. *Pearl Harbor Reexamined: Prologue to the Pacific War.* Honolulu, 1989.

———. *Going to War with Japan, 1937–1941.* Knoxville, TN, 1985.

———. "The United States Enters World War II." In John M. Carroll and George C. Herring, eds. *Modern American Diplomacy.* Wilmington, DE, 1986.

Vogel, Ezra F. *Japan as Number One: Lessons for America.* New York, 1979, 1980.

———. "Japanese-American Relations After the Cold War." In Aspen Strategy Group. *Harness the Rising Sun.* Lanham, MD, 1993.

Walker, J. Samuel. "The Decision to Use the Bomb: A Historiographical Update." *Diplomatic History,* 14 (Winter 1990).

Ward, Robert E. "Presurrender Planning: Treatment of the Emperor and Constitutional Changes." In Robert E. Ward and Sakamoto Yoshikazu, eds. *Democratizing Japan: The Allied Occupation.* Honolulu, 1987.

Watanabe Akio, ed. *Sengo Nihon no taigai sesaku: kokusai kankei no hen'yo to Nihon no yakuwari* [Postwar Japanese Foreign Policy: The Changes in International Relations and Japan's Role]. Tokyo, 1985.

Weingartner, James J. "Trophies of War: U.S. Troops and the Mutilation of Japanese War Dead, 1941–1945." *Pacific Historical Review,* 61 (February 1992).

Weinstein, Martin E. *The Human Face of Japan's Leadership: Twelve Portraits.* New York, 1989.

Welfield, John. *An Empire in Eclipse; Japan in the Postwar American Alliance System: A Study in the Interaction of Domestic Politics and Foreign Policy.* London, 1988.

White, John Albert. *Diplomacy of the Russo-Japanese War.* Princeton, 1964.

White, Theodore H. "The Danger from Japan." *New York Times Magazine,* July 28, 1985.

Whiting, Allen S. *The Chinese Calculus of Deterrence: India and Indochina.* Ann Arbor, MI, 1975.

Whiting, Robert. *The Chrysanthemum and the Bat: Baseball Samurai Style.* New York, 1977.

Whitney, Major General Courtney. *MacArthur. His Rendezvous with History.* New York, 1956.

Widenor, William C. *Henry Cabot Lodge and the Search for an American Foreign Policy.* Berkeley, 1980.

Wiley, Peter Booth, with Korigi Ichiro. *Yankees in the Land of the Gods.* New York, 1990.

Wilkins, Myra. "The Role of U.S. Business." In Dorothy Borg and Shumpei Okamoto, eds. *Pearl Harbor as History: Japanese-American Relations, 1931–1941.* New York, 1973.

Williams, Justin, Sr., John W. Dower, and Howard Schonberger. "A Forum: American Democratization Policy for Occupied Japan." *Pacific Historical Review,* 57 (May 1988).

Willoughby, Major General Charles, and John Chamberlain. *MacArthur, 1941–1951.* New York, 1954.

Wiltz, John Edward. "Did the United States Betray Korea in 1905?" *Pacific Historical Review,* 54 (August 1985).

Wolf, Charles, Jr. *Perspectives on Economic and Foreign Policies.* Santa Monica, CA, 1995.

Wolferen, Karl van. *The Enigma of Japanese Power: People and Politics in a Stateless Nation.* New York, 1990.

———. "Japan's Non-Revolution." *Foreign Affairs,* 72 (September–October 1993).

Woodward, Sir Ernest Llewellyn. *British Foreign Policy in the Second World War.* London, 1962.

Wray, Harry, and Hilary Conroy, eds. *Japan Examined: Perspectives on Modern Japanese History.* Honolulu, 1983.

Wright, Quincy, and Carl J. Nelson. "American Attitudes Toward Japan and China, 1937–1938." *Public Opinion Quarterly,* 3 (January 1939).

Yamamoto Mitsuru. *Fumo no gensetsu: Kokkai toben no naka no Nichi-Bei kankei* [The Barren Discourse: The Diet's Response to the Japan-U.S. Relationship]. Tokyo, 1992.

Yardley, Herbert O. *The Chinese Black Chamber. An Adventure in Espionage.* Introduction by James Bamford. Boston, 1983.

Yasuba Yasukichi. "Anatomy of the Debate on Japanese Capitalism." *Journal of Japanese Studies,* 2 (Autumn 1975).

Yasuhara Yoko. "Japan, Communist China, and Export Controls in Asia, 1948–1952." *Diplomatic History,* 10 (Winter 1986).

"Yasuhiro Nakasone: The Statesman as CEO." Interviewed by Alan M. Webber. *Harvard Business Review,* 67 (March–April 1989).

Yoshida Shigeru. *The Yoshida Memoirs; The Story of Japan in Crisis.* Westport, CT, 1973.

Yoshikazu Sakamoto. "The International Context of the Occupation of Japan." In Robert E. Ward and Sakamoto Yoshikazu, eds. *Democratizing Japan: The Allied Occupation.* Honolulu, 1987.

Yoshino, M. Y. *Japan's Multinational Enterprises.* Cambridge, MA, 1976.

Yoshitsu, Michael M. *Japan and the San Francisco Peace Settlement.* New York, 1983.

Yui Daizaburo. "From Exclusion to Integration: Asian Americans' Experiences in World War II." *Hitotsubashi Journal of Social Studies,* 24 (December 1992).

Yutaka Kosai. "The Postwar Japanese Economy, 1945–1973." Translated by Andrew Goble. In Peter Duus, ed. *The Cambridge History of Japan.* Vol. 6. *The Twentieth Century.* Cambridge, UK, 1988.

Acknowledgments

AS THIS PROJECT, planned to be completed in two and a half years, stretched to five, the debts also multiplied. It is a cliché for a tardy author to thank the long-suffering editor, but in this case the cliché has force. Ed Barber, Vice President of W. W. Norton, has been not only patient and supportive, but a trusted friend. His red pen robbed the world of many noble phrases, but he was invariably right, especially when he suggested cuts for a runaway manuscript. As the copy editor for a rather complex work, Ann Adelman was extraordinary. I am greatly indebted to her. Gerry McCauley placed the manuscript, and has also been a most supportive and valued friend.

Akira Iriye and Michael Barnhart read the entire manuscript. Their knowledge of Japan, as well as of U.S. foreign relations, saved me from many errors. In addition, Akira's friendship has long been valued, as have his many contributions to the writing of history. Frank Costigliola also read a large portion of the manuscript and over twenty-five years has provided good advice and close friendship. Gabriela Lopez, Mark Anderson, and Lu Yan were indispensable, for they translated most of the Japanese-language sources used in the book. Lu Yan, despite a pressing deadline for her doctoral dissertation, also was most kind in going over the final manuscript to check for usage. Professor Sayuri Shimizu was a new Ph.D. at Cornell when she translated sources and introduced me to many important Japanese materials, including her own work on the 1950s. I value her, Danny's, and her parents' friendship.

A number of other friends and former students helped with material and insights. David Langbart of the National Archives once again was unsurpassed in his knowledge of the documents and in his determination to make them legitimately available for researchers. Barry Eisler of California and Tokyo read parts of the manuscript and provided personal insights. David Maisel, Evan Stewart, Eric Edelman, Mark Lytle, Robert Hannigan, Doug Little, Catheryn Obern, Arthur Kaminsky, Carol Kuntz, and Hirschel and Elaine Abelson have been counsellors, on academic as well as other matters, and friends. Milton Leitenberg, Michael Schaller, Ronald McGlothlen, and Tom Schoonover, as well as Ambassador Frank McNeill, sent materials and demonstrated an enthusiasm for U.S. diplomatic history that was catching. I am grateful to Robert W. Barnett and James Morley for permission to quote them.

Stephen Weiss not only made certain research for this book possible, but over the years has helped make Cornell a stimulating place for teaching and scholarship. So has Marie Underhill Noll, a longtime teacher-of-history and personal friend. This book is dedicated to four persons who, since the 1960s, led in the building of the present Cornell. Among other accomplishments, they helped make it possible to have such colleagues as Robert Smith—whose distinguished work on Japan as well as thirty-six years of friendship helped shape this book—Joel Silbey, Dick Polenberg, Michael Kammen, Takashi Sharaishi, Tom Christensen, Peter Katzenstein, Tim Borstelmann, Glenn Altschuler, Mary Beth Norton, Larry Moore, Sherman Cochran, Ted Lowi, David Wyatt, and Vic Koschmann. Some of the best ideas in this book were stolen from Lloyd Gardner, Tom McCormick, and Marty Sklar, but that has long been the case.

Carmen Blankinship, Caroline Spicer, Janie Harris, and Mary Wesche of the Cornell Libraries, as well as their directors, Alain Seznec and David Corson, especially helped make this book better. LizAnn Rogovoy, Rebecca Gaslow, Kathryn Comerford, and Karen Tanis used the libraries in providing vital research help. That three of them are on their way to successful careers in law reveals their talent as well as the length of time it has taken to finish this work. Dennis Hilger of the Truman Library, Steve Branch of the Reagan Library, E. Philip Scott of the Johnson Library, and David Humphrey, formerly of the Johnson Library and now with the State Department Historical Office, were most kind in expediting the availability of documents and photos. Bob Wampler, head of the post-1960 U.S.-Japan project at the National Security Archive, has provided hundreds of pages of invaluable documents that otherwise would have been held back from researchers—and needlessly so—for years to come. A number of Japanese friends are valued for their friendship and thanked for their interest and help: Sato Kinya and Funabashi Yoichi of *Asahi Shimbun,* Aruga Tadashi, Homma Nagayo, Hosoya Chihiro, Nagata Akifumi, Asada Sadao, Kubo Fumiaki, Takahara Takao, Kurosawa Fumitaka, Ishii Osamu, Inoue Toshikazu, Abe Hitoshi, Matsuda Takeshi—all distinguished contributors to U.S.-Japan studies—Maruyama Isamu of the International House of Japan; and two Cornellians, Professor Okada Yasuo and Matsunobu Yohei.

Once again, Scott LaFeber, Suzanne, Tom, and Matthew Kahl, Bill and Hilde Kahl, Peg and Hurley Gould, and—above all—Sandy have made it all worthwhile as well as possible.

—WALTER LaFEBER,
July 1996

Index